Second Grade Math with Confidence

Instructor Guide

Second Grade Math with Confidence

Instructor Guide

KATE SNOW

WELL-TRAINED MIND PRESS

Publisher's Cataloging-In-Publication Data
(Prepared by The Donohue Group, Inc.)

Names: Snow, Kate (Teacher), author.
Title: Second grade math with confidence. Instructor guide / Kate Snow.
Description: [Charles City, Virginia] : Well-Trained Mind Press, [2022] | Series: [Math with confidence] ; [7]
Identifiers: ISBN 9781952469312 (paperback) | ISBN 9781952469329 (ebook)
Subjects: LCSH: Mathematics--Study and teaching (Elementary) | LCGFT: Teachers' guides.
Classification: LCC QA107.2 .S662 2022 (print) | LCC QA107.2 (ebook) | DDC 372.7--dc23

Reprinted May 2026 at Bradford and Bigelow

9 10 11 12 13 B&B 30 29 28 27 26

Table of Contents

Welcome to Second Grade Math with Confidence!

Second Grade Math with Confidence is a complete math curriculum that will give your child a solid foundation in math. It's playful, hands-on, and fun with thorough coverage of second-grade math skills:

- reading, writing, and comparing numbers to 1000
- adding and subtracting 2- and 3-digit numbers
- solving addition and subtraction word problems
- telling time, counting money, and measuring length
- reading graphs, identifying 2-D and 3-D shapes, and understanding simple fractions

The carefully-sequenced and confidence-building lessons will help your child develop a strong understanding of math, step by step. Daily review ensures that she will fully master what she has learned in previous lessons. With this blend of **deep conceptual understanding** and **traditional skill practice**, you'll give your child a thorough second-grade math education.

Fun activities like Pretend Restaurant, Measurement Tag, and Fraction Bump will help your child develop a **positive attitude** toward math. You'll also find optional weekly enrichment lessons, with suggestions for delightful math picture books and real-world math activities that help your child appreciate the importance of math in real life.

Besides this Instructor Guide, *Second Grade Math with Confidence* also includes a **colorful, engaging Student Workbook** to reinforce what your child has learned. These short, straightforward workbook pages both reinforce new skills and review previous lessons so that your child remembers what he's learned.

If you're like most parents, you've probably never taught math before. You may even feel a little anxious. But don't worry: I promise to guide you every step of the way! *Second Grade Math with Confidence* is full of features that will help you teach math with confidence all year long:

- **Scripted, open-and-go lessons**
- **Clear goals** at the beginning of each lesson so you know exactly what you're trying to accomplish
- **Explanatory notes** help you understand more deeply how children learn math so you feel well-equipped to teach your child
- **Checkpoints** at the end of each unit give you specific guidance on whether to spend more time on the current unit or move on to the next one

In the next section, you'll learn how the curriculum is organized and how to get your materials ready. Invest a little time reading this section now (and getting your Math Kit ready), and you'll be ready to teach math like a pro all year long.

Wishing you a joyful year of second grade math!

Kate Snow

Introduction

The Goals of *Second Grade Math with Confidence*

Second Grade Math with Confidence aims to help children become confident and capable math students, with a deep understanding of math concepts, proficiency and fluency with fundamental skills, and a positive attitude toward math.

Deep conceptual understanding

You'll focus on one concept at a time for several weeks so your child can build deep, connected knowledge of each new topic. (Educators call this a *mastery approach* to new content.) Each new lesson builds on the previous one so your child gradually develops thorough understanding and makes connections between concepts.

Proficiency with fundamental skills

Children need lots of practice in order to master the basic skills necessary for proficiency in math. *Second Grade Math with Confidence* provides continual, ongoing review of these core skills so your child fully grasps them by the end of the year. (Educators call this a *spiral approach* to review, because children periodically revisit topics, just as the curve of a spiral returns to the same point on a circle.)

Positive attitude

The lessons in *Second Grade Math with Confidence* include games, movement, pretend activities, and lots of hands-on learning so your child enjoys and even looks forward to math time. Optional enrichment lessons each week (with a picture book suggestion and math extension activity) provide a break from the usual routine and help your child appreciate how math is used in real life.

Overview

Second Grade Math with Confidence is organized into units, weeks, and lessons. Each section has clear goals so you know exactly what you're trying to accomplish.

Units

Second Grade Math with Confidence is divided into 14 units. Each unit focuses on developing thorough understanding of one core topic, such as graphs, mental addition, or numbers to 1000.

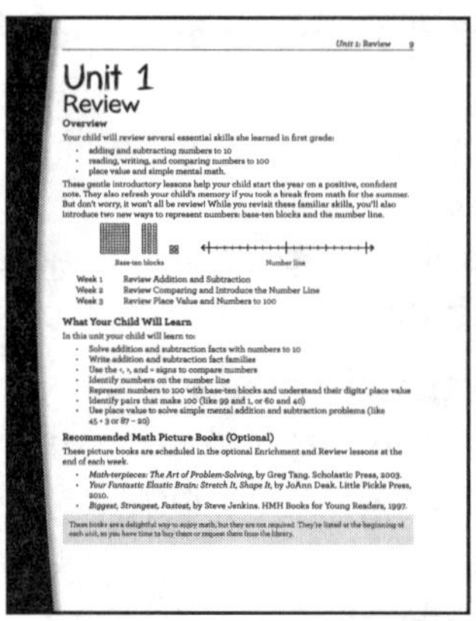

Unit 1: Review 9

Unit 1
Review

Overview

Your child will review several essential skills she learned in first grade:

- adding and subtracting numbers to 10
- reading, writing, and comparing numbers to 100
- place value and simple mental math.

These gentle introductory lessons help your child start the year on a positive, confident note. They also refresh your child's memory if you took a break from math for the summer. But don't worry, it won't all be review! While you revisit these familiar skills, you'll also introduce two new ways to represent numbers: base-ten blocks and the number line.

Base-ten blocks Number line

Week 1 Review Addition and Subtraction
Week 2 Review Comparing and Introduce the Number Line
Week 3 Review Place Value and Numbers to 100

What Your Child Will Learn

In this unit your child will learn to:

- Solve addition and subtraction facts with numbers to 10
- Write addition and subtraction fact families
- Use the <, >, and = signs to compare numbers
- Identify numbers on the number line
- Represent numbers to 100 with base-ten blocks and understand their digits' place value
- Identify pairs that make 100 (like 99 and 1, or 60 and 40)
- Use place value to solve simple mental addition and subtraction problems (like 45 + 3 or 87 − 20)

Recommended Math Picture Books (Optional)

These picture books are scheduled in the optional Enrichment and Review lessons at the end of each week.

- *Math-terpieces: The Art of Problem-Solving*, by Greg Tang. Scholastic Press, 2003.
- *Your Fantastic Elastic Brain: Stretch It, Shape It*, by JoAnn Deak. Little Pickle Press, 2010.
- *Biggest, Strongest, Fastest*, by Steve Jenkins. HMH Books for Young Readers, 1997.

These books are a delightful way to enjoy math, but they are not required. They're listed at the beginning of each unit, so you have time to buy them or request them from the library.

Weeks

Each unit is divided into 2–3 weeks (with a total of 32 weeks of lessons). Each week focuses on a specific topic, such as telling time to the minute or developing fluency with written addition. These groups of lessons are called weeks, but you don't have to finish each one in a calendar week—it's fine to have your "week" begin on Wednesday and end on the following Friday.

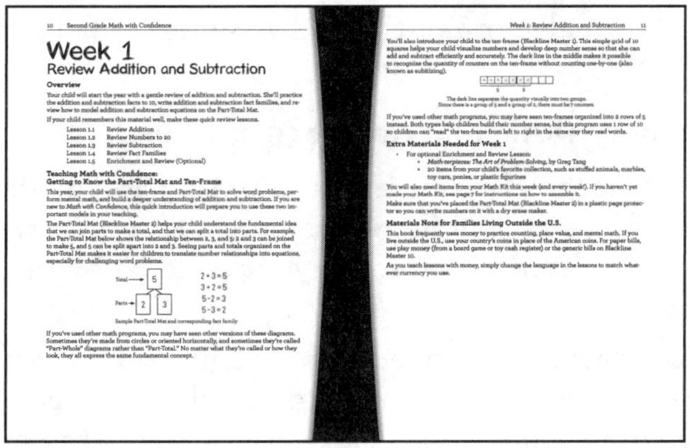

Week 1
Review Addition and Subtraction

The preview for each week includes the following:

- **Overview.** A brief summary of what you'll teach that week, along with a list of the lessons.
- **Teaching Math with Confidence.** These notes will help you understand more deeply how children learn math so that you'll be well prepared to teach the new concepts.
- **Extra Materials.** You'll sometimes need to supplement your regular math materials with a few everyday household items, such as small toys, tape, or scissors. This section will give you a heads-up if you need any extra materials for the week. (See below for more information on materials.)

Two Types of Lessons

Each week includes five lessons: four required core lessons and one optional enrichment lesson. The core lessons teach and review essential second-grade concepts and skills, while the enrichment lessons provide extra fun and real-life math applications.

Both types of lessons follow a consistent three-part format, with the purpose and materials listed at the top for easy reference. Plan for your child to spend a total of 20-30 minutes on each lesson, with 15-20 minutes of parent-led instruction.

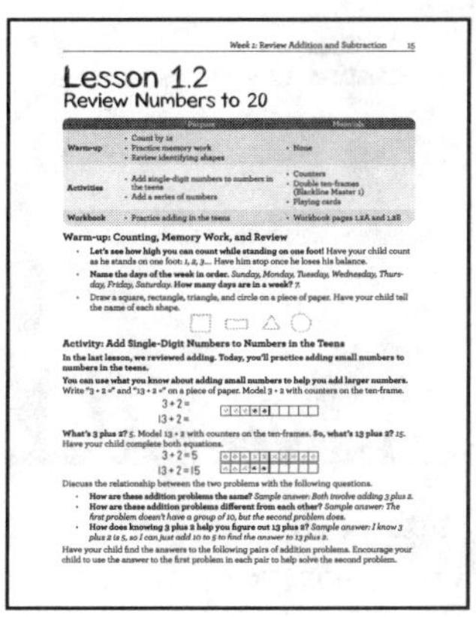

Lesson 1.2
Review Numbers to 20

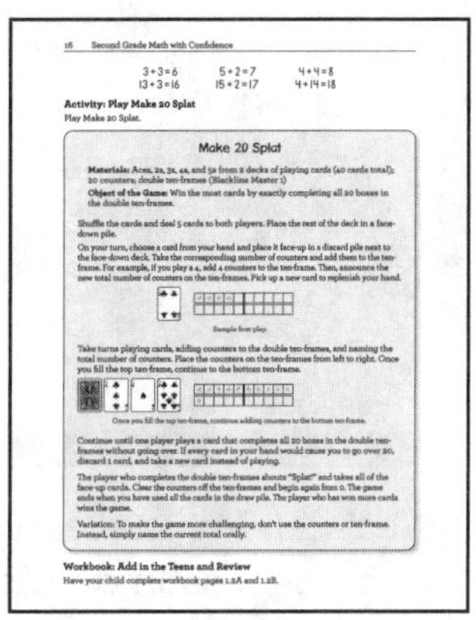

Make 20 Splat

Within the lessons:

- **Bold** text indicates what you are to say.
- *Italic* text provides sample answers.
- Gray-highlighted text indicates explanatory notes.

If possible, try to plan a consistent time for teaching math each day. Many families find it best to do math first thing in the morning when everyone's fresh. If you have younger children, you might find it works better to teach math in the afternoon while your younger children are napping.

Core Lessons (Required)

Each core lesson includes several short and varied activities to help keep your child engaged and attentive:

Warm-up: counting, memory work, and review (5 minutes)

The warm-up provides regular, brief practice with counting and memory work. It also includes a quick review activity so your child remembers and retains what he has learned. Try to keep this part of the lesson short and sweet so your child isn't worn out before the new learning later in the lesson.

Children vary in how much review they need. If your child already knows a particular fact or skill, you do not need to review it every time it is listed in the Instructor Guide. Or, if your child needs more practice than suggested, feel free to add more review.

Hands-on activities (10-15 minutes)

These parent-directed activities are the most important part of each lesson. You'll teach your child the new concepts and skills through conversation, hands-on materials, and games. The lessons are scripted so you can just open the book and start reading, but you're welcome to rephrase the words to fit your own teaching style better.

Feel free to inject your own personality into your teaching, and personalize the lessons for your child. You might use your child's favorite objects for counting, change the names in word problems to match your family members, or take your math lesson outside to enjoy a beautiful day.

Workbook (5-10 minutes)

Your child will complete a two-sided workbook page at the end of each core lesson. (These workbook pages are included in the separate Student Workbook.) Side A gives your child written practice with the lesson's new material. Side B reviews skills your child has already learned.

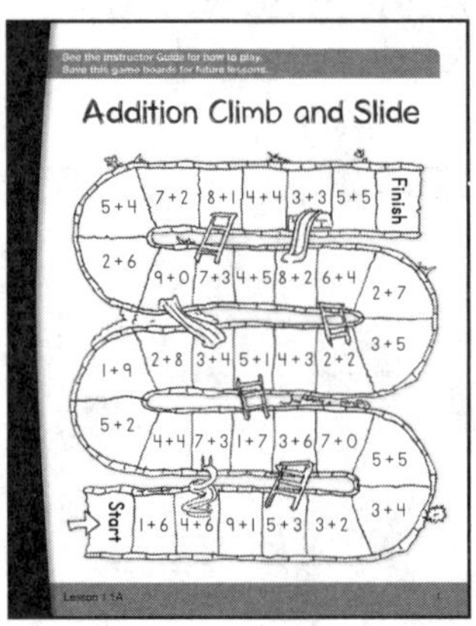

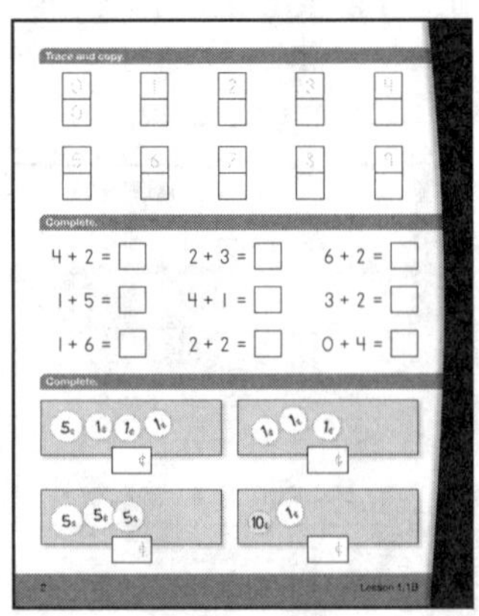

You'll occasionally use Side A during the lesson, but your child will usually complete the workbook pages at the end of the lesson on his own. Most second-graders will be able to complete the worksheets independently, but many will need their parent to help read and interpret the directions. If writing is difficult for your child, feel free to have your child complete part or all of the worksheets orally rather than writing out the answers.

Have your child use a pencil for the workbook pages so it's easy to erase mistakes. You'll also occasionally need crayons or markers for coloring activities, so make sure you have them available. And, try to check the workbook pages as soon as your child finishes them. This immediate feedback shows your child that you value his work, and it helps prevent mistakes from becoming ingrained habits.

Enrichment Lessons (Optional)

Enrichment lessons are scheduled on the fifth day of each week. Many parents and children find that these enrichment lessons are their favorite part of the week. (Siblings often enjoy participating in them, too!) However, these enrichment lessons are completely optional. You are free to choose the ones that sound the most fun for your family, or skip them entirely if your schedule is too full.

Warm-up: counting, memory work, and review (5 minutes)

The enrichment lessons give your child a chance to show off her counting skills and recite all of the memory work she has learned so far. If you have time, you can also revisit one of her favorite or most challenging activities from the week.

Picture book (10 minutes)

Reading math picture books together is a fun, cozy, and delightful way to enjoy math. Most of the suggested books relate to the main concept studied that week, but some expose your child to other interesting math topics. **The picture books are not required.** You do not need to buy every book or track down every book in your library system. It's also perfectly fine to use a book on a similar topic as a substitute.

Enrichment activity (varies)

The enrichment activities help your child understand and appreciate how math is used in everyday life. You'll find suggestions for art projects, field trips, physical activities, and more to make math come alive for your child.

Pacing and Checkpoints

Just as children learn to crawl, walk, and talk at different times, they are developmentally ready to learn math at different times, too. *Second Grade Math with Confidence* provides lots of flexibility so your child can learn at his own pace. You know your child best, and you are always welcome to slow down or speed up the pace of the lessons based on your child's needs. Use the information below to help make decisions about pacing.

Is My Child Ready to Start *Second Grade Math with Confidence*?

Most children are ready to start *Second Grade Math with Confidence* when they are 7 years old. Your child is ready to begin this program if she can:

- Count to 100 by 1s, 2s, 5s, and 10s.
- Read, write, and compare 2-digit numbers.
- Understand the meaning of the tens-place and ones-place in 2-digit numbers.
- Write simple addition and subtraction equations, and solve simple word problems with single-digit numbers.
- Know most of the addition facts up to 9 + 9.
- Know most of the subtraction facts that involve subtracting from numbers up to 10 (for example, 7 – 4 or 10 – 6).
- Know the names and values of coins and identify combinations of a few coins.

All of these skills are reviewed in the first few units, so don't worry if your child needs a refresher on a few of them.

If your child is not fluent with the addition facts up to 9 + 9 or the subtraction facts up to 10, you may need to spend a little extra time on them in Units 2 and 4. Notes throughout the lessons and Checkpoints at the end of each unit will help you decide whether to continue on to the next unit or spend more time solidifying these essential skills. (See the next question for more on Checkpoints.)

How Do I Know Whether to Stick with a Lesson or Move On?

Each lesson in *Second Grade Math with Confidence* gently builds on the previous one, but your child doesn't need to completely master every lesson before moving on to the next. The program includes many opportunities for review and practice before your child is expected to achieve full proficiency with any topic.

As a general principle, continue teaching new lessons until you reach the end of a unit. At the end of each unit, you'll find a Checkpoint that will help you assess how your child is doing. The Checkpoints will also give you guidance on whether to move on to the next unit or give your child more practice with the current unit.

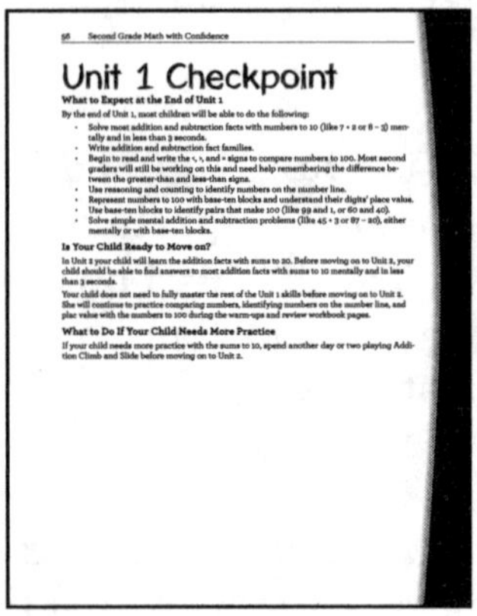
56 Second Grade Math with Confidence

Unit 1 Checkpoint

What to Expect at the End of Unit 1

By the end of Unit 1, most children will be able to do the following:

- Solve most addition and subtraction facts with numbers to 10 (like 7 + 2 or 8 − 3) mentally and in less than 3 seconds.
- Write addition and subtraction fact families.
- Begin to read and write the <, >, and = signs to compare numbers to 100. Most second graders will still be working on this and need help remembering the difference between the greater-than and less-than signs.
- Use reasoning and counting to identify numbers on the number line.
- Represent numbers to 100 with base-ten blocks and understand their digits' place value.
- Use base-ten blocks to identify pairs that make 100 (like 99 and 1, or 60 and 40).
- Solve simple mental addition and subtraction problems (like 45 + 3 or 87 − 20), either mentally or with base-ten blocks.

Is Your Child Ready to Move on?

In Unit 2 your child will learn the addition facts with sums to 20. Before moving on to Unit 2, your child should be able to find answers to most addition facts with sums to 10 mentally and in less than 3 seconds.

Your child does not need to fully master the rest of the Unit 1 skills before moving on to Unit 2. She will continue to practice comparing numbers, identifying numbers on the number line, and plac value with the numbers to 100 during the warm-ups and review workbook pages.

What to Do If Your Child Needs More Practice

If your child needs more practice with the sums to 10, spend another day or two playing Addition Climb and Slide before moving on to Unit 2.

Each Checkpoint is divided into three parts:

- **What to Expect at the End of the Unit** This list of skills tells you what second-graders typically are able to do at the end of each unit.
- **Is Your Child Ready to Move On?** This section tells you what your child needs to have mastered before moving on to the next unit.
- **What to Do if Your Child Needs More Practice** If your child isn't quite ready to move on, this section gives you options for reviewing and practicing the skills she needs to master before the next unit. (This section is omitted if no specific skills are necessary for the next unit.)

For many units, your child does not need to master all of the material from the current unit before moving on. For example, in Unit 6, your child will learn to add two-digit numbers. He'll continue to practice this skill as he learns to tell time in Unit 7, but he does not need to be completely fluent at adding two-digit numbers before starting the new unit.

What Should I Do If My Child is Crying or Frustrated?

Extra tiredness, oncoming illness, or just plain grumpiness can make for a less-than-cheerful day of math. Don't worry if your child occasionally gets frustrated or cries during lesson time. If emotions rise during math, it's usually best to cut the lesson short and resume later in the day or the next day.

However, if your child is continually frustrated, resisting math lessons, or crying during math time, it's a clear sign you should take a break from the current topic, do some gentle review, and then try the topic again in a few weeks. If your child shows these signs frequently, this book may be too challenging for his current maturity level, no matter how old he is. It may be wiser to use *First Grade Math with Confidence* instead. Every child's brain matures at a different rate, and you and your child will both find math time much more enjoyable when your child is developmentally ready for the concepts.

What Should I Do If the Lessons are Taking Too Long?

The lessons in this program are meant to take no more than 20-30 minutes and include a variety of activities so your child can stay engaged and attentive. If you find a particular lesson takes longer than 30 minutes or if your child gets restless, stop and resume the lesson the next day. Or, break the lesson into two parts: do the hands-on activities during one part of the day, and then have your child do the workbook page at a different time. The rest of the lesson will probably go much more smoothly once your child is fresh.

What Should I Do If My Child Flies Through the Lessons?

If you have a child who picks up math quickly, you can condense lessons or skip some of the warm-up activities and review workbook pages. If you go this route, occasionally double-check whether your child still remembers these skills. Just because she knew a skill at one point doesn't mean she still knows it, and periodic checks will help cement that information in her memory.

What You'll Need

You'll use simple household items to make math hands-on, concrete, and fun in *Second Grade Math with Confidence*. Most lessons only require materials from your Math Kit, but you'll also sometimes use everyday objects to enhance the lessons. No need for an expensive shopping trip, though! You likely already own nearly everything you need.

How to Create Your Math Kit

You'll use materials from your Math Kit in every core lesson. Stick the following materials in a box or basket so they're always ready to go, and keep them handy when you're teaching.

- **Base-ten blocks.** Base-ten blocks provide a concrete way for children to understand place value. Each block represents a different value in our number system (ones, tens, hundreds, or thousands). Look for a set with at least 100 units, 20 rods, 10 flats, and 1 large cube. They're generally available for about $25 online or at school supply stores. You can also photocopy and color Blackline Master 11 (page 557) instead, although children usually find real blocks easier to maneuver.

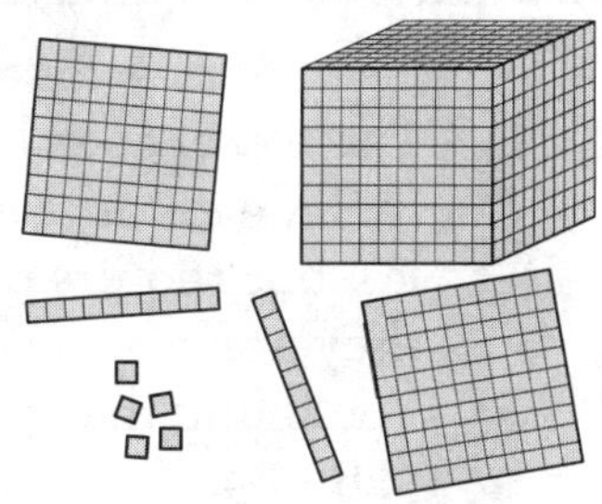
Base-ten blocks

- **50 small counters.** Any type of small object (such as plastic tiles, Legos, blocks, plastic bears, coins, or dried beans) is fine. These work best (and fit the Blackline Masters) if they are less than .75" (or 2 cm) across. You can also use the units from your set of base-ten blocks. You'll occasionally need 2 colors, so make sure at least 10 of the counters are a different color than the rest.
- **Coins (20 pennies, 20 nickels, 10 dimes, 8 quarters).** You can use toy coins, but children often enjoy using real coins more. (If you live outside the U.S., you can use your local currency's coins instead. See the materials note on page 11 for more details.)

- **Play money (10 each of one-dollar bills, five-dollar bills, ten-dollar bills, twenty-dollar bills, and hundred-dollar bills).** Play money from a toy cash register or board game works well, or you can copy and cut out the play money on Blackline Master 10.
- **Clock with hands.** Your clock should have clear, easy-to-read numbers, tick marks along the edge for each minute, and hands your child can easily move. If your family's clocks don't meet these criteria, you may want to buy an inexpensive plastic teaching clock (sometimes called a "Judy clock") to make these lessons easier to teach.
- **1-foot (or 30-centimeter) ruler.** You will teach your child to measure in both inches and centimeters this year, so make sure your ruler is labeled with both units.
- **Two packs of playing cards and two dice.** You'll use playing cards and dice for some of the games in this book. Any standard 52-card decks and regular, six-sided dice will work fine.
- **Blank paper.** Any kind of paper is fine, including plain copy paper.
- **Pencils.** Keep sharp pencils on hand for lessons and workbook pages.
- **3 page protectors.** You will need a page protector for the Part-Total Mat (Blackline Master 2) and both pages of the Place-Value Chart (Blackline Master 5) so you can write on them with a dry-erase marker.

- **Dry-erase marker.** You will use this to write numbers on the Part-Total Mat and Place-Value Chart.
- **Binder with about 25 plastic page protectors. (Recommended, but not required.)** Blackline Masters and game boards are an important part of the program and are often reused. Many pilot-test families found it easiest to keep track of these papers in plastic page protectors in a binder.

You will occasionally need to save items for future lessons. This symbol will alert you if you need to save anything.

Other Supplies Needed

You'll need only your Math Kit for most lessons, but occasionally you'll need a few other common household items. You'll find these items listed in three different places in the curriculum to make sure you always know what you need:

- The preview for each week lists all extra household items needed.
- The top of each lesson lists all supplies you'll need to teach that lesson. These lists include items from your Math Kit as well as extra household items. (Note that many lessons require paper, slips of paper, pencils, or a dry-erase marker. To save space, they are not listed unless you need more than 3 slips of paper.)
- You'll find the complete list of household items needed throughout the year on pages 528-529.

Don't feel you have to gather the extra household items now. Most are common things like tape, scissors, or small toys you can grab right before you begin the lesson.

Helpful Resources

You'll find an appendix of helpful resources at the back of this book:

- Scope and Sequence
- Complete Memory Work List
- Complete Picture Book List
- Materials List
- Game List
- Blackline Masters

Unit 1 Review

Overview

Your child will review several essential skills she learned in first grade:

- adding and subtracting numbers to 10
- reading, writing, and comparing numbers to 100
- place value and simple mental math.

These gentle introductory lessons help your child start the year on a positive, confident note. They also refresh your child's memory if you took a break from math for the summer. But don't worry, it won't all be review! While you revisit these familiar skills, you'll also introduce two new ways to represent numbers: base-ten blocks and the number line.

Base-ten blocks Number line

Week 1	Review Addition and Subtraction
Week 2	Review Comparing and Introduce the Number Line
Week 3	Review Place Value and Numbers to 100

What Your Child Will Learn

In this unit your child will learn to:

- Solve addition and subtraction facts with numbers to 10
- Write addition and subtraction fact families
- Use the <, >, and = signs to compare numbers
- Identify numbers on the number line
- Represent numbers to 100 with base-ten blocks and understand their digits' place value
- Identify pairs that make 100 (like 99 and 1, or 60 and 40)
- Use place value to solve simple mental addition and subtraction problems (like 45 + 3 or 87 – 20)

Recommended Math Picture Books (Optional)

These picture books are scheduled in the optional Enrichment and Review lessons at the end of each week.

- *Math-terpieces: The Art of Problem-Solving,* by Greg Tang. Scholastic Press, 2003.
- *Your Fantastic Elastic Brain: Stretch It, Shape It,* by JoAnn Deak. Little Pickle Press, 2010.
- *Biggest, Strongest, Fastest,* by Steve Jenkins. HMH Books for Young Readers, 1997.

These books are a delightful way to enjoy math, but they are not required. They're listed at the beginning of each unit, so you have time to buy them or request them from the library.

Week 1
Review Addition and Subtraction

Overview

Your child will start the year with a gentle review of addition and subtraction. She'll practice the addition and subtraction facts to 10, write addition and subtraction fact families, and review how to model addition and subtraction equations on the Part-Total Mat.

If your child remembers this material well, make these quick review lessons.

Lesson 1.1	Review Addition
Lesson 1.2	Review Numbers to 20
Lesson 1.3	Review Subtraction
Lesson 1.4	Review Fact Families
Lesson 1.5	Enrichment and Review (Optional)

Teaching Math with Confidence: Getting to Know the Part-Total Mat and Ten-Frame

This year, your child will use the ten-frame and Part-Total Mat to solve word problems, perform mental math, and build a deeper understanding of addition and subtraction. If you are new to *Math with Confidence*, this quick introduction will prepare you to use these two important models in your teaching.

The Part-Total Mat (Blackline Master 2) helps your child understand the fundamental idea that we can join parts to make a total, and that we can split a total into parts. For example, the Part-Total Mat below shows the relationship between 2, 3, and 5: 2 and 3 can be joined to make 5, and 5 can be split apart into 2 and 3. Seeing parts and totals organized on the Part-Total Mat makes it easier for children to translate number relationships into equations, especially for challenging word problems.

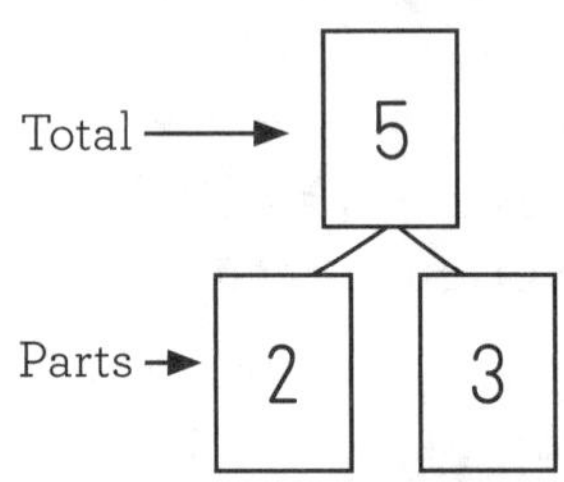

$2 + 3 = 5$

$3 + 2 = 5$

$5 - 2 = 3$

$5 - 3 = 2$

Sample Part-Total Mat and corresponding fact family

If you've used other math programs, you may have seen other versions of these diagrams. Sometimes they're made from circles or oriented horizontally, and sometimes they're called "Part-Whole" diagrams rather than "Part-Total." No matter what they're called or how they look, they all express the same fundamental concept.

You'll also introduce your child to the ten-frame (Blackline Master 1). This simple grid of 10 squares helps your child visualize numbers and develop deep number sense so that she can add and subtract efficiently and accurately. The dark line in the middle makes it possible to recognize the quantity of counters on the ten-frame without counting one-by-one (also known as subitizing).

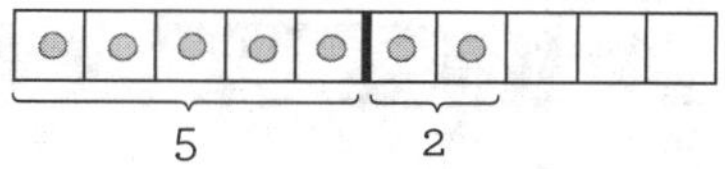

The dark line separates the quantity visually into two groups.
Since there is a group of 5 and a group of 2, there must be 7 counters.

If you've used other math programs, you may have seen ten-frames organized into 2 rows of 5 instead. Both types help children build their number sense, but this program uses 1 row of 10 so children can "read" the ten-frame from left to right in the same way they read words.

Extra Materials Needed for Week 1

- For optional Enrichment and Review Lesson:
    - *Math-terpieces: The Art of Problem-Solving,* by Greg Tang
    - 20 items from your child's favorite collection, such as stuffed animals, marbles, toy cars, ponies, or plastic figurines

You will also need items from your Math Kit this week (and every week!). If you haven't yet made your Math Kit, see page 7 for instructions on how to assemble it.

Make sure that you've placed the Part-Total Mat (Blackline Master 2) in a plastic page protector so you can write numbers on it with a dry erase maker.

Materials Note for Families Living Outside the U.S.

This book frequently uses money to practice counting, place value, and mental math. If you live outside the U.S., use your country's coins in place of the American coins. For paper bills, use play money (from a board game or toy cash register) or the generic bills on Blackline Master 10.

As you teach lessons with money, simply change the language in the lessons to match whatever currency you use.

Lesson 1.1
Review Addition

	Purpose	Materials
Warm-up	• Count by 1s • Practice memory work • Review coin combinations	• Coins
Activities	• Set a positive tone for the year and preview what your child will learn • Review recognizing quantities by sight on the ten-frame • Review addition facts with sums to 10	• Double ten-frames (Blackline Master 1) • Counters • Addition Climb and Slide game board (from workbook page 1.1A) • Die
Workbook	• Review writing numbers and addition facts with sums to 10	• Workbook page 1.1B

The Week 1 lessons assume that your child already knows these skills and simply needs a quick review. If your child remembers this material well, condense the lessons or skim through them quickly. If any of the material is new to your child, spend some extra time practicing it and review it regularly until she masters it. You know your child best, so always feel free to adjust the amount of practice and review based on what your child needs.

Warm-up: Counting, Memory Work, and Review

Each day, we'll begin with a warm-up. In the warm-up, you'll practice counting, work on memorizing important information, and review skills you've already learned so that you don't forget them. The warm-up gets your brain into math mode and prepares you to learn new skills.

Show your child the Memory Work list on page 523. **You'll memorize these important facts this year. During Unit 1, we'll review some of the memory work that you learned in first grade.**

- Place a handful of pennies on the table (about 25-30). **About how much do you think these coins are worth?** *Answers will vary.* Have your child count by 1s to find their value.
- Show your child a penny, nickel, dime, and quarter. Have her tell the name of each coin and how much its worth.

  If you live outside the U.S., see page 11 to learn how to modify lessons to match your local currency.

- Have your child tell the value of the following coin combinations.
  - × 4 pennies *(4¢)*
  - × 1 nickel and 2 pennies *(7¢)*
  - × 1 nickel and 4 pennies *(9¢)*
  - × 1 dime and 3 pennies *(13¢)*
  - × 1 dime, 1 nickel, and 1 penny *(16¢)*
  - × 2 dimes *(20¢)*

Activity: Introduce the Workbook and Math Kit

Today, you'll begin your new math book. You already know a lot about math! Discuss what your child learned and enjoyed in her first-grade math program. For example: **What was your favorite part of math last year? How high do you think you can count now? Do you remember all those fun addition and subtraction games we played?**

This year, you will build on what you already know to learn even more about numbers, shapes, and measurement. Let's take a look at your workbook and see what you'll learn this year. Briefly page through the workbook with your child. **What are you most excited to learn about in math this year?** *Answers will vary.*

We'll use the Math Kit to help you learn and understand math. Show your child your Math Kit and talk about the items in it. For example: **We'll use base-ten blocks to add and subtract 2- and 3-digit numbers. You'll learn more about telling time and counting coins this year.**

> If you haven't gathered the supplies for your Math Kit yet, work with your child now to collect the necessary materials. See page 7 for the full list.

Activity: Introduce the Ten-Frame (For Families New to Math with Confidence)

> If your child did not use *First Grade Math with Confidence*, use this quick activity to introduce the ten-frame. See the Week 1 **Teaching Math with Confidence** for more on ten-frames' benefits.

Show your child Blackline Master 1. **You'll use these ten-frames to help master all the addition and subtraction facts this year.**

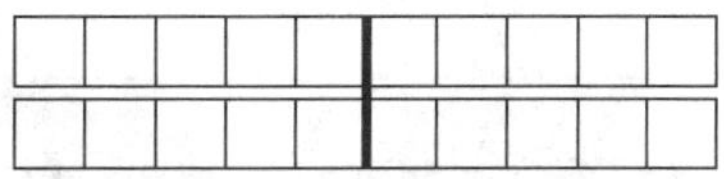

Cover the bottom ten-frame with a piece of paper. Discuss the top ten-frame with these questions:

- **How many boxes are to the left of the dark line?** *5.*
- **How many boxes are to the right of the dark line?** *5.*
- **How many boxes are there in all?** *10.*

Place 6 counters on the ten-frame. **How many counters are there?** *6.* If your child starts to count them one-by-one, say: **There's a shortcut for finding the number of counters without counting. I see a group of 5, plus one more counter. So, there must be 6.**

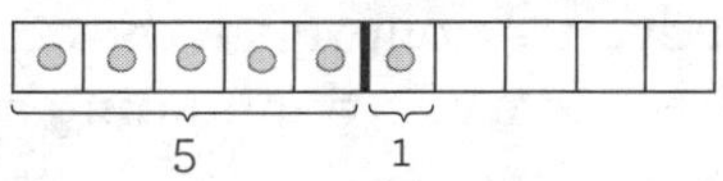

> Always fill the ten-frame from left to right, without skipping any boxes, so your child can tell at a glance how many counters there are.

Secretly place 9 counters on the ten-frame and cover the counters with a piece of paper. **I'm going to show you some counters for just a second. When I lift the paper, tell me how many counters there are, as fast as you can.** Briefly lift the piece of paper, then replace it. **How many counters?** *9.* After your child responds, lift the paper and allow her to check her answer.

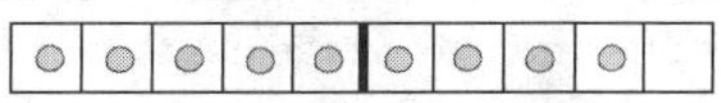

Repeat with 5, 6, 7, 8, and 10 counters, in random order. Encourage your child to look for combinations of "5 and some more" rather than counting one-by-one.

Activity: Review Addition

Last year, you learned a lot about addition. What does it mean to add two numbers together? *Sample answer: It means to join them.*

Write "4 + 3 =" on a piece of paper. **Let's put counters on the ten-frame to show what this problem means.** Have your child help you place 4 counters of one color and 3 counters of another color on the ten-frame.

4 + 3 = 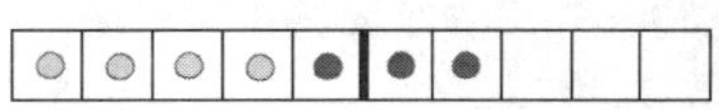

So, what's 4 + 3? *7.* Have your child complete the written equation: 4 + 3 = 7.

> If your child starts to count, encourage her to use the dividing line on the ten-frame to "see" the answer: **There are 5 counters on the left side of the dark line, plus 2 more counters on the right side. So, there are 7.**

Briefly review addition vocabulary with the following questions:

- Point to the plus sign. **What do we call this sign?** *The plus sign.* **It stands for the word plus, and it means we join two groups together.**
- Point to the equals sign. **What do we call this sign?** *The equals sign.* **It tells us two amounts are equal to each other or are the same as each other.**
- Point to the 4 and 3. **What do we call the numbers that we add together?** *The addends.* **Here's how to remember this word: we add the addends.**
- Point to the 7. **What do we call this number?** *The sum.*

$$4 + 3 = 7$$

addends sum

Activity: Play Addition Climb and Slide

Play Addition Climb and Slide.

Addition Climb and Slide

Materials: Addition Climb and Slide game board (from workbook page 1.1A); 2 different-colored counters to use as game tokens; die

Object of the Game: Be the first player to reach the Finish square.

Each player chooses a counter to use as a game token and places it on the Start Square.

On your turn, roll the die, and advance your token the corresponding number of squares. Say the answer to the problem on your landing square.

If you land on a square at the bottom of a ladder, "climb" the ladder and place your game token on the square at the top of the ladder. If you land on a square at the top of a slide, slide down the slide and place your game token on the square at the bottom of the slide.

The first player to reach Finish wins the game.

> If your child has trouble finding the sums, have her place counters on the ten-frame to find the answer. Stop her if she starts to count one-by-one and encourage her to look for a combination of "5 and some more" instead.

Save this game board with your math materials so you can play again.

Workbook: Review Writing Numbers and Addition Facts

Have your child complete workbook page 1.1B.

> Your child will usually complete 2 workbook pages at the end of every lesson. Side A provides practice with the new lesson material, while Side B provides review. In this lesson, side A has a game board, so your child will only complete side B.

Lesson 1.2
Review Numbers to 20

	Purpose	Materials
Warm-up	• Count by 1s • Practice memory work • Review identifying shapes	• None
Activities	• Add single-digit numbers to numbers in the teens • Add a series of numbers	• Counters • Double ten-frames (Blackline Master 1) • Playing cards
Workbook	• Practice adding in the teens	• Workbook pages 1.2A and 1.2B

Warm-up: Counting, Memory Work, and Review

- **Let's see how high you can count while standing on one foot!** Have your child count as he stands on one foot: *1, 2, 3....* Have him stop once he loses his balance.
- **Name the days of the week in order.** *Sunday, Monday, Tuesday, Wednesday, Thursday, Friday, Saturday.* **How many days are in a week?** *7.*
- Draw a square, rectangle, triangle, and circle on a piece of paper. Have your child tell the name of each shape.

Activity: Add Single-Digit Numbers to Numbers in the Teens

In the last lesson, we reviewed adding. Today, you'll practice adding small numbers to numbers in the teens.

You can use what you know about adding small numbers to help you add larger numbers. Write "3 + 2 =" and "13 + 2 =" on a piece of paper. Model 3 + 2 with counters on the ten-frame.

3 + 2 =

13 + 2 =

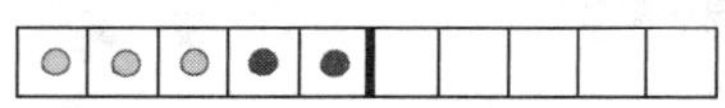

What's 3 plus 2? *5.* Model 13 + 2 with counters on the ten-frames. **So, what's 13 plus 2?** *15.* Have your child complete both equations.

3 + 2 = 5

13 + 2 = 15

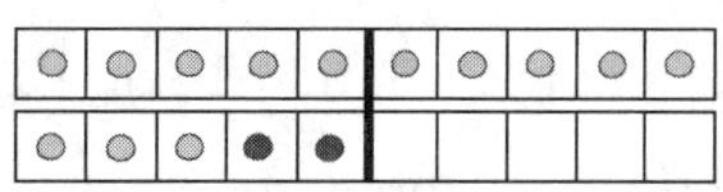

Discuss the relationship between the two problems with the following questions.

- **How are these addition problems the same?** *Sample answer: Both involve adding 3 plus 2.*
- **How are these addition problems different from each other?** *Sample answer: The first problem doesn't have a group of 10, but the second problem does.*
- **How does knowing 3 plus 2 help you figure out 13 plus 2?** *Sample answer: I know 3 plus 2 is 5, so I can just add 10 to 5 to find the answer to 13 plus 2.*

Have your child find the answers to the following pairs of addition problems. Encourage your child to use the answer to the first problem in each pair to help solve the second problem.

$3 + 3 = 6$ $\quad$ $5 + 2 = 7$ $\quad$ $4 + 4 = 8$

$13 + 3 = 16$ $\quad$ $15 + 2 = 17$ $\quad$ $4 + 14 = 18$

Activity: Play Make 20 Splat

Play Make 20 Splat.

Make 20 Splat

Materials: Aces, 2s, 3s, 4s, and 5s from 2 decks of playing cards (40 cards total); 20 counters; double ten-frames (Blackline Master 1)

Object of the Game: Win the most cards by exactly completing all 20 boxes in the double ten-frames.

Shuffle the cards and deal 5 cards to both players. Place the rest of the deck in a face-down pile.

On your turn, choose a card from your hand and place it face-up in a discard pile next to the face-down deck. Take the corresponding number of counters and add them to the ten-frame. For example, if you play a 4, add 4 counters to the ten-frame. Then, announce the new total number of counters on the ten-frames. Pick up a new card to replenish your hand.

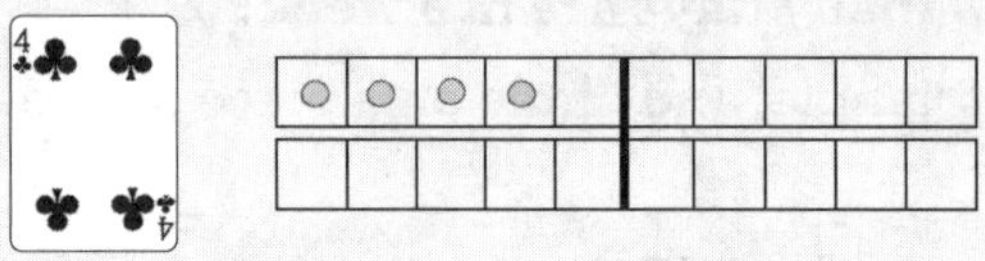

Sample first play.

Take turns playing cards, adding counters to the double ten-frames, and naming the total number of counters. Place the counters on the ten-frames from left to right. Once you fill the top ten-frame, continue to the bottom ten-frame.

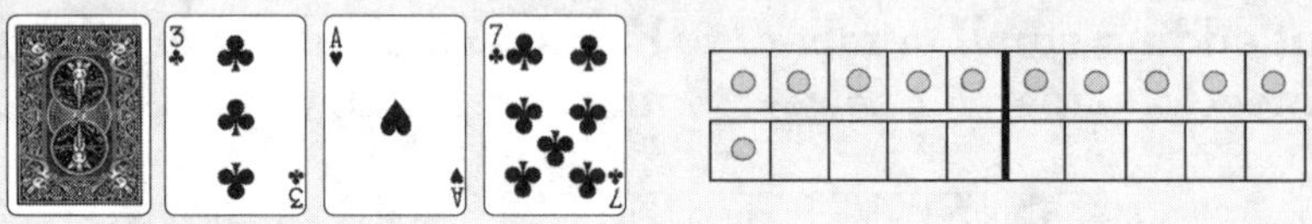

Once you fill the top ten-frame, continue adding counters to the bottom ten-frame.

Continue until one player plays a card that completes all 20 boxes in the double ten-frames without going over. If every card in your hand would cause you to go over 20, discard 1 card, and take a new card instead of playing.

The player who completes the double ten-frames shouts "Splat!" and takes all of the face-up cards. Clear the counters off the ten-frames and begin again from 0. The game ends when you have used all the cards in the draw pile. The player who has won more cards wins the game.

Variation: To make the game more challenging, don't use the counters or ten-frame. Instead, simply name the current total orally.

Workbook: Add in the Teens and Review

Have your child complete workbook pages 1.2A and 1.2B.

Lesson 1.3
Review Subtraction

	Purpose	Materials
Warm-up	• Count by 1s • Practice memory work • Review halves and fourths	• Play money
Activities	• Review subtracting numbers to 10	• Counters • Double ten-frames (Blackline Master 1) • Subtraction Climb and Slide game board (from workbook page 1.3A) • Die
Workbook	• Practice subtraction facts	• Workbook page 1.3B

Warm-up: Counting, Memory Work, and Review

- Place a handful of one-dollar bills on the table (about 20-25). **About how much do you think these bills are worth?** *Answers will vary.* Have your child count by 1s to find their value.
- **Name the months in order.** *January, February, March, April, May, June, July, August, September, October, November, December.* **How many months are in a year?** *12.*
- Draw two circles on a piece of paper. For one circle, have your child draw a line that splits the circle into halves. For the other circle, have her draw lines that split the circle into fourths.

Activity: Review Subtraction

In the last two lessons, we reviewed addition. Today, we'll review subtraction. Subtracting is the opposite of adding. When we add, we join parts to make a total. When we subtract, we split a total into parts.

Write "8 - 2 =" on a piece of paper. **Let's put counters on the ten-frame to show what this problem means.** Place 8 counters on the ten-frame. Then, remove 2 of the counters.

8 - 2 =

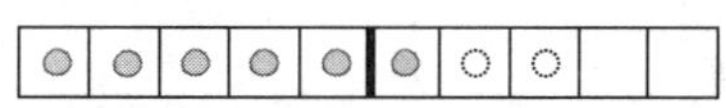

So, what does 8 minus 2 equal? *6.* Have your child complete the written equation: 8 - 2 = 6.

Briefly review subtraction vocabulary with the following questions:

- Point to the minus sign. **What do we call this sign?** *The minus sign.* **It stands for the word minus, and it means we subtract one number from another.**
- Point to the equals sign. **What do we call this sign?** *The equals sign.* **It tells us two amounts are equal to each other or are the same as each other.**
- Point to the 6. **What do we call this number?** *The difference.*

8 - 2 = 6

↑ difference

Always read the subtraction sign as minus rather than take away, since we use subtraction for more than just take-away situations. Your child will learn more about the many ways to use subtraction in Unit 4.

Children often mistakenly believe the equals sign means "the answer is coming." To help prevent this misunderstanding, always emphasize the equals sign means the amounts on either side of the equals sign are the same as each other.

Activity: Review Subtracting on the Ten-Frame

Write "7 – 3 =" on a piece of paper and place 7 counters on the ten-frame. **Imagine if I subtracted 3 counters. First, I'd take away the 2 counters on the right side of the dark line.** Point to these 2 counters.

7 - 3 =

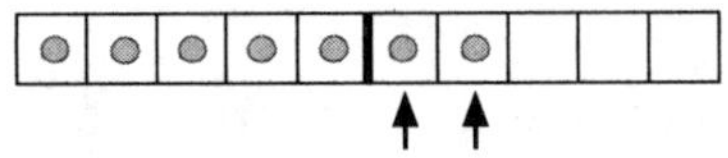

Then, I'd still need to take away 1 more counter on the other side of the dark line. Point to this counter. **How many counters would be left?** *4.*

7 - 3 =

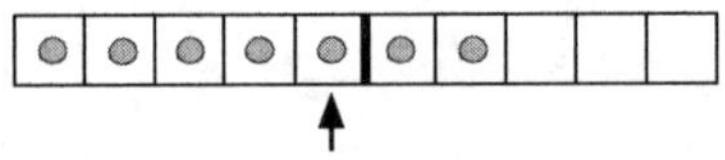

Visualizing removing the counters before physically removing them helps your child learn to solve the problems mentally.

Remove the 3 counters. Have your child complete the written equation and read it aloud: *7 minus 3 equals 4.*

7 - 3 = 4

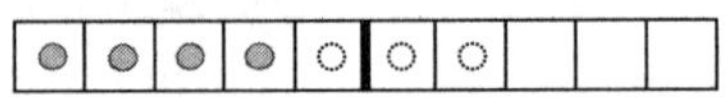

Have your child solve the following problems. Model the problems with counters on the ten-frame as needed. Encourage her to use the dark line in the middle of the ten-frame to "see" the answers rather than counting.

- 8 - 3 = *5*
- 9 - 4 = *5*
- 8 - 4 = *4*
- 8 - 1 = *7*
- 7 - 4 = *3*
- 9 - 3 = *6*
- 10 - 1 = *9*
- 7 - 2 = *5*
- 10 - 2 = *8*

Activity: Play Subtraction Climb and Slide

Play Subtraction Climb and Slide.

Subtraction Climb and Slide

Materials: Subtraction Climb and Slide game board (from workbook page 1.3A); 2 different-colored counters to use as game tokens; die

Object of the Game: Be the first player to reach the Finish square.

Each player chooses a counter to use as a game token and places it on the Start square.

On your turn, roll the die and advance your token the corresponding number of squares. Say the answer to the problem on your landing square.

If you land on a square at the bottom of a ladder, "climb" the ladder and place your game token on the square at the top of the ladder. If you land on a square at the top of a slide, slide down the slide and place your game token on the square at the bottom of the slide.

The first player to reach Finish wins the game.

If your child has trouble solving any of the problems, have her place counters on the ten-frame to find the answer. Stop her if she starts to count one-by-one.

Save this game board with your math materials so you can play again.

You may want to place your game boards and blackline masters in plastic page protectors in a binder so that you don't lose them. There are black-and-white versions available at welltrainedmind.com/mwc in case one goes missing.

Workbook: Practice Subtraction Facts and Review

Have your child complete workbook page 1.3B.

If possible, check your child's work as soon as she finishes, and have her correct any mistakes. Children tend to benefit more from immediate feedback, and your prompt attention shows that you value your child's work and effort.

Second-graders' reading and writing abilities vary widely. As your child completes the worksheets, support her as needed so that she can learn math without reading or writing holding her back. If necessary, read the directions aloud, scribe your child's answers, or have your child complete the workbook pages orally.

Don't worry if your child sometimes reverses her written numbers. This is quite common for second-graders, especially with 3s and 5s. If your child has trouble writing numbers correctly, write the numbers 1 to 9 on a card. Keep the card visible for your child to look at as she completes the workbook pages.

Lesson 1.4
Review Fact Families

	Purpose	Materials
Warm-up	• Count by 2s • Practice memory work • Review subtraction facts to 10	• Subtraction Climb and Slide game board (from workbook page 1.3A) • Die • Counters
Activities	• Review addition and subtraction fact families • Understand the relationship between addition and subtraction • Review the Part-Total Mat	• Counters • Part-Total Mat (Blackline Master 2)
Workbook	• Write fact families to match the Part-Total Mat	• Workbook pages 1.4A and 1.4B

You will review the Part-Total Mat in this lesson. In *First Grade Math with Confidence,* you placed Number Cards in the boxes on the mat. This year, you will keep the mat in a plastic page protector and write the numbers with dry-erase marker since your child will be working with greater numbers.

Warm-up: Counting, Memory Work, and Review

- **Let's see how high you can count by 2s while standing on one foot!** Have your child count by 2s as he stands on one foot: *2, 4, 6...* Have him stop once he loses his balance.
- **How many sides does a triangle have?** *3.* **A square?** *4.* **A rectangle?** *4.*
- Play Subtraction Climb and Slide. See Lesson 1.3 (page 19) for directions.

If you forgot to save the game board, you'll find extra copies at welltrainedmind.com/mwc.

Activity: Review Fact Families

In the last lesson, we reviewed subtraction. Today, we'll review the connection between addition and subtraction.

Addition and subtraction are opposites. Have your child name a few pairs of opposites. **When we add, we join two parts to make a total.** Place 5 counters of one color and 3 counters of another color on the table. Push the two groups of counters together.

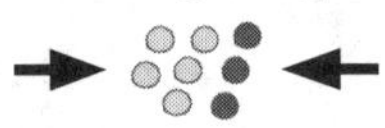

When we subtract, we split a total into parts. Separate the 8 counters back into a group of 5 and a group of 3.

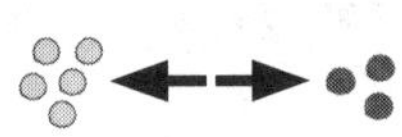

Let's pretend the counters are candies. You have 5 candies of one color and 3 candies of another color. Push the two groups of counters together again. **What two addition equations describe joining the two parts to make a total?** *5 + 3 = 8 and 3 + 5 = 8.* Have your child write the 2 equations on a piece of paper.

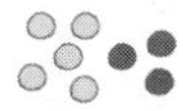

$$5 + 3 = 8$$
$$3 + 5 = 8$$

Both equations describe joining a group of 5 and a group of 3. It doesn't matter which order we join the two parts, because we get a total of 8 either way.

> The fact that we can add numbers in any order is called the commutative property of addition. Your second-grader does not need to memorize the name of this property; he only needs to be able to use it.

Separate the 8 counters again into a group of 5 and a group of 3. **When you separate a total into two parts, you subtract. What 2 subtraction equations describe splitting the total into two parts?** *8 – 3 = 5 and 8 – 5 = 3.* Have your child write the 2 equations on a piece of paper.

$$8 - 3 = 5$$
$$8 - 5 = 3$$

> If your child writes the numbers in the wrong order, say: **Mathematicians have agreed that we always start subtraction problems with the total. That way, it is clear which number is the total and which number is the part.** Avoid saying that subtraction equations must always begin with the greater number, since this rule breaks down later for negative numbers.

Point to the list of equations. **This group of addition and subtraction facts is a fact family. The fact family shows the relationships between the numbers.**

Activity: Review the Part-Total Mat

We can use the Part-Total Mat to show how we join and split groups, too. Show your child the Part-Total Mat (Blackline Master 2).

> See the Week 1 **Teaching Math with Confidence** for more on the benefits of the Part-Total Mat.

This time let's pretend you have 8 candies of one color and 2 candies of another color. Place 8 counters of one color and 2 counters of another color on the table. **Here's how we use the Part-Total Mat to show the parts and total.**

- **You have 8 candies of one color. That's one part.** Use a dry-erase marker to write 8 on the mat.
- **You have 2 candies of a different color. That's the other part.** Write 2 on the mat.
- **When you join the parts, how many candies do you have?** *10.* **So, the total is 10.** Write 10 on the mat.

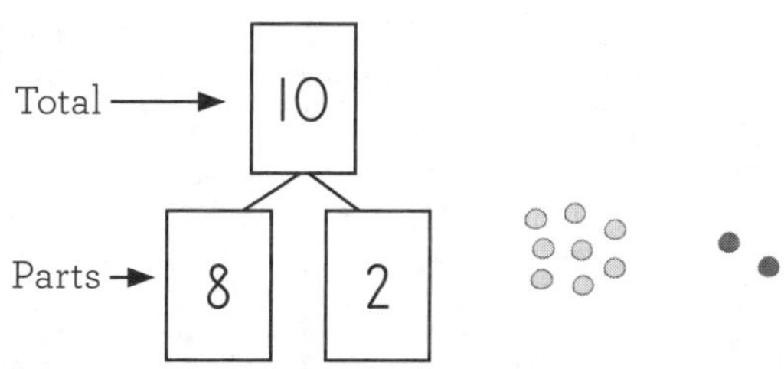

> The parts on the Part-Total Mat can be written in any order, but the total always goes in the box at the top.

Have your child write the matching fact family. If he's not sure what to write, join or separate the counters to prompt him.

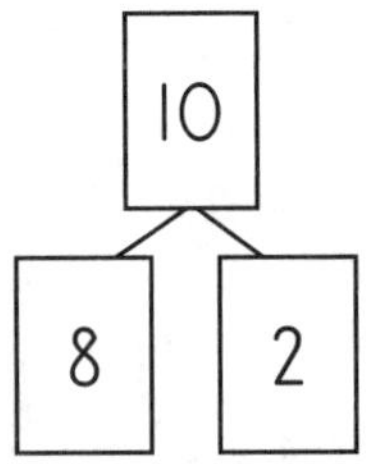

8 + 2 = 10
2 + 8 = 10
10 - 8 = 2
10 - 2 = 8

Place 4 counters of one color and 4 counters of another color on the table. Write 4, 4, and 8 on the Part-Total Mat. Have your child write the matching fact family. **If the parts are the same, the fact family has only two equations.**

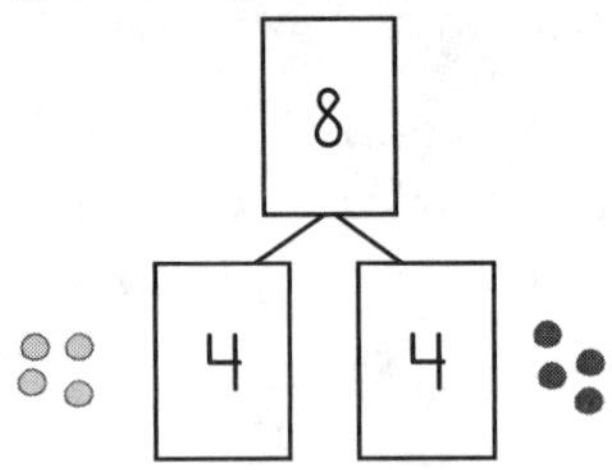

4 + 4 = 8
8 - 4 = 4

It might feel silly to use the Part-Total Mat for small numbers, since you already know how to add and subtract with these numbers. But, knowing how to use the Part-Total Mat will help you solve word problems with larger numbers later in the year.

Workbook: Write Fact Families and Review

Have your child complete workbook pages 1.4A and 1.4B.

Lesson 1.5
Enrichment and Review (Optional)

	Purpose	Materials
Warm-up	• Count to 100 • Review your child's favorite or most challenging activities from Week 1	• Varies, depending on the activities you choose
Picture Book	• Find multiple combinations that equal a given number	• *Math-terpieces: The Art of Problem-Solving*, by Greg Tang
Enrichment Activity	• Create number riddles about a favorite collection	• 20 items from your child's favorite collection, such as stuffed animals, marbles, toy cars, ponies, or plastic figurines

The final lesson each week is an optional enrichment and review lesson. If you prefer to teach math 4 days per week, skip this lesson entirely or incorporate the picture book and enrichment activity into your week at another time. See page 5 in the Introduction for more information.

Note there are no workbook pages for Enrichment and Review lessons.

Warm-up: Counting, Memory Work, and Review

- Have your child count to 100.
- Review the following memory work facts that your child learned in first grade:
    - Show your child a penny, nickel, dime, and quarter. Have her tell the name of each coin and how much it's worth.
    - **Name the days of the week in order.** *Sunday, Monday, Tuesday, Wednesday, Thursday, Friday, Saturday.* **How many days are in a week?** *7.*
    - **Name the months in order.** *January, February, March, April, May, June, July, August, September, October, November, December.* **How many months are in a year?** *12.*
    - **How many sides does a triangle have?** *3.* **A square?** *4.* **A rectangle?** *4.*
- If you have time, repeat one or two of the activities from this week's lessons. Choose activities your child especially enjoyed or found challenging.

Math Picture Book: *Math-terpieces: The Art of Problem-Solving*

Read *Math-terpieces: The Art of Problem-Solving*, by Greg Tang. As you read, enjoy the famous artworks, and have your child solve the number riddles on each page. (You can find suggested problem-solving strategies and answers at the back of the book.)

These riddles can take some time. If your child's attention lags, break up the reading and do a few pages each day for several days.

Enrichment Activity: Make Your Own Number Riddles

Have your child choose about 20 objects from one of her favorite collections and sort the objects into smaller groups. (See Materials for examples.)

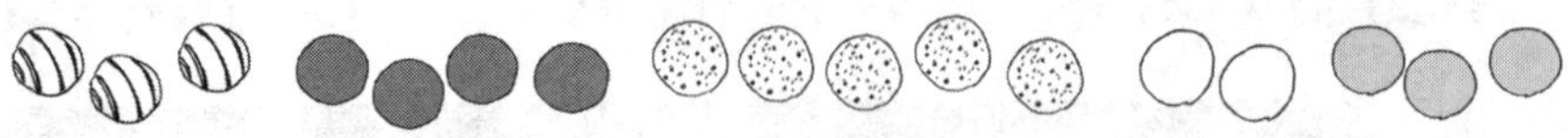

Sample collection, sorted into smaller groups

Pose some number riddles about the collection. For example, for the above marble collection, you might ask: **How many ways can you make 6?** *2 ways.*

2 ways to make 6 with the sample collection

Or, **How many ways can you make 9?** *3 ways.*

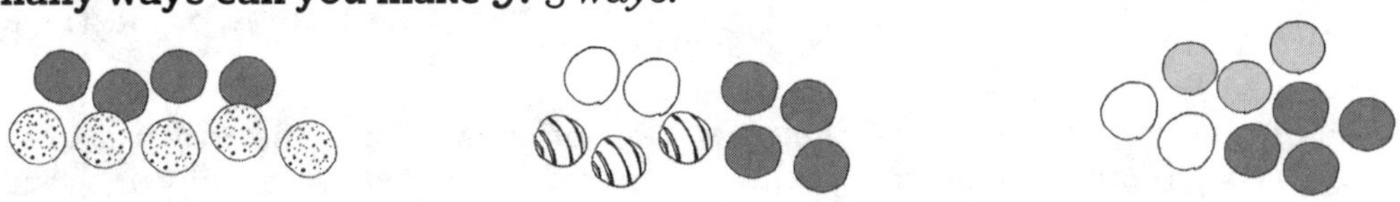

3 ways to make 9 with the sample collection

Have your child create some number riddles for you to solve, too.

The purpose of the enrichment lessons is to help your child enjoy math, develop a positive attitude toward math, and appreciate how math is used in everyday life. Feel free to adapt the enrichment activity directions to fit your family. Simplify them if you're short on time, or use different materials if you don't have the exact items listed. Or, if your child is particularly excited about a project, make the project more elaborate and spend more time on it.

Week 1 Answer Key

1.1A

See the Instructor Guide for how to play.
Save this game board for future lessons.

Addition Climb and Slide

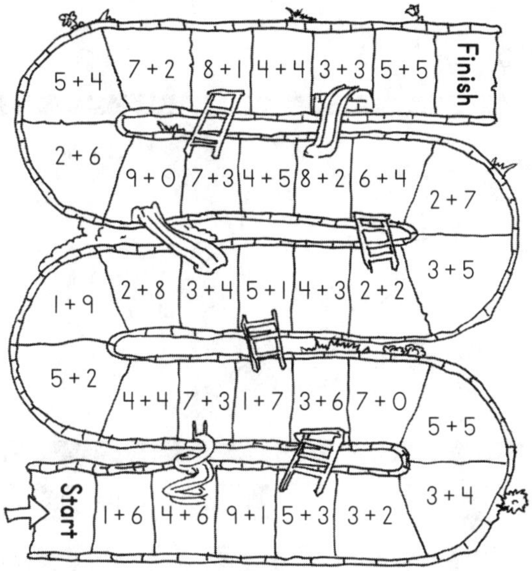

1.1B

Trace and copy.

0	1	2	3	4
0	1	2	3	4

5	6	7	8	9
5	6	7	8	9

Complete.

4 + 2 = 6　　2 + 3 = 5　　6 + 2 = 8

1 + 5 = 6　　4 + 1 = 5　　3 + 2 = 5

1 + 6 = 7　　2 + 2 = 4　　0 + 4 = 4

Complete.

5¢ 1¢ 1¢ 1¢ — 8 ¢

1¢ 1¢ 1¢ — 3 ¢

5¢ 5¢ 5¢ — 15 ¢

10¢ 1¢ — 11 ¢

1.2A

Complete.

7 + 2 = 9 17 + 2 = 19	4 + 5 = 9 14 + 5 = 19
3 + 6 = 9 13 + 6 = 19	1 + 6 = 7 11 + 6 = 17
4 + 4 = 8 14 + 4 = 18	5 + 5 = 10 15 + 5 = 20

Write the sum of each row of cards.

4 5 0 6 1 — Sum: 16

8 3 0 2 4 — Sum: 17

7 5 0 4 3 — Sum: 19

1.2B

Ava made a tally chart of the weather each day. Use the chart to answer the questions.

How many days were cloudy? 7

How many days were sunny? 9

How many days were rainy? 3

Weather Tally Chart

Cloudy Days	~~||||~~ ||
Sunny Days	~~||||~~ ||||
Rainy Days	|||

Circle the greater number in each pair.

(7) 5	4 (8)	10 (11)
(20) 2	11 (15)	12 (18)

Color the numbers you say when you count by 2s.

1	2	3	4	5	6	7	8	9	10
11	12	13	14	15	16	17	18	19	20
21	22	23	24	25	26	27	28	29	30
31	32	33	34	35	36	37	38	39	40

Week 1 Answer Key

1.3A

See the Instructor Guide for how to play. Save this game board for future lessons.

Subtraction Climb and Slide

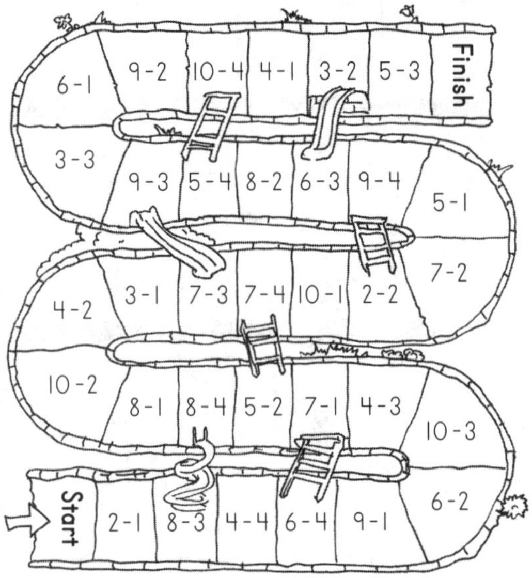

1.3B

Complete.

5 - 1 = 4 4 - 4 = 0 10 - 2 = 8

8 - 0 = 8 8 - 1 = 7 5 - 2 = 3

10 - 3 = 7 4 - 3 = 1 8 - 3 = 5

Color the triangles. X the shapes that are not triangles.

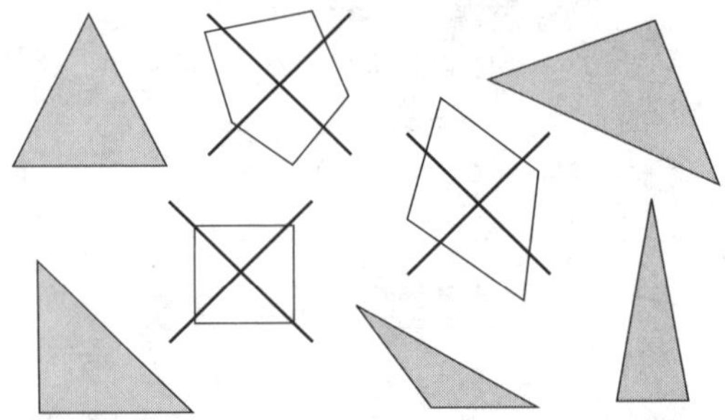

Write the number that comes before and after.

4 5 6 9 10 11 6 7 8

18 19 20 12 13 14 15 16 17

1.4A

Complete.

7: 4 and 3 — 4 + 3 = 7

9: 1 and 8 — 1 + 8 = 9

9: 7 and 2 — 7 + 2 = 9

Complete the fact families to match the Part-Total Diagrams.

10: 3 and 7

3 + 7 = 10
7 + 3 = 10
10 - 3 = 7
10 - 7 = 3

9: 4 and 5

4 + 5 = 9
5 + 4 = 9
9 - 4 = 5
9 - 5 = 4

1.4B

Draw a line that splits each cookie in half.

Sample answers. Many answers are possible.

Complete.

9 - 1 = 8 6 - 2 = 4 9 - 4 = 5

10 - 4 = 6 5 - 4 = 1 3 - 1 = 2

7 - 2 = 5 5 - 3 = 2 9 - 0 = 9

Complete.

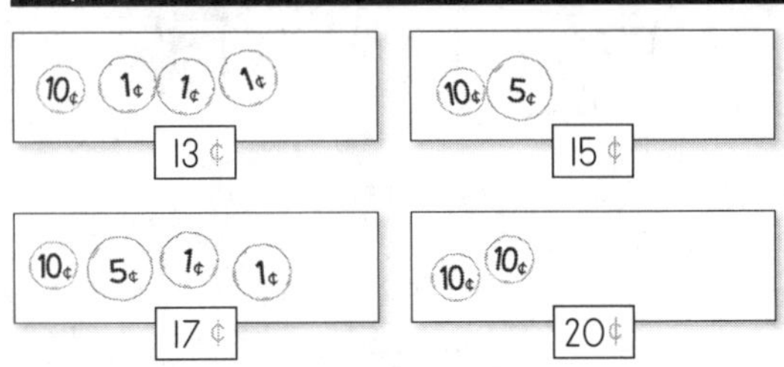

Week 2
Review Comparing and Introduce the Number Line

Overview

In first grade, your child learned how to compare numbers to 100. This week, he will learn how to put comparisons in written form with the <, >, or = signs. You'll also introduce the number line and teach him how to identify numbers on the number line.

Lesson 2.1	Write <, >, and = Signs
Lesson 2.2	Read <, >, and = Signs
Lesson 2.3	Introduce the Number Line
Lesson 2.4	Count Forwards and Backwards on the Number Line
Lesson 2.5	Enrichment and Review (Optional)

Teaching Math with Confidence: How to Use the Blank Number Line

This week, you'll introduce your child to a new way to represent numbers: the number line. You'll use the Blank Number Line (Blackline Master 3) for all number line activities in *Second Grade Math with Confidence.*

Since this number line is unlabeled, you can use it represent any set of 20 counting numbers. You'll use small slips of paper or sticky notes to label the decades, and then your child will use his number sense to identify the other numbers. For example, in Lesson 2.3, you'll label the number line with 0, 10, and 20 and challenge him to identify the unlabeled tick marks.

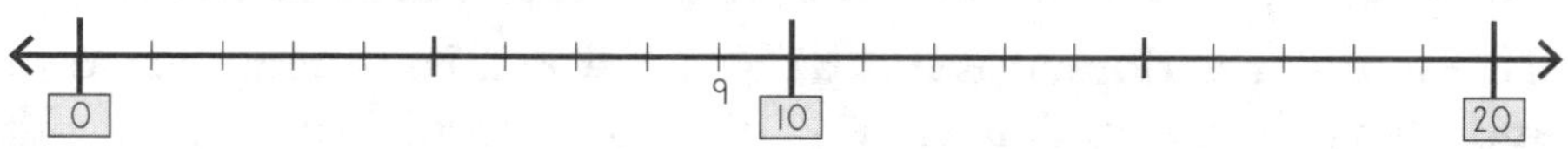

Since this number is 1 less than 10, it must be 9.

Reasoning about numbers on the number line helps your child develop deeper number sense and better understand the relationships between numbers. But the number line's benefits don't stop there. Working with number lines also lays the groundwork for many more advanced topics.

This year, your child will build on his number line knowledge to read bars on bar graphs, tell time to the minute, and measure length in inches and centimeters. In future grades, he'll broaden his understanding of number lines to fractions, decimals, negative numbers, and even coordinate grids. So, as you play Number Line Crash this week, give yourself a pat on the back for preparing your child for many future years of math!

Extra Materials Needed for Week 2

- 2 toothpicks, narrow strips of paper, or crayons
- Scissors
- Tape
- For optional Enrichment and Review Lesson:
    - *Your Fantastic Elastic Brain: Stretch It, Shape It,* by JoAnn Deak
    - Chalk, masking tape, or a long strip of paper

Lesson 2.1
Write <, >, and = Signs

	Purpose	Materials
Warm-up	• Count by 2s • Practice memory work • Review comparing numbers	• Counters
Activities	• Learn the meaning of the < and > signs • Compare numbers with the <, >, and = signs	• 2 toothpicks, narrow strips of paper, or crayons
Workbook	• Compare numbers with the <, >, and = signs	• Workbook pages 2.1A and 2.1B

Warm-up: Counting, Memory Work, and Review

- Place a handful of counters on the table (about 30-40). **About how many counters do you think there are?** *Answers will vary.* Have your child count by 2s to find the total.
- **What do we call the result when we add numbers together?** *The sum.* **What do we call the result when we subtract a number from another number?** *The difference.*
- Secretly choose a number between 1 and 100. **I'm thinking of a number that's greater than 1 and less than 100.** Have your child guess your number. After each guess, tell whether your secret number is more or less than her guess. Continue until she figures out your secret number.

Activity: Introduce < and > Signs

Mathematicians have invented many signs so that they don't have to write everything in words. What are some math signs you already know? *Sample answers: plus sign, minus sign, equals sign.* **Today, you'll learn two signs we use to compare numbers.**

We often describe family relationships in 2 different ways. For example, we say that I am your mother, and that you are my daughter. (Adjust this wording based on your relationship with your child.) Discuss other examples of relationships that can be described in two ways, such as grandfather/grandson, uncle/niece, or father/son.

When we compare 2 numbers, we can describe the numbers' relationship in 2 different ways, too. Let's use 6 and 7 as an example. 7 is greater than 6, and 6 is less than 7. Write both statements in words on a piece of paper.

7 is greater than 6. 6 is less than 7.

These are the signs mathematicians use to mean *is greater than* and *is less than*. Write 7 > 6 and 6 < 7 below the previous statements.

7 is greater than 6. 6 is less than 7.
7 > 6 6 < 7

Point to the greater-than sign. **This is called the greater-than sign.**

7 > 6
↑
greater than sign

Point to the less-than sign. **This is called the less-than sign.**

6 < 7

less than sign

People often get confused by the greater-than and less-than signs since they look so much alike! It helps if you remember that the small, pointy part of the sign always points to the lesser number, and the big, wide part of the sign always opens toward the greater number. Sometimes kids like to pretend that the sign is an alligator's mouth that wants to chomp the bigger number!

7 > 6 　　　 6 < 7

The small, pointy part always points to the lesser number.

7 > 6 　　　 6 < 7

The wider part always opens toward the greater number.

> Children often love the alligator image and find it helpful for remembering the signs' meanings. Have fun pretending to chomp the numbers with your child, but make sure you don't neglect the signs' official names so that your child isn't confused down the road when she sees inequalities with variables in pre-algebra or algebra. You'll teach her how to read both signs in Lesson 2.2, and then she'll practice their names for memory work in Week 4.

Write 8 twice on a piece of paper, with a little space between the two numbers. **Which number is greater?** *Neither!*

8 　 8

8 is equal to 8. Write an equals sign between the two numbers. **The equals sign has 2 lines like the greater than and less than signs. But the two lines open equally wide on both sides, just like the amounts on either side are equal to each other.**

8 = 8

Activity: Write <, >, and = Signs

Write 15 and 12 on a piece of paper with a little space between them. Give your child 2 toothpicks, narrow strips of paper, or crayons and have her use them to construct the correct sign between the two numbers.

15 > 12

Then, have her remove the toothpicks and write the greater-than sign in its place.

15 > 12

> Writing these signs can be very difficult for second graders. Creating the < and > signs with hands-on materials helps your child visualize the correct sign before trying to write it. If she needs more support, have her draw a dot at the end of each toothpick, remove the toothpicks, and then connect the dots.

Repeat with the following pairs of numbers. For each, have your child first construct the correct sign with toothpicks. Then, have her remove the toothpicks and write the sign.

26 < 46 　　 85 = 85 　　 85 > 68

97 > 90 　　 97 < 100 　　 28 < 45

Have your child write several pairs of numbers of her own choosing and write the correct symbol between them.

Workbook: Compare Numbers with the <, >, and = Signs and Review

Have your child complete workbook pages 2.1A and 2.1B.

Lesson 2.2
Read <, >, and = Signs

	Purpose	Materials
Warm-up	• Count by 5s • Practice memory work • Review adding small numbers	• Coins • Playing cards
Activities	• Learn to read the < and > signs • Compare ages with the <, >, and = signs	• None
Workbook	• Compare numbers with the <, >, and = signs	• Workbook pages 2.2A and 2.2B

Some children find review activities confidence-building and affirming. Others feel insulted when asked to revisit skills they've already learned. If you have a child who hates review, focus your warm-up time on the topics your child most needs to practice and skip reviewing material that he already knows well. Or, save these warm-up exercises for the end of the lesson so that his dislike of them doesn't ruin the entire session.

Warm-up: Counting, Memory Work, and Review

- Place about 12-15 nickels on the table. **About how many cents do you think the coins are worth?** *Answers will vary.* Have your child count the nickels by 5s to find their value.
- Show your child a penny, nickel, dime, and quarter. Have him tell the name of each coin and how much it's worth.
- Play Make 20 Splat. See Lesson 1.2 (page 16) for directions.

Activity: Read the < and > Signs

In the last lesson, you learned how to write the greater-than and less-than signs. Today, you'll learn how to read these signs.

Write 14 and 17 on a piece of paper. **Describe the relationship between the numbers two ways.** *14 is less than 17. 17 is greater than 14.* Write both statements on a piece of paper, and write the corresponding inequality below each.

14 is less than 17. 17 is greater than 14.

14 < 17 17 > 14

Mathematical statements that use the = sign are called *equations,* while statements that use the < and > signs are called *inequalities.* Your child does not need to memorize these terms, but this Instructor Guide will use them for clarity's sake.

Remember, the small, pointy part of the sign always points to the lesser number, and the wide-open part of the sign always opens toward the greater number.

We read mathematical statements from left to right, just like sentences. But it can be hard to remember whether to say "less than" or "greater than" since the two signs look so much alike.

If you see the pointy part first, say "is less than," because you know you have already said the lesser number. If you see the wide-open part first, say "is greater than," because you know you've already said the greater number.

Secretly write 5 < 6 on a piece of paper and cover it with a slip of paper. Gradually slide the slip of paper from left to right and read each number or symbol as you uncover it: **5 is less than 6.**

5 5 < 5 < 6

Children often find it more difficult to read the < and > signs than to write them. Covering part of the inequality with paper focuses your child's attention on the left-most part of the sign so that he can read it correctly.

Secretly write 8 > 0 and cover it with a slip of paper. Have your child gradually slide the slip of paper from left to right and read the inequality: **8 is greater than 0.**

8 8 > 8 > 0

Have your child read the following inequalities. Use the slip of paper as needed.

15 > 14 37 < 53 50 = 50

15 is greater than 14. 37 is less than 53. 50 equals 50.

Activity: Compare Ages with the <, >, and = Signs

Make a simple chart with the names and ages of 5-6 of your child's siblings, neighbors, or friends. Include your child, and try to include children who are younger, older, and the same age as your child.

Name	Age
Lily	3
Noah	15
William	7
Ava	6
Maya	11
Me	7

Sample chart

Have your child write several inequalities about the ages with the <, >, and = signs and discuss the real-world meaning of each statement.

3 < 15 7 = 7

3 is less than 15. Lily is younger than Noah. 7 equals 7. William and I are the same age.

Workbook: Compare Numbers with the <, >, and = Sign and Review

Have your child complete workbook pages 2.2A and 2.2B. After your child completes 2.2A, have him read several of the inequalities or equations to you. For example: *72 is greater than 49.*

Many answers are possible for the problems at the bottom of page 2.2A. For example, for the first problem (6 > __), your child can write any number less than 6 to make the statement true.

Lesson 2.3
Introduce the Number Line

	Purpose	Materials
Warm-up	• Count by 10s • Practice memory work • Review reading inequalities	• Play money
Activities	• Introduce the number line • Identify unlabeled numbers on the number line	• Blank Number Line (Blackline Master 3) • Scissors • Tape • Counters
Workbook	• Identify unlabeled numbers on the number line	• Workbook pages 2.3A and 2.3B

This lesson directs you to label the Blank Number Line (Blackline Master 3) with small sticky notes or slips of paper. If you prefer, you can instead laminate the Blank Number Line (or cover it with packing tape) and then write the numbers with dry-erase marker.

Warm-up: Counting, Memory Work, and Review

- Place about 6-8 ten-dollar bills on the table. **About how many dollars do you think the money is worth?** *Answers will vary.* Have your child count the bills by 10s to find their value.
- **What do we call the result when we add numbers together?** *The sum.* **What do we call the result when we subtract a number from another number?** *The difference.*
- Write the following inequalities on a piece of paper and have your child read them.
    - 86 > 51. *86 is greater than 51.*
    - 24 < 25. *24 is less than 25.*
    - 73 = 73. *73 equals 73.*

Activity: Introduce the Number Line

Today, you'll learn a new way to represent numbers: the number line. Show your child the Blank Number Line (Blackline Master 3). Cut the page apart on the dotted line and tape the two pieces together.

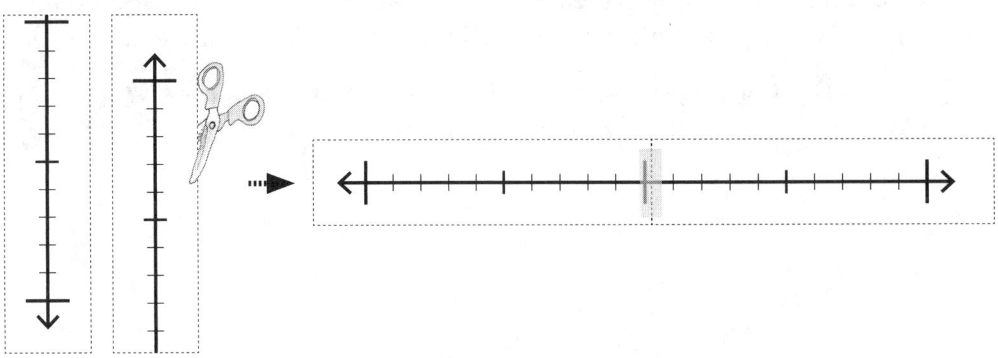

Try to line up the two edges without overlapping the paper, and place a piece of transparent tape on both the front and back of the joined edges. This will make it easier to fold the number line for storage.

Write 0, 10, and 20 on small slips of paper or sticky notes and place them on the number line.

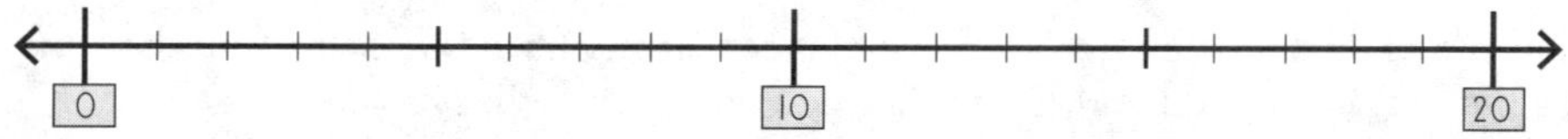

On this number line, each tick mark stands for the next counting number. It takes a long time to write every number, so we'll label only a few numbers. I bet you can figure out where the other numbers are.

Point to 10. **If this mark is 10, where is 11?** *Child points to next tick mark.*

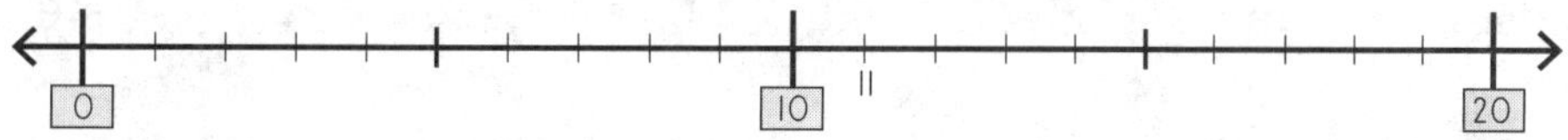

Make sure your child points directly at the tick mark, not the space to the left or right of the tick mark. In third grade, your child will learn how to identify fractions and mixed numbers in the spaces between tick marks.

Where is 9? *Child points to tick mark before 10.*

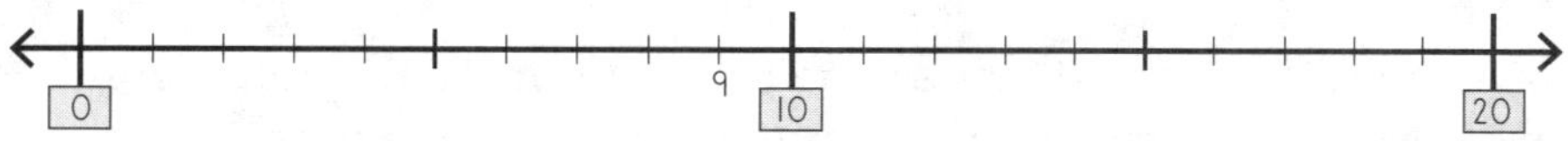

Have your child point to 0, 1, 2, 20, and 19 (one at a time).

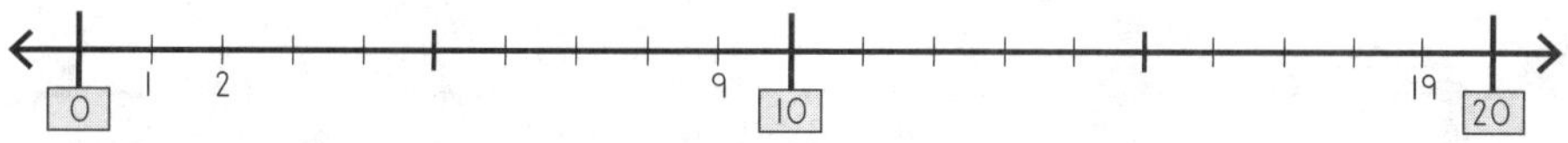

Then, reverse the process. Point to 13. **What number is this?** *13.* **How do you know?** *Possible answer: It's 3 tick marks after 10.*

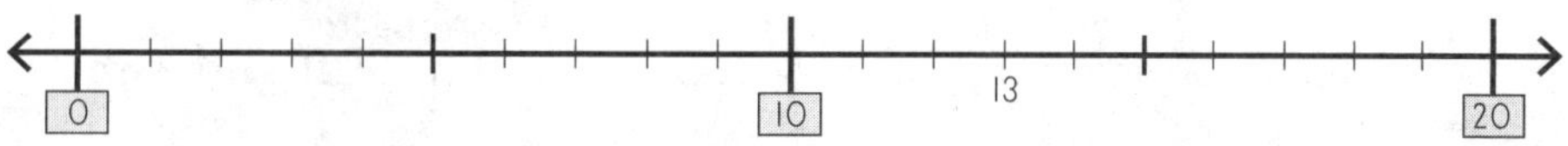

Point to 5. **What number is this?** *5.* **How do you know?** *Possible answers: It's 5 tick marks after 0. It's 5 tick marks before 10.*

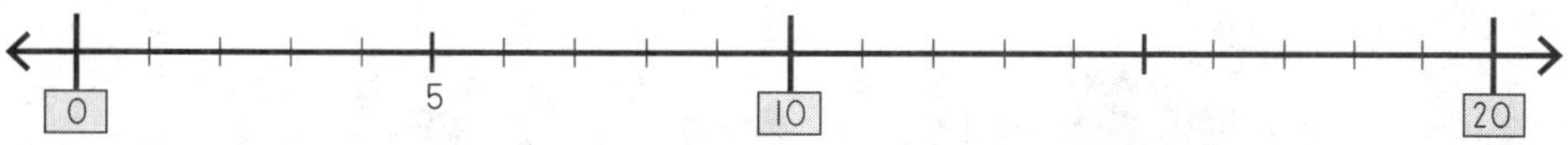

5 is halfway between 0 and 10. Do you notice how this tick mark is a little longer and darker than most of the others? That makes it easier to see, just like the dark bar in the middle of the ten-frame.

Point to 6, 7, 15, and 16 (one at a time) and have your child identify them.

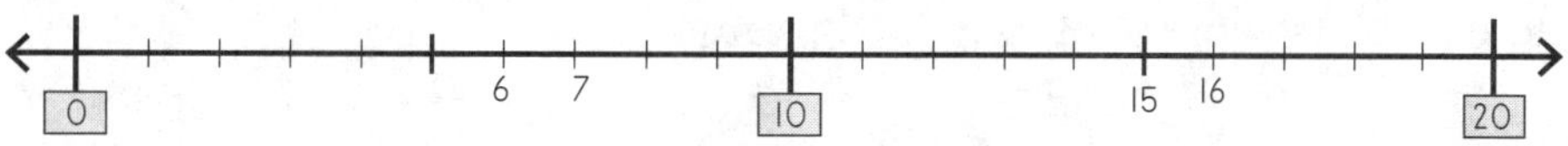

There are infinitely many numbers, so no number line could ever show all of them. Point out the arrows at either end of the number line. **These arrows help remind us that the numbers continue further.**

See the Week 2 **Teaching Math with Confidence** for more information about number lines.

Activity: Play Number Line Bump

Play several rounds of Number Line Bump with the Blank Number Line labeled with 0, 10, and 20.

The game helps your child become more comfortable identifying numbers on the number line. It also previews using the number line to add and subtract, which your child will explore more in future grades.

Number Line Bump

Materials: Blank Number Line (Blackline Master 3); 4 counters of 2 different colors, 1 die

Object of the Game: Bump all of your opponent's counters off of the number line.

Give each player 4 counters, and take turns placing your counters on the number line. Each counter must be on one of the tick marks, and there may only be one counter on each tick mark.

The first player rolls the die and moves one of her counters the corresponding number of tick marks. For example, if your counter is on a 5 and you roll a 3, you can move your counter to either 2 or 8.

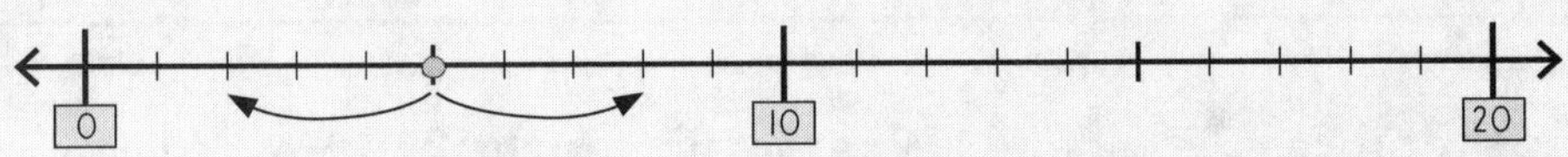

Two possible moves if you roll a 3.

If your opponent has a counter on your landing spot, "bump" it and remove it from the game.

Take turns rolling and moving your counters. The player who removes all of the other player's counters first wins.

Make sure your child announces her landing spot after each move so that she practices identifying numbers on the number line as she plays.

Workbook: Identify Numbers on the Number Line and Review

Have your child complete workbook pages 2.3A and 2.3B.

Lesson 2.4
Count Forwards and Backwards on the Number Line

	Purpose	Materials
Warm-up	• Count starting at numbers other than 1 • Practice memory work • Review addition facts to 10	• Counters • Addition Climb and Slide game board (from workbook page 1.1A) • Die
Activities	• Count by 2s, 5s, and 10s on the number line • Count backwards on the number line • Understand more and less with numbers on the number line	• Blank Number Line (Blackline Master 3)
Workbook	• Count by 1s, 2s, and 5s • Solve number line riddles with *more* and *less*	• Workbook pages 2.4A and 2.4B

Warm-up: Counting, Memory Work, and Review

- Have your child count forward from the following numbers. Stop him after he reaches the last number listed in the sample answers.
    - **Count forward from 77:** *77, 78, 79, 80, 81.*
    - **Count forward from 58:** *58, 59, 60, 61, 62.*
    - **Count forward from 96:** *96, 97, 98, 99, 100.*

> Children often have trouble switching decades when counting (for example, going from 79 to 80). This activity reinforces this important skill. If your child has trouble, have him point to each number on the 100 Chart (Blackline Master 4).

- **Name the days of the week in order.** *Sunday, Monday, Tuesday, Wednesday, Thursday, Friday, Saturday.* **How many days are in a week?** *7.*
- Play Addition Climb and Slide. See Lesson 1.1 (page 14) for directions.

Activity: Count Forwards on the Number Line

In the last lesson, we used the number line to show the numbers from 0 to 20. Today, you'll learn how to count forwards and backwards on the number line and solve number line riddles.

We can choose which part of the number line we want to show. Today, we'll show the numbers from 30 to 50. Write 30, 40, and 50 on small slips of paper or sticky notes and place them on the number line. Have your child point to the following numbers: 32, 35, 36, 44, 45, 49.

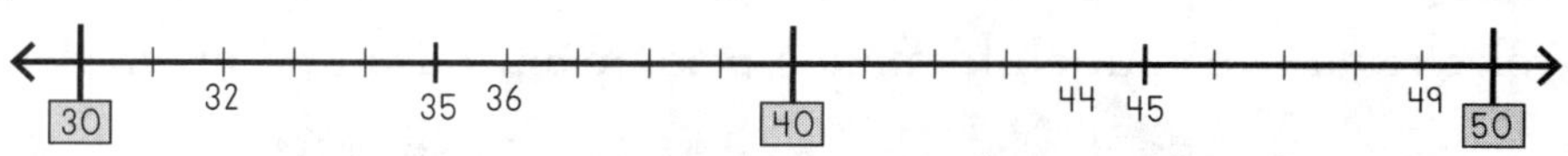

We can count on the number line, just like the 100 Chart. Have your child count by 1s from 30 to 50 on the number line. Stop him several times as he counts and have him check that his finger is touching the right tick mark.

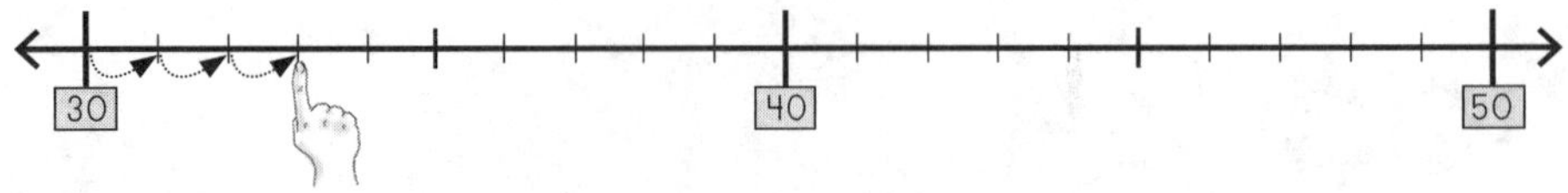

30, 31, 32, 33...

> Your child may find counting forward on the number line very easy. Do these exercises anyway, as they prepare him for a more difficult skill: counting backwards by 1s, 2s, 5s, and 10s.

Repeat with 2s, 5s, and 10s. Occasionally stop your child and have him check that his finger is touching the correct tick mark.

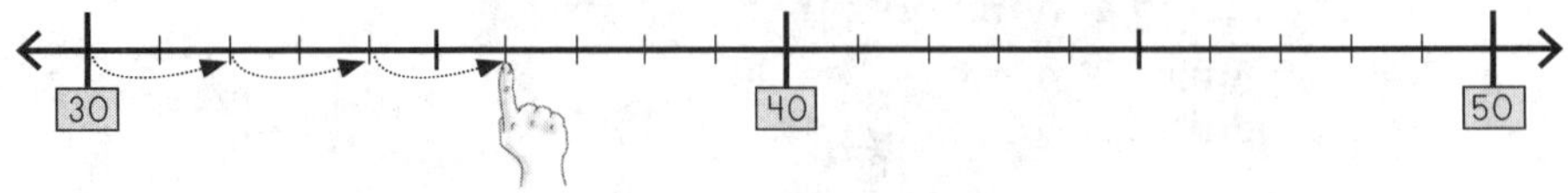

30, 32, 34, 36...

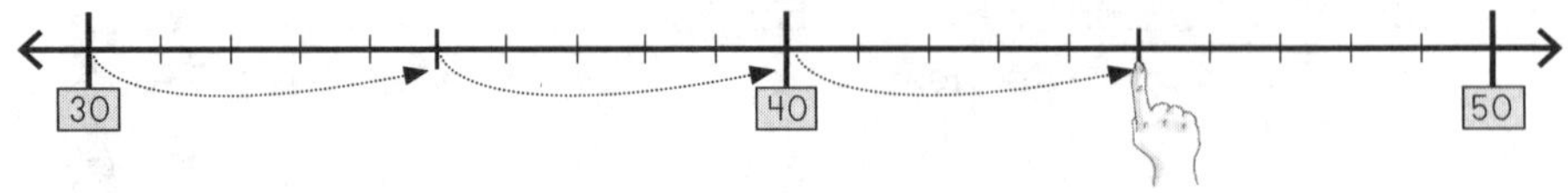

30, 35, 40, 45...

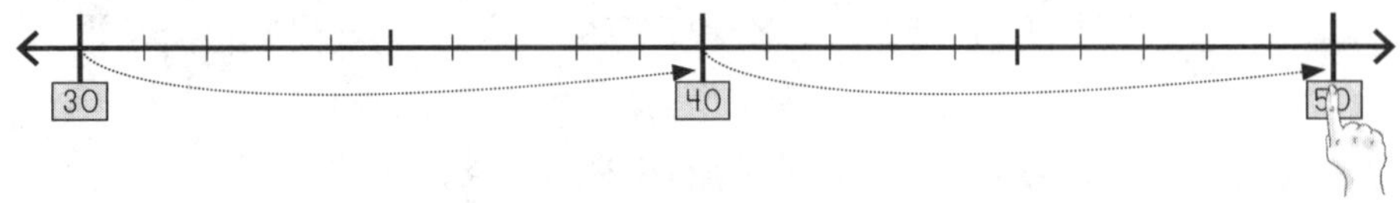

30, 40, 50...

Activity: Count Backwards on the Number Line

We can count backwards on the number line, too. Start at 50 and count backward by 1s. Have your child count backward by 1s. Again, have him touch each tick mark as he says the matching number and stop him a few times to check that his finger is in the right place.

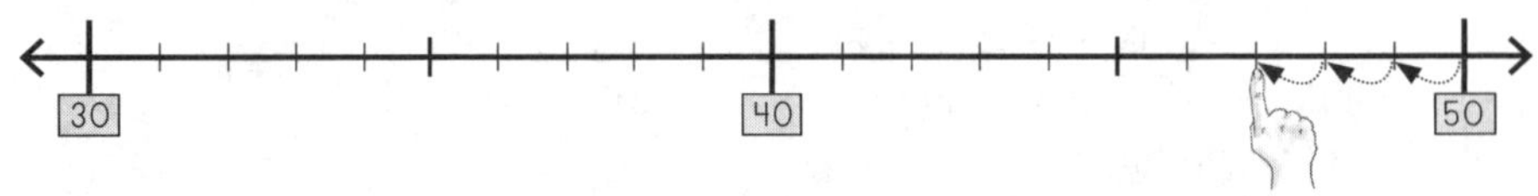

50, 49, 48, 47...

Have your child also count backwards from 50 by 2s, 5s, and 10s. Occasionally stop your child and have him check that his finger is touching the correct tick mark.

Activity: More/Less Number Line Riddles

Ask your child the following number line riddles.

- **I'm thinking of a number that is 1 more than 32. What's my number?** *33.*
- **I'm thinking of a number that is 5 more than 35. What's my number?** *40.*
- **I'm thinking of a number that is 2 more than 48. What's my number?** *50.*
- **I'm thinking of a number that is 2 less than 36. What's my number?** *34.*
- **I'm thinking of a number that is 1 less than 40. What's my number?** *39.*
- **I'm thinking of a number that is 5 less than 45. What's my number?** *40.*

Then, switch roles and have your child make up some similar number riddles to ask you.

> These riddles prepare your child to solve word problems that involve more and less later in the year.

Workbook: Number Line Riddles and Review

Have your child complete workbook pages 2.4A and 2.4B.

Lesson 2.5
Enrichment and Review (Optional)

	Purpose	Materials
Warm-up	• Count to 100 • Review memory work • Review your child's favorite or most challenging activities from Week 2	• Varies, depending on the activities you choose
Picture Book	• Learn that practicing and making mistakes helps brains grow	• *Your Fantastic Elastic Brain: Stretch It, Shape It,* by JoAnn Deak
Enrichment Activity	• Create a life-size number line	• Chalk, masking tape, or a long strip of paper

Warm-up: Counting, Memory Work, and Review

- Have your child count to 100.
- Quiz your child on the memory work through Week 2. See page 523 for the full list.
- If you have time, repeat one or two of the activities from this week's lessons. Choose activities your child especially enjoyed or found challenging.

Math Picture Book: *Your Fantastic Elastic Brain: Stretch It, Shape It*

Read *Your Fantastic Elastic Brain: Stretch It, Shape It,* by JoAnn Deak. After you read, share with your child times in your life when trying new things or making mistakes has helped you grow. Talk about how learning new concepts in math helps your child's brain grow, even when it feels hard or he makes mistakes.

Enrichment Activity: Make a Life-Size Number Line

With your child, make a large number line that shows the numbers from 0 to 100. If the weather permits and you have easy access to a large expanse of pavement, use chalk to draw the number line outside. If that's not an option, you can make your number line from a long strip of paper or a long piece of masking tape on the floor in a hallway.

Follow these steps to make a number line with 100 evenly spaced tick marks, labeled on the decades.

1. Mark your starting point with a tick mark. Have your child take 10 steps in a straight line, and make a new tick mark after each step (so that you end up with 10 roughly-equal spaces between the tick marks). Draw a straight line from the first tick mark to the last tick mark.

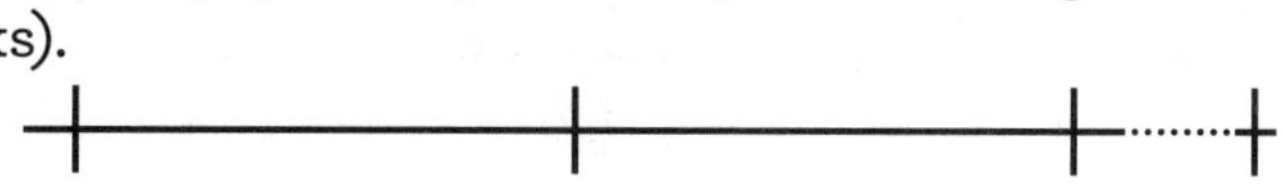

2. Label the tick marks from 0 to 100, counting by 10s. (0, 10, 20, etc.) up to 100.

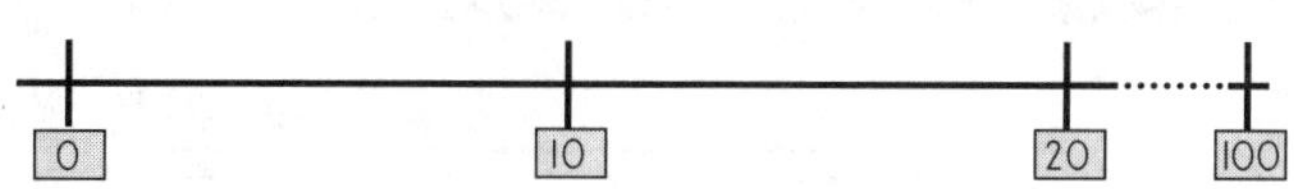

3. Divide each of the spaces in half.

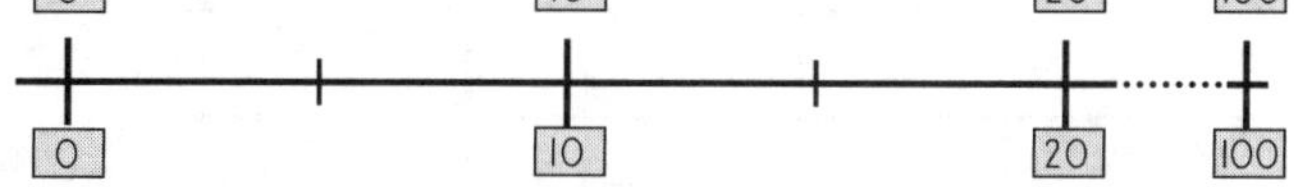

4. Draw 4 tick marks in each of the resulting spaces.

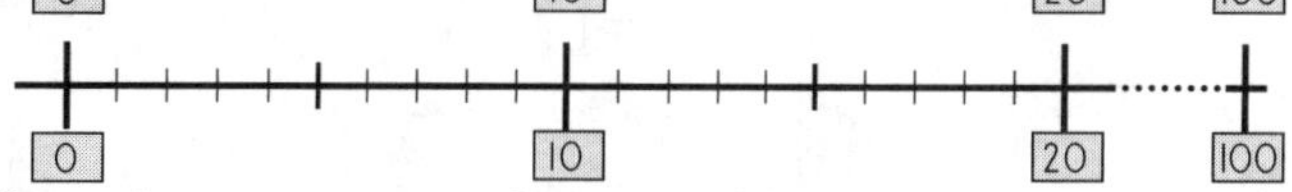

After you finish the number line, call out numbers between 0 and 100 and have your child run to the corresponding tick mark on the number line. Or, ask him some number line riddles involving more or less as in Lesson 2.4.

Week 2 Answer Key

2.1A

Complete the circles with <, >, or =

4 (<) 5	8 (>) 2	6 (=) 6
7 (=) 7	6 (>) 5	10 (>) 9
17 (>) 16	8 (<) 18	80 (>) 18
36 (<) 63	40 (<) 42	50 (=) 50
64 (<) 67	95 (=) 95	83 (>) 82

Complete the missing numbers on the 100 Chart.

51	52	53	54	55	56	57	58	59	60
61	62	63	64	65	66	67	68	69	70
71	72	73	74	75	76	77	78	79	80
81	82	83	84	85	86	87	88	89	90
91	92	93	94	95	96	97	98	99	100

2.1B

Complete the fact family to match the Part-Total Diagram.

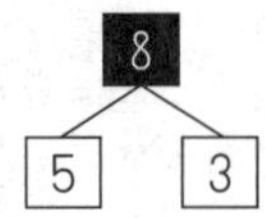

5 + 3 = 8
3 + 5 = 8
8 - 5 = 3
8 - 3 = 5

Complete. Use the ten-frame to help.

10 - 1 = 9	10 - 9 = 1
10 - 4 = 6	10 - 6 = 4
10 - 2 = 8	10 - 8 = 2
10 - 3 = 7	10 - 7 = 3
10 - 5 = 5	10 - 0 = 10

Draw lines that split each cookie into fourths.

Sample answers. Many answers are possible.

2.2A

Complete the circles with <, >, or =.

42 (>) 41	35 (<) 36	40 (=) 40
7 (<) 17	38 (>) 20	43 (>) 40
55 (<) 60	100 (>) 99	82 (<) 83
6 (<) 60	50 (=) 50	100 (>) 10
11 (>) 10	17 (<) 71	74 (>) 54

Complete each box with a number that makes the statement true.

6 > ☐	4 < ☐	5 = ☐
3 > ☐	10 < ☐	19 < ☐
26 < ☐	48 > ☐	73 = ☐
☐ > 40	☐ < 75	☐ > 82
99 < ☐	99 > ☐	99 = ☐

Many answers are possible.

2.2B

Match.

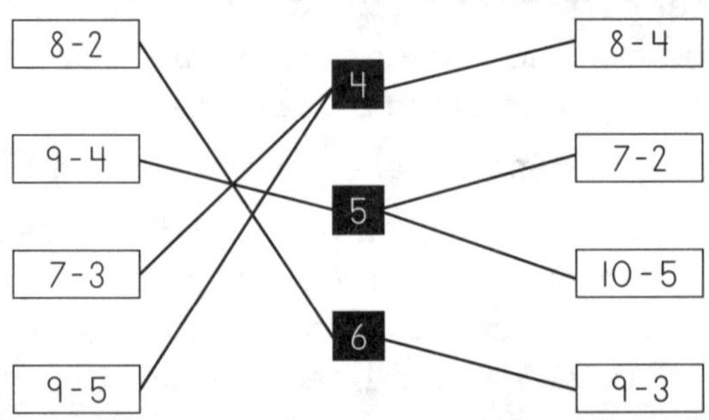

Liam flipped a coin. He made a bar graph to show how many times he flipped heads and how many times he flipped tails. Use the bar graph to answer the questions.

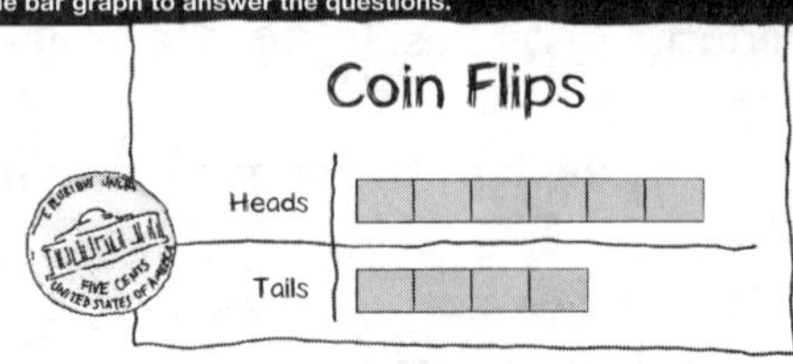

How many heads did he flip?	6	How many more heads than tails did he flip?	2
How many tails did he flip?	4	How many times did he flip the coin in all?	10

Week 2 Answer Key

2.3A

Connect each number to its spot on the number line.

Number line 0–10: 1, 4, 5, 6, 9

Number line 10–20: 12, 13, 17, 18, 20

Number line 20–30: 20, 22, 24, 26, 28

Number line 30–40: 31, 33, 35, 37, 39

2.3B

Complete.

6 + 3 = 9	3 + 1 = 4	1 + 7 = 8
2 + 6 = 8	4 + 4 = 8	3 + 2 = 5
3 + 7 = 10	2 + 5 = 7	0 + 6 = 6
5 + 4 = 9	2 + 8 = 10	1 + 9 = 10

X the shape that doesn't belong in each row.

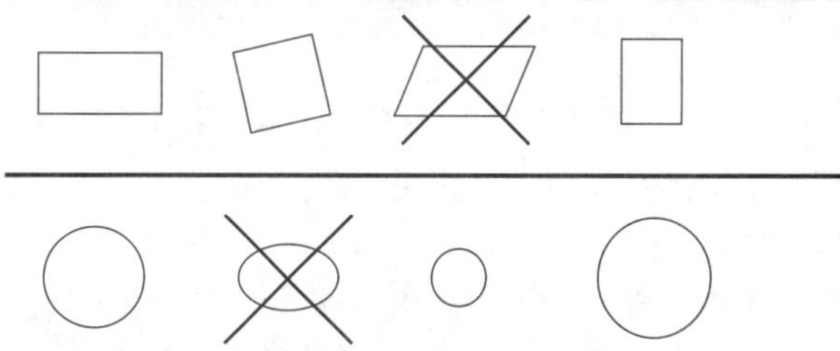

Complete.

\$10 \$10 \$5 \$5 — \$ 30

\$10 \$10 \$10 \$1 — \$ 31

2.4A

Complete the missing numbers in the sequences.

Count by 2s: 50, 52, 54, 56, 58, 60

Count by 5s: 50, 55, 60, 65, 70, 75

Count by 1s: 58, 59, 60, 61, 62, 63

Use the number line to complete.

Number line: 70, 80, 90

What number is 1 more than 80? 81	What number is 1 less than 80? 79
What number is 3 more than 75? 78	What number is 3 less than 84? 81
What number is 5 more than 70? 75	What number is 5 less than 80? 75

2.4B

Complete.

10¢ 10¢ 5¢ — 25 ¢

10¢ 10¢ 10¢ — 30 ¢

10¢ 10¢ 5¢ 1¢ — 26 ¢

10¢ 10¢ 1¢ 1¢ 1¢ — 23 ¢

Complete the circles with <, >, or =.

14 > 12	90 < 100	37 > 36
85 > 75	75 < 85	75 = 75

Complete.

6 + 3 = 9	5 + 5 = 10
1 + 8 = 9	9 + 1 = 10
0 + 9 = 9	7 + 3 = 10
7 + 2 = 9	4 + 6 = 10
5 + 4 = 9	8 + 2 = 10

Week 3
Review Place Value and Numbers to 100

Overview

This week, you'll review the numbers to 100 with base-ten blocks. You'll introduce the blocks with a fun design activity and then use the blocks to review place value, perform mental math, and find pairs that equal 100.

Lesson 3.1	Introduce Base-Ten Blocks
Lesson 3.2	Review Place Value
Lesson 3.3	Review Mental Math
Lesson 3.4	Review Pairs That Make 100
Lesson 3.5	Enrichment and Review (Optional)

Teaching Math with Confidence: Introducing Base-Ten Blocks

You'll introduce your child to base-ten blocks this week. You'll use these blocks all year long to model place value, demonstrate mental math strategies, and teach your child to add and subtract two- and three-digit numbers.

Base-ten blocks come in 4 different sizes: units, rods, flats, and large cubes. Each block is 10 times the size of the next-smaller block, just as each place in our base-ten number system has 10 times the value of the next-smaller place.

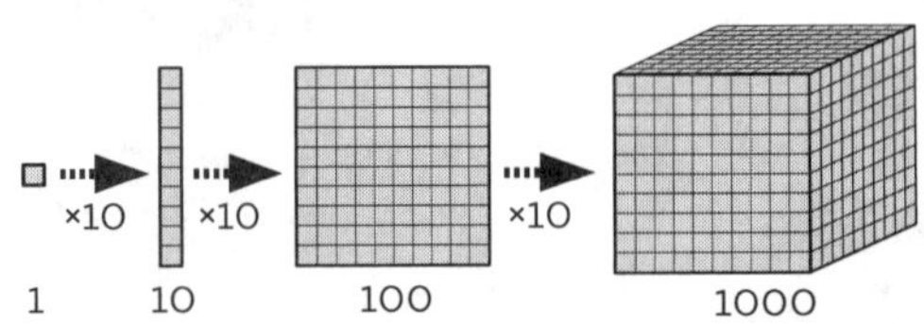

For example, here's how you'll use base-ten blocks to model the number 145:

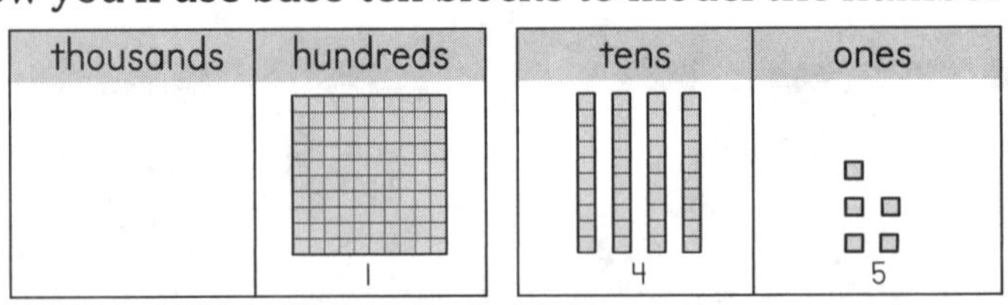

You'll use base-ten blocks to model place value in second grade.

Base-ten blocks provide a concrete way for your child to understand the abstract concept of place value. This week, your child will get to know base-ten blocks in the context of the numbers to 100 so that she's ready to use them to model larger numbers (and more complex problems) later in the year.

Extra Materials Needed for Week 3

- Napkin
- For optional Enrichment and Review Lesson:
  - *Biggest, Strongest, Fastest,* by Steve Jenkins
  - Chutes and Ladders, Rack-O, or 100 Chart (Blackline Master 4), die, and counters

Make sure that you've placed the Place-Value Chart (Blackline Master 5) in a plastic page protector so you can write numbers on it with a dry erase maker.

You will also need base-ten blocks for this week's lessons. If you do not have real base-ten blocks, you can use the paper versions on Blackline Master 11 instead.

Lesson 3.1
Introduce Base-Ten Blocks

	Purpose	Materials
Warm-up	• Count coins • Practice memory work • Review subtraction facts to 10	• Coins • Counters • Subtraction Climb and Slide game board (from workbook page 1.3A) • Die
Activities	• Introduce base-ten blocks • Find the value of combinations of tens and ones	• Base-ten blocks
Workbook	• Find the value of combinations of tens and ones	• Workbook pages 3.1A and 3.1B

Warm-up: Counting, Memory Work, and Review

- Place 6 dimes and 2 pennies on the table. **How much are the coins worth?** *62¢.*
- **What do we call the result when we add numbers together?** *The sum.* **What do we call the result when we subtract a number from another number?** *The difference.*
- Play Subtraction Climb and Slide. See Lesson 1.3 (page 19) for directions.

Activity: Introduce Base-Ten Blocks

This week, we'll review place value and mental math with the numbers to 100. We'll use a new math tool: base-ten blocks! Today, you will make designs with the blocks and count to find the value of the blocks in each design.

> See the Week 3 **Teaching Math with Confidence** for an introduction to base-ten blocks.

Show your child the set of base-ten blocks. Tell your child the name of each type of block.

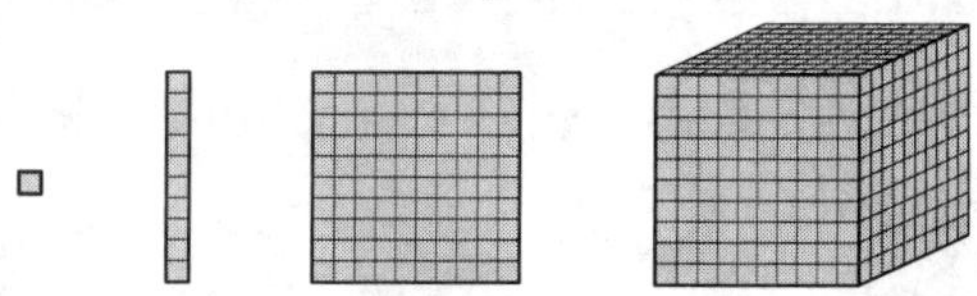

unit rod flat large cube

> These names are nicknames, not important mathematical terms, and your child does not need to memorize them.

The smallest block is the unit. The other blocks are made of these units connected together. How many units are in 1 rod? *10.* Have your child line up 10 units to confirm that they are the same size as 1 rod. **Ten ones equal 1 ten.**

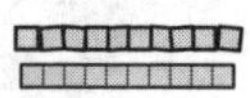

Show your child that 10 rods equal 1 flat, and that 10 flats equal 1 large cube.

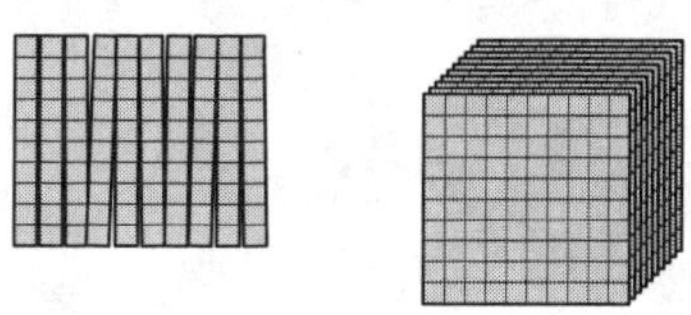

Can you guess why these blocks are called base-ten blocks? *Sample answer: Each bigger block is made of 10 of the next-smaller blocks.* **The number 10 is the base of our number system. It's the foundation for place value and for how we read and write numbers.**

Activity: Identify Quantities of Base-Ten Blocks

Place 3 rods and 5 units on the table. **Each unit has a value of 1. So, each rod has a value of 10. I can count these blocks by 10s and 1s to find their value.** Demonstrate how to count the blocks by 10s and 1s: **10, 20, 30, 31, 32, 33, 34, 35.**

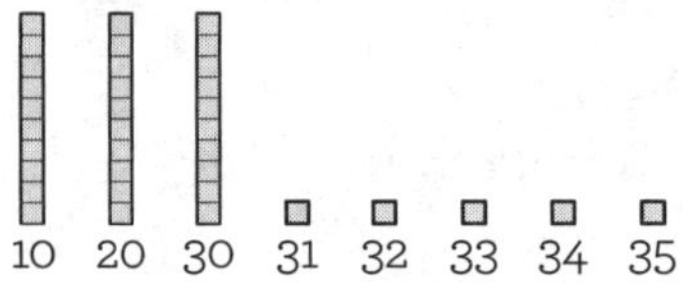

Counting by 10s and 1s to find the blocks' value

Or, I can use place-value thinking: There are 3 tens and 5 ones. 3 tens equal 30 and 5 ones equal 5. So, the blocks have a value of 35.

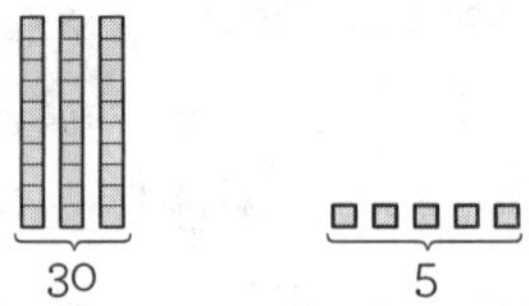

Using place-value thinking to find the blocks' value

Show your child the following block arrangements. Have her identify the value of each set of blocks, either by counting by 10s and 1s or by using place-value thinking.

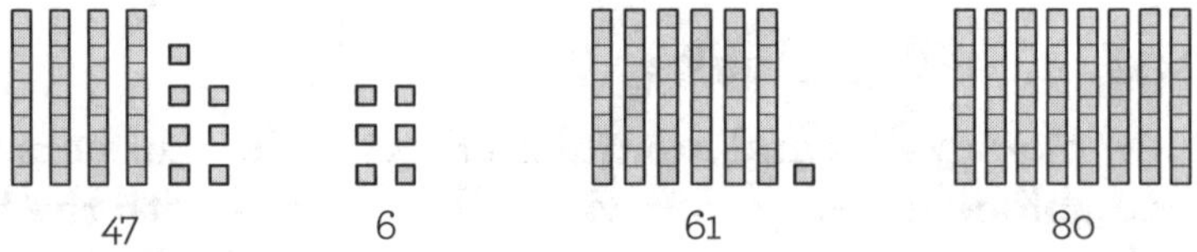

Activity: Make Designs with Base-Ten Blocks

Leave 8 rods and 19 units on the table, and put away the rest of the base-ten blocks.

> Leaving just these blocks on the table ensures your child's designs will have a value less than 100.

Let's use the blocks to build your initials. Have your child build her initials with units and rods.

Sample initials made from base-ten blocks

What's the value of the blocks in your design? *Answers will vary.*

> If your child's design has 10 or more unit blocks, she can either trade 10 units for 1 rod or count the units by 1s. You'll explore trading in Lesson 3.2.

Have your child make 2 more designs of her own choosing and find the value of the blocks in each design. If she's stuck, suggest she make a house, sun, or stick-figure person.

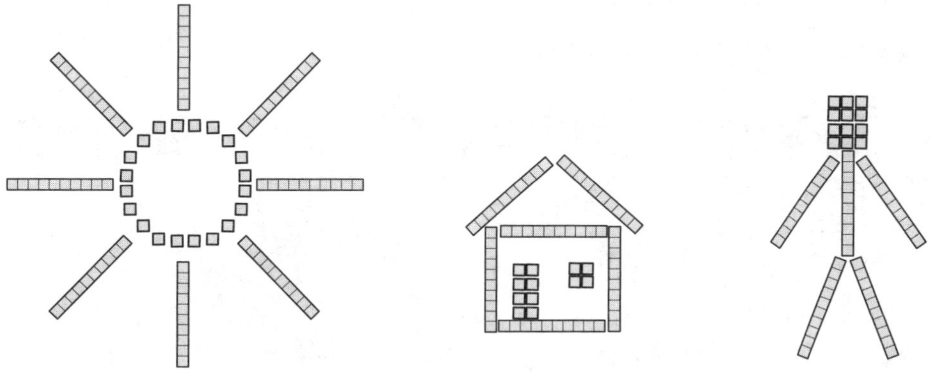

Workbook: Identify Combinations of Tens and Ones and Review

Have your child complete workbook pages 3.1A and 3.1B.

Workbook page 3.1B directs your child to color the leaves according to the key. If your child doesn't enjoy coloring or finds it tiring, she can draw an X of the appropriate color instead of coloring the entire shape.

Lesson 3.2
Review Place Value

	Purpose	Materials
Warm-up	• Count money • Practice memory work • Review missing addends	• Play money
Activities	• Review place value with tens and ones • Review writing two-digit numbers • Understand that you can trade 10 ones for 1 ten	• Place-Value Chart (Blackline Master 5) • Base-ten blocks • Playing cards
Workbook	• Write two-digit numbers to match combinations of tens and ones	• Workbook pages 3.2A and 3.2B

Warm-up: Counting, Memory Work, and Review

- Place 7 ten-dollar bills and 3 one-dollar bills on the table. **How much are the bills worth?** *$73.*
- **Name the months in order.** *January, February, March, April, May, June, July, August, September, October, November, December.* **How many months are in a year?** *12.*
- Secretly write each of the following equations on a piece of paper and hide the addend indicated with a slip of paper. Have your child pretend to use "x-ray vision" to identify the hidden number in each equation.

$10 + \boxed{5} = 15$ $\quad$ $10 + 1 = \boxed{11}$ $\quad$ $\boxed{10} + 3 = 13$

$10 + 6 = \boxed{16}$ $\quad$ $10 + 20 = \boxed{30}$

Activity: Review Place Value

In the last lesson, you made base-ten block designs and found the value of the blocks in your designs. Today, we'll use base-ten blocks to review place value.

Show your child both pages of the Place-Value Chart (Blackline Master 5.) **When we write a number, the Place-Value Chart helps write each digit in the place that matches its value. This year, we'll use a place-value chart with places for thousands, hundreds, tens, and ones.**

thousands	hundreds

tens	ones

We'll use just the page with the tens-place and ones-place today. Put away the page with the hundreds-place and thousands-place. Place 7 rods and 2 units on the table. **What is the value of the blocks?** *72.*

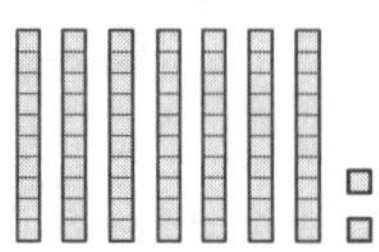

Let's use the Place-Value Chart to help write the number 72. Place the 7 rods in the tens-place and the 2 units in the ones-place on the Place-Value Chart.

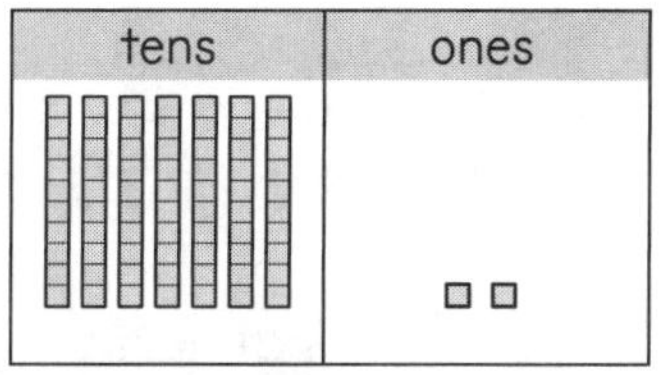

There are 7 tens, so I write 7 in the tens-place. Write 7 in the tens-place on the Place-Value Chart. **There are 2 ones, so I write 2 in the ones-place.** Write 2 in the ones-place on the Place-Value Chart. **So, that's the number 72.**

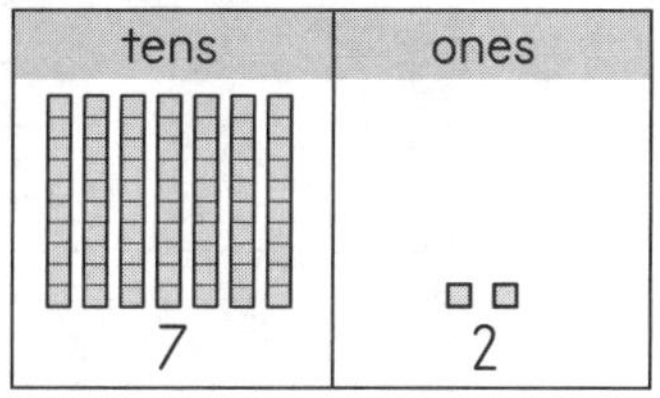

We call 7 and 2 the *digits* in the number 72. The number 72 has 2 digits, so we call it a two-digit number.

Show your child the following sets of blocks. For each arrangement, have him identify the blocks' value and write the corresponding digits on the Place-Value Chart.

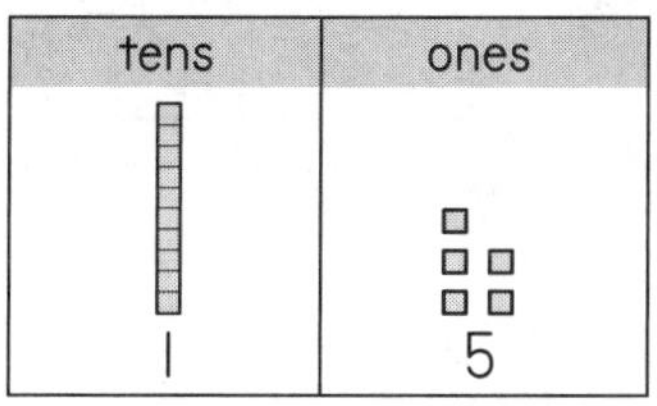

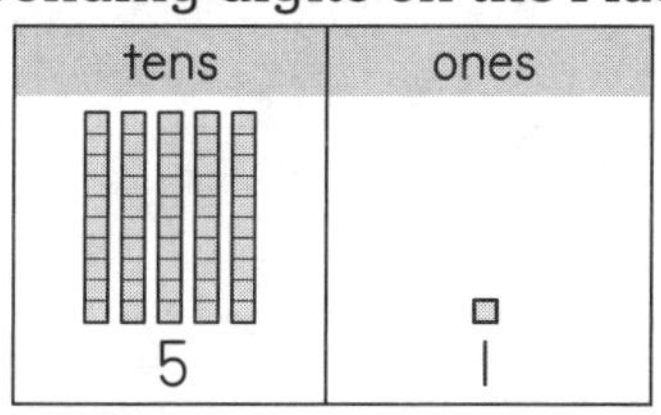

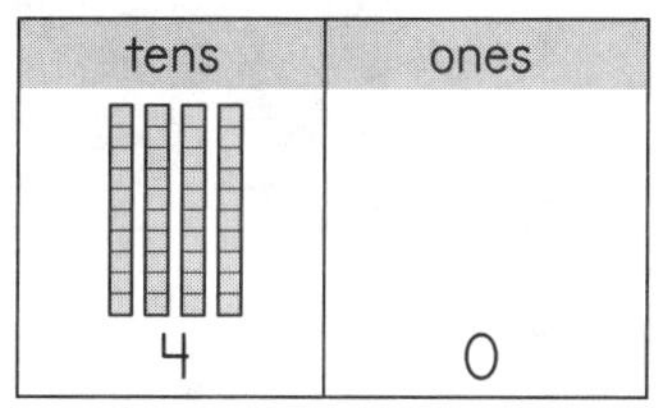

Activity: Trade 10 Ones for 1 Ten

> This activity and the following game preview the trading your child will do later in the year when he adds 2- or 3-digit numbers.

Place 2 rods and 15 units on the Place-Value Chart. **When we write numbers, we can only use the digits from 0 to 9. If there are any groups of 10 on the Place-Value Chart, we have to trade before we record the digits.** Help your child trade 10 units for 1 rod and write the digits in the Place-Value Chart.

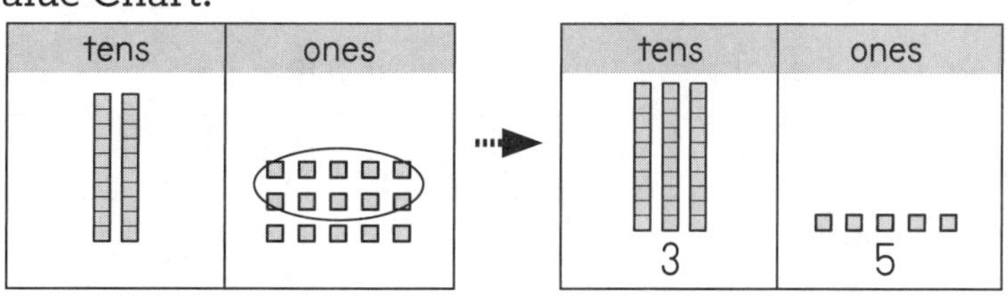

So, what's the value of the blocks? *35.*

Activity: Play Race to 100

Play Race to 100.

Race to 100

Materials: Aces, 5s, and 10s from 2 decks of cards (24 cards total); base-ten blocks
Object of the Game: Be the first player to reach 100.

Shuffle the cards and place them in a face-down pile. Make a simple scorecard to record the score.

Louise	
Mom	

On your turn flip over a card. If you flip over a 1, take 1 unit. If you flip over a 5, take 5 units. If you flip over a 10, take 1 rod.

Find the total value of your blocks and record this score in the chart.

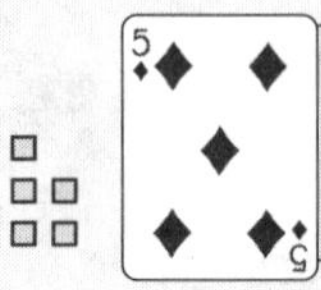

Louise	5
Mom	

Sample first play

Take turns flipping over a card, taking the corresponding blocks, and recording the total value of your blocks. If you have ten units at the end of a turn, trade them for a rod.

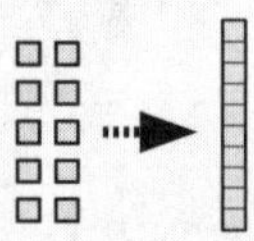

Trade 10 units for 1 rod if possible.

If you run out of cards, shuffle and reuse the discard pile.

Continue until one player reaches 100 or goes over 100.

Louise	5	15	16	26	36	41	42	52	57	67	68	78	88	98	103
Mom	5	6	16	17	22	23	24	29	39	44	45	50	60	65	

Sample final scorecard

Workbook: Write Two-Digit Numbers and Review

Have your child complete workbook pages 3.2A and 3.2B.

Lesson 3.3
Review Mental Math

	Purpose	Materials
Warm-up	• Count by 10s starting at a number other than 0 • Practice memory work • Review addition facts to 10	• Base-ten blocks • Counters • Addition Climb and Slide game board (from workbook page 1.1A) • Die
Activities	• Understand the purpose of mental math • Solve simple mental addition or subtraction problems	• Base-ten blocks • Napkin
Workbook	• Solve simple mental addition or subtraction problems	• Workbook pages 3.3A and 3.3B

Warm-up: Counting, Memory Work, and Review

- **Count with me by 10s, starting at 5. We'll model the numbers with base-ten blocks as we count.** Begin with 5 units on the table, and add a rod as you say each new number: **5, 15, 25....** Continue until you reach 95.
- **What do we call the result when we add numbers together?** *The sum.* **What do we call the result when we subtract a number from another number?** *The difference.*
- Play Addition Climb and Slide. See Lesson 1.1 (page 14) for directions.

Activity: Review Mental Addition and Subtraction

In first grade, you learned how to add and subtract numbers in your head. This kind of math is called mental math. Mental math is important because it helps you understand numbers, place value, and addition and subtraction more deeply. It also helps get you ready to solve more complicated written addition and subtraction problems. Today, we'll review some of the mental math skills you learned in first grade with a mental math magic show.

Write "34 + 20 =" on a piece of paper. Have your child model the problem with base-ten blocks. **Place-value thinking makes it easier to add 34 plus 20 in your head. 34 is 3 tens and 4 ones. 20 is 2 tens. When I add them together, I have 5 tens and 4 ones.** Have your child complete the written equation: 34 + 20 = 54.

34 + 20 = 54

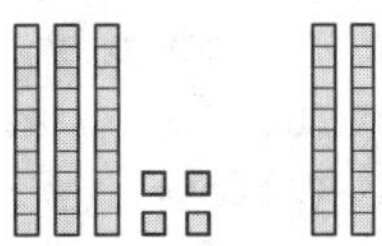

Write the following problems on paper. Model each problem with base-ten blocks and have your child use place-value thinking to solve them.

- 34 + 2 = *36*
- 34 - 2 = *32*
- 34 - 20 = *14*
- 34 - 4 = *30*
- 34 + 6 = *40*

For 34 + 6, remind your child to trade the 10 units for 1 rod.

34 + 6 = 40

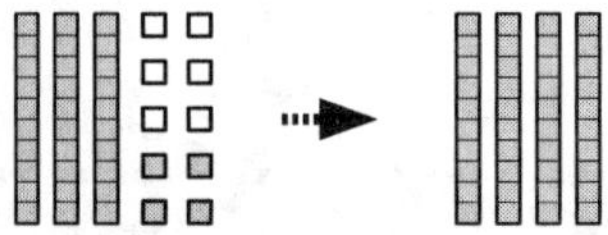

Activity: Mental Math Magic with Addition

We'll do lots of mental math this year, and we'll use many different activities to make it fun. Today, we'll play Mental Math Magic. We'll pretend I'm a magician, but I'm not very good at it! I need you, my trusty assistant, to help make the show a success.

> Always feel free to adjust activities to better fit you and your child. If you and your child enjoy pretending, you can ham it up, add props, and make the activity as elaborate as you like. But if you don't enjoy pretend activities or are pressed for time, simply model the problems as directed and have your child answer the questions without the pretend context.

Pretend you're facing an audience, and use your "magician voice" to announce: **I have 10.** Put 1 rod on the table, then cover it with a napkin or piece of paper.

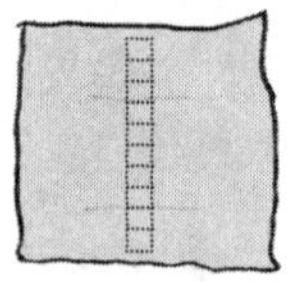

Then, I add 20. Slide 2 rods under the napkin (so that all 3 rods are covered).

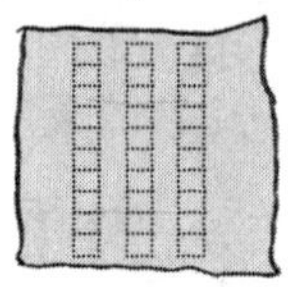

Whisper to your child: **How many do I have now, trusty assistant?** *30.* Remove the napkin with a flourish, and announce loudly to the pretend audience: **Now there are 30!**

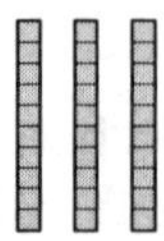

> If your child isn't sure, encourage her to visualize the rods under the napkin and use place-value thinking to find the total. If she's still not sure, briefly remove the napkin and allow her to peek.

Continue the "magic show" with the following questions. Keep the pace brisk, but adjust as needed for your child.

- **I have 30. Then, I add 7. How many do I have now, trusty assistant?** *37.*
- **I have 37. Then, I add 1. How many do I have now?** *38.*
- **I have 38. Then, I add 2. How many do I have now?** *40.* Trade the 10 units for 1 rod.
- **I have 40. Then, I add 10. How many do I have now?** *50.*
- **I have 50. Then, I add 5. How many do I have now?** *55.*
- **I have 55. Then, I add 30. How many do I have now?** *85.*
- **I have 85. Then, I add 5. How many do I have now?** *90.*
- **I have 90. Then, I add 10. How many do I have now?** *100.*

Activity: Mental Math Magic with Subtraction

Now, I will make all of the blocks disappear! Continue the "magic show" with the following questions.

- **I have 100. Then, I take away 30. How many do I have now?** *70.*
- **I have 70. Then, I take away 20. How many do I have now?** *50.*
- **I have 50. Then, I take away 10. How many do I have now?** *40.*
- **I have 40. Then, I take away 20. How many do I have now?** *20.*
- **I have 20. Then, I take away 10. How many do I have now?** *10.*
- **I have 10. Then, I take away 10. How many do I have now?** *0.*

Thank you, assistant! Let's take a bow!

Workbook: Mental Addition and Subtraction and Review

Have your child complete workbook pages 3.3A and 3.3B.

Lesson 3.4
Review Pairs That Make 100

	Purpose	Materials
Warm-up	• Count coins • Practice memory work • Review counting out coins	• Coins • 3 small school items (i.e., pencil, ruler, eraser)
Activities	• Understand that you can trade 10 tens for 1 hundred • Introduce the hundreds-place • Use base-ten blocks to find pairs that make 100	• Base-ten blocks • Place-Value Chart (Blackline Master 5) • Part-Total Mat (Blackline Master 2)
Workbook	• Use base-ten blocks to find pairs that make 100	• Workbook pages 3.4A and 3.4B

Warm-up: Counting, Memory Work, and Review

- Place 2 dimes, 1 nickel, and 5 pennies on the table. **How much are the coins worth?** *30¢.*
- **How many sides does a triangle have?** *3.* **A square?** *4.* **A rectangle?** *4.*
- Write 17¢, 40¢, 65¢ on separate slips of paper. Place each next to a small school item (like a pencil, ruler, and eraser). Give your child coins and have him pretend to buy the items.

Activity: Trade 10 Tens for 1 Hundred

In the last lesson, we reviewed the tens-place and ones-place. Today, you'll learn about the hundreds-place and use base-ten blocks to find pairs that make 100.

Place 9 rods and 9 units on the Place-Value Chart. (Use both pages of the Place-Value Chart for this lesson.) **How much are the blocks worth?** *99.*

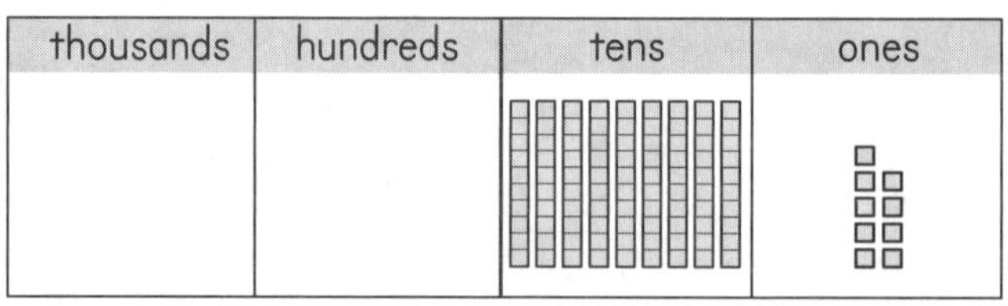

What number comes after 99? *100.* Have your child add 1 unit to the Place-Value Chart.

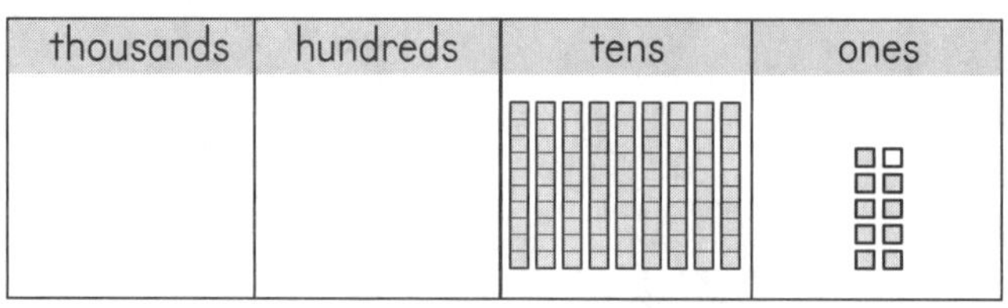

How many ones do you have now? *10.* **Remember, if we have a group of 10, we have to trade.** Help your child trade the 10 units for 1 rod.

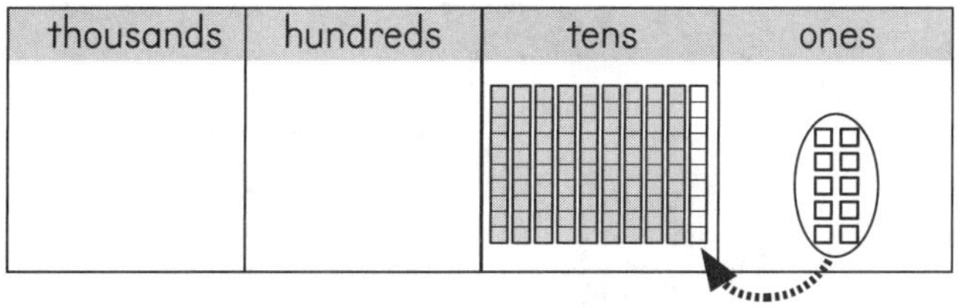

How many tens do you have now? *10.* Help your child trade the 10 rods for 1 flat and place it in the hundreds-place. **10 tens make 1 hundred.**

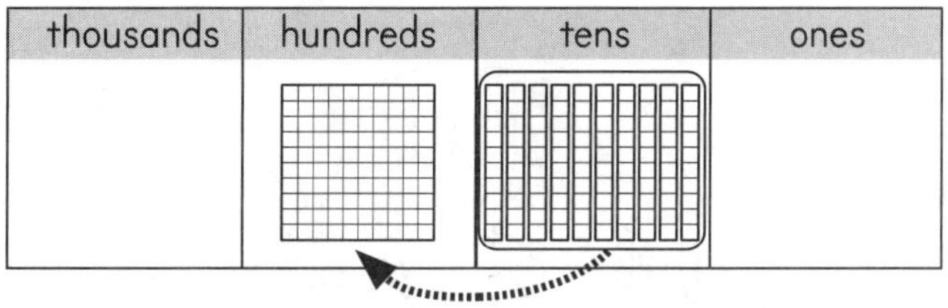

Now we're ready to write the digits in the Place-Value Chart. Demonstrate how to write 100 on the Place-Value Chart. **Why is there a zero in the tens-place and ones-place?** *Because there are zero ones and zero tens.*

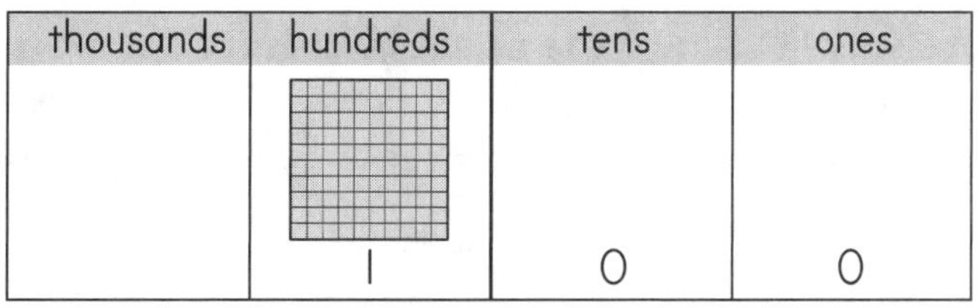

What would happen if I didn't write the zeros in 100? *Sample answers: The number would look like 1. The 1 would be in the wrong place.*

If I don't write the zeros, the 1 will be in the wrong place. We call zeros like these place-holders, because they hold the tens-place and ones-place for the 1. Make sure you always write zeros if they're holding a place for another digit.

Activity: Find Pairs That Make 100

Place the Part-Total Mat and 10 rods on the table. **Let's pretend we have 10 bars of chocolate to share. We'll pretend each rod is 1 bar, and that each bar of chocolate has 10 pieces. How many pieces of chocolate are in the 10 bars?** *100.* **How do you know?** *10 tens make 100.* Write 100 in the total box on the Part-Total Mat.

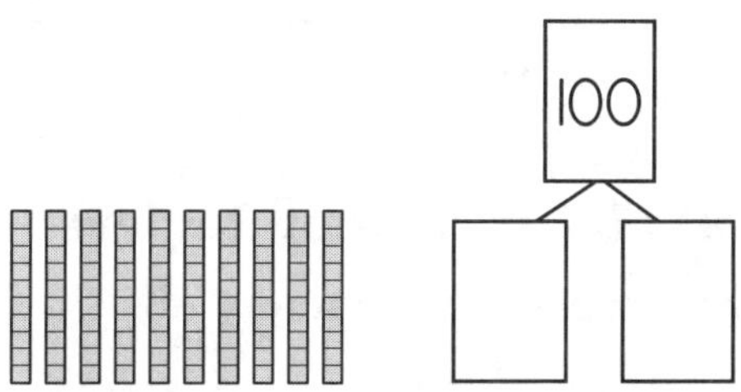

Real-life contexts make math more meaningful and interesting, so you'll often find pretend activities involving food in this book. Always feel free to use a different food than the one suggested to better match your family's eating habits.

Give 5 rods to your child. **Let's pretend we share the chocolate equally. How many pieces of chocolate do each of us get?** *50.* Have your child write 50 and 50 on the Part-Total Mat.

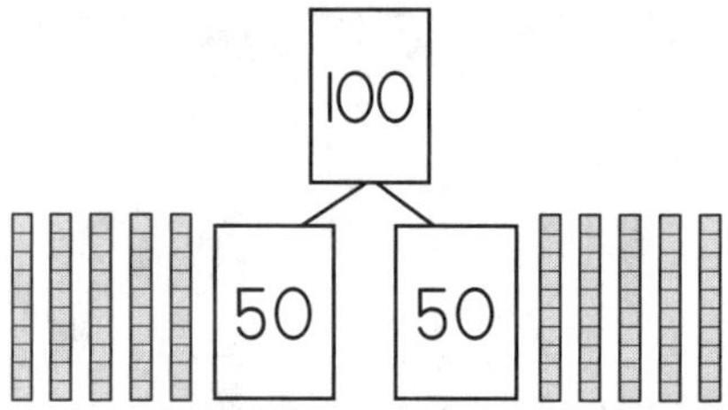

What's another way we could share the bars? *Answers will vary.* Have your child find several ways to share the 10 rods and record each on the Part-Total Mat.

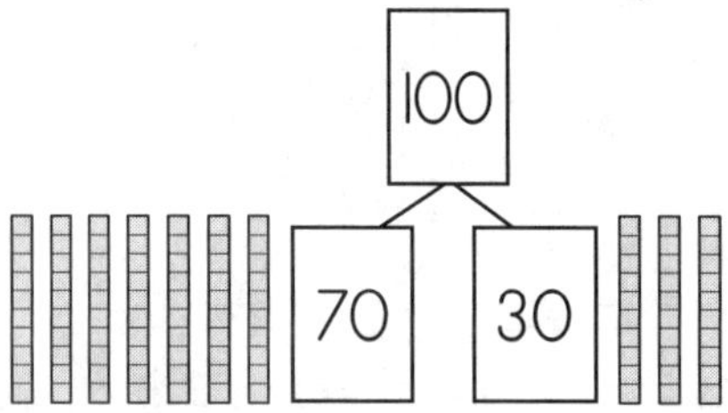

We could also pretend to break 1 of the chocolate bars into 10 pieces. Trade 1 of the rods for 10 units.

Now we have many more ways to share the chocolate! Here's one way. Give your child 1 unit and keep 9 rods and 9 units for yourself. **How many pieces of chocolate do each of us get?** *I get 1 piece, but you get 99!* Have your child record the amounts on the Part-Total Mat.

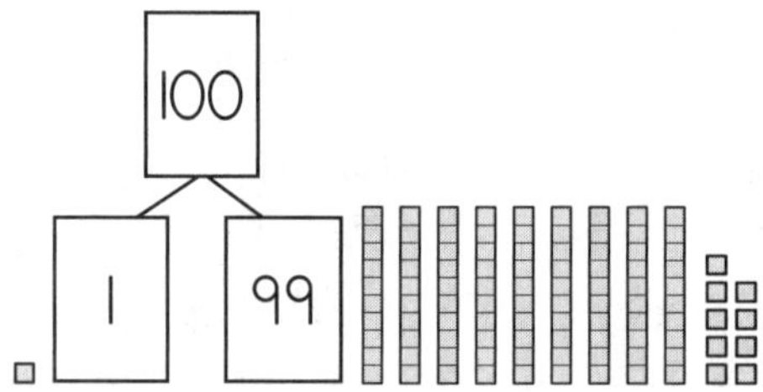

Have your child find and record several more ways to share the rods and units.

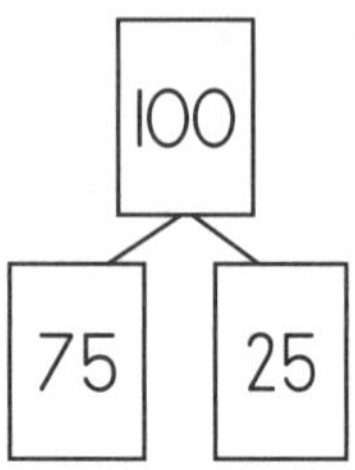

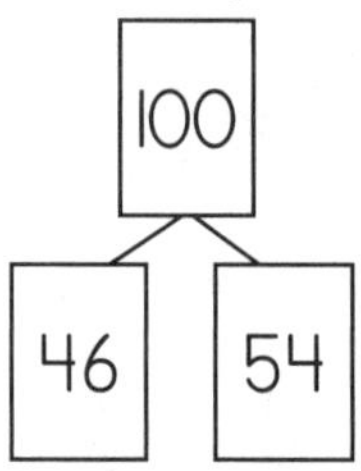

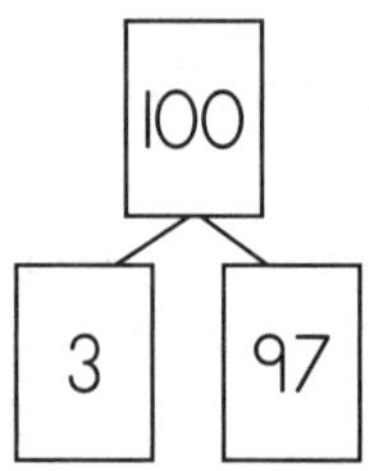

There are 101 different ways to share 100 pieces of chocolate, so we don't have to find all of them!

Workbook: Find Pairs That Make 100 and Review

Have your child complete workbook pages 3.4A and 3.4B.

Lesson 3.5
Enrichment and Review (Optional)

	Purpose	Materials
Warm-up	• Count backward from 100 to 1 • Review memory work • Review your child's favorite or most challenging activities from Week 3	• Varies, depending on the activities you choose
Picture Book	• Understand large numbers in the context of animals	• *Biggest, Strongest, Fastest,* by Steve Jenkins
Enrichment Activity	• Play a classic board game with the numbers to 100	• Chutes and Ladders, Rack-O, or 100 Chart (Blackline Master 4), die, and counters

Warm-up: Counting, Memory Work, and Review

- Have your child count backward from 100 to 1.
- Quiz your child on the memory work through Week 2. See page 523 for the full list.

> Your child will gradually memorize the full list of memory work on page 523 over the course of the year. New memory work is introduced every 2 weeks, so there is no new memory work on the odd-numbered weeks.

- If you have time, repeat one or two of the activities from this week's lessons. Choose activities your child especially enjoyed or found challenging.

Math Picture Book: *Biggest, Strongest, Fastest*

Read *Biggest, Strongest, Fastest,* by Steve Jenkins. As you read, marvel at the animals and discuss the numbers you and your child encounter in the book.

Enrichment Activity: Play a Classic Game

Play a classic board game with your child that uses the numbers to 100, such as Chutes and Ladders or Rack-O.

If you don't own either of these games, make a simple Chutes and Ladders board from your 100 Chart. To make the board, place the 100 Chart in a plastic page protector and use a dry-erase marker to draw a few ladders and chutes.

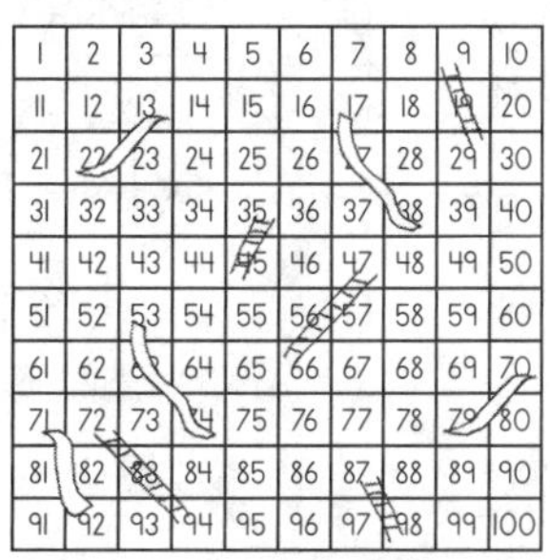

To play, have each player place a counter on the box labeled 100. Take turns rolling a die and moving backwards the corresponding number of spaces. If you land on a chute, slide your piece down it to the box at the bottom of the chute. If you land on a ladder, slide your piece up the ladder to the box at the top. Continue until one player reaches 100.

Week 3 Answer Key

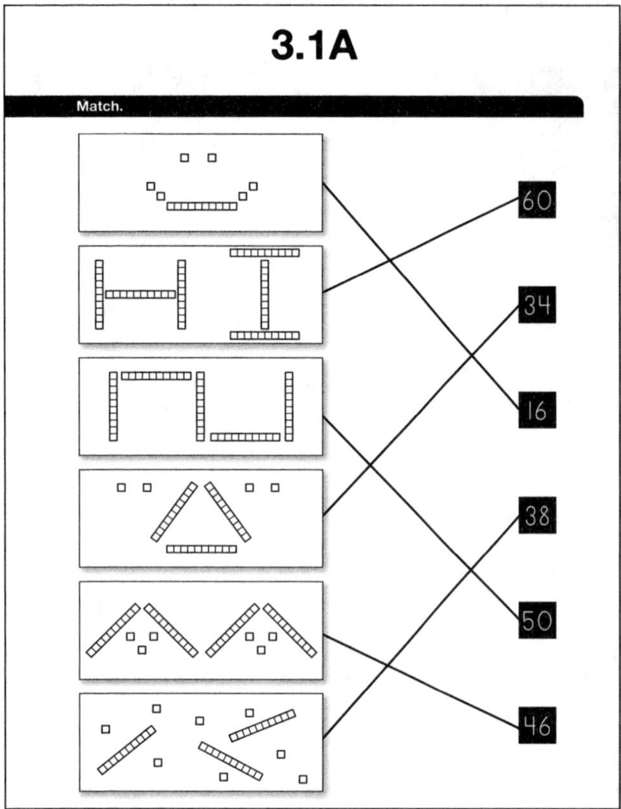

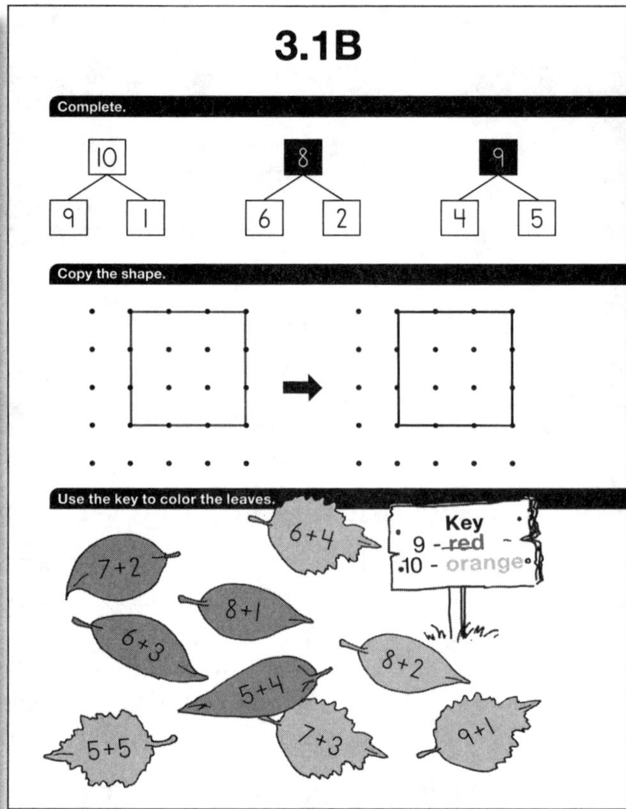

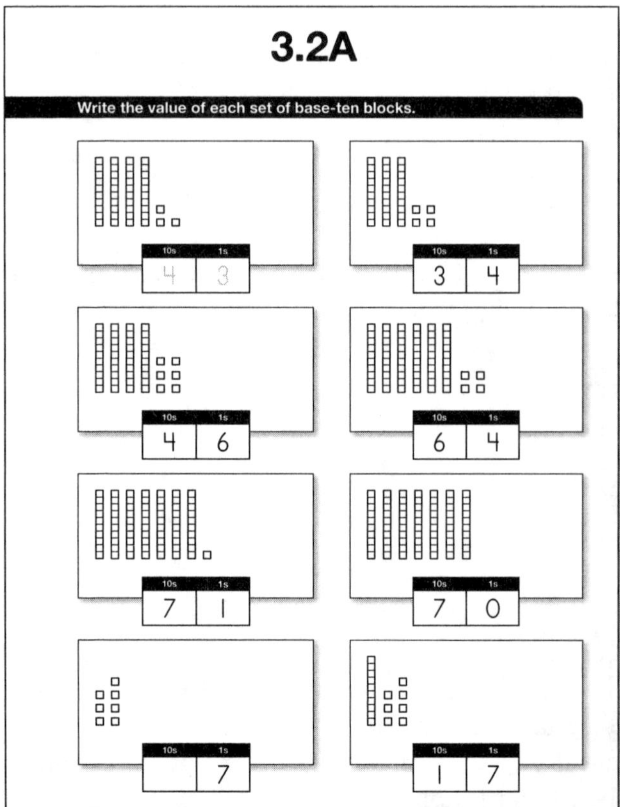

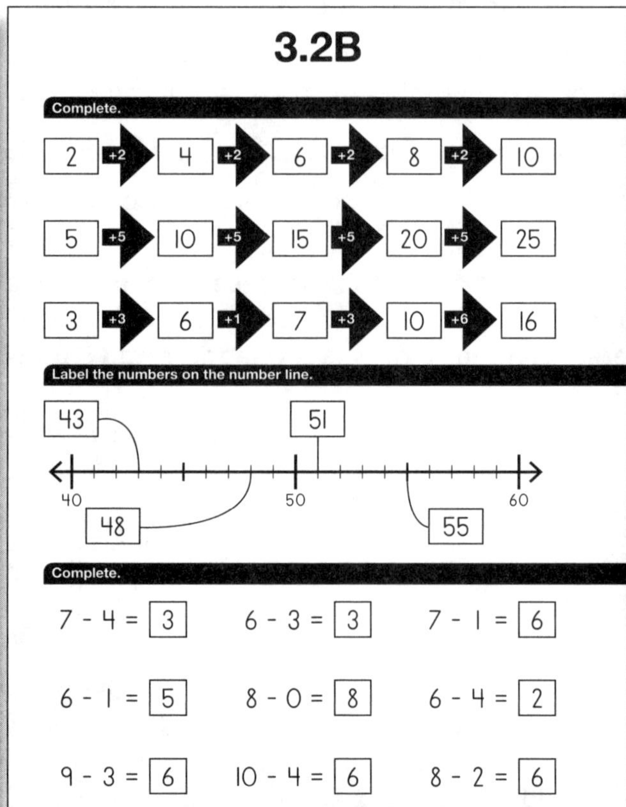

Week 3 Answer Key

3.3A

Complete.

50 + 3 = 53

40 + 20 = 60

35 + 30 = 65

75 + 20 = 95

46 - 3 = 43

60 - 20 = 40

32 - 2 = 30

71 - 30 = 41

3.3B

Color the addition facts that equal the number in the star.

7	8	9	10
4 + 3	7 + 2	3 + 6	3 + 7
6 + 2	4 + 4	9 + 0	9 + 1
2 + 5	6 + 1	5 + 4	6 + 5
7 + 0	3 + 5	1 + 8	8 + 2

Complete the missing numbers in the sequences.

Count by 2s: 60, 62, 64, 66, 68, 70

Count by 5s: 20, 25, 30, 35, 40, 45

Count by 10s: 50, 60, 70, 80, 90, 100

3.4A

Complete.

100: 30, 70

100: 10, 90

100: 45, 55

100: 25, 75

100: 5, 95

100: 85, 15

3.4B

Sarah made a bar graph about the children in her swim class. Use the bar graph to answer the questions.

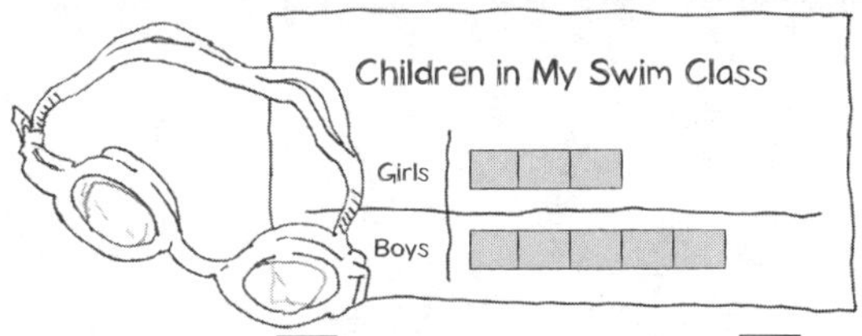

How many girls are in the class? 3

How many more boys than girls are in the class? 2

How many boys are in the class? 5

How many children are in the class? 8

Complete.

4 - 1 = 3 7 - 3 = 4 8 - 4 = 4

9 - 2 = 7 10 - 2 = 8 4 - 2 = 2

3 - 3 = 0 10 - 1 = 9 5 - 0 = 5

Complete the circles with <, >, or =.

42 > 36	87 > 85	39 < 79
7 < 70	15 < 50	94 = 94

Unit 1 Checkpoint

What to Expect at the End of Unit 1

By the end of Unit 1, most children will be able to do the following:

- Solve most addition and subtraction facts with numbers to 10 (like 7 + 2 or 8 – 3) mentally and in less than 3 seconds.
- Write addition and subtraction fact families.
- Begin to read and write the <, >, and = signs to compare numbers to 100. Most second graders will still be working on this and need help remembering the difference between the greater-than and less-than signs.
- Use reasoning and counting to identify numbers on the number line.
- Represent numbers to 100 with base-ten blocks and understand their digits' place value.
- Use base-ten blocks to identify pairs that make 100 (like 99 and 1, or 60 and 40).
- Solve simple mental addition and subtraction problems (like 45 + 3 or 87 – 20), either mentally or with base-ten blocks.

Is Your Child Ready to Move on?

In Unit 2 your child will learn the addition facts with sums to 20. Before moving on to Unit 2, your child should be able to find answers to most addition facts with sums to 10 mentally and in less than 3 seconds.

Your child does not need to fully master the rest of the Unit 1 skills before moving on to Unit 2. She will continue to practice comparing numbers, identifying numbers on the number line, and place value with the numbers to 100 during the warm-ups and review workbook pages.

What to Do If Your Child Needs More Practice

If your child needs more practice with the sums to 10, spend another day or two playing Addition Climb and Slide before moving on to Unit 2.

Unit 2
Addition Facts and Word Problems

Overview

In Unit 1, your child reviewed the meaning of addition and the addition facts with sums to 10. In this unit, he will practice and review the addition facts with sums to 20. He'll also review addition and subtraction word problems, learn to double numbers, and solve word problems with three addends.

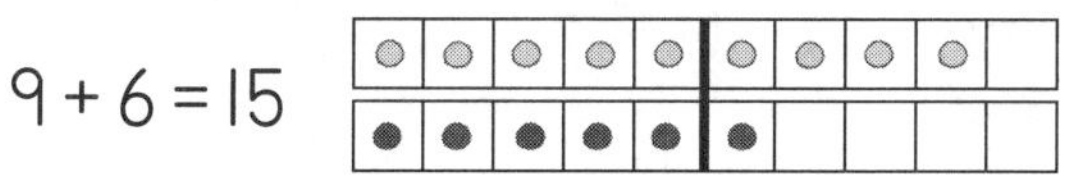

Addition facts to 20

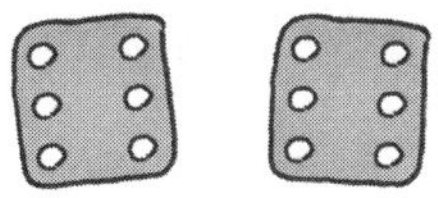

Doubling

You have 4 round crackers, 5 square crackers, and 4 triangle crackers. How many crackers do you have?

Word problem with three addends

Knowing the addition facts by heart lays a solid foundation for many other second grade math skills: mastering the subtraction facts, mental addition, and solving vertical addition problems with the traditional written process. But, don't worry if your child isn't fully fluent with the addition facts by the end of this unit. He'll have many more opportunities for more practice. The Unit 2 Checkpoint (page 88) will help you gauge whether to move on or not.

You know your child best, so feel free to adjust the pacing in this unit (and in all units!) depending on your child's needs. If your child already knows the addition facts to 20, zip through the unit and combine lessons to give your child a quick refresher. If your child didn't learn the addition facts in first grade (or doesn't remember them well), spend an extra day or so practicing each set of facts.

Week 4	+9 and +8 Facts
Week 5	+7 and +6 Facts

What Your Child Will Learn

In this unit your child will learn to:

- Solve addition facts up to 10 + 10
- Write and solve equations to match simple addition and subtraction word problems
- Solve word problems that involve finding how many more of an item is needed
- Solve word problems with 3 or more addends

Recommended Math Picture Books (Optional)

These picture books are scheduled in the optional Enrichment and Review lessons at the end of each week.

- *If You Were a Plus Sign*, written by Trisha Sue Speed Shaskan and illustrated by Francesca Carabelli. Picture Window Books, 2008.
- *Each Orange Had 8 Slices*, written by Paul Giganti Jr. and illustrated by Donald Crews. Greenwillow Books, 1992.

Week 4
+9 and +8 Facts

Overview

Your child will practice the +9 and +8 addition facts with strategies, games, and written exercises on the workbook pages. He will also review addition and subtraction word problems and learn how to double numbers to 10.

If your child already knows the answers immediately for the +9 and +8 facts, make Lessons 4.1 and 4.3 quick review lessons.

Lesson 4.1 Review +9 Facts
Lesson 4.2 Review Addition and Subtraction Word Problems
Lesson 4.3 Review +8 Facts
Lesson 4.4 Doubles
Lesson 4.5 Enrichment and Review (Optional)

Teaching Math with Confidence: Why Not Just Memorize the Math Facts?

In Unit 2 and Unit 4, your child will practice the addition and subtraction facts so that he knows them by heart. But that doesn't mean you have to break out the flash cards and timed tests! Instead, you'll teach your child simple strategies for finding the answers. For example, this week, you'll teach your child to complete a group of 10 to find the answers to the +9 and +8 facts.

9 + 7 = 16

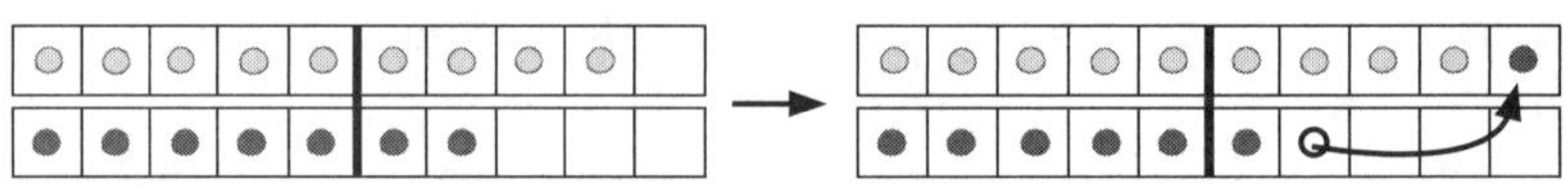

10 + 6 = 16, so 9 + 7 = 16.

Then, you'll practice the facts with fun games and have your child complete short written practice exercises in the workbook pages. With repeated practice, your child will become faster and faster until he "just knows" the answers.

Using a strategy approach (rather than rote memorization) has many benefits:

- Learning strategies makes the math facts feel less overwhelming. Instead of memorizing every math fact individually, all it takes is a few simple strategies to master all of them.
- Focusing on strategies is more efficient. Children learn the facts more quickly–and remember them better–when they use strategies to find the answers rather than memorizing each fact separately.
- Strategies help build children's overall number sense and understanding of the relationships between numbers.
- Using strategies helps children understand that math is a subject to be understood, not just memorized.

Some children will know all the addition facts by heart by the end of this unit, while others will need more practice (and many reminders to "use your strategies") to become fully fluent. Aim to have your child know the answers to most of the addition facts within 3 seconds by the end of Week 13. That way, he'll be ready to use the facts to solve mental addition problems in Week 14. You'll find plenty of addition fact practice in the warm-ups and review workbook pages before then to make sure he's ready!

Extra Materials Needed for Week 4

- 5 small toys
- 5 slips of paper
- Mirror (hand mirror preferred, but wall-mounted is fine)
- For optional Enrichment and Review Lesson:
    - *If You Were a Plus Sign*, written by Trisha Sue Speed Shaskan and illustrated by Francesca Carabelli
    - 20 small snack items, such as raisins, pieces of cereal, or blueberries

Lesson 4.1
Review +9 Facts

	Purpose	Materials
Warm-up	• Count backward • Practice memory work • Review reading inequalities	• 100 Chart (Blackline Master 4), optional
Activities	• Review the "complete a 10" strategy for the +9 facts • Practice the +9 facts	• Double ten-frames (Blackline Master 1) • Addition Crash game board (from workbook page 4.1A) • Counters • Playing cards
Workbook	• Practice the +9 facts	• Workbook page 4.1B

If your child already knows the answers immediately for the +9 and +8 facts, make this a quick review lesson.

Warm-up: Counting, Memory Work, and Review

- Have your child count backward from the following numbers. Stop her after she reaches the last number listed. Allow her to use the 100 Chart if needed.
    - **Count backward from 58:** *58, 57, 56, 55, 54.*
    - **Count backward from 34:** *34, 33, 32, 31, 30.*
    - **Count backward from 91:** *91, 90, 89, 88, 87.*
- Write the < sign. **What does this sign mean?** *Less than.*
  Write the > sign. **What does this sign mean?** *Greater than.*
- Write the following inequalities on a piece of paper and have your child read them.
    - 34 < 99. *34 is less than 99.*
    - 80 = 80. *80 equals 80.*
    - 98 > 89. *98 is greater than 89.*

Activity: Review +9 Facts

In this unit, you'll practice the addition facts so that you know them by heart. The addition facts are the addition problems from 1 + 1 up to 9 + 9. It 's important that you know them by heart so that you can use them to solve more difficult problems.

When you know something by heart, it means you know it right off the top of your head without having to think about it. What are some things that you know by heart? *Sample answers: The alphabet. Songs or poems. How to count to 20.*

It takes a lot of practice to learn something by heart! When you first learned to count to 10, you had to listen to me say the numbers many times and practice it over and over. You made a lot of mistakes while you were learning, too! But, now you can count to 10 without even thinking about it.

You already know lots of the addition facts by heart. What's 1 plus 1? *2.* **See, that's an addition fact you know by heart! We'll play lots of fun games in this unit to help you know the harder addition facts by heart, too. Today, you'll review the +9 addition facts.**

Write "9 + 7 =" on a piece of paper. Place 9 counters of one color on the top ten-frame and 7 counters of another color on the bottom ten-frame.

9 + 7 =

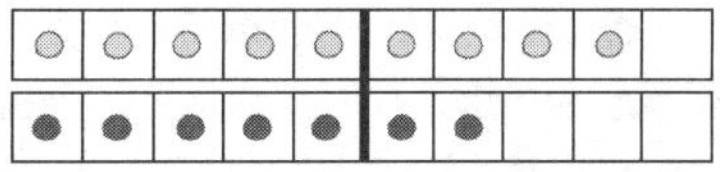

It's easier to see the answer if I move 1 counter to complete the 10. Move 1 counter as shown.

How many counters are on the top ten-frame now? *10.* **How many counters are on the bottom ten-frame now?** *6.* **So, how many counters are there in all?** *16.*

9 + 7 =

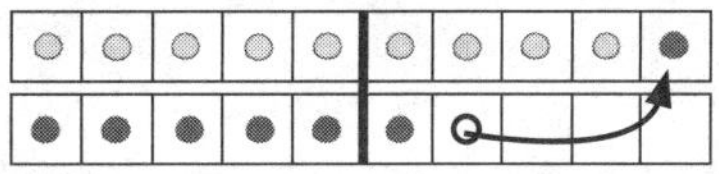

Completing the 10 makes it a lot easier to find the answer. Instead of adding 9 plus 7, I can just add 10 and 6. Have your child complete the written addition problem: 9 + 7 = 16.

Strategies like completing the 10 are a stepping stone to knowing the addition facts by heart. Use the strategy as much as you need to, but it's great if you "just know" the answers, too!

> See the Week 4 **Teaching Math with Confidence** for more on the benefits of a strategy approach to the math facts.

Repeat with the other +9 addition facts. Encourage your child to complete the 10 on the top row of the ten-frame to make the problems easier to solve.

- 9 + 2 = *11*
- 9 + 8 = *17*
- 9 + 4 = *13*
- 9 + 3 = *12*
- 9 + 5 = *14*
- 9 + 9 = *18*
- 9 + 6 = *15*

> Remind your child to use the combinations of "10 and some more" (and not counting) as she finds the total number of counters on the ten-frames. If your child can find the answers mentally, don't require her to use the ten-frame and counters.

Activity: Play Addition Crash (+9 Version)

If you don't have time for a particular game (or if your child is resistant), it's fine to skip the game and simply practice the skill instead. For example, if you don't have time to play Addition Crash, do some oral drill with the +9 addition facts instead.

We're going to play a game called Addition Crash to practice addition facts this week. Today, we'll play the +9 version. Play Addition Crash. Allow your child to use the ten-frame and counters to find the sums as needed.

Addition Crash (+9 Version)

Materials: Addition Crash game board (from workbook page 4.1A); deck of playing cards with aces, 10s, and face cards removed (32 cards total); 7 counters of two different colors each

Object of the Game: Place all 7 of your counters on the game board.

Shuffle the cards and place the stack face down on the table. Give 7 counters of one color to one player and 7 counters of a different color to the other player.

On your turn, flip over the top card. Add 9 to the number on the card and place a counter on a matching square. For example, if you flip over a 7, place a counter on a square with a 16, since 9 + 7 = 16.

If the other player already has a counter on a square with your sum, you may "crash" into their counter, remove it, and place your own counter on the square. Continue until one player places all 7 counters on the board.

Crashing into your opponent isn't required—you can put your counter in an empty box instead—but it makes the game more competitive and fun.

Save this game board with your math materials so you can play again.

Workbook: Practice +9 Facts and Review

Have your child complete workbook page 4.1B.

Lesson 4.2
Review Addition and Subtraction Word Problems

	Purpose	Materials
Warm-up	• Count base-ten blocks • Practice memory work • Review +9 addition facts	• Base-ten blocks • Addition Crash game board (from workbook page 4.1A) • Counters • Playing cards
Activities	• Review simple addition and subtraction word problems • Learn how to solve written word problems	• Play money • 5 small toys • 5 slips of paper • Part-Total Mat (Blackline Master 2) • Workbook page 4.2A
Workbook	• Solve addition and subtraction word problems	• Workbook pages 4.2A and 4.2B

Warm-up: Counting, Memory Work, and Review

- Place 5 rods and 8 units on the table. **What is the value of these blocks?** *58.*
- Write the < sign. **What does this sign mean?** *Less than.*
  Write the > sign. **What does this sign mean?** *Greater than.*
- Play Addition Crash (+9 Version). See Lesson 4.1 (page 62) for directions.

Activity: Review Word Problems at the Pretend Store

Learning how to use numbers in real life is one of the most important reasons to learn math. We'll spend lots of time on real-life math problems this year. We call these problems word problems because they are math problems we say in words. Today, we'll play Pretend Store to review addition and subtraction word problems.

Write $3, $4, $5, $9, and $10 on small slips of paper to make price tags. Lay 5 small toys in a row and have your child place a price tag next to each toy.

Pretend to be the customer: **I'd like to buy the toy that costs $4 and the toy that costs $5, please. How much do I owe you?** *$9.* **How did you figure that out?** *I added 4 plus 5.*

Have your child write the numbers on the Part-Total Mat and then write the matching equation. Pretend to pay him $9.

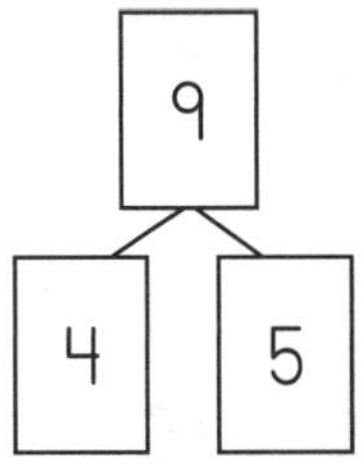

4 + 5 = 9

When we add, we join two parts to make a total. You joined the \$4 and \$5 to make a total of \$9.

Take 7 one-dollar bills. **I have \$7. I'd like to buy the toy that costs \$5. How much money will I have left?** *\$2.* **How did you figure that out?** *I subtracted 5 from 7.* Have your child write the numbers on the Part-Total Mat and then write the matching equation. Pretend to pay him \$5, and check that you have \$2 left.

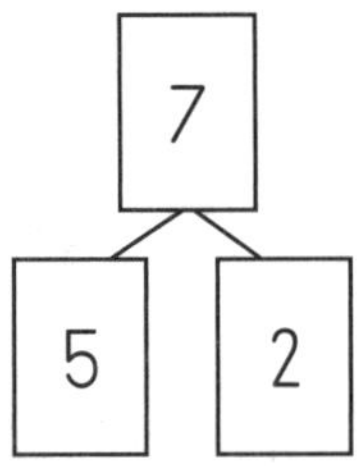

7 - 5 = 2

When we subtract, we split a total into parts. You split the \$7 to find that I'd have \$2 after I spend \$5.

> Most second-graders won't have any trouble deciding whether to add or subtract for these problems. But, later in the year, your child will learn to solve word problems in which it's not so obvious. Using the Part-Total Mat now equips him to solve these more-challenging problems later. If your child resists using the Part-Total Mat because he already knows how to write the equations, simply write the numbers yourself on the mat and move on.

Act out the following word problems with play money. Have your child complete the Part-Total Mat and write an equation to match each problem.

- **I'd like to buy the toy that costs \$3 and the toy that costs \$10, please. How much do I owe you?** *\$13.*

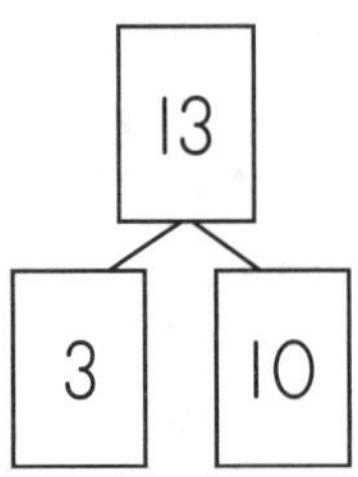

3 + 10 = 13

- **I have \$10, and I'd like to buy the toy that costs \$4. How much money will I have left?** *\$6.*

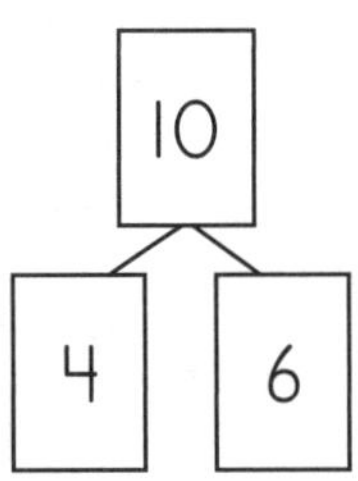

10 - 4 = 6

- **I have \$15, and I'd like to buy the toy that costs \$10. How much money will I have left?** *15 – 10 = 5. \$5.*
- **I'd like to buy the toy that costs \$9 and the toy that costs \$5, please. How much do I owe you?** *9 + 5 = 14. \$14.*

Activity: Solve Written Word Problems

Show your child workbook page 4.2A. **Let's solve the first problem together, and then you can solve the rest on your own when you do the workbook page.**

There are 3 main steps for solving word problems. The first step is to read the problem slowly and carefully. Have your child read aloud the first problem (or read it aloud to him). Briefly discuss your child's experiences with treat bags at parties.

You put 4 red lollipops and 3 purple lollipops in the treat bag.
How many lollipops are in the bag?

If your child is not yet a proficient reader, it may be too much of a cognitive load for him to both read the word problems and solve them. In that case, read the problems aloud to him so that he can focus on the math skills.

The next step is to write an equation to match the problem. Have your child write an equation to match the problem in the space provided on the worksheet.

[4] (+) [3] = [ ]

If your child has trouble writing the equation, have him first write the numbers on the Part-Total Mat. **We know the parts, and we're trying to find the total. So, we need to add the 4 and 3 together.**

The final step is to complete the equation and write the answer in the answer box.

[4] (+) [3] = [7]

[7] lollipops

Workbook: Solve Addition Word Problems and Review

Have your child complete workbook pages 4.2A and 4.2B. If your child has trouble with any of the word problems, have him write the numbers on the Part-Total Mat before completing the equations.

Lesson 4.3
Review +8 Facts

	Purpose	Materials
Warm-up	• Count coins • Practice memory work • Review place-value terms	• Coins
Activities	• Review the "complete the 10" strategy for the +8 facts • Practice the +8 facts	• Double ten-frames (Blackline Master 1) • Addition Crash game board (from workbook page 4.1A) • Counters • Playing cards
Workbook	• Practice the +8 and +9 facts	• Workbook pages 4.3A and 4.3B

If your child already knows the answers immediately for the +8 facts, make this a quick review lesson.

Warm-up: Counting, Memory Work, and Review

- Place 5 dimes, 1 nickel, and 4 pennies on the table. **How much are the coins worth?** *59¢.*
- Write the < sign. **What does this sign mean?** *Less than.*
  Write the > sign. **What does this sign mean?** *Greater than.*
- Write the number 87 on a piece of paper. **How many digits does this number have?** *2.* **Which digit is in the ones-place?** *7.* **Which digit is in the tens-place?** *8.*

Activity: Introduce +8 Addition Facts

In the last two lessons, you reviewed the +9 facts. Today, you'll review how to complete a 10 to solve the +8 facts.

Write "8 + 5 =" on a piece of paper. Place 8 counters of one color on the top ten-frame and 5 counters of another color on the bottom ten-frame.

8 + 5 =

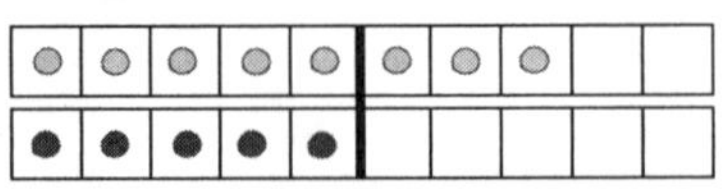

When you added 9, you moved 1 counter to complete the 10. But when you add 8, you move 2 counters to complete the 10. Move 2 counters as shown. **How many counters are on the top ten-frame?** *10.* **How many counters are on the bottom ten-frame?** *3.* **So, how many counters are there in all?** *13.*

8 + 5 =

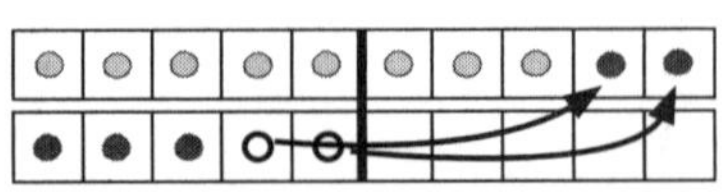

Moving 2 counters to complete the 10 helps find the answer. Instead of adding 8 plus 5, you can just add 10 plus 3. *Have your child complete the written addition problem: 8 + 5 = 13.*

Repeat with the other +8 addition facts. Encourage your child to complete the 10 on the top row of the ten-frame to make the problems easier to solve.

- 8 + 3 = 11
- 8 + 7 = 15
- 8 + 4 = 12
- 8 + 8 = 16
- 8 + 6 = 14

Parents often wonder how quickly their child should be able to recall the answers to the math facts. As a general rule, aim for no more than 3 seconds per fact, and less if possible. Children who process information quickly may rattle off answers automatically, but children who are slower processors may always need several seconds. You're the parent and know your child best, so adjust your expectations to your individual child.

Activity: Play Addition Crash (+8 Version)

Today we'll play the +8 version of Addition Crash. Play Addition Crash. See Lesson 4.1 (page 62) for the general directions.

To play the +8 version, use a deck of playing cards with the aces, 2s, 10s, and face cards removed (28 cards total). Add 8 to the number on your card. For example, if you flip over a 7, place a counter on a square with a 15 since 8 + 7 = 15.

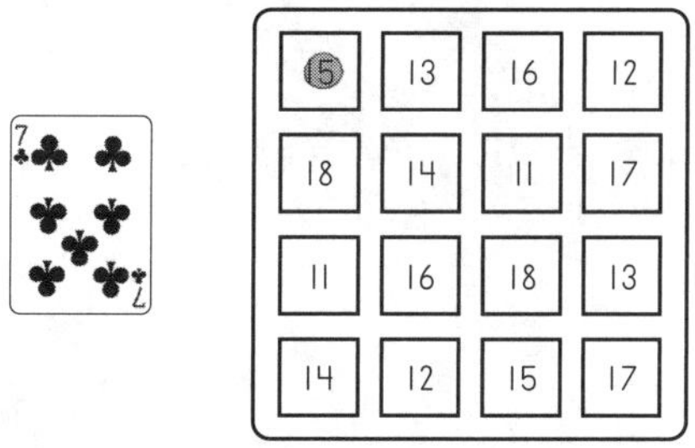

Workbook: Practice +8 Facts and Review

Have your child complete workbook page 4.3A and 4.3B.

Lesson 4.4
Doubles

	Purpose	Materials
Warm-up	• Count base-ten blocks • Practice memory work • Review +8 facts	• Base-ten blocks • Addition Crash game board (from workbook page 4.1A) • Counters • Playing cards
Activities	• Double numbers to 10 • Introduce column addition and learn to write the digits in the correct place	• 2 dice • Counters • Double ten-frames (Blackline Master 1) • Mirror • Workbook page 4.4A
Workbook	• Double numbers to 10 • Solve column addition problems	• Workbook pages 4.4A and 4.4B

Warm-up: Counting, Memory Work, and Review

- Place 3 rods and 17 units on the table. Remind him to trade 10 units for 1 rod when he reaches 40. **What is the value of these blocks?** *47.*
- Write the < sign. **What does this sign mean?** *Less than.*
  Write the > sign. **What does this sign mean?** *Greater than.*
- Play Addition Crash (+8 Version). See Lesson 4.3 (page 67) for full directions.

Activity: Find Doubles with Dice

In the last lesson, you reviewed the +8 addition facts. Today, you'll learn how to double the numbers from 1 to 10.

What does it mean to double something? *Sample answer: Make it twice as much.* Discuss your child's experiences with doubling. For example: **Remember when we went to the arcade and you doubled your tickets? A double cheeseburger has 2 patties on it!**

We often talk about doubles when we use dice for board games. In some games, you get an extra turn if you roll doubles. Place 2 dice on the table. Turn them so that both dice show 1 dot. **1 plus 1 equals 2, so double 1 is 2.** Write "1 + 1 = 2" to begin a list of doubles.

1 + 1 = 2 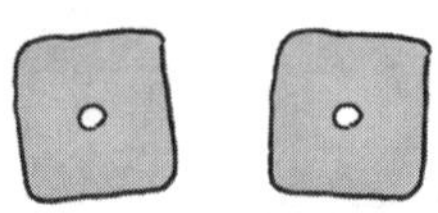

Turn the dice so that 2 dots show on each die. **What's double 2?** *4.* Add "2 + 2 = 4" to the list of doubles.

2 + 2 = 4 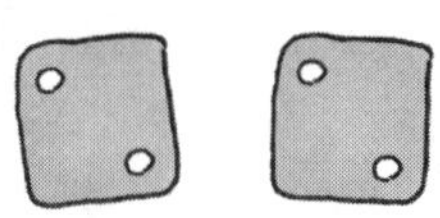

Repeat with 3, 4, 5, and 6 dots on each die. Your finished list should look like this:

$$1 + 1 = 2$$
$$2 + 2 = 4$$
$$3 + 3 = 6$$
$$4 + 4 = 8$$
$$5 + 5 = 10$$
$$6 + 6 = 12$$

Activity: Find Doubles with a Mirror

Have your child look in a mirror. **I see two of you. You're doubled! Let's use the mirror to double 7, 8, 9, and 10.**

> This activity works best with a hand mirror. If you don't have one, place the ten-frame on a sturdy surface (like a book) so that you can hold it next to a bathroom mirror.

Put 7 counters on the ten-frame. Then hold the mirror next to the ten-frame so that the counters appear doubled. Point out the groups of 10 and 4. **How many counters can you see?** *14.* **So, what's double 7?** *14.* Add "7 + 7 = 14" to the list of doubles.

$$7 + 7 = 14$$

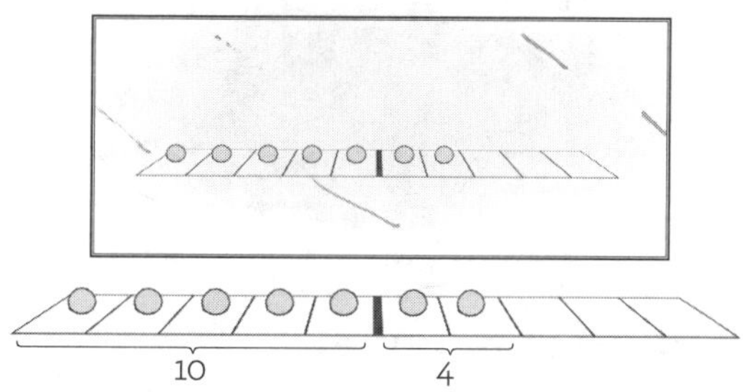

Repeat with 8, 9, and 10 counters.

$$8 + 8 = 16$$
$$9 + 9 = 18$$
$$10 + 10 = 20$$

> This activity previews the strategy your child will use for the +7 and +6 facts in Week 5.

Activity: Introduce Column Addition

In English, we always write words from left to right across the page. But people who speak Japanese write words from top to bottom down the page. Have your child try writing his name both horizontally and vertically.

Blake

B
l
a
k
e

Even though we always write words from left to right, we sometimes write math problems from top to bottom. Show your child the column addition problems at the bottom of workbook page 4.4A.

$$\begin{array}{r} 8 \\ +\ 1 \\ \hline \\ \end{array} \qquad \begin{array}{r} 8 \\ +\ 4 \\ \hline \\ \end{array} \qquad \begin{array}{r} 8 \\ +\ 8 \\ \hline \\ \end{array}$$

This is called column addition because the numbers are written in a column. Discuss places your child has seen columns, perhaps in her history book or on a local civic building. **Column addition problems are always lined up nice and straight, like a column in a building.**

When you write the answer for a column addition problem, write the ones-place for the sum directly below the ones-place for the addends. This habit will help you later in the year when you solve problems with greater numbers.

Have your child solve the first problem on workbook page 4.4A. Watch to make sure that he writes each digit in the correct place and help as needed.

Always read column addition problems from top to bottom. They don't have an equals sign, but we say equals when we get to the line that separates the addends from the sum. Point to the first problem (8 + 1). **This problem says 8 plus 1 equals 9.**

$$\begin{array}{r} 8 \\ +\ 1 \\ \hline 9 \end{array}$$

Workbook: Find Doubles and Review

Have your child complete workbook pages 4.4A and 4.4B.

Lesson 4.5
Enrichment and Review (Optional)

	Purpose	Materials
Warm-up	• Count backward from 100 to 1 • Review memory work • Review your child's favorite or most challenging activities from Week 4	• Varies, depending on the activities you choose
Picture Book	• Review addition concepts and vocabulary in real-life contexts	• *If You Were a Plus Sign*, written by Trisha Sue Speed Shaskan and illustrated by Francesca Carabelli
Enrichment Activity	• Identify pairs that make 20	• 20 small snack items, such as raisins, pieces of cereal, or blueberries • Double ten-frames (Blackline Master 1) • Paper

Warm-up: Counting, Memory Work, and Review

- Have your child count backward from 100 to 1.
- Quiz your child on the memory work through Week 4. See page 523 for the full list.
- If you have time, repeat one or two of the activities from this week's lessons. Choose activities your child especially enjoyed or found challenging.

Math Picture Book: *If You Were a Plus Sign*

Read *If You Were a Plus Sign*, written by Trisha Sue Speed Shaskan and illustrated by Francesca Carabelli. As you read, discuss the addition concepts and vocabulary in the book.

Enrichment Activity: Eat a Snack with 20 Pieces

Have your child place 20 small snack items (such as raisins, pieces of cereal, or blueberries) in each of the boxes on the double ten-frames.

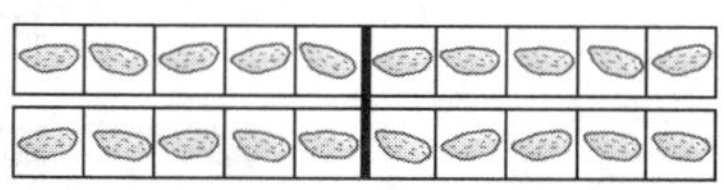

Start a simple chart showing how many pieces your child has eaten and how many pieces are left.

Raisins eaten	0
Raisins left	20

Sample chart

As your child eats each item, have him identify how many he's eaten and how many are left. Also have him write the corresponding numbers in the chart (or write them in the chart yourself).

Raisins eaten	0	1	2	3	4	5	6	7	8	9	10	11	12	13	14	15	16	17	18	19	20
Raisins left	20	19	18	17	16	15	14	13	12	11	10	9	8	7	6	5	4	3	2	1	0

Sample final chart

Week 4 Answer Key

4.1A

See the Instructor Guide for how to play.
Save this game board for future lessons.

Addition Crash

Game Board

15	13	16	12
18	14	11	17
11	16	18	13
14	12	15	17

4.1B

Complete.

9 + 3 = 12 9 + 1 = 10 9 + 6 = 15

9 + 8 = 17 9 + 2 = 11 9 + 5 = 14

9 + 4 = 13 9 + 9 = 18 9 + 7 = 16

Complete.

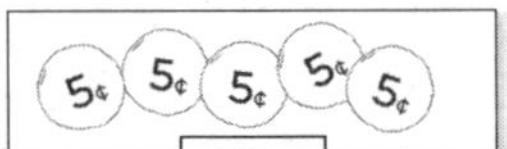

25 ¢

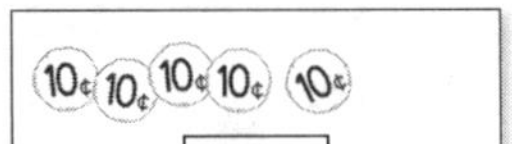

50 ¢

Complete.

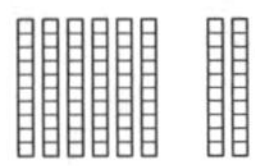

60 + 20 = 80

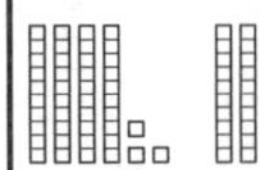

43 + 20 = 63

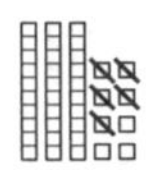

38 - 5 = 33

76 - 40 = 36

4.2A

Solve.

You put 4 red lollipops and 3 purple lollipops in the treat bag.
How many lollipops are in the bag?

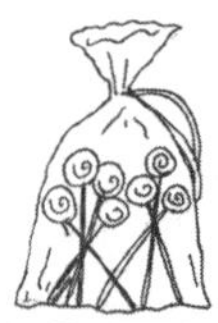

4 + 3 = 7

7 lollipops

You put 9 bouncy balls in the treat bag. Then, you take out 5.
How many bouncy balls are left?

9 - 5 = 4

4 bouncy balls

You put 6 erasers and 3 pencils in the treat bag.
How many things are in the bag?

6 + 3 = 9

9 things

You have 8 lollipops in the treat bag. Then, you eat 2.
How many are left?

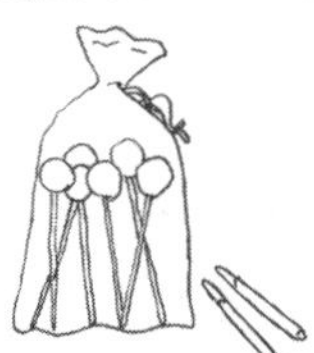

8 - 2 = 6

6 lollipops

4.2B

Complete.

4 + 9 = 13 6 + 9 = 15 3 + 9 = 12

8 + 9 = 17 1 + 9 = 10 9 + 9 = 18

2 + 9 = 11 7 + 9 = 16 5 + 9 = 14

X the shape that doesn't belong in each row.

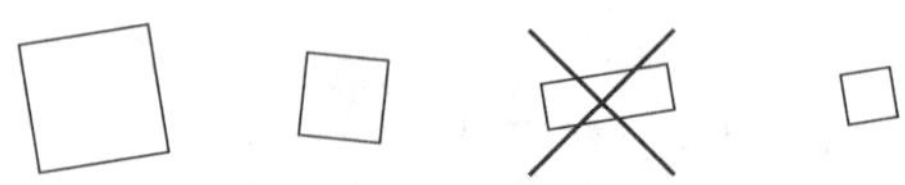

Complete.

65: 60, 5

31: 30, 1

78: 70, 8

47: 40, 7

26: 20, 6

84: 80, 4

Week 4 Answer Key

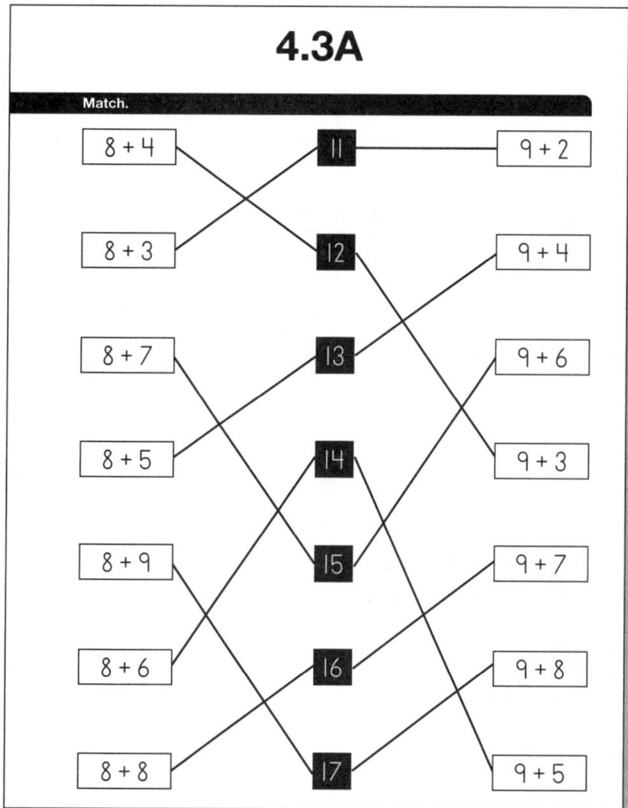

4.3A

Match.

8 + 4	11	9 + 2
8 + 3	12	9 + 4
8 + 7	13	9 + 6
8 + 5	14	9 + 3
8 + 9	15	9 + 7
8 + 6	16	9 + 8
8 + 8	17	9 + 5

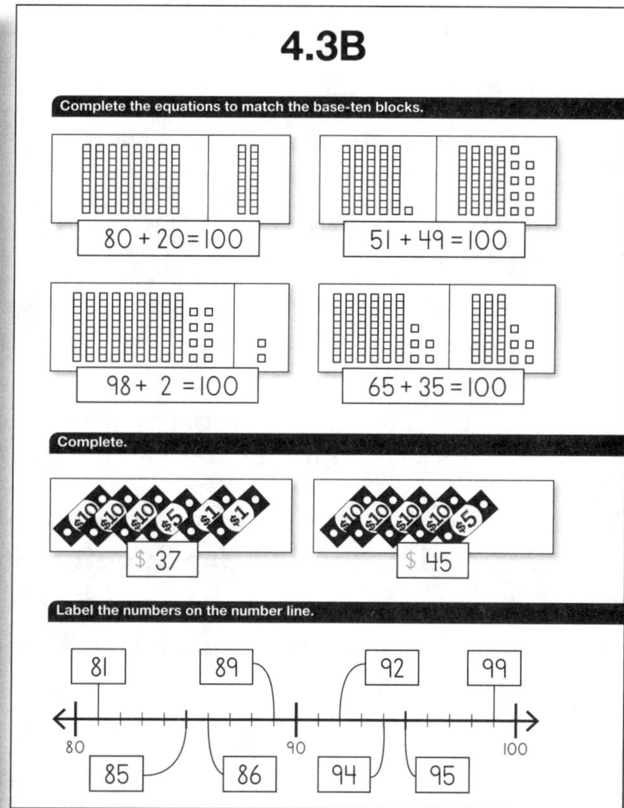

4.3B

Complete the equations to match the base-ten blocks.

80 + 20 = 100

51 + 49 = 100

98 + 2 = 100

65 + 35 = 100

Complete.

$10 $10 $10 $5 $1 $1 — $ 37

$10 $10 $10 $10 $5 — $ 45

Label the numbers on the number line.

80, 90, 100

81, 85, 86, 89, 92, 94, 95, 99

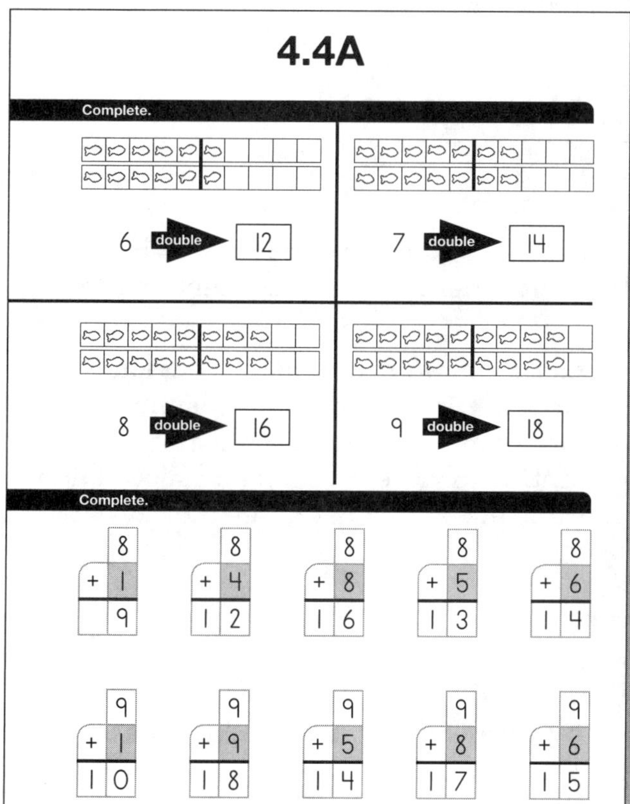

4.4A

Complete.

6 double 12

7 double 14

8 double 16

9 double 18

Complete.

8 + 1 = 9; 8 + 4 = 12; 8 + 8 = 16; 8 + 5 = 13; 8 + 6 = 14

9 + 1 = 10; 9 + 9 = 18; 9 + 5 = 14; 9 + 8 = 17; 9 + 6 = 15

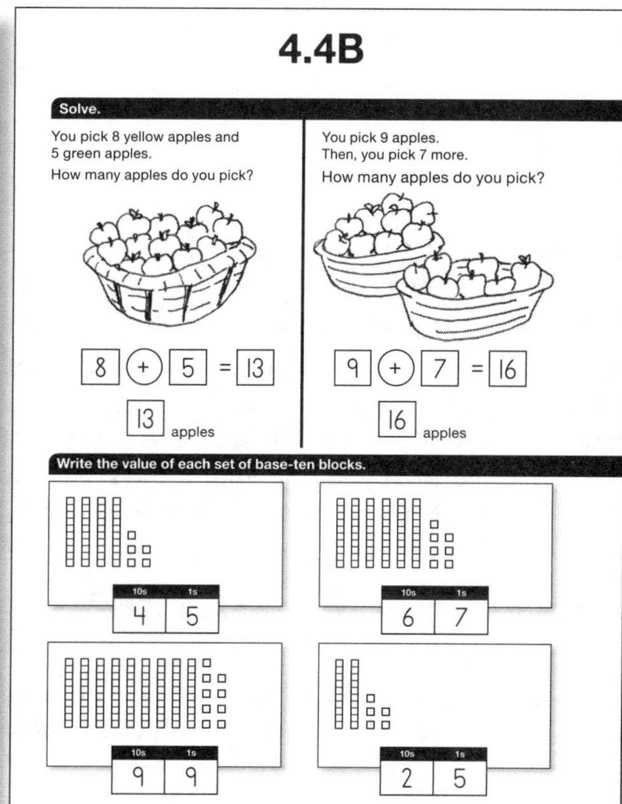

4.4B

Solve.

You pick 8 yellow apples and 5 green apples. How many apples do you pick?

8 + 5 = 13

13 apples

You pick 9 apples. Then, you pick 7 more. How many apples do you pick?

9 + 7 = 16

16 apples

Write the value of each set of base-ten blocks.

10s	1s
4	5
6	7
9	9
2	5

Week 5
+7 and +6 Facts

Overview

Your child will practice the +7 and +6 addition facts. She will also learn to solve two new types of addition word problems.

If your child already knows the answers immediately for the +7 and +6 facts, make Lessons 5.1 and 5.3 quick review lessons.

Lesson 5.1	Review +7 Facts
Lesson 5.2	How Many More Do I Need? Word Problems
Lesson 5.3	Review +6 Facts
Lesson 5.4	Word Problems with 3 Addends
Lesson 5.5	Enrichment and Review (Optional)

Teaching Math with Confidence: Does My Child Have to Use Specific Strategies for Math Facts?

This week, your child will practice the +6 and +7 facts. You'll teach her to look for a group of 10 on the ten-frame and then add on the remaining counters.

$7 + 5 =$

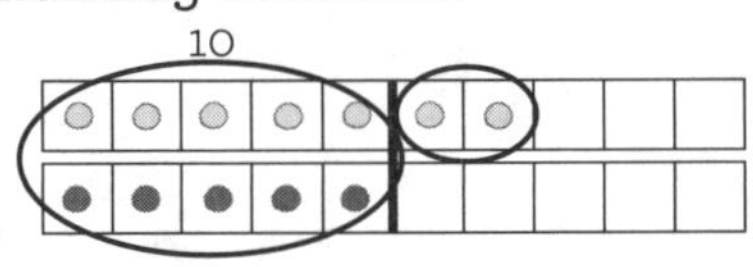

2 groups of 5 make 10. 10 + 2 = 12, so 7 + 5 = 12.

However, your child may prefer to complete a 10 to solve these problems, like she did in Week 4 for the +9 and +8 facts.

$7 + 5 =$

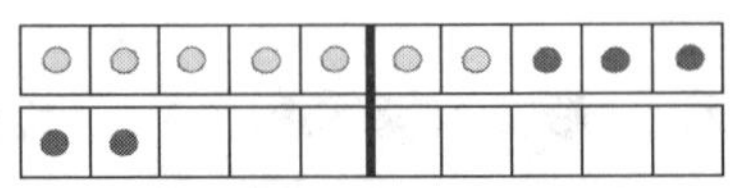

Completing a 10 to add.

Different strategies appeal to different children. Your child might use either of the above strategies, or she might even make up her own. It's fine for her to use any efficient and accurate strategy that makes sense to her.

But, don't allow your child to count one-by-one to find the answers, whether it's out loud, in her head, on her fingers, or with counters. Counting is error-prone and time-consuming, and it prevents children from developing the deeper number sense that more sophisticated strategies help build. If you find your child frequently counting to solve addition and subtraction problems, continue to use counters on the ten-frame and encourage her to see the answers rather than count them.

Extra Materials Needed for Week 5

- 6 forks
- For optional Enrichment and Review Lesson:
  - *Each Orange Had 8 Slices,* written by Paul Giganti Jr. and illustrated by Donald Crews

Lesson 5.1
Review +7 Facts

	Purpose	Materials
Warm-up	• Count by 2s, 5s, and 10s on the number line • Practice memory work • Review doubling numbers to 10	• Blank Number Line (Blackline Master 3) • Double ten-frames (Blackline Master 1), optional • Counters, optional
Activities	• Practice the +7 facts	• Double ten-frames (Blackline Master 1) • Addition Bingo game boards (from workbook page 5.1A) • Counters • Playing cards
Workbook	• Practice the +7 facts	• Workbook page 5.1B

Warm-up: Counting, Memory Work, and Review

- Label the Number Line with 80, 90, and 100. Have your child count from 80 to 100 by 2s, 5s, and 10s. Have her point to each corresponding tick mark as she counts.
- **What do we call the result when we add numbers together?** *The sum.* **What do we call the result when we subtract a number from another number?** *The difference.*
- **What's double 1?** *2.* **What's double 2?** Continue to 10. If your child has trouble, model the number with counters on the top ten-frame and then double the counters on the bottom ten-frame.

Activity: Introduce +7 Addition Facts

Last week, we reviewed the +9 and +8 facts. You only have a few addition facts left to practice! Today, we'll practice the +7 facts.

Write "7 + 5 =" on a piece of paper. Place 7 counters of one color on the top ten-frame and 5 counters of another color on the bottom ten-frame. Point out the groups of 10 and 2 as shown below. **How many counters are on the left side?** *10.* **How many counters are on the right side?** *2.* **So, how many counters are there in all?** *12.*

7 + 5 =

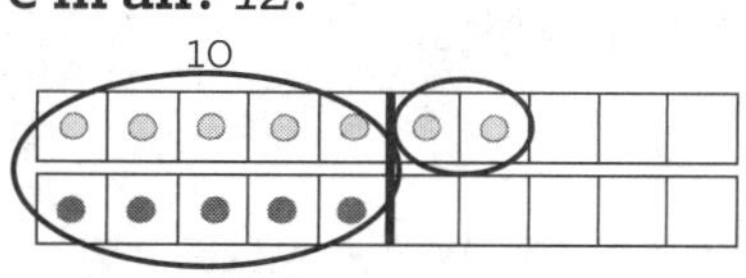

Instead of adding 7 plus 5, you can just add 10 plus 2. Have your child complete the written addition problem: 7 + 5 = 12.

How is this strategy different from the strategy you used to solve the +8 and +9 addition facts? *Sample answer: We don't move any counters.* **How are the strategies similar?** *Sample answer: We make a 10, just in a different way.*

> Some children prefer to solve the +7 and +6 problems by completing a 10, as in Lessons 4.1 and 4.3. Your child can use whichever approach makes the most sense to her, as long as it's efficient and reliable. See the Week 5 **Teaching Math with Confidence** for more details.

Repeat with the other +7 addition facts.

7 + 7 = 14

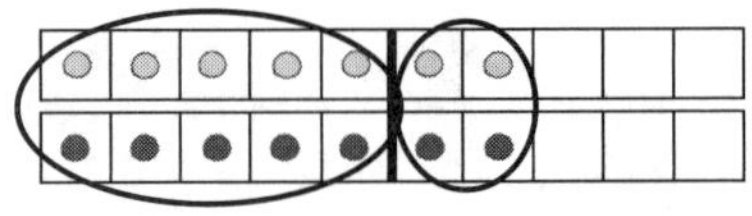

7 + 6 = 13

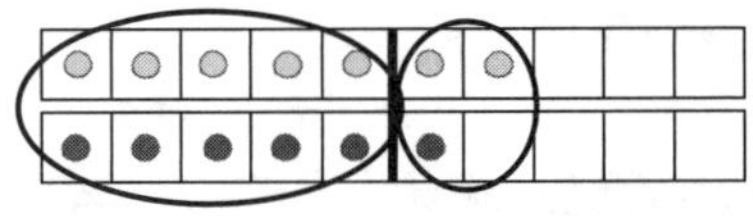

For 7 + 4, have your child imagine taking 1 counter from the 7 and adding it to the row of 4 to make a 5.

7 + 4 = 11

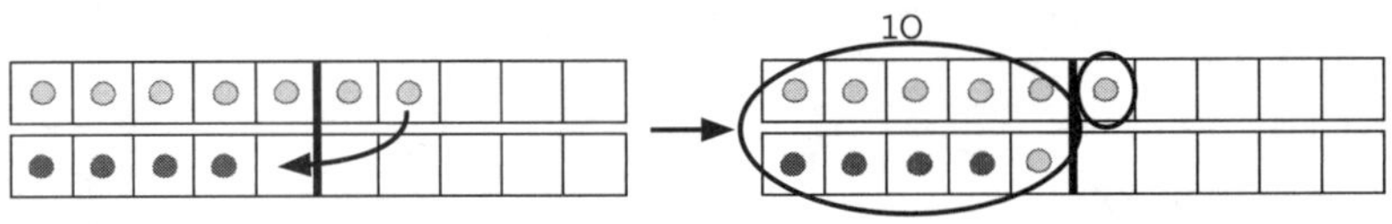

How to visualize 7 + 4

Activity: Play Addition Bingo (+7 Version)

Play Addition Bingo (+7 Version).

This game is like traditional Bingo with your child as the "caller."

Addition Bingo (+7 Version)

Materials: Addition Bingo game boards (from workbook page 5.1A); 4s, 5s, 6s, 7s, 8s, and 9s from a deck of playing cards (24 cards total); counters

Object of the Game: Be the first player to fill in an entire column, row, or diagonal.

Shuffle the cards and place the stack face down on the table. Have each player choose which game board to use.

Have your child turn over the top card and say the sum of the card plus 7. For example, if the card is a 5, your child says, "5 + 7 equals 12." Then, each of you uses a counter to cover a square containing that sum on your game board.

B	I	N	G	O
13	14	15	16	12
16	11	15	12	11
13	15	FREE	11	14
11	16	12	14	13
14	12	13	16	15

B	I	N	G	O
12	13	11	16	12
15	11	16	11	14
13	14	FREE	12	15
11	15	13	14	16
16	12	15	13	14

Continue until one of you wins by filling an entire column, row, or diagonal.

If your counters do not fit on the game board, place the game board in a plastic page protector and mark your plays with dry-erase marker instead.

Save this game board with your math materials so you can play again.

Workbook: Practice +7 Facts and Review

Have your child complete workbook page 5.1B.

Lesson 5.2
How Many More Do I Need? Word Problems

	Purpose	Materials
Warm-up	• Count backwards by 2s, 5s, and 10s on the number line • Practice memory work • Review +7 facts	• Blank Number Line (Blackline Master 3) • Addition Bingo game boards (from workbook page 5.1A) • Counters • Playing cards
Activities	• Model "How many more do I need?" word problems on the Part-Total Mat and write equations to match • Solve "How many more do I need?" word problems	• 6 forks • Part-Total Mat (Blackline Master 2)
Workbook	• Solve addition word problems	• Workbook pages 5.2A and 5.2B

Warm-up: Counting, Memory Work, and Review

- Label the Number Line with 80, 90, and 100. Have your child count backwards from 100 to 80 by 2s, 5s, and 10s. Have him point to each corresponding tick mark as he counts.
- Write the < sign. **What does this sign mean?** *Less than.*
  Write the > sign. **What does this sign mean?** *Greater than.*
- Play Addition Bingo, +7 Version. See Lesson 5.1 (page 76) for directions.

Activity: Model "How Many More Do I Need?" Word Problems on the Part-Total Mat

In the last lesson, you reviewed the +7 addition facts. Today, you'll solve word problems where you find how many more you need of something. We'll do a problem with easier numbers before we tackle some harder ones.

> Solving word problems with easy numbers helps children better understand the problem structure and prepares them to solve problems with more challenging numbers.

Let's pretend we're setting the table for a party. Briefly discuss your child's experiences with setting the table.

Put 6 forks on the table. **Let's pretend you have 6 forks, but you need 10. How many more do you need?** *4.* **How do you know?** *Sample answer: 6 plus 4 equals 10.*

Discuss how to represent the problem on the Part-Total Mat:

- **You have 6 forks. That's one of the parts.** Write 6 on the mat.
- **You need a total of 10 forks.** Write 10 on the mat.
- **You need to find the other part.** Point to the blank box.

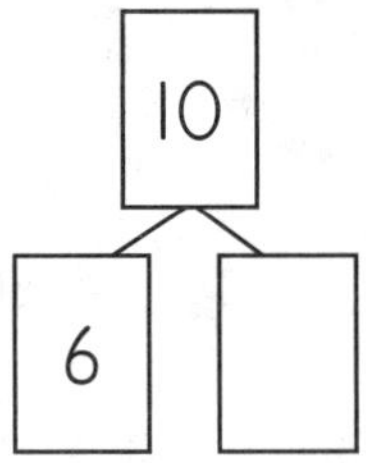

What missing addend equation matches the Part-Total Mat? *6 + __ = 10.* Have your child write the equation on a piece of paper.

$6 + \_\_\_ = 10$

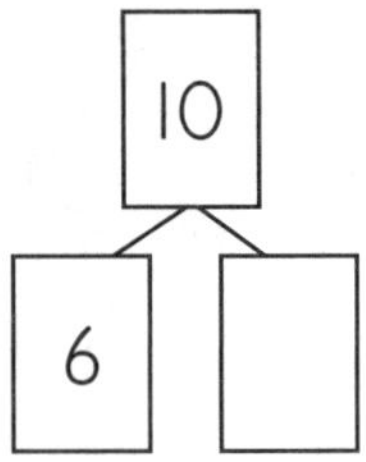

What number completes the equation? *4.* Have your child complete the blank in the equation and write 4 on the Part-Total Mat.

$6 + \underline{4} = 10$

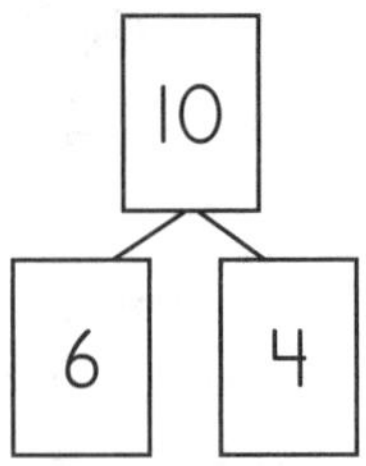

We could also write a subtraction equation. What subtraction equation matches the Part-Total Mat? *10 – 6 = 4.* Have your child write the equation below the previous equation.

$6 + \underline{4} = 10$
$10 - 6 = 4$

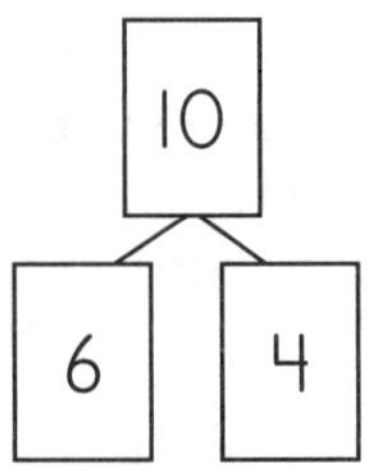

You can use either a missing addend equation or a subtraction problem to solve this problem! In math, there's often more than one way to find an answer.

Activity: Solve Word Problems

Let's solve some more word problems. Watch out: some of them will be similar to the problem you just solved, but there may be some other types mixed in, too!

> When children expect word problems to all follow the same format, they're often tempted to mindlessly follow the pattern. Telling your child in advance that the word problems will vary nudges him to pay closer attention.

Ask your child to listen to the following word problems. Have him model each problem on the Part-Total Mat and then write and solve an equation to match.

If your child has trouble visualizing these problems, act them out with real kitchenware.

- **You have 9 knives, and you need 12. How many more do you need?** *3.*

$9 + \underline{3} = 12$

$12 - 9 = 3$

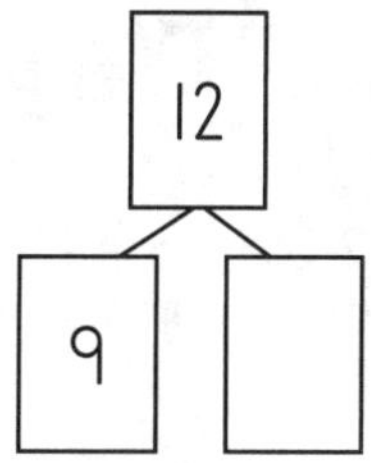

- **You have 7 big spoons and 9 small spoons. How many spoons do you have?** *16.*

$7 + 9 = 16$

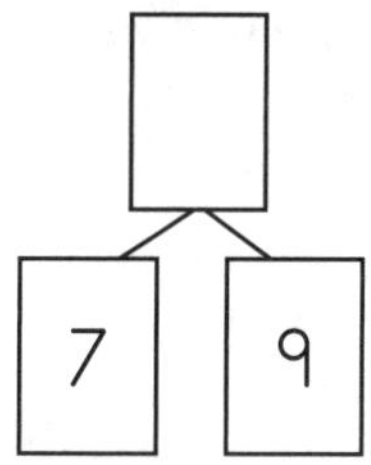

- **You have 9 plates, and you need 15. How many more do you need?** *6.*

$9 + \underline{6} = 15$

$15 - 9 = 6$

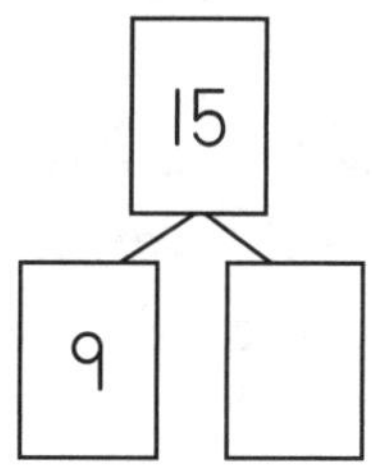

- **You have 9 cups, and then you put 4 back. How many do you have now?** *5.*

$9 - 4 = 5$

$4 + \underline{5} = 9$

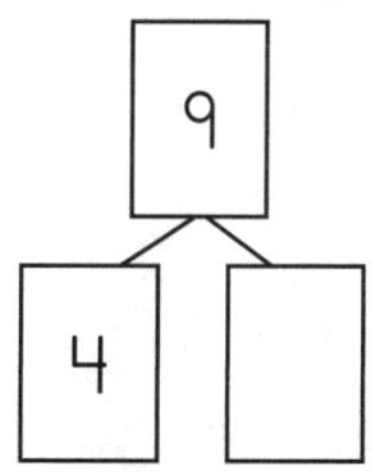

If your child "just knows" the answer and resists completing the Part-Total Mat or writing an equation, write the numbers on the Part-Total Mat yourself as a quick demonstration. Then, have your child orally tell you an equation that matches the numbers on the mat so that he gets practice with translating parts and totals into equations.

Workbook: Solve Word Problems and Review

Have your child complete workbook pages 5.2A and 5.2B.

Lesson 5.3
Review +6 Facts

	Purpose	Materials
Warm-up	• Count money • Practice memory work • Review counting out paper bills	• Play money • 3 small school items (i.e., pencil, ruler, eraser)
Activities	• Practice the +6 facts	• Double ten-frames (Blackline Master 1) • Addition Bingo game boards (from workbook page 5.1A) • Counters • Playing cards
Workbook	• Practice the +6 facts	• Workbook pages 5.3A and 5.3B

Warm-up: Counting, Memory Work, and Review

- Place 8 ten-dollar bills, 1 five-dollar bill, and 1 one-dollar bill on the table. **How much are the bills worth?** *$86.*
- **What do we call the result when we add numbers together?** *The sum.* **What do we call the result when we subtract a number from another number?** *The difference.*
- Write $32, $50, and $19 on separate slips of paper. Place each next to a small school item (like a pencil, ruler, and eraser). Give your child paper bills and have her pretend to buy the items.

Activity: Review +6 Addition Facts

In the last two lessons, you reviewed the +7 facts. Today, you'll use the same strategy for the final +6 addition facts.

Write "6 + 5 =" on a piece of paper. Place 6 counters of one color on the top ten-frame and 5 counters of another color on the bottom ten-frame. Point out the groups of 10 and 1 as shown below. **How many counters are on the left side?** *10.* **How many counters are on the right side?** *1.* **So, how many counters are there in all?** *11.* Have your child complete the written addition problem: 6 + 5 = 11.

6 + 5 = 11

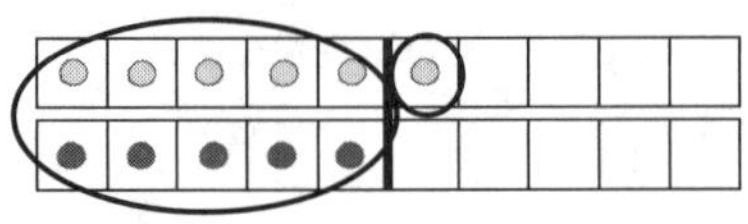

Repeat with 6 + 6 = 12.

As in Lesson 5.1, your child may also solve these problems by completing the 10.

Activity: Play Addition Bingo (+6 Version)

Today we'll play the +6 version of Addition Bingo. Play Addition Bingo. See Lesson 5.1 (page 76) for the general directions.

To play the +6 version, use the 5s, 6s, 7s, 8s, 9s, and 10s from a deck of playing cards (24 cards total). Add 6 to the number on your card. For example, if you flip over a 5, your child says, "5 + 6 equals 11." Each of you covers a square with an 11.

B	I	N	G	O
13	14	15	16	12
16	11	15	12	
13	15	FREE	11	14
11	16	12	14	13
14	12	13	16	15

B	I	N	G	O
12	13	11	16	12
15	11	16		14
13	14	FREE	12	15
11	15	13	14	16
16	12	15	13	14

Workbook: Practice +6 Facts and Review

Have your child complete workbook pages 5.3A and 5.3B.

Lesson 5.4
Word Problems with 3 Addends

	Purpose	Materials
Warm-up	• Count base-ten blocks • Practice memory work • Review +6 facts	• Base-ten blocks • Addition Bingo game boards (from workbook page 5.1A) • Counters • Playing cards
Activities	• Solve word problems with 3 or more addends • Solve word problems with equal groups	• Counters
Workbook	• Solve addition word problems	• Workbook pages 5.4A and 5.4B

Warm-up: Counting, Memory Work, and Review

- Place 8 rods and 20 units on the table. Remind him to trade 10 units for 1 rod every time he counts a group of 10. When he reaches 100, help him trade 10 rods for 1 flat. **What is the value of these blocks?** *100.*
- Write the < sign. **What does this sign mean?** *Less than.*
  Write the > sign. **What does this sign mean?** *Greater than.*
- Play Addition Bingo, +6 Version. See Lesson 5.3 (page 81) for directions.

Activity: Solve Word Problems with 3 Addends

When we solve real-life problems, we often need to add 3 or more numbers. Today, you'll learn how to solve word problems with 3 or more addends.

Let's pretend we want to invite 2 other families over for a party. What two other families should we pretend to invite? *Answers will vary.* Make a simple chart that shows the number of people in each family. Include your own family as well.

Family	Number of People
Snows	4
Brewers	5
Johnsons	6

Sample chart

Let's figure out how many people would be at the party. Help your child write an equation that shows the sum of the number of people in your family and the 2 other families.

$$4 + 5 + 6 =$$

Sample equation

To solve the equation, add the numbers in order from left to right. Have your child add the numbers in order from left to right to find the sum: *4 plus 5 equals 9. 9 plus 6 equals 15.* Have him complete the written equation.

Another way to solve the equation is to add the numbers in pairs. This method can be easier, especially if there are any pairs that equal 10. If your equation has a pair of numbers that equal 10, demonstrate how to solve the problem this way. For example, for the above equation: **We can add numbers in any order. 4 and 6 make 10, so I'll add them first. 4 plus 6 equals 10. 10 plus 5 equals 15.**

Repeat with 2 more families.

$5 + 2 + 6 = 13$

Family	Number of People
Our family	5
Grandma and Grandpa	2
Uncle Paul and Aunt Karen's family	6

Sample chart and equation

Activity: Solve Word Problems with Equal Groups

We can also use addition equations to solve word problems with equal groups. Let's pretend you buy 3 packs of gum, and each pack has 5 pieces of gum. Draw 3 large rectangles on a piece of paper to represent the packs. Have your child place 5 counters in each rectangle to represent the pieces of gum.

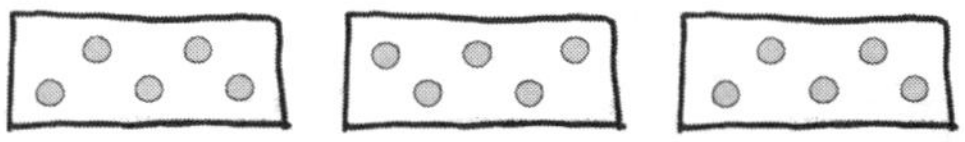

How can you find the total number of pieces of gum in all the packs? *Add up the pieces of gum in all the packs.* Have your child write the matching addition equation: 5 + 5 + 5 = 15.

Have your child model each of the following problems with counters, write a matching addition equation, and solve.

- **You have 5 packs of toy cars. Each pack has 2 cars. How many toy cars do you have?** *10.*

$2 + 2 + 2 + 2 + 2 = 10$

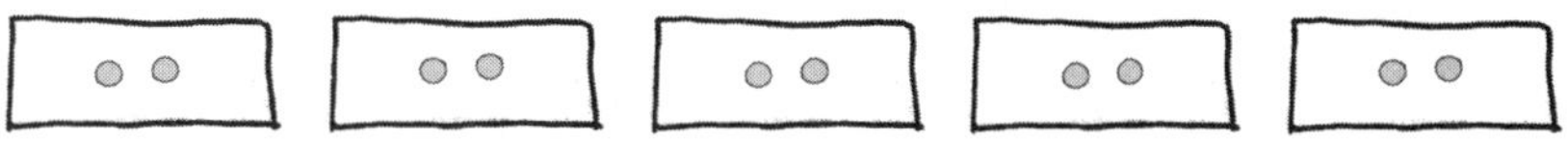

- **You have 4 packs of cookies. Each pack has 3 cookies. How many cookies do you have?** *12.*

$3 + 3 + 3 + 3 = 12$

Workbook: Solve Word Problems and Review

Have your child complete workbook pages 5.4A and 5.4B.

Lesson 5.5
Enrichment and Review (Optional)

	Purpose	Materials
Warm-up	• Count by 2s to 100 • Review memory work • Review your child's favorite or most challenging activities from Week 5	• Varies, depending on the activities you choose
Picture Book	• Solve real-life problems involving equal groups	• *Each Orange Had 8 Slices,* written by Paul Giganti Jr. and illustrated by Donald Crews
Enrichment Activity	• Use addition to calculate future ages	• None

Warm-up: Counting, Memory Work, and Review

- Have your child count by 2s to 100.
- Quiz your child on the memory work through Week 4. See page 523 for the full list.
- If you have time, repeat one or two of the activities from this week's lessons. Choose activities your child especially enjoyed or found challenging.

Math Picture Book: *Each Orange Had 8 Slices*

Read *Each Orange Had 8 Slices,* written by Paul Giganti Jr. and illustrated by Donald Crews. As you read, discuss how the numbers in the text match the illustrations, and have your child answer the questions on each page.

Enrichment Activity: How Old Will I Be?

Write an addition equation that shows how old your child will be in 1 year. For example, if your child is 7, write 7 + 1 = 8. **In 1 more year, you'll be 8.**

$$7 + 1 = 8$$

↑ age

Sample equation. Use your child's actual age as the first addend in the equation and adjust the sum accordingly.

With your child, make a list of similar addition equations showing how old he will be in 2, 3, 4, 5, 6, 7, 8, 9, and 10 years. If your child is 7, your finished list should look like this.

$$7 + 1 = 8$$
$$7 + 2 = 9$$
$$7 + 3 = 10$$
$$7 + 4 = 11$$
$$7 + 5 = 12$$
$$7 + 6 = 13$$
$$7 + 7 = 14$$
$$7 + 8 = 15$$
$$7 + 9 = 16$$
$$7 + 10 = 17$$

Look over the list together and discuss future milestones. For example:

- **In 3 years, you'll be 10 and have 2 digits in your age.**
- **In 6 years, you'll be a teenager.**
- **In 9 years, you'll be old enough to drive!**

Week 5 Answer Key

5.1A

See the Instructor Guide for how to play.
Save these game boards for future lessons.

Addition Bingo

B	I	N	G	O
13	14	15	16	12
16	11	15	12	11
13	15	FREE	11	14
11	16	12	14	13
14	12	13	16	15

B	I	N	G	O
12	13	11	16	12
15	11	16	11	14
13	14	FREE	12	15
11	15	13	14	16
16	12	15	13	14

5.1B

Complete.

7 + 4 = 11 | 7 + 7 = 14 | 7 + 5 = 12 | 7 + 8 = 15 | 7 + 6 = 13

3 + 8 = 11 | 8 + 8 = 16 | 8 + 4 = 12 | 6 + 8 = 14 | 5 + 8 = 13

Complete.

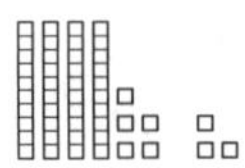
45 + 3 = 48

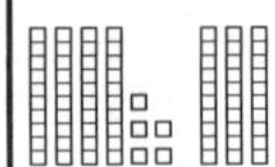
45 + 30 = 75

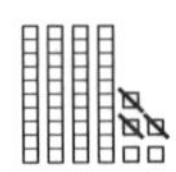
45 - 3 = 42

45 - 30 = 15

5.2A

Solve.

You pick 5 sunflowers. You want 10 sunflowers to make a bouquet.
How many more sunflowers do you need?

10 − 5 = 5

5 sunflowers

Your child may write 5+5=10.

You pick 9 sunflowers. You want 14 to make a bouquet.
How many more sunflowers do you need?

14 − 9 = 5

5 sunflowers

Your child may write 9+5=14.

Complete.

7 + 4 = 11 | 7 + 6 = 13 | 7 + 5 = 12 | 7 + 7 = 14 | 7 + 8 = 15

9 + 7 = 16 | 8 + 8 = 16 | 6 + 8 = 14 | 9 + 4 = 13 | 5 + 8 = 13

5.2B

Complete.

1 double → 2
5 double → 10
10 double → 20
3 double → 6
4 double → 8
6 double → 12

Color the rectangles. X the shapes that are not rectangles.

Match the pairs that make 100.

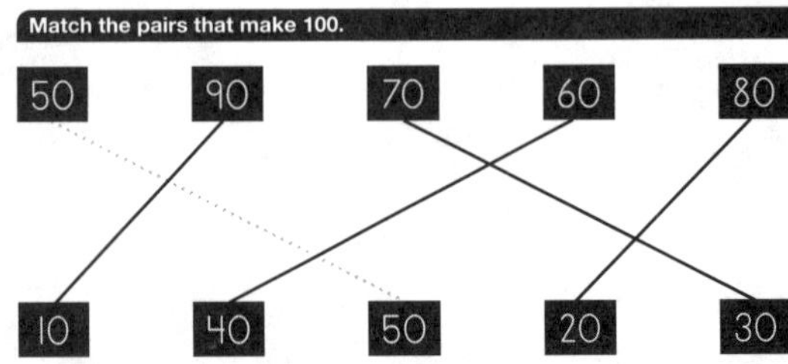

Week 5 Answer Key

5.3A

Complete.

$6 + 6 = 12$ $6 + 4 = 10$ $6 + 5 = 11$ $6 + 7 = 13$ $6 + 8 = 14$

$7 + 5 = 12$ $7 + 8 = 15$ $7 + 7 = 14$ $7 + 4 = 11$ $7 + 6 = 13$

Color the addition facts that equal the number in the star.

13	14	15	16
5 + 8	7 + 7	9 + 6	9 + 9
9 + 3	9 + 4	8 + 7	8 + 8
7 + 7	6 + 8	4 + 8	6 + 5
7 + 6	5 + 7	8 + 8	7 + 9

5.3B

Ethan made a bar graph about the animals he saw at the zoo. Use the bar graph to answer the questions.

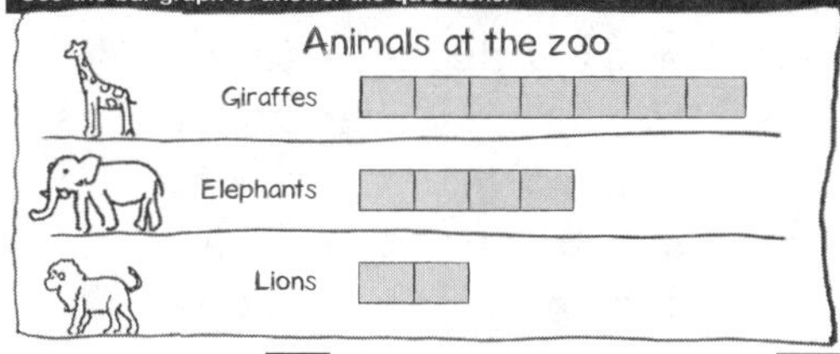

How many giraffes did he see? 7

How many elephants did he see? 4

How many lions did he see? 2

How many more giraffes than elephants did he see? 3

How many more giraffes than lions did he see? 5

Complete the circles with <, >, or =.

35 < 36	34 < 35	30 = 30
76 > 46	92 > 27	50 < 83

Complete the fact family to match the Part-Total Diagram.

Total: 13; Parts: 6, 7

6 + 7 = 13
7 + 6 = 13
13 - 6 = 7
13 - 7 = 6

5.4A

Solve.

You have 4 round crackers,
5 square crackers, and 4 triangle crackers.
How many crackers do you have?

4 + 5 + 4 = 13

13 crackers

You see 3 cardinals, 5 blue jays, and 7 robins.
How many birds do you see?

3 + 5 + 7 = 15

15 birds

You buy 3 packs of pencils.
Each pack has 6 pencils.
How many pencils do you buy?

6 + 6 + 6 = 18

18 pencils

5.4B

Complete.

5 + 6 = 11	7 + 4 = 11	6 + 7 = 13
6 + 9 = 15	6 + 6 = 12	9 + 9 = 18
4 + 7 = 11	9 + 5 = 14	7 + 7 = 14
8 + 8 = 16	6 + 5 = 11	8 + 6 = 14

Color the squares. X the shapes that are not squares.

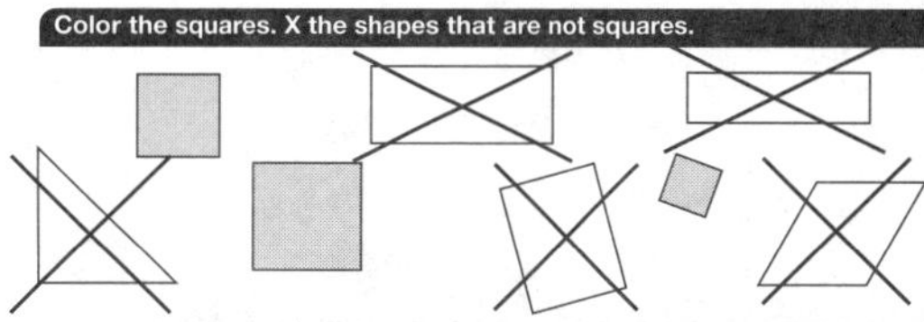

Complete the missing numbers in the sequences.

Unit 2 Checkpoint

What to Expect at the End of Unit 2

By the end of Unit 2, most children will be able to do the following:

- Find most single-digit sums mentally and in less than 3 seconds. Some children will still need a little more time (or counters on ten-frames) to solve some of the more difficult problems, especially the +6 and +7 facts.
- Write and solve equations to match addition word problems. Most second-graders will have no trouble with simple joining problems, but some will need more practice with the "How many more do I need?" problems from Lesson 5.2.

Is Your Child Ready to Move on?

In Unit 3, your child will learn to count to 200 and read, write, and compare numbers to 200. Before moving on to Unit 3, your child should have mastered the following skills:

- Represent numbers to 100 with base-ten blocks.
- Read and write numbers to 100.
- Know the value of coins and count small combinations of coins or paper bills.

Your child does not need to have fully mastered the addition facts with sums to 20. He'll have more opportunities to practice them throughout Unit 3. You'll find an informal addition fact assessment at the end of Unit 3 to help assess your child's progress.

What to Do If Your Child Needs More Practice

If your child is having trouble with the skills listed above, spend a day or two practicing the corresponding review activities below before moving on to Unit 3.

Activities for representing numbers to 100 with base-ten blocks

- Make Designs with Base-Ten Blocks (Lesson 3.1)
- Race to 100 (Lesson 3.2)

Activities for reading and writing numbers to 100

- Guess the Secret Number (Warm-up, Lesson 2.1)
- Race to 100 (Lesson 3.2)

Activity for counting combinations of coins or paper bills

- Pretend Store with Coins (Warm-up, Lesson 3.4)
- Pretend Store with Paper Bills (Warm-up, Lesson 5.3)

Unit 3
Numbers to 200

Overview

Your child will build on what she knows about the numbers to 100 to read, write, and compare numbers to 200. She'll reinforce her understanding of place value and strengthen her number sense as she doubles and finds halves of numbers, identifies the number of objects in arrays, writes numbers in expanded form, and counts paper bills and coins.

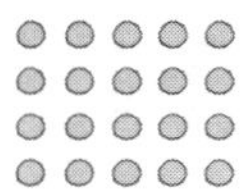

Arrays

137 = 100 + 30 + 7

Expanded form of numbers to 200

Counting money

Throughout the unit, your child will continue to practice the addition facts. If she often takes more than 3 seconds to find the answers to the addition facts, make sure to prioritize addition fact practice so that she is ready to use the addition facts to help master the subtraction facts in Unit 4.

Week 6	Equal Groups
Week 7	Numbers to 200
Week 8	Money

What Your Child Will Learn

In this unit your child will learn to:

- Use base-ten blocks to double or find half of numbers
- Identify even and odd numbers
- Use repeated addition to find the number of objects in an array
- Read, write, and compare numbers to 200
- Understand place value in numbers to 200
- Write numbers to 200 in expanded form
- Solve simple mental addition and subtraction problems with the numbers to 200
- Write money amounts with a dollar sign and decimal point, or with a cents sign
- Count combinations of bills and coins (including twenty-dollar bills and quarters)

Recommended Math Picture Books (Optional)

These picture books are scheduled in the optional Enrichment and Review lessons at the end of each week.

- *One Grain of Rice: A Mathematical Folktale*, by Demi. Scholastic Press, 1997.
- *How Many Seeds in a Pumpkin?*, written by Margaret McNamara and illustrated by G. Brian Karas. Schwartz & Wade, 2007.
- *Lemonade in Winter*, written by Emily Jenkins and illustrated by G. Brian Karas. Schwartz & Wade, 2012.

Week 6
Equal Groups

Overview

In Unit 2, your child doubled numbers to 10 and solved word problems with equal groups. This week, he'll learn more about equal groups as he doubles numbers greater than 10, finds halves of quantities, and uses repeated addition to find the number of objects in an array. He'll also learn how to identify even and odd numbers to 100.

Lesson 6.1	Double Numbers to 100
Lesson 6.2	Find Half of Numbers to 100
Lesson 6.3	Identify Even and Odd Numbers
Lesson 6.4	Repeated Addition and Arrays
Lesson 6.5	Enrichment and Review (Optional)

Teaching Math with Confidence: Laying the Foundation for Multiplication

Throughout second grade, your child will work with equal groups so that he is well-prepared to learn multiplication in third grade. He already began to work with equal groups in Unit 2, when he learned how to double numbers to 10 and solve equal-group word problems.

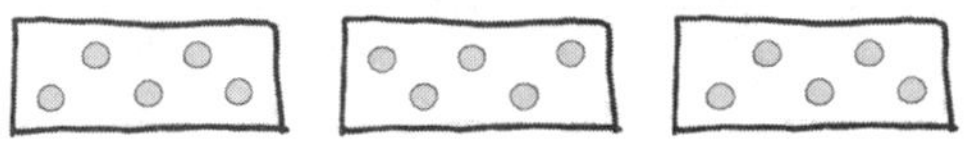

In Lesson 5.4, your child added 5 + 5 + 5 to find how many pieces of gum are in 3 packs of gum (with 5 pieces in each pack). In third grade, he'll discover he can multiply 3 × 5 to find the total.

This week, your child will extend that learning as he doubles numbers to 100. He'll also organize blocks into rows and columns and use repeated addition to find the total number of blocks.

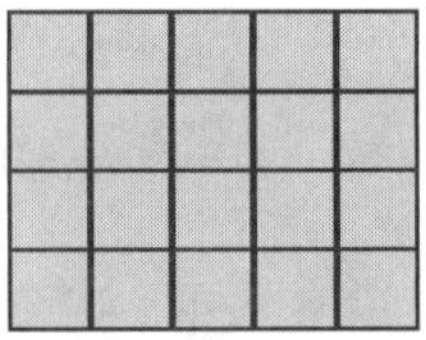

In Lesson 6.4, your child will count by 5s or add 5 + 5 + 5 + 5 to find the total number of blocks. Next year, he'll find the total by multiplying 4 × 5.

Your child will continue to practice equal-groups problems in the warm-ups and workbook review pages. By the end of second grade, he'll be familiar with many of the combinations up to 5 × 5 and ready to master the multiplication facts in third grade.

Extra Materials Needed for Week 6

- Construction paper or cardstock
- 30-40 slips of paper (or index cards or sticky notes)
- Crayons or colored pencils
- 25 square or rectangular blocks, any size or material
- For optional Enrichment and Review Lesson:
    - *One Grain of Rice: A Mathematical Folktale,* by Demi
    - Paper
    - Scissors

Lesson 6.1
Double Numbers to 100

	Purpose	Materials
Warm-up	• Count base-ten blocks by 1s, starting at 100 • Practice memory work • Review mental addition	• Base-ten blocks
Activities	• Use base-ten blocks to double numbers • Practice trading 10 ones for 1 ten	• Construction paper or cardstock • About 10 slips of paper • Base-ten blocks • Place-Value Chart (Blackline Master 5)
Workbook	• Double numbers	• Workbook pages 6.1A and 6.1B

In this lesson, your child will discover that the mysterious Number Machine doubles numbers. Make sure to hide the lesson title while you teach so as not to spoil the surprise.

Warm-up: Counting, Memory Work, and Review

- Place 1 flat and a small handful of unit blocks on the table. Help your child count to find the value of the blocks, starting at 100: 100, 101.... Help her trade 10 units for 1 rod every time she counts a group of 10.

  This week's counting activities introduce the counting sequence beyond 100 so that your child is ready to learn to read and write numbers to 200 in Week 7.

- **How many tens equal 1 hundred?** *10.*
- Write the following problems on paper and have your child solve them mentally. Allow her to use base-ten blocks as needed.
  - × 52 + 4 = *56*
  - × 79 + 1 = *80*
  - × 40 + 40 = *80*
  - × 30 + 55 = *85*
  - × 70 + 30 = *100*

  Most second graders will need to think hard to solve these problems. Writing the problems on paper helps reduce the cognitive load so that your child doesn't have to simultaneously remember the numbers and solve the problems.

Activity: Introduce the Number Machine

You have already learned how to use place-value thinking to add in your head. Today, we'll make a Number Machine to help you learn how to use place-value thinking in a new way.

Write *Number Machine* on a horizontal piece of construction paper or cardstock. Have your child draw a few mechanical parts on it, like gears, dials, or switches.

Fold the paper in half. Stand it on the table between you and your child so that your child faces the paper's decorated side.

This activity works best if you sit across from your child, with the folded paper between you.

Here's how the Number Machine works: We put a number into the machine. Then, the machine changes the number and tells us the result. There are many different ways to set the Number Machine. But, once it's set, it always does the same thing to every number we put into it.

Pretend to turn a knob on the front of the machine to set it. **Let's see what happens when I put 4 into the Number Machine on this setting.** Write 4 on a slip of paper, show it to your child, and slide it behind the Number Machine screen. Secretly write 8 on the back of the slip and slide it out from behind the other side of the screen.

Hmm, when 4 goes in, 8 comes out. What do you think the Number Machine did? *Sample answers: It added 4 to the number. It doubled it.*

Accept any answer that fits the numbers.

Let's try a few more numbers to learn more about how the machine works on this setting. Demonstrate the following numbers.

- **When 3 goes in, 6 comes out.**

- **When 7 goes in, 14 comes out.**
- **When 10 goes in, 20 comes out.**

If 5 goes in, what number do you think will come out? *10.* Have your child write 5 on a slip of paper and slide it behind the Number Machine. Secretly write 10 on the back of the slip and slide it out.

What does the Number Machine do to the numbers on this setting? *Sample answers: It doubles the number. It makes the number twice as much. It adds the number to itself.*

On this setting, the Number Machine doubles the number that we put into it, just like we used a mirror to double counters in Lesson 4.4. It adds the number to itself, so the new number is always twice as much as the original number.

Activity: Double Numbers with Base-Ten Blocks

Let's try some larger numbers. We'll use base-ten blocks to predict what number will come out of the Number Machine.

Write 32 on a paper slip. Have your child model it with base-ten blocks on the Place-Value Chart.

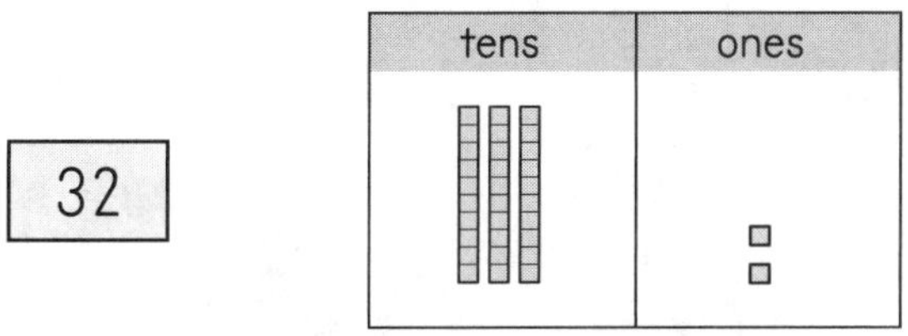

To double 32, we have to double both the tens and the ones. Add 3 rods and 2 units to the Place-Value Chart. **So, what's double 32?** *64.*

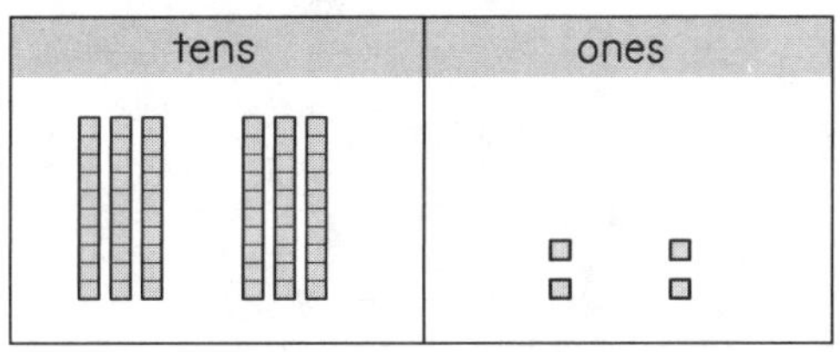

Slide 32 behind the Number Machine. Write 64 on the back and slide it out the other side.

Let's try another one. Write 15 on a slip of paper. Have your child model it with base-ten blocks on the Place-Value Chart and then double the blocks. **Looks like we have a group of 10 in the ones-place!** Have your child trade the 10 units for 1 rod. **So, what's double 15?** *30.*

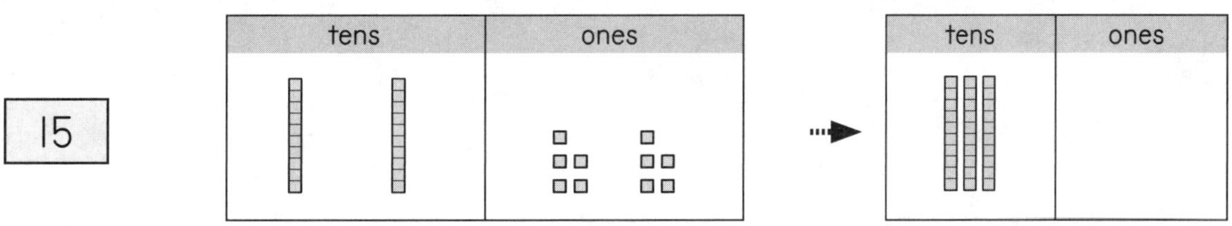

Slide 15 behind the Number Machine. Write 30 on the back and slide it out the other side.

Activity: Practice Doubling Numbers

Have your child predict the Number Machine's results for the following numbers. She can model the numbers with base-ten blocks or find the answers mentally.

- **If 7 goes into the Number Machine, what number will come out?** *14.*
- **If 11 goes in, what number will come out?** *22.*
- **If 13 goes in, what number will come out?** *26.*
- **If 21 goes in, what number will come out?** *42.*
- **If 25 goes in, what number will come out?** *50.*
- **If 26 goes in, what number will come out?** *52.*

Save the Number Machine for future lessons.

Workbook: Double Numbers and Review

Have your child complete workbook pages 6.1A and 6.1B.

Lesson 6.2
Find Half of Numbers to 100

	Purpose	Materials
Warm-up	• Count by 1s starting at 100 • Practice memory work • Review doubling	• Number Machine (from Lesson 6.1) • 6 slips of paper
Activities	• Understand what it means to find half of a quantity • Use base-ten blocks to find half of numbers • Practice trading 1 ten for 10 ones	• Number Machine (from Lesson 6.1) • 12 slips of paper • Base-ten blocks • Place-Value Chart (Blackline Master 5)
Workbook	• Find halves of numbers	• Workbook pages 6.2A and 6.2B

Your child will use the Number Machine again in this lesson, but you'll pretend to put it on a different setting than you used in Lesson 6.1. Again, hide the lesson title so your child has the opportunity to figure out for himself how the Number Machine works on this new setting.

Warm-up: Counting, Memory Work, and Review

- **Let's see how high you can count while standing on one foot and starting at 100!** Have your child count as he stands on one foot: *100, 101...* Have him stop once he loses his balance.
- **How many tens equal 1 hundred?** *10.*
- Set up the Number Machine and pretend to set it to the Double setting.
    - **If 7 goes in, what number will come out?** *14.*
    - **If 8 goes in, what number will come out?** *16.*
    - **If 9 goes in, what number will come out?** *18.*
    - **If 10 goes in, what number will come out?** *20.*
    - **If 12 goes in, what number will come out?** *24.*
    - **If 40 goes in, what number will come out?** *80.*

Model the questions with base-ten blocks as needed.

Activity: Introduce Finding Half with the Number Machine

In the last lesson, I set the Number Machine to double numbers. What does it mean to double a number? *Sample answer: Find twice as much.*

Today, we'll set the Number Machine to a different setting. Stand the Number Machine on the table between you and your child. Pretend to turn a knob on the front of the machine to set it.

Let's see what happens when I put 4 into the Number Machine on this setting. Write 4 on a slip of paper and slide it behind the Number Machine screen. Secretly write 2 on the back of the slip and slide it out from behind the other side of the screen.

4 → 2

Hmm, when 4 goes in, 2 comes out. What do you think the Number Machine did? *Sample answers: It subtracted 2 from 4. It split 2 in half.*

Accept any answer that fits the numbers.

Let's try a few more numbers to see how the machine works on this setting. Demonstrate the following numbers.

- **When 6 goes in, 3 comes out.**

- **When 20 goes in, 10 comes out.**
- **When 10 goes in, 5 comes out.**

These input numbers are all even so that they can be evenly divided in half without a remainder or fraction. You will discuss even and odd numbers in Lesson 6.3.

What does the Number Machine do to the numbers on this setting? *It splits the numbers in half.* **On this setting, the Number Machine splits the number in half. It splits the quantity into 2 equal groups, just like when you split a cookie in half into 2 equal pieces.**

Activity: Find Half of Numbers with Counters

Put 8 counters on the table and have your child split them into two equal groups. **If 8 goes in, what number do you think will come out?** *4.* Have your child write 8 on a slip of paper and slide it behind the Number Machine. Secretly write 4 on the back of the slip and slide it out.

To find half of a number, you can use counters and split the counters into two equal groups. Or, you can think, "What plus itself equals this number?" 4 plus 4 equals 8, so 4 is half of 8.

Have your child predict the Number Machine's results for the following numbers. He can model the numbers with counters or use addition to find the answers.

- **If 12 goes in, what number will come out?** *6.*
- **If 14 goes in, what number will come out?** *7.*
- **If 18 goes in, what number will come out?** *9.*

Activity: Find Half of Numbers with Base-Ten Blocks

Let's leave the Number Machine set to the Half setting and try some larger numbers. We'll use base-ten blocks to predict what number will come out of the Number Machine.

Write 24 on a paper slip. Have your child model it with base-ten blocks on the Place-Value Chart.

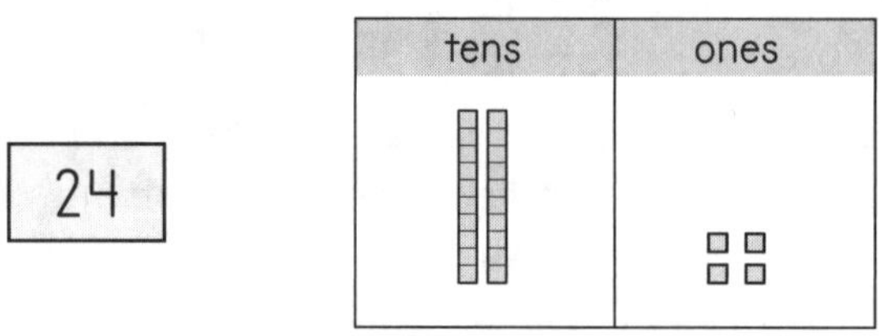

To find half of 24, we have to split the blocks into 2 equal groups. Split the base-ten blocks into 2 equal groups. **So, what's half of 24?** *12.*

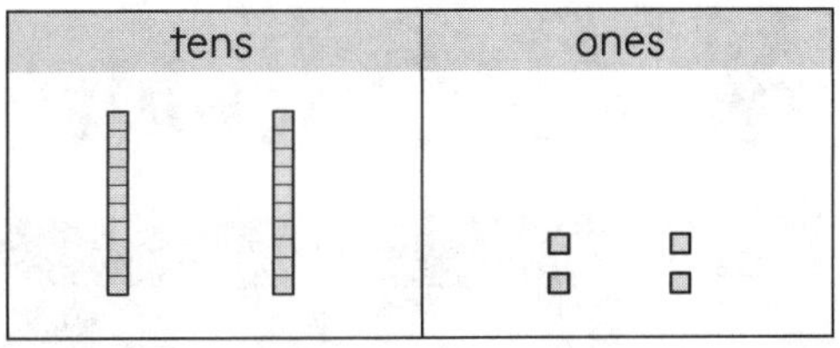

Slide 24 behind the Number Machine. Write 12 on the back and slide it out the other side.

24 → 12

Have your child use base-ten blocks to predict the Number Machine's results for the following numbers.

- **If 28 goes in, what number will come out?** *14.*
- **If 42 goes in, what number will come out?** *21.*
- **If 30 goes in, what number will come out?** *15.*

For 30, have your child trade 1 rod for 10 units so that he can split the blocks in half.

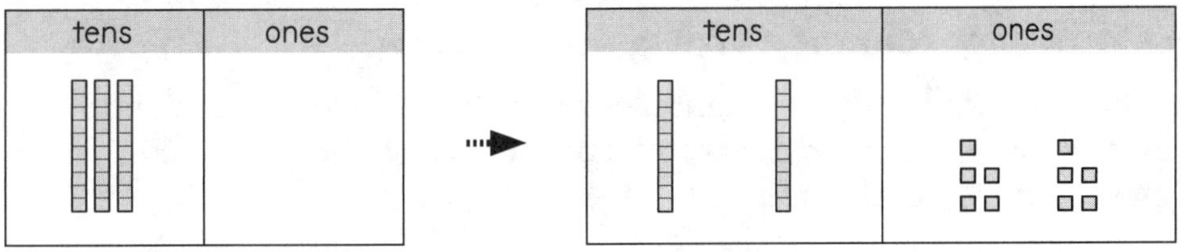

Workbook: Find Half and Review

Have your child complete workbook pages 6.2A and 6.2B.

Lesson 6.3
Identify Even and Odd Numbers

	Purpose	Materials
Warm-up	• Count base-ten blocks by 1s, starting at 100 • Practice memory work • Review finding half	• Base-ten blocks • Number Machine (from Lesson 6.1) • 5 slips of paper
Activities	• Learn the definitions of even and odd numbers • Use patterns to identify even and odd numbers to 100	• Number Machine (from Lesson 6.1) • Base-ten blocks • Workbook page 6.3A • Crayons or colored pencils
Workbook	• Identify even and odd numbers	• Workbook pages 6.3A and 6.3B

Warm-up: Counting, Memory Work, and Review

- Place 1 flat and two handfuls of unit blocks on the table. Help your child count to find the value of the blocks, starting at 100: **100, 101...** Help her trade 10 units for 1 rod every time she counts a group of 10.
- **How many tens equal 1 hundred?** *10.*
- Set up the Number Machine and pretend to set it to the Half setting. Model the questions with base-ten blocks as needed.
  - **If 6 goes in, what number comes out?** *3.*
  - **If 10 goes in, what number comes out?** *5.*
  - **If 18 goes in, what number comes out?** *9.*
  - **If 20 goes in, what number comes out?** *10.*
  - **If 28 goes in, what number will come out?** *14.*

Activity: Review Even and Odd Numbers

In first grade, you memorized the even and odd numbers up to 20. Today, you'll learn how to tell whether any number up to 100 is even or odd.

In the last lesson, we set the Number Machine to the Half setting. What does it mean to find half of a number? *Sample answer: split it into two equal parts.*

When we can split a number into 2 equal groups, we call it an even number. 6, 10, and 20 can all be split evenly in half, so they are even numbers.

Let's see what happens if I put 5 into the Number Machine. Write 5 on a slip of paper and slide it behind the Number Machine. **Error, error!** Pretend that the Number Machine rejects the slip of paper, and slide it back out the same way you put it in the machine.

The Number Machine can't find half of 5! Why do you think that is? *Answers will vary.*

Give your child 5 counters and have her try to split them into 2 equal groups. **It's not possible to split the 5 counters into 2 equal groups unless we cut one of them in half. The Number Machine only uses whole numbers, so it can't find half of 5.**

When a number of blocks can't be split evenly into 2 equal groups, we call it an odd number. So, 5 is an odd number.

> If your child is interested, discuss real life situations in which it is possible to find half of a quantity. For example: **Let's pretend that you and I had 5 cookies to share equally. How many cookies would each of us get?** *2 and a half.* Your child will learn more about fractions in Unit 11.

Activity: Identify Even and Odd Numbers on the 100 Chart

Show your child the 100 Chart at the top of workbook page 6.3 and read the directions aloud. **Let's figure out which numbers from 1 to 100 are odd and which are even.**

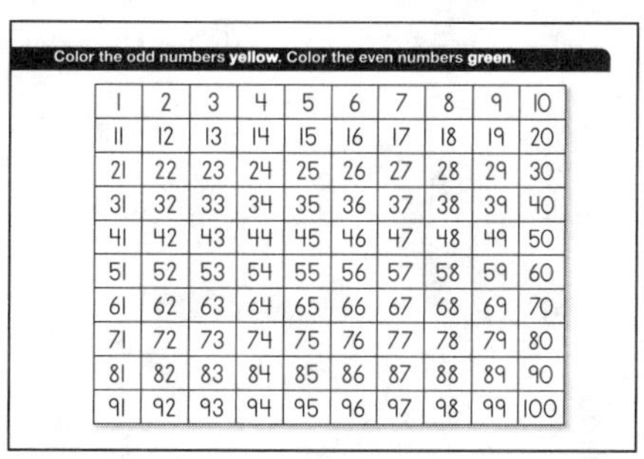

Color the odd numbers **yellow**. Color the even numbers **green**.

1	2	3	4	5	6	7	8	9	10
11	12	13	14	15	16	17	18	19	20
21	22	23	24	25	26	27	28	29	30
31	32	33	34	35	36	37	38	39	40
41	42	43	44	45	46	47	48	49	50
51	52	53	54	55	56	57	58	59	60
61	62	63	64	65	66	67	68	69	70
71	72	73	74	75	76	77	78	79	80
81	82	83	84	85	86	87	88	89	90
91	92	93	94	95	96	97	98	99	100

> If your child immediately knows which numbers are even and odd, allow her to simply color the columns of the 100 Chart to match the directions. Then, have her choose a few numbers and use base-ten blocks to prove to you that they are even or odd. For example: *I can split 42 into 2 equal groups, so it's even. I have 1 unit left over when I try to split 67 into 2 equal groups, so it's odd.*

Point to 1 on the 100 Chart. Can you split 1 counter into 2 equal groups? *No.* **So, is 1 even or odd?** *Odd.* Have your child color the square purple.

Point to 2 on the 100 Chart. **Can you split 2 counters into 2 equal groups?** *Yes.* **So, is 2 even or odd?** *Even.* Have your child color the square with the 2 green.

Continue in this way with the numbers through 20. If your child isn't sure about a number, have her model the number with counters and see if she can split the counters into two equal groups.

1	2	3	4	5	6	7	8	9	10
11	12	13	14	15	16	17	18	19	20

What patterns do you notice? *Possible answers: The numbers go even-odd-even-odd. The even numbers are in the columns below 2, 4, 6, 8, and 10. The odd numbers are in the columns below 1, 3, 5, 7, and 9.*

Do you think 42 is even or odd? *Even.* Encourage your child to find 42 on the 100 Chart and look at the pattern to help make her prediction. Then, have her model 42 with base-ten blocks and split them into two groups to check that the number is even.

1	2	3	4	5	6	7	8	9	10
11	12	13	14	15	16	17	18	19	20
21	22	23	24	25	26	27	28	29	30
31	32	33	34	35	36	37	38	39	40
41	42	43	44	45	46	47	48	49	50
51	52	53	54	55	56	57	58	59	60
61	62	63	64	65	66	67	68	69	70
71	72	73	74	75	76	77	78	79	80
81	82	83	84	85	86	87	88	89	90
91	92	93	94	95	96	97	98	99	100

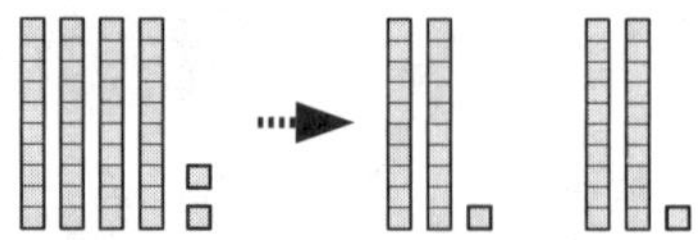

Repeat with 43, 66, 67, 90, 91 and 100. Have your child color each square after she identifies whether the number is even or odd.

For 90, 91, and 100, your child will need to trade 1 rod for 10 units or 1 flat for 10 rods as she tries to split the blocks into equal groups.

The even/odd pattern that you found with the numbers to 20 holds true for all numbers! If a number has 1, 3, 5, 7, or 9 in the ones-place, the number is odd. Have your child color the rest of the odd numbers on the 100 Chart purple. **If a number has 0, 2, 4, 6, or 8 in the ones-place, the number is even.** Have your child color the rest of the even numbers on the 100 Chart green.

1	2	3	4	5	6	7	8	9	10
11	12	13	14	15	16	17	18	19	20

Workbook: Identify Even and Odd Numbers and Review

Have your child complete workbook pages 6.3A and 6.3B.

Lesson 6.4
Repeated Addition and Arrays

	Purpose	Materials
Warm-up	• Count from 100 to 120 on the number line • Practice memory work • Review identifying even and odd numbers	• Blank Number Line (Blackline Master 3)
Activities	• Write addition equations to match arrays • Identify the total number of objects in an array	• Counters • 25 square or rectangular blocks, any size or material • Dot array and L-cover (Blackline Master 6)
Workbook	• Find the total number of objects in an array	• Workbook pages 6.4A and 6.4B

You will need the Dot Array and L-cover (Blackline Master 6) for the first time in this lesson. Cut out the L-cover along the dotted lines before the lesson.

Warm-up: Counting, Memory Work, and Review

- Label the Number Line with 100, 110, and 120. Have your child count from 100 to 120. Have him point to each corresponding tick mark as he counts.
- **How many tens equal 1 hundred?** *10.*
- Have your child tell whether each of the following numbers is even or odd.
  - × 6. *Even.*
  - × 7. *Odd.*
  - × 15. *Odd.*
  - × 16. *Even.*
  - × 30. *Even.*
  - × 54. *Even.*
  - × 83. *Odd.*
  - × 100. *Even.*

Activity: Add to Find the Number of Objects in an Array

You have learned a lot about doubling and finding half this week! Today, you'll learn about arrays. An array is a group of objects arranged in rows and columns. Arrange 12 counters in 3 rows of 4.

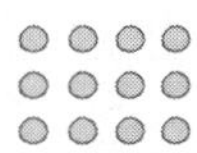

See the Week 6 **Teaching Math with Confidence** to learn how arrays preview multiplication.

Bakers often arrange doughnuts and muffins in arrays. Let's pretend the counters are muffins. How many rows of muffins are there? *3.* **How many muffins are in each row?** *4.*

Let's write an addition equation that shows the sum of the muffins in each row. Write 4 + 4 + 4 = on a piece of paper. Discuss how each 4 in the equation corresponds to one row of muffins. Have your child find the sum and complete the equation. **What does the 12 stand for?** *The total number of muffins.*

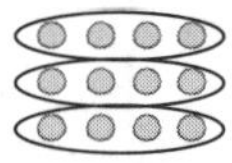

4 + 4 + 4 = 12

How many columns of muffins are there? *4.* **How many muffins are in each column?** *3.* **We can also write an equation that shows the sum of the muffins in each column.** Help your child write this equation: 3 + 3 + 3 + 3 = 12. Emphasize that each 3 corresponds to the muffins in one column.

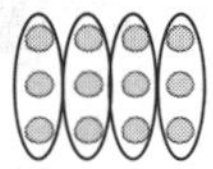

3 + 3 + 3 + 3 = 12

What does the 12 stand for? *The total number of muffins.* **We get the same total whether we add the rows or the columns.**

Activity: Build Block Arrays

Builders often create arrays when they stack bricks, lay tiles, or install windows. Let's pretend that you're a builder making a tile floor from these blocks. Place about 25 square or rectangular blocks on the table.

Have you child create an array with 4 rows and 5 columns. **Each row has 5 blocks, so we can count by 5s to find the total number of blocks.** Point to each row as you count it: 5, 10, 15, 20.

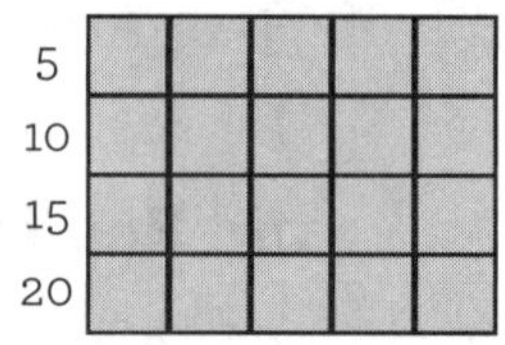

Have your child create an array with 2 rows and 7 columns. **How many blocks are in the array?** *14.* **How did you find the total?** *Answers will vary.*

Point out that you could add 7 plus 7 or count by 2s to find the total, if your child doesn't mention these methods. **There's lots of ways to find the number of objects in array! You can use whatever method makes the most sense to you. Just don't count every block one-by-one, because that takes a long time!**

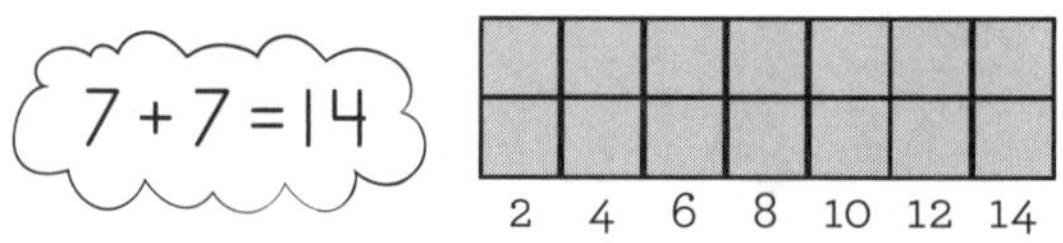

Two ways to find the number of blocks.

Have your child build the following arrays and tell how many blocks are in each. Encourage him to use addition or skip-counting to find the totals rather than counting one-by-one.

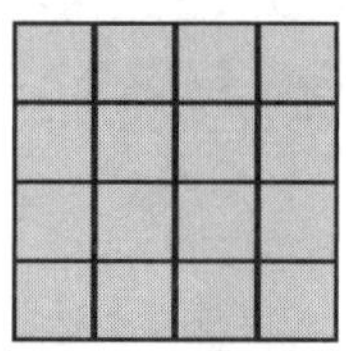

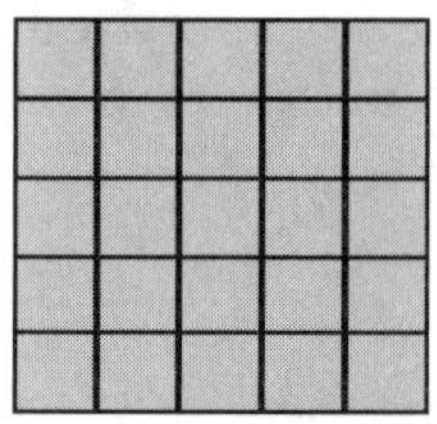

If your child is interested, look around your house for bricks, tiles, windows, or other objects arranged in arrays.

Activity: Introduce the Dot Array

Show your child the dot array and L-cover (Blackline Master 6). **These dots are arranged in an array.**

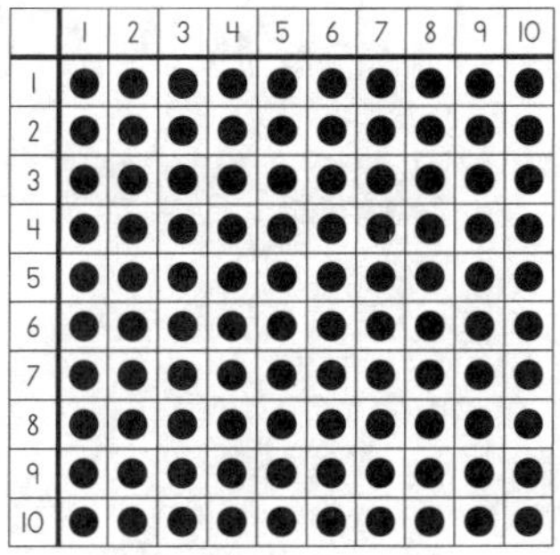

Slide the L-cover over the dot array so that 3 rows of 6 are showing. **The numbers on the top and side tell how many rows and columns are showing so that you don't have to count. How many rows are in this array?** *3.* **How many columns are in this array?** *6.*

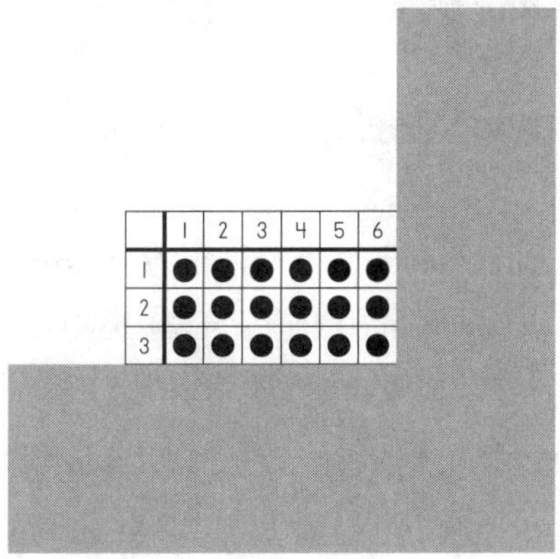

How many dots are in the array? *18.* If your child starts to count each dot individually, encourage her to add 6 + 6 + 6 instead.

Have your child find the total number of dots in the following arrays.

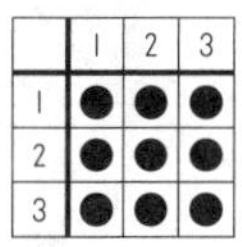

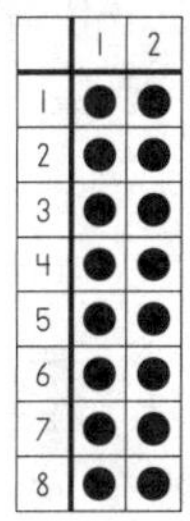

Workbook: Find the Number of Objects in Arrays and Review

Have your child complete workbook pages 6.4A and 6.4B.

Lesson 6.5
Enrichment and Review (Optional)

	Purpose	Materials
Warm-up	• Count from 100 to 150 • Review memory work • Review your child's favorite or most challenging activities from Week 6	• Varies, depending on the activities you choose
Picture Book	• Understand doubling in the context of a folktale • Discover that repeated doubling increases	• *One Grain of Rice: A Mathematical Folktale,* by Demi
Enrichment Activity	• Explore finding half repeatedly	• Paper • Scissors

Warm-up: Counting, Memory Work, and Review

- Have your child count from 100 to 150.
- Quiz your child on the memory work through Week 6. See page 523 for the full list.
- If you have time, repeat one or two of the activities from this week's lessons. Choose activities your child especially enjoyed or found challenging.

Math Picture Book: *One Grain of Rice: A Mathematical Folktale*

Read *One Grain of Rice: A Mathematical Folktale,* by Demi. As you read, discuss how the number of grains of rice double each day and marvel at how quickly the total number increases.

Enrichment Activity: Cut Paper in Half Repeatedly

This activity is the opposite of the doubling in *One Grain of Rice: A Mathematical Folktale.* Instead of repeated doubling, your child will cut a piece of paper in half over and over.

Have your child fold a piece of paper in half. Then, have her cut along the fold line.

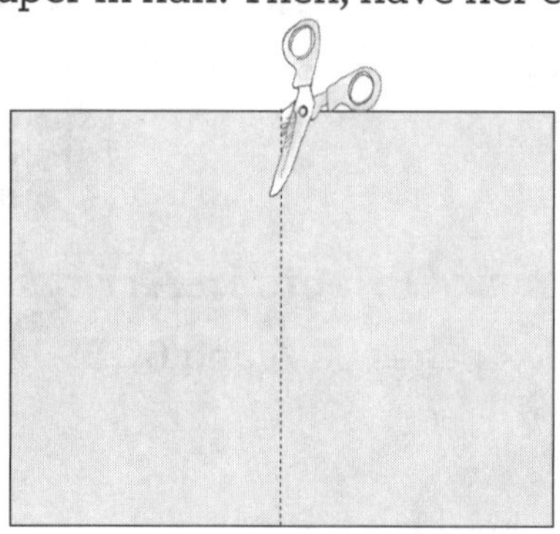

Set aside one of the halves, and have her repeat the process with the other half.

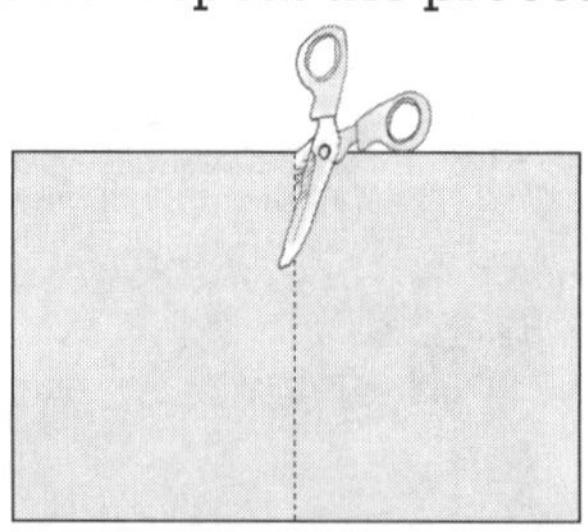

Have her repeat this folding and cutting process as many times as she can. Then, arrange the pieces of paper in order and discuss how small the pieces become after cutting the paper only a few times.

If your child enjoys puzzles, she can try to put the pieces back together in the shape of the original piece of paper.

Week 6 Answer Key

6.1A

Complete.

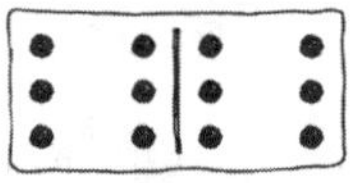

6 double → 12

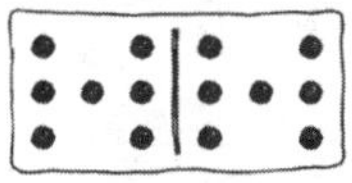

7 double → 14

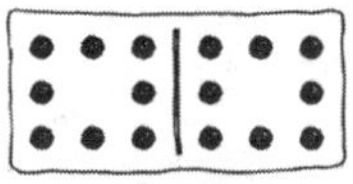

8 double → 16

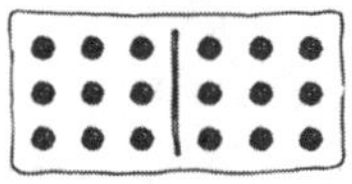

9 double → 18

Complete.

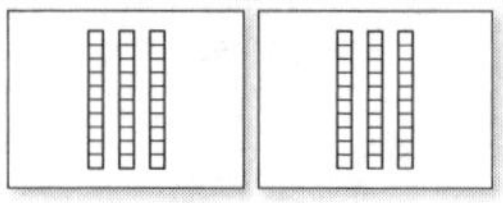

30 double → 60

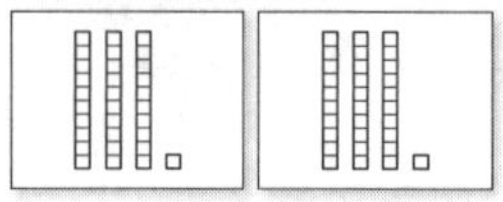

31 double → 62

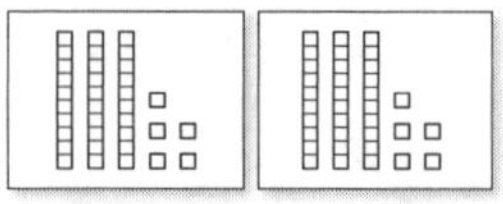

35 double → 70

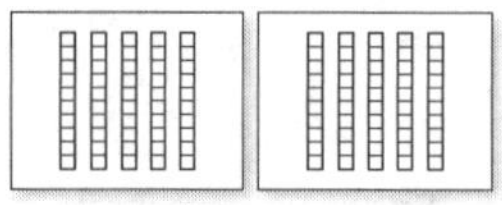

50 double → 100

6.1B

Complete.

5 + 1 = 6	7 + 5 = 12	4 + 9 = 13
6 + 7 = 13	4 + 2 = 6	8 + 8 = 16
5 + 4 = 9	9 + 6 = 15	1 + 6 = 7

Complete.

80 → 40, 40

50 → 20, 30

60 → 20, 40

100 → 50, 50

100 → 10, 90

100 → 80, 20

Draw lines to cut each pizza into halves.

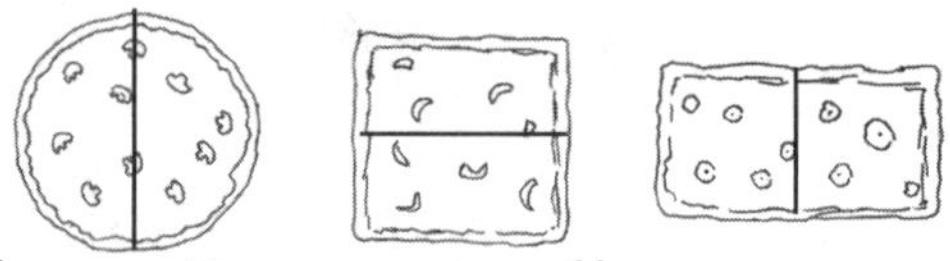

Sample answers. Many answers are possible.

6.2A

Complete.

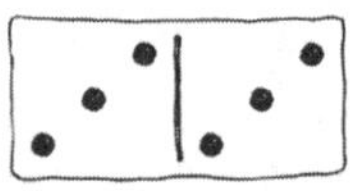

6 half → 3

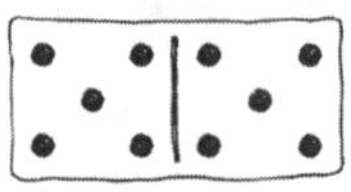

10 half → 5

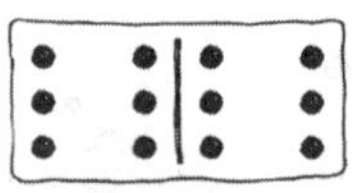

12 half → 6

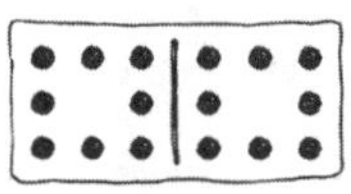

16 half → 8

Complete.

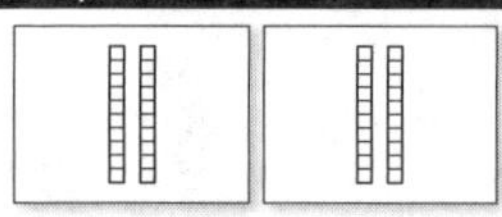

40 half → 20

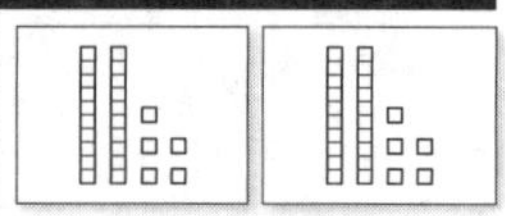

50 half → 25

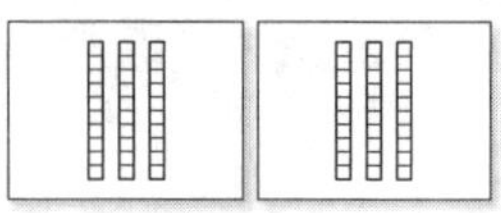

60 half → 30

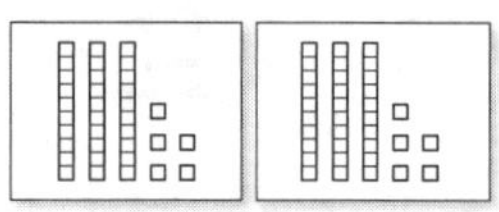

70 half → 35

6.2B

Complete.

8 + 6 = 14	3 + 5 = 8	9 + 2 = 11
2 + 8 = 10	8 + 4 = 12	7 + 9 = 16
7 + 4 = 11	6 + 6 = 12	8 + 7 = 15

Complete.

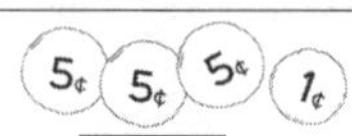

16 ¢

30 ¢

Solve.

You pick 4 apples. You need 8 apples to make a pie.
How many more apples do you need?

8 − 4 = 4

4 apples

You pick 9 apples. You need 12 apples to make applesauce.
How many more apples do you need?

12 − 9 = 3

3 apples

Your child may write 9+3=12.

Week 6 Answer Key

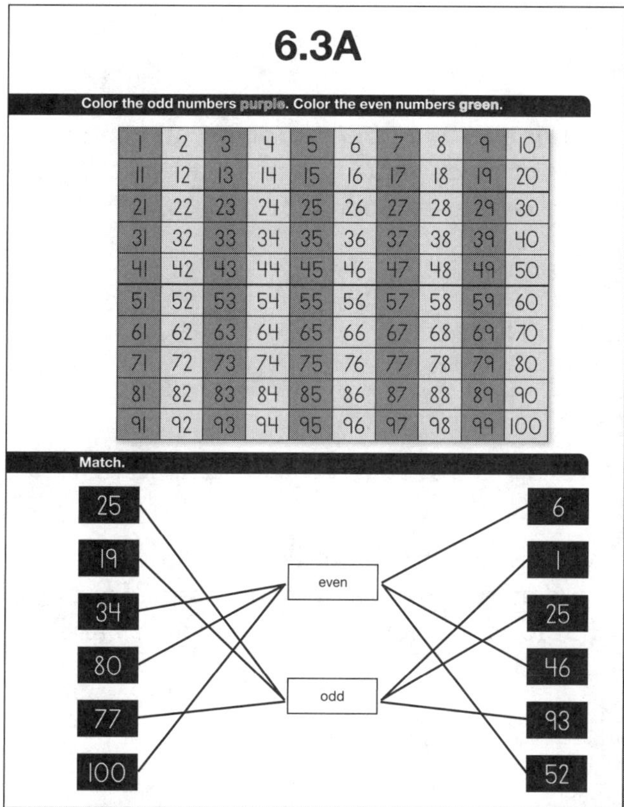

6.3A

Color the odd numbers purple. Color the even numbers green.

1	2	3	4	5	6	7	8	9	10
11	12	13	14	15	16	17	18	19	20
21	22	23	24	25	26	27	28	29	30
31	32	33	34	35	36	37	38	39	40
41	42	43	44	45	46	47	48	49	50
51	52	53	54	55	56	57	58	59	60
61	62	63	64	65	66	67	68	69	70
71	72	73	74	75	76	77	78	79	80
81	82	83	84	85	86	87	88	89	90
91	92	93	94	95	96	97	98	99	100

Match.

25, 19, 34, 80, 77, 100

even

odd

6, 1, 25, 46, 93, 52

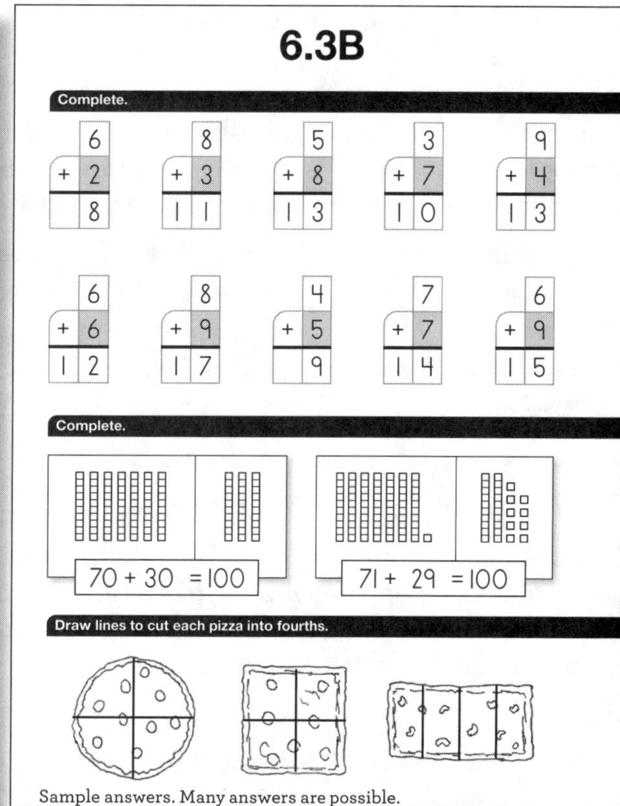

6.3B

Complete.

6 + 2 = 8

8 + 3 = 11

5 + 8 = 13

3 + 7 = 10

9 + 4 = 13

6 + 6 = 12

8 + 9 = 17

4 + 5 = 9

7 + 7 = 14

6 + 9 = 15

Complete.

70 + 30 = 100

71 + 29 = 100

Draw lines to cut each pizza into fourths.

Sample answers. Many answers are possible.

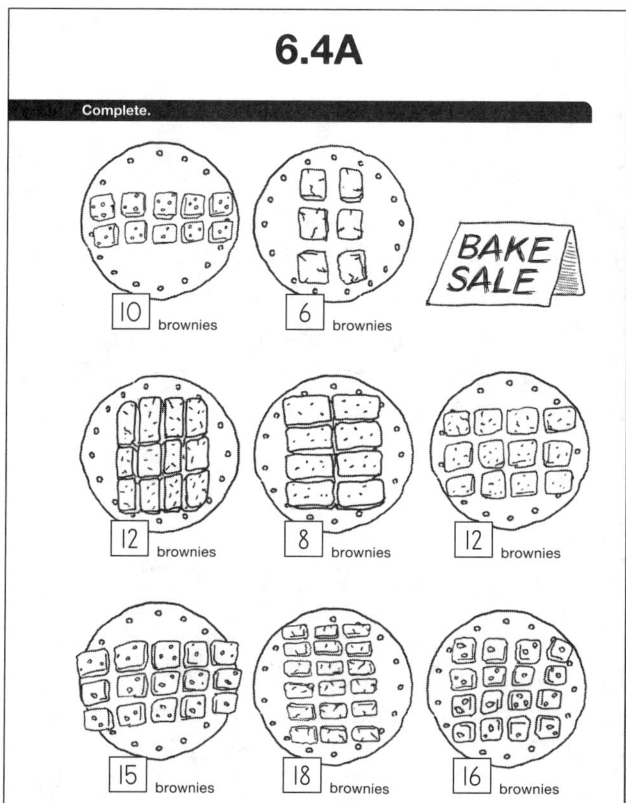

6.4A

Complete.

10 brownies

6 brownies

12 brownies

8 brownies

12 brownies

15 brownies

18 brownies

16 brownies

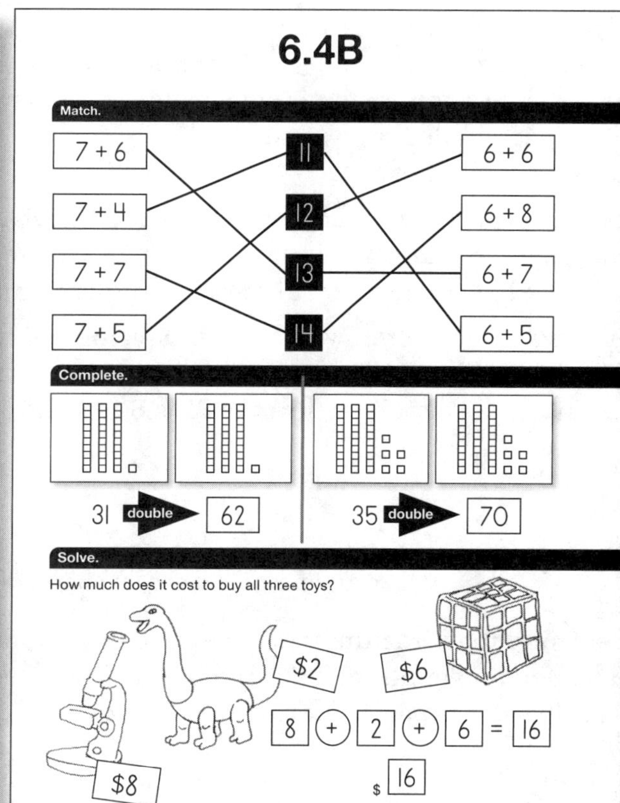

6.4B

Match.

7 + 6 → 13

7 + 4 → 11

7 + 7 → 14

7 + 5 → 12

6 + 6 → 12

6 + 8 → 14

6 + 7 → 13

6 + 5 → 11

Complete.

31 double → 62

35 double → 70

Solve.

How much does it cost to buy all three toys?

8 + 2 + 6 = 16

$ 16

Week 7
Numbers to 200

Overview

Your child will build on what she knows about the numbers to 100 to read, write, and compare numbers to 200. She'll also deepen her understanding of place value as she performs simple mental math with the numbers to 200 and writes numbers in expanded form.

Teaching Math with Confidence: How Writing Numbers in Expanded Form Builds Your Child's Number Sense

One of the most important goals of elementary math education is for children to develop number sense: deep knowledge of numbers and the relationships between numbers. For example, before you read on, think about the number 81 for a moment. What can you say about it? How is it related to other numbers?

Here are just a few ways to think of the number 81:

- It is between 80 and 82 in the counting sequence.
- It is odd.
- It is less than 100.
- It is 1 more than 80 and 9 less than 90.
- It equals 8 tens and 1 one.
- It equals 40 + 41, 5 + 76, or 200 – 119.
- It is a square number, because it equals 9 × 9.
- It equals 3 × 3 × 3 × 3.
- It is half of 162.

Don't worry—your child doesn't need to know all this by the end of second grade! But this is a sample of the deep number sense you'll help your child build during her elementary years, so that she has an in-depth understanding of numbers and can use them fluently.

This week, your child will further develop her number sense as she learns to write numbers in expanded form. The expanded form of a number is the sum of the value of the digits. For example, the expanded form of 81 is 80 + 1, and the expanded form of 143 is 100 + 40 + 3.

The expanded form of a number shows the sum of the value of each digit.

Learning to write numbers in expanded form prepares your child to use place value to mentally add and subtract later in the year. You'll use the Number Machine this week to provide examples of expanded form and help your child learn to take apart numbers in this way.

Extra Materials Needed for Week 7

- Rubber band
- 7 slips of paper
- For optional Enrichment and Review Lesson:
    - *How Many Seeds in a Pumpkin?,* written by Margaret McNamara and illustrated by G. Brian Karas
    - 100-200 small food items (such as macaroni, grains of rice, or sunflower seeds) or seeds from a fresh pumpkin

Lesson 7.1
Read and Write Numbers to 200

	Purpose	Materials
Warm-up	• Count money • Practice memory work • Review +8 facts	• Play money • Addition Crash game boards (from workbook page 4.1A) • Counters • Playing cards
Activities	• Use place-value thinking to identify quantities • Read and write numbers to 200	• Base-ten blocks • Place-Value Chart (Blackline Master 5)
Workbook	• Read and write numbers to 200	• Workbook pages 7.1A and 7.1B

Warm-up: Counting, Memory Work, and Review

- Place 3 ten-dollar bills, 2 five-dollar bills, and 4 one-dollar bills on the table. **How much are the bills worth?** *$44.*
- Write the < sign. **What does this sign mean?** *Less than.*
  Write the > sign. **What does this sign mean?** *Greater than.*
- Play Addition Crash (+8 Version). See Lesson 4.3 (page 67) for full directions.

Activity: Write Numbers to 200

In Unit 1, you reviewed place value and the numbers to 100. Today, you'll use what you know about place value to read and write numbers to 200.

Place 1 flat, 2 rods, and 5 units on the Place-Value Chart. **I can count the blocks by 100s, 10s, and 1s to find their value.** Demonstrate how to count the blocks this way: **100, 110, 120, 121, 122, 123, 124, 125.**

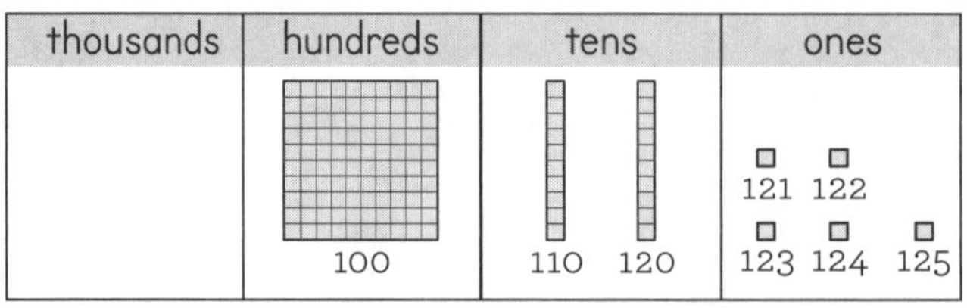

Counting by 100s, 10s and 1s to find the total.

Or, I can use place-value thinking. Point to each column of the Place-Value Chart as you name the value of the blocks in it: **100...20...5. So, the blocks have a value of 125.**

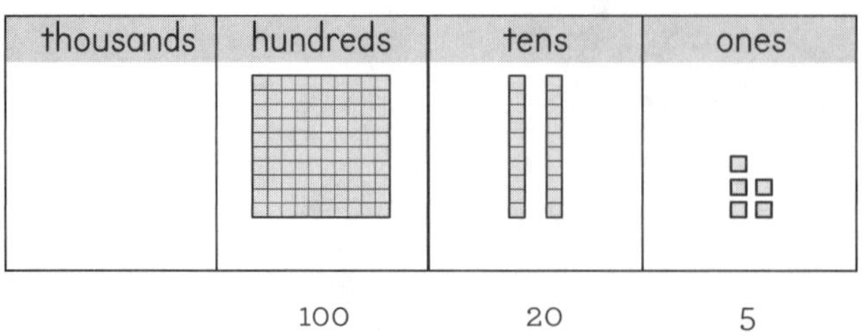

We write numbers from left to right, in the same order that we say the parts of the number. Here's how to write 125.

- **There is 1 hundred, so I write a 1 in the hundreds-place.** Write 1 in the hundreds-place.
- **There are 2 tens, so I write a 2 in the tens-place.** Write 2 in the tens-place.
- **There are 5 ones, so I write a 5 in the ones-place.** Write 5 in the ones-place on the Place-Value Chart.

thousands	hundreds	tens	ones
	1	2	5

Show your child the following block arrangements. For each arrangement, have her identify the blocks' value and write the corresponding digits on the Place-Value Chart.

thousands	hundreds	tens	ones
	1	6	5

thousands	hundreds	tens	ones
	1	0	4

thousands	hundreds	tens	ones
	2	0	0

Activity: Read Numbers to 200

Secretly write 142 on a piece of paper and cover it with a slip of paper. **We read numbers from left to right, just like we read words.**

Slide the piece of paper to the right, so that only the 1 is visible. **I see a 1, but I don't know what place the 1 is in. It might be in the tens-place, hundreds-place, or even the millions-place! I need to see the whole number to know its place and its value.**

Remove the slip of paper so that the entire number is visible. **I know the ones-place is the place furthest to the right.** Point to the ones-place. **Which digit is in the ones-place?** *2.*

142
↑
ones-place

That means the 4 is in the tens-place and the 1 is in the hundreds-place.

- **What's the value of the 1?** *100.*
- **What's the value of the 4?** *40.*
- **What's the value of the 2?** *2.*

If your child can't easily answer these questions, write the digits on the Place-Value Chart and have her place matching base-ten blocks on the chart before answering.

Now that I know the value of each digit, I can read the number: 142. Point to each digit as you read it.

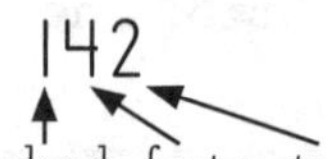

"One hundred...forty....two"

Write the following numbers on a piece of paper, one at a time. Have your child identify the value of each digit and then read the number. Model the numbers with base-ten blocks as needed.

- 173
- 119
- 190
- 109
- 200

Workbook: Read and Write Numbers to 200 and Review

Have your child complete workbook pages 7.1A and 7.1B.

Lesson 7.2
Compare Numbers to 200

	Purpose	Materials
Warm-up	• Count coins • Practice memory work • Review reading numbers to 200	• Coins • 200 Chart (Blackline Master 7) • Counters
Activities	• Use place value to compare numbers to 200 • Use the counting sequence to compare numbers to 200	• Base-ten blocks • 200 Chart (Blackline Master 7) • Counters
Workbook	• Compare numbers to 200	• Workbook pages 7.2A and 7.2B

Warm-up: Counting, Memory Work, and Review

- Place 4 dimes, 1 nickel, and 6 pennies on the table. **How much are the coins worth?** *51¢.*
- **How many tens equal 1 hundred?** *10.*
- **I'm going to read some numbers. Cover each number on the 200 Chart with a counter as I say it. The final design will look like a letter. See if you can tell which one!** Read the following numbers one at a time, and have your child cover each number with a small counter: **136, 146, 169, 110, 137, 128, 176, 147, 106, 180, 126, 166, 119, 158, 116, 156.** The final arrangement of counters should look like a K.

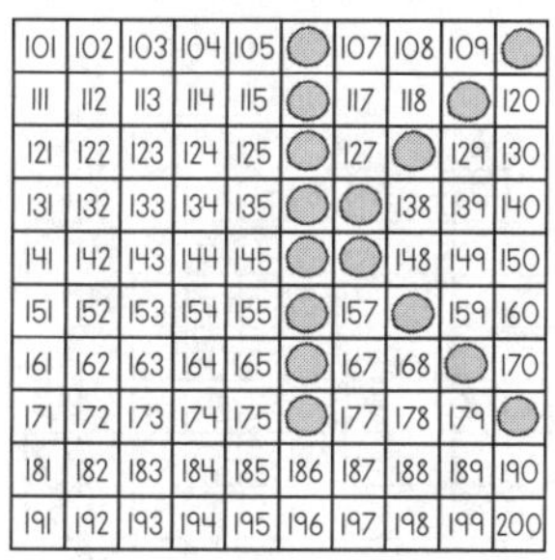

Activity: Compare Numbers to 200

In the last lesson, you have learned how to read and write numbers to 200. Today, you'll learn how to compare them.

Write 137 and 173 on a piece of paper. Have your child model both numbers with base-ten blocks.

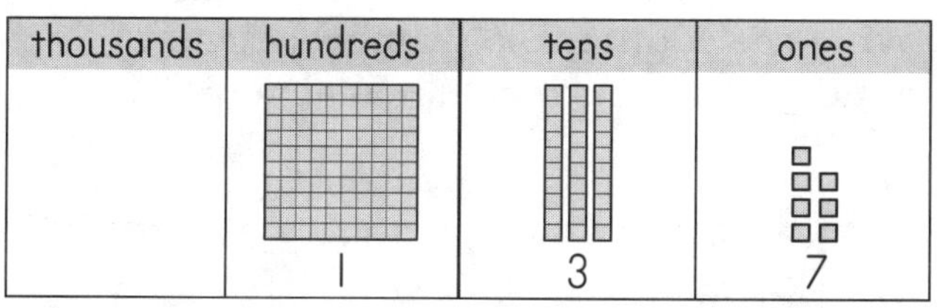

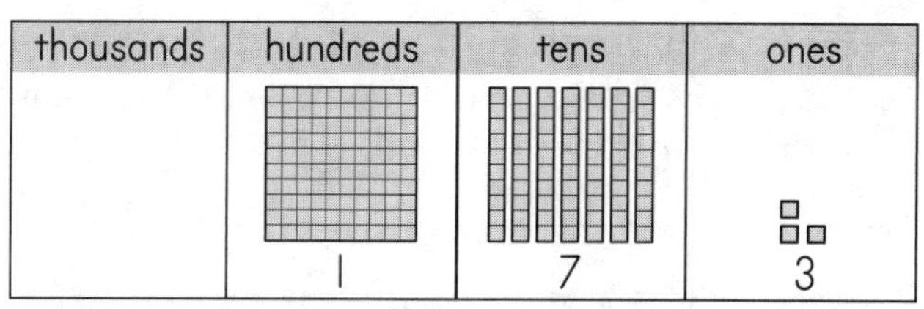

Which number is greater, 173 or 137? *173.* **How do you know?** *Sample answers: Both numbers have 1 hundred. 173 has 7 tens, but 137 only has 3 tens. Or, 173 comes after 137 when you count.*

Repeat with the following pairs of numbers.

- **145 and 146.** *146 is greater than 145.*
- **132 and 99.** *132 is greater than 99.*
- **106 and 160.** *160 is greater than 106.*

Make sure to have your child model each number with base-ten blocks, even if he can immediately tell which number is greater. This reinforces his understanding of place value and prepares him to write numbers in expanded form in Lesson 7.4.

Activity: Play Guess the Secret Number (101-200)

Play Guess the Secret Number (101-200) several times. Take turns with your child choosing the secret number.

The previous activity emphasized using place value to compare numbers. In this next game, your child will focus on the numbers' positions in the counting sequence. These two ways of thinking about numbers complement each other and help your child develop a thorough understanding of the numbers to 200.

Guess the Secret Number (101-200)

Materials: 200 Chart (Blackline Master 7), counters

Object of the Game: Guess the secret number.

Secretly choose a number between 101 and 200, and write it on a slip of paper.

Place a counter on the 101 and the 200 on the 200 Chart. **My secret number is greater than 101 and less than 200.**

	102	103	104	105	106	107	108	109	110
111	112	113	114	115	116	117	118	119	120
121	122	123	124	125	126	127	128	129	130
131	132	133	134	135	136	137	138	139	140
141	142	143	144	145	146	147	148	149	150
151	152	153	154	155	156	157	158	159	160
161	162	163	164	165	166	167	168	169	170
171	172	173	174	175	176	177	178	179	180
181	182	183	184	185	186	187	188	189	190
191	192	193	194	195	196	197	198	199	

The other player guesses the secret number. If the guess is incorrect, move one counter to the number he guesses, so the secret number is still between the two counters. For example, if the secret number is 174, and your child guesses 140, move the counter from 101 to 140 and say: My secret number is greater than 140.

Have your child continue guessing. Keep moving the counters so your secret number is between the two counters. Once your child guesses correctly, reveal your written number.

Workbook: Compare Numbers to 200 and Review

Have your child complete workbook pages 7.2A and 7.2B.

Lesson 7.3
Counting and Mental Math with Numbers to 200

	Purpose	Materials
Warm-up	• Count by 1s from numbers other than 1 • Practice memory work • Review +7 facts	• 200 Chart (Blackline Master 7), optional • Addition Bingo game boards (from workbook page 5.1A) • Counters • Playing cards
Activities	• Count by 2s, 5s, and 10s to 200 • Mentally add single-digit numbers or multiples of 10 to numbers to 200	• 100 Chart (Blackline Master 4) • 200 Chart (Blackline Master 7) • Counters • Play money • Place-Value Chart (Blackline Master 5)
Workbook	• Add single-digit numbers or multiples of 10 to numbers to 200 • Count by 2s, 5s, and 10s to 200	• Workbook pages 7.3A and 7.3B

Warm-up: Counting, Memory Work, and Review

- Have your child count forward from the following numbers. Stop her after she reaches the last number listed in the sample answers, and allow her to use the 200 Chart as needed.
    - **Count forward from 170:** *170, 171, 172, 173, 174.*
    - **Count forward from 152:** *152, 153, 154, 155, 156.*
    - **Count forward from 189:** *189, 190, 191, 192, 193.*
- **What do we call the result when we add numbers together?** *The sum.* **What do we call the result when we subtract a number from another number?** *The difference.*
- Play Addition Bingo (+7 Version). See Lesson 5.1 (page 76) for directions.

Activity: Count by 1s, 2s, 5s, and 10s to 200

In the last lesson, you learned how to compare numbers to 200. Today, you'll learn how to count by 2s, 5s, and 10s to 200. You'll also learn how to solve mental math problems with numbers to 200.

The numbers to 200 follow the same patterns as the numbers to 100. So, you can use what you know about counting to 100 to help you count to 200. Let's use the 100 Chart and 200 Chart to show you what I mean. Put the 100 Chart and 200 Chart on the table.

Give your child 5 counters. **Start at 37 and count by 1s. Put a counter on each number as you say it.** *37, 38, 39, 40, 41.*

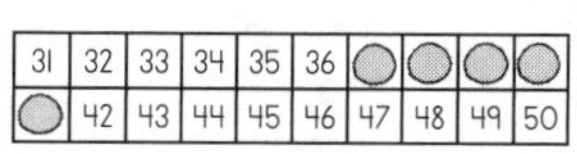

Give your child 5 counters. **Now, start at 137 and count by 1s. Put a counter on each number as you say it.** *137, 138, 139, 140, 141.*

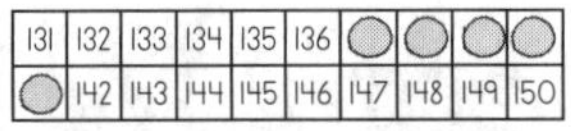

What do you notice? *Sample answer: The numbers sound the same, but you say "one hundred" before the ones in the second group.*

This works for counting by other numbers, too! Have your child count by 2s from 40 to 50. Then, have her count by 2s from 140 to 150.

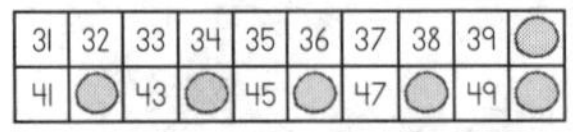

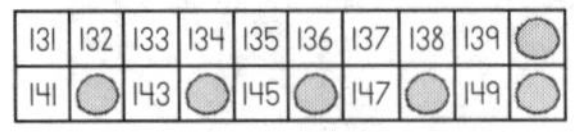

Have your child count by 5s from 25 to 45. Then, have her count by 5s from 125 to 145.

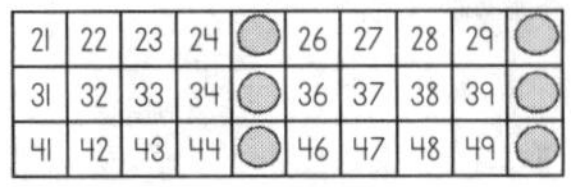

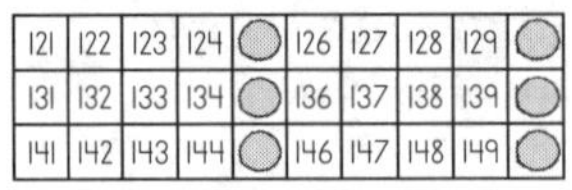

Have your child count by 10s from 60 to 100. Then, have her count by 10s from 160 to 200.

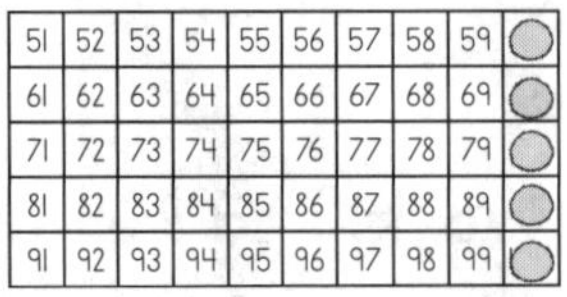

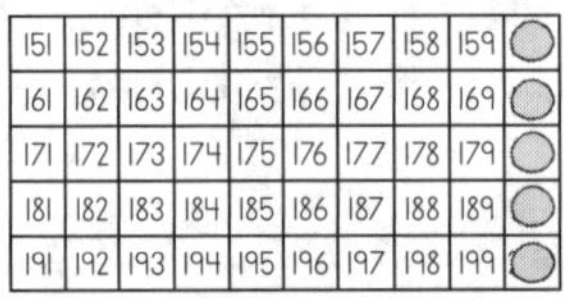

This lesson is only an introduction to counting by 1s, 2s, 5s, and 10s to 200. Your child will practice more in the lesson warm-ups.

Activity: Mental Math with Numbers to 200

You can also use what you know about numbers to 100 to help you add and subtract numbers to 200. Let's pretend you have $34, and then you earn $2 more. Write "34 + 2 =" on a piece of paper and model the equation with play money on the Place-Value Chart. Have your child complete the equation: 34 + 2 = 36.

34 + 2 = 36

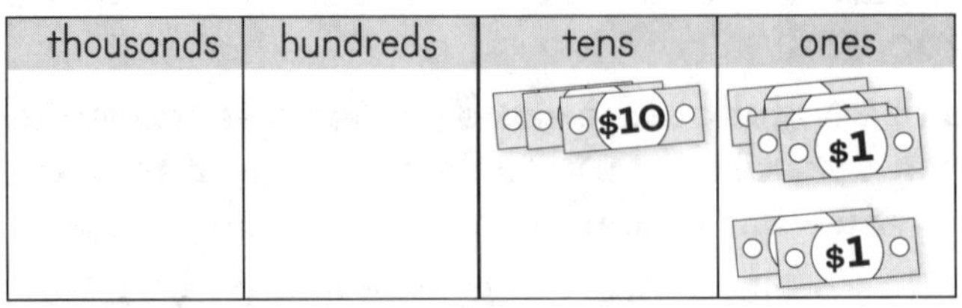

Now, let's pretend you have $134 and earn $2 more. Write "134 + 2 =" on a piece of paper and add 1 hundred-dollar bill to the Place-Value Chart. Have your child complete the equation: 134 + 2 = 136.

134 + 2 = 136

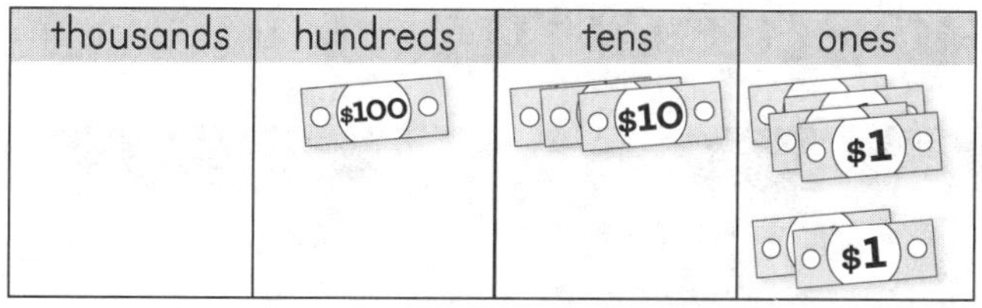

Have your child find the answers to the following pairs of addition problems. For each problem, encourage her to use the answer to the first problem to help solve the second problem. Model the problems with money on the Place-Value Chart as needed.

37 + 40 = 77	27 - 3 = 24	75 - 30 = 45
137 + 40 = 177	127 - 3 = 124	175 - 30 = 145

Workbook: Mental Math with Numbers to 200 and Review

Have your child complete workbook pages 7.3A and 7.3B.

Lesson 7.4
Expanded Form

	Purpose	Materials
Warm-up	• Count backward • Practice memory work • Review place-value terms	• 200 Chart (Blackline Master 7), optional
Activities	• Learn how to write numbers to 200 in expanded form • Reinforce understanding of place value	• Number Machine (from Lesson 6.1) • 7 slips of paper • Rubber band • Base-ten blocks • Place-Value Chart (Blackline Master 5)
Workbook	• Write numbers to 200 in expanded form	• Workbook pages 7.4A and 7.4B

Warm-up: Counting, Memory Work, and Review

- Have your child count backward from the following numbers. Stop him after he reaches the last number listed. Allow him to use the 200 Chart if needed.
  - **Count backward from 158:** *158, 157, 156, 155, 154.*
  - **Count backward from 134:** *134, 133, 132, 131, 130.*
  - **Count backward from 191:** *191, 190, 189, 188, 187.*
- **How many tens equal 1 hundred?** *10.*
- Write 150 on a piece of paper. **How many digits does this number have?** *3.* **Which digit is in the ones-place?** *0.* **Which digit is in the tens-place?** *5.* **Which digit is in the hundreds-place?** *1.*

Activity: Introduce Expanded Form with the Number Machine

In the last lesson, you learned how to count and solve mental math problems with the numbers to 200. Today, the Number Machine is back! Stand the Number Machine on the table between you and your child. Pretend to turn a knob on the front of the machine to set it.

Let's see what happens when I put 18 into the Number Machine on this setting. Write 18 on a slip of paper and slide it behind the Number Machine screen. Secretly write "10 + 8" on the back of the slip and slide it out from behind the other side.

Interesting! Let's try a few more before you tell me what you think the Number Machine is doing. Demonstrate the following numbers.

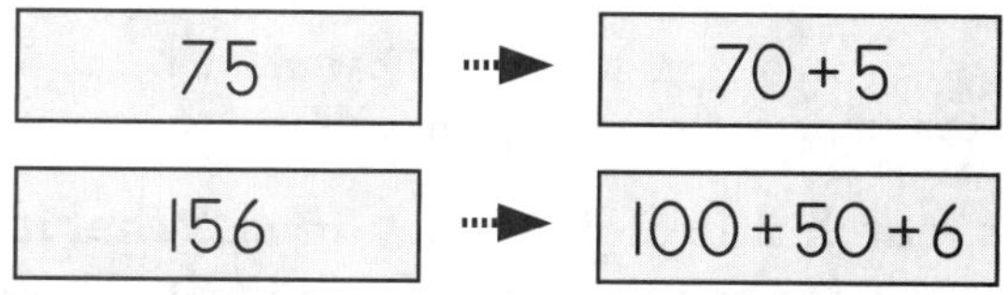

What do you think the Number Machine is doing to the numbers on this setting? *Answers will vary.*

On this setting, the Number Machine writes the numbers in expanded form. What does it mean for something to expand? *Answers will vary.* Briefly have your child stretch a rubber band. **When the rubber band expands, it stretches and takes up more space.**

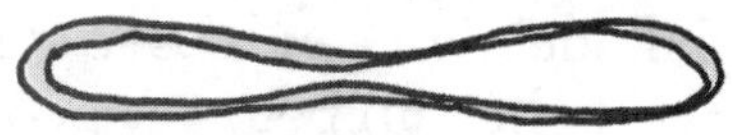

Let's expand our bodies! With your child, stand and stretch to make yourself take up as much space as possible. **The Number Machine is s-t-r-e-t-c-h-i-n-g the numbers to show the value of their digits. Today, you'll learn how to write numbers in expanded form.**

See the Week 7 **Teaching Math with Confidence** to learn how writing numbers in expanded form deepens children's number sense.

Activity: Write Numbers in Expanded Form

Write 27 on a piece of paper. Have your child write the digits in the correct places on the Place-Value Chart and model them with base-ten blocks. **To write a number in expanded form, I look at each digit and think about how much it is worth.**

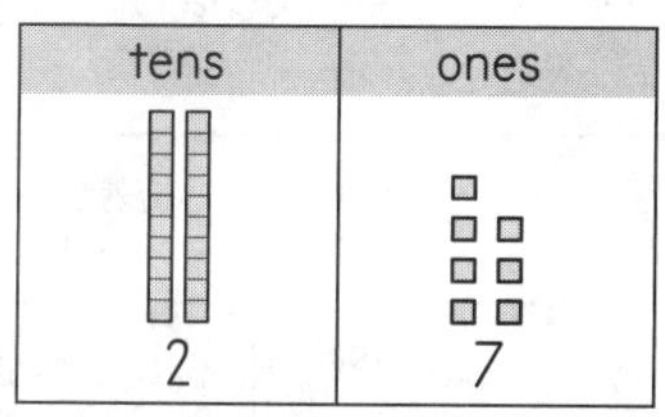

Point to the 2. **The 2 is in the tens-place, so it has a value of 20.** Write 20 below the 2. Point to the 7. **The 7 is in the ones-place, so it has a value of 7.** Write 7 below the 7. **So, the expanded form of 27 is 20 plus 7.** Write "20 + 7" on the paper.

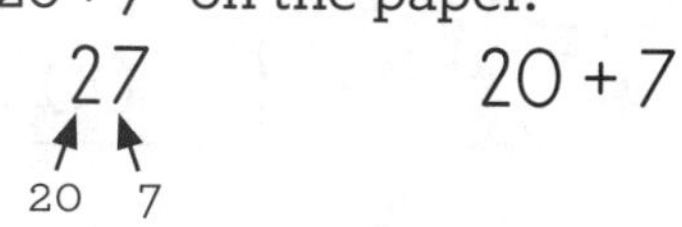

20 + 7 is the expanded form of 27.

Write the addends in expanded form in the same order as the digits, beginning with the digit with the greatest value. Even though 7 + 20 shows the value of each digit in 27, it is not the "official" expanded form of the number.

Write 65 on a piece of paper. Have your child write the digits on the Place-Value Chart and model them with base-ten blocks.

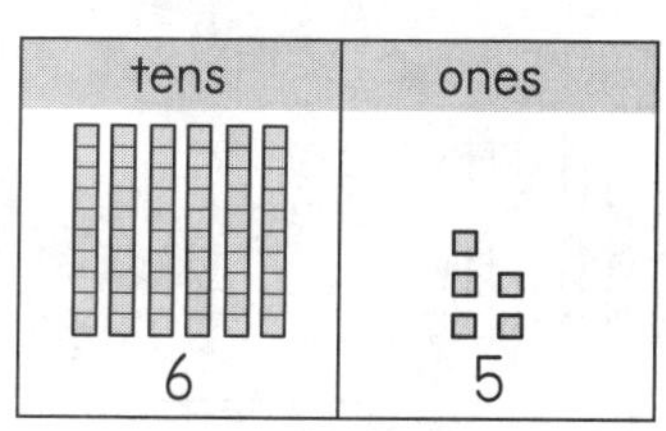

Point to the 6. **Which blocks match this digit?** *The 6 rods.* **What is the value of the 6?** *60.* Write 60 below the 6.

If your child is confused by the word "value," instead ask: **How much is the 6 worth?** Or, to make the question even more concrete: **How much are the 6 rods worth?**

Point to the 5. **Which blocks match this digit?** *The 5 units.* **What is the value of the 5?** *5.* Write 5 below the 5. **So, 60 plus 5 is the expanded form of 65.** Have your child write "60 + 5" on a piece of paper.

65 → 60 5

60 + 5

Now, let's try a three-digit number. Write 143 on a piece of paper. Have your child write the digits on the Place-Value Chart and model them with base-ten blocks. Have your child identify the value of each digit and then write the number in expanded form: 100 + 40 + 3.

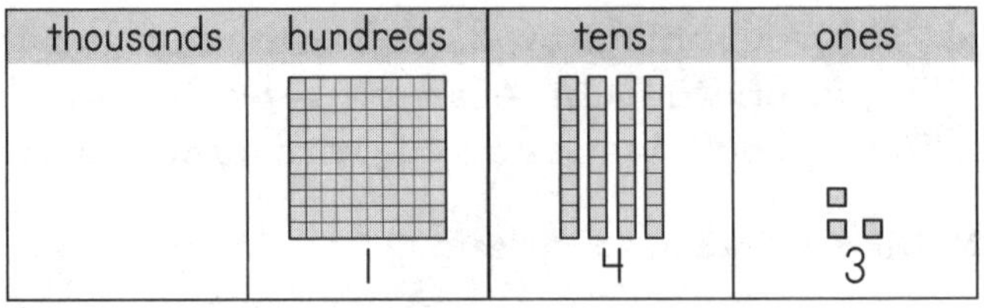

Activity: Practice Writing Numbers in Expanded Form

Let's leave the Number Machine on the expanded form setting and put some more numbers into it. This time, you'll predict the Number Machine's results before I show them to you.

Have your child predict the Number Machine's results for the following numbers before you slide the answer out. Use base-ten blocks as needed to help your child identify the value of each digit in the numbers.

82 → 80 + 2

193 → 100 + 90 + 3

128 → 100 + 20 + 8

107 → 100 + 7

Your child does not need to write the value of any placeholder zeros in the number. For example, the expanded form of 107 is 100 + 7, not 100 + 0 + 7.

Workbook: Write Numbers in Expanded Form and Review

Have your child complete workbook pages 7.4A and 7.4B.

If your child is confused by the equals sign in the exercises, remind him that the equals sign means that the amounts on either side are the same as each other. The expanded form of a number is the same amount as the original number, so it can be written on the right-hand side of the equals sign.

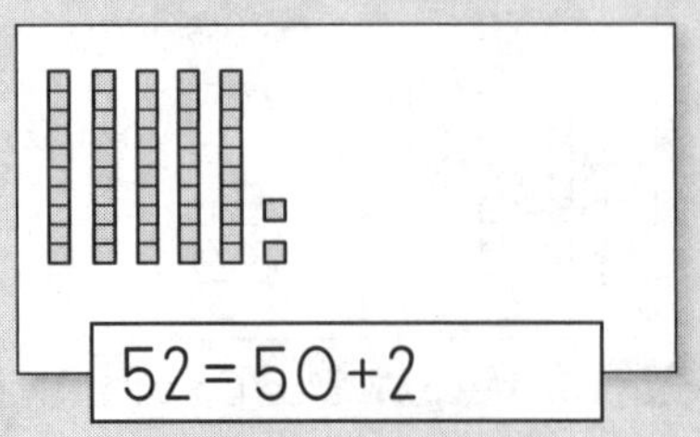

Lesson 7.5
Enrichment and Review (Optional)

	Purpose	Materials
Warm-up	• Count by 2s from 100 to 150 • Review memory work • Review your child's favorite or most challenging activities from Week 7	• Varies, depending on the activities you choose
Picture Book	• Understand counting by 2s, 5s, or 10s in real life	• *How Many Seeds in a Pumpkin?*, written by Margaret McNamara and illustrated by G. Brian Karas
Enrichment Activity	• Estimate the quantity for 100-200 items • Count 100-200 items by 2s, 5s, or 10s	• 100-200 small food items (such as macaroni, grains of rice, or sunflower seeds) or seeds from a fresh pumpkin

Warm-up: Counting, Memory Work, and Review

- Have your child count by 2s from 100 to 150.
- Quiz your child on the memory work through Week 6. See page 523 for the full list.
- If you have time, repeat one or two of the activities from this week's lessons. Choose activities your child especially enjoyed or found challenging.

Math Picture Book: *How Many Seeds in a Pumpkin?*

Read *How Many Seeds in a Pumpkin?*, written by Margaret McNamara and illustrated by G. Brian Karas. Demonstrate how to count the illustrated groups of pumpkin seeds by 2s, 5s, or 10s, and have your child join you as much as possible.

Enrichment Activity: Estimate and Count

Show your child 100-200 of a small food item, like macaroni, grains of rice, or sunflower seeds. (Or, scoop out the seeds from a fresh pumpkin as in the suggested picture book.)

Pile the items on the table and ask your child to estimate how many there are. Then, decide together whether to count the items by 2s, 5s, or 10s. Group the items by that number, then count together to find the total number. Discuss how close your child's estimate was to the actual number.

Week 7 Answer Key

7.1A

Match.

124 — 1 hundred, 2 tens, 4 ones

115 — 1 hundred, 1 ten, 5 ones

130 — 1 hundred, 3 tens

Write the value of each set of base-ten blocks.

100s	10s	1s
1	2	7
1	4	1
1	2	0
1	0	6

7.1B

Complete.

4 + 4 = 8	7 + 6 = 13	9 + 4 = 13	2 + 6 = 8	9 + 7 = 16
4 + 7 = 11	8 + 2 = 10	9 + 9 = 18	8 + 5 = 13	3 + 9 = 12
5 + 5 = 10	6 + 6 = 12	7 + 7 = 14	8 + 8 = 16	9 + 9 = 18

Color the even numbers yellow. Color the odd numbers red.

34 26 72

81 19

82 30

57 35

50 94 46

7.2A

Complete the circles with <, >, or =.

148 < 149	196 > 112	134 < 175
146 > 142	177 < 187	140 = 140
163 > 136	148 < 149	185 > 118
107 > 105	97 < 101	199 < 200
29 < 129	100 < 200	86 < 142

Complete the missing numbers on the 200 Chart.

101	102	103	104	105	106	107	108	109	110
111	112	113	114	115	116	117	118	119	120
121	122	123	124	125	126	127	128	129	130
131	132	133	134	135	136	137	138	139	140
141	142	143	144	145	146	147	148	149	150

7.2B

Complete.

7: 4 and 3

4 + 3 = 7

7 - 4 = 3

9: 7 and 2

7 + 2 = 9

9 - 7 = 2

Complete.

9 tiles

12 tiles

15 tiles

Color the subtraction facts that equal the number in the star.

0	1	2	3
8 - 8	7 - 6	10 - 5	6 - 3
9 - 5	8 - 7	9 - 6	10 - 7
6 - 6	9 - 8	10 - 8	8 - 4
10 - 3	10 - 7	8 - 6	9 - 5

Week 7 Answer Key

7.3A

Complete.

55 + 3 = 58
155 + 3 = 158

48 + 30 = 78
148 + 30 = 178

68 - 2 = 66
168 - 2 = 166

39 - 20 = 19
139 - 20 = 119

20 + 17 = 37
120 + 17 = 137

34 - 4 = 30
134 - 4 = 130

Complete the missing numbers in the sequences.

Count by 10s: 150, 160, 170, 180, 190, 200

Count by 5s: 150, 155, 160, 165, 170, 175

Count by 2s: 150, 152, 154, 156, 158, 160

7.3B

Use the key to color the apples.

Key
12 - red
13 - yellow
14 - green

9+5, 11+2, 12+1, 10+2, 7+7, 8+5, 9+3, 4+8, 5+7, 9+4, 10+4, 6+8, 10+3, 7+6

Complete.

28 half 14

46 half 23

Solve.

85: 80, 5

39: 30, 9

42: 40, 2

7.4A

Write the expanded form of each number.

52 = 50+2

41=40+1

78=70+8

65=60+5

156=100+50+6

115=100+10+5

131=100+30+1

104=100+4

7.4B

Complete.

8 + 7 = 15

6 + 8 = 14

9 + 6 = 15

2 + 9 = 11

9 + 4 = 13

7 + 4 = 11

3 + 8 = 11

6 + 5 = 11

9 + 1 = 10

7 + 8 = 15

Complete.

$10 $10 $10 $10 $10 → $ 50

$10 $10 $5 $5 → $ 30

Solve.

The ball costs $5.
The bat costs $7.
How much does it cost to buy both the ball and the bat?

$5 $7

5 + 7 = 12

$ 12

You have $8.
You need $11 to buy the toy.
How much more money do you need?

$5 $1 $1 $1 $11

11 - 8 = 3

$ 3

Your child may write 8+3=11.

Week 8
Money

Overview

Your child will learn how to count money combinations that include twenty-dollar bills or quarters. He'll also learn how to use either a decimal point or a cents sign to write money amounts.

Lesson 8.1	Write Dollars with a Decimal Point
Lesson 8.2	Write Dollars and Cents with a Decimal Point
Lesson 8.3	Read Prices in Dollars and Cents
Lesson 8.4	Practice Counting Money
Lesson 8.5	Enrichment and Review (Optional)

Teaching Math with Confidence: Rules for Writing Money Amounts

This week, you'll teach your child to write money amounts with the cents sign, dollar sign, and decimal point. (If your family's currency uses different symbols, you will teach your child how to use these symbols instead.)

Although this skill may seem simple, writing money amounts is surprisingly complex. You'll teach your child the following 4 rules this week so that he knows how to write money amounts correctly:

- Write the dollar sign before the number, but write the cents sign after the number. For example, \$7.43 or 95¢.
- If there are no dollars, write a placeholder zero before the decimal point. For example, \$0.56.
- If there are no cents, you can write 2 placeholder zeros after the decimal point—but it's optional. For example, 17 dollars can be written as \$17 or \$17.00.
- If there are fewer than 10 cents, write a placeholder zero after the decimal point and before the number of cents. For example, 5 cents is written as \$0.05.

Several of these rules have connections to decimal place value, but your child is not expected to understand decimal place value in second grade. For now, you will simply explain that the decimal point separates the dollars from the cents. Your child will build on this to understand decimal place value in future years.

Extra Materials Needed for Week 8

- For optional Enrichment and Review Lesson:
  - *Lemonade in Winter,* written by Emily Jenkins and illustrated by G. Brian Karas
  - Bills and coins to spend

Materials Note for Families Living Outside the U.S.

If your family does not use American currency, look for notes throughout the week for suggestions on how to modify the lessons to match your currency. If your currency does not use quarters (coins worth 25¢), you'll find ways to include twenty-cent or fifty-cent coins instead.

Lesson 8.1
Write Dollars with a Decimal Point

	Purpose	Materials
Warm-up	• Count by 2s • Practice memory work • Review subtraction facts	• Subtraction Climb and Slide game board (from workbook page 1.3A) • Counters • Die
Activities	• Write dollar values with a dollar sign and decimal point • Sort, order, and count combinations of twenty-dollar, ten-dollar, five-dollar, and one-dollar bills	• Play money
Workbook	• Count combinations of twenty-dollar, ten-dollar, five-dollar, and one-dollar bills	• Workbook pages 8.1A and 8.1B

Note for Families Living Outside the U.S.

The money lessons this week teach children to use the dollar-sign, cent-sign, and decimal point to write money amounts. If your family writes money amounts differently, simply change the language and signs in these lessons to match your currency.

Warm-up: Counting, Memory Work, and Review

- Have your child count by 2s from 120 to 140.
- **If a number has 1, 3, 5, 7, or 9 in the ones-place, is the number even or odd?** *Odd.* **If a number has 0, 2, 4, 6, or 8 in the ones-place, is the number even or odd?** *Even.*
- Play Subtraction Climb and Slide. See Lesson 1.3 (page 19) for directions.

Activity: Review Sorting, Ordering, and Counting Bills

Today, we'll review how to count combinations of paper bills. You'll learn how to count combinations with twenty-dollar bills and write dollars with a decimal point.

Let's pretend you work at a farmer's market selling fruit and vegetables. Briefly discuss your child's experiences with farmer's markets or farm stands. **What kind of fruit or vegetables would you want to sell?** *Answers will vary.*

One day a customer pays you with these bills. Mix up 2 ten-dollar bills, 3 five-dollar bills, and 6 one-dollar bills, and give them to your child.

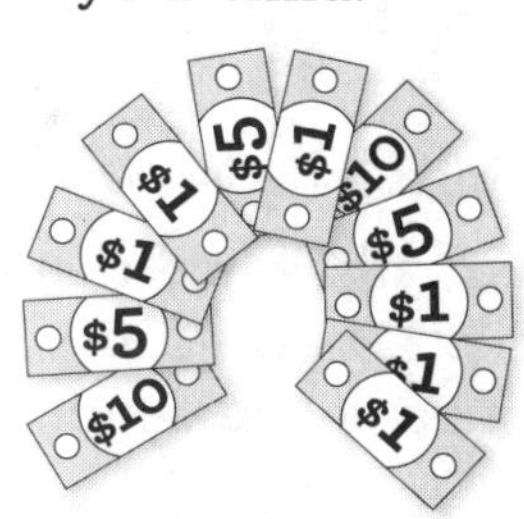

Salespeople usually follow 3 steps when a customer gives them a pile of bills: sort, order, and count. This helps them count the money quickly. Demonstrate how to sort the bills by type, put the piles in order from greatest value to least value, and then count them: **10, 20, 25, 30, 35, 36, 37, 38, 39, 40, 41.**

Count the ten-dollar bills first, then the five-dollar bills, and finally the one-dollar bills. Also make sure to point to each bill as you count it.

Activity: Write Dollars with a Decimal Point

Show your child how to write a dollar sign: **First, you make a capital S. Then, you draw a vertical line through it.** Have your child write several dollar signs on a piece of paper.

The dollar sign always comes before the number. Write $41 on a piece of paper. Have your child write the following dollar amounts with a dollar sign: 6 dollars, 50 dollars, 79 dollars, 100 dollars.

$41 $6 $50 $79 $100

Have you ever seen written amounts of money with a dot in the middle? *Answers will vary.* **The little dot is called a decimal point. It separates the dollars from the cents.**

Here's how we write 41 dollars with a decimal point. Write $41.00 on a piece of paper. **The zeros show that there aren't any extra cents.** Have your child write the previous money amounts with a dollar sign and decimal.

$41.00 $6.00 $50.00 $79.00 $100.00

See the Week 8 **Teaching Math with Confidence** for more on teaching your child to write money amounts.

Activity: Count Paper Bill Combinations with Twenty-Dollar Bills

Place 5 twenty-dollar bills on the table. **Each twenty-dollar bill is worth 20 dollars.** Write $20 below the first bill.

What's 20 plus 20? *40.* **So, 2 twenty-dollar bills are worth 40 dollars.** Write $40 below the second bill. Repeat until you've labeled all the bills.

Have your child practice counting the bills by 20s: *20, 40, 60, 80, 100.*

Mix up 2 twenty-dollar bills, 3 ten-dollar bills, 2 five-dollar bills, and 1 one-dollar bill. Have your child sort, order, and count the bills: *20, 40, 50, 60, 70, 75, 80, 81.* Also have her write the amount two ways, both with and without a decimal point.

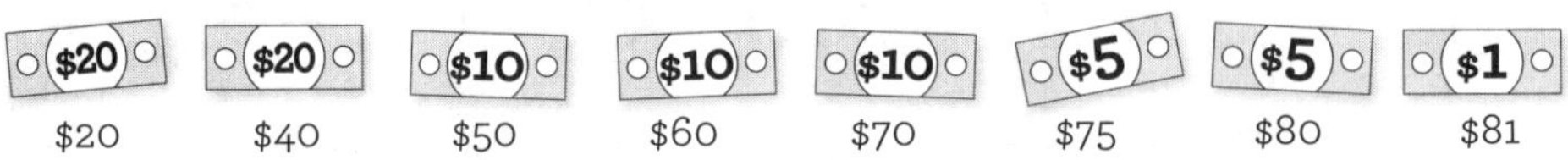

$81 $81.00

Pretend to be a customer at the farmer's market and pay your child with the following combinations of bills. For each amount, have her sort, order, and count the bills. Then, have her write their value, both with and without a decimal point.

- 1 twenty-dollar bill, 3 ten-dollar bills, 3 five-dollar bills, and 2 one-dollar bills. *20, 30, 40, 50, 55, 60, 65, 66, 67. $67 and $67.00.*
- 3 twenty-dollar bills, 1 ten-dollar bill, 1 five-dollar bill, and 3 one-dollar bills. *20, 40, 60, 70, 75, 76, 77, 78. $78 and $78.00.*
- 4 twenty-dollar bills and 4 five-dollar bills. *20, 40, 60, 80, 85, 90, 95, 100. $100 and $100.00.*

Workbook: Write Dollar Amounts with a Decimal Point and Review

Have your child complete workbook pages 8.1A and 8.1B. If your child has trouble counting the printed bills, have her touch each bill or cross it off as she counts it.

Lesson 8.2
Write Dollars and Cents with a Decimal Point

	Purpose	Materials
Warm-up	• Count by 2s • Practice memory work • Review identifying the total number of objects in an array	• Dot array and L-cover (Blackline Master 6)
Activities	• Write cents with a cents sign or dollar sign and decimal point • Write dollars and cents with a dollar sign and decimal point • Sort, order, and count combinations of paper bills and coins	• Play money • Coins • Die
Workbook	• Write cents with a cents sign or dollar sign and decimal point • Count combinations of paper bills and coins	• Workbook pages 8.2A and 8.2B

This lesson includes dimes, nickels, and pennies. Your child will learn to count quarters in Lesson 8.3.

Warm-up: Counting, Memory Work, and Review

- Have your child count by 2s from 140 to 160.
- **If a number has 1, 3, 5, 7, or 9 in the ones-place, is the number even or odd?** *Odd.* **If a number has 0, 2, 4, 6, or 8 in the ones-place, is the number even or odd?** *Even.*
- Use the dot array and L-cover to show your child the following dot arrangements. Have him find the total number of dots in each array.

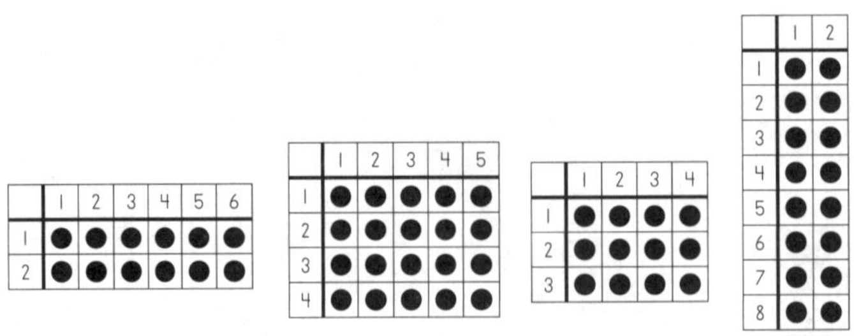

12 20 12 16

If your child starts to count each dot individually, encourage him to use repeated addition (or skip-count by 2s or 5s) instead.

Activity: Review Sorting, Ordering, and Counting Coins

In the last lesson, you learned how to write dollar amounts with a decimal point. Today, you'll review counting coins and learn to write cents with a cents sign or dollar sign and decimal point.

We follow the same 3 steps when we count coins as when we count paper bills: sort, order, and count. Mix up 5 dimes, 4 nickels, and 2 pennies on the table. Demonstrate how to sort the coins by type, put the piles in order from greatest value to least value, and then count the coins: **10, 20, 30, 40, 50, 55, 60, 65, 70, 71, 72.**

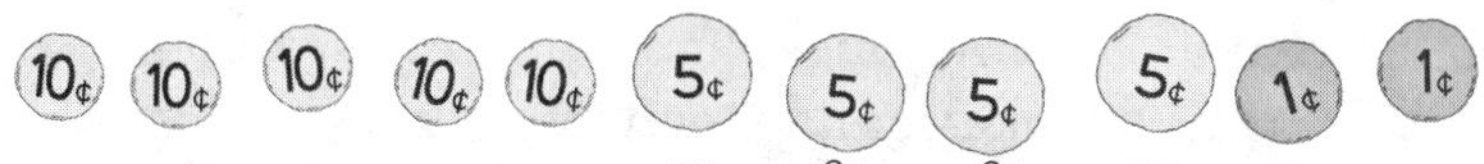

10 20 30 40 50 55 60 65 70 71 72

> Count the dimes first, then the nickels, and finally the pennies. Also make sure to point to each coin as you count it.

Activity: Write Cents Two Ways

Show your child how to write a cents sign: **First, you write a lowercase c. Then, you draw a vertical line through it.** Have your child write several cents signs on a piece of paper.

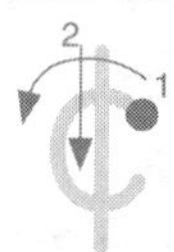

The cents sign always comes after the number. Write 72¢ on a piece of paper. Have your child write the following amounts with a cents sign: 45 cents, 37 cents, 50 cents, 8 cents.

72¢ 45¢ 37¢ 50¢ 8¢

We can also write cents with a dollar sign and decimal point. Write $0.72 on a piece of paper. **The decimal point separates the dollars from the cents. The zero shows that there aren't any dollars.** Have your child write the previous money amounts with a dollar sign and decimal.

$0.72 $0.45 $0.37 $0.50 $0.08

For $0.08, explain that the zero before the 8 is a place-holder zero: **The number of cents can be any number from 0 to 99. Putting a place-holder zero before the 8 makes the number of cents easier to read. Make sure you always include a place-holder zero if there are fewer than 10 cents.**

> Your child is not expected to fully understand decimal points or decimal place value in second grade. He'll learn more about decimals in future grades, including the tenths-place and hundredths-place.

Activity: Write Dollars and Cents with a Decimal Point

Give your child 1 five-dollar bill, 3 one-dollar bills, 2 dimes, 1 nickel, and 2 pennies. Let's pretend you saved up this money. **How much are the paper bills worth?** *$8.* **How much are the coins worth?** *27¢.*

> If needed, remind your child to sort and order the money before counting.

You have 8 dollars and 27 cents! Write $8.27 on a piece of paper.

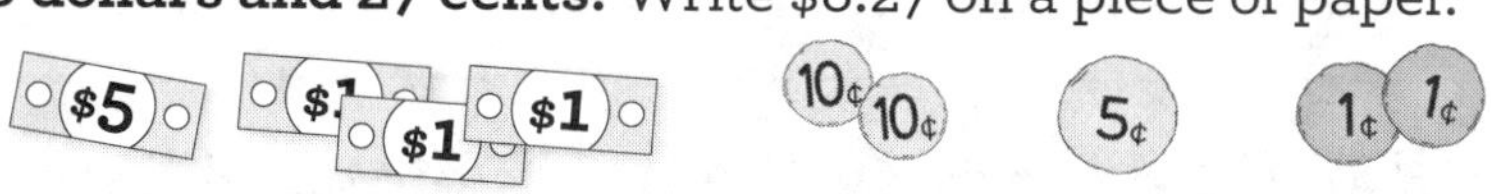

$8.27

Here's how you read this amount: 8 dollars and 27 cents. Point to each number as you read it, and point to the decimal point when you say "and."

$8.27

8 dollars and 27 cents

Mix up the following money combinations and give them to your child. Have him find the value of each combination and write it with a dollar sign and decimal point.

- 2 one-dollar bills, 3 dimes, 2 nickels, and 1 penny. *$2.41.*
- 1 five-dollar bill, 1 one-dollar bill, 1 nickel and 4 pennies. *$6.09.*
- 1 ten-dollar bill, 5 dimes, 5 nickels, and 5 pennies. *$10.80.*

Activity: Play Money War

Play Money War.

Money War

Materials: Play money (one-dollar bills, dimes, nickels, and pennies); die

Object of the Game: Win the most rounds.

Set the play money in piles in front of both players, in order from greatest value to lowest value.

In each round, both players take turns rolling the die 4 times.

- For your first roll, take as many one-dollar bills as dots on the die. (For example, if you roll a 4, take 4 one-dollar bills.)
- For your second roll, take as many dimes as dots on the die.
- For your third roll, take as many nickels as dots on the die.
- For your fourth roll, take as many pennies as dots on the die.

Count the money you have collected and record the value. The player whose money is worth more wins the round.

	Round 1
Gabriel	$4.38
Dad	$2.52

Sample scoring record.

Play 5 rounds. Whoever wins more rounds wins.

Workbook: Write Dollars and Cents with a Decimal Point and Review

Have your child complete workbook pages 8.2A and 8.2B.

Lesson 8.3
Read Prices in Dollars and Cents

	Purpose	Materials
Warm-up	• Count by 2s • Practice memory work • Review pairs that make 100	• None
Activities	• Read prices in dollars and cents • Count out money to match a price • Count quarters by 25s	• Play money • Coins
Workbook	• Count money with quarters • Assess addition fact mastery	• Workbook pages 8.3A and 8.3B

Warm-up: Counting, Memory Work, and Review

- Have your child count by 2s from 160 to 180. Allow her to use the 200 Chart if needed.
- **If a number has 1, 3, 5, 7, or 9 in the ones-place, is the number even or odd?** *Odd.* **If a number has 0, 2, 4, 6, or 8 in the ones-place, is the number even or odd?** *Even.*
- Secretly write each of the following equations on a piece of paper and hide the addend indicated with a slip of paper. Have your child pretend to use her "x-ray vision" to identify the hidden number in each equation.

$98 + \boxed{2} = 100 \qquad 95 + \boxed{5} = 100 \qquad 90 + \boxed{10} = 100$

$89 + \boxed{11} = 100 \qquad 85 + \boxed{15} = 100$

Activity: Read Menu Prices at the Pretend Restaurant

In the last two lessons, you learned how to write dollars and cents with a dollar sign and decimal point. Today, you'll practice reading dollars and cents and learn to count quarters.

We're going to make a menu for a Pretend Restaurant today. First, I'll write the prices, and then you can choose the foods. Fold a piece of paper in half to create 2 columns. Write the following prices in the right-hand column:

	\$4.50
	\$1.25
	\$0.50
	\$3.00
	\$0.75
	\$0.05

If your family's currency includes 20-cent coins rather than 25-cent coins, use the following prices instead: \$4.50, \$1.20, \$0.50, \$3.00, \$0.80, \$0.05.

Point to \$4.50. **Here's how you read this amount: 4 dollars and 50 cents.** Point to each number as you read it, and point to the decimal point when you say "and."

$4.50

4 dollars and 50 cents

Have your child read the rest of the menu prices aloud. *1 dollar and 25 cents. 50 cents. 3 dollars. 75 cents. 5 cents.*

For $0.50, $0.75, and $0.05, it's fine if your child says "0 dollars" before reading each number of cents. For $3.00, it's fine if she says "3 dollars and zero cents."

Have your child choose food for each price, and write the dishes on the menu.

Pizza	$4.50
Cookie	$1.25
Apple	$0.50
Sandwich	$3.00
Chips	$0.75
Piece of candy	$0.05

Sample menu

Activity: Count Out Money at the Pretend Restaurant

Give your child one-dollar bills, dimes, nickels, and pennies. **Let's pretend you're the customer, and I'm the waiter. What would you like to eat?** *Answers will vary.* Have your child count out the correct amount of money and pay you for the item.

Pizza	$4.50

Pretend to serve your child the food she chose. Repeat until your child has selected all the items on the menu.

Encourage your child to first count out the correct number of dollars and then the correct number of cents. Also encourage her to use the fewest coins possible. For example, if she starts to count out 50 cents in nickels, ask: **Is there a different coin you could use so that you don't have to count so many nickels?** *Dimes.*

Activity: Use Quarters at the Pretend Restaurant

It can take a while to count the right number of coins, especially if you use a lot of pennies and nickels. Dimes make it easier, but quarters make it even faster! Show your child a quarter. **How much is a quarter worth?** *25 cents.* **So, we count quarters by 25s.**

Place 4 quarters on a piece of paper. **1 quarter is worth 25 cents.** Write 25¢ below the first quarter. **25 plus 25 equals 50. So, 2 quarters are worth 50 cents.** Write 50¢ below the second quarter. Repeat until you've labeled all the quarters.

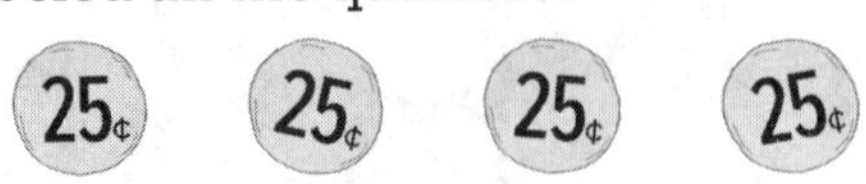

25¢ 50¢ 75¢ 100¢

Have your child practice counting the quarters by 25s: *25, 50, 75, 100.*

If your family's currency includes twenty-cent coins rather than quarters, place 5 twenty-cent coins on the table and have your child count them by 20s: *20, 40, 60, 80, 100*. If your family's currency commonly includes fifty-cent coins, place 2 fifty-cent coins on the table and demonstrate how to count them by 50s. Include these coins as your child pays for the menu items.

Have your child use one-dollar bills and quarters to pay for each of the items on the menu. Encourage her to look at the labeled quarters if she needs help counting out the correct number of quarters for an item.

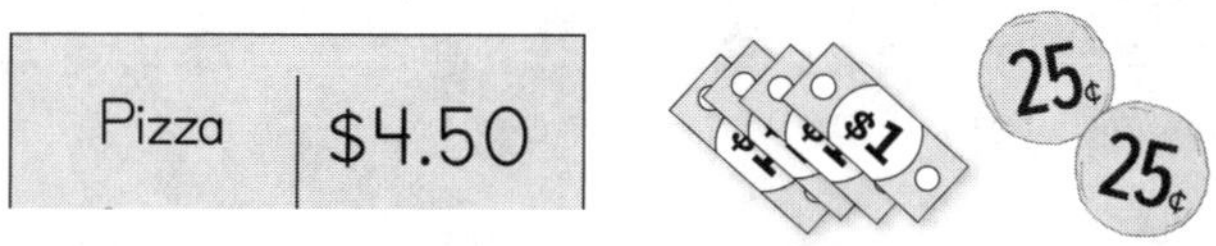

Workbook: Count Money with Quarters and Assess Addition Fact Mastery

Have your child complete workbook pages 8.3A and 8.3B. Have her work horizontally across the rows of problems on 8.3B.

If your child is overwhelmed by the number of problems on workbook page 8.3B, ask her the problems orally instead. Note whether she knows the correct answer, and give her at least 3 seconds to respond to each question.

Workbook pages 8.3B and 8.4B together provide an informal assessment of how well your child has mastered the addition facts. See the Unit 3 Checkpoint for guidance for assessing your child's progress.

Save workbook page 8.3B so that you can look at it with workbook page 8.4B to assess your child's addition fact mastery.

Lesson 8.4
Practice Counting Money

	Purpose	Materials
Warm-up	• Count by 2s • Practice memory work • Review word problems	• None
Activities	• Count money combinations that include quarters	• Play money • Coins • Savings Game game board (from workbook page 8.4A) • Die • Counters
Workbook	• Assess addition fact mastery	• Workbook page 8.4B

Warm-up: Counting, Memory Work, and Review

- Have your child count by 2s from 180 to 200.
- **If a number has 1, 3, 5, 7, or 9 in the ones-place, is the number even or odd?** *Odd.* **If a number has 0, 2, 4, 6, or 8 in the ones-place, is the number even or odd?** *Even.*
- Have your child write a matching equation for each of the following word problems and solve.
    - **You earn $6 on Monday and $8 on Tuesday. How much do you earn in all?** *6 + 8 = 14. $14.*
    - **You have $12, and you want to buy something that costs $15. How much more money do you need?** *12 + _3_ = 15, or 15 − 12 = 3. $3.*
    - **You earn $8. Then, you spend $4. How much money do you have left?** *8 − 4 = 4. $4.*

Activity: Count Coin Combinations with Quarters

This week, you've learned how to count money and use a decimal point to write dollars and cents. Today, you'll practice counting money combinations that include quarters.

Mix up 2 quarters, 3 dimes, 1 nickel, and 4 pennies on the table. Have your child sort the coins by type, put the piles in order by coin value, and count them: *25, 50, 60, 70, 80, 85, 86, 87, 88, 89.* Have him write the amount two ways: with a cents sign, and with a dollar sign and decimal point.

25 50 60 70 80 85 86 87 88 89

$0.89 89¢

> If your family's currency includes twenty-cent coins rather than quarters, use them instead of quarters in this activity.

Mix up the following money combinations and give them to your child. Have him find the value of each combination and write it with a dollar sign and decimal point.

- 1 five-dollar bill, 1 quarter, 3 nickels, 6 pennies. *$5.46.*
- 3 one-dollar bills, 2 quarters, 1 dime, 1 nickel, 3 pennies. *$3.68*
- 5 ten-dollar bills, 2 one-dollar bills, 3 quarters, 1 nickel, and 4 pennies. *$52.84*

Activity: Play the Savings Game

We're going to play the Savings Game to practice counting money. Play the Savings Game.

The Savings Game

Materials: The Savings Game game board (from workbook page 8.4A); play money and coins (twenty-dollar bills, ten-dollar bills, five-dollar bills, one-dollar bills, and quarters); die; counters

Object of the Game: Be the first person to save $100.

Have each player choose a different-colored counter to use as a game token and place it on one of the Start squares. Give each player 2 twenty-dollar bills, 2 ten-dollar bills, 2 five-dollar bills, 2 one-dollar bills, and 2 quarters to start. This is your "savings" that you will add to or spend from during the game.

Place the rest of the play money and coins on the table, in order from greatest value to lowest value. When you "earn" money in the game, take it from these piles. When you "spend" money in the game, take it from your savings and return it to these piles.

On your turn, roll the die and advance your token the corresponding number of squares clockwise around the path. Follow the directions on the square (by either "earning" or "spending" money). Count your savings and announce your current total. Play then passes to the other player.

The first player to have $100 wins the game.

If your child needs extra practice reading and writing money with a dollar sign and decimal point, record your scores on a simple scorecard after each turn.

Trade your quarters and bills as needed to make counting and "spending" simpler. For example, if you land on the square that directs you to spend 75¢ but only have 1 quarter, trade a one-dollar bill for 4 quarters.

Workbook: Assess Addition Fact Mastery

Have your child complete workbook page 8.4B. Have him work horizontally across each row.

If your child is overwhelmed by the number of problems on the page, ask him the problems orally instead. Note whether he knows the correct answer, and give him at least 3 seconds to respond to each question.

Workbook pages 8.3B and 8.4B together provide an informal assessment of how well your child has mastered the addition facts. See the Unit 3 Checkpoint for guidance for assessing your child's progress.

Lesson 8.5
Enrichment and Review (Optional)

	Purpose	Materials
Warm-up	• Count from 150 to 200 by 2s • Review memory work • Review your child's favorite or most challenging activities from Week 8	• Varies, depending on the activities you choose
Picture Book	• Practice counting money in the context of a lemonade stand	• *Lemonade in Winter*, written by Emily Jenkins and illustrated by G. Brian Karas • Coins
Enrichment Activity	• Use money in real life	• Bills and coins to spend

Warm-up: Counting, Memory Work, and Review

- Have your child count from 150 to 200 by 2s.
- Quiz your child on the memory work through Week 8. See page 523 for the full list.
- If you have time, repeat one or two of the activities from this week's lessons. Choose activities your child especially enjoyed or found challenging.

Math Picture Book: *Lemonade in Winter*

Read *Lemonade in Winter*, written by Emily Jenkins and illustrated by G. Brian Karas. As you read, use quarters to model the children's lemonade sales.

Enrichment Activity: Use Money at the Store

Take a field trip to a store. Have your child use cash to pay for your transaction.

> You may want to go at a time when the store isn't busy (and look for a patient-looking cashier or a self-check-out!) so that your child isn't rushed while counting out the bills and coins.

Week 8 Answer Key

8.1A

Write how much money is in each coin purse.
Use a dollar sign and decimal point.

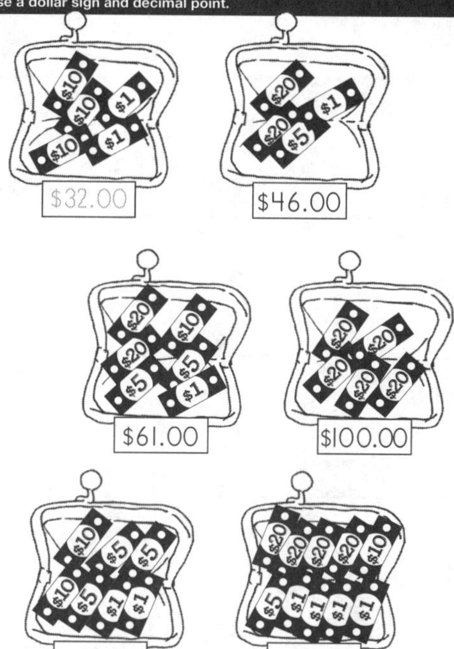

$32.00 | $46.00 | $61.00 | $100.00 | $37.00 | $99.00

8.1B

5 + 6 = 11	7 + 6 = 13	7 + 3 = 10	9 + 8 = 17	7 + 7 = 14
4 + 6 = 10	8 + 7 = 15	2 + 9 = 11	8 + 6 = 14	5 + 9 = 14

Complete the circles with <, >, or =.

139 < 155	146 = 146	150 > 99
111 > 110	101 > 100	193 < 194

Complete.

35 + 4 = 39 135 + 4 = 139	62 + 20 = 82 162 + 20 = 182
58 - 4 = 54 158 - 4 = 154	71 - 30 = 41 171 - 30 = 141

8.2A

Match.

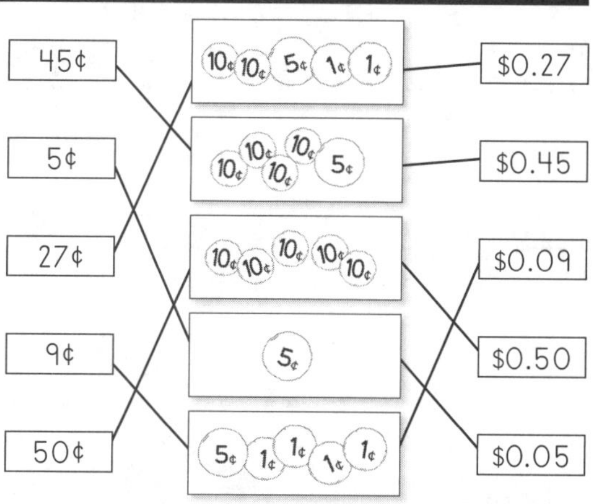

Write how much money is in each coin purse two ways.

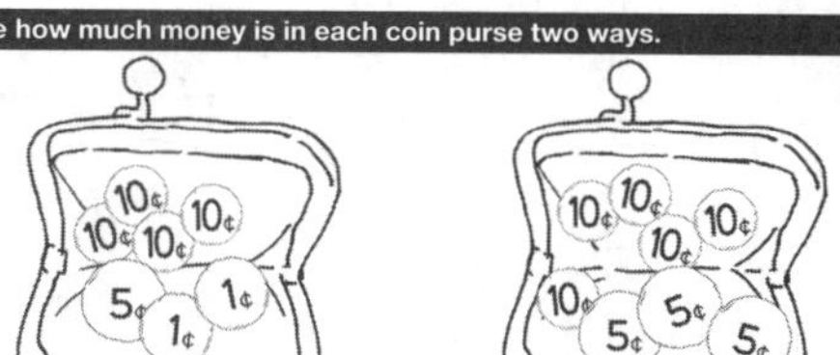

47 ¢ $0.47 | 65 ¢ $0.65

8.2B

Complete.

8 → 6, 2 6 + 2 = 8 8 - 6 = 2	10 → 9, 1 9 + 1 = 10 10 - 9 = 1

Complete.

9 - 4 = 5	7 - 2 = 5	10 - 3 = 7
8 - 1 = 7	9 - 6 = 3	7 - 4 = 3
10 - 5 = 5	8 - 4 = 4	10 - 8 = 2

Write the expanded form of each number.

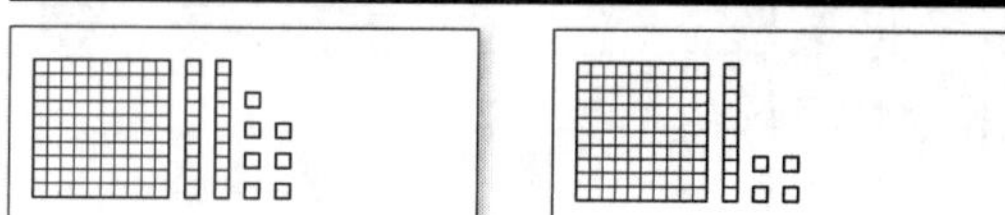

127=100+20+7 | 114=100+10+4

Week 8 Answer Key

8.3A

Write how much money is in each coin purse. Use a dollar sign and decimal point.

8.3B

Complete.

4 + 9 = 13	8 + 2 = 10	9 + 7 = 16	6 + 2 = 8	9 + 5 = 14
9 + 9 = 18	1 + 8 = 9	7 + 7 = 14	5 + 6 = 11	5 + 1 = 6
0 + 9 = 9	8 + 6 = 14	2 + 7 = 9	6 + 7 = 13	3 + 5 = 8
9 + 6 = 15	7 + 8 = 15	7 + 5 = 12	1 + 6 = 7	5 + 5 = 10
1 + 9 = 10	8 + 0 = 8	3 + 7 = 10	6 + 8 = 14	6 + 5 = 11

8.4A

See the Instuctor Guide for how to play. Save this game board for future lessons.

8.4B

Complete.

9 + 5 = 14	3 + 8 = 11	7 + 1 = 8	6 + 6 = 12	5 + 0 = 5
7 + 9 = 16	8 + 8 = 16	8 + 7 = 15	6 + 9 = 15	4 + 5 = 9
9 + 2 = 11	9 + 8 = 17	7 + 6 = 13	3 + 6 = 9	5 + 8 = 13
8 + 9 = 17	8 + 4 = 12	0 + 7 = 7	6 + 4 = 10	2 + 5 = 7
9 + 3 = 12	5 + 8 = 13	7 + 4 = 11	0 + 6 = 6	5 + 7 = 12

Unit 3 Checkpoint

What to Expect at the End of Unit 3

By the end of Unit 3, most children will be able to do the following:

- Double or find halves of numbers, either mentally or with base-ten blocks.
- Identify even and odd numbers to 100.
- Use repeated addition or skip-counting to find the number of objects in an array.
- Read, write, and compare numbers to 200. Some children will still need to use the Place-Value Chart to make sure they write the digits in the correct place.
- Represent numbers to 200 with base-ten blocks and understand their digits' place value.
- Write numbers to 200 in expanded form. Many children will need to be reminded what expanded form means or need to construct numbers with base-ten blocks before writing the expanded form.
- Solve simple mental addition and subtraction problems with the numbers to 200, either mentally or with base-ten blocks.
- Write money amounts with a dollar sign and decimal point. Many children will still forget to include place-holder zeros when writing money amounts with fewer than 10 cents, such as $12.04.
- Count combinations of bills and coins (including twenty-dollar bills and quarters). Some children will still be working on counting by 20s or 25s.

Is Your Child Ready to Move on?

Your child does not need to have mastered all of the skills from Unit 3 before moving on. However, she should know how to find the answers to most of the addition facts (up to 10 + 10) without counting on fingers or counting one-by-one. It's fine if she still takes a bit to think through some of the facts or has a few facts that she struggles with.

Use workbook pages 8.3B and 8.4B to assess your child's progress with the addition facts. They're organized to make it easy for you to see which facts your child has mastered and which facts she still needs to practice.

For example, if your child has several problems wrong in Column 3 (or took longer than 3 seconds to answer many of the problems), she needs more practice with the +7 facts.

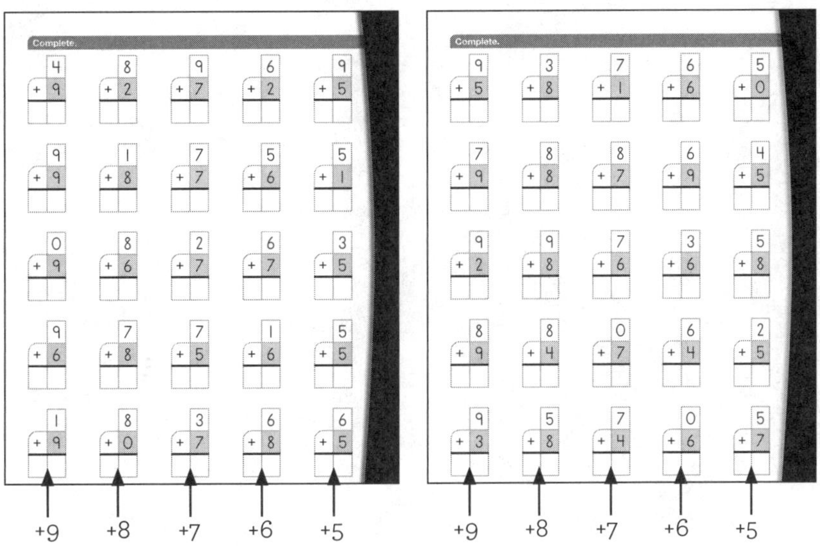

What to Do If Your Child Needs More Practice

If your child needs more practice with some of the addition facts, spend a few days practicing the corresponding games before moving on to Unit 4.

Activities for Mastering the Addition Facts

- Addition Crash (+9 Version) (Lesson 4.1)
- Addition Crash (+8 Version) (Lesson 4.3)
- Addition Bingo (+7 Version) (Lesson 5.1)
- Addition Bingo (+6 Version) (Lesson 5.3)

The +5 facts are incorporated into the games for the +6, +7, +8, and +9 facts.

If you practice the addition facts for several days and find that your child does not have them fully mastered, move on to Unit 4 anyway. Children vary in how long it takes them to develop speed and fluency with the addition facts, and your child will continue to reinforce them as she studies subtraction in Unit 4.

Unit 4
Subtraction Facts and Word Problems

Overview

In Unit 1, your child reviewed the meaning of subtraction and the subtraction facts to 10. In this unit, he will practice and review the subtraction facts to 20. He'll also review take-away, take-apart, and comparison word problems, and he'll begin to solve subtraction word problems involving more or fewer.

You have 10 balloons. 2 are blue, and the rest are yellow. How many are yellow?	You found 11 eggs, and I found 6 eggs. How many more eggs did you find than me?	You have 7 candies. I have 3 fewer than you. How many do I have?

Samples of some of the word problem types your child will tackle in this unit

You'll alternate between lessons focused on fact mastery and lessons focused on word problems. The word problem lessons all include subtraction fact practice in the warm-up. If your child is still working on subtraction fact fluency, make sure not to skip these warm-ups! But, just as in Unit 1, don't worry if your child isn't fully fluent with the subtraction facts by the end of this unit. He'll have many more opportunities to practice. The Unit 4 Checkpoint (page 188) will help you gauge whether or not to move on.

If your child already knows the subtraction facts to 20 well, zip through the fact mastery lessons and instead focus on the word problem lessons.

Week 9	-9 and -8 Facts
Week 10	-7 and -6 Facts
Week 11	-2, -3, -4, and -5 Facts

What Your Child Will Learn

In this unit your child will learn to:

- Solve subtraction facts with numbers to 20
- Solve take-away and take-apart word problems
- Use subtraction to compare quantities and ages
- Solve word problems involving *more* or *fewer*

Recommended Math Picture Books (Optional)

These picture books are scheduled in the optional Enrichment and Review lessons at the end of each week.

- *If You Were a Minus Sign*, written by Trisha Sue Speed Shaskan and illustrated by Francesca Carabelli. Picture Window Books, 2009.
- *What's the Difference? An Endangered Animal Subtraction Story*, written by Suzanne Slade and illustrated by Joan Waites. Sylvan Dell Publishing, 2010.
- *Subtraction Action*, by Loreen Leedy. Holiday House, 2000.

Week 9
-9 and -8 Facts

Overview

Your child will review the relationship between addition and subtraction. Then, she'll use that relationship to subtract 8 and 9 from numbers in the teens. She'll also review take-away subtraction word problems. Next week, she'll practice more challenging subtraction word problems.

Lesson 9.1	Use Addition to Solve Subtraction Problems
Lesson 9.2	Practice -9 Facts
Lesson 9.3	Take-Away Subtraction Word Problems
Lesson 9.4	Practice -8 Facts
Lesson 9.5	Enrichment and Review (Optional)

Teaching Math with Confidence: Using Addition to Solve Subtraction Equations

This week, you'll teach your child to use addition to find the answers to the −9 and −8 facts. For example, to solve 13 – 9, she'll think "9 plus what equals 13?" Most children find this much easier than trying to visualize removing 9 counters.

$13 - 9 = ?$

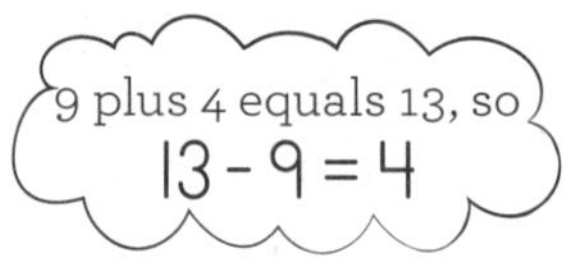

However, for subtraction facts that involve subtracting smaller numbers, many children find it easier to simply imagine removing the matching number of counters from the ten-frame. For example, in Week 11, you'll teach your child to imagine removing 5 counters from the ten-frames to solve 14 – 5.

$14 - 5 = 9$

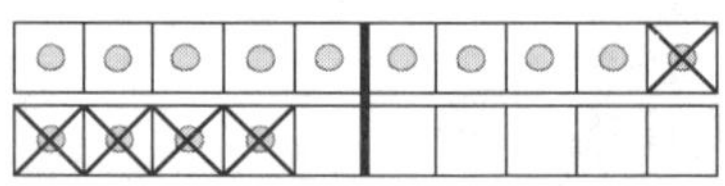

Different numbers lend themselves better to different strategies, whether they're single-digit subtraction facts or multi-digit mental subtraction problems. To experience this difference yourself, think about how you would solve 100 – 12 versus 100 – 97. For 100 – 12, you'd likely think about taking 1 ten and 2 ones away from 100. But for 100 – 97, most adults think: 97 plus what equals 100?

$100 - 11 = ?$

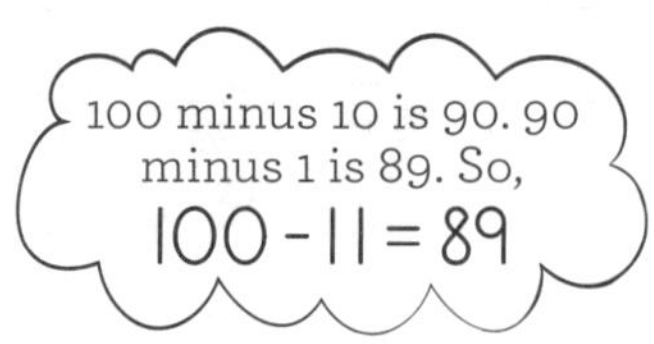

$100 - 97 = ?$

Flexible problem-solvers adjust their mental strategy based on the numbers in the problem.

This week's lessons on using addition to solve subtraction will help your child become a more flexible problem-solver. Throughout the unit, the lessons will guide you as you teach your child specific strategies for the subtraction facts. But, just as with addition, your child may use whatever approach makes the most sense to her, as long as her strategy is efficient, is accurate, and doesn't require counting one-by-one.

Extra Materials Needed for Week 9

- For optional Enrichment and Review Lesson:
    - *If You Were a Minus Sign,* written by Trisha Sue Speed Shaskan and illustrated by Francesca Carabelli

Lesson 9.1
Use Addition to Solve Subtraction Problems

	Purpose	Materials
Warm-up	• Count by 20s • Practice memory work • Review fact families	• Play money
Activities	• Understand how to use addition to solve subtraction problems • Practice subtracting numbers to 10	• Double ten-frames (Blackline Master 1) • Counters • Part-Total Mat (Blackline Master 2) • Playing cards
Workbook	• Practice subtracting numbers to 10	• Workbook pages 9.1A and 9.1B

Warm-up: Counting, Memory Work, and Review

- Place 5 twenty-dollar bills on the table. Have your child count by 20 to find the bills' value.
- Write the $<$ sign. **What does this sign mean?** *Less than.*
  Write the $>$ sign. **What does this sign mean?** *Greater than.*
- Write the numbers 2, 6, and 8 on a piece of paper. Have your child write the matching fact family.

$$2 + 6 = 8$$
$$6 + 2 = 8$$
$$8 - 6 = 2$$
$$8 - 2 = 6$$

Activity: Use Addition to Solve Subtraction Problems

You learned how to subtract in first grade. In this unit, you'll practice the subtraction facts so that you know them by heart.

Some of the subtraction facts are easier if you use addition to solve them. Today, we'll review the connection between addition and subtraction so that you can use addition to help find answers to the subtraction facts.

Write "8 – 7 =" on a piece of paper. Place 8 counters on the ten-frame. **To solve this problem, you could imagine taking away 7 counters.** Remove 7 of the counters and complete the equation: 8 – 7 = 1.

$$8 - 7 = 1$$

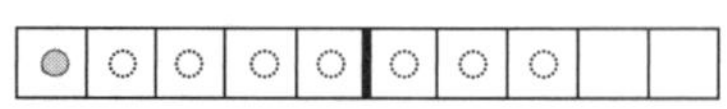

That's a lot of counters to keep track of, though! Many kids find it easier to use addition to solve this problem. Write 8 – 7 = on a piece of paper again. **8 is the total, and 7 is one of the parts. We need to find the other part.** Write 7 and 8 on the Part-Total Mat.

8 - 7 =

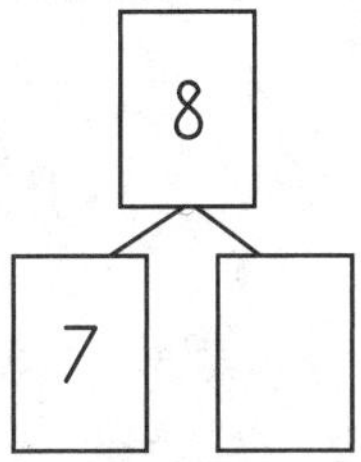

To find the other part, I can think addition: 7 plus what equals 8? Write "7 + ___ = 8" below the previous equation.

8 - 7 =

7 + __ = 8

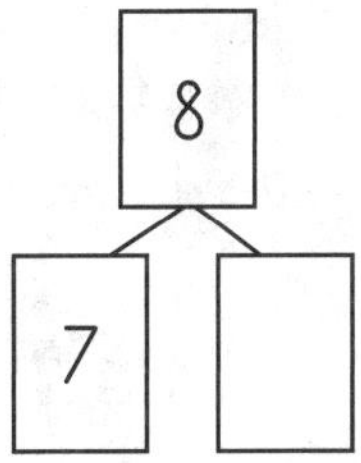

7 plus what equals 8? *1.* **Since 7 plus 1 equals 8, 8 minus 7 equals 1.** Have your child write 1 on the Part-Total Mat and complete the equations.

8 - 7 = 1

7 + 1 = 8

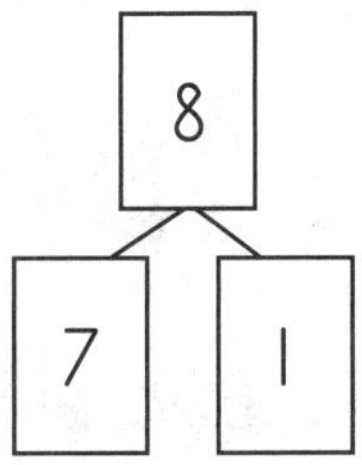

How do you like using addition to solve that problem? *Answers will vary.* **Many kids find it easier to think addition when they solve subtraction problems. But you can use whatever strategy makes the most sense to you, as long as it's quick and works every time. It's great if you "just know" the answers, too!**

Have your child solve the following subtraction problems. If she doesn't know the answers by heart, encourage her to try thinking of them as missing addend problems. Use the Part-Total Mat to demonstrate as needed.

- 7 - 6 = *1*
- 9 - 7 = *2*
- 9 - 5 = *4*
- 9 - 8 = *1*
- 9 - 6 = 3
- 10 - 8 = *2*

You can also use counters to model the missing addend problems if your child has trouble. For example, for 9 - 5, place 5 counters on the ten-frame. **How many more counters would you need to have 9?** *4.* **So, 5 plus what equals 9?** *4.*

9 - 5 =

5 + __ = 9

If your child needs counters for these problems, spend another day practicing them and playing Difference War (below) before you move on to Lesson 9.2.

Activity: Play Difference War

We call the answer to a subtraction problem the difference. In this game, we'll subtract to find the difference between numbers.

Difference War

Materials: 4s, 5s, 6s, 7s, 8s, 9s, and 10s from one deck of cards (28 cards total)

Object of the Game: Win the most cards.

Shuffle the cards and deal them face down in two piles. Each player flips over the top two cards in their pile. Then, each player subtracts to find the difference between their two cards. For example, if you turn over a 10 and an 8, the difference is 2, since 10 – 8 = 2.

The player with the greater difference wins all 4 cards.

Difference: 2 Difference: 3

The player with the 6 and 9 wins, since 3 is more than 2.

If the differences are equal, leave the cards face-up on the table and have both players play again. Whoever has the greater difference in the next round wins all the face-up cards.

Play until the piles run out. Whoever has won more cards wins the game.

Workbook: Practice Subtraction Facts and Review

Have your child complete workbook pages 9.1A and 9.1B.

Lesson 9.2
Practice -9 Facts

	Purpose	Materials
Warm-up	• Count quarters by 25s • Practice memory work • Review +9 facts	• Coins
Activities	• Use addition to solve subtraction problems • Practice -9 facts	• Part-Total Mat (Blackline Master 2) • Counters • Double ten-frames (Blackline Master 1) • Subtraction Race game board (from workbook page 9.2A) • Coin
Workbook	• Practice -9 facts	• Workbook page 9.2B

If your child already knows the answers immediately for the -9 facts, make this a quick review lesson.

Warm-up: Counting, Memory Work, and Review

- Place 4 quarters on the table. Have your child count by 25s to find their value.
- **If a number has 1, 3, 5, 7, or 9 in the ones-place, is the number even or odd?** *Odd.* **If a number has 0, 2, 4, 6, or 8 in the ones-place, is the number even or odd?** *Even.*
- Do a brief oral review of the +9 facts. Have your child give each answer as quickly as possible.
  - 9 + 2 = *11*
  - 5 + 9 = *14*
  - 8 + 9 = *17*
  - 6 + 9 = *15*
  - 9 + 9 = *18*
  - 3 + 9 = *12*
  - 9 + 7 = *16*
  - 4 + 9 = *13*

Reviewing the +9 facts prepares your child to use them to solve the -9 facts.

Activity: Practice -9 Facts

In the last lesson, you learned how to use addition to solve subtraction problems. Today, you'll use that approach to practice the -9 facts.

Write "13 – 9 =" on a piece of paper. **You could put 13 counters on the ten-frames and try to imagine taking 9 counters away. But it's usually easier to use addition for the –9 facts.**

13 is the total, and 9 is one of the parts. We need to find the other part. Have your child write 13 and 9 on the Part-Total Mat.

13 - 9 =

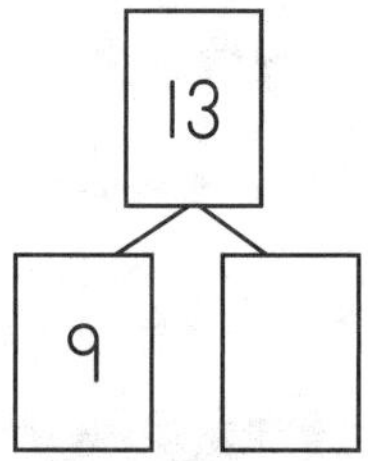

To find the other part, we can use addition: 9 plus what equals 13?

If your child immediately knows the answer to this question, skip placing the counters on the ten-frame and go straight to the practice problems below.

Here's how we can figure it out. Write "9 + ___ = 13" below the previous equation. Put 9 counters on the ten-frame.

13 - 9 =
9 + __ = 13

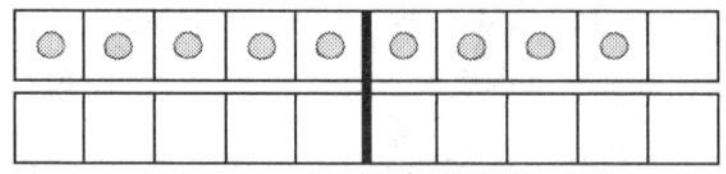

We want to know how many more counters we need to reach 13. We'll do it in two steps. First, I add 1 counter to complete the 10. Add 1 counter to the top ten-frame.

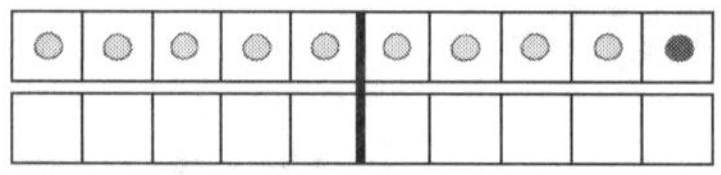

How many more counters do I need to add to make 13? *3*. Add 3 more counters.

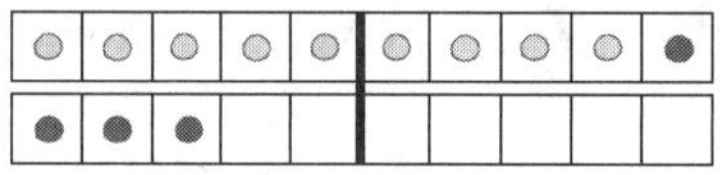

So, 9 plus what equals 13? *4*. Have your child write 4 on the Part-Total Mat and complete the missing addend equation: 9 + _4_ = 13.

Since 9 plus 4 equals 13, 13 minus 9 equals 4. Have your child complete the written subtraction equation: 13 – 9 = 4.

13 - 9 = 4
9 + 4 = 13

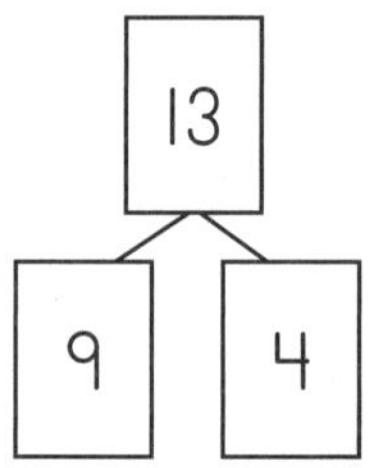

Encourage your child to use addition to solve the rest of the -9 facts, listed below. Write missing addend problems and place counters on the ten-frame to model the problems as needed.

- 11 – 9 = *2*
- 15 – 9 = *6*
- 12 – 9 = *3*
- 14 – 9 = *5*
- 16 – 9 = *7*
- 18 – 9 = *9*
- 17 – 9 = *8*

If you find that this method doesn't "click" for your child, he may instead visualize taking away the counters in two steps. For example, to solve 13 – 9, he can first take away the 3 counters on the bottom ten-frame. Then, he can remove 6 more counters to see that the answer is 4. See the Week 9 **Teaching Math with Confidence** for more on these two strategies.

13 - 9 = 4

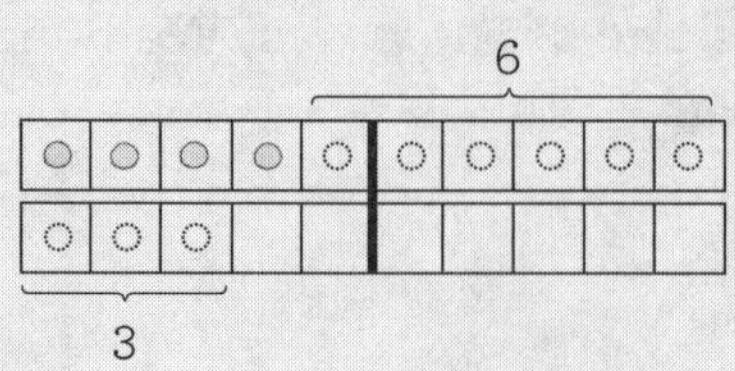

Activity: Play Subtraction Race (-9 Version)

Play Subtraction Race (-9 Version). Keep the ten-frame and counters available and encourage him to think addition to find the answers.

This fast-moving, luck-based game provides lots of practice with the -9 facts. If you have time, play it several times.

Subtraction Race (-9 Version)

Materials: Subtraction Race game board (from workbook page 9.2A); counters; coin

Object of the Game: Be the first player to reach the end of the race course.

Choose which player will be heads and which will be tails. Have each player choose a counter as a game token and place it on the matching starting space.

Have one player flip the coin. (Either you or your child can do this.) If the coin shows heads, the "heads" player moves his game token to the next space and subtracts 9 from the number on the space. For example, if you land on 14: 14 minus 9 equals 5.

If the coin shows tails, the "tails" player moves his game token to the next space and subtracts 9 from the number on the space.

Continue flipping the coin and moving the counters until one player reaches the final space on the race course. The first player to reach the end wins.

Save this game board with your math materials so you can play again.

Workbook: Practice -9 Facts and Review

Have your child complete workbook page 9.2B. Remind him to use the addition equations to solve the corresponding subtraction equations.

Lesson 9.3
Take-Away Subtraction Word Problems

	Purpose	Materials
Warm-up	• Count by 5s • Practice memory work • Review -9 subtraction facts	• Play money • Subtraction Race game board (from workbook page 9.2A) • Coin • Counters
Activities	• Write equations to match take-away subtraction word problems • Create take-away subtraction word problems	• Counters • Part-Total Mat (Blackline Master 2)
Workbook	• Solve take-away subtraction word problems	• Workbook pages 9.3A and 9.3B

This lesson focuses on using subtraction in take-away situations, where items are consumed, removed, or used up. Your child will learn about other types of subtraction word problems in Lessons 10.1, 10.3, and 11.2.

Warm-up: Counting, Memory Work, and Review

- Place 1 hundred-dollar bill and 7 five-dollar bills on the table. Have your child count the bills by 5s, starting at 100.
- **What do we call the result when we add numbers together?** *The sum.* **What do we call the result when we subtract a number from another number?** *The difference.*
- Play Subtraction Race (-9 Version). See Lesson 9.2 (page 149) for directions. Encourage your child to use addition to find the answers.

  If your child takes more than 3 seconds to find the answers to many of the subtraction problems in this game, spend another day or two practicing the -9 facts before moving on to Lesson 9.4.

Activity: Review Take-Away Subtraction Word Problems

In the last lesson, you practiced the -9 facts. Today, we'll review how to use subtraction to solve word problems. You'll also practice the -9 facts some more.

Imagine this word problem as I read it: You have 10 stickers. Then, you use 6. How many stickers do you have left? Model the problem with counters: Place 10 counters on the table, and then remove 6.

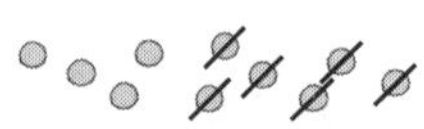

What is the total in this problem? *10.* **What part do we know?** *6.* Have your child write 10 and 6 on the Part-Total Mat. **What's the missing part?** *4.* Have your child write 4 on the Part-Total Mat.

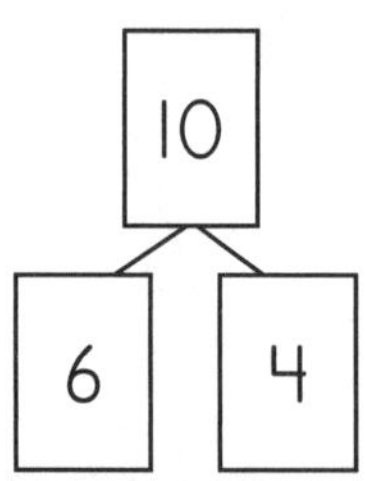

What subtraction equation matches the problem? *10 – 6 = 4.* Have your child write the equation on paper.

10 - 6 = 4

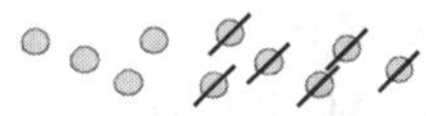

If your child writes a missing addend equation, show her how to write the corresponding subtraction equation as well. If your child writes the numbers in the equation in the wrong order, remind her that subtraction equations begin with the total.

Have your child write numbers on the Part-Total Mat to match the following word problems. Then, have her write and solve a subtraction equation to match.

If your child has trouble writing the numbers on the Part-Total Mat, use counters to model each problem first.

The numbers in these word problems are small so that your child can focus on understanding the word problems, not the numbers. If your child would like more of a challenge, substitute larger numbers in the problems.

- **You have 10 balloons. Then 2 pop. How many do you have left?** *8.*

10 - 2 = 8

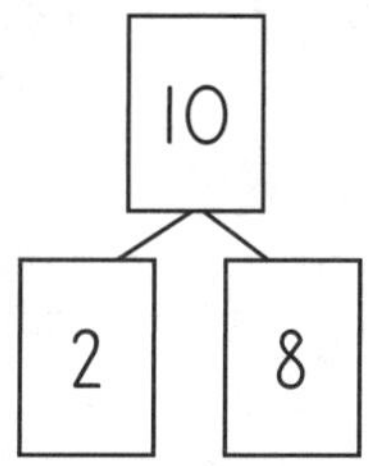

- **You have 9 crackers. Then you eat 4. How many do you have left?** *5.*

9 - 4 = 5

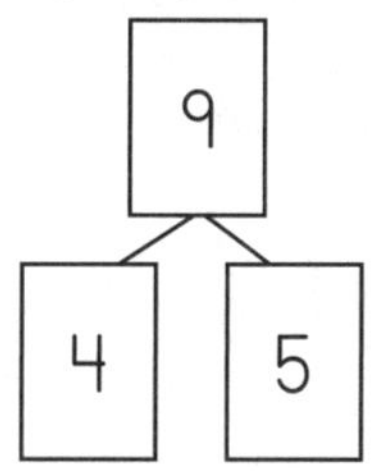

- **You have 8 ice cubes. Then 1 melts. How many do you have left?** *7.*

8 - 1 = 7

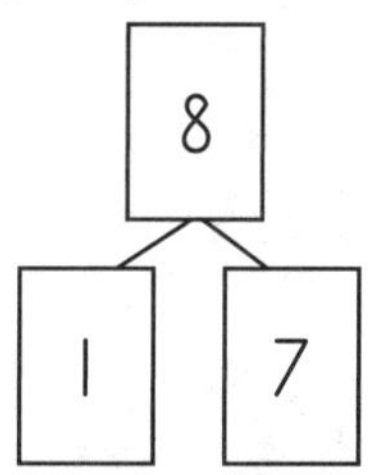

What do these stories have in common? *Sample answers: We know the total and one of the parts. We have to find one part. You can use subtraction to solve all of them. All of them are about taking things away.*

All of these word problems involve taking something away. The stickers get used up, the balloons pop, you eat the crackers, and the ice cubes melt. The total is split into two parts, and one part is removed or taken away.

Take-away situations aren't the only situations where we use subtraction. You'll learn about more subtraction situations in Weeks 10 and 11.

Activity: Create Take-Away Subtraction Word Problems

Write "8 – 6 = 2" on a piece of paper. Have your child make up several take-away subtraction word problems that match the equation. If she has trouble getting started, suggest she think about real-life situations where something gets used up or removed.

$$8 - 6 = 2$$

Sample answers:

- *I had $8, and then I spent $6. How much money did I have left?*
- *I had 8 crackers, and then I ate 6. How many did I have left?*
- *I had 8 cupcakes. I gave 6 to my friends. How many did I have left?*

Workbook: Solve Word Problems and Review

Have your child complete workbook pages 9.3A and 9.3B.

On 9.3B, encourage your child to imagine adding counters to the ten-frames in two steps to solve the missing addend problems. For example, for 9 + __ = 12: **First, you'd add 1 counter to complete the group of 10. Then, you'd need 2 more on the bottom ten-frame. So, 9 plus 3 equals 12.** If your child finds this difficult to visualize, she can use real counters on ten-frames instead.

Lesson 9.4
Practice -8 Facts

	Purpose	Materials
Warm-up	• Count by 5s • Practice memory work • Review +8 facts	• Play money
Activities	• Practice -8 facts	• Part-Total Mat (Blackline Master 2) • Counters • Double ten-frames (Blackline Master 1) • Subtraction Race game board (from workbook page 9.2A) • Coin
Workbook	• Practice -8 facts	• Workbook pages 9.4A and 9.4B

If your child already knows the answers immediately for the -8 facts, make this a quick review lesson.

Warm-up: Counting, Memory Work, and Review

- Place 1 hundred-dollar bill and about 15 five-dollar bills on the table. Have your child count the bills by 5s, starting at 100.
- **How many tens equal 1 hundred?** *10.*
- Do a brief oral review of the +8 facts. Have your child give each answer as quickly as possible.
    - 8 + 8 = *16*
    - 5 + 8 = *13*
    - 6 + 8 = *14*
    - 9 + 8 = *17*
    - 3 + 8 = *11*
    - 8 + 7 = *15*
    - 4 + 8 = *12*

Activity: Practice -8 Subtraction Facts

In the last two lessons, you practiced the -9 subtraction facts. Today, you'll think addition to practice the -8 facts.

Write "14 – 8 =" on a piece of paper. **14 is the total, and 8 is one of the parts. We need to find the other part.** Have your child write 14 and 8 on the Part-Total Mat.

14 - 8 =

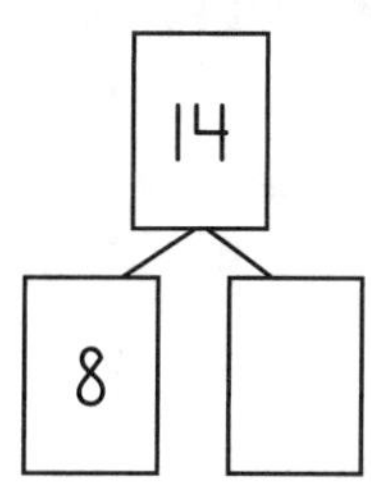

To find the other part, we can think of it as addition: 8 plus what equals 14?

If your child immediately knows the answer to this question, skip placing the counters on the ten-frame and go straight to the practice problems below.

Here's how we can figure it out. Write "8 + ___ = 14" below the previous equation. Put 8 counters on the ten-frame.

14 - 8 =
8 + ___ = 14

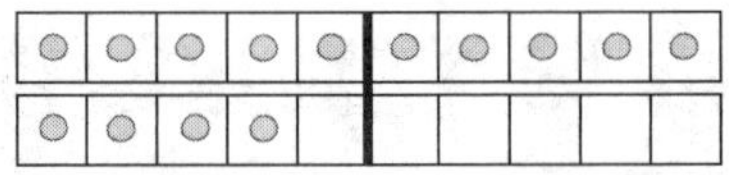

We want to know how many more counters we need to reach 14. We'll do it in two steps. First, I add 2 counters to complete the 10. Add 2 counters to the top ten-frame.

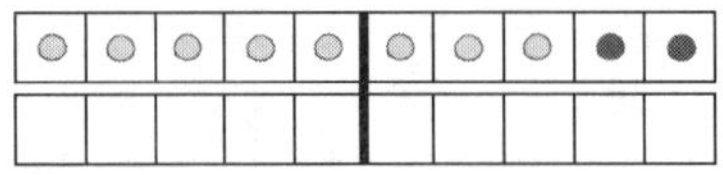

How many more counters do I need to add to make 14? *4.* Add 4 more counters.

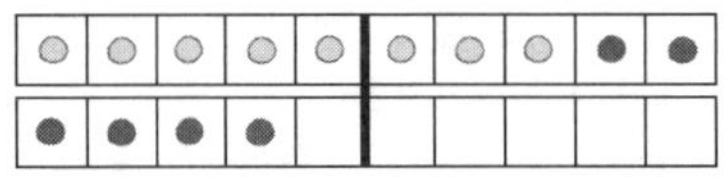

So, 8 plus what equals 14? *6.* Have your child write 6 on the Part-Total Mat and complete the missing addend problem: 8 + _6_ = 14.

Since 8 plus 6 equals 14, 14 minus 8 equals 6. Have your child complete the written subtraction problem: 14 – 8 = 6.

14 - 8 = 6
8 + 6 = 14

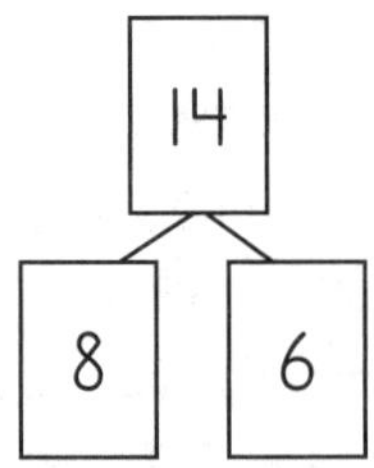

Encourage your child to think addition to solve the rest of the -8 facts, listed below. Write missing addend problems and place counters on the ten-frame to model the problems as needed.

- 11 - 8 = *3*
- 15 - 8 = *7*
- 12 - 8 = *4*
- 13 - 8 = *5*
- 16 - 8 = *8*
- 17 - 8 = *9*

As in Lesson 9.2, if this method doesn't "click" for your child, he may visualize taking away counters in two steps instead. For example, to solve 14 - 8, he can first take away the 4 counters on the bottom ten-frame. Then, he can remove 4 more counters to see that the answer is 6.

14 - 8 = 6

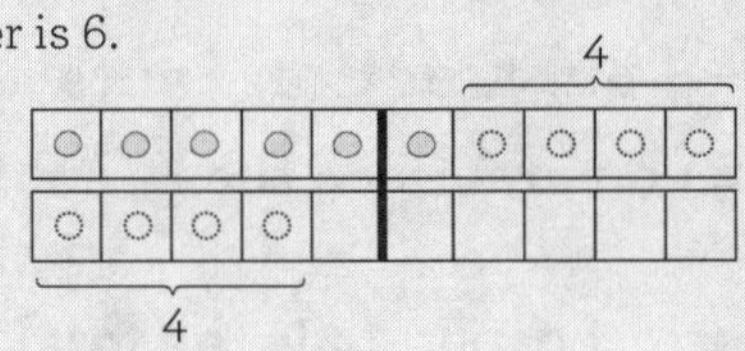

Activity: Play Subtraction Race (-8 Version)

Today, we'll play the -8 version of Subtraction Race. See Lesson 9.2 (page 149) for the general directions. To play the -8 version, subtract 8 from the number that you land on. For example, if you land on 14: 14 minus 8 equals 6.

If you have time, play the game several times.

Workbook: Practice -8 Subtraction Facts and Review

Have your child complete workbook page 9.4A and 9.4B.

Lesson 9.5
Enrichment and Review (Optional)

	Purpose	Materials
Warm-up	• Count from 100 to 200 by 5s • Review memory work • Review your child's favorite or most challenging activities from Week 9	• Varies, depending on the activities you choose
Picture Book	• Review subtraction concepts and vocabulary in real-life contexts	• *If You Were a Minus Sign*, written by Trisha Sue Speed Shaskan and illustrated by Francesca Carabelli
Enrichment Activity	• Create and solve addition and subtraction word problems during errands	• None

Warm-up: Counting, Memory Work, and Review

- Have your child count from 100 to 200 by 5s.
- Quiz your child on the memory work through Week 8. See page 523 for the full list.
- If you have time, repeat one or two of the activities from this week's lessons. Choose activities your child especially enjoyed or found challenging.

Math Picture Book: *If You Were a Minus Sign*

Read *If You Were a Minus Sign*, written by Trisha Sue Speed Shaskan and illustrated by Francesca Carabelli. As you read, discuss the subtraction concepts and vocabulary in the book.

Enrichment Activity: Subtraction on the Go

While you run errands this week, have your child make up addition and subtraction word problems to match the items around you. For example, she might make up problems about books at the library, fruit at the grocery store, or the number of people in line at the drive-thru. Encourage her to create many different types of word problems. For example:

- *I checked out 8 books from the library, and then I returned 4. How many do I have left?* (Take-away subtraction.)
- *I checked out 9 books. 5 are chapter books, and the rest are picture books. How many picture books did I check out?* (Take-apart subtraction.)
- *There are 6 people in this line. The other line is 3 people longer. How many people are in the other line?* (Comparison with *more*.)
- *This line has 10 people, and the other line has 7 people. How many fewer people are in the other line?* (Comparison with *how many fewer*.)

If you don't typically take your child on errands, consider a field trip to the pet store for this activity. Your child can make up word problems about fish, hamsters, or guinea pigs. Or, if you'd rather do this activity at home, have your child create a pretend grocery store, book store, or toy store and create subtraction problems about his pretend store.

Week 9 Answer Key

9.1A

Match.

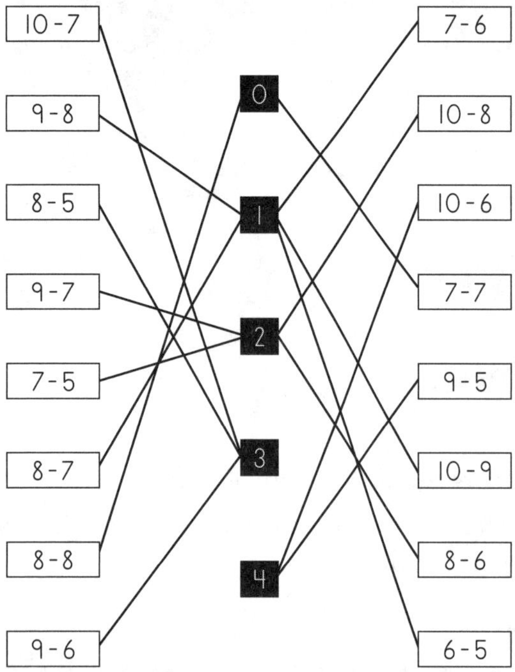

9.1B

Write how much money is in each coin purse.
Use a dollar sign and decimal point.

Complete the circles with <, >, or =.

48 < 84	72 > 27	172 > 170
60 = 60	60 < 160	200 > 120
117 > 71	99 < 105	106 > 104

9.2A

See the Instructor Guide for how to play.
Save this game board for future lessons.

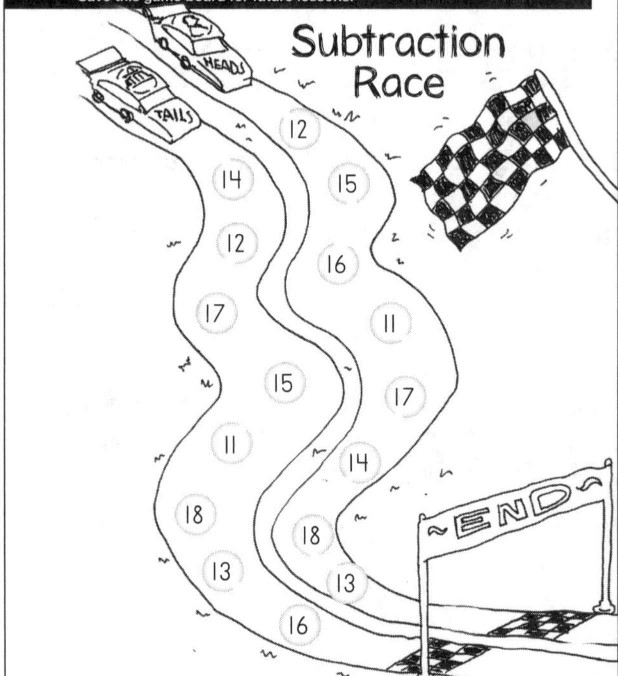

9.2B

Use the ten-frames to complete the equations.

9 + 2 = 11 11 - 9 = 2	9 + 5 = 14 14 - 9 = 5
9 + 4 = 13 13 - 9 = 4	9 + 6 = 15 15 - 9 = 6
9 + 3 = 12 12 - 9 = 3	9 + 8 = 17 17 - 9 = 8
9 + 7 = 16 16 - 9 = 7	9 + 9 = 18 18 - 9 = 9

Week 9 Answer Key

9.3A

Solve.

You have 8 apples.
You eat 5.
How many are left?

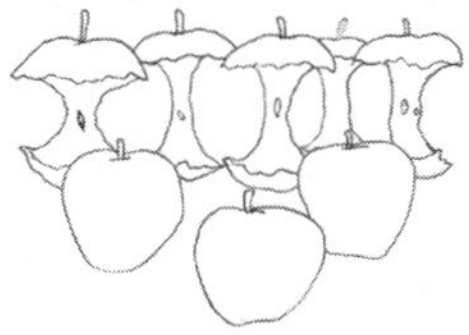

8 − 5 = 3

3 apples

You have 7 lollipops.
You eat 2.
How many are left?

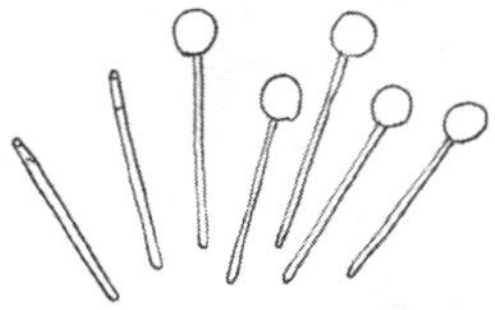

7 − 2 = 5

5 lollipops

You have 10 pencils.
1 pencil breaks.
How many whole pencils are left?

10 − 1 = 9

9 pencils

You have 10 stickers.
You use 3.
How many do you have left?

10 − 3 = 7

7 stickers

9.3B

Complete. Look at the ten-frame to help find the answers.

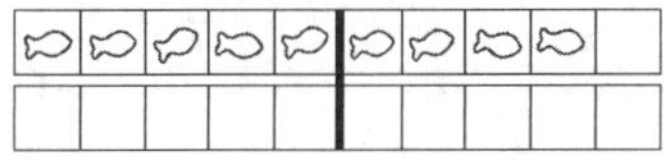

9 + 3 = 12
12 - 9 = 3

9 + 5 = 14
14 - 9 = 5

9 + 9 = 18
18 - 9 = 9

9 + 2 = 11
11 - 9 = 2

9 + 8 = 17
17 - 9 = 8

9 + 7 = 16
16 - 9 = 7

9 + 6 = 15
15 - 9 = 6

9 + 4 = 13
13 - 9 = 4

9.4A

Use the ten-frames to complete the equations.

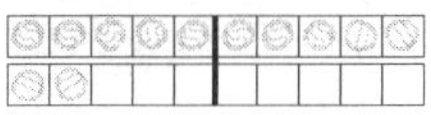

8 + 4 = 12
12 - 8 = 4

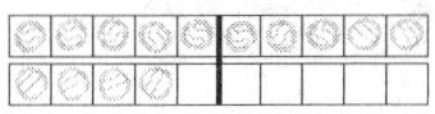

8 + 6 = 14
14 - 8 = 6

8 + 8 = 16
16 - 8 = 8

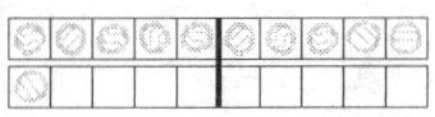

8 + 3 = 11
11 - 8 = 3

8 + 5 = 13
13 - 8 = 5

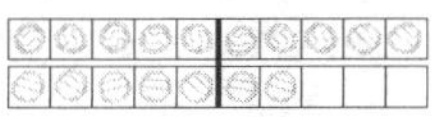

8 + 9 = 17
17 - 8 = 9

8 + 7 = 15
15 - 8 = 7

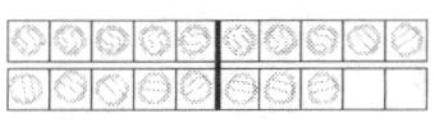

8 + 10 = 18
18 - 8 = 10

9.4B

Write the expanded form for each number.

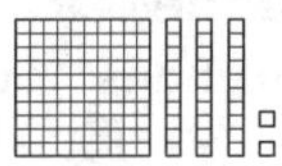

132 = 100 + 30 + 2

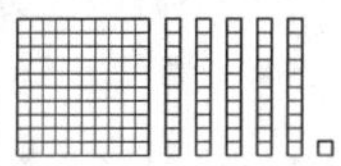

151 = 100 + 50 + 1

Lucia made a bar graph about the animals she saw at the pet store. Use the bar graph to answer the questions.

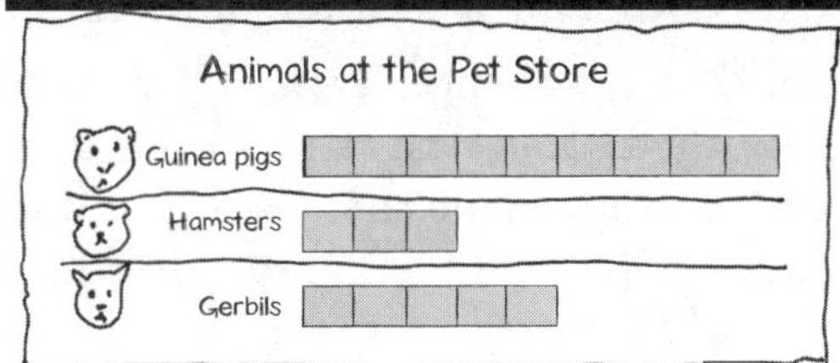

How many guinea pigs did she see? 9

How many hamsters did she see? 3

How many gerbils did she see? 5

How many more guinea pigs than gerbils did she see? 4

How many more gerbils than hamsters did she see? 2

How many guinea pigs, gerbils, and hamsters did she see in all? 17

Week 10
-7 and -6 Facts

Overview

Your child will learn to subtract 6 or 7 from numbers in the teens. He will review take-apart subtraction word problems, and he'll learn how to use subtraction to compare quantities or ages.

Lesson 10.1	Take-Apart Subtraction Word Problems
Lesson 10.2	Practice -6 and -7 Facts
Lesson 10.3	Use Subtraction to Compare Quantities
Lesson 10.4	Use Subtraction to Compare Ages
Lesson 10.5	Enrichment and Review (Optional)

Teaching Math with Confidence: The Challenges of Writing Equations for Comparison Subtraction Situations

This week, you'll teach your child to use subtraction to compare quantities and find the difference between two numbers. You'll pretend that you and your child collect eggs at a farm, and you'll use subtraction to find how many more eggs one of you collected. For example, if you collect 8 eggs, and your child collects 5 eggs, he can subtract 8 – 5 to find that you collected 3 more eggs than him.

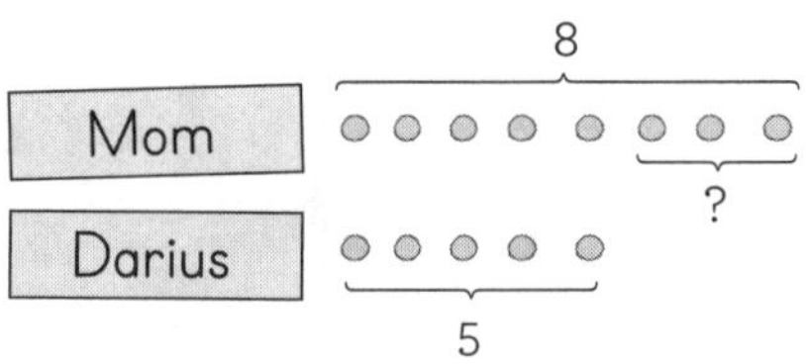

8 - 5 = 3

Children sometimes resist writing equations for these problems, because they "just know" or can easily see the answers. If your child does this, praise him for his excellent number sense and explain that we often need to find the difference between numbers that are much greater (for example, when we compare the price of two cars, or two houses). So, it's important he know how to subtract to find differences, too.

Second-graders also sometimes find it confusing that the numbers in comparison problems don't neatly correspond to parts and totals in the same way as the numbers in take-away and take-apart subtraction situations. To prevent this confusion, Lessons 10.3 and 10.4 use familiar contexts and lines of counters (and not the Part-Total Mat) to model these problems.

If your child wants to model these problems on the Part-Total Mat (or you think he might find it helpful), explain that he can think of the greater number as the total. He's trying to find what number plus the lesser number equals the total, so the difference and lesser number are the parts. For example, here's how to model the above problem about eggs on the Part-Total Mat:

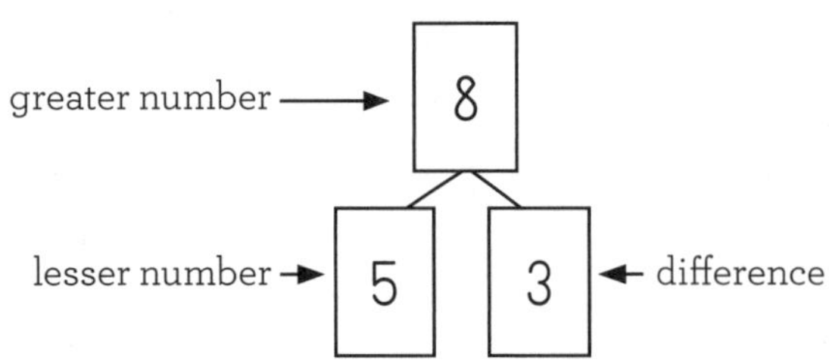

8 - 5 = 3

How to use the Part-Total Mat to model comparison problems.

Don't be concerned if it takes your child a little time before he understands how these subtraction equations match the real-life situations. He'll solve comparison problems in many different contexts this year and will gradually develop deeper understanding of them.

Extra Materials Needed for Week 10

- Crayons or markers
- For optional Enrichment and Review Lesson:
  - *What's the Difference? An Endangered Animal Subtraction Story,* written by Suzanne Slade and illustrated by Joan Waites
  - Art supplies, such as construction paper, paint, markers, crayons, or colored pencils

Lesson 10.1
Take-Apart Subtraction Word Problems

	Purpose	Materials
Warm-up	• Count by 20s • Practice memory work • Review the -8 facts	• Play money • Subtraction Race game board (from workbook page 9.2A) • Coin • Counters
Activities	• Draw pictures and write equations to match take-apart subtraction word problems • Create take-apart subtraction word problems	• Crayons or markers • Part-Total Mat (Blackline Master 2)
Workbook	• Read and write numbers to 200	• Workbook pages 10.1A and 10.1B

This lesson focuses on using subtraction in take-apart situations, where a larger group is split into two smaller groups without removing anything.

Warm-up: Counting, Memory Work, and Review

- Place 6-8 twenty-dollar bills on the table. Have your child count by 20 to find the bills' value. Prompt her as needed if she has trouble counting.
- **How many cents equal 1 dollar?** *100.*
- Play Subtraction Race (-8 Version). See Lesson 9.4 (page 154) for directions.

> If your child takes more than 3 seconds to find the answers to many of the subtraction problems in this game, spend another day or two practicing the -8 facts before moving on to Lesson 10.2.

Activity: Review Take-Apart Subtraction

In Week 9, you solved take-away subtraction word problems. In every problem, the total was split into two parts, and then one part was removed or taken away. The stickers got used up, the balloons popped, the crackers got eaten, and the ice cubes melted.

Today, you'll solve take-apart subtraction word problems. In these problems, we take the total apart into smaller parts, but we don't take away any of the parts.

Imagine this word problem as I read it. You have 7 stickers. 1 sticker is red, and the rest are green. How many are green?

Have your child draw 7 circles on a piece of paper to stand for the 7 stickers. Have her color 1 circle red. **If 1 sticker is red, how many must be green?** *6.* Have your child color the remaining 6 circles green.

What is the total in this problem? *7.* **What part do we know?** *1.* Have your child write 7 and 1 on the Part-Total Mat. **What's the missing part?** *6.* Have your child write 6 on the Part-Total Mat.

What subtraction equation matches the problem? *7 – 1 = 6.* Have your child write the equation on paper.

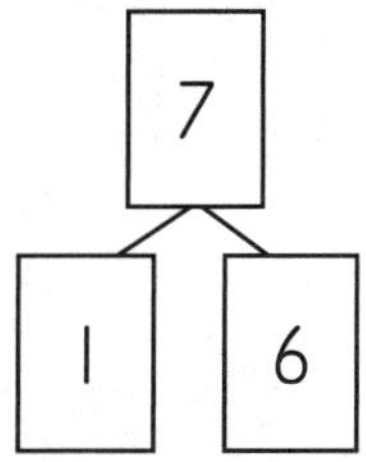

7 - 1 = 6

> If your child writes the numbers in the equation in the wrong order, remind her that subtraction equations begin with the total.

No one takes away any stickers in this story. Instead, we split the stickers into two parts and use subtraction to find the part we don't know.

Have your child draw a simple picture to match each of the following word problems. Then, have her write numbers on the Part-Total Mat and write a subtraction equation to match.

- **You have 10 balloons. 2 are blue, and the rest are yellow. How many are yellow?** *8.*

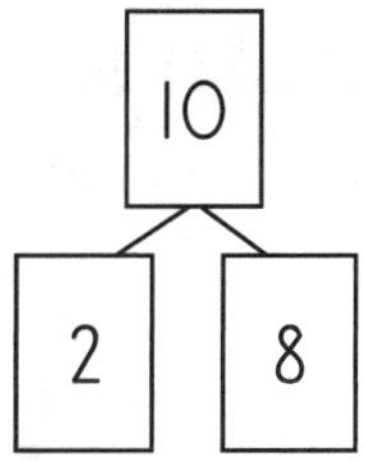

10 - 2 = 8

- **You have 9 crackers. 4 crackers have seeds on them, and the rest are plain. How many are plain?** *5.*

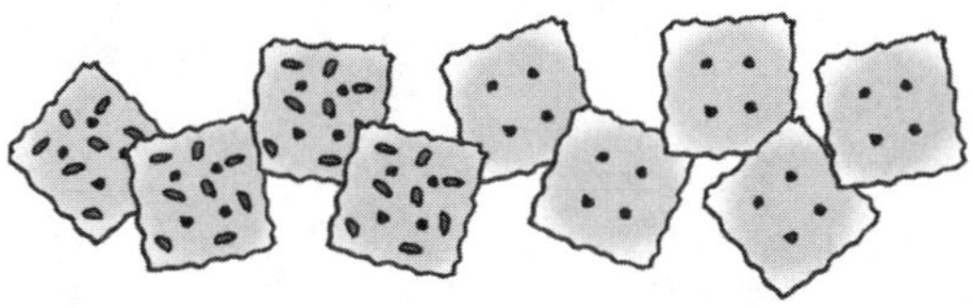

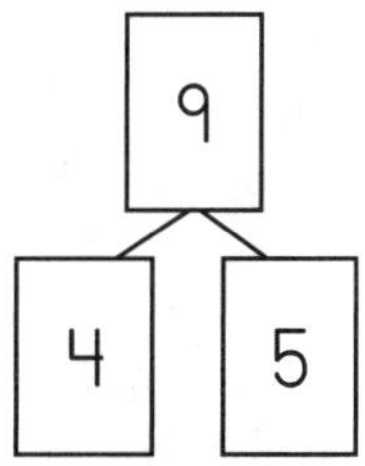

9 - 4 = 5

- **You have 8 ice cubes. You put 1 in my glass and the rest in your glass. How many do you put in your glass?** *7.*

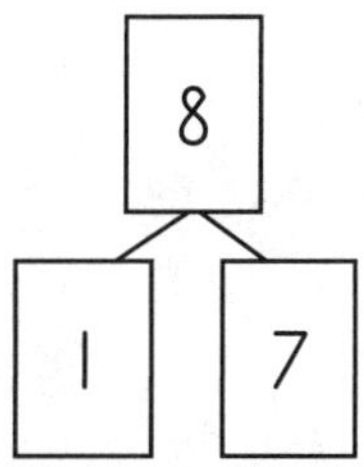

8 - 1 = 7

> These numbers and objects are the same as in Lesson 9.3 to highlight the similarities and differences between take-away and take-apart problems.

What do these stories have in common? *Sample answer: We know the total and one of the parts. We have to find one part. You can use subtraction to solve all of them. Nothing gets taken away in any of the stories.*

In all of these word problems, the total gets split into two parts. We know one part, so we use subtraction to find the other part. Nothing gets removed or taken away.

Activity: Create Take-Apart Subtraction Word Problems

Write "8 – 6 = 2" on a piece of paper. Have your child make up several take-apart subtraction word problems that match the equation. If she has trouble getting started, suggest she think about real-life situations where a group gets split into two parts.

$$8 - 6 = 2$$

Sample answers:

- *I spent $8 at the garage sale. I spent $6 on books and the rest on clothes. How much did I spend on clothes?*
- *There are 8 children in the swim class. 6 are girls, and the rest are boys. How many are boys?*
- *I made 8 cards. I gave 6 to my brother and the rest to my sister. How many did I give my sister?*

> Children usually find it more difficult to create take-apart problems than take-away problems, so help your child as needed.

Workbook: Solve Word Problems and Review

Have your child complete workbook pages 10.1A and 10.1B.

Lesson 10.2
Practice -6 and -7 Facts

	Purpose	Materials
Warm-up	• Count by 10s • Practice memory work • Review +6 and +7 facts	• Base-ten blocks
Activities	• Practice -6 and -7 facts	• Counters • Double ten-frames (Blackline Master 1) • Treasure Hunt game board (from workbook page 10.2A) • Die
Workbook	• Practice -6 and -7 facts	• Workbook page 10.2B

If your child already knows the answers immediately for the -6 and-7 facts, make this a quick review lesson.

Warm-up: Counting, Memory Work, and Review

- Place 1 flat and 6-8 rods on the table. Have your child count by 10s, starting at 100, to find the blocks' value.
- **How many cents equal 1 dollar?** *100.*
- Do a brief oral review of the +6 and +7 facts. Have your child give each answer as quickly as possible.

× 5 + 6 = *11*
× 6 + 8 = *14*
× 7 + 5 = *12*
× 9 + 7 = *16*
× 7 + 7 = *14*
× 6 + 6 = *12*
× 7 + 8 = *15*
× 7 + 6 = *13*
× 4 + 7 = *11*

Activity: Introduce -6 and -7 Facts

Last week, you practiced the -8 and -9 facts. Today, you'll practice the -6 and -7 facts.

Write "13 - 6 =" on a piece of paper and place 13 counters on the ten-frame. **Some children like to imagine taking away counters for the -6 and -7 facts, and some like to use addition to solve them. We'll talk about both ways and then you can decide which way works better for you.**

First, let's try taking away the counters in two steps. Take away the 3 counters on the bottom ten-frame.

13 - 6 =

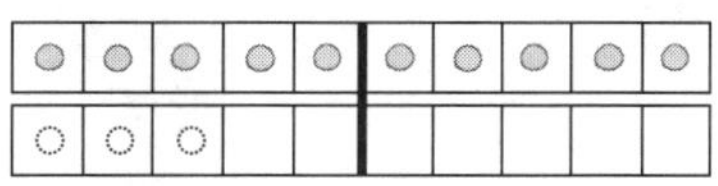

How many more counters do I need to take away? *3*. Remove 3 more counters. **How many counters are left?** *7*. Have your child complete the written equation and read it aloud: *13 minus 6 equals 7.*

13 - 6 = 7

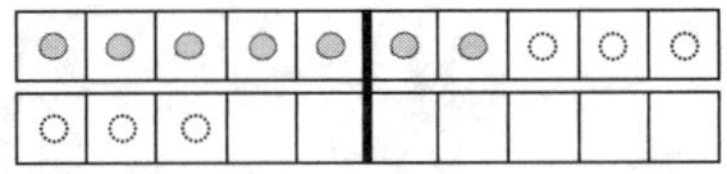

Now, let's try using addition to solve the same problem. Write "13 - 6 =" on a piece of paper again. **What missing addend equation matches this subtraction problem?** *6 plus what equals 13*. Write "6 + ___ = 13" and put 6 counters on the ten-frame.

13 - 6 =

6 + __ = 13

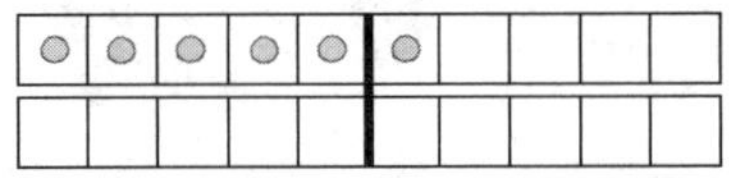

How many more counters do we need to add to reach 13? *7*. Encourage your child to think about how many counters it takes to fill in the top ten-frame (4), and then how many more are needed on the bottom ten-frame to reach 13 (3). Have your child complete both equations.

13 - 6 = 7

6 + 7 = 13

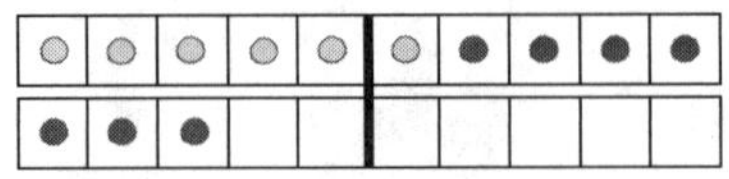

Which strategy do you like better: taking away the counters in two steps or using addition? *Answers will vary.*

> There's no right answer to this question, since different strategies "click" better for different children. See the Week 10 **Teaching Math with Confidence** for more on the benefits of math fact strategies.

Have your child use whichever strategy he prefers to find the answers to the rest of the -6 and -7 subtraction facts.

- 11 - 6 = *5*
- 12 - 7 = *5*
- 14 - 6 = *8*
- 16 - 7 = *9*
- 15 - 6 = *9*
- 14 - 7 = *7*
- 12 - 6 = *6*
- 15 - 7 = *8*
- 13 - 7 = *6*
- 11 - 7 = *4*

Activity: Play Treasure Hunt

We're going to play a game called Treasure Hunt to practice the -6 and -7 facts. Play Treasure Hunt. Keep the ten-frame and counters available as you play.

Treasure Hunt

Materials: Treasure Hunt game board (from workbook page 10.2A); counters; die

Object of the Game: Win the most counters.

Have each player choose a different-colored counter to use as a game token and place it on one of the Start squares. Place 12 other counters in the treasure chest in the middle of the game board.

On your turn, roll the die and advance your token the corresponding number of squares clockwise around the path. If you land on a square with a subtraction problem, say the answer to the problem and take 1 counter from the treasure chest. Otherwise, follow the directions on the square.

Play until all of the counters are gone from the treasure chest. The player who has more counters wins the game.

Save this game board with your math materials so you can play again.

Workbook: Practice -6 and -7 Facts and Review

Have your child complete workbook page 10.2B. Encourage your child to use the printed ten-frames to help find the answers, either with a two-step take-away strategy or by thinking addition.

Lesson 10.3
Use Subtraction to Compare Quantities

	Purpose	Materials
Warm-up	• Count by 25s • Practice memory work • Review -6 and -7 subtraction facts	• Coins • Counters • Treasure Hunt game board (from workbook page 10.2A) • Die
Activities	• Learn how to subtract to find the difference between two quantities • Solve *how many more* and *how many fewer* word problems	• Counters
Workbook	• Solve *how many more* and *how many fewer* word problems • Practice -9 facts	• Workbook pages 10.3A and 10.3B

Warm-up: Counting, Memory Work, and Review

- Place 8 quarters on the table. Have your child count by 25s to find their value.
- **How many cents equal 1 dollar?** *100.*
- Play Treasure Hunt. See Lesson 10.2 (page 165) for directions.

Activity: Use Subtraction to Compare Amounts

You already know how to solve take-away and take-apart subtraction word problems. Today, you'll learn about another kind of subtraction word problem: comparison word problems.

Let's pretend that we collect eggs on a farm. One day, I found 5 eggs, and you found 8 eggs. Arrange 5 counters in a row. Have your child arrange 8 counters in a row below yours. Label each row with your names.

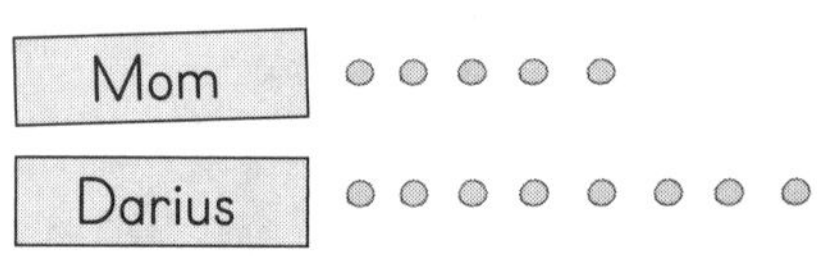

Make sure all the counters are equally spaced.

Who found more eggs? *I did!* **Who found fewer eggs?** *You did.* **How many more eggs did you find than me?** *3.* **How do you know?** *Sample answer: My row is 3 eggs longer than yours.*

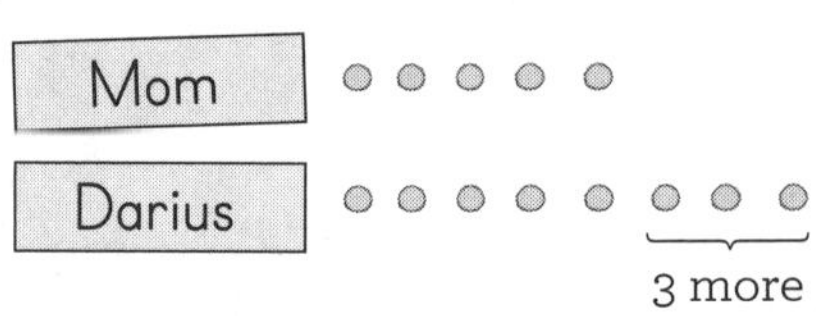

You just solved a comparison word problem! I told you two amounts, and you found how much greater one amount is than the other. In this problem, it's easy to see how many more eggs you found than I did. But, in real life, the numbers are often too big to just see the answer. That's why you need to know how to use subtraction to solve comparison problems.

To compare two numbers, start with the greater number and then subtract the lesser number. What do we call an answer to a subtraction problem? *The difference.* **That's because the answer to a subtraction problem tells how "different" the numbers are from each other!** Write "greater number – lesser number = difference" on a piece of paper.

What's the greater number in this problem? *8.* **What's the lesser number?** *5.* Write "8 – 5 =" on a piece of paper and have your child complete the equation: 8 – 5 = 3.

greater number – lesser number = difference

8 - 5 = 3

> If your child is confused by the terms *greater* and *lesser,* you may use *bigger* and *smaller* instead. *Bigger number* and *smaller number* are not precise mathematical terms, but they're more familiar to children.

Once you know the difference between the numbers, you can tell both how many more eggs you collected, and how many fewer eggs I collected. You found 3 more eggs than I did. So, how many fewer eggs did I find than you? *3.*

Activity: Solve Comparison Word Problems

Have your child model each problem with counters, write a matching subtraction equation, and solve. Remind him as needed to start with the greater number and subtract the lesser number from it.

- **You found 11 eggs, and I found 6 eggs. How many more eggs did you find than me?** *5.* **How many fewer eggs did I find than you?** *5.*

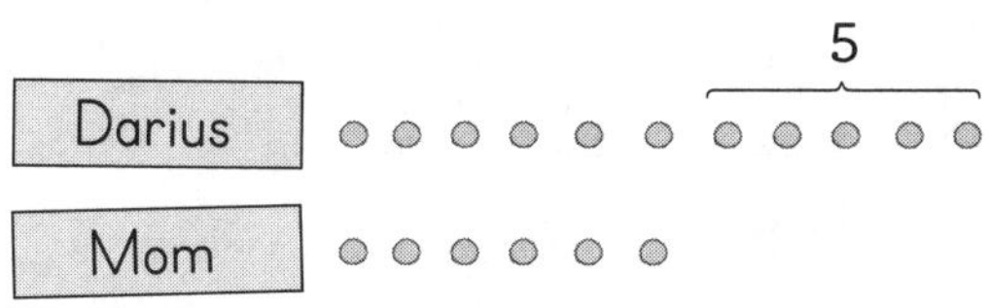

11 – 6 = 5

- **I found 13 eggs. You found 9 eggs. How many more eggs did I find than you?** *4.* **How many fewer eggs did you find than me?** *4.*

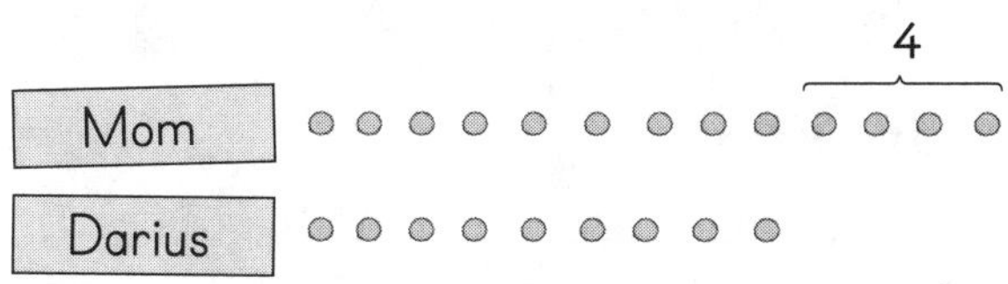

13 - 9 = 4

- **I found 8 eggs. You found 8 eggs. How many more eggs did I find than you?** *0!*

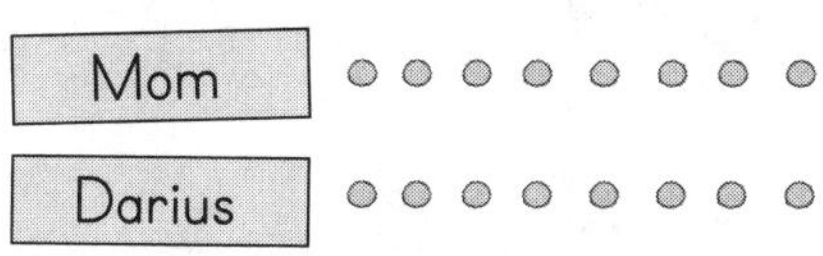

8 - 8 = 0

> Second graders often find comparison subtraction challenging, so don't worry if your child doesn't fully grasp this skill yet. She'll work on it in many different contexts this year (including bar graphs and length) so that she fully understands comparison subtraction by the end of the year.

Workbook: Solve Word Problems and Review

Have your child complete workbook pages 10.3A and 10.3B.

Lesson 10.4
Use Subtraction to Compare Ages

	Purpose	Materials
Warm-up	• Count by 5s • Practice memory work • Review -6 and -7 facts	• 200 Chart (Blackline Master 7), optional • Counters • Treasure Hunt game board (from workbook page 10.2A) • Die
Activities	• Use subtraction to compare ages	• None
Workbook	• Use subtraction to compare ages • Practice subtraction facts	• Workbook pages 10.4A and 10.4B

In the last lesson, your child used concrete objects to model comparison problems. In this lesson, he'll use more abstract reasoning to compare ages.

Warm-up: Counting, Memory Work, and Review

- Have your child count by 5s from the following numbers. Stop him after he reaches the last number listed, and allow him to use the 200 Chart as needed.
  - **Count by 5s from 170:** *170, 175, 180, 185, 190.*
  - **Count by 5s from 125:** *125, 130, 135, 140, 145.*
  - **Count by 5s from 90:** *90, 95, 100, 105, 110.*
- **How many cents equal 1 dollar?** *100.*
- Play Treasure Hunt. See Lesson 10.2 (page 165) for directions.

If your child takes more than 3 seconds to find the answers to many of the subtraction problems in this game, spend another day or two practicing the -6 and -7 facts before moving on to Lesson 11.1.

Activity: Use Subtraction to Compare Ages

In the last lesson, you learned how to subtract to compare quantities of eggs. Today, you'll learn how to use subtraction to compare ages. Make a quick chart with the names and ages of 5-6 of your child's siblings, neighbors, or friends.

Name	Age
Lily	3
Noah	15
William	7
Ava	6
Maya	11
Me	7

Sample chart

Who is the youngest? *Sample answer: Lily.* **Who is the oldest?** *Sample answer: Noah.*

Let's find out how much older the oldest child is than you. Remember, to compare two numbers, start with the greater number and then subtract the lesser number. Write "greater number – lesser number = difference" on a piece of paper.

greater number – lesser number = difference

Help your child write a subtraction equation that shows the difference between the two ages. Start with the oldest child's age, and then subtract your child's age from it. For example: **Noah is 15, and you are 7. So, we subtract 15 minus 7 to find the difference between your ages.** Have your child subtract to complete the equation.

$$15 - 7 = 8$$

Oldest child's age → 15; Your child's age → 7; Difference in ages → 8

Sample equation. "Noah is 8 years older than me, and I'm 8 years younger than him."

Repeat with several other children on the chart.

$$11 - 7 = 4$$

"I'm 4 years younger than Maya, and she's 4 years older than me."

$$7 - 3 = 4$$

"I'm 4 years older than Lily, and she's 4 years younger than me."

> Many children will be able to find the difference in ages mentally, without writing the matching equations. Make sure to have your child write the equation anyway so that he connects his intuitive understanding of ages to the written symbols. This prepares him to solve comparison subtraction problems with larger numbers later in the year.

Workbook: Practice -6 and -7 Facts and Review

Have your child complete workbook pages 10.4A and 10.4B.

Lesson 10.5
Enrichment and Review (Optional)

	Purpose	Materials
Warm-up	• Count from 100 to 200 by 5s • Review memory work • Review your child's favorite or most challenging activities from Week 10	• Varies, depending on the activities you choose
Picture Book	• Understand take-away subtraction in the context of animals	• *What's the Difference? An Endangered Animal Subtraction Story*, written by Suzanne Slade and illustrated by Joan Waites
Enrichment Activity	• Create an art project that shows subtraction with animals	• Art supplies, such as construction paper, paint, markers, crayons, or colored pencils

Warm-up: Counting, Memory Work, and Review

- Have your child count from 100 to 200 by 5s.
- Quiz your child on the memory work through Week 10. See page 523 for the full list.
- If you have time, repeat one or two of the activities from this week's lessons. Choose activities your child especially enjoyed or found challenging.

Math Picture Book: *What's the Difference? An Endangered Animal Story*

Read *What's the Difference? An Endangered Animal Story*, written by Suzanne Slade and illustrated by Joan Waites. As you read, discuss how the illustrations and text match the printed subtraction equations.

Enrichment Activity: Animal Subtraction Art Project

Have your child choose a subtraction equation with the numbers to 10 and then paint or draw an animal picture that illustrates the equation. Your child can choose either a take-away or a take-apart situation. For example, to illustrate $7 - 4 = 3$ as a take-away situation, he might draw 4 whales swimming away and 3 whales remaining. Or, to illustrate the equation as a take-apart situation, he might draw 4 whales in one pod and 3 in another pod.

Week 10 Answer Key

10.1A

Color the pictures to match the word problems and solve.

You have 8 apples.
5 are green, and the rest are red.
How many are red?

8 − 5 = 3

3 apples

You have 7 lollipops.
6 are purple, and the rest are yellow.
How many are yellow?

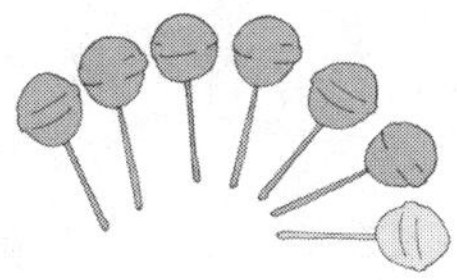

7 − 6 = 1

1 lollipops

You have 10 pencils.
7 are yellow, and the rest are green.
How many are green?

10 − 7 = 3

3 pencils

You have 9 pompoms.
1 is blue, and the rest are orange.
How many are orange?

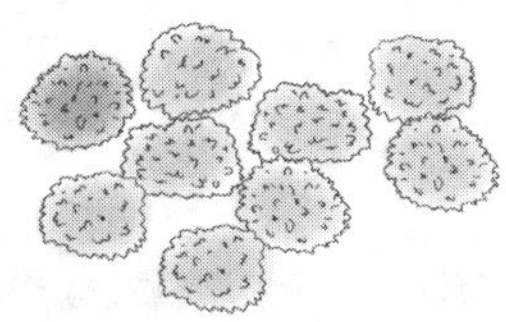

9 − 1 = 8

8 pompoms

10.1B

Match.

17 − 9 → 8
13 − 9 → 4
14 − 9 → 5
16 − 9 → 7
15 − 9 → 6

4 → 12 − 8
5 → 13 − 8
6 → 14 − 8
7 → 15 − 8
8 → 16 − 8

Match.

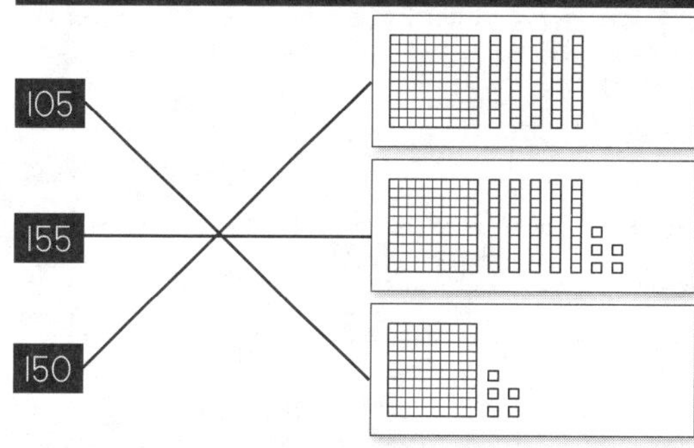

10.2A

**See the Instructor Guide for how to play.
Save this game board for future lessons.**

10.2B

Use the ten-frames to complete.

11 − 6 = 5
11 − 7 = 4

13 − 6 = 7
13 − 7 = 6

14 − 6 = 8
14 − 7 = 7

16 − 6 = 10
16 − 7 = 9

15 − 6 = 9
15 − 7 = 8

12 − 6 = 6
12 − 7 = 5

Use the key to color the leaves.

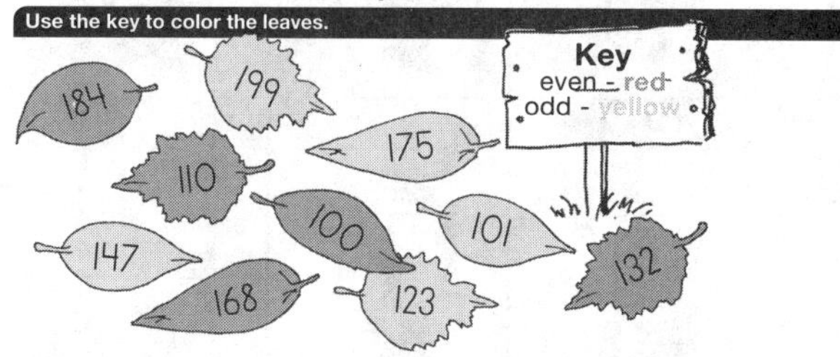

Week 10 Answer Key

10.3A

Solve.

You have 10 blue marbles and 8 green marbles.
How many more blue marbles than green marbles do you have?

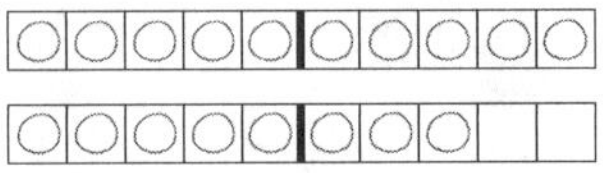

10 − 8 = 2

2 marbles

You have 6 purple marbles and 9 orange marbles.
How many fewer purple marbles than orange marbles do you have?

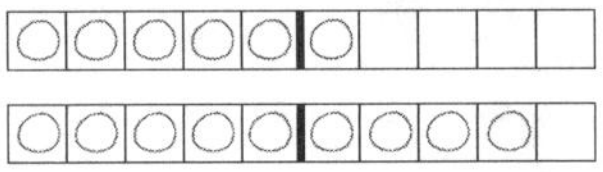

9 − 6 = 3

3 marbles

You have 12 red marbles and 7 rainbow marbles.
How many more red marbles than rainbow marbles do you have?

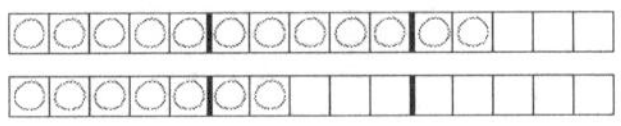

12 − 7 = 5

5 marbles

You have 15 yellow marbles and 9 striped marbles.
How many fewer striped marbles than yellow marbles do you have?

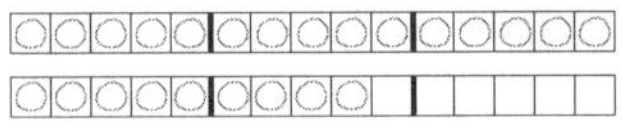

15 − 9 = 6

6 marbles

10.3B

Complete.

11 − 6 = 5	15 − 6 = 9	14 − 6 = 8
16 − 7 = 9	13 − 6 = 7	12 − 7 = 5
12 − 6 = 6	11 − 7 = 4	13 − 7 = 6
14 − 7 = 7	10 − 6 = 4	15 − 7 = 8

X the shape that doesn't belong.

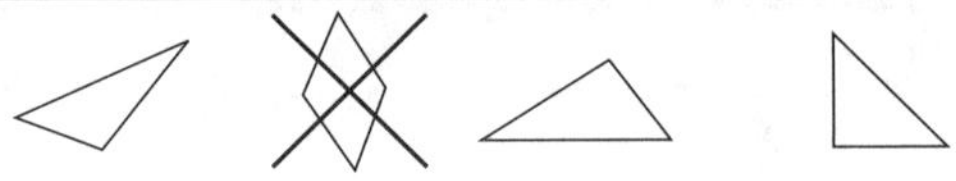

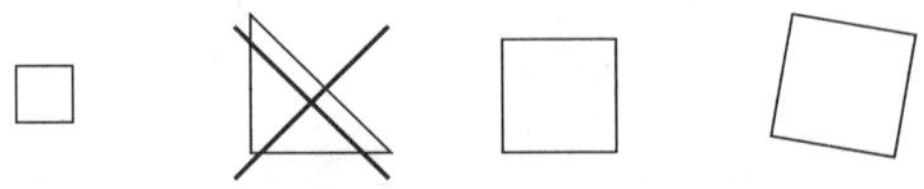

Complete.

73 ¢

10.4A

Use the chart to solve.

Name	Age
Dylan	5
Jasmine	11
Titus	14

How much older is Jasmine than Dylan?

11 − 5 = 6

6 years

How much younger is Dylan than Titus?

14 − 5 = 9

9 years

How much older is Titus than Jasmine?

14 − 11 = 3

3 years

Color the subtraction facts that equal the number in the star.

4	5	6
11-7	12-9	12-6
12-8	13-8	14-7
14-8	11-6	13-7
13-9	14-9	15-9

10.4B

Label the numbers on the number line.

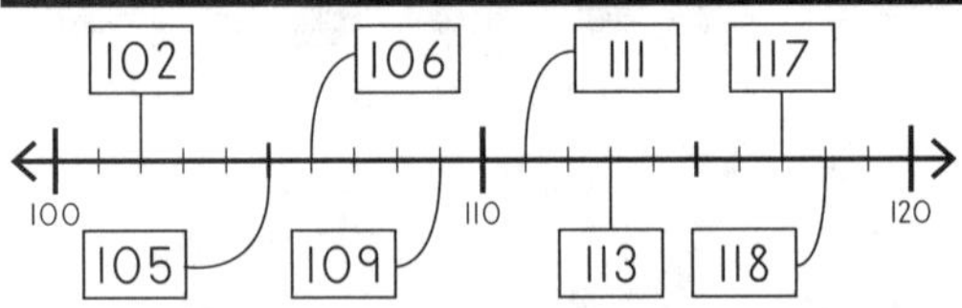

Complete.

10 + 60 = 70	76 + 2 = 78
110 + 60 = 170	176 + 2 = 178
50 − 30 = 20	97 − 5 = 92
150 − 30 = 120	197 − 5 = 192
24 + 40 = 64	28 − 20 = 8
124 + 40 = 164	128 − 20 = 108

Complete.

10 muffins | 15 muffins | 20 muffins

Week 11

-2, -3, -4, and -5 Facts

Overview

Your child will learn to subtract 2, 3, 4, and 5 from numbers in the teens. She will also learn how to solve subtraction word problems involving more or fewer.

Lesson 11.1 Practice -2, -3, -4, and -5 Facts
Lesson 11.2 More/Fewer Word Problems, Part 1
Lesson 11.3 More/Fewer Word Problems, Part 2
Lesson 11.4 Subtraction Word Problems at the Pretend Store
Lesson 11.5 Enrichment and Review (Optional)

Teaching Math with Confidence: Solving Word Problems with *More* or *Fewer*

In Week 10, your child learned to solve comparison word problems. She knew both quantities, and her goal was to find the difference between them. For example: **I found 8 eggs. You found 6 eggs. How many fewer eggs did you find than me?**

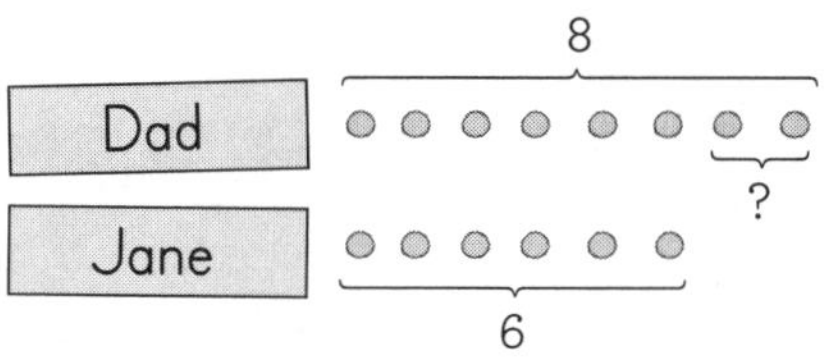

$8 - 6 = 2$

This week, you'll teach your child how to solve a different kind of comparison word problem. These problems are similar to the problems your child solved in Week 10, but with one key twist. In the new problems this week, you know one quantity and the difference between the two quantities. Your goal is to find the other quantity.

These problems usually involve the words *more* or *fewer*. For example: **I found 7 eggs. You found 1 more egg than me. How many did you find?** In this problem you know the lesser quantity and the difference. You add to find the greater quantity.

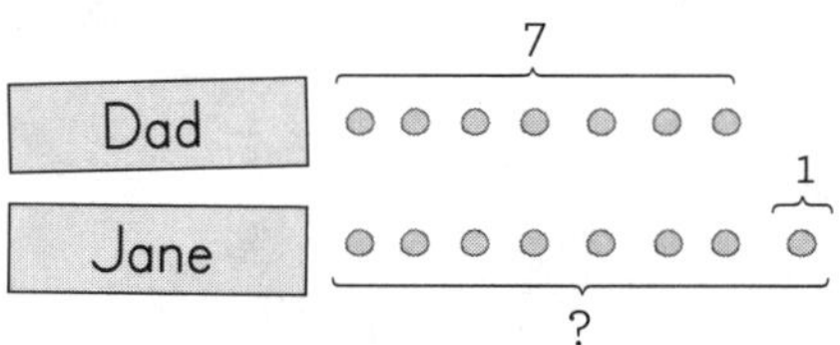

$7 + 1 = 8$

Or: **I found 6 eggs. You found 2 fewer eggs than me. How many did you find?** In this problem you know the greater quantity and the difference. You subtract to find the lesser quantity.

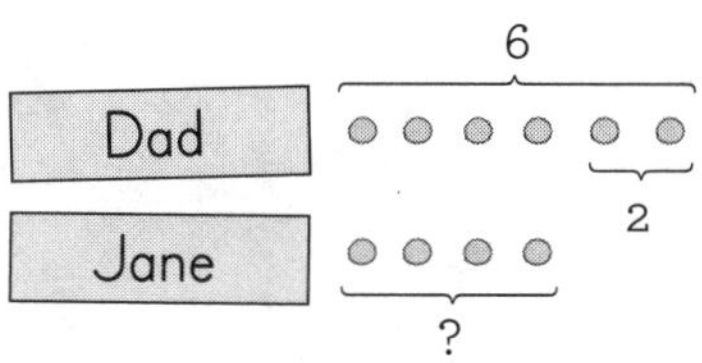

$6 - 2 = 4$

It can be tempting to teach your child to simply add if they see the word *more* or subtract if they see the word *fewer.* But this keyword approach short-circuits the process of deeply understanding the structure of these problems. (It also doesn't always work. For example: **I have 9 eggs. I have 3 more than you. How many do you have?** Even though this problem has the word more, you subtract 3 from 9 to find the answer.) The lessons this week include a variety of word problems involving *more* and *fewer* so that your child learns to actively think about whether to add or subtract.

Extra Materials Needed for Week 11

- 6 small toys
- 10 slips of paper
- For optional Enrichment and Review Lesson:
    - *Subtraction Action,* by Loreen Leedy
    - Small slips of paper and tape. or sticky notes

Lesson 11.1
Practice -2, -3, -4, and -5 Facts

	Purpose	Materials
Warm-up	• Count money combinations • Practice memory work • Review addition facts	• Play money • Coins
Activities	• Practice -2, -3, -4, -5 facts	• Counters • Four in a Row game board (from workbook page 11.1A)
Workbook	• Practice -2, -3, -4, -5 facts	• Workbook page 11.1B

If your child already knows the answers immediately for the -2, -3, -4, and -5 facts, make this a quick review lesson.

Warm-up: Counting, Memory Work, and Review

- Place 2 ten-dollar bills, 1 five-dollar bill, and 3 quarters on the table. **How much is the money worth?** *$25.75.*
- **If a number has 1, 3, 5, 7, or 9 in the ones-place, is the number even or odd?** *Odd.* **If a number has 0, 2, 4, 6, or 8 in the ones-place, is the number even or odd?** *Even.*
- Do a brief oral review of the following addition facts. Have your child give each answer as quickly as possible.
    - 9 + 2 = *11*
    - 8 + 5 = *13*
    - 9 + 3 = *12*
    - 5 + 6 = *11*
    - 9 + 5 = *14*
    - 8 + 4 = *12*
    - 9 + 4 = *13*
    - 8 + 3 = *11*
    - 7 + 5 = *12*
    - 7 + 4 = *11*

Activity: Practice -2, -3, -4, and -5 Facts

You have already practiced the -9, -8, -7, and -6 facts. This week, you'll practice -2, -3, -4, and -5 facts. Most children find these problems easier to solve if they imagine taking away counters on the ten-frame.

Write "14 - 5 =" on a piece of paper and place 14 counters on the ten-frame. **Let's take away 5 counters. We'll do it in two steps. First, I take away the 4 counters on the bottom ten-frame.** Take away the 4 counters on the bottom ten-frame.

14 - 5 =

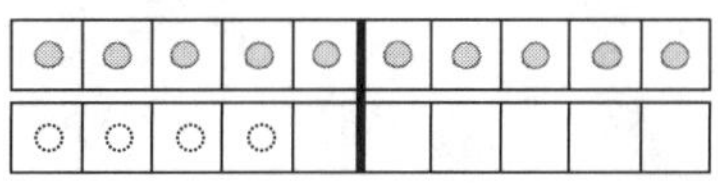

How many more counters do I need to take away? *1.* Remove 1 more counter. **How many counters are left?** *9.* Have your child complete the written equation and read it aloud: *14 minus 5 equals 9.*

14 - 5 = 9

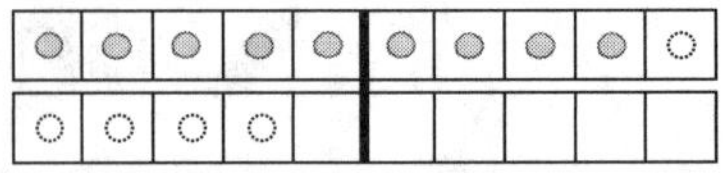

Encourage your child to use similar reasoning to complete the follow equations. Place counters on the ten-frame as needed, and remind her to remove the counters in two steps rather than counting one-by-one.

- 11- 2 = 9
- 12 - 4 = 8
- 11 - 5 = 6
- 12 - 3 = 9
- 13 - 5 = 8
- 11 - 4 = 7
- 12 - 5 = 7
- 11 - 3 = 8
- 13 - 4 = 9

Activity: Play Four in a Row (–2, –3, –4, –5 Facts)

Play Four in a Row. Allow your child to use the ten-frame and counters as needed.

Four in a Row

Materials: Four in a Row game board (from workbook page 11.1A); 20 counters per player, with a different color for each player

Object of the Game: Be the first player to place counters in 4 squares in a row, either horizontally, vertically, or diagonally.

On your turn, choose one subtraction problem on the board and say its answer. Use a counter to cover the box with the problem you chose.

Play then passes to the other player. Continue until one player covers 4 boxes in a row, either horizontally, vertically, or diagonally.

Save this game board with your math materials so you can play again.

Workbook: Practice –2, –3, –4, and –5 Facts and Review

Have your child complete workbook page 11.1B.

Lesson 11.2
More/Fewer Word Problems, Part 1

	Purpose	Materials
Warm-up	• Count by 2s, 5s, and 10s • Practice memory work • Review -2, -3, -4, -5 facts	• Four in a Row game board (from workbook page 11.1A) • Number Line (Blackline Master 3) • Counters
Activities	• Use counters to solve more/fewer word problems • Write equations to match more/fewer word problems	• Counters
Workbook	• Practice -2, -3, -4, -5 facts	• Workbook pages 11.2A and 11.2B

In Lessons 11.2 and 11.3, your child will learn to solve word problems that involve *more* or *fewer*. Children often find the language in these problems very confusing, so you'll start with concrete examples before writing equations.

Warm-up: Counting, Memory Work, and Review

- Label the Number Line with 100, 110, and 120. Have your child count from 100 to 120 by 2s, 5s, and 10s. Have him point to each corresponding tick mark as he counts.
- **How many cents equal 1 dollar?** *100.*
- Play Four in a Row. See Lesson 11.1 (page 176) for directions.

Activity: Solve More/Fewer Riddles with Counters

Last week, you learned to subtract to compare quantities or ages. Let's pretend you have 9 candies, and I have 4. Give your child 9 counters, and take 4 for yourself. **How many more pieces do you have than me?** *5.* **How did you find the difference?** *Sample answer: I subtracted 4 from 9.*

Have your child write the matching subtraction equation: 9 – 4 = 5. Remind him if needed to start with the greater number and subtract the lesser number from it.

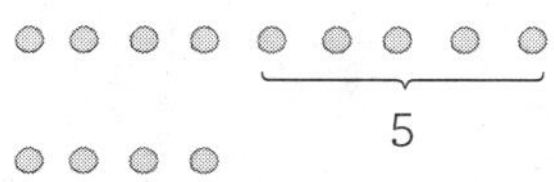

9 - 4 = 5

In this problem, you knew how many candies each of us had. Then, you subtracted the lesser number from the greater number to find the difference.

Today, you'll learn how to solve word problems where you know the difference and how many one person has. In these problems, you want to find how many the other person has. We'll start with some riddles!

Give your child 4 counters. Secretly take 6 counters and place them under a piece of paper. **Let's pretend you have 4 candies. I have 2 more candies than you. How many do I have?** *6.* Remove the paper so your child can check his answer.

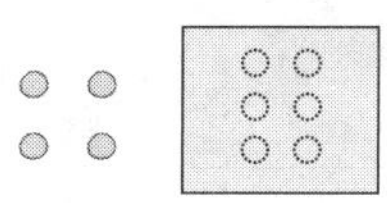

Give your child 8 counters. Secretly take 7 counters and place them under a piece of paper. **You have 8 candies. I have 1 fewer candy than you. How many candies do I have?** *7.* Remove the paper so your child can check his answer.

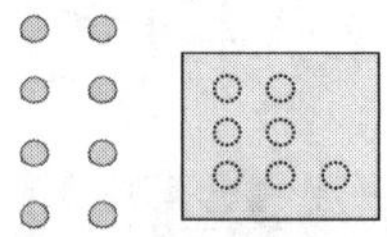

If you typically use the word *less* instead of *fewer* in everyday conversation, you can substitute it to make the dialogue feel more natural.

Repeat with the following questions. Model each question with counters, and hide your counters until your child figures out how many you have.

- **You have 9 candies. I have 1 more than you. How many do I have?** *10.*
- **You have 9 candies. I have 3 more than you. How many do I have?** *12.*
- **You have 7 candies. I have 3 fewer than you. How many do I have?** *4.*
- **You have 10 candies. I have 4 more than you. How many do I have?** *14.*
- **You have 10 candies. I have 5 fewer than you. How many do I have?** *5.*
- **You have 10 candies. I have 9 fewer than you. How many do I have?** *1.*

Reverse roles, and have your child make up several similar riddles.

These questions use small quantities so your child can focus on the meaning of the problems. If he finds these very easy, adjust the difficulty level by using more challenging numbers.

Activity: Write Equations to Match More/Fewer Word Problems

Let's pretend again that we collect eggs on a farm. One day, you find 6 eggs. Give your child 6 counters. **I find 3 more eggs than you.** Secretly take 9 counters and place them under a piece of paper. **How many eggs did I find?** *9.* Remove the paper so your child can check his answer.

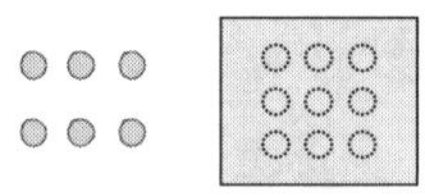

How did you find the answer? *Sample answer: I added 6 plus 3.* Write "6 + 3 = 9" on a piece of paper. Arrange the counters in two evenly-spaced rows so that it is easy to see that 9 is 3 more than 6.

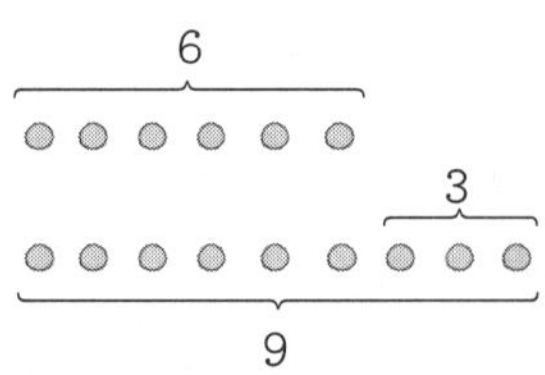

$$6 + 3 = 9$$

You knew the lesser number and the difference between the two numbers, so you added to find the greater number.

Don't teach your child to automatically add when he hears the word *more* or subtract when he hears the word *less* in these problems. See the Week 11 **Teaching Math with Confidence** for more on why it's best to avoid a keyword approach to word problems.

One day, you find 10 eggs. Give your child 10 counters. **On this day, I find 3 fewer eggs than you.** Secretly take 7 counters and place them under a piece of paper. **How many eggs did I find?** *7.* Remove the paper so your child can check his answer.

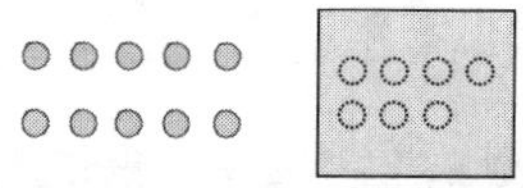

How did you find the answer? *Sample answer: I subtracted 3 from 10.* Write "10 - 3 = 7" on a piece of paper. Arrange the counters in two evenly-spaced rows so that it is easy to see that 7 is 3 less than 10.

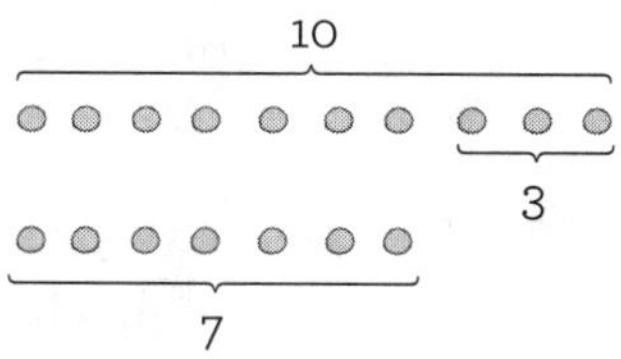

10 - 3 = 7

You knew the greater number and the difference, so you subtracted to find the lesser number.

> This activity is meant as an introduction to writing equations for more/fewer word problems. Your child will practice more in Lesson 11.3.

Workbook: Practice -2, -3, -4, and -5 Facts and Review

Have your child complete workbook pages 11.2A and 11.2B. Point out that the subtraction problems are written vertically for the first time, and check that your child writes the digits in the correct places in the problems.

Lesson 11.3
More/Fewer Word Problems, Part 2

	Purpose	Materials
Warm-up	• Count by 10s starting at a number other than 0 • Practice memory work • Review -2, -3, -4, -5 facts	• Base-ten blocks • Four in a Row game board (from workbook page 11.1A) • Counters
Activities	• Solve more/fewer word problems in the context of ages and prices	• Counters • 4 small toys • 4 slips of paper
Workbook	• Solve more/fewer word problems	• Workbook pages 11.3A and 11.3B

Warm-up: Counting, Memory Work, and Review

- **Count with me by 10s, starting at 6. We'll model the numbers with base-ten blocks as we count.** Begin with 6 units on the table, and add a rod as you say each new number: **6, 16, 26...** Continue until you reach 96.
- Write the < sign. **What does this sign mean?** *Less than.* Write the > sign. **What does this sign mean?** *Greater than.*
- Play Four in a Row. See Lesson 11.1 (page 176) for directions.

Activity: Review More/Fewer Riddles

In the last lesson, you learned to solve riddles that involved *more* or *fewer*. Let's warm up with a couple of these riddles. Give your child 11 counters. Secretly take 8 counters and place them under a piece of paper. **I have 3 fewer counters than you. How many do I have?** *8.* Remove the paper so your child can check her answer.

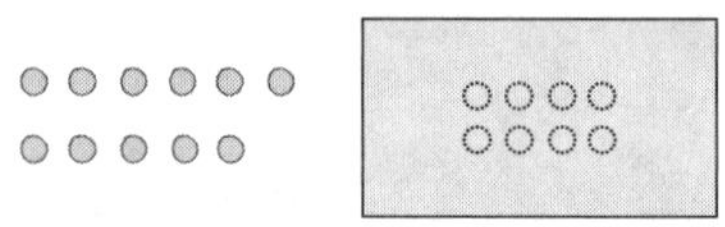

You knew that I had fewer counters than you, so you subtracted 11 minus 3 to find how many I had.

Give your child 9 counters. Secretly take 14 counters and place them under a piece of paper. **I have 5 more counters than you. How many do I have?** *14.* Remove the paper so your child can check her answer.

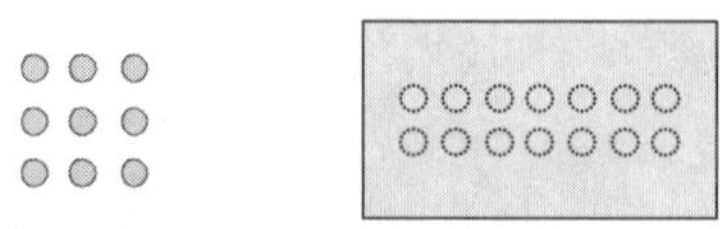

You knew that I had more counters than you, so you added 9 plus 5 to find how many I had.

Problems like this often come up in real life, but we don't always use the words *more* or *fewer* to describe them. Today, you'll learn to solve these kinds of real-life word problems with ages and prices.

Activity: Solve More/Fewer Word Problems with Ages

When we compare ages, we don't usually say that one person has lived "more years" or "fewer years" than another person. We say that one person is older or younger than another person. Make a simple chart like the following:

Name	Age
Stella	7
Daniel	
Parker	
Gabriella	

I'm going to give you some clues so you can figure out how old each child is. Tell your child each clue and complete the chart as your child finds the answers.

- **Stella is 7. Daniel is 5 years older than Stella. How old is Daniel?** *12.* **How do you know?** *I added 7 plus 5.* Write "7 + 5 = 12" on a piece of paper.

> If your child isn't sure, ask: **Is Daniel older or younger than Stella?** *Older.* **When you know the smaller number, you add to find the bigger number. So, add 7 plus 5.**

- **Parker is 3 years younger than Daniel. How old is Parker?** *9.* **How do you know?** *I subtracted 12 minus 3.* Write "12 – 3 = 9" on a piece of paper.

> If your child isn't sure, ask: **Is Parker older or younger than Daniel?** *Younger.* **When you know the greater number, you subtract to find the lesser number. So, subtract 12 minus 3.**

- **Gabriella is 7 years younger than Parker. How old is Gabriella?** *2.* **How do you know?** *I subtracted 9 minus 7.* Write "9 – 7 = 2" on a piece of paper.

Name	Age
Stella	7
Daniel	12
Parker	9
Gabriella	2

7 + 5 = 12
12 - 3 = 9
9 - 7 = 2

Completed chart

Activity: Solve More/Fewer Word Problems with Prices

When we compare prices, we say that an item costs more or less than another item. Place 4 small toys on the table. Place a blank slip of paper in front of each toy. Write $10 on the leftmost slip of paper.

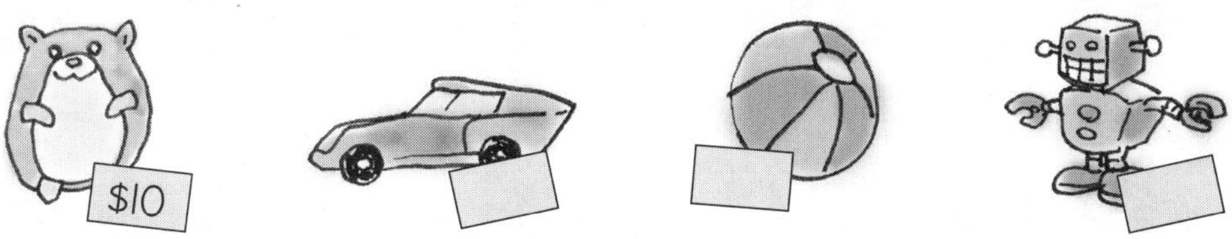

Let's pretend the first toy costs $10. I'm going to give you some clues so you can figure out the other toys' prices. Tell your child each clue and complete the price tags as your child finds the answers.

- **The second toy costs $4 less than the first toy. How much does the second toy cost?** *$6.* **How did you find the answer?** *I subtracted 10 minus 4.*
- **The third toy costs $9 more than the second toy. How much does the third toy cost?** *$15.* **How did you find the answer?** *I added 6 plus 9.*
- **The fourth toy costs $7 less than the third toy. How much does the fourth toy cost?** *$8.* **How did you find the answer?** *I subtracted 15 minus 7.*

Completed price tags

Workbook: Solve More/Fewer Word Problems and Review

Have your child complete workbook pages 11.3A and 11.3B.

Lesson 11.4
Subtraction Word Problems at the Pretend Store

	Purpose	Materials
Warm-up	• Count money • Practice memory work • Review -2, -3, -4, -5 facts	• Play money • Four in a Row game board (from workbook page 11.1A) • Counters
Activities	• Review addition and subtraction word problems in the context of money	• 6 small toys • 6 slips of paper • Play money
Workbook	• Solve money word problems	• Workbook pages 11.4A and 11.4B

Warm-up: Counting, Memory Work, and Review

- Place 5 twenty-dollar bills, 1 ten-dollar bill, 4 five-dollar bills, and 2 one-dollar bills on the table. **How much is the money worth?** *$132.*
- **What do we call the result when we add numbers together?** *The sum.* **What do we call the result when we subtract a number from another number?** *The difference.*
- Play Four in a Row. See Lesson 11.1 (page 176) for directions.

> If your child already knows the -2, -3, -4, and -5 facts well, you can play a different subtraction game from this unit instead.

Activity: Solve Word Problems at the Pretend Store

You have learned how to use addition and subtraction to solve many different types of word problems. Today, you're going to practice solving word problems at the pretend store.

Write $7, $9, $10, $12, $13, and $15 on small slips of paper to make price tags. Lay 6 small toys in a row and have your child place a price tag next to each toy. Also place play money on the table to use.

Act out each of the following problems with the toys in your pretend store. Have your child write an equation to match each problem and solve. He may take bills from the piles of play money as needed.

- Give your child 1 ten-dollar bill, 1 five-dollar bill, and 2 one-dollar bills. **You have $17. Then, you buy the item that costs $10.** Have your child pay $10. **How much money do you have left?** *$7.*

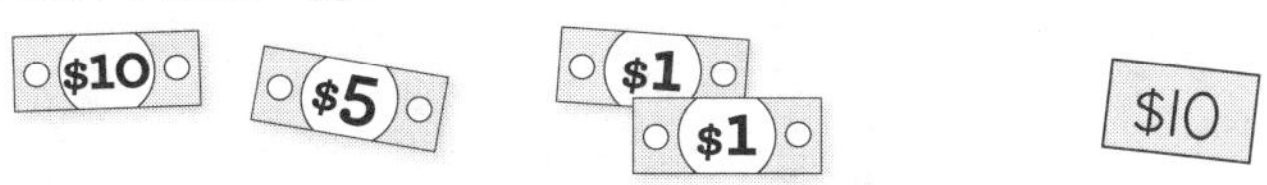

17 - 10 = 7

- **You buy the item that costs \$7 and the item that costs \$12. How much do you pay?** *\$19.*

\$7 \$12 $7 + 12 = 19$

- **Which item costs \$3 more than the \$12 item?** *The \$15 item.*

\$12 $12 + 3 = 15$

- **How much more does the \$13 item cost than the \$9 item?** *\$4.*

\$13 \$9 $13 - 9 = 4$

- Give your child 1 five-dollar bill and 3 one-dollar bills. **You have \$8. You want to buy the item that costs \$13. How much more money do you need?** *\$5.*

\$5 \$1 \$1 \$1 \$13

$13 - 8 = 5$

$8 + \underline{5} = 13$

- **How much less does the \$7 item cost than the \$12 item?** *\$5.*

\$7 \$12 $12 - 7 = 5$

- **You spend \$16 to buy 2 items. One costs \$9. How much does the other item cost?** *\$7.*

\$10 \$5 \$1 \$9 $16 - 9 = 7$

- **Which item costs \$5 less than the \$15 item?** *The \$10 item.*

\$15 $15 - 10 = 5$

If you have time, invite your child to make up some word problems about the pretend store, too.

Workbook: Subtraction Word Problems and Review

Have your child complete workbook pages 11.4A and 11.4B.

Lesson 11.5
Enrichment and Review (Optional)

	Purpose	Materials
Warm-up	• Count from 100 to 200 by 10s • Review memory work • Review your child's favorite or most challenging activities from Week 11	• Varies, depending on the activities you choose
Picture Book	• Understand subtraction in a variety of real-life contexts	• *Subtraction Action*, by Loreen Leedy
Enrichment Activity	• Make a lift-the-flap craft to practice the subtraction facts	• Small slips of paper and tape, or sticky notes

Warm-up: Counting, Memory Work, and Review

- Have your child count from 100 to 200 by 10s.
- Quiz your child on the memory work through Week 10. See page 523 for the full list.
- If you have time, repeat one or two of the activities from this week's lessons. Choose activities your child especially enjoyed or found challenging.

Math Picture Book: *Subtraction Action*

Read *Subtraction Action*, by Loreen Leedy. As you read, have your child solve the subtraction problems and check the answers in the back of the book.

This book includes an introduction to subtracting two-digit numbers and money. Your child will learn more about these topics later in the year.

Enrichment Activity: Subtraction Lift-the-Flap

Fold a piece of paper (or draw lines on a piece of paper) to make a 3x3 grid. Have your child tape a small slip of paper or place a sticky note in each box. Have her write a subtraction fact that she finds challenging on each slip of paper or sticky note, and then have her write the answer underneath.

Encourage your child to use the subtraction facts that she finds most difficult so she can use this lift-the-flap craft to practice them.

Week 11 Answer Key

11.1A

See the Instructor Guide for how to play. Save this game board for future lessons.

Four in a Row

12 - 3	11 - 4	14 - 5	13 - 4	11 - 5
13 - 5	12 - 4	11 - 5	11 - 4	13 - 5
11 - 3	11 - 3	12 - 3	11 - 2	11 - 3
11 - 2	12 - 4	12 - 5	13 - 5	13 - 4
12 - 5	11 - 5	13 - 4	14 - 5	12 - 4

11.1B

Complete.

11 - 4 = 7

13 - 5 = 8

12 - 3 = 9

12 - 5 = 7

13 - 4 = 9

11 - 2 = 9

11 - 3 = 8

14 - 5 = 9

12 - 4 = 8

11 - 5 = 6

Complete the missing numbers in the sequence.

11.2A

Complete. Use the ten-frames to help.

11 - 2 = 9

11 - 3 = 8

11 - 4 = 7

11 - 5 = 6

12 - 2 = 10

12 - 3 = 9

12 - 4 = 8

12 - 5 = 7

13 - 2 = 11

13 - 3 = 10

13 - 4 = 9

13 - 5 = 8

14 - 2 = 12

14 - 3 = 11

14 - 4 = 10

14 - 5 = 9

11.2B

Complete.

30 → +10 → 40 → +20 → 60 → +30 → 90 → +10 → 100

100 → -20 → 80 → -30 → 50 → -20 → 30 → -30 → 0

50 → +40 → 90 → -30 → 60 → -30 → 30 → +20 → 50

Write the expanded form for each number.

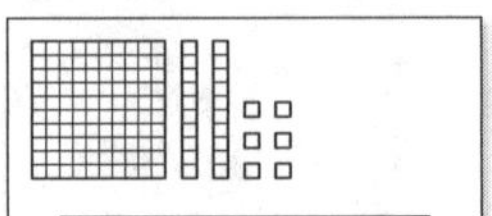

126=100+20+6

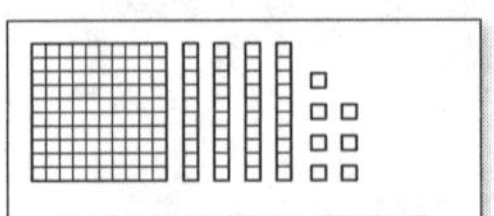

147=100+40+7

Write how much money is in each coin purse in two ways.

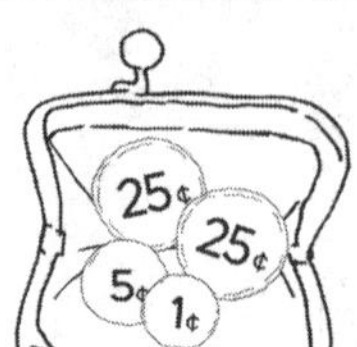

56 ¢ | $0.56

70 ¢ | $0.70

Week 11 Answer Key

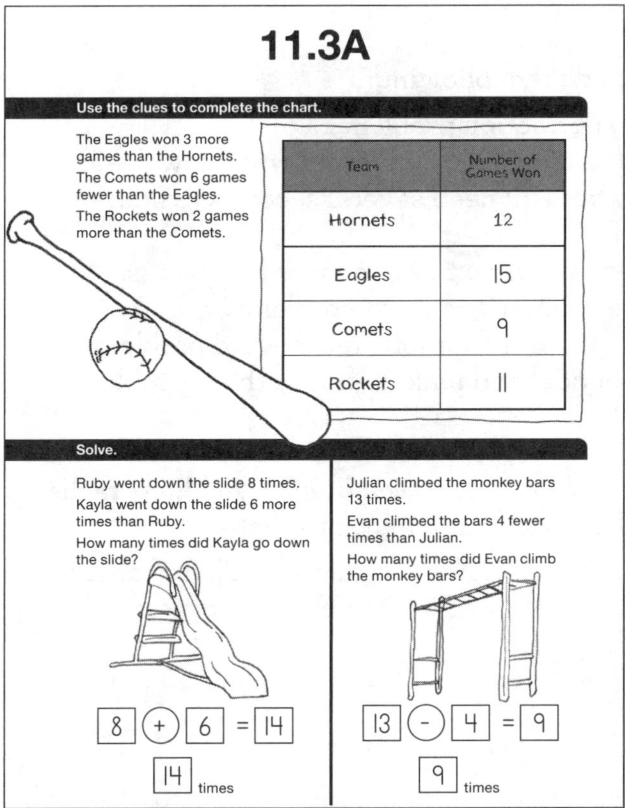

11.3A

Use the clues to complete the chart.

The Eagles won 3 more games than the Hornets.
The Comets won 6 games fewer than the Eagles.
The Rockets won 2 games more than the Comets.

Team	Number of Games Won
Hornets	12
Eagles	15
Comets	9
Rockets	11

Solve.

Ruby went down the slide 8 times. Kayla went down the slide 6 more times than Ruby. How many times did Kayla go down the slide?

8 + 6 = 14

14 times

Julian climbed the monkey bars 13 times. Evan climbed the bars 4 fewer times than Julian. How many times did Evan climb the monkey bars?

13 − 4 = 9

9 times

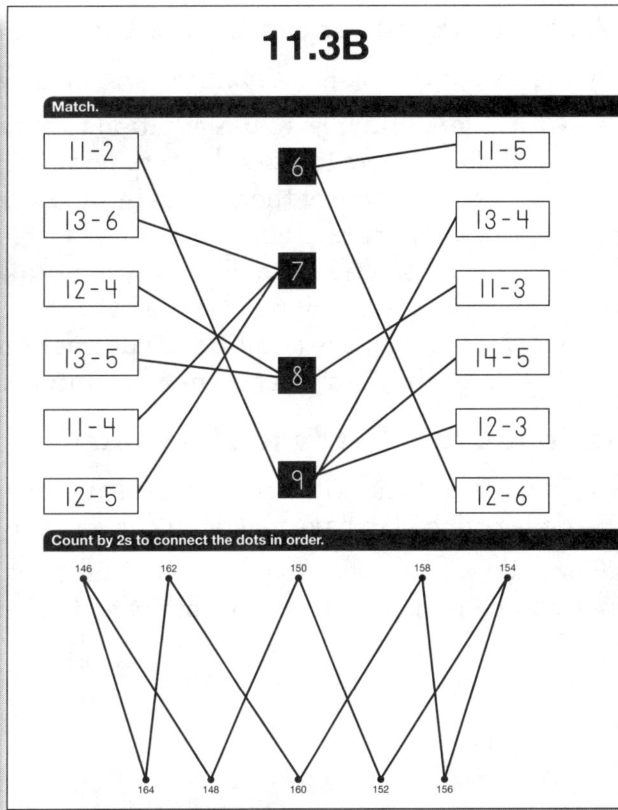

11.3B

Match.

11-2 — 9
13-6 — 7
12-4 — 8
13-5 — 8
11-4 — 7
12-5 — 7

11-5 — 6
13-4 — 9
11-3 — 8
14-5 — 9
12-3 — 9
12-6 — 6

Count by 2s to connect the dots in order.

146, 148, 150, 152, 154, 156, 158, 160, 162, 164

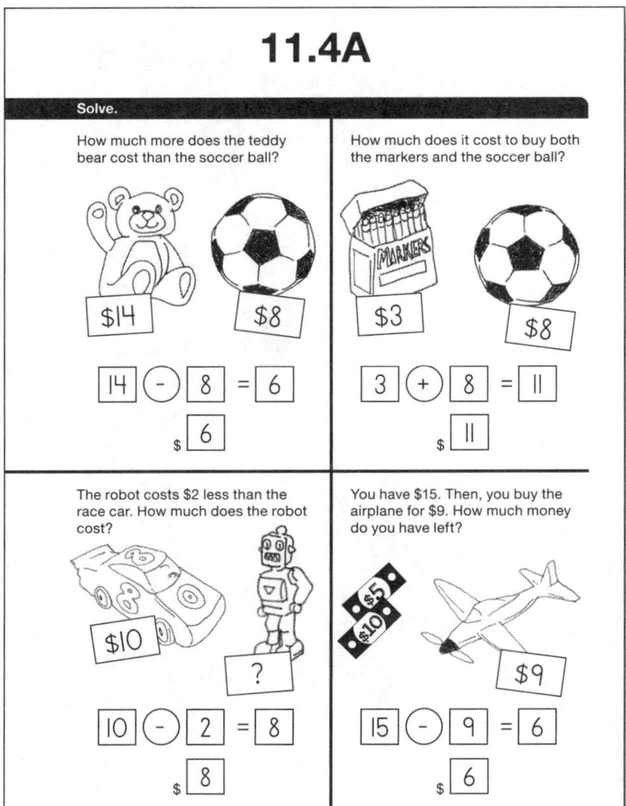

11.4A

Solve.

How much more does the teddy bear cost than the soccer ball?

$14, $8

14 − 8 = 6

$ 6

How much does it cost to buy both the markers and the soccer ball?

$3, $8

3 + 8 = 11

$ 11

The robot costs $2 less than the race car. How much does the robot cost?

$10, ?

10 − 2 = 8

$ 8

You have $15. Then, you buy the airplane for $9. How much money do you have left?

$9

15 − 9 = 6

$ 6

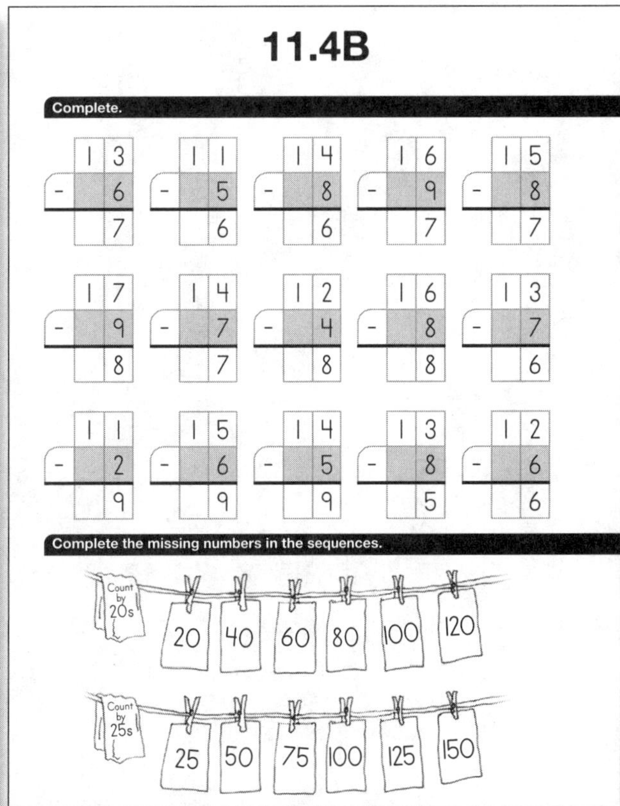

11.4B

Complete.

13 − 6 = 7
11 − 5 = 6
14 − 8 = 6
16 − 9 = 7
15 − 8 = 7

17 − 9 = 8
14 − 7 = 7
12 − 4 = 8
16 − 8 = 8
13 − 7 = 6

11 − 2 = 9
15 − 6 = 9
14 − 5 = 9
13 − 8 = 5
12 − 6 = 6

Complete the missing numbers in the sequences.

Count by 20s: 20, 40, 60, 80, 100, 120

Count by 25s: 25, 50, 75, 100, 125, 150

Unit 4 Checkpoint

What to Expect at the End of Unit 4

By the end of Unit 4, most children will be able to do the following:

- Understand how to use addition to solve subtraction problems.
- Find answers to the subtraction facts in the teens. Most children will know the answers to some of these facts immediately but will need several seconds to figure out the answers to others.
- Use subtraction to solve take-away, take-apart, or comparison word problems. Many children will still need some help to solve comparison word problems.
- Write and solve addition or subtraction equations for more/fewer word problems. Some children will still need counters to model and make sense of these problems..

Is Your Child Ready to Move on?

In Unit 5, your child will learn to create and interpret bar graphs, pictographs, and line graphs. He does not need to have mastered any specific skills before moving on to Unit 5.

Your child will continue to practice the subtraction facts in Units 5, 6, and 7. You'll find an informal subtraction fact assessment at the end of Unit 7 to help assess your child's progress.

Unit 5
Graphs

Overview

Your child will learn how to create and interpret bar graphs, pictographs, and line graphs in a variety of contexts. She'll gather data with dice, coins, and a survey, and she'll use her addition and subtraction skills to draw conclusions about all three types of graphs.

Bar graph.

Pictograph.

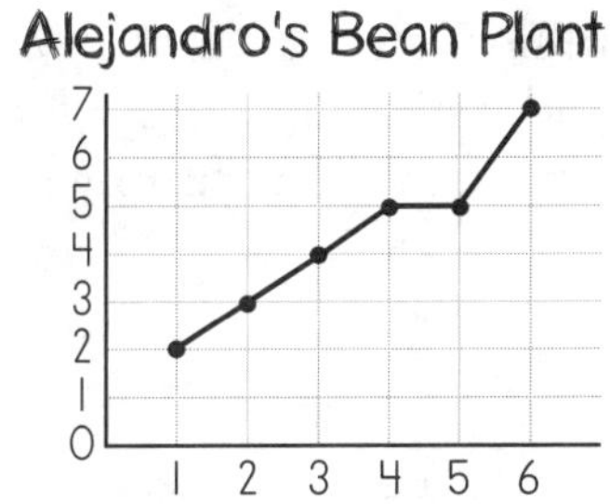

Line graph.

Many families find this unit a refreshing break after the intense focus on the subtraction facts. Your child will continue to practice the subtraction facts during warm-ups and on worksheets to increase her speed and fluency.

Week 12	Bar Graphs
Week 13	Pictographs and Line Graphs

What Your Child Will Learn

In this unit your child will learn to:

- Create bar graphs, pictographs, and line graphs
- Interpret bar graphs, pictographs, and line graphs with increments of 1 or 10
- Use addition and subtraction to draw conclusions from graphs

Recommended Math Picture Books (Optional)

These picture books are scheduled in the optional Enrichment and Review lessons at the end of each week.

- *Lemonade for Sale*, written by Stuart J. Murphy and illustrated by Tricia Tusa. HarperCollins, 1998.
- *The Great Graph Contest*, by Loreen Leedy. Holiday House, 2006.

Week 12
Bar Graphs

Overview

Your child will learn how to create and interpret bar graphs based on dice rolls, coin flips, and a survey. He'll begin by shading boxes one-by-one and then advance to using the numbers on the axes to draw the bars.

In Lessons 12.3 and 12.4, your child will create his own survey question, gather responses, and make a bar graph of his results. You may want to plan a time for him to gather responses from friends or family between Lessons 12.3 and 12.4.

Lesson 12.1	Shade Boxes to Make a Bar Graph
Lesson 12.2	Draw Bars to Make a Bar Graph
Lesson 12.3	Interpret a Survey Bar Graph
Lesson 12.4	Make a Survey Bar Graph
Lesson 12.5	Enrichment and Review (Optional)

Teaching Math with Confidence: Counted versus Measured Quantities

In first grade, your child learned how to shade boxes to make bar graphs. He shaded one box for each data point and then counted how many boxes were in each category.

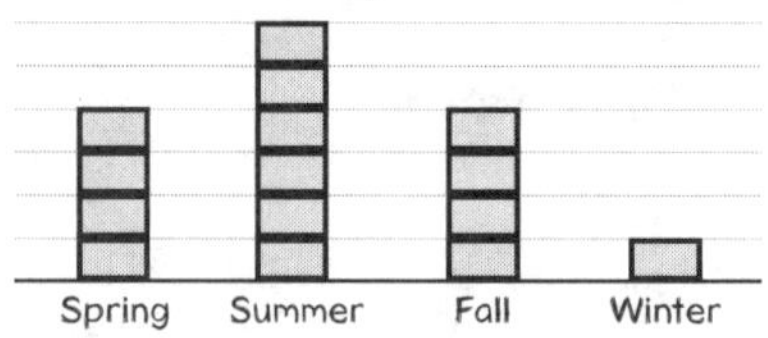

In this bar graph, each box represents one person. Since there are 4 boxes for spring, 4 people chose spring.

This week, your child will learn to create and interpret bar graphs in which the bars are continuous and not subdivided into individual boxes. Instead of counting, he'll learn to use the numbers on the vertical axis to find the height of each bar. He'll also use addition and subtraction to draw conclusions based on the bar graphs.

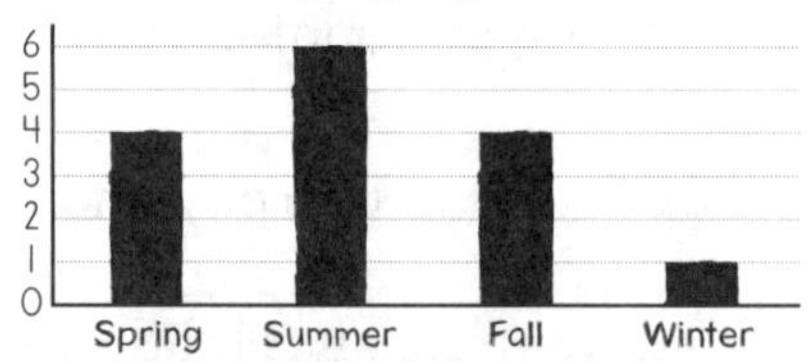

In this bar graph, the labels along the vertical axis tell the height of each bar.
Since the bar for spring is 4 units tall, 4 people chose spring.

Throughout second grade, your child will gradually learn to add and subtract quantities that are measured rather than counted, such as inches, centimeters, or minutes. Using the labels on the vertical axis to measure and reason about the bars on the bar graphs this week will provide a gentle introduction to thinking about quantities in this new way.

Extra Materials Needed for Week 12

- 6 slips of paper
- Cup
- For optional Enrichment and Review Lesson:
    - *Lemonade for Sale*, written by Stuart J. Murphy and illustrated by Tricia Tusa

Lesson 12.1
Shade Boxes to Make a Bar Graph

	Purpose	Materials
Warm-up	• Count by 1s, 2s, and 5s on the number line • Practice memory work • Review subtraction facts	• Blank Number Line (Blackline Master 3) • Subtraction Race game board (from workbook page 9.2A) • Coin • Counters
Activities	• Shade boxes to make a bar graph • Interpret a bar graph	• Workbook page 12.1A • 2 dice
Workbook	• Interpret a bar graph	• Workbook pages 12.1A and 12.1B

Drawing graphs by hand can be time-consuming and frustrating for second graders, so you will use blank graph templates on side A of the workbook pages for many lessons in this unit.

Warm-up: Counting, Memory Work, and Review

- Label the Blank Number Line with 160, 170, and 180. Have your child count from 160 to 180 by 1s, then 2s, and then 5s. Have her point to each corresponding tick mark as she counts.
- **How many months are in a year?** *12.* **How many days are in a week?** *7.*
- Play Subtraction Race (-8 Version). See Lesson 9.4 (page 154) for directions.

Activity: Introduce Graph Vocabulary

Today, we will begin a unit on graphs. We use graphs to organize information and make it easier to understand. When do you see graphs in everyday life? *Sample answers: The TV news has graphs about how much rain has fallen. The doctor showed me a graph with my height on it.*

Show your child workbook page 12.1A. **We'll make a bar graph on your workbook page today. To make the graph, you'll roll 2 dice and color in a square that matches their sum. So, if you roll a 3 and 5, you'll color in the first empty square above the 8.**

Before you start rolling the dice, let's talk about the different parts of the graph.

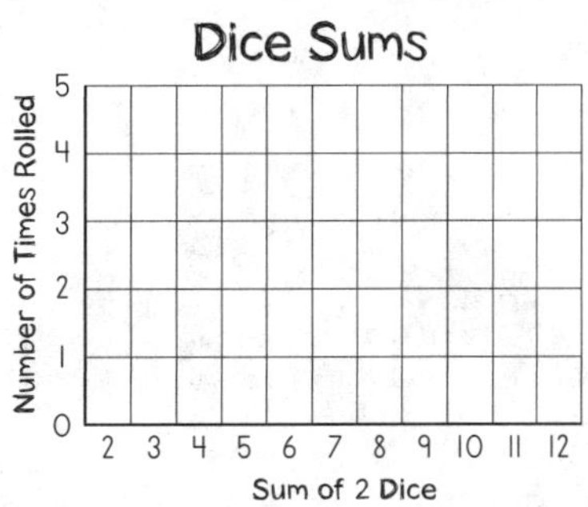

- Point to the title. **What's the title of the graph?** *Dice Sums.*
- Run your finger along the graph's horizontal axis. **This line is called the graph's horizontal axis. What's this axis labeled?** *Sum of 2 Dice.*

- Run your finger along the graph's vertical axis. **This line is called the graph's vertical axis. What's this axis labeled?** *Number of Times Rolled.*

Help your child as needed with reading these labels. Your child does not need to memorize the terms *horizontal axis* or *vertical axis*, although she'll likely learn them as you use them in context.

What's the least number on the horizontal axis? *2.* **Why do you think the numbers start at 2?** *Answers will vary.* **The least number possible on each die is 1. So, the least sum possible is 1 plus 1, or 2.**

What's the greatest number on the horizontal axis? *12.* **Why do you think the numbers end at 12?** *Answers will vary.* **The greatest number possible on each die is 6. So, the greatest sum possible is 6 plus 6, which equals 12.**

The least sum possible is 2. The greatest sum possible is 12.

This vertical axis starts at 0 and goes up to 5, because we'll stop after you roll one of the sums 5 times.

Activity: Make a Dice Sum Bar Graph

Have your child roll 2 dice and color the square that matches their sum until one column is completely full. For example, if she rolls a 2 and a 4, she should color the first empty box above the 6. Make sure she colors the boxes from bottom to top without skipping any.

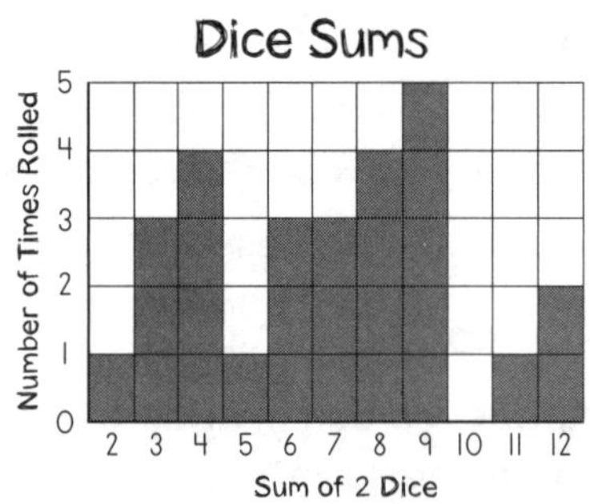

Sample final bar graph

If you're short on time (or patience!), have your child roll the dice and find the sum while you shade the squares, or vice versa.

If your child rolled the dice many more times, her graph would begin to take this general shape, with many more 6s, 7s, and 8s than 2s or 12s.

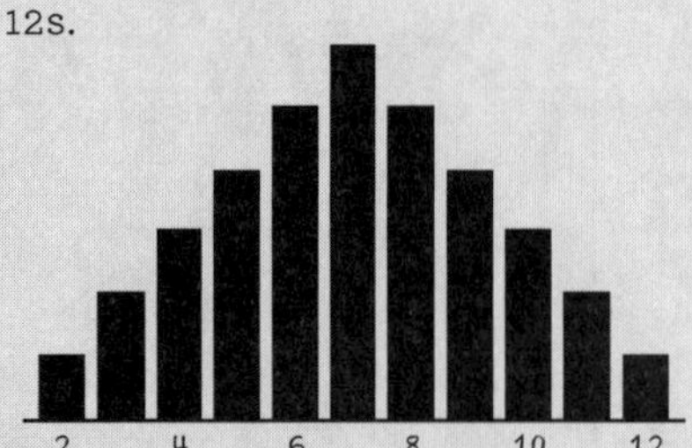

That's because there are many more ways for the dice to have these sums. For example, there are 6 different dice combinations that equal 7 (1 and 6, 2 and 5, 3 and 4, 4 and 3, 5 and 2, 6 and 1) but only 1 combination that equals 2 (1 and 1). Your child will learn more about the probability theory that underlies this graph in future years.

Activity: Discuss the Bar Graph

Have your child go through each number from 2 to 12 and identify how many times she rolled each sum. **How many times did you roll each sum?** *Answers will vary.*

What do you notice about your bar graph? *Sample answer: I rolled 9 the most and 10 the least. I rolled the sums in the middle of the graph a lot more than the sums at the edges of the graph.*

Are these results surprising to you? Why or why not? *Sample answer: I didn't think I would get so many 3s. I'm surprised that I didn't roll any 10s, because I roll 10s a lot when I play board games.*

> Asking open-ended questions gives your child the chance to draw her own conclusions about the graph before she answers the more-specific questions printed on the workbook page. Some children love these types of questions, while others freeze up. If your child is in the second category, save these two open-ended questions for after your child completes workbook page 12.1A.

Workbook: Interpret a Bar Graph and Review

Have your child complete workbook pages 12.1A and 12.1B.

> For the final question on workbook page 12.1A, your child can count the number of total boxes she colored on the graph.

Lesson 12.2
Draw Bars to Make a Bar Graph

	Purpose	Materials
Warm-up	• Count combinations of base-ten blocks • Practice memory work • Review doubling	• Base-ten blocks • Number Machine (from Lesson 6.1) • 6 slips of paper
Activities	• Organize information and draw bars to make a bar graph • Interpret a bar graph	• Coins • Cup • Workbook page 12.2A
Workbook	• Review previously-learned material	• Workbook page 12.2B

Warm-up: Counting, Memory Work, and Review

- Place 1 flat and 8 units on the table. **What is the value of these blocks?** *108.*
- **How many months are in a year?** *12.* **How many days are in a week?** *7.*
- Set up the Number Machine and pretend to set it to the Double setting. Model the questions with base-ten blocks as needed.
  - × **If 5 goes in, what number will come out?** *10.*
  - × **If 8 goes in, what number will come out?** *16.*
  - × **If 12 goes in, what number will come out?** *24.*
  - × **If 15 goes in, what number will come out?** *30.*
  - × **If 41 goes in, what number will come out?** *82.*
  - × **If 100 goes in, what number will come out?** *200.*

Activity: Flip Coins and Record Results

In the last lesson, you made a bar graph about dice. Today, you'll make a bar graph about coins.

When scientists do experiments, they usually collect the results first and then make a graph to show it. That's what we'll do today with coins. You'll shake 10 coins in a cup, dump them out, and count how many coins show tails. You'll record your results on your workbook page, and then later you'll make a bar graph. Show your child workbook page 12.2A.

Have your child shake 10 coins in a cup, dump them out, and count how many show tails. Have him record the number of tails in one of the blank boxes at the top of 12.2A. Repeat until he has filled in all of the boxes.

Have your child dump the coins onto a small towel or into a tray to prevent them from rolling away.

Activity: Draw Bars to Make a Bar Graph

Now that you have all your results, we'll count them up and draw bars on the bar graph to match. What's the graph's title? *Number of Tails Flipped.* **What's the horizontal axis labeled?** *Number of Tails.* **What's the vertical axis labeled?** *Number of Times.*

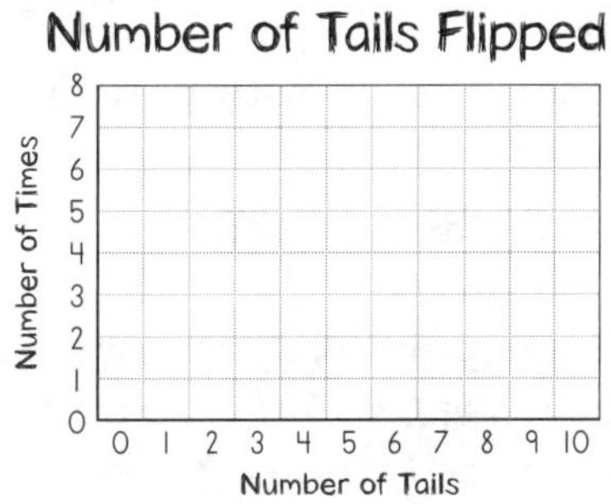

Have your child count how many times he flipped each number of tails and draw a corresponding bar on the bar graph. If he did not flip a certain number of tails, have him leave the column above that number blank.

As your child works, point out that he can use the numbers on the vertical axis to draw the tops of the bars without counting each box one-by-one. For example: **You flipped 5 tails 7 times. So, you can draw the top of the bar on the line marked 7.** Encourage him to draw the outline of the bar and then shade the entire bar.

The final bar graph should look something like this:

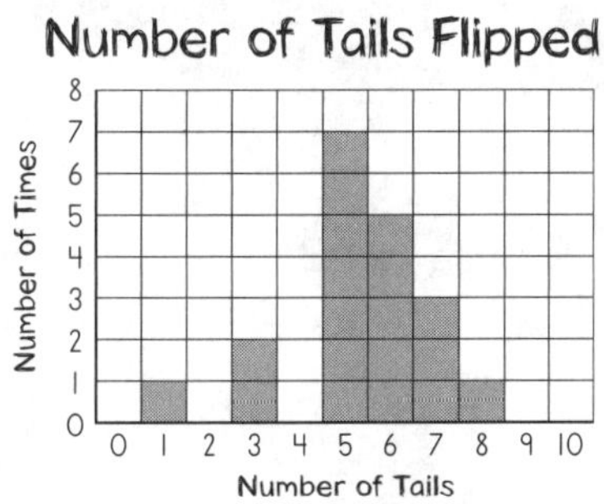

If your child flipped the coins many more times, his graph would begin to take this general shape with many more 4s, 5s, and 6s than 0s, 1s, 9s, or 10s.

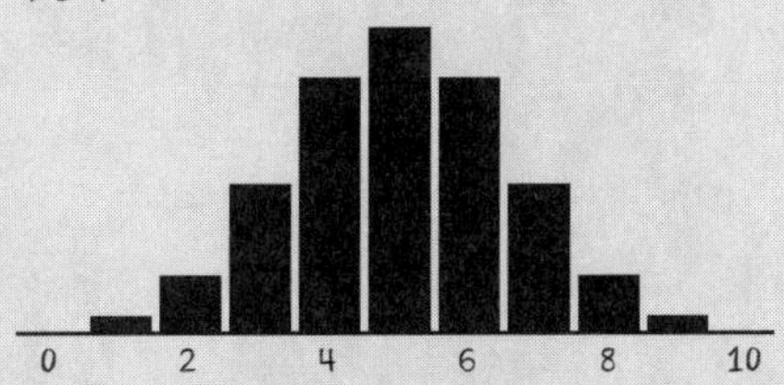

That's because there are many more ways for 10 coins to show these numbers of tails. If you imagine each coin having a different color, there are 1,024 different ways they can land—and 252 of these ways have 5 tails! Your child's results may look quite different, however, since he only flipped the coins 20 times.

Activity: Interpret the Bar Graph

Have your child go through each number from 0 to 10 and identify how many times he flipped that number of tails. **How many times did you flip each number of tails?** *Answers will vary.*

Then, use the following questions to discuss your child's bar graph. (These sample answers are based on the sample graph above. Your child's answers should be based on his own graph.)

- **What do you notice about your bar graph?** *Sample answer: I flipped 5 tails a lot! I didn't ever flip all heads or all tails.*
- **Are these results surprising to you? Why or why not?** *Sample answer: It makes sense that I got a lot of 5s, because 5 is half of 10 and you usually get tails about half the time. I wish I had gotten 10 tails, but it doesn't seem very likely that they would all be the same.*
- **Which number of tails did you flip the most?** *Sample answer: 5.*
- **Which number of tails did you flip the least?** *Sample answer: I didn't ever flip 0, 2, 4, 9, or 10 tails.*
- Choose a few pairs of numbers and have your child tell how many more times (or how many fewer times) he flipped one number of tails than another. For example: **How many more times did you flip 5 tails than 6 tails?** *Sample answer: 2.*

Most second graders will find the answer to the final question by visually comparing the heights of the bars. If your child isn't sure, have him subtract the lesser number from the greater number to find the difference.

Workbook: Review

Have your child complete workbook page 12.2B.

Lesson 12.3
Interpret a Survey Bar Graph

	Purpose	Materials
Warm-up	• Count by 10s • Practice memory work • Review adding a series of numbers	• Playing cards
Activities	• Interpret a bar graph in which the bars are not subdivided • Plan and conduct a survey	• Workbook page 12.3A
Workbook	• Review previously-learned material	• Workbook page 12.3B

Warm-up: Counting, Memory Work, and Review

- Have your child count forward by 10s from the following numbers. Stop her after she reaches the last number listed in the sample answers.
    - **Count forward by 10s from 20:** *20, 30, 40, 50, 60.*
    - **Count forward by 10s from 90:** *90, 100, 110, 120, 130.*
    - **Count forward by 10s from 75:** *75, 85, 95, 105, 115.*

> Encourage your child to count from memory, but allow her to use the 100 and 200 Charts if needed.

- **How many months are in a year?** *12.* **How many days are in a week?** *7.*
- Play Make 20 Splat. See Lesson 1.2 (page 16) for directions.

Activity: Interpret a Bar Graph Based on a Survey

In the last two lessons, you created bar graphs based on dice and coins. Today, you'll learn how to read a bar graph based on a survey and plan a survey of your own.

Show your child workbook page 12.3A. Read aloud the directions at the top and briefly discuss your child's favorite season. Have your child identify the title, horizontal axis and label, and vertical axis and label.

The bars on this bar graph aren't divided into smaller boxes. Instead of counting boxes to see how many people chose each season, we'll use the numbers on the vertical axis.

> See the Week 12 **Teaching Math with Confidence** for more on this shift from counting boxes to measuring bars with the numbers on the axis.

Which bar shows how many people chose spring? *Child points to corresponding bar.* **To find the bar's height, I can point to the top of the bar and then slide my finger until it reaches the vertical axis.** Demonstrate how to do this.

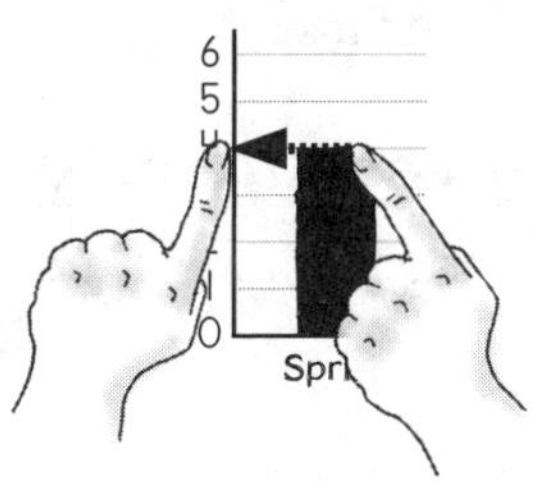

The bar for spring has a height of 4, so I know 4 people chose spring. Have your child fill in the corresponding box in the chart. Then, have her use the same method to complete the rest of the chart.

Season	Spring	Summer	Fall	Winter
Number of people	4	6	4	1

Sliding her finger along the graph helps your child understand the meaning of the numbers on the vertical axis. It also helps her visually track the lines on the graph. Many second graders are still developing their visual tracking skills, and the extra support of the moving finger helps prevent mistakes.

Use the following questions to discuss the bar graph and chart.

- **What do you notice about the graph?** *Sample answer: Lots of people like summer!*
- **Are these results surprising to you? Why or why not?** *Sample answer: Yes, because I thought more people would choose winter.*
- **What was the most popular season?** *Summer.*
- **What was the least popular season?** *Winter.*
- **Which two seasons were equally popular?** *Spring and fall.*
- **How many people chose fall or winter?** *5.*
- **How many fewer people chose spring than summer?** *2.*

Your child will complete the questions at the bottom of 12.3A later in the lesson.

Activity: Plan and Conduct a Survey

The girl who made the bar graph on the workbook page wanted to know which season people like best. Now, you get to plan a survey about something you'd like to find out! You'll make a bar graph of your results in the next lesson.

What would you like to survey people about? *Answers will vary.* Discuss possibilities with your child and help her choose a question with 3-5 well-defined options. For example:

- Which of these kinds of pie do you like best: pumpkin, apple, or pecan?
- Which of these holidays is your favorite: Christmas, Easter, Fourth of July, or Thanksgiving?
- Which winter activity do you like best: ice-skating, sledding, snowball fights, or skiing?

Help her create a list of 10-15 people to survey and plan how she will conduct her survey. Choose people who are easy to reach, such as family members or neighbors, and help your child contact them and record their answers.

Save the survey results for Lesson 12.4.

Your child will make a bar graph with her results in Lesson 12.4. If your child needs several days to complete the survey, skip Lesson 12.4 until you have the results. Move on to Lesson 12.5 or Week 13 in the meantime and then return to Lesson 12.4 once you have 10-15 responses.

Workbook: Interpret a Bar Graph and Review

Have your child complete workbook pages 12.3A and 12.3B.

Lesson 12.4
Make a Survey Bar Graph

	Purpose	Materials
Warm-up	• Count combinations of base-ten blocks • Practice memory work • Review subtraction facts	• Base-ten blocks • Counters • Treasure Hunt game board (from workbook page 10.2A) • Die
Activities	• Organize survey results to make a bar graph • Interpret a bar graph	• Survey results from Lesson 12.3 • Workbook page 12.4A
Workbook	• Interpret a bar graph	• Workbook pages 12.4A and 12.4B

You will need the results from your child's survey in Lesson 12.3 to complete this lesson. If your child needs more time to complete the survey, skip this lesson until you have the results and move on to Lesson 12.5 or 13.1 in the meantime.

Warm-up: Counting, Memory Work, and Review

- Place 5 rods and 12 units on the table. **What is the value of these blocks?** *62.*
- **How many months are in a year?** *12.* **How many days are in a week?** *7.*
- Play Treasure Hunt. See Lesson 10.2 (page 165) for directions.

Activity: Organize Survey Data

In the last lesson, you took a survey. Today, we'll organize your results and show them on a bar graph.

Have your child count how many responses he had in each category in his survey and make a simple chart showing the results.

Ice-skating	4
Sledding	7
Skiing	2

Sample chart of survey results

Activity: Make a Survey Bar Graph

Show your child the blank bar graph on workbook page 12.4A. **What would be a good title for your graph?** *Answers will vary.* Have him write the title at the top of the graph. Also have him write the name of each category along the bottom of the graph and label each axis.

Sample title and category labels

> Help your child as needed with spelling or writing the words.

Have your child draw bars on the graph to match his results. Encourage him to draw the outline of the entire bar before shading it in. His final bar graph should look something like this:

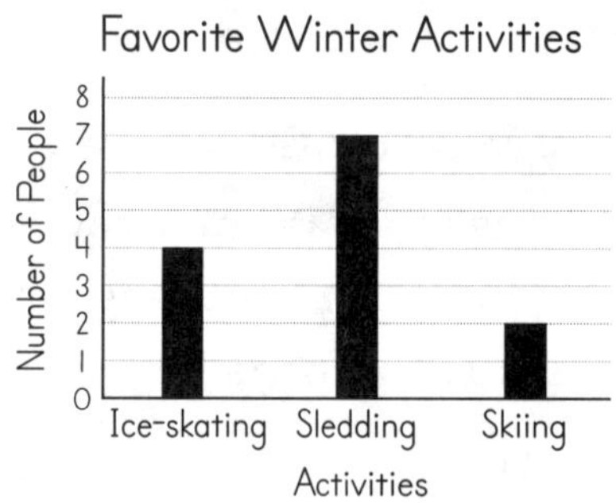

Sample bar graph

Activity: Interpret the Survey Bar Graph

Use questions like the following to discuss your child's bar graph. Adjust the wording as needed based on your child's survey question.

- **How many people chose each of the options in your survey?** *Answers will vary.*
- **What do you notice about your bar graph?** *Answers will vary.*
- **Are these results surprising to you? Why or why not?** *Answers will vary.*

Workbook: Interpret a Bar Graph and Review

Have your child complete workbook pages 12.4A and 12.4B.

Lesson 12.5
Enrichment and Review (Optional)

	Purpose	Materials
Warm-up	• Count from 100 to 200 by 10s • Review memory work • Review your child's favorite or most challenging activities from Week 12	• Varies, depending on the activities you choose
Picture Book	• Understand how bar graphs can be used to record sales	• *Lemonade for Sale,* written by Stuart J. Murphy and illustrated by Tricia Tusa
Enrichment Activity	• Make a bar graph of animals observed on a nature walk	• None

Warm-up: Counting, Memory Work, and Review

- Have your child count from 100 to 200 by 10s.
- Quiz your child on the memory work through Week 12. See page 523 for the full list.
- If you have time, repeat one or two of the activities from this week's lessons. Choose activities your child especially enjoyed or found challenging.

Math Picture Book: *Lemonade for Sale*

Read *Lemonade for Sale,* written by Stuart J. Murphy and illustrated by Tricia Tusa. As you read, help your child understand how the lemonade sales match the bars on the graphs.

> The bar graphs in this book have an increment of 10 along the vertical axis. Your child will learn more about reading graphs with increments other than 1 during Week 13.

Enrichment Activity: Record and Graph Animals on a Nature Walk

Go on a nature walk with your child, either around your neighborhood or at a local park or nature preserve. Before you start the walk, have your child choose 3 or 4 animals common to your area. As you walk, have your child keep track of how many of each kind of animal he sees.

Chipmunks	𝍸 |
Robins	𝍸 ||
Turtles	||

After you return home, help your child make a simple bar graph showing the animals he saw. Make sure he includes a title for the graph and labels for the axes.

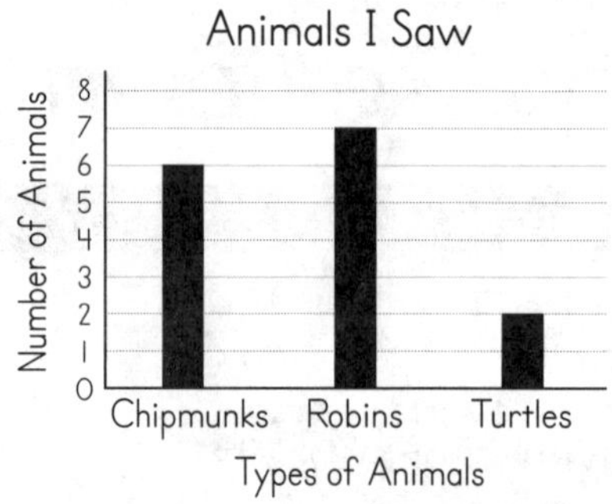

Drawing the graph on graphing or lined paper makes it easier to keep the bars evenly spaced, but don't worry if your child's bars aren't precise.

Week 12 Answer Key

12.1A

See the Instructor Guide for directions.

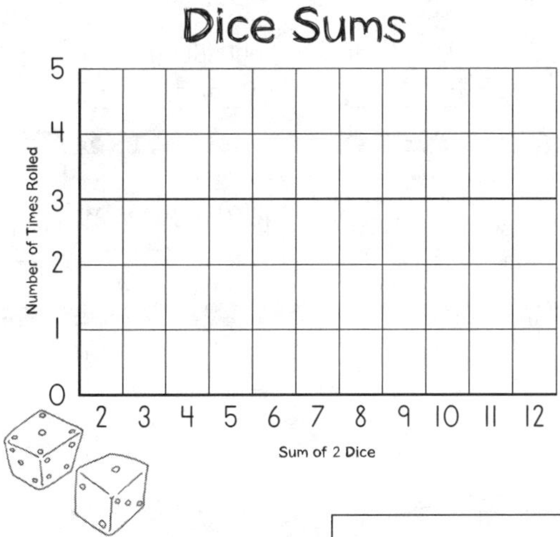

Which sum (or sums) did you roll the most? ______

Which sum (or sums) did you roll the least? ______

How many more times did you roll 7 than 2? ______ times

How many times did you roll in all? ______ times

12.1B

Complete.

12 − 5 = 7

13 − 4 = 9

11 − 2 = 9

13 − 5 = 8

11 − 4 = 7

11 − 3 = 8

14 − 5 = 9

11 − 5 = 6

12 − 4 = 8

12 − 3 = 9

Use the chart to answer the questions.

Name	Age
Isabella	12
Alex	14
Mia	7
Jacob	9

Who is the oldest? Alex

Who is the youngest? Mia

How much older is Alex than Jacob?

14 − 9 = 5

5 years

How much younger is Mia than Isabella?

12 − 7 = 5

5 years

12.2A

See the Instructor Guide for directions.

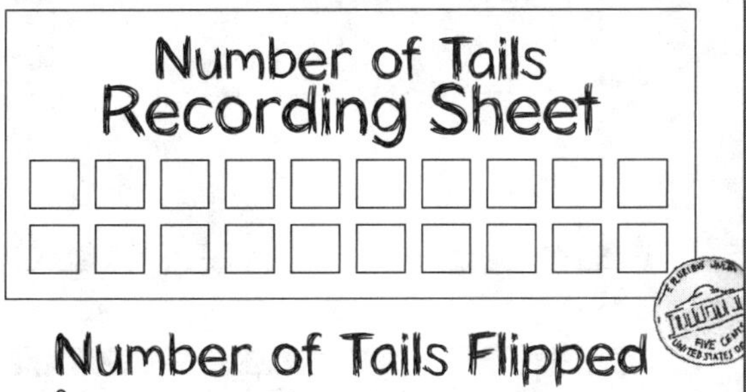

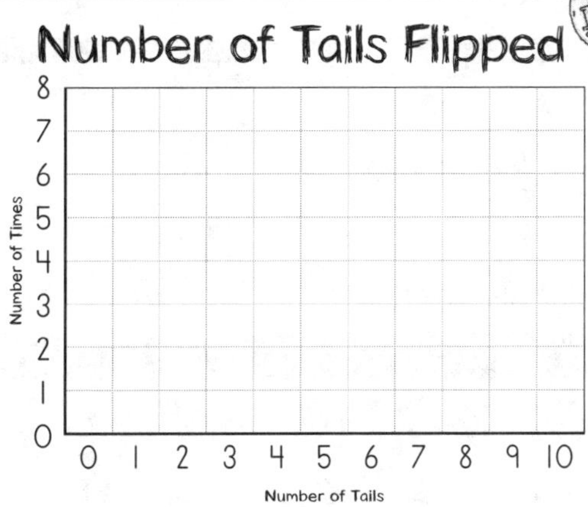

12.2B

Complete.

11 − 6 = 5

12 − 7 = 5

14 − 6 = 8

14 − 5 = 9

13 − 7 = 6

12 − 6 = 6

16 − 7 = 9

15 − 6 = 9

14 − 7 = 7

11 − 7 = 4

13 − 6 = 7

15 − 7 = 8

Solve.

You earn \$12 on Monday and \$5 on Tuesday.
How much do you earn in all?

12 + 5 = 17

\$ 17

You earn \$12 on Monday and \$5 on Tuesday.
How much less do you earn on Tuesday than Monday?

12 − 5 = 7

\$ 7

Week 12 Answer Key

12.3A

Rebecca surveyed her family and friends about their favorite season. She made a bar graph of the results. Use the bar graph to complete the chart.

Season	Spring	Summer	Fall	Winter
Number of people	4	6	4	1

Use the bar graph and chart to complete.

How many people chose spring or summer?

4 + 6 = 10

10 people

How many more people chose summer than spring?

6 - 4 = 2

2 people

How many fewer people chose winter than fall?

4 - 1 = 3

3 people

How many people did Rebecca survey? Write your own equation.

4 + 6 + 4 + 1 = 15

15 people

12.3B

Complete.

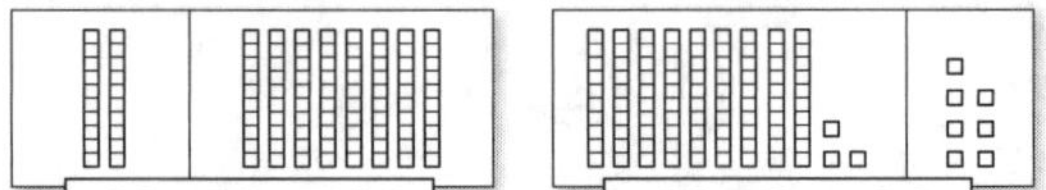

20 + 80 = 100

93 + 7 = 100

Complete.

55 ¢

37 ¢

Match.

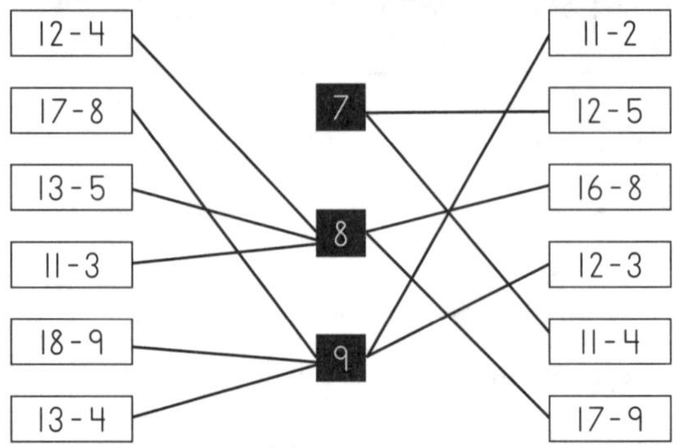

12.4A

Use this page to make a bar graph based on your survey results. See the Instructor Guide for directions.

Use your bar graph to answer the questions.

What was the most popular answer?

What was the least popular answer?

How many more people chose the most-popular answer than the least-popular answer? ___ people

How many people did you survey? ___ people

12.4B

Complete.

$11 - 9 = 2$

$12 - 8 = 4$

$11 - 5 = 6$

$13 - 9 = 4$

$13 - 8 = 5$

$12 - 9 = 3$

$11 - 8 = 3$

$14 - 9 = 5$

Complete.

6 + 3 = 9	8 - 4 = 4
96 + 3 = 99	38 - 4 = 34
106 + 3 = 109	108 - 4 = 104
196 + 3 = 199	138 - 4 = 134

Circle the sandwiches that are split in half. X the sandwiches that are not split in half.

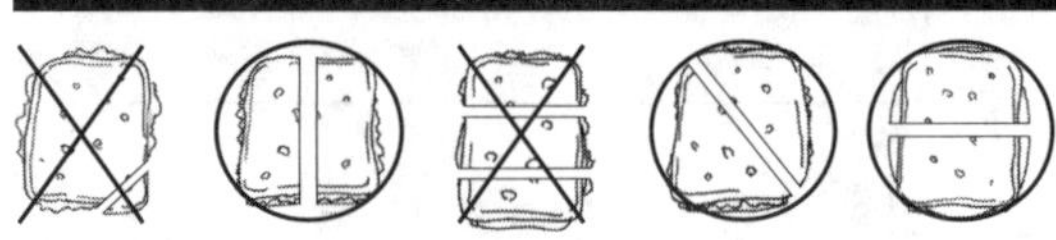

Week 13
Pictographs and Line Graphs

Overview

Your child will learn how to create and interpret pictographs and line graphs with increments of 1, 2, or 10. She will also compare and contrast these graphs with bar graphs.

Lesson 13.1	Pictographs with Increments of 1 or 2
Lesson 13.2	Pictographs and Bar Graphs with Increments of 10
Lesson 13.3	Make and Interpret Line Graphs
Lesson 13.4	Compare and Contrast Different Kinds of Graphs
Lesson 13.5	Enrichment and Review (Optional)

Teaching Math with Confidence: How to Help Your Child Understand Pictographs

Your child will learn how to create and interpret pictographs this week. A pictograph is a graph in which the quantities are expressed with pictures. These graphs always include a key that tells the value of each picture. For example, in this pictograph, 1 circle equals 1 cookie.

Oatmeal Raisin	○○○○
Chocolate Chip	○○○○○○○○○

→ ○ = 1 cookie

But the pictures can also stand for other numbers. In this pictograph, 1 soccer ball equals 10 minutes of playing soccer.

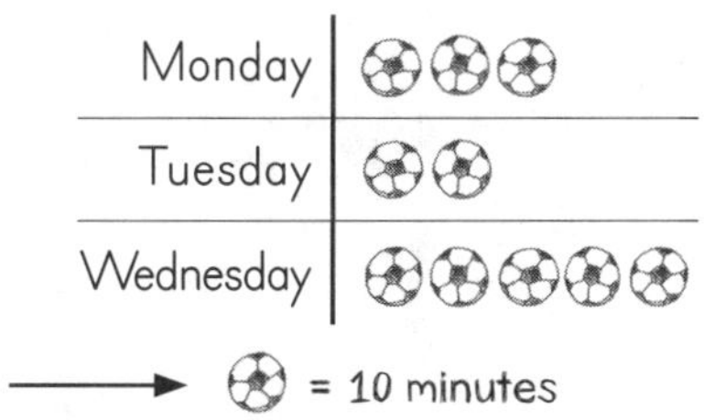

Children run into two common problems with pictographs. First, they often find it confusing that 1 picture can represent multiple objects. In the lessons this week, you'll help your child understand this concept through the familiar context of coins. Just as 1 dime is worth 10 cents, 1 picture of a soccer ball can be worth 10 minutes.

Second, even after they understand that 1 picture can represent multiple objects, children often forget to check the key. As your child reads pictographs this week and in future review activities, don't be surprised if you often have to remind him to check what each picture is worth.

All of the pictographs in Second Grade Math with Confidence use increments that your child already knows how to count by (like 1s, 2s, 5s, or 10s) so that he can easily use skip-counting to find the total number of objects represented. For example, you'll teach your child to count by 2s to count the gifts in this pictograph.

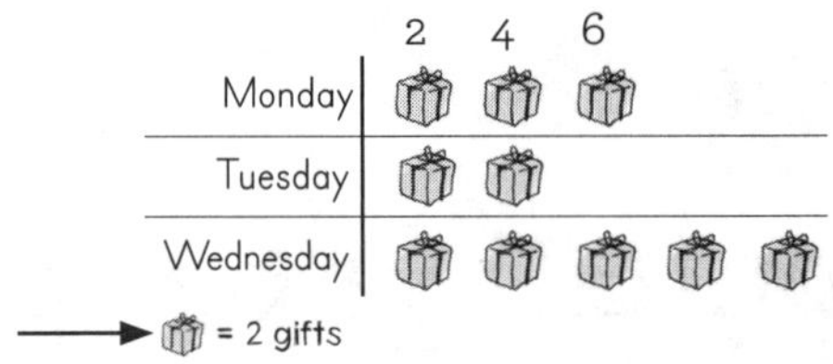

"2, 4, 6. She wrapped 6 gifts on Monday."

Skip-counting to find the totals in pictographs gently previews multiplication which your child will learn in third grade.

Extra Materials Needed for Week 13

- 5 slips of paper
- For optional Enrichment and Review Lesson:
    - *The Great Graph Contest,* by Loreen Leedy
    - Graph of your town's average monthly rainfall, either printed or online

Lesson 13.1
Pictographs with Increments of 1 or 2

	Purpose	Materials
Warm-up	• Count nickels by 5s • Practice memory work • Review finding half of numbers	• Coins • Number Machine (from Lesson 6.1) • 5 slips of paper • Base-ten blocks, optional
Activities	• Draw a pictograph with an increment of 1 • Interpret a pictograph with an increment of 2	• Workbook page 13.1A
Workbook	• Use addition and subtraction to answer questions about a pictograph	• Workbook pages 13.1A and 13.1B

Warm-up: Counting, Memory Work, and Review

- Place a handful of nickels on the table. **About how many cents do you think the coins are worth?** *Answers will vary.* Have your child count the nickels by 5s to find their value.
- Write the < sign. **What does this sign mean?** *Less than.*
  Write the > sign. **What does this sign mean?** *Greater than.*
- Set up the Number Machine and pretend to set it to the Half setting. Model the questions with base-ten blocks as needed.
  - **If 10 goes in, what number will come out?** *5.*
  - **If 12 goes in, what number will come out?** *6.*
  - **If 18 goes in, what number will come out?** *9.*
  - **If 40 goes in, what number will come out?** *20.*
  - **If 60 goes in, what number will come out?** *30.*

Activity: Make a Pictograph with an Increment of 1

Last week, you learned how to draw and interpret bar graphs. Today, you'll learn about pictographs. The word is a combination of "picture" and "graph." A pictograph is like a bar graph, but it uses pictures or symbols instead of bars.

Let's pretend you have a bake sale and sell oatmeal raisin and chocolate chip cookies. Briefly discuss your child's experience with bake sales. **You sell 4 oatmeal raisin cookies and 9 chocolate chip cookies. We'll make a pictograph to show your sales.** Write the amounts on a piece of paper and set up a simple pictograph.

Oatmeal Raisin	
Chocolate Chip	

> You can also allow your child to choose the cookie varieties and use them in place of oatmeal raisin and chocolate chip.

First, we have to decide what picture to use and how many cookies each picture will stand for. In this pictograph, we'll use circles to stand for the cookies. Each circle will stand for 1 cookie. Write the following below your pictograph. **This part is called the *key*, because it's key to understanding the pictograph.**

○ = 1 cookie

Next, we draw pictures to match the information. You sold 4 oatmeal cookies, so draw 4 circles in the oatmeal raisin row. *Child draws 4 circles.* **How many circles do you need to draw in the chocolate chip row?** *9.* Have your child draw 9 circles.

Oatmeal Raisin	OOOO
Chocolate Chip	OOOOOOOOO

Encourage your child to draw all the circles roughly the same size and to space them as evenly as possible so the circles in the top row are aligned with the circles in the bottom row.

Last, we write a title. What is a good title for this pictograph? *Sample answer: Cookie Sales.* Have your child add a title to the graph.

How many cookies did you sell in all? *13.* Have your child write an addition equation to match: 9 + 4 = 13.

How many more chocolate chip cookies did you sell than oatmeal raisin? *5.* **How do you know?** *Sample answer: 9 minus 4 equals 5.*

There are two different ways to find how many more chocolate chip cookies you sold than oatmeal raisin. You can count how many more circles are in the chocolate chip row than the oatmeal row. Or, you can use subtraction. What subtraction equation tells the difference between the two numbers of cookies? *9 minus 4 equals 5.*

Oatmeal Raisin	OOOO
Chocolate Chip	OOOOOOOOO

5

9 - 4 = 5

Activity: Interpret a Pictograph with an Increment of 2

Show your child workbook page 13.1A. Read aloud the directions at the top and briefly discuss your child's experiences with wrapping gifts.

Can you find the pictograph's key? *Child points to key.* **In this pictograph, each picture equals 2 gifts. Maybe Riley didn't want to have to draw so many gifts!**

It can be confusing to have 1 picture stand for 2 things! Think of the pictures like coins. A nickel is only 1 coin, but it stands for 5 cents. So, we count nickels by 5s to find how much a pile of nickels is worth.

Since each picture stands for 2 gifts, we count the pictures by 2s to find how many gifts Riley wrapped each day. Point to the Monday row and count by 2s as you touch each picture: **2, 4, 6. Riley wrapped 6 gifts on Monday.** Have your child write 6 in the Monday column of the chart.

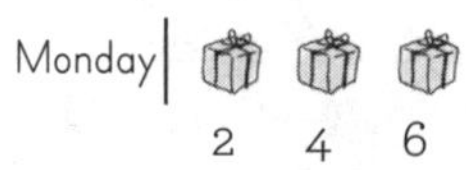

If your child doesn't understand why you counted by 2s, use counters to represent the gifts. Place 2 counters on top of (or next to) each picture, and then have your child count them by 2s.

Have your child count the pictures by 2s to complete the rest of the chart.

Day	Monday	Tuesday	Wednesday
Number of Gifts	6	4	10

Workbook: Interpret a Pictograph and Review

Have your child complete workbook pages 13.1A and 13.1B.

Lesson 13.2
Pictographs and Bar Graphs with Increments of 10

	Purpose	Materials
Warm-up	• Count dimes by 10s • Practice memory work • Review subtraction facts	• Coins • Four in a Row game board (from workbook page 11.1A) • Counters
Activities	• Interpret pictographs and bar graphs with an increment of 10 • Use addition and subtraction to answer questions about pictographs	• Workbook page 13.2A
Workbook	• Review previously-learned material	• Workbook page 13.2B

Warm-up: Counting, Memory Work, and Review

- Place a handful of dimes on the table. **About how many cents do you think the coins are worth?** *Answers will vary.* Have your child count the dimes by 10s to find their value.
- **If a number has 1, 3, 5, 7, or 9 in the ones-place, is the number even or odd?** *Odd.* **If a number has 0, 2, 4, 6, or 8 in the ones-place, is the number even or odd?** *Even.*
- Play Four in a Row. See Lesson 11.1 (page 176) for directions.

Activity: Interpret a Pictograph with an Increment of 10

In the last lesson, you learned how to draw and interpret pictographs. In one of the pictographs, each circle stood for 1 cookie. In the other pictograph, each picture stood for 2 gifts. Today, you'll learn about pictographs where each picture stands for 10.

Show your child workbook page 13.2A and read aloud the directions at the top. Point to the key on the pictograph. **What does each soccer ball stand for?** *10 minutes of playing soccer.*

 = 10 minutes

Each soccer ball stands for 10 minutes. So, what number should we count by to find how much time Tommy spent playing soccer? *10.* Have your child count the soccer balls by 10s to complete the chart.

Day	Minutes
Monday	30
Tuesday	20
Wednesday	50

See the Week 13 **Teaching Math with Confidence** for more on using increments other than 1 in graphs.

Briefly discuss the pictograph and chart with these questions.

- **Which day did Tommy play soccer the most?** *Wednesday.*

- **Which day did Tommy play soccer the least?** *Tuesday.*
- **How many minutes did Tommy play soccer on Monday and Tuesday?** *50 minutes.* Have your child write an addition equation to match: *30 + 20 = 50.*
- **How many minutes more did Tommy play soccer on Monday than on Tuesday?** *10 minutes.* Have your child write a subtraction equation to match: *30 – 20 = 10.*
- **Tommy played soccer 10 minutes longer on Monday than Tuesday, but the difference between the rows on the pictograph is just 1 soccer ball. Why?** *Sample answer: Each soccer ball stands for 10 minutes.*
- **How many minutes less did Tommy play soccer on Tuesday than on Wednesday?** *30 minutes.* Have your child write a subtraction equation to match: 50 – 20 = 30.

Even if your child finds the answer to the last question visually, have him write the matching subtraction equation anyway. This solidifies his understanding of how to use subtraction to compare and also prepares him to solve comparison problems with greater numbers.

Activity: Interpret a Bar Graph with an Increment of 10

Tommy liked seeing how much time he spent playing soccer, so he decided to keep recording his minutes for the rest of the week. This time, he made a bar graph. Read your child the directions at the bottom of workbook page 13.2A.

What number did Tommy count by when he wrote the numbers on the horizontal axis? *10.* **Why do you think he did that?** *Sample answer: It would take a long time to write all the numbers to 60!*

Which bar shows how long he played soccer on Thursday? *Child points to bar for Thursday.* Show your child how to point to the end of the bar and then slide his finger down to find the corresponding number of minutes.

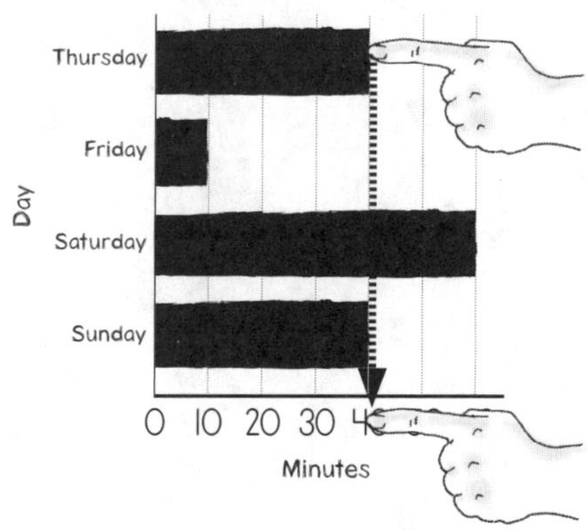

How many minutes did Tommy play soccer on Thursday? *40.* Have your child write 40 in the corresponding spot on the chart. Then have him read the bar graph to complete the rest of the chart.

Day	Minutes
Thursday	40
Friday	10
Saturday	60
Sunday	40

Briefly discuss the bar graph and matching chart with these questions.

- **Which day did Tommy play soccer the most?** *Saturday.*
- **Which day did Tommy play soccer the least?** *Friday.*
- **Which two days did Tommy play soccer the same amount of time?** *Thursday and Sunday.* Point out that the bars for these two days are the same length.
- **How many minutes did Tommy play soccer on Thursday and Friday?** *50 minutes.* Have your child write an addition equation to match: *40 + 10 = 50.*
- **How many minutes more did Tommy play soccer on Thursday than Friday?** *30 minutes.* Have your child write a subtraction equation to match: *40 −10 = 30.*
- **How many minutes less did Tommy play soccer on Friday than on Saturday?** *50 minutes.* Have your child write a subtraction equation to match: *60 − 10 = 50.*

Workbook: Review

Have your child complete workbook page 13.2B.

Lesson 13.3
Make and Interpret Line Graphs

	Purpose	Materials
Warm-up	• Count quarters by 25s • Practice memory work • Review subtraction word problems	• Coins
Activities	• Interpret a line graph • Draw a line graph	• Workbook page 13.3A
Workbook	• Review previously-learned material	• Workbook page 13.3B

Children often find line graphs confusing, so you'll show your child an example of a line graph before helping her create one. Don't worry if she has trouble at first grasping the idea that a dot can represent a measurement. You'll discuss line graphs more in Lesson 13.4, and she will see more examples of line graphs over the course of the year in her review workbook pages.

Warm-up: Counting, Memory Work, and Review

- Place 7 quarters on the table. Have your child count by 25s to find their value. **What's the value of the coins?** *175¢, or 1 dollar and 75 cents.*
- **What do we call the result when we add numbers together?** *The sum.* **What do we call the result when we subtract a number from another number?** *The difference.*
- Have your child write a matching equation for each of the following word problems and solve. Model the problems with play money as needed.
  - **You have $14, and I have $8. How much more money do you have than me?** *14 − 8 = 6. $6.*
  - **I have $8. You have $3 more than me. How much money do you have?** *8 + 3 = 11. $11.*
  - **You have $9. I have $6 less than you. How much money do I have?** *9 − 6 = 3. $3.*

Activity: Interpret a Line Graph

You have learned about bar graphs and pictographs. Today, you'll learn about line graphs. Show your child workbook page 13.3A and read the directions at the top aloud. Briefly discuss your child's experiences with growing plants from seed. Have your child identify the graph's title, horizontal axis and label, and vertical axis and label.

Line graphs are made from dots and lines. Each dot stands for one measurement, and the lines connect the dots.

Here's how to find how tall the bean plant was on Day 1. First, I find Day 1 on the horizontal axis. Point to 1 on the horizontal axis. **Then, I slide my finger up to the dot for Day 1.** Point to the dot for Day 1. **Last, I slide my finger to the left to find how tall the plant was on Day 1.** Slide your finger to the left until it touches the vertical axis. **The plant was 2 inches tall on Day 1.**

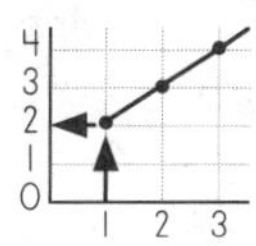

Day	Height (inches)
1	2

Use your fingers to show your child approximately how tall 2 inches is. Then, have your child write 2 in the corresponding spot on the chart.

Showing your child the approximate height helps her understand concretely what the graph means. She will learn more about measuring length in Unit 9.

Have her slide her fingers along the graph in the same way to complete the rest of the chart.

Day	Height (inches)
1	2
2	3
3	4
4	5
5	5
6	7

Second-graders usually find the idea of a "Day 0" very confusing, so this day is left off the chart and graph. If your child would like to include it, draw a dot at the bottom left corner of the graph to show that the plant was 0 inches tall on Day 0 (the day before it sprouted).

Activity: Make a Line Graph

Show your child the bottom part of workbook page 13.3A and read the directions. **To make a line graph, first we draw dots to match the information. Then we connect the dots with straight lines.** Point to the top row of the chart. **How tall was the plant on day 1?** *1 inch.*

Here's how we find where to draw the dot for this measurement. I put one finger on Day 1 and another finger on 1 inch. Point to each of these spots on the horizontal and vertical axes. **Then, I slide my fingers along the lines to the place where the two lines cross.** Show your child how to do this, and draw a dot.

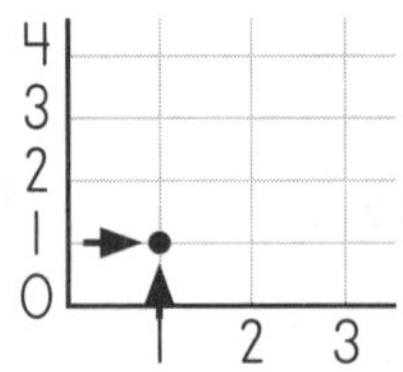

Help your child use this method to graph a point for each measurement on the chart. Then, have her connect the points with straight lines.

Day	Height (inches)
1	1
2	2
3	3
4	5
5	7
6	7

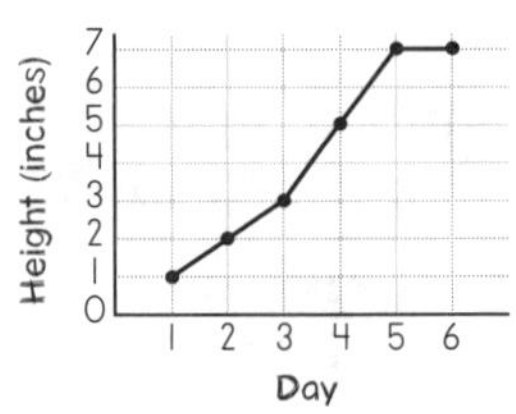

Your child can draw the lines freehand or with a ruler. It's fine if her lines are a little crooked.

Whose plant was taller on day 6, Sofia's or Alejandro's? *They were both the same height.*

Workbook: Review

Have your child complete workbook page 13.3B.

Lesson 13.4
Compare and Contrast Different Kinds of Graphs

	Purpose	Materials
Warm-up	• Count by 1s, 2s, and 5s on the number line • Practice memory work • Review expanded form	• Blank Number Line (Blackline Master 3)
Activities	• Review pictographs, bar graphs, and line graphs • Compare and contrast different kinds of graphs • Identify change on different kinds of graphs	• Workbook page 13.4A
Workbook	• Review previously-learned material	• Workbook page 13.4B

Warm-up: Counting, Memory Work, and Review

- Label the Blank Number Line with 180, 190, and 200. Have your child count from 180 to 200 by 1s, then 2s, and then 5s. Have him point to each corresponding tick mark as he counts.
- **How many tens equal 1 hundred?** *10.*
- Have your child tell the expanded form of the following numbers.
  - 74. *70 + 4.*
  - 39. *30 + 9.*
  - 61. *60 + 1.*
  - 175. *100 + 70 + 5.*
  - 102. *100 + 2.*

Activity: Make Different Graphs for the Same Data

You have learned how to make and interpret bar graphs, pictographs, and line graphs. Today, you'll make all 3 kinds of graphs. We'll also talk about what they have in common and how they are different from each other.

Show your child workbook page 13.4A and read aloud the directions at the top. Have your child draw a pictograph, bar graph, and line graph on the worksheet to match the chart. Encourage him to work independently, but help as needed.

This activity provides an informal assessment of your child's graphing skills.

Activity: Compare and Contrast Different Kinds of Graphs

Discuss the similarities and differences between the graphs with the following questions.

- **What do all 3 graphs have in common?** *Possible answers: They all show the same information. They all show that the bakery sold the most pies during week 4, and the fewest pies during week 1. They all have the same title. They all measure in 10s.*
- **How are the 3 graphs different from each other?** *Possible answers: They use pictures, bars, and lines. The pictograph shows the information horizontally, but the bar graph and line graph show the information vertically.*

- **Is there one kind of graph that you like best? If so, why?** *Answers will vary.*

Activity: Identify Change on Different Kinds of Graphs

Did the bakery sell more pies during week 1 or week 2? *Week 2.* **How many more?** *20 pies.* Have your child write a subtraction problem to match: *30 – 10 = 20.*

> The following discussion is meant as an introduction to identifying change on graphs. It's fine if your child doesn't fully grasp the concept.

Look at each graph with your child and discuss how it shows the difference between the sales for week 1 and the sales for week 2.

- **How does the pictograph show the difference between week 1 and week 2?** *Sample answer: Week 2 has 2 more circles than week 1. Each circle equals 10 pies, so that's 20 pies.*
- **How does the bar graph show the difference between week 1 and week 2?** *Sample answer: The bar for week 2 is taller than the bar for week 1.*
- **How does the line graph show the difference between week 1 and week 2?** *Sample answer: The line between Week 1 and Week 2 goes up 20.*

All of the graphs show that sales increased and went up from week 1 to week 2.

Did the bakery sell more pies during week 2 or week 3? *Week 2.* **How many more?** *10 pies.* Have your child write a subtraction problem to match: *30 – 20 = 10.*

Again, look at each graph and discuss how each graph shows the difference between the sales for the two weeks.

Did the bakery sell more pies during week 3 or week 4? *Week 4.* **How many more?** *50 pies!* Have your child write a subtraction problem to match: *70 – 20 = 50.*

> If you live in the U.S., point out that pie sales might increase during the fourth week of November as families prepare to celebrate Thanksgiving.

Workbook: Review

Have your child complete workbook page 13.4B.

Lesson 13.5
Enrichment and Review (Optional)

	Purpose	Materials
Warm-up	• Count from 100 to 200 by 1s, 2s, 5s, or 10s • Review memory work • Review your child's favorite or most challenging activities from Week 13	• Varies, depending on the activities you choose
Picture Book	• Introduce a variety of different types of graphs	• *The Great Graph Contest,* by Loreen Leedy
Enrichment Activity	• Interpret a weather graph	• Graph of your town's average monthly rainfall, either printed or online

To find a graph of your town's average monthly precipitation, try searching online for "average monthly rainfall graph" along with the name of your town. You may find a bar graph or line graph (or both!) Depending on your area's climate and your child's interests, you might also want to look for a graph of the average monthly high and low temperatures, or the average monthly snowfall.

Warm-up: Counting, Memory Work, and Review

- Have your child count from 100 to 200 by 1s, 2s, 5s, or 10s. (Choose whichever counting sequence your child needs to practice the most.)
- Quiz your child on the memory work through Week 12. See page 523 for the full list.
- If you have time, repeat one or two of the activities from this week's lessons. Choose activities your child especially enjoyed or found challenging.

Math Picture Book: *The Great Graph Contest*

Read *The Great Graph Contest,* by Loreen Leedy. As you read, discuss the different kinds of graphs that the characters create.

Enrichment Activity: Interpret a Rainfall Graph

Look at a graph of the average monthly rainfall for your area. Discuss the title and labels on each axis. Then, use questions like the following to discuss and interpret the graph.

- **How much rain do we get on average in January? February?** (Continue through all of the months.)
- **Which month is usually the wettest?**
- **Which month is usually the driest?**
- **Do we get about the same amount of rain each month, or does it change a lot?**

Week 13 Answer Key

13.1A

Riley helped her parents wrap gifts. She made a pictograph of how many gifts she wrapped. Use the pictograph to complete the chart.

Day	Monday	Tuesday	Wednesday
Number of Gifts	6	4	10

Use the pictograph and chart to complete.

How many different gifts did she wrap on Monday and Tuesday?

6 + 4 = 10

10 gifts

How many more gifts did she wrap on Monday than Tuesday?

6 − 4 = 2

2 gifts

How many fewer gifts did she wrap on Tuesday than Wednesday?

10 − 4 = 6

6 gifts

How many gifts did she wrap in all? Write your own equation.

6 + 4 + 10 = 20

20 gifts

13.1B

Color the subtraction facts that equal the number in the star.

7	8	9
14 - 7 (colored)	12 - 3	13 - 4 (colored)
16 - 9 (colored)	14 - 6 (colored)	14 - 6
12 - 5 (colored)	13 - 4	18 - 9 (colored)
15 - 7	15 - 7 (colored)	15 - 6 (colored)

Write the value of each set of base-ten blocks.

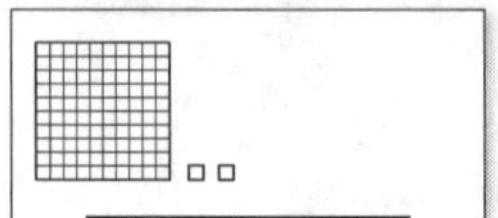

100s	10s	1s
1	0	2

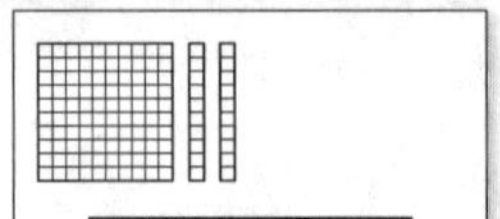

100s	10s	1s
1	2	0

Copy the shape.

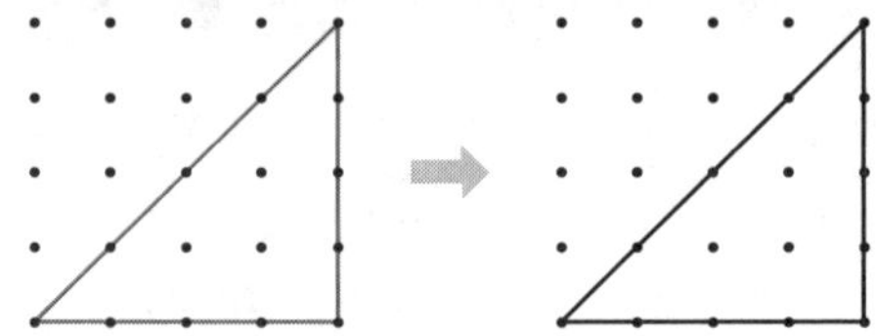

13.2A

Tommy made a pictograph about how much time he spent playing soccer each day. Use the pictograph to complete the chart.

Day	Minutes
Monday	30
Tuesday	20
Wednesday	50

Then, Tommy also made a bar graph about how much time he spent playing soccer the rest of the week. Use the bar graph to complete the chart.

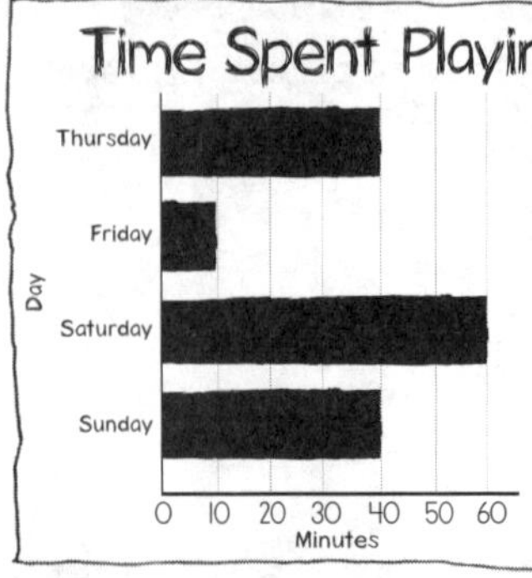

Day	Minutes
Thursday	40
Friday	10
Saturday	60
Sunday	40

13.2B

Complete.

11 - 3 = 8	12 - 8 = 4	14 - 5 = 9
12 - 7 = 5	13 - 9 = 4	12 - 6 = 6
15 - 9 = 6	12 - 3 = 9	14 - 9 = 5
14 - 8 = 6	13 - 5 = 8	16 - 7 = 9

Complete.

$80

$40

Match.

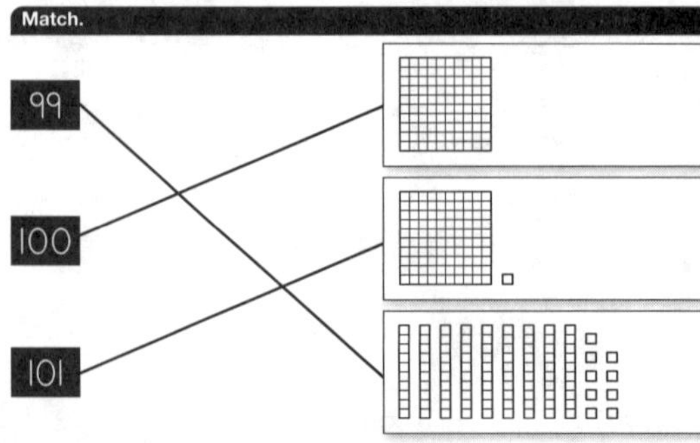

Week 13 Answer Key

13.3A

Alejandro planted a bean seed. He made a line graph to show how his plant grew. Use his line graph to complete the chart.

Day	Height (inches)
1	2
2	3
3	4
4	5
5	5
6	7

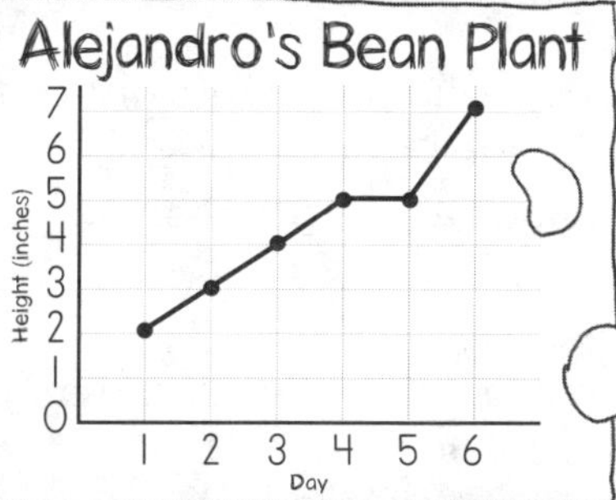

Sofia planted a bean seed, too. Once it sprouted, she measured its height every day. Use her chart to complete the line graph.

Day	Height (inches)
1	1
2	2
3	3
4	5
5	7
6	7

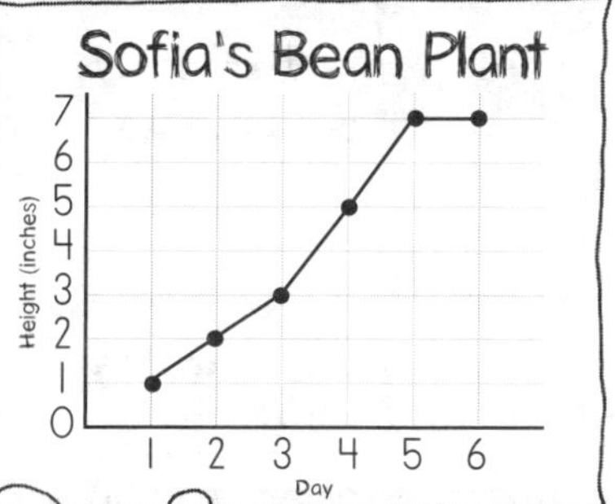

13.3B

Color the subtraction facts that equal the number in the star.

9	8	7
11 - 2	16 - 9	**13 - 6**
15 - 7	**12 - 4**	**15 - 8**
17 - 8	**14 - 6**	**16 - 9**
14 - 5	**13 - 5**	11 - 5

Complete the missing numbers in the sequences.

Count by 10s: 130, 140, 150, 160, 170, 180

Count by 20s: 80, 100, 120, 140, 160, 180

Count by 25s: 100, 125, 150, 175, 200, 225

13.4A

James helps his parents at their bakery. He made a chart of how many pies the bakery sold each week in November. Use the chart to complete the graphs.

November Pie Sales

Week	Pies Sold
1	10
2	30
3	20
4	70

November Pie Sales Pictograph

Week 1	◎
Week 2	◎◎◎
Week 3	◎◎
Week 4	◎◎◎◎◎◎◎

◎ = 10 pies

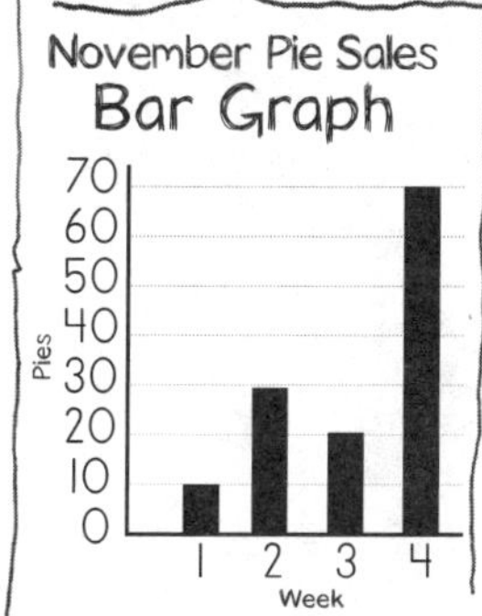

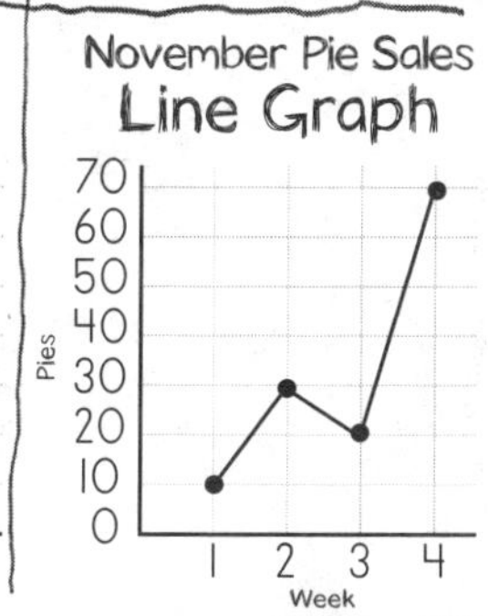

13.4B

Complete.

17 - 9 = 8   14 - 7 = 7   12 - 9 = 3

11 - 5 = 6   15 - 8 = 7   12 - 6 = 6

13 - 7 = 6   11 - 2 = 9   13 - 8 = 5

8 + 4 = 12   6 + 7 = 13   5 + 9 = 14

Complete the circles with <, >, or =.

48 < 58	148 < 158	148 = 148
58 > 48	158 > 148	158 = 158

Count by 10s to connect the dots in order.

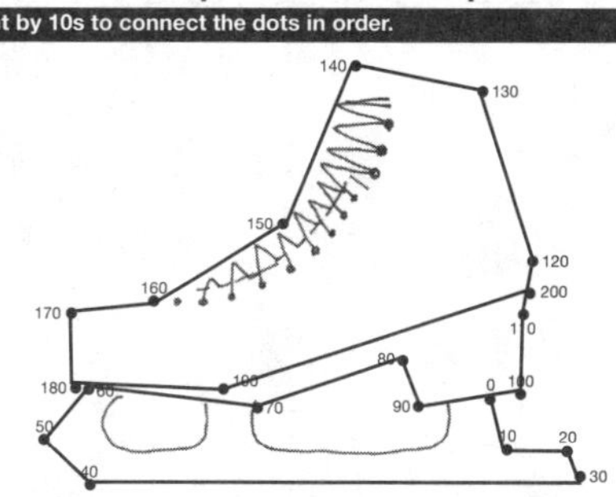

Unit 5 Checkpoint

What to Expect at the End of Unit 5

By the end of Unit 5, most children will be able to do the following:

- Create bar graphs, pictographs, or line graphs. Many children will still need help placing the dots correctly on line graphs.
- Read bar graphs, pictographs, and line graphs with increments of 1 or 10. Many children will need to be reminded to look at the key for pictographs.
- Use addition and subtraction to draw conclusions about graphs.

Is Your Child Ready to Move on?

In Unit 6, your child will learn to add two-digit numbers mentally. Before moving on to Unit 6, your child should have already mastered the following skills:

- Understand place value in numbers to 100 and that you can trade 10 ones for 1 ten, or 10 tens for 1 hundred.
- Solve simple mental addition problems with two-digit numbers (such as 42 + 3 or 30 + 20).
- Find answers to most of the addition facts with sums to 20 mentally and in less than 3 seconds.

What to Do If Your Child Needs More Practice

If your child is having trouble with any of the above skills, spend a few days practicing the corresponding review activities below before moving on to Unit 6.

Activities for understanding place value and trading in numbers to 100

- Make Designs with Base-Ten Blocks (Lesson 3.1)
- Race to 100 (Lesson 3.2)

Activities for solving simple mental addition problems

- Mental Math Magic with Addition (Lesson 3.3)

Activities for practicing addition facts to 20

- Addition Climb and Slide (Lesson 1.1)
- Addition Crash (+9 Version) (Lesson 4.1)
- Addition Crash (+8 Version) (Lesson 4.3)
- Addition Bingo (+7 Version) (Lesson 5.1)
- Addition Bingo (+6 Version) (Lesson 5.3)

If you practice the addition facts for several days and find that your child does not have them fully mastered, move on to Unit 6 anyway. Children vary in how long it takes them to develop speed and fluency with the addition facts, and your child will continue to practice them in the context of mental math in Unit 6.

Unit 6
Mental Addition to 100

Overview

In Unit 2, your child reviewed and practiced the single-digit addition facts. In this unit, he'll build on the addition facts and his place-value knowledge to solve mental addition problems. First, he'll work on adding one-digit numbers to two-digit numbers. Then, he'll learn to add two-digit numbers to two-digit numbers.

$37 + 4 = 41 \qquad 39 + 23 = 62$

Your child will learn to solve addition problems like these in his head.

The overall goal of this unit is for children to move from using base-ten blocks to finding the sums completely mentally. Some children will make this transition quickly, while others will need to use the blocks for nearly every problem in the unit. As always, feel free to adjust your pace to your child, and use the base-ten blocks to help your child make sense of these problems.

Week 14	Mental Addition, Part 1
Week 15	Mental Addition, Part 2

What Your Child Will Learn

In this unit your child will learn to:

- Mentally add one- or two-digit numbers to two-digit numbers (with sums less than 100)

Recommended Math Picture Books (Optional)

These picture books are scheduled in the optional Enrichment and Review lessons at the end of each week.

- *Night Noises,* written by Mem Fox and illustrated by Terry Denton. HMH Books for Young Readers, 1989.
- *A Fair Bear Share,* written by Stuart J. Murphy and illustrated by John Speirs. HarperCollins, 1998.

Week 14
Mental Addition, Part 1

Overview

Your child will learn how to add one-digit numbers to two-digit numbers in his head. You'll use base-ten blocks to help him master this foundational mental math skill.

Lesson 14.1	Use Related Addition Facts to Add One-Digit Numbers
Lesson 14.2	Complete a 10 to Add One-Digit Numbers
Lesson 14.3	Practice Adding One-Digit Numbers to Two-Digit Numbers
Lesson 14.4	Add One-Digit Numbers to Two-Digit Numbers without Base-Ten Blocks
Lesson 14.5	Enrichment and Review (Optional)

Teaching Math with Confidence: What's the Point of Mental Math?

In Unit 3, your child reviewed mental math strategies for simple problems like 25 + 3 or 36 + 40. In this unit, he'll learn how to solve more difficult problems like 48 + 5 or 37 + 56. Mental math is often useful in real life, but the main goal of this unit is to help your child develop stronger number sense. As he breaks numbers apart and puts them together again, he'll develop a deeper understanding of place value and the relationships between numbers.

This week, you'll teach your child two different strategies for adding a one-digit number to a two-digit number. Your child might prefer one strategy over the other, or he may even come up with his own strategy to solve these problems. Model the strategies presented in the lesson to demonstrate these options, but allow him to use any efficient and accurate strategy that makes sense to him—as long he doesn't count one by one to find the answers.

Also, keep in mind that the goal of mental math isn't to develop a memory champion. If your child has trouble keeping track of the numbers in his head, it's fine for him to write down any in-between steps in his solving process. But, don't show him how to write the numbers vertically and solve the problems with the traditional written process. If he's already learned to add this way, make sure to teach him the mental math skills in this unit as well.

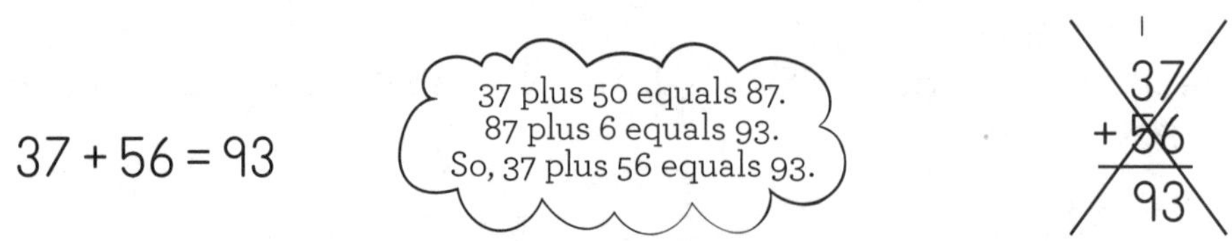

Focus on mental math strategies in this unit, not the written process for vertical addition.

Skipping right to the standard algorithm short-circuits all the number sense growth that mental math provides. It also can develop the bad habit of mindlessly following steps in math without attempting to understand what they mean. Once your child has developed strong mental math skills, he'll be well-prepared to learn how to carry out the steps in the written process and also understand why the steps work. You'll teach him how to use this method to add in Unit 10.

Extra Materials Needed for Week 14

- Paper clip
- For optional Enrichment and Review Lesson:
    - *Night Noises*, written by Mem Fox and illustrated by Terry Denton

Lesson 14.1
Use Related Addition Facts to Add One-Digit Numbers

	Purpose	Materials
Warm-up	• Count money • Practice memory work • Review mental addition	• Play money • Base-ten blocks, optional
Activities	• Use related addition facts to add one-digit numbers to two-digit numbers	• Base-ten blocks • Double ten-frames (Blackline Master 1) • Workbook page 14.1A • Die
Workbook	• Review previously-learned material	• Workbook page 14.1B

Warm-up: Counting, Memory Work, and Review

- Place 3 twenty-dollar bills, 3 five-dollar bills, and 6 one-dollar bills on the table. **How much is this money worth?** *$81.*
- **How many hours are in a day?** *24.* **How many minutes are in an hour?** *60.* **How many seconds are in a minute?** *60.*
- Write the following problems on paper and have your child solve them mentally. Allow her to use base-ten blocks as needed.
  - × 43 + 4 = *47*
  - × 47 + 3 = *50*
  - × 50 + 28 = *78*
  - × 78 + 2 = *80*
  - × 80 + 20 = *100*

Activity: Use Related Addition Facts to Add One-Digit Numbers to Two-Digit Numbers

You already know how to solve mental addition problems like 42 + 3 or 37 + 20. In this unit, you'll learn how to solve more difficult addition problems in your head.

This week, we'll focus on mentally adding one-digit numbers to two-digit numbers. You'll learn two different strategies for these problems, and you can use whichever strategy works best for you.

See the Week 14 **Teaching Math with Confidence** for more on using multiple strategies to solve mental math problems.

Today, you'll learn how to use related addition facts to add one-digit numbers to two-digit numbers. Show your child the first problem at the top of workbook page 14.1A (37 + 4). Model the problem with base-ten blocks and the ten-frames as shown.

37 + 4 = ☐

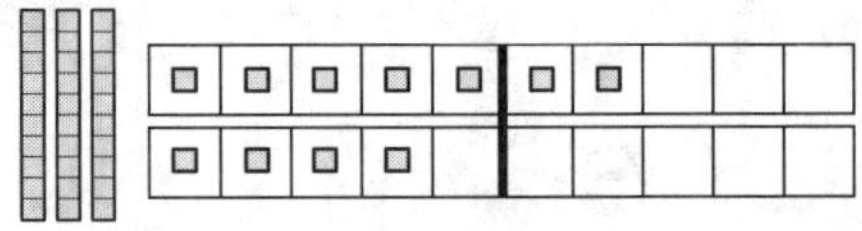

Before we add, let's split 37 into tens and ones. That will make it easier to use a related addition fact to find the sum. What's the expanded form of 37? *30 plus 7.* Draw part-total lines below 37 to split it into 30 and 7.

37 + 4 = ☐

30 7

Now, you can use the related addition fact to add the ones. Point to the unit blocks on the ten-frames. **What's 7 plus 4?** *11.*

What's 30 plus 11? *41.* **So, 37 plus 4 equals 41.** Have your child complete the written equation: *37 + 4 = 41.*

37 + 4 = 41

30 7

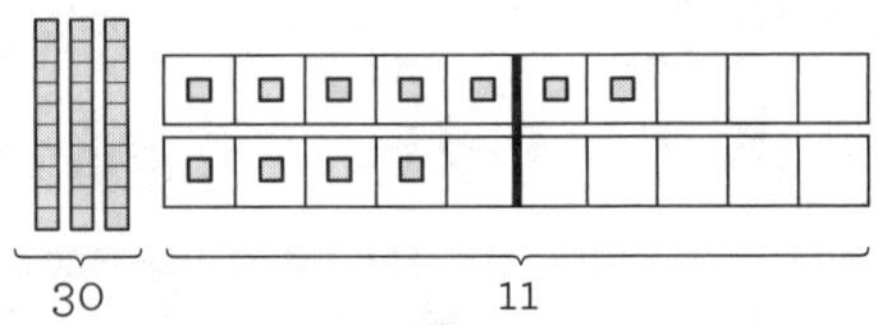

Your child does not need to trade 10 units for 1 rod, but she may if she'd like to verify the blocks' value.

Have your child solve the rest of the problems at the top of workbook page 14.1A in the same way.

59 + 6 = 65

50 9

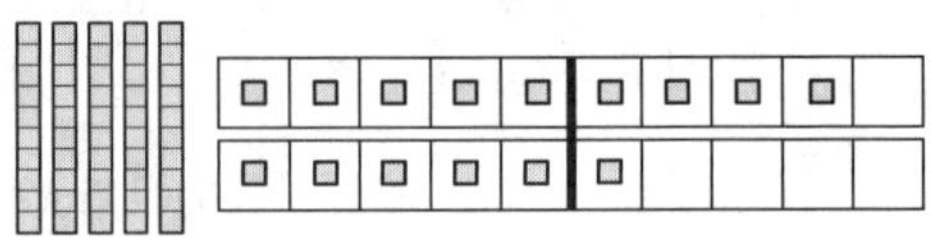

48 + 2 = 50

40 8

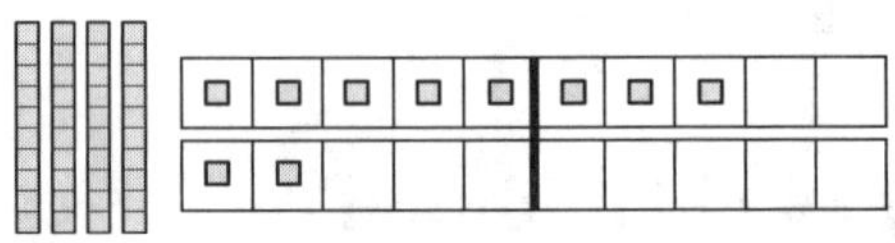

47 + 5 = 52

40 7

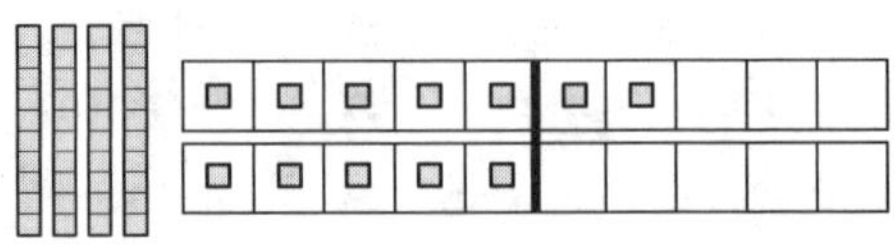

Activity: Play Roll and Add

Play Roll and Add.

If your child is still beginning to understand how to add these numbers, model every problem with base-ten blocks. If your child is ready for more challenge, encourage her to find the sums in the game mentally. She will practice mental addition more throughout Week 14.

Roll and Add

Materials: Die; Roll and Add game board from workbook page 14.1

Object of the Game: Win the most points.

Roll and Add has 5 rounds. In each round, both players roll the die, write the corresponding number in the blank on the scorecard, and find the sum of the printed number and written number. Whoever has the greater sum wins a point. If the sums are equal, both players win a point.

For example, if Player 1 rolls a 4 and Player 2 rolls a 2 in the first round:

Player 1	Player 2
29 + [4] = [33]	29 + [2] = [31]

Player 1 wins the point, since 33 is greater than 31.

Play until you have completed the entire scorecard. Whoever has won more points wins the game.

Workbook: Review

Have your child complete workbook page 14.1B.

Lesson 14.2
Complete a 10 to Add One-Digit Numbers

	Purpose	Materials
Warm-up	• Count coins • Practice memory work • Review identifying missing addends	• Coins
Activities	• Add one-digit numbers to two-digit numbers by completing a 10	• Base-ten blocks • Double ten-frames (Blackline Master 1) • Workbook page 14.2A • Paper clip
Workbook	• Review previously-learned material	• Workbook page 14.2B

Warm-up: Counting, Memory Work, and Review

- Place 2 quarters, 3 dimes, and 3 nickels on the table. **How much are these coins worth?** *95¢.*
- **How many hours are in a day?** *24.* **How many minutes are in an hour?** *60.* **How many seconds are in a minute?** *60.*
- Secretly write each of the following equations on a piece of paper and hide the addend indicated with a slip of paper. Have your child use his "x-ray vision" to identify the hidden numbers.

65 + [5] = 70   59 + [1] = 60   87 + [3] = 90

94 + [6] = 100   76 + [4] = 80

Activity: Complete a 10 to Add One-Digit Numbers

In the last lesson, you used related addition facts to mentally add one-digit numbers to two-digit numbers. Today, you'll learn how to complete a 10 to solve these problems, just like you did with the +9 and +8 facts in Unit 2.

Show your child the first problem at the top of workbook page 14.2A (39 + 6). Model the problem with base-ten blocks and the double-ten frames as shown.

39 + 6 = [ ]

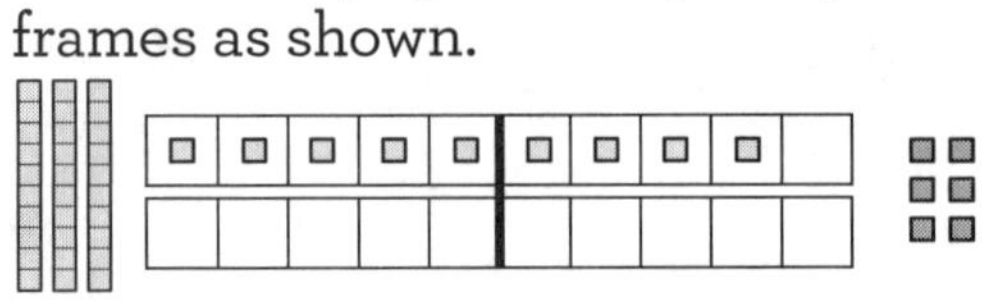

To find 39 plus 6, I add in two steps. First, I add 1 block to complete the group of 10. Add 1 unit to the top ten-frame. **39 plus 1 equals 40.**

39 + 6 = [ ]

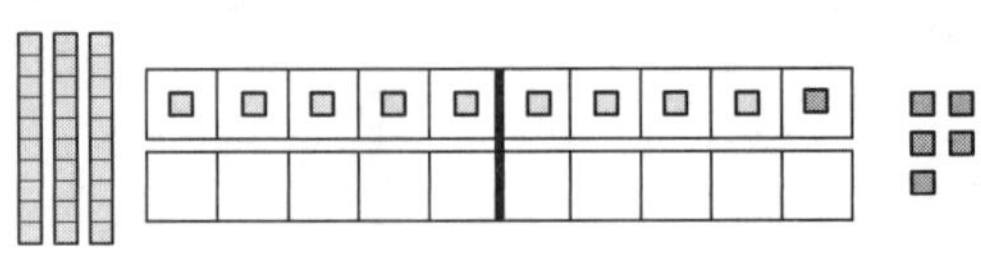

Then, I add the other 5 blocks. Place the remaining 5 units on the bottom-ten frame. **40 plus 5 equals 45**. Have your child complete the equation: 39 + 6 = 45.

39 + 6 = [45]

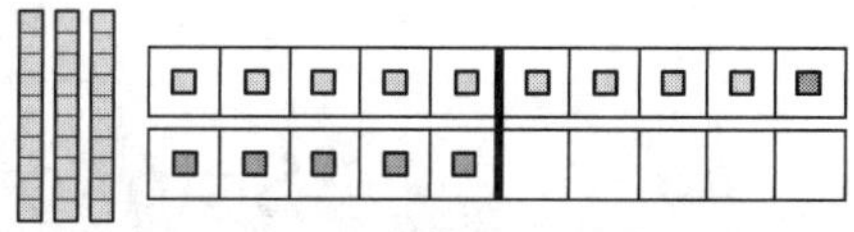

Have your child use this method to solve the rest of the problems on the top of workbook page 14.2A.

48 + 7 = [55]

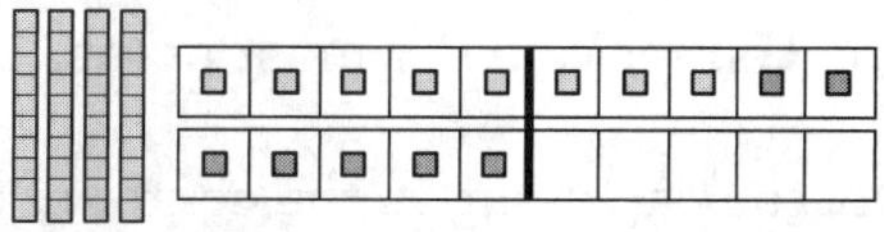

48 plus 2 equals 50. 50 plus 5 equals 55.

76 + 5 = [81]

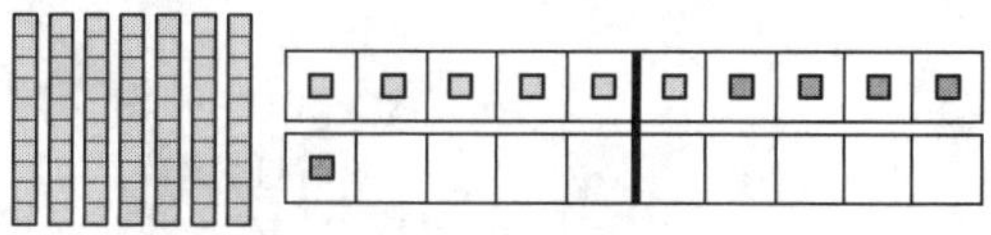

76 plus 4 equals 80. 80 plus 1 equals 81.

87 + 4 = [91]

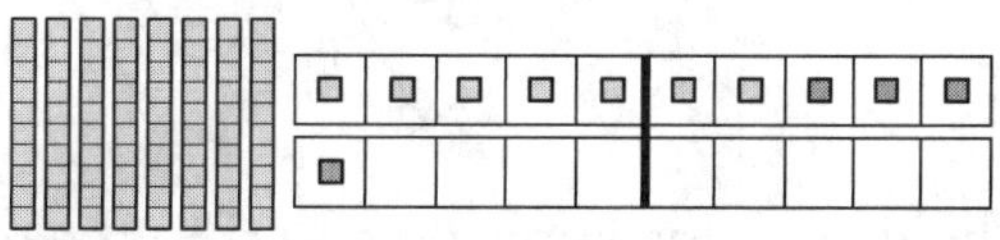

87 plus 3 equals 90. 90 plus 1 equals 91.

> If your child has trouble keeping track of the numbers in his head, draw part-total lines below the one-digit number to show how you split it.
>
> 48 + 7 = 55
>
> 2 5

Which strategy do you like better for these problems: completing the 10 or using related addition facts? *Answers will vary.* **Either way is fine!**

> There's no right answer to this question. Different strategies "click" better for different children, and your child can use whichever strategy makes more sense to him.

Activity: Play Spin to Win

Play Spin to Win. Model the problems with base-ten blocks as needed.

Spin to Win

Materials: Paper clip; Spin to Win game board from workbook page 14.2A

Object of the Game: Win the most points.

Place one end of the paper clip in the center of the top spinner on the game board. Place the point of a pencil through the paper clip so that it touches the very center of the circle.

On your turn, hold the pencil upright and spin the paper clip so that it spins freely around the circle. Write the number it lands on in the first box in the first blank equation. Then, move the paper clip and pencil to the bottom spinner. Spin again, and write this number in the next box in the blank equation. Add to find the sum of the two spins.

For example, if you spin 57 on the top spinner and 7 on the bottom spinner:

57 + 7 = 64

Then, have the other player spin twice, write the value of each spin in the next blank equation, and find the sum. Whoever has the greater sum wins a point.

Continue until you have filled in all the blank equations. Whoever has won more points wins the game.

Workbook: Review

Have your child complete workbook page 14.2B.

Lesson 14.3
Practice Adding One-Digit Numbers to Two-Digit Numbers

	Purpose	Materials
Warm-up	• Count backward by 5s • Practice memory work • Review place-value vocabulary	• None
Activities	• Practice adding 1-digit numbers to 2-digit numbers	• Playing cards • Base-ten blocks, optional • Workbook page 14.3A
Workbook	• Practice adding 1-digit numbers to 2-digit numbers	• Workbook pages 14.3A and 14.3B

Warm-up: Counting, Memory Work, and Review

- Have your child count backward by 5s from the following numbers. Prompt her as needed, and stop her after she reaches the last number listed.
    - × **Count backward by 5s from 135:** *135, 130, 125, 120, 115.*
    - × **Count backward by 5s from 200:** *200, 195, 190, 185, 180.*
    - × **Count backward by 5s from 110:** *110, 105, 100, 95, 90.*

  If your child has trouble, have her point to each number on the 200 Chart.

- **How many hours are in a day?** *24.* **How many minutes are in an hour?** *60.* **How many seconds are in a minute?** *60.*
- Write the number 146 on a piece of paper. **How many digits does this number have?** *3.* **Which digit is in the ones-place?** *6.* **The tens-place?** *4.* **The hundreds-place?** *1.*

Activity: Prepare to Play Two-Digit Plus One-Digit War

This week, you have learned how to add one-digit numbers to two-digit numbers in your head. Today, we'll practice more with a game called Two-Digit Plus One-Digit War.

In this game, you use 3 cards to make a two-digit number and a one-digit number. Then, you find the sum of your two numbers. Whoever has the greater sum wins all the cards.

Before we play, we'll first investigate how to arrange the cards to make the greatest sum possible. Show your child workbook page 14.3A, and place a 2, 5, and 8 from a deck of playing cards on the table. (Any suit is fine.)

Here's one way to arrange the cards. Arrange the cards as shown below. **What's the sum?** *60.* Have your child write "52 + 8 = 60" in the first blank equation at the top of workbook page 14.3A.

5 2 + 8 = 6 0

There are 5 more ways to arrange the cards. I wonder how many of them you can find! Have your child find as many different ways as she can. For each arrangement, have her write the matching equations on the workbook page and find the sum.

Below are all possible ways to arrange the cards. If your child misses any, demonstrate the arrangement and have her write the matching equation.

52 + 8 = 60	25 + 8 = 33
82 + 5 = 87	28 + 5 = 33
85 + 2 = 87	58 + 2 = 60

Even though there are 6 equations, there are only 3 different sums! Discuss the equations with the following questions:

- **Which equations have the greatest possible sum?** *82 + 5 and 85 + 2.*
- **Which equations have the least possible sum?** *28 + 5 and 25 + 8.*
- **82 plus 5 and 85 plus 2 both have the same sum, even though the digits are arranged in different ways. Why?** *Sample answer: The 2 and 5 are both in the ones-place. So, they add up to 7 ones, even if you switch them.*
- **What do you think is the best strategy for arranging your cards in Two-Digit Plus One-Digit War?** *Sample answer: Put the greatest number in the tens-place.*

Some children will grasp this strategy immediately, but others will need to actually play the game before they'll be able to articulate it. If your child has trouble with this final question, try discussing it again after you play the game.

Activity: Play Two-Digit Plus One-Digit War

Play Two-Digit Plus One-Digit War. Encourage your child to find the sums mentally as she plays, but allow her to use base-ten blocks if needed.

Two-Digit Plus One-Digit War

Materials: Aces, 2s, 3s, 4s, 5s, 6s, 7s, 8s, and 9s from one deck of playing cards (36 cards total)

Object of the Game: Win the most cards by creating the greater sum.

Shuffle the cards and deal them face down in a pile. Each player flips over 3 cards from the top of the pile. Then, they use the cards to create a two-digit number and a one-digit number and find the sum of these numbers.

For example, if you turn over a 1, 4, 9, you can make 14 + 9, 19 + 4, 41 + 9, 49 + 1, 91 + 4, or 94 + 1. The best play is either 91 + 4 or 94 + 1, since these combinations create the greatest possible sum (95). Whoever has the greater sum wins all the cards.

If the sums are equal, leave the cards face-up on the table and have both players play again. Whoever creates the greater sum in the next round wins all the face-up cards.

Play until the piles run out. Whoever has won more cards wins the game.

Workbook: Add One-Digit Numbers to Two-Digit Numbers and Review

Have your child complete workbook pages 14.3A and 14.3B.

Lesson 14.4
Add One-Digit Numbers to Two-Digit Numbers without Base-Ten Blocks

	Purpose	Materials
Warm-up	• Count backward by 1s, 2s, and 5s on the number line • Practice memory work • Review more and less with numbers on the number line	• Blank Number Line (Blackline Master 3)
Activities	• Add one-digit numbers to two-digit numbers without base-ten blocks	• Base-ten blocks • Double ten-frames (Blackline Master 1) • Workbook page 14.4A
Workbook	• Add one-digit numbers to two-digit numbers	• Workbook pages 14.4A and 14.4B

Warm-up: Counting, Memory Work, and Review

- Label the Blank Number Line with 30, 40, 50. Have your child count backward from 50 to 30, by 1s, then 2s, and then 5s. Have him point to each corresponding tick mark as he counts.

  Leave the number line out for the review activity below.

- **How many hours are in a day?** *24.* **How many minutes are in an hour?** *60.* **How many seconds are in a minute?** *60.*
- Ask your child the following number line riddles:
  - Point to 32 on the labeled number line. **I'm thinking of a number that is 7 more than 32. What's my number?** *39.*

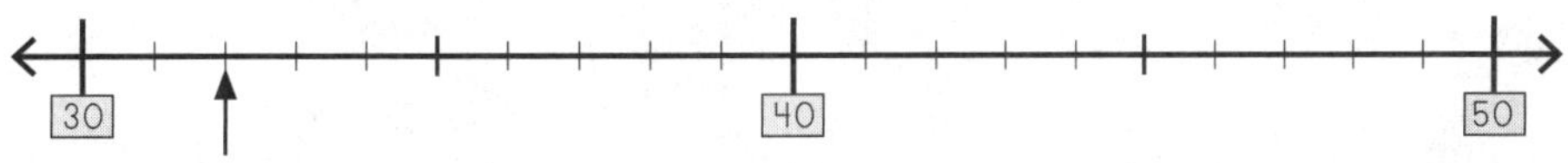

  - **I'm thinking of a number that is 5 less than 35. What's my number?** *30.*
  - **I'm thinking of a number that is 8 less than 48. What's my number?** *40.*
  - **I'm thinking of a number that is 1 less than 40. What's my number?** *39.*
  - **I'm thinking of a number that is 6 more than 39. What's my number?** *45.*

Activity: Add One-Digit Numbers to Two-Digit Numbers without Base-Ten Blocks

This week, you have used base-ten blocks to add one-digit numbers to two-digit numbers. Today, you'll try solving these problems in your head, without base-ten blocks.

Point to the first exercise on workbook page 14.4A (39 + 4). **Try solving this problem in your head. While you work, I'll model the problem with base-ten blocks. Once we finish, we'll compare our answers and make sure they match.**

Have your child solve the problem. While he works, secretly model the problem with base-ten blocks and the double ten-frames. Cover the blocks with a piece of paper.

39 + 4 = [43]

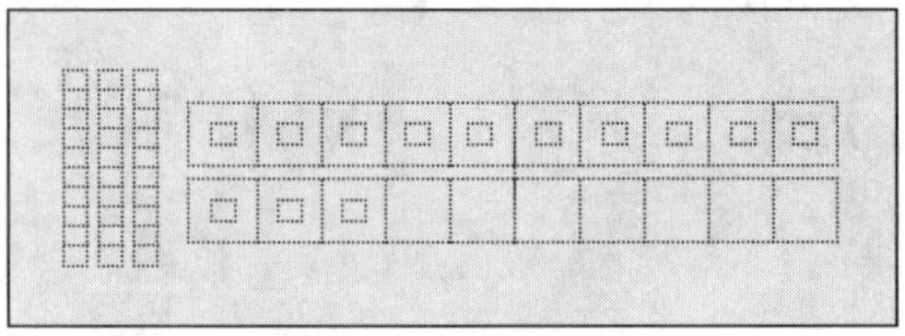

So, what's 39 + 4? *43*. Remove the cover from the blocks so your child can check whether his answer matches the blocks. If his answer does not match, have him use the blocks to find the correct sum.

Continue in the same way with the other 3 problems at the top of the page.

65 + 7= [72] 46 + 6 = [52] 78 + 9 = [87]

Activity: Play Two-Digit Plus One-Digit War

Play Two-Digit Plus One-Digit War. See Lesson 14.3 (page 230) for directions.

Workbook: Add One-Digit Numbers to Two-Digit Numbers and Review

Have your child complete workbook pages 14.4A and 14.4B. Encourage your child to solve the addition problems on workbook page 14.4A without using base-ten blocks, but allow him to use them if needed.

> This workbook page provides an informal assessment of how well your child can mentally add one-digit numbers to two-digit numbers. If your child has trouble solving these problems without base-ten blocks, spend another day or two playing Two-Digit Plus One-Digit War before moving on to Week 15.

Lesson 14.5
Enrichment and Review (Optional)

	Purpose	Materials
Warm-up	• Count from 100 to 200 by 1s, 2s, 5s, or 10s • Review memory work • Review your child's favorite or most challenging activities from Week 14	• Varies, depending on the activities you choose
Picture Book	• Use mental addition to find the number of guests at a family party	• *Night Noises,* written by Mem Fox and illustrated by Terry Denton • Base-ten blocks
Enrichment Activity	• Use mental addition to find the number of guests at a pretend party	• None

Warm-up: Counting, Memory Work, and Review

- Have your child count from 100 to 200 by 1s, 2s, 5s, or 10s. (Choose whichever counting sequence your child needs to practice the most.)
- Quiz your child on the memory work through Week 14. See page 523 for the full list.
- If you have time, repeat one or two of the activities from this week's lessons. Choose activities your child especially enjoyed or found challenging.

Math Picture Book: *Night Noises*

Read *Night Noises,* written by Mem Fox and illustrated by Terry Denton. After you read, write an addition equation to show how many people come to the birthday party in the book. Have your child model the addends with base-ten blocks and count the blocks to find their sum.

> This book previews adding two-digit numbers, which your child will learn in Week 15. Your child is not expected to be able to add these numbers mentally yet.

Enrichment Activity: Plan a Big Party

Pretend that you're planning a big party (like a wedding, milestone birthday, or other special occasion). Have your child make a list of 10-15 families that he would like to invite, along with the number of people in each family. Then, have him use mental addition to find the total number of people represented on the list.

Family	Number of People
Uncle Todd and Aunt Jill's family	6
The Walkers	4
The Nguyens	5

Week 14 Answer Key

14.1A

See the Instructor Guide for directions.

37 + 4 = 41	59 + 6 = 65
48 + 2 = 50	47 + 5 = 52

Roll and Add

Player 1	Player 2
29 + ☐ = ☐	29 + ☐ = ☐
38 + ☐ = ☐	38 + ☐ = ☐
47 + ☐ = ☐	47 + ☐ = ☐
56 + ☐ = ☐	56 + ☐ = ☐
79 + ☐ = ☐	79 + ☐ = ☐

14.1B

Tiana made a graph of the money she earned at the craft fair. Use the graph to complete the chart and answer the questions.

My Earnings

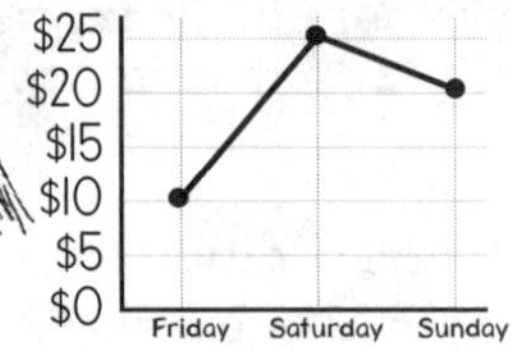

Day	Money
Friday	$ 10
Saturday	$ 25
Sunday	$ 20

Which day did she earn the most? Saturday

Which day did she earn the least? Friday

How much more did she earn on Saturday than Friday?

25 − 10 = 15

$ 15

How much money did Tiana earn in all? Write your own equation.

10 + 25 + 20 = 55

$ 55

Complete.

$ 98

14.2A

See the Instructor Guide for directions.

39 + 6 = 45	48 + 7 = 55
76 + 5 = 81	87 + 4 = 91

SPIN TO WIN!

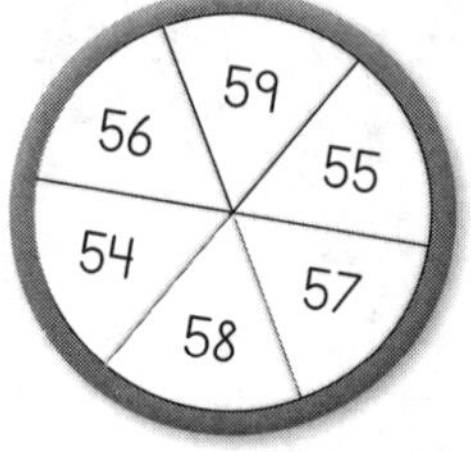

☐ + ☐ = ☐
☐ + ☐ = ☐
☐ + ☐ = ☐
☐ + ☐ = ☐
☐ + ☐ = ☐
☐ + ☐ = ☐
☐ + ☐ = ☐
☐ + ☐ = ☐
☐ + ☐ = ☐
☐ + ☐ = ☐

14.2B

Complete the missing numbers in the sequences.

Count by 2s: 96, 98, 100, 102, 104

Count by 10s: 90, 100, 110, 120, 130

Count by 5s: 90, 95, 100, 105, 110

Solve. For the second problem, color the picture to match.

You have 15 stickers.
You use 7.
How many do you have left?

15 − 7 = 8

8 stickers

You have 16 stickers.
9 are green, and the rest are blue.
How many are blue?

16 − 9 = 7

7 stickers

Week 14 Answer Key

14.3A

See the Instructor Guide for directions.

Match.

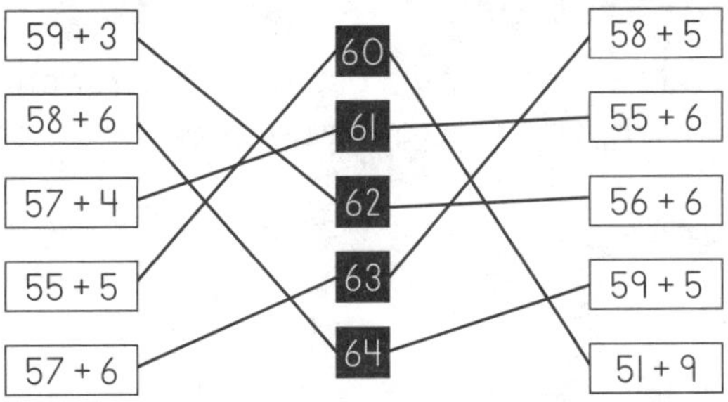

14.3B

Jackson counted some of his toys. Use his chart to make a bar graph.

My Toys

Toy	Number
Cars	40
Trucks	20
Airplanes	10

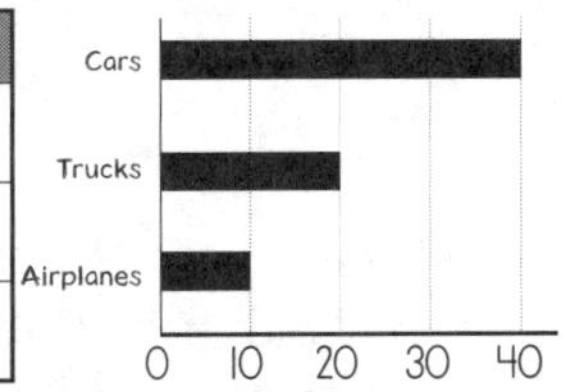

Match pairs that equal 100.

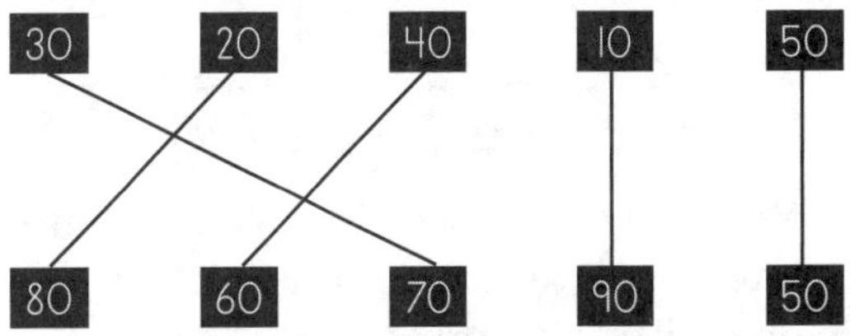

Complete.

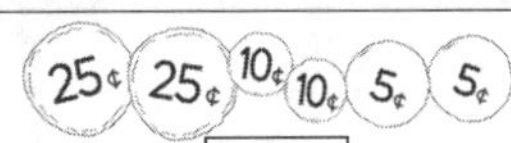

80 ¢

14.4A

See the Instructor Guide for directions.

39 + 4 = 43

65 + 7 = 72

46 + 6 = 52

78 + 9 = 87

Color the addition problems that equal the number in the star.

44: 39 + 5, 40 + 4, 38 + 6

31: 25 + 6, 28 + 3, 27 + 5

50: 47 + 2, 45 + 5, 49 + 1

62: 56 + 8, 59 + 3, 57 + 6

73: 68 + 5, 69 + 2, 65 + 8

84: 78 + 6, 77 + 5, 75 + 9

14.4B

Raj went on a nature walk. He made a pictograph about the animals he saw. Use the pictograph to complete the chart.

Animals I Saw

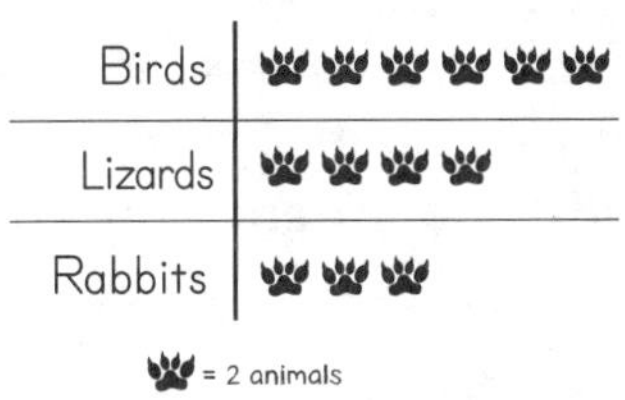

Animal	Number
Birds	12
Lizards	8
Rabbits	6

How many more birds than lizards did he see?

12 − 8 = 4

4 birds

How many animals did he see? Write your own equation.

12 + 8 + 6 = 26

26 animals

Label the numbers on the number line.

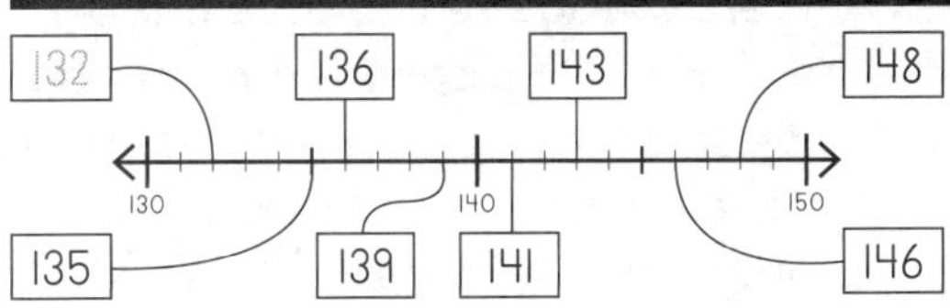

Week 15
Mental Addition, Part 2

Overview

Your child will learn how to add two-digit numbers mentally by breaking the numbers into tens and ones. Your child will gradually develop this skill over the course of the week, beginning with easier numbers and progressing to more challenging numbers.

Lesson 15.1	Add Easier Two-Digit Numbers
Lesson 15.2	Add Two-Digit Numbers with a 5 in the Ones-Place
Lesson 15.3	Add More Challenging Two-Digit Numbers
Lesson 15.4	Add Two-Digit Numbers at the Pretend Store
Lesson 15.5	Enrichment and Review (Optional)

Teaching Math with Confidence: Why Add the Tens First in Mental Addition Problems?

This week, your child will learn how to mentally add two-digit numbers. You'll first show her how to break both addends into expanded form and add the tens and ones separately before combining them.

Adding the tens and ones separately before combining them.

This method makes intuitive sense to most children. However, it can be a bit cumbersome to juggle this many different numbers when adding numbers in real-life situations like the grocery store. So, you'll also show your child a more streamlined method.

Instead of breaking both numbers into their expanded forms, you'll show her how to break just the second addend into expanded form and then add in two steps. Besides being more efficient, this method also better prepares your child for mental subtraction. (See the Week 19 Teaching Math with Confidence for an explanation of why.)

A more efficient way to add mentally.

If your child resists using this more-efficient method, demonstrate it as described in the lessons and encourage her to give it a try. But, don't worry if she continues to prefer breaking both addends into expanded form and adding the tens and ones separately. She may even develop her own approach to solving these problems. Allow her to use the strategy that makes the most sense to her, and she'll gradually transition to more efficient strategies as she becomes more comfortable with mental math.

Extra Materials Needed for Week 15

- 14 slips of paper
- 4 small toys
- For optional Enrichment and Review Lesson:
    - *A Fair Bear Share,* written by Stuart J. Murphy and illustrated by John Speirs
    - Large piece of posterboard (or 9 sheets of paper and tape)
    - 2 beanbags, crumpled wads of paper, or soft, unbreakable toys

Lesson 15.1
Add Easier Two-Digit Numbers

	Purpose	Materials
Warm-up	• Count coins • Practice memory work • Review mental addition	• Coins
Activities	• Add two-digit numbers with base-ten blocks	• Base-ten blocks • Workbook page 15.1A
Workbook	• Add two-digit numbers	• Workbook pages 15.1A and 15.1B

None of the problems in this lesson require combining ones to make a ten. This ensures that that your child only has to compute easy sums as she tackles this new and challenging mental math skill. She will solve problems with more difficult numbers in Lessons 15.2 and 15.3.

Warm-up: Counting, Memory Work, and Review

- Place 3 quarters, 2 nickels, and 3 pennies on the table. **How much are these coins worth?** *88¢.*
- Write the < sign. **What does this sign mean?** *Less than.*
  Write the > sign. **What does this sign mean?** *Greater than.*
- Write the following problems on paper and have your child solve them mentally. Allow her to use base-ten blocks as needed.
  - 31 + 20 = *51*
  - 43 + 30 = *73*
  - 62 + 20 = *82*
  - 25 + 30 = *55*

Activity: Split Both Numbers to Add with Base-Ten Blocks

Last week, you learned how to add one-digit numbers to two-digit numbers in your head. This week, you'll learn how to mentally add two-digit numbers to two-digit numbers. We'll start with easier numbers today and then work up to harder numbers in the next two lessons.

Show your child the first problem at the top of workbook page 15.1A (31 + 25). Model the problem with base-ten blocks as shown.

31 + 25 = ☐

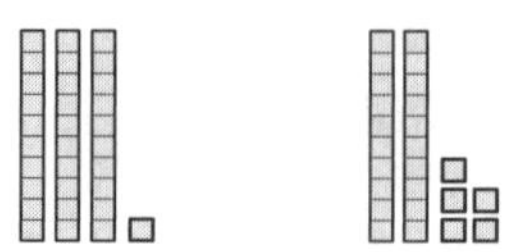

Before we add, let's split the numbers into tens and ones. What's the expanded form of 31? *30 plus 1.* **What's the expanded form of 25?** *20 plus 5.* Have your child draw part-total lines to show the expanded form of both numbers.

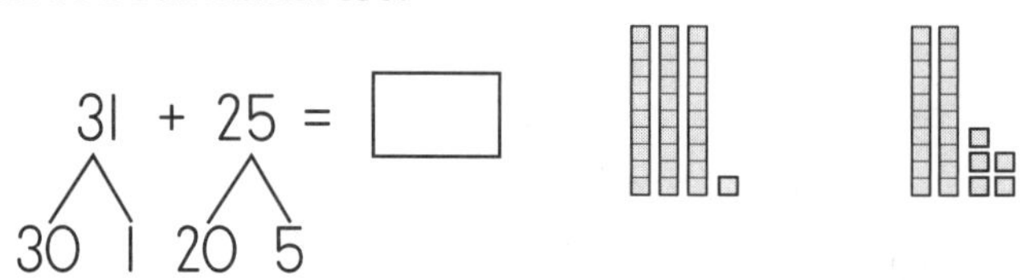

We can add numbers in any order and still get the same sum. Let's add the tens and ones separately. Then, we'll combine them to find the answer.

What's 30 plus 20? *50.*

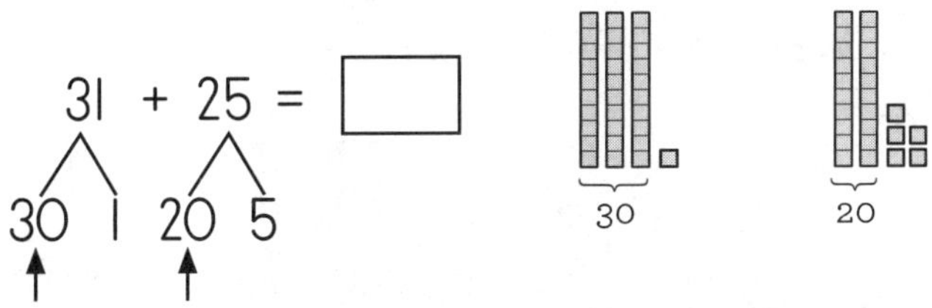

What's 1 plus 5? *6.* **So, what's 31 plus 25?** *56.* Have your child complete the written equation: 31 + 25 = 56.

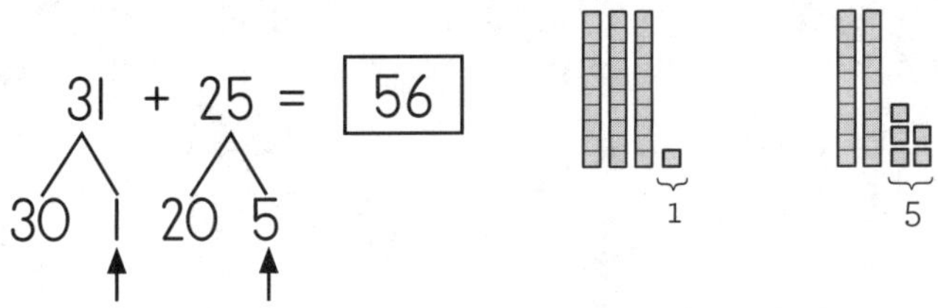

Have your child solve the next problem (43 + 32) in the same way. Guide her to add the tens and ones separately and then combine them to find the answer.

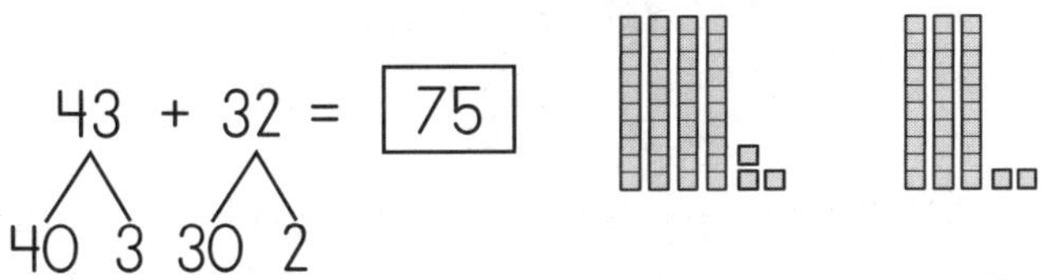

Activity: Split Only One Number to Add with Base-Ten Blocks

Show your child the next problem (62 + 24). Model the problem with base-ten blocks.

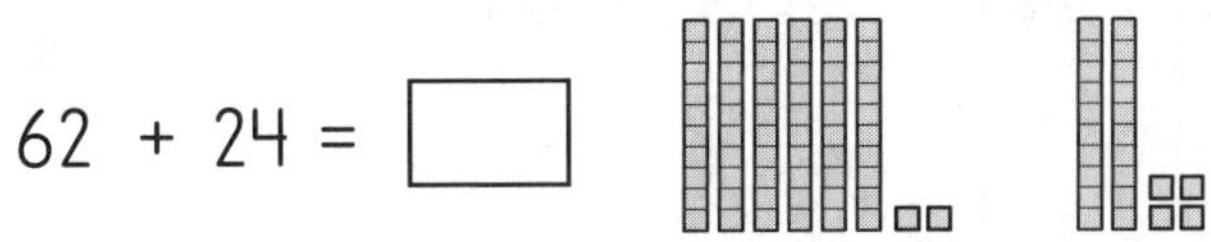

When we split both addends, we have to remember four different numbers as we add! Many people find adding in their heads easier when they break up just the second addend.

> Breaking both addends apart also doesn't translate well to mental subtraction, so it's better for your child to develop the habit of only breaking apart the second addend. See the Week 19 **Teaching Math with Confidence** for more on why.

What's the expanded form of 24? *20 plus 4.* Have your child draw part-total lines to show the expanded form of 24.

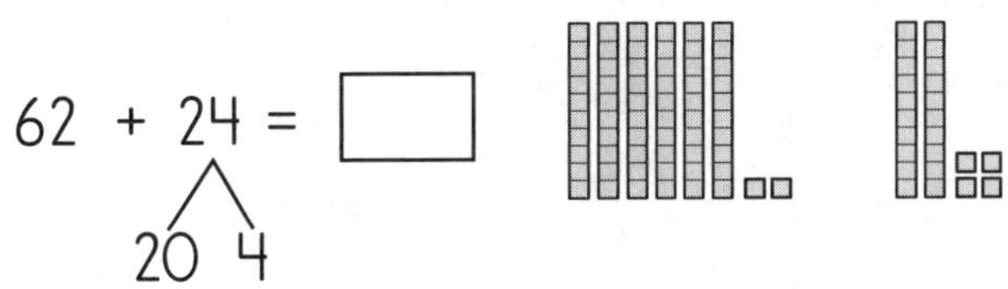

Let's add in two steps. Cover the 4 unit blocks with a piece of paper. **What's 62 plus 20?** *82.*

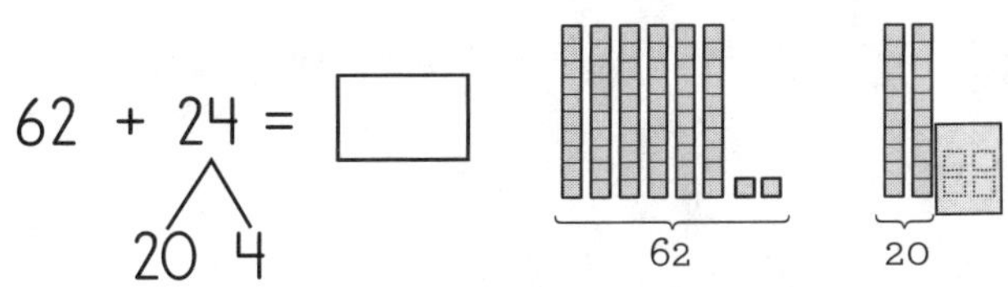

Covering the unit blocks helps your child break the problem into steps and focus on adding the tens first. See the Week 15 **Teaching Math with Confidence** for an explanation of why you begin with the tens in these mental math problems.

Uncover the 4 unit blocks. **What's 82 plus 4?** *86.* Have your child complete the equation: 62 + 24 = 86.

$$62 + 24 = \boxed{86}$$

20 4

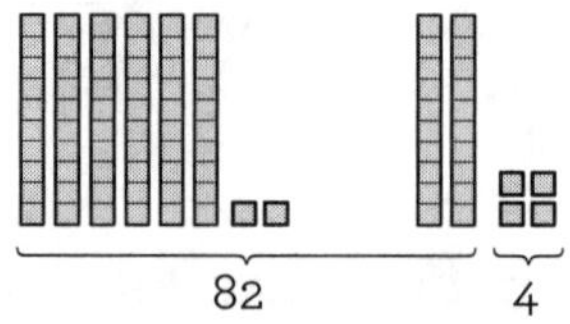

The goal of mental math is to deepen your child's number sense and problem-solving ability, not test her memory, so it's fine to provide written support whenever needed. For example, for the above problem, write out each step if it helps to make the process clearer:

$$62 + 20 = 82 \qquad 82 + 4 = 86$$

Have your child solve the next problem (25 + 34) in the same way.

$$25 + 34 = \boxed{59}$$

30 4

25 plus 30 equals 55. 55 plus 4 equals 59.

Workbook: Add Two-Digit Numbers Mentally and Review

Have your child complete workbook pages 15.1A and 15.1B. Allow her to model the addition problems on 15.1A with base-ten blocks as needed.

Lesson 15.2
Add Two-Digit Numbers with 5 in the Ones-Place

	Purpose	Materials
Warm-up	• Count by 25s to 200 • Practice memory work • Review identifying the total number of objects in an array	• Counters • Dot array and L-cover (Blackline Master 6)
Activities	• Add two-digit numbers with 5 in the ones-place (for example, 45 + 25)	• Play money • Workbook page 15.2A
Workbook	• Add two-digit numbers with 5 in the ones-place	• Workbook pages 15.2A and 15.2B

This lesson increases the difficulty level slightly from Lesson 15.1. All of the problems in this lesson have 5 in the ones-place (such as 35 + 15 or 25 + 35) so that your child begins to mentally combine the ones into a ten. Your child will tackle more challenging numbers in Lesson 15.3.

Warm-up: Counting, Memory Work, and Review

- Have your child count by 25s from 25 to 200.
- **If a number has 1, 3, 5, 7, or 9 in the ones-place, is the number even or odd?** *Odd.* **If a number has 0, 2, 4, 6, or 8 in the ones-place, is the number even or odd?** *Even.*
- Use the dot array and L-cover to show your child the following dot arrangements. Have him find the total number of dots in each array.

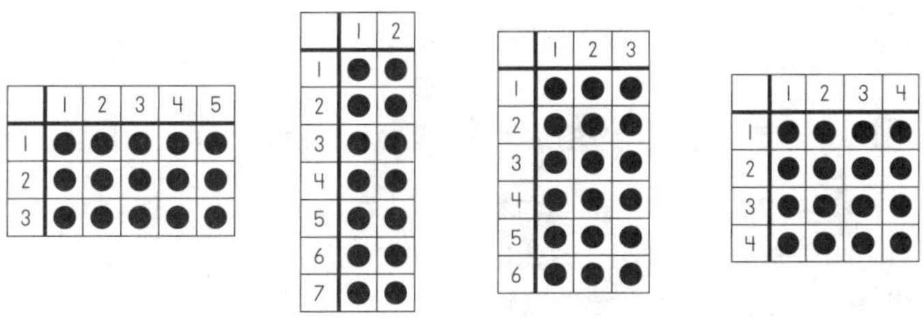

15 14 18 16

Activity: Add Two-Digit Numbers with 5 in the Ones-Place with Base-Ten Blocks

In the last lesson, you learned how to mentally add two-digit numbers. Today, you'll learn how to add two-digit numbers that have a 5 in the ones-place.

Show your child the first problem on workbook page 15.2A (35 + 15). **Let's pretend you have $35, and then you earn $15.** Model each addend with ten-dollar bills and five-dollar bills.

35 + 15 = ☐

Using ten-dollar bills and five-dollar bills in this lesson reinforces place value and prevents having lots of bills to manage.

What's the expanded form of 15? *10 plus 5.* Have your child draw part-total lines to show the expanded form of 15.

35 + 15 = ☐

10 5

Now, we add in two steps. Cover the second five-dollar bill with a piece of paper. **What's 35 plus 10?** *45.*

35 + 15 = ☐

10 5

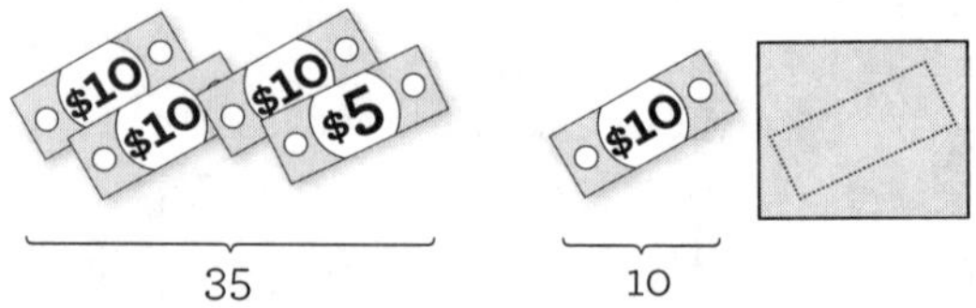

Uncover the five-dollar bill. **What's 45 plus 5?** *50.* Have your child complete the written equation: 35 + 15 = 50.

35 + 15 = 50

10 5

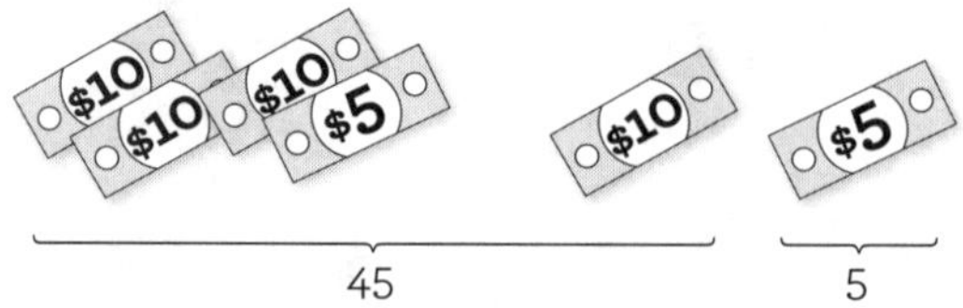

If your child has trouble with this question, ask: **What's 5 plus 5?** *10.* **So, you can add 40 plus 10 to find the total, just like you did last week when you used related addition facts to add one-digit numbers to two-digit numbers.**

Have your child solve the next problem (45 + 35) in the same way.

45 + 35 = 80

30 5

45 plus 30 equals 75. 75 plus 5 equals 80.

Activity: Add Two-Digit Numbers with 5 in the Ones-Place Mentally

Let's try the next two problems without acting them out with money. Show your child the next problem (55 + 25). **What's the expanded form of 25?** *20 plus 5.* Have your child draw part-total lines to show the expanded form of 25.

55 + 25 = ☐

20 5

Point to the 55 and 20. **What's 55 plus 20?** *75.*

55 + 25 = ☐

20 5

Point to the 5. **What's 75 plus 5?** *80.* Have your child complete the written equation: 55 + 25 = 80.

55 + 25 = 80

20 5

Have your child try the next problem (25 + 25) in the same way.

25 + 25 = 50

20 5

25 plus 20 equals 45. 45 plus 5 equals 50.

> If your child has trouble, model the problem with play money. Don't require your child to draw part-total lines if he can solve the problem without them.

Workbook: Add Two-Digit Numbers with 5 in the Ones-Place and Review

Have your child complete workbook pages 15.2A and 15.2B. Allow him to model the addition problems on 15.2A with play money as needed.

Lesson 15.3
Add More Challenging Two-Digit Numbers

	Purpose	Materials
Warm-up	• Count by 20s • Practice memory work • Review reading numbers to 200	• 200 Chart (Blackline Master 7) • Counters
Activities	• Use base-ten blocks to solve more challenging two-digit mental addition problems	• Base-ten blocks • Workbook page 15.3A • 10 slips of paper
Workbook	• Review previously-learned material	• Workbook pages 15.3A and 15.3B

Warm-up: Counting, Memory Work, and Review

- Have your child count by 20s to 100.
- **What do we call the result when we add numbers together?** *The sum.* **What do we call the result when we subtract a number from another number?** *The difference.*
- Read the following numbers one at a time, and have your child cover each number with a small counter: **193, 133, 127, 155, 104, 163, 103, 123, 146, 183, 173, 113, 154, 116, 137, 153, 147, 143.** The final arrangement of counters should look like a P.

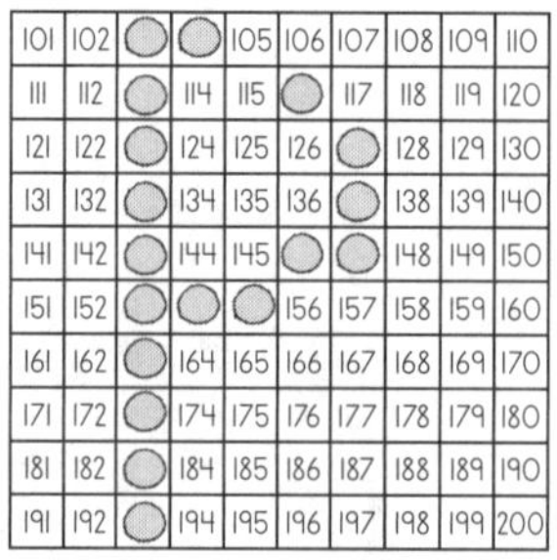

Activity: Add Two-Digit Numbers with Base-Ten Blocks

In the last lesson, you learned how to add two-digit numbers with a 5 in the ones-place.

Today, you'll learn how to add two-digit numbers that have greater digits in the ones-place. We'll use the same approach for these problems and add in two steps.

Show your child the first problem on workbook page 15.3A (39 + 23). Have your child model the problem with base-ten blocks. **What's the expanded form of 23?** *20 plus 3.* Have your child draw part-total lines to show the expanded form of 23.

39 + 23 = ☐

20 3

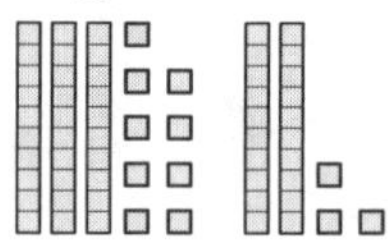

Now, we add in two steps. Cover the 3 unit blocks. **What's 39 plus 20?** *59.*

39 + 23 = ☐

20 3

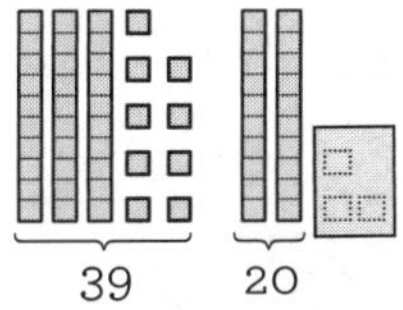

Uncover the 3 unit blocks. **What's 59 plus 3?** *62.* Have your child complete the written equation: 39 + 23 = 62.

39 + 23 = 62

20 3

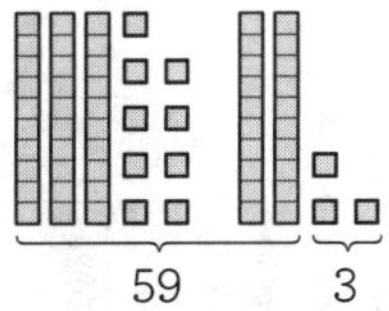

Have your child solve the rest of the problems on the top of workbook page 15.3A in the same way.

68 + 14 = 82

10 4

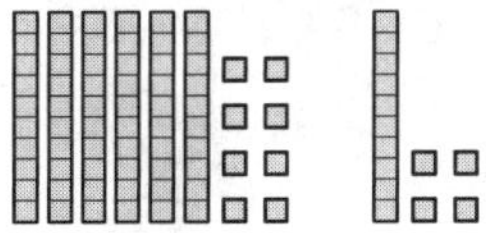

68 plus 10 equals 78. 78 plus 4 equals 82.

25 + 37 = 62

30 7

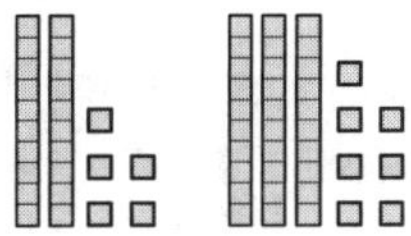

25 plus 30 equals 55. 55 plus 7 equals 62.

56 + 24 = 80

20 4

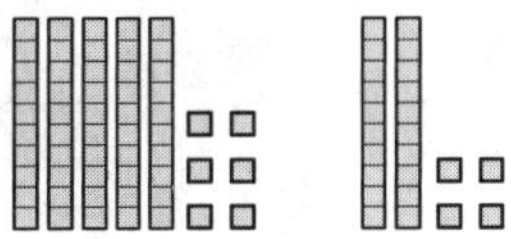

56 plus 20 equals 76. 76 plus 4 equals 80.

If your child needs the support of the part-total lines but resists drawing them, encourage her to point to the tens-place in the second number as she adds the tens, and the ones-place as she adds the ones. For example:

68 + 14 = (arrow under the tens digit)	68 + 14 = (arrow under the ones digit)
68 + 10 = 78.	78 + 4 = 82.

Activity: Play Snowball Fight

Play Snowball Fight. Model the problems with base-ten blocks as needed.

The silliness of this activity makes solving these challenging problems feel more relaxed and fun. But, if you'd rather not encourage throwing (or if you're teaching this lesson in a place where it's not practical), put the paper wads in a bowl and draw 2 wads each turn instead. Replace the wads in the bowl after each turn.

Snowball Fight

Materials: 10 slips of paper; workbook page 15.3A

Object of the Game: Win the most points.

Write numbers listed at the bottom of the workbook page on slips of paper. Crumple the slips of paper and place them on the table.

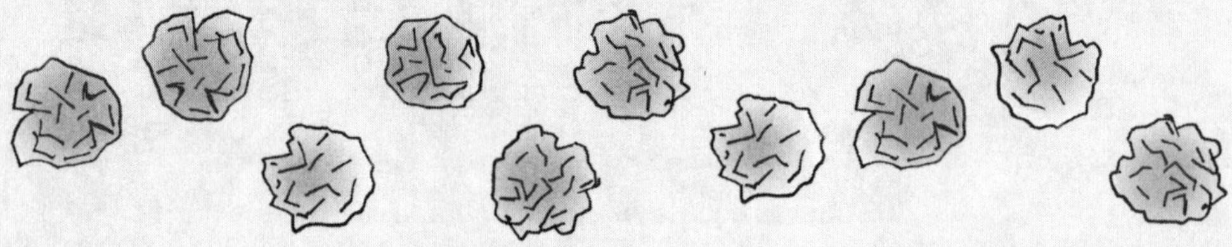

Both players count down in unison from 10 while throwing the crumpled wads of paper at each other. When you reach 1, both players stop and pick up the 2 closest wads of paper.

Both players unfold their paper wads and write their numbers in neighboring blank equations on 15.3A. Then, they find the sum. Whoever has the greater sum wins a point.

19 + 38 = 57

35 + 26 = 61

Crumple up your numbers and add them back to the pile of "snowballs." Continue until you have filled in all of the blank equations. Whoever wins more points wins the game.

Workbook: Review

Have your child complete workbook page 15.3B.

Lesson 15.4
Add Two-Digit Numbers at the Pretend Store

	Purpose	Materials
Warm-up	• Count money • Practice memory work • Review identifying even and odd numbers	• Play money
Activities	• Practice adding two-digit numbers mentally • Solve money word problems	• Workbook page 15.4A • 4 small toys • 4 slips of paper • Play money
Workbook	• Add two-digit numbers mentally	• Workbook pages 15.4A and 15.4B

Warm-up: Counting, Memory Work, and Review

- Place 2 twenty-dollar bills, 3 ten-dollar bills, and 3 five-dollar bills on the table. **How much is this money worth?** *$85.*
- **How many tens equal 1 hundred?** *10.*
- Have your child tell whether the following numbers are even or odd.
  - 8. *Even.*
  - 11. *Odd.*
  - 23. *Odd.*
  - 34. *Even.*
  - 80. *Even.*

Activity: Add Two-Digit Numbers to Two-Digit Numbers without Base-Ten Blocks

This week, you have used base-ten blocks to add two-digit numbers to two-digit numbers. Today, you'll try solving these problems in your head, without base-ten blocks.

Point to the first exercise on workbook page 15.4A (28 + 56). **Try solving this problem in your head. While you work, I'll model the problem with base-ten blocks. Once we finish, we'll compare our answers and make sure they match.**

Have your child solve the problem. While he works, secretly model the problem with base-ten blocks. Cover the blocks with a piece of paper.

28 + 56 = 84

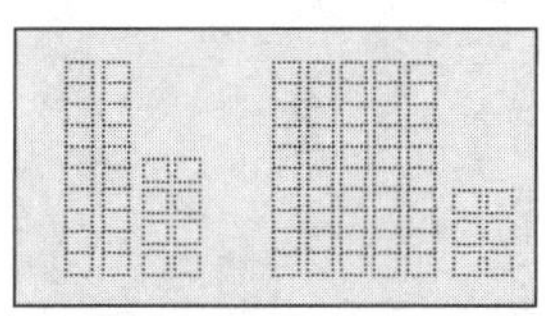

So, what's 28 + 56? *84.* Remove the cover from the blocks so your child can check whether his answer matches the blocks. If his answer does not match, have him use the blocks to find the correct sum.

Continue in the same way with the other problems at the top of the page.

Activity: Add Two-Digit Numbers at the Pretend Store

We often need to do mental math when we're shopping to find the total cost of our items and check if we have enough money. Write \$37, \$29, \$46, and \$18 on slips of paper to make price tags. Lay 4 small toys in a row and have your child place a price tag next to each toy. Also place play money on the table to use.

Have your child write an equation to match each of the following problems and solve. Encourage him to solve the problems mentally as much as possible.

- **How much does it cost to buy the item that costs \$18 and the item that costs \$37?** *\$55.*

  \$18 \$37   18 + 37 = 55

- **How much does it cost to buy the item that costs \$37 and the item that costs \$29?** *\$66.*

  \$37 \$29   37 + 29 = 66

- Give your child 6 ten-dollar bills. **You have \$60. Do you have enough to buy the item that costs \$46 and the item that costs \$18?** *No.* **How do you know?** *Sample answer: They cost \$64 in all, and that's more than \$60.*

  \$46 \$18   46 + 18 = 64

- Give your child 5 ten-dollar bills. **You have \$50. Do you have enough to buy the item that costs \$29 and the item that costs \$18?** *Yes.* **How do you know?** *Sample answer: They cost \$47 in all, and that's less than \$50.*

  \$29 \$18   29 + 18 = 47

If you have time, have your child make up and solve some word problems of his own. For example: *If I buy the two most expensive items, how much will I pay? If I buy two of the \$37 items, how much will they cost?*

Workbook: Add Two-Digit Numbers and Review

Have your child complete workbook pages 15.4A and 15.4B.

Lesson 15.5
Enrichment and Review (Optional)

	Purpose	Materials
Warm-up	• Count from 100 to 200 by 1s, 2s, 5s, or 10s • Review memory work • Review your child's favorite or most challenging activities from Week 15	• Varies, depending on the activities you choose
Picture Book	• Understand how forming groups of 10 makes adding easier	• *A Fair Bear Share*, written by Stuart J. Murphy and illustrated by John Speirs
Enrichment Activity	• Use mental math to calculate scores in a carnival game	• Large piece of posterboard (or 9 sheets of paper and tape) • 2 beanbags, crumpled wads of paper, or soft, unbreakable toys

Warm-up: Counting, Memory Work, and Review

- Have your child count from 100 to 200 by 1s, 2s, 5s, or 10s. (Choose whichever counting sequence your child needs to practice the most.)
- Quiz your child on the memory work through Week 14. See page 523 for the full list.
- If you have time, repeat one or two of the activities from this week's lessons. Choose activities your child especially enjoyed or found challenging.

Math Picture Book: *A Fair Bear Share*

Read *A Fair Bear Share*, written by Stuart J. Murphy and illustrated by John Speirs. As you read, discuss how the bears make groups of 10 to help them find the totals.

Enrichment Activity: Make a Carnival Game

Help your child divide a sheet of poster board into 9 rectangles. Have her label each rectangle as shown.

38	25	46
19	24	35
47	36	27

If you don't have posterboard on hand, tape 9 sheets of paper into a grid instead.

Use the board to play a simple carnival-style game. Stand about 10 feet away from the board. Take turns throwing 2 beanbags, crumpled wads of paper, or soft toys onto the board. Look to see what number your beanbags landed on, and add the two numbers together to find your score. Whoever's score is greater wins the round.

Play 5 rounds in this way. Whoever wins more rounds wins.

Week 15 Answer Key

15.1A

See the Instructor Guide for directions.

31 + 25 = 56	43 + 32 = 75
62 + 24 = 86	25 + 34 = 59

Complete. Then, use the key to color the stripes on the scarf.

Key
Even sum - Purple
Odd sum - Green

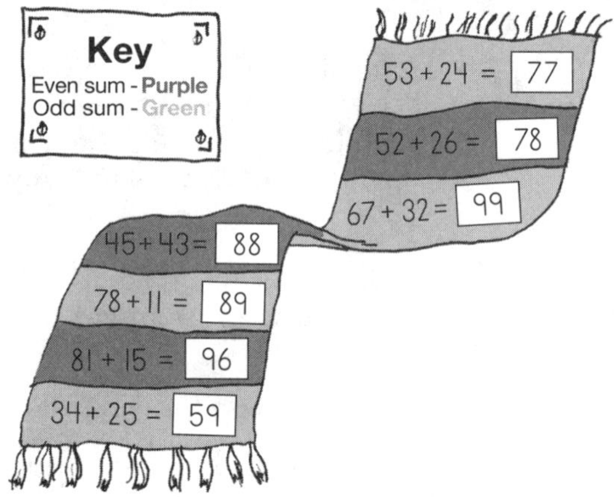

15.1B

Match.

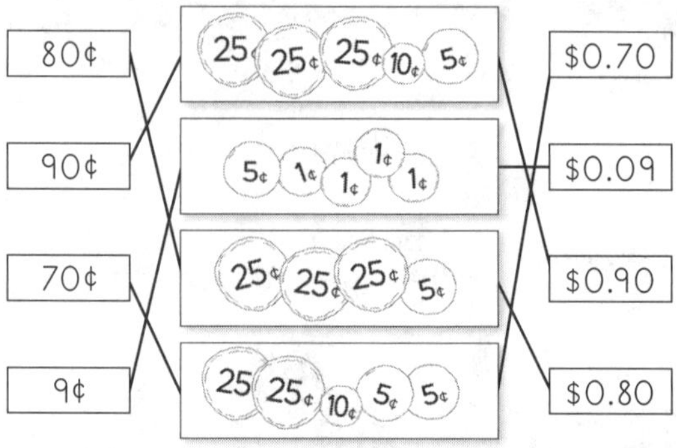

Solve.

You have $30.
Then, you spend $10.
How much money do you have left?

30 − 10 = 20

$20

You have $20.
You spend $9 on a shirt and the rest on a hat.
How much does the hat cost?

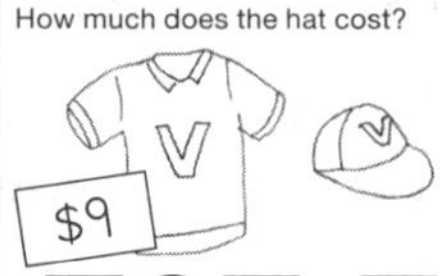

20 − 9 = 11

$11

15.2A

See the Instructor Guide for directions.

35 + 15 = 50	45 + 35 = 80
55 + 25 = 80	25 + 25 = 50

Match.

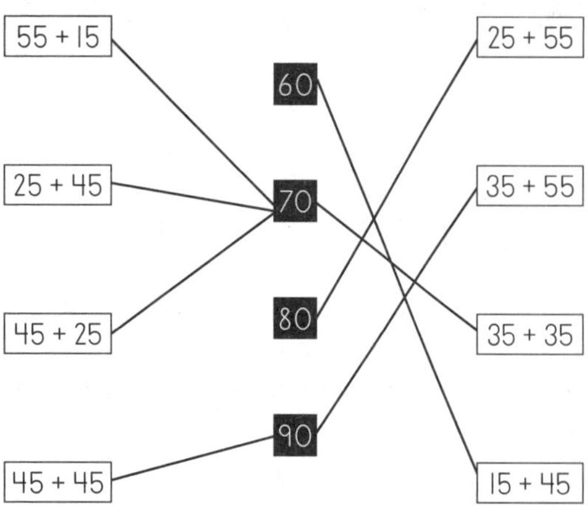

15.2B

Complete the circles with <, >, or =.

165 > 156	101 < 107	135 = 135
38 < 60	102 < 120	150 > 149

Complete the fact family to match the Part-Total Diagram.

Total: 15; Parts: 8, 7

8 + 7 = 15
7 + 8 = 15
15 − 8 = 7
15 − 7 = 8

Count by 5s to connect the dots in order.

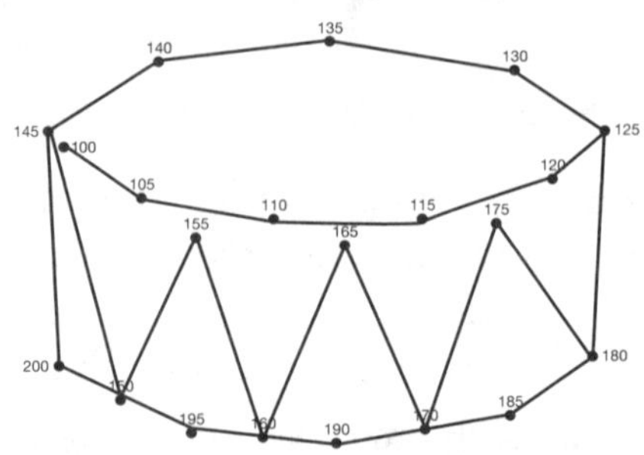

Week 15 Answer Key

15.3A

See the Instructor Guide for directions.

39 + 23 = 62	68 + 14 = 82
25 + 37 = 62	56 + 24 = 80

Snowball Fight

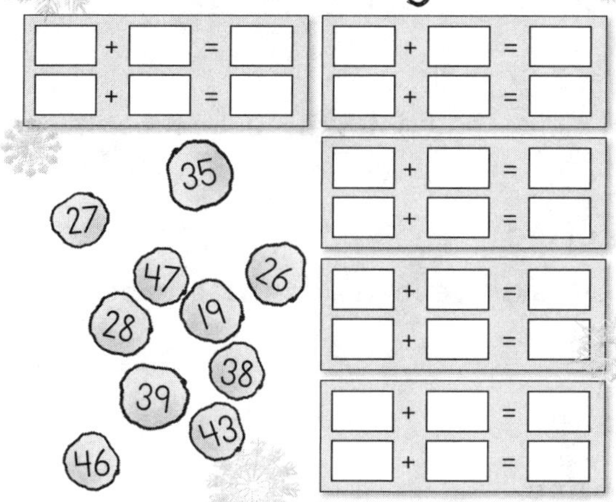

15.3B

Samantha made a pictograph about how much time she spent practicing the piano. Use the pictograph to complete the chart and answer the questions.

Piano Practice

Monday	♪ ♪ ♪
Tuesday	♪ ♪ ♪ ♪ ♪
Wednesday	♪ ♪ ♪ ♪
Thursday	♪ ♪

♪ = 5 minutes

Day	Minutes
Monday	15
Tuesday	25
Wednesday	20
Thursday	10

Which day did she practice the most? Tuesday

Which day did she practice the least? Thursday

How much less did she practice on Monday than Tuesday? Write your own equation.
25 - 15 = 10
10 minutes

How much did she practice in all? Write your own equation.
15 + 25 + 20 + 10 = 70
70 minutes

Copy the shape.

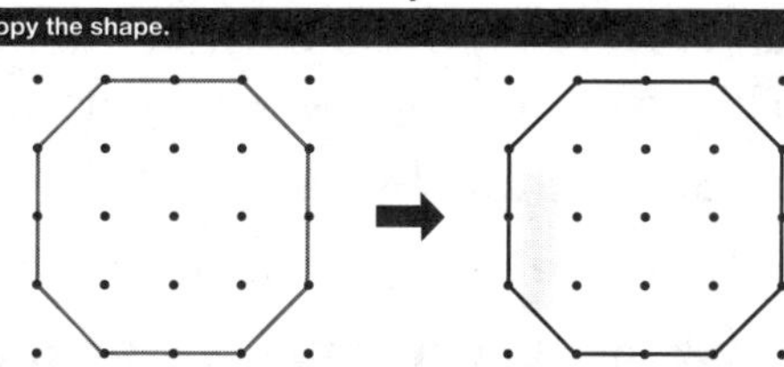

15.4A

See the Instructor Guide for directions.

28 + 56 = 84	37 + 49 = 86
65 + 25 = 90	74 + 17 = 91

Match.

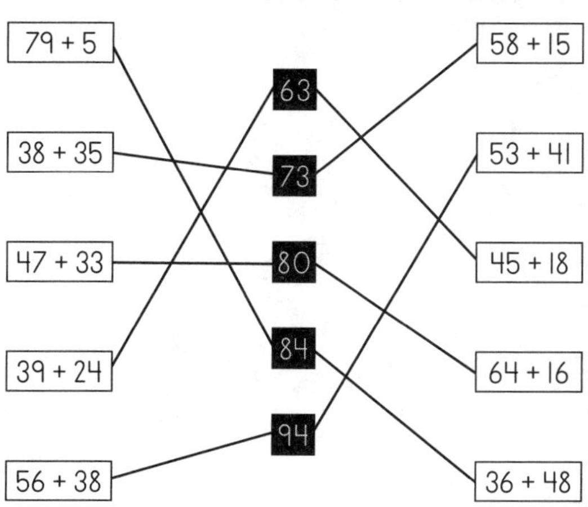

15.4B

Lucy made a bar graph about her art supplies.
Use the bar graph to complete the chart and answer the questions.

Art Supplies

Item	Number
Markers	30
Colored Pencils	20
Crayons	60

How many more markers than colored pencils does she have?
30 - 20 = 10
10 markers

How many more crayons than colored pencils does she have?
60 - 20 = 40
40 crayons

Draw a line that splits each shape in half.

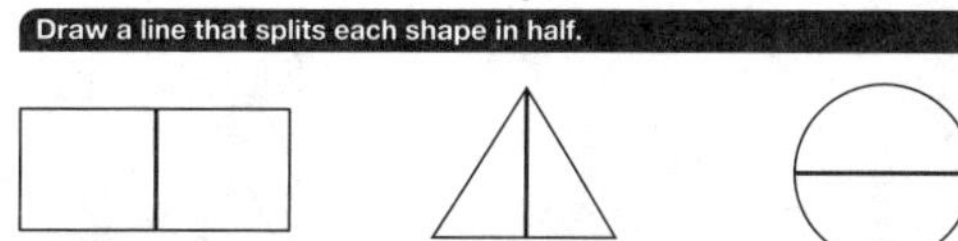

Sample answers. Many answers are possible.

Draw lines that split each shape into fourths.

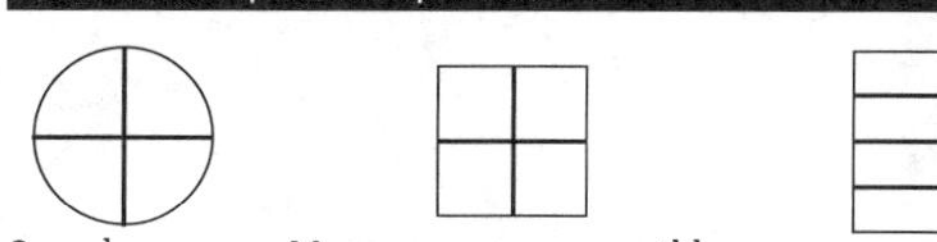

Sample answers. Many answers are possible.

Unit 6 Checkpoint

What to Expect at the End of Unit 6

By the end of Unit 6, most children will be able to do the following:

- Mentally add one-digit or two-digit numbers, with sums less than 100. Some children will be able to solve these problems completely mentally, but many will still need to use base-ten blocks in order to find the answers.

Is Your Child Ready to Move on?

In Unit 7, your child will learn how to tell time to the minute. Before moving on to Unit 7, your child should have already mastered the following skills:

- Count by 5s to 100.
- Identify numbers on the number line.

Your child does not need to have mastered the Unit 6 mental addition skills before moving on to Unit 7.

What to Do If Your Child Needs More Practice

If your child is having trouble with either of the above skills, spend a day practicing the corresponding review activities below before moving on to Unit 7.

Activities for counting by 5s

- Count nickels by 5s (Warm-up, Lesson 2.2)

Activities for identifying numbers on the number line

- Number Line Bump (Lesson 2.3)
- Count Forward and Backward on the Number Line (Lesson 2.4)
- More/Less Number Line Riddles (Lesson 2.4)

Unit 7
Time

Overview

In first grade, your child learned to tell time to the hour and half-hour. In this unit, she'll build on these skills and learn to tell time to the minute. She'll also learn to describe times of the day with a.m. and p.m. and identify quarter-hours and half-hours.

If your child already knows how to tell time, feel free to condense these lessons and skip activities that she has already mastered. But, don't skip this unit entirely! You may find that your child has forgotten some of the details of telling time, especially identifying hour-hand positions. Most children need lots of practice to fully master telling time. Plus, the warm-up activities and review worksheets will help your child consolidate her mental addition skills and prepare her to tackle mental subtraction in Unit 8.

Week 16 Tell Time to the Hour
Week 17 Tell Time to the Minute

What Your Child Will Learn

In this unit your child will learn to:

- Identify times of day as a.m. and p.m.
- Be familiar with half-hours and quarter-hours
- Identify the hour and tell time to the minute on clocks with hands

Recommended Math Picture Books (Optional)

These picture books are scheduled in the optional Enrichment and Review lessons at the end of each week.

- *It's About Time, Max!*, written by Kitty Richards and illustrated by Gioia Flammenghi. Kane Press, 2000.
- *Pigs on a Blanket*, written by Amy Axelrod and illustrated by Sharon McGinley-Nally. Aladdin, 1998.

Week 16
Tell Time to the Hour

Overview

You'll review telling time to the hour and teach your child to identify the hour hand's position. This thorough understanding of the hour hand will help prevent confusion when he learns to tell time to the minute in Week 17.

Lesson 16.1	Introduce a.m. and p.m.
Lesson 16.2	Identify the Hour Hand's Position
Lesson 16.3	Tell Time to the Hour
Lesson 16.4	Identify 5-Minute Marks on the Clock
Lesson 16.5	Enrichment and Review (Optional)

Teaching Math with Confidence: The Challenge of Identifying the Hour on Clocks with Hands

As children learn to tell time, they often have trouble identifying the hour, especially if the hour hand is between numbers. For example, many children mistakenly think that the following clock shows a time in the 7 o'clock hour, since the hour hand is closer to the 7 than the 6.

Since the hour hand is closer to the 7, children often mistakenly think the time is 7:50 rather than 6:50.

To help your child master identifying the hour, you'll teach him that each hour "owns" a segment of the clock. If the hour hand is in that hour's part of the clock, that hour wins! So, since the hour hand is in the 6 o'clock hour's part of the clock, the time is 6:50 (and not 7:50).

You'll teach your child that the 6 o'clock hour "owns" this part of the clock.

Extra Materials Needed for Week 16

- Timer
- Crayons or colored pencils
- 12 slips of paper
- For optional Enrichment and Review Lesson:
    - *It's About Time, Max!*, written by Kitty Richards and illustrated by Gioia Flammenghi
    - Timer

You will use a clock with hands to teach your child to tell time this week. Your clock should have:

- Clear, easy-to-read numbers (No Roman numerals!)
- Tick marks along the edge for each minute
- Hands your child can easily move

If your family's clocks don't meet these criteria, you may want to buy an inexpensive plastic teaching clock (sometimes called a "Judy clock") to make these lessons easier to teach.

Lesson 16.1
Introduce a.m. and p.m.

	Purpose	Materials
Warm-up	• Count by 1s for 1 minute • Practice memory work • Review subtraction facts	• Timer • Subtraction Race game board (from workbook page 9.2A) • Coin • Counters
Activities	• Review how to read written times • Review how clock hands move • Learn to describe times with a.m. and p.m.	• Clock
Workbook	• Label parts of a clock • Identify a.m. and p.m.	• Workbook pages 16.1A and 16.1B

Warm-up: Counting, Memory Work, and Review

- **How many jumping jacks do you think you can do in 1 minute?** *Answers will vary.* Set a timer for 1 minute. Have your child do jumping jacks (and count them) for 1 minute. Discuss how her results compare with her prediction.

  This activity helps your child grasp the length of a minute.

- **How many hours are in a day?** *24.* **How many minutes are in an hour?** *60.* **How many seconds are in a minute?** *60.*
- Play Subtraction Race (-9 Version). See Lesson 9.2 (page 149) for directions.

Activity: Review How to Read Written Times

In first grade, you learned how to tell time to the hour and half-hour. This year, you'll learn how to tell time to the minute. Today, we'll review how to write and read times. You'll also learn how to use a.m. and p.m. to describe times.

Let's write down today's schedule. With your child, make a list of 5-6 events in your child's day. Include both "o'clock" times without minutes (such as 9:00 or 11:00) and times with minutes (such as 8:45 or 2:30).

Time	Event
7:00	Wake up
8:45	School lessons
12:00	Eat lunch
2:30	Play outside
6:00	Eat dinner
8:00	Go to bed

Sample chart. Adjust the times and events to fit your own family.

Written times have 3 parts: the hour, the number of minutes past the hour, and the colon that separates them. Have your child read the times written in the list. If necessary, remind your child to say "o'clock" for times like 9:00 or 11:00.

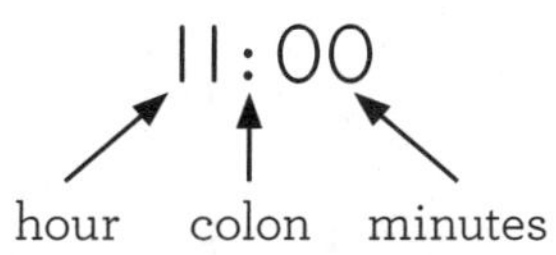

Activity: Connect Real-Life Times and Clock Hands' Movements

Show your child a clock with hands. Point to the shorter hand. **The shorter hand tells the hour. It's called the hour hand.**

Point to the longer hand. **The longer hand is the minute hand. It tells how many minutes have passed since the start of the hour.**

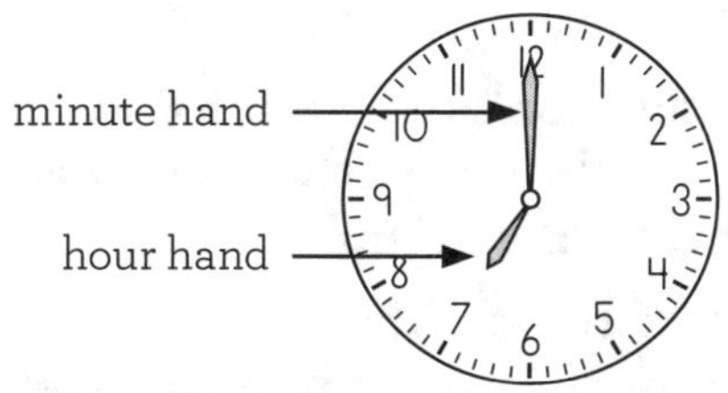

Have your child investigate turning the clock's hands. **Which hand moves faster?** *The minute hand.* **Which hand moves slower?** *The hour hand.*

> If your clock has a second hand, explain that this hand measures seconds. Tell your child to ignore this hand when reading the time.

Each day is divided into 24 hours. Each day begins at 12:00 a.m., or midnight. Set the clock to 12:00.

What are you usually doing at midnight? *Sleeping!* **While you sleep, the hours pass. The hour hand slowly turns around the clock and moves from one hour to the next.** Turn the clock's hands through the morning hours. Name each hour as the hands pass it, and discuss each time on your list (from the previous activity) as you reach it. For example: **You usually wake up around 7 o'clock.**

Time	Event
7:00	Wake up

> Focus on the hour hand's movement, not on teaching your child to read the clock. You will teach her to identify the hour hand's position in Lessons 16.2 and 16.3.

When the clock reaches 12:00 again, say: **12 o'clock p.m. is the middle of the day. We also call it noon. The hour hand has now gone all the way around the clock once. It still has to go all the way around the clock again before the day is over.**

Continue turning the hands on the clock until you have discussed every time on your list and reached midnight. **Once the hour hand goes around the clock twice and returns to the 12, it is midnight again. 24 hours have passed, and a new day begins.**

Activity: Introduce a.m. and p.m.

The hour hand goes all the way around the clock twice each day. So, each time occurs twice per day. That can be confusing! If I tell a friend that I will meet her at 8:30, I might mean 8:30 in the morning, or I might mean 8:30 at night.

We use the abbreviations a.m. or p.m. to tell the difference. We use a.m. for times that happen before noon. We use p.m. for times that are at noon or later. Look at your chart and have your child label each time with a.m. or p.m.

Time	Event
7:00 a.m.	Wake up
8:45 a.m.	School lessons
12:00 p.m.	Eat lunch
2:30 p.m.	Play outside
6:00 p.m.	Eat dinner
8:00 p.m.	Go to bed

Both a.m. and p.m. come from Latin. The abbreviation a.m. stands for "ante meridiem," which means before midday, while p.m. stands for "post meridiem," which means after midday. Midnight (the official start to the day) is 12:00 a.m., while noon is 12:00 p.m.

Name a few more events from your child's day and have your child identify their times as a.m. or p.m. For example:

- **You usually eat your morning snack at 10:00. Is that 10:00 a.m. or 10:00 p.m.?** *10:00 a.m.*
- **You take your bath around 7:30 in the evening. Is that 7:30 a.m. or 7:30 p.m.?** *7:30 p.m.*
- **Some days you watch a show after lunch, around 12:30. Is that 12:30 a.m. or 12:30 p.m.?** *12:30 p.m.*

Workbook: Identify a.m. and p.m. and Review

Have your child complete workbook pages 16.1A and 16.1B.

Lesson 16.2
Identify the Hour Hand's Position

	Purpose	Materials
Warm-up	• Count money • Practice memory work • Review money word problems	• Play money • Coins
Activities	• Use the hour hand to approximate the time • Identify the hour hand's position	• Clock • Workbook page 16.2A • Crayons or colored pencils
Workbook	• Identify the hour hand's position	• Workbook pages 16.2A and 16.2B

Warm-up: Counting, Memory Work, and Review

- Place 2 twenty-dollar bills, 4 one-dollar bills, 1 quarter, and 3 dimes on the table. **How much is this money worth?** *$44.55.*
- **Are times in the morning a.m. or p.m.?** *A.m.*
  Are times in the afternoon and evening a.m. or p.m.? *P.m.*
- Have your child write a matching equation for each of the following word problems and solve. Model with play money as needed.
  - **You have $29. Then, you earn $25 more. How much do you have then?** *29 + 25 = 54. $54.*
  - **You have $54, and you want to buy something that costs $60. How much more money do you need?** *54 + _6_ = 60. $6.*
  - **You have $50. Then, you spend $20. How much money do you have left?** *50 – 20 = 30. $30.*

Activity: Use the Hour Hand to Approximate the Time

In the last lesson, you learned about a.m. and p.m. and reviewed how clock hands move. Today, you'll learn how to identify the hour hand's position.

Set the clock to 7:00 and have your child identify the hour hand and minute hand. **Every hour begins with the minute hand pointing to the 12 at the top of the clock.**

When the hour hand points to the 7 and the minute hand points to 12, it is 7 o'clock.

As the hour passes, the minute hand moves around the clock. It shows how many minutes have passed since the start of the hour. Once the minute hand returns to the 12, an hour has passed.

I'm going to turn the minute hand all the way around the clock, from 7 o'clock to 8 o'clock. Watch the hour hand to see what it does. Turn the minute hand forward until the clock is set to 8:00.

What did the hour hand do? *It moved from the 7 to the 8.* **Did it move from the 7 to the 8 gradually or all at once?** *Gradually.*

Since the hour hand moves gradually, it tells us whether a little or a lot of the hour has passed. Turn the minute hand until the clock is set to 8:10. **Where is the hour hand pointing now?** *A little past the 8.* **Even if the minute hand fell off, the hour hand shows that it's a little bit past 8 o'clock.**

Approximating the time with the hour hand helps your child pay close attention to the hand's movement. Your child will learn to tell time to the minute later in this unit, so you do not need to teach him to read minutes in this lesson.

Turn the minute hand until the clock is set to 8:35. **Where is the hour hand pointing now?** *Halfway between the 8 and 9.* **Since the hour hand is about halfway between the 8 and 9, we know it's about half an hour after 8 o'clock.**

Turn the minute hand until the clock is set to 8:50. **Where is the hour hand pointing now?** *Almost to the 9.* **Since the hour hand is almost to the 9, we know it's almost 9 o'clock.**

Turn the minute hand until the clock is set to 9:00. **Where is the hour hand pointing now?** *To the 9.* **Since the hour hand is pointing directly to the 9 and the minute hand is pointing to the 12, it's exactly 9 o'clock.**

Activity: Identify the Hour

Show your child the printed clock at the top of workbook page 16.2A. **It can be tricky to tell the hour. It helps if you think of each hour as owning a part of the clock. The 9 o'clock hour owns this part of the clock.** Lightly draw lines on the printed clock as shown. Have your child color in this part of the clock.

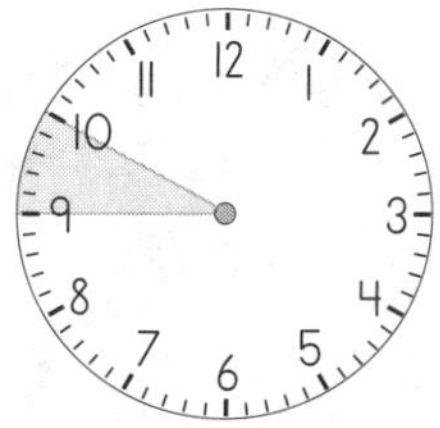

Put the clock next to the workbook page. Slowly turn the hour hand through the 9 o'clock hour and point out how the hour hand is always in the shaded portion of the clock. **If the hour hand is in this part of the clock, the hour is 9.**

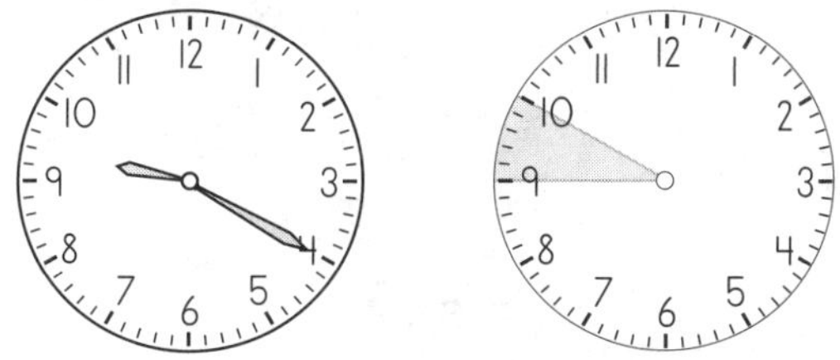

Turn the clock's hour hand until it points to 10. **Once the hour hand points to 10, the hour is 10. The 10 o'clock hour owns the next part of the clock.** Have your child draw a line on the printed clock as shown and color this wedge with a different color.

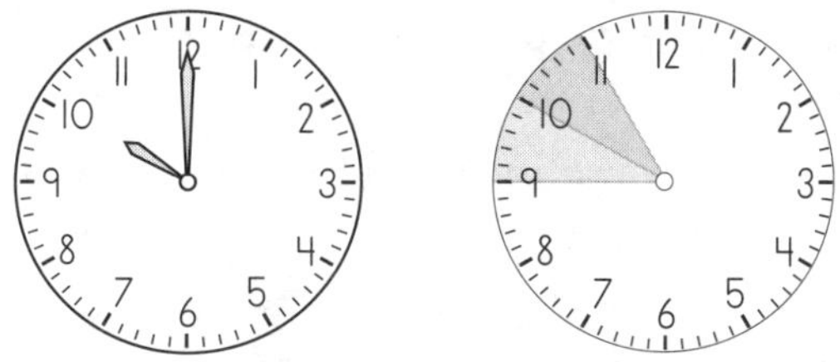

Have your child draw lines and color the rest of the clock in the same way. Discuss which hour "owns" each part of the clock as your child works.

> If your child has trouble understanding this idea, explain that it is similar to telling a person's age: After you turn 7, you're 7 years old until you turn 8. In the same way, after the hour hand passes 7 o'clock, the hour remains 7 until the hour hand reaches 8 o'clock.

Workbook: Identify the Hour and Review

Have your child complete workbook pages 16.2A and 16.2B.

Lesson 16.3
Tell Time to the Hour

	Purpose	Materials
Warm-up	• Count backward by 1s, 2s, and 5s on the number line • Practice memory work • Review mental subtraction	• Blank Number Line (Blackline Master 3) • Base-ten blocks, optional
Activities	• Tell time to the hour on a clock with hands • Make a schedule with one-hour increments	• Clock
Workbook	• Tell time to the hour	• Workbook pages 16.3A and 16.3B

If your child is already proficient at telling time to the hour, use the activities in this lesson to provide some quick review and then move on to the next lesson.

Warm-up: Counting, Memory Work, and Review

- Label the Blank Number Line with 50, 60, and 70. Have your child count backward from 70 to 50, by 1s, then 2s, and then 5s. Have her point to each corresponding tick mark as she counts.
- **Are times in the morning a.m. or p.m.?** *A.m.* **Are times in the afternoon and evening a.m. or p.m.?** *P.m.*
- Write the following problems on paper and have your child solve them mentally. Allow her to use base-ten blocks as needed.
    - × 45 - 5 = *40*
    - × 78 - 3 = *75*
    - × 40 - 20 = *20*
    - × 46 - 20 = *26*
    - × 87 - 70 = *17*

Activity: Tell Time to the Hour on a Clock with Hands

In the last lesson, you learned how to tell which hour the hour hand is in. Today, you'll learn how to tell time to the hour.

Set the clock to 5:00. Have your child identify the hour hand and minute hand. **To what number is the hour hand pointing?** *5.* **To what number is the minute hand pointing?** *12.*

Every hour begins with the minute hand pointing to the 12 at the top of the clock. So, this clock shows 5 o'clock. Write 5:00 on a piece of paper.

Set the clock to the following times. Have your child name each time and write it on a piece of paper.

10 o'clock. 10:00.

2 o'clock. 2:00.

9 o'clock. 9:00.

6 o'clock. 6:00.

12 o'clock. 12:00.

1 o'clock. 1:00.

Activity: Make a Schedule with Hours

Let's pretend we're in charge of a soccer league. Our job is to make a schedule for 6 games on a Saturday morning. Each game lasts an hour, and the first game is at 8:00. Is that 8:00 a.m. or 8:00 p.m.? *8:00 a.m.* Start a simple chart, and have your child set a clock to 8:00.

If your child participates in an hour-long activity other than soccer (such as dance class or hockey), use that activity as your example instead.

Game	Time
1	8:00 a.m.
2	
3	
4	
5	
6	

Each game lasts an hour. So, when does the next game start? *9 o'clock.* Have your child turn the minute hand one full turn around the clock to 9:00, and have her add the time to your chart.

Continue in this way until your child has completed the chart. Emphasize that an hour passes each time the minute hand goes all the way around the clock.

Game	Time
1	8:00 a.m.
2	9:00 a.m.
3	10:00 a.m.
4	11:00 a.m.
5	12:00 p.m.
6	1:00 p.m.

Workbook: Tell Time to the Hour and Review

Have your child complete workbook pages 16.3A and 16.3B.

Lesson 16.4
Identify 5-Minute Marks on the Clock

	Purpose	Materials
Warm-up	• Count forward and backward by 5s • Practice memory work • Review telling time to the hour	• Clock
Activities	• Understand that each tick mark on a clock stands for 1 minute • Learn to count by 5s to identify minutes on a clock	• Clock • 12 slips of paper
Workbook	• Count by 5s to identify minutes on a clock	• Workbook pages 16.4A and 16.4B

Many teaching clocks have the numbers for minutes printed along the edge of the clock (:00, :05, :10, etc.). These printed numbers can become a crutch and prevent your child from learning them by heart. If your clock has numbers for minutes printed on it, either cover them with small sticky notes or black them out with a permanent marker.

Warm-up: Counting, Memory Work, and Review

- Have your child count by 5s to 100. Then, have him count backwards by 5s from 100 to 0.

  Counting by 5s in the warm-up prepares your child to count by 5s to identify minutes on the clock.

- **Are times in the morning a.m. or p.m.?** *A.m.*
  Are times in the afternoon and evening a.m. or p.m.? *P.m.*
- Set the clock to the following times: 4:00, 6:00, 11:00, 12:00, 1:00. Have your child tell each time.

Activity: Label Minutes on the Clock

In the last two lessons, you learned how to read the hour on a clock. Today, you'll learn about minutes.

The minute hand tells us how many minutes have passed since the start of the hour. But the tricky part is that the numbers for minutes aren't printed on the clock! Instead, each tick mark stands for 1 minute.

Set the clock to 8:00. **What time is it?** *8:00.* **When the minute hand points to the 12, it is zero minutes past the hour.** Write :00 on a slip of paper and place it above the 12.

As each minute passes, the minute hand moves to the next tick mark. Turn the minute hand so it points to the first tick mark past 12. **The minute hand is now 1 tick mark past the 12, so the clock shows 1 minute past 8 o'clock.**

Have your child move the minute hand forward to the next tick mark. **How many minutes past 8 o'clock does the clock show now?** *2 minutes.* Continue moving forward 1 tick mark at a time until the minute hand points to the 1.

The minute hand moved forward 5 tick marks to get to the 1. So, when the minute hand points to the 1, it is 5 minutes past the hour. Have your child write :05 on a slip of paper and place it next to the 1.

Continue moving the minute hand forward one tick mark at a time until it points to the 2. **How many minutes past 8 o'clock does the clock show now?** *10.* Have your child write :10 on a slip of paper and place it next to the 2.

Continue in the same way until the minute hand points to the 3. **How many minutes past 8 o'clock does the clock show now?** *15.* Have your child write :15 on a slip of paper and place it next to the 3.

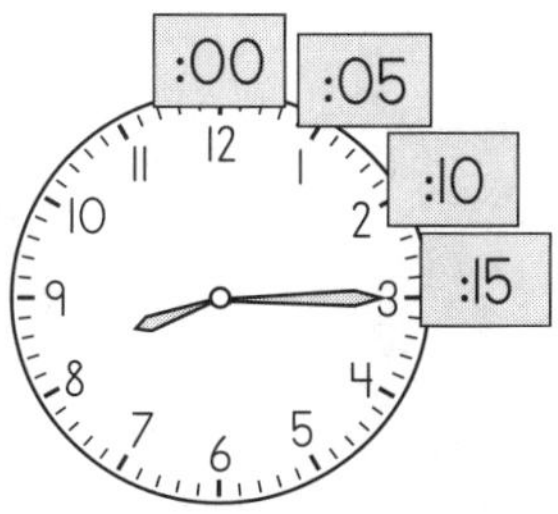

It takes a long time to count every tick mark! Do you notice a pattern we can use to make it easier to tell the minutes? *Sample answer: The numbers are the same numbers we say when we count by 5s.*

> If your child doesn't recognize the pattern, point to the slips of paper and read them aloud: **5, 10, 15. What counting sequence is that?** *The count-by-5s sequence.*

Move the minute hand to each printed number on the clock (in order). Have your child count by 5s to label the minutes for each printed number.

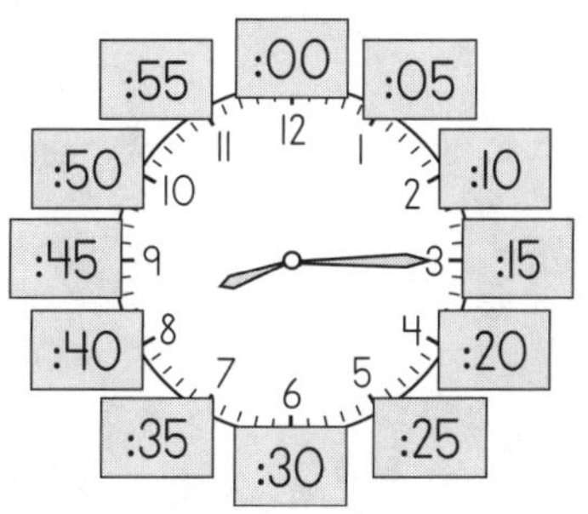

When the minute hand reaches the 12, say: **60 minutes have passed, so a new hour begins.**

Activity: Practice Identifying Minutes

With your child looking away, secretly turn the :40 slip of paper face-down. Point to the 8 on the clock. **When the minute hand points to the 8, how many minutes past the hour is it?** *40.* If your child's not sure, have him start at the previous number and count by 5s: *35, 40.*

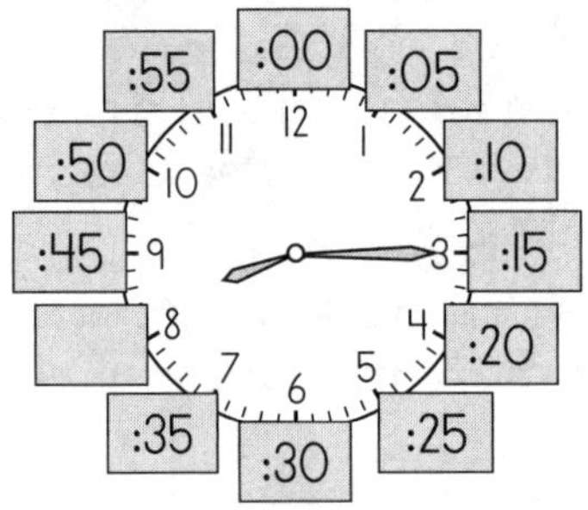

Turn the slip face-up. Repeat with the rest of the slips of paper, in random order.

> If your child is ready for more challenge, turn all the labels face-down. Point to one and have your child identify it. Then, have him turn the label face-up to check his answer.

Now that you know about the hour hand and minute hand, you're ready to tell the time with hours and minutes! You'll learn how next week.

Save these Minute Labels for future lessons.

Workbook: Label Minutes on a Clock and Review

Have your child complete workbook pages 16.4A and 16.4B.

Lesson 16.5
Enrichment and Review (Optional)

	Purpose	Materials
Warm-up	• Count backward by 1s, 2s, 5s, or 10s • Review memory work • Review your child's favorite or most challenging activities from Week 16	• Varies, depending on the activities you choose
Picture Book	• Understand telling time in a real-life context	• *It's About Time, Max!*, written by Kitty Richards and illustrated by Gioia Flammenghi
Enrichment Activity	• Estimate seconds	• Timer

Warm-up: Counting, Memory Work, and Review

- Have your child count backward from 200 to 100 by 1s, 2s, 5s, or 10s. (Choose whichever counting sequence your child needs to practice the most.)
- Quiz your child on the memory work through Week 16. See page 523 for the full list.
- If you have time, repeat one or two of the activities from this week's lessons. Choose activities your child especially enjoyed or found challenging.

Math Picture Book: *It's About Time, Max!*

Read *It's About Time, Max!*, written by Kitty Richards and illustrated by Gioia Flammenghi. As you read, point out the clocks in the illustrations and discuss how Max finds the times.

Enrichment Activity: Estimate Seconds While Balancing on One Foot

Seconds are very short! It takes about a second to say the word Mississippi. Have your child balance on one foot for as long as he can. Have him count "Mississippis" to estimate how long he balances: *1 Mississippi, 2 Mississippi, 3 Mississippi...*

At the same time, use a timer to measure how long he balances. Then, compare his estimate with the actual length of time and discuss how close the measurements are. For example: **The timer measured 12 seconds, and you counted 11 Mississippis. That's pretty close!**

Repeat several times. Have your child try balancing on both the left and right foot, and also have him try balancing with his eyes closed.

> If your family typically uses a different word to estimate seconds (such as "thousand" or "potato"), feel free to use that word instead.

Week 16 Answer Key

16.1A

Label the hours on the clock.
Color the hour hand blue and the minute hand green.

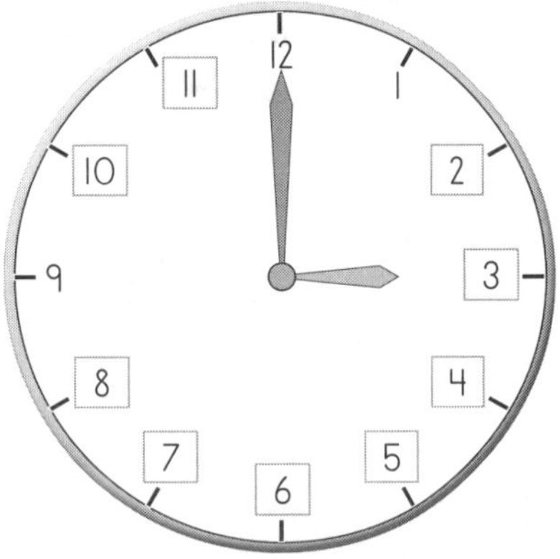

Write a.m. or p.m. for each time.

Sunrise 7:00 a.m.	Breakfast 7:30 a.m.	Lunch 12:30 p.m.
Play outside 2:00 p.m.	Dinner 6:00 p.m.	Bedtime 8:00 p.m.

16.1B

Complete.

48 + 27 = 75	29 + 33 = 62
52 + 38 = 90	75 + 16 = 91
61 + 24 = 85	19 + 36 = 55

Solve.

You have $38.
Then, you earn $5.
How much do you have now?

38 + 5 = 43

$ 43

You have $29.
Then, you earn $7.
How much do you have now?

29 + 7 = 36

$ 36

16.2A

See the Instructor Guide for directions.

What hour does the hour hand show?

3, 8, 10
5, 7, 12

16.2B

Match.

75 + 7	79	45 + 36
72 + 7	80	62 + 20
74 + 6	81	26 + 54
78 + 3	82	34 + 45

75 + 7 — 82; 72 + 7 — 79; 74 + 6 — 80; 78 + 3 — 81
79 — 34 + 45; 80 — 26 + 54; 81 — 45 + 36; 82 — 62 + 20

Solve.

How much less do the mittens cost than the scarf?

15 − 9 = 6

$ 6

Ethan earned $9 on Monday, $7 on Tuesday, and $5 on Wednesday. How much did he earn in all?

9 + 7 + 5 = 21

$ 21

Week 16 Answer Key

16.3A

Write the time.

Complete the sequence.

16.3B

Complete.

25 → +15 → 40 → +17 → 57 → +8 → 65 → +9 → 74

47 → +6 → 53 → +28 → 81 → +12 → 93 → +6 → 99

68 → +14 → 82 → +7 → 89 → +5 → 94 → +6 → 100

Write how many.

16.4A

Label the minutes.

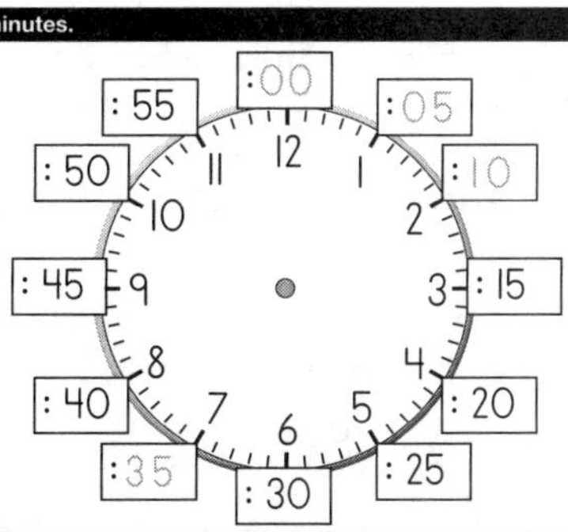

Write the time.

16.4B

Complete.

42 + 4 = 46	37 + 9 = 46
52 + 4 = 56	57 + 9 = 66
72 + 4 = 76	87 + 9 = 96
26 + 18 = 44	45 + 45 = 90
26 + 38 = 64	35 + 55 = 90
46 + 18 = 64	25 + 65 = 90

Complete. Use a decimal point and dollar sign.

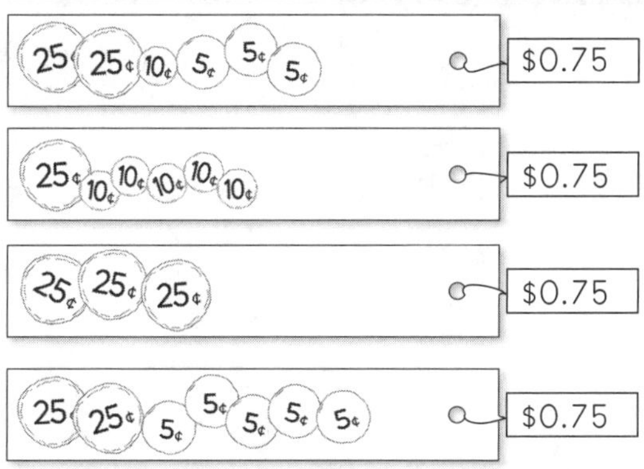

Week 17
Tell Time to the Minute

Overview

Now that your child understands the hour hand well, she'll learn to tell time to the minute. She'll begin by telling time with the 5-minute marks on the clock and progress to reading any time on the clock.

Lesson 17.1 Tell Time with 5-Minute Marks
Lesson 17.2 Half-Hours and Quarter-Hours
Lesson 17.3 Tell Time to the Minute
Lesson 17.4 Practice Telling Time
Lesson 17.5 Enrichment and Review (Optional)

Teaching Math with Confidence: Clocks and Number Lines

This week, you'll teach your child to tell time to the minute. First, she'll count by 5s to tell the minutes for the numbered tick marks on the clock. Then, you'll teach her how to read any time on the clock.

Telling time to the minute is very similar to identifying numbers on the number line. For example, in Unit 1, your child found that 9 is 4 tick marks past 5, or 1 tick mark before 10. In the same way, she'll find that the 9-minute mark on the clock is 4 minutes past the 5-minute mark, and 1 minute before the 10-minute mark.

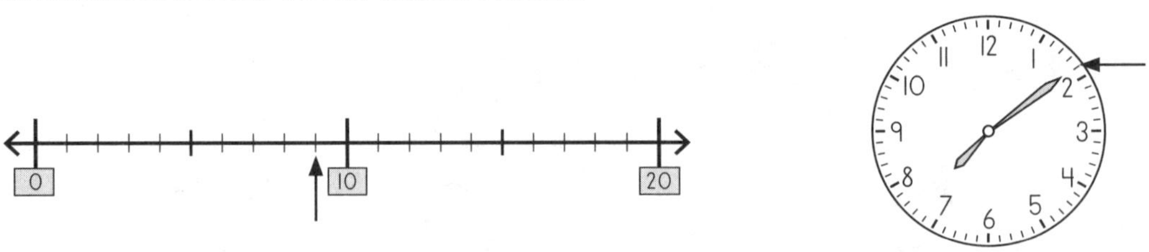

Finding 9 on the number line and 9 minutes past the hour on the clock.
Both skills require a similar thought process.

You and your child will compare and contrast the number line and clock in Lesson 17.3 to make this connection clear. In Unit 9, you and your child will explore how rulers are similar to the number line, too. All three provide examples of quantities that are measured rather than counted. Like the bars on the bar graphs in Unit 5, these representations help your child understand that there's more to using numbers than just counting individual objects.

Extra Materials Needed for Week 17

- For optional Enrichment and Review Lesson:
  - *Pigs on a Blanket,* written by Amy Axelrod and illustrated by Sharon McGinley-Nally
  - Online or streaming video with child-appropriate content, any length

Lesson 17.1
Tell Time with 5-Minute Marks

	Purpose	Materials
Warm-up	• Count by one-hour intervals • Practice memory work • Review finding half of numbers	• Clock • Number Machine (from Lesson 6.1) • Base-ten blocks
Activities	• Practice identifying 5-minute marks on the clock • Tell time with 5-minute marks on a clock	• Clock • Minute Labels (from Lesson 16.4)
Workbook	• Tell time with 5-minute marks • Assess subtraction fact mastery	• Workbook pages 17.1A and 17.1B

If your child can already tell time with 5-minute marks, make this lesson a quick review and combine it with Lesson 17.2.

Warm-up: Counting, Memory Work, and Review

- Set the clock to 6:00. **We can count by units of time just like we count by numbers. Today, we'll count by hours.** Have your child turn the minute hand around the clock and count each hour as the clock shows it: *6 o'clock, 7 o'clock, 8 o'clock....* Stop her when she reaches 6:00 again.
- **How many cents equal one dollar?** *100.*
- Set up the Number Machine and pretend to set it to the Half setting. Model the questions with base-ten blocks as needed.
    - **If 10 goes in, what number will come out?** *5.*
    - **If 20 goes in, what number will come out?** *10.*
    - **If 30 goes in, what number will come out?** *15.*
    - **If 40 goes in, what number will come out?** *20.*
    - **If 50 goes in, what number will come out?** *25.*
    - **If 60 goes in, what number will come out?** *30.*
    - **If 70 goes in, what number will come out?** *35.*
    - **If 80 goes in, what number will come out?** *40.*
    - **If 90 goes in, what number will come out?** *45.*
    - **If 100 goes in, what number will come out?** *50.*

Activity: Practice Identifying 5-Minute Marks on the Clock

In the last lesson, you learned how to count by 5s to tell the minutes on a clock with hands. Today, you'll learn how to tell time with hours and minutes.

Place the clock on the table. Mix up the Minute Labels from Lesson 16.4. Have your child place each label next to the corresponding printed number on the clock. Remind her to count by 5s to find the correct order.

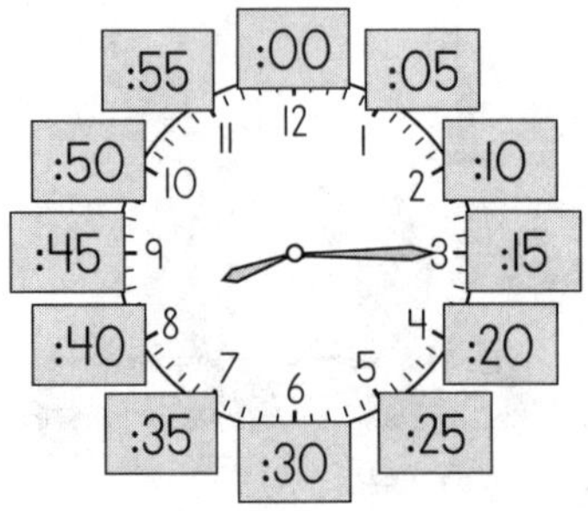

Turn the labels face-down. Point to the slip of paper next to the 4. **When the minute hand points to the 4, how many minutes past the hour is it?** *20*. Have your child flip the label over to check.

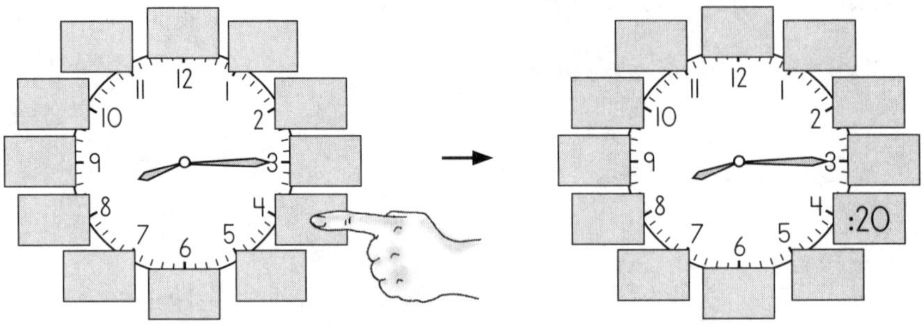

Leave the slip face-up. Point to the rest of the Minute Labels in random order until your child has identified them and flipped all of them over.

Activity: Tell Time with 5-Minute Marks

Put away the Minute Labels. Set the clock to 9:20. **What is the hour?** *9*. **How many minutes have passed since the start of the hour?** *20*. **So, what's the time?** *9:20*. Have your child write 9:20 on a piece of paper.

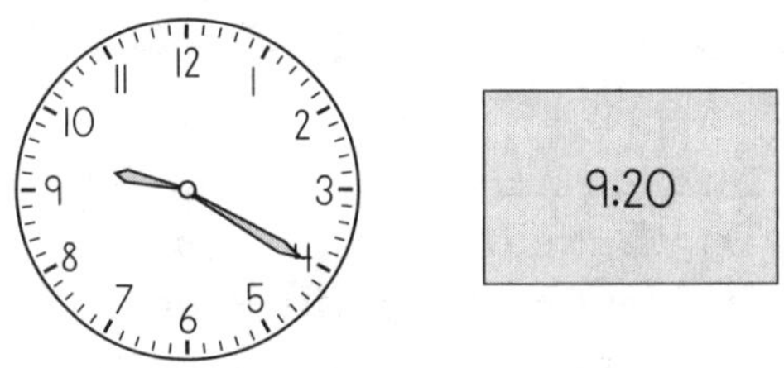

Set the clock to the following times and have your child read and write each time.

10:30

10:55

11:00

11:05

11:45

12:00

As needed, remind your child to think about which hour "owns" each section of the clock. Encourage her to count by 5s to find the minutes.

Workbook: Tell Time with 5-Minute Marks and Review

Have your child complete workbook pages 17.1A and 17.1B. Have her work horizontally across the rows of subtraction problems on 17.1B.

If your child is overwhelmed by the number of subtraction problems on workbook page 17.1B, ask her the problems orally instead. Note whether she knows the correct answer, and give her at least 3 seconds to respond to each question.

Workbook pages 17.1B, 17.2B, 17.3B, and 17.4B together provide an informal assessment of how well your child has mastered the subtraction facts. See the Unit 7 Checkpoint for guidance on assessing your child's progress.

Save workbook page 17.1B so that you can look at it with workbook pages 17.2B, 17.3B, and 17.4B to assess your child's subtraction fact mastery.

Lesson 17.2
Half-Hours and Quarter-Hours

	Purpose	Materials
Warm-up	• Count by 5s • Practice memory work • Review identifying halves and fourths	• None
Activities	• Learn that 30 minutes equal half an hour and that 15 minutes equal a quarter-hour • Use half-hours and quarter-hours to figure out other times	• Clock • Minute Labels (from Lesson 16.4)
Workbook	• Tell time with five-minute marks • Assess subtraction fact mastery	• Workbook pages 17.2A and 17.2B

This lesson provides a brief introduction to half- and quarter-hours. Focus on how the half- and quarter-hour numbers on the clock (12, 3, 6, and 9) provide benchmarks for identifying the minute hand's position, and don't worry if your child doesn't fully understand the fractional parts. Your child will learn more about fractions in Unit 11.

Warm-up: Counting, Memory Work, and Review

- Have your child count forward by 5s from the following numbers. Stop him after he reaches the last number listed.
  - **Count forward by 5s from 15:** *15, 20, 25, 30, 35.*
  - **Count forward by 5s from 40:** *40, 45, 50, 55, 60.*
  - **Count forward by 5s from 90:** *90, 95, 100, 105, 110.*
- **Are times in the morning a.m. or p.m.?** *A.m.*
  Are times in the afternoon and evening a.m. or p.m.? *P.m.*
- Draw a circle, rectangle, and square on a piece of paper. Have your child draw a line that splits each shape in half.

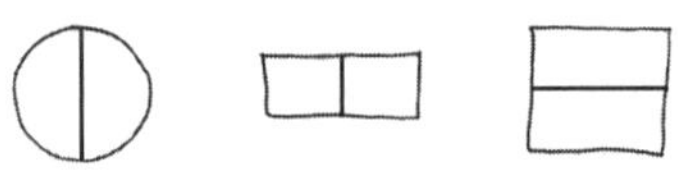

Many answers are possible.

Draw another circle, rectangle, and square. Have your child draw lines that split each shape into fourths.

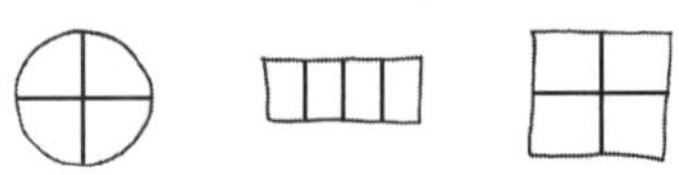

Many answers are possible.

Reviewing halves and fourths prepares your child to learn about half-hours and quarter-hours in this lesson.

Activity: Introduce Half-Hours

In the last lesson, you learned how to tell time with hours and minutes. Today, you'll practice telling time. You'll also learn about half-hours and quarter-hours.

How many minutes are in an hour? *60.* **What is half of 60?** *30.* **So, 30 minutes are half of an hour.** Discuss several half-hour-long activities that your family does. For example: **It takes about half an hour to drive to Grandma's.**

Set a clock to 2:00. Show your child the printed clock at the top of workbook page 17.2A. **When the minute hand points to the 12, it's the start of the hour.** Have your child write 00 in the box above the 12.

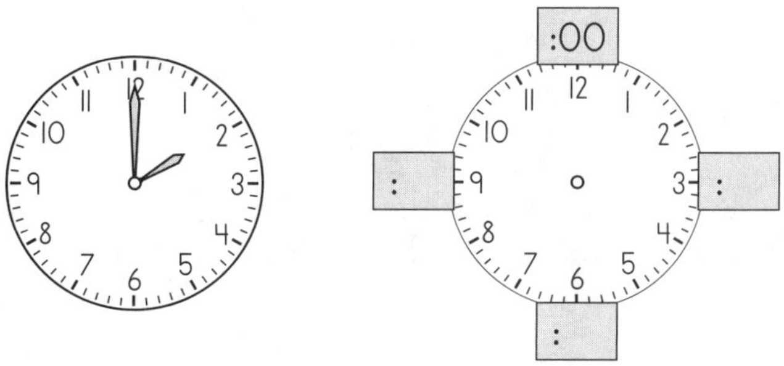

Turn the minute hand on the clock to show 30 minutes past the hour. *Child turns minute hand so that it points to the 6.* Have your child write 30 in the box below the 6.

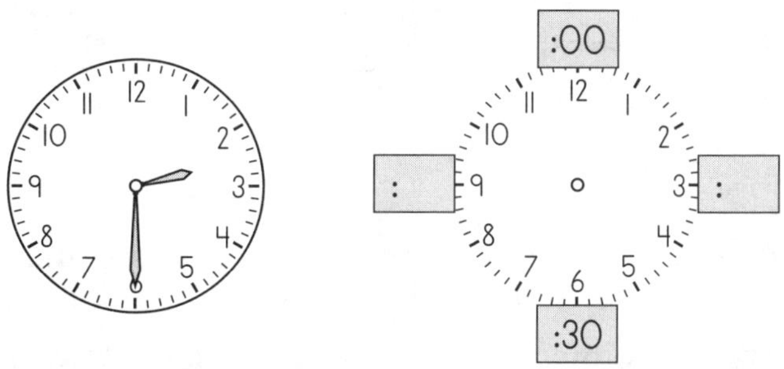

The minute hand traveled half of the way around the clock! Draw a light line vertically across the printed clock to show that the minute hand turned halfway around the clock.

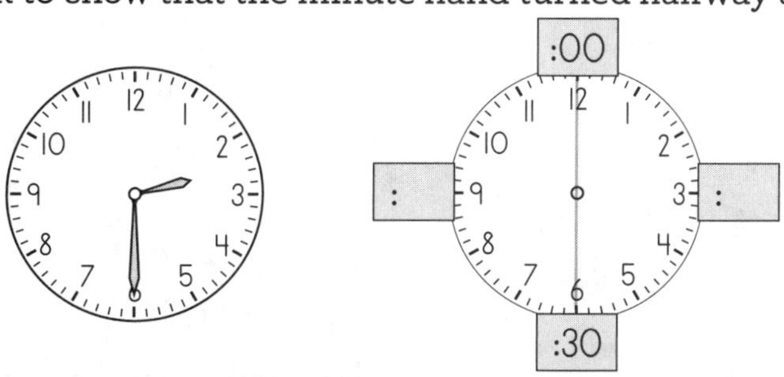

Sometimes, people use the word *half* to tell the time. If someone tells you that it is half past 4, what time do you think they mean? *4:30.* Set the clock to 4:30 to show your child that the minute hand is half an hour past 4 o'clock.

Half past 4.

Activity: Introduce Quarter-Hours

People also sometimes talk about "quarter past" an hour or "quarter to" an hour. A quarter is one-fourth of an hour, just like a quarter coin is one-fourth of a dollar.

Draw a second light line across the printed clock as shown. **These lines split the clock into 4 equal parts. Each part is one-fourth, or one-quarter of the clock.**

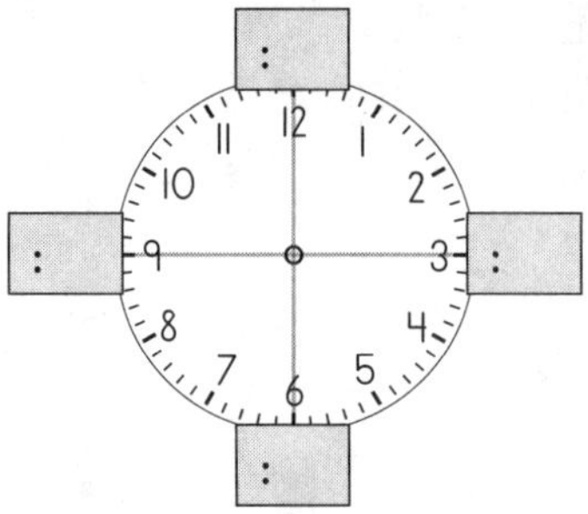

Set the clock to 5:00. Then, turn the minute hand so that it points to the 3. **The minute hand traveled one-fourth of the way around the clock! How many minutes passed?** *15.* Have your child write 15 in the box next to the 3.

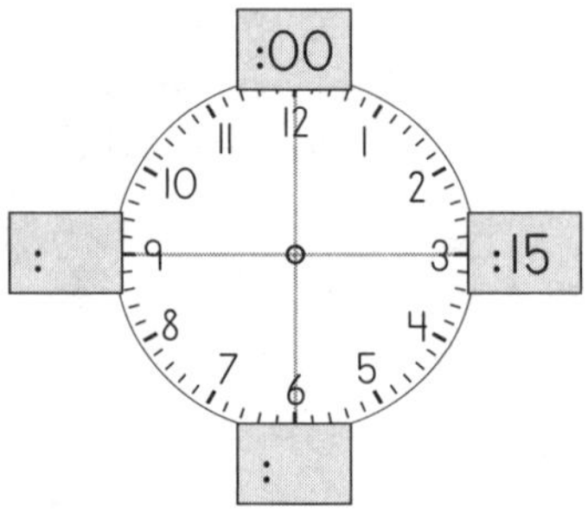

15 minutes is a fourth, or a quarter, of an hour. Discuss several quarter-hour-long activities that your family does. For example: **You usually practice piano for a quarter-hour each day.**

Turn the minute hand so that it points to the 6. **The minute hand traveled another fourth of the way around the clock. Another 15 minutes passed, and now it's 30 minutes past the hour.**

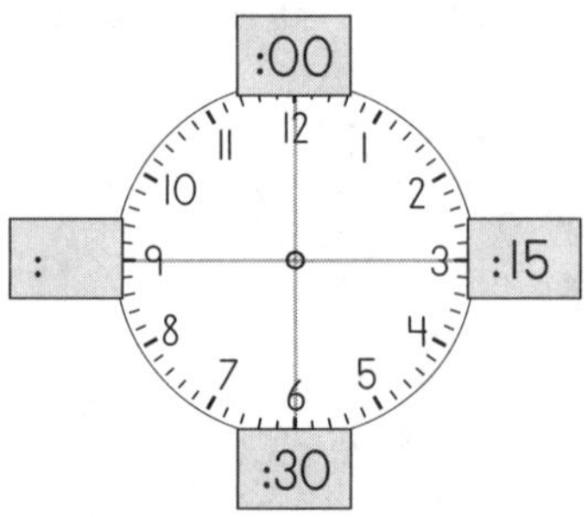

Turn the minute hand so that it points to the 9. **The minute hand traveled another fourth of the way around the clock. Another 15 minutes passed, and now it's 45 minutes past the hour.** Have your child write 45 in the box next to the 9.

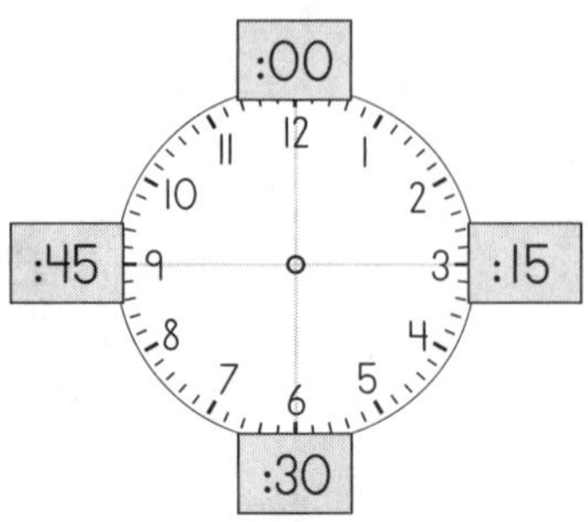

Turn the minute hand so that it points to the 12. **The minute hand traveled another fourth of the way around the clock. Another 15 minutes passed, and now the minute hand has traveled all the way around the clock.**

The 12, 3, 6, and 9 are called the quarter-hour positions for the minute hand. If someone tells you that it is quarter past 6, what time do you think they mean? *6:15.* Set the clock to 6:15 to show your child that the minute hand is one-quarter of the way around the clock and 15 minutes past 6 o'clock.

Quarter past 6.

Activity: Use Half-Hours and Quarter-Hours as Benchmarks

Once you know the quarter-hour minute marks, you can use them to figure out other times, too. Set the clock to 8:30. **What time does the clock show?** *8:30.*

Set the clock to 8:35. **What time does the clock show now?** *8:35.* **How do you know?** *Sample answer: 35 is 5 more than 30.* If your child starts to count by 5s starting with the 12, point out that the time is 5 minutes past 8:30, so it must be 8:35.

5 minutes

Set the clock to 8:50. **What time does the clock show now?** *8:50.* **How do you know?** *Sample answer: 50 is 5 more than 45.*

Repeat with 8:25. If your child doesn't mention it, point out that the time is 5 minutes before 8:30, so it must be 8:25.

5 minutes

Workbook: Tell Time with 5-Minute Marks and Review

Have your child complete workbook pages 17.2A and 17.2B. Have him work horizontally across the rows of subtraction problems on 17.2B.

Save workbook page 17.2B so that you can look at it with workbook pages 17.1B, 17.3B, and 17.4B to assess your child's subtraction fact mastery.

Lesson 17.3
Tell Time to the Minute

	Purpose	Materials
Warm-up	• Count backward by 1s, 2s, and 5s on the number line • Practice memory work • Review telling time with 5-minute marks	• Blank Number Line (Blackline Master 3) • Clock
Activities	• Compare the number line with the clock • Identify minutes on the clock • Tell time to the minute	• Minute Labels (from Lesson 16.4) • Blank Number Line (Blackline Master 3) • Clock
Workbook	• Tell time to the minute • Assess subtraction fact mastery	• Workbook pages 17.3A and 17.3B

Warm-up: Counting, Memory Work, and Review

- Label the Blank Number Line with 70, 80, and 90. Have your child count backward from 90 to 70, by 1s, then 2s, and then 5s. Have her point to each corresponding tick mark as she counts.

  Leave the number line out for the first lesson activity.

- **How many months are in a year?** *12.* **How many days are in a week?** *7.*
- Set the clock to the following times: 6:00, 6:05, 6:30, 6:35, 6:55, 7:00, 7:15, 7:25. Have your child tell each time.

Activity: Compare the Clock and Number Line

In the last few lessons, you learned how to tell the time with the 5-minute marks on the clock. Today, you'll learn how to read any number of minutes on the clock.

Identifying the minutes on a clock is a lot like finding numbers on the number line. Place the clock and Blank Number Line on the table. Label the number line with 0, 10, and 20. Have your child place the Minute Labels in their correct positions around the clock.

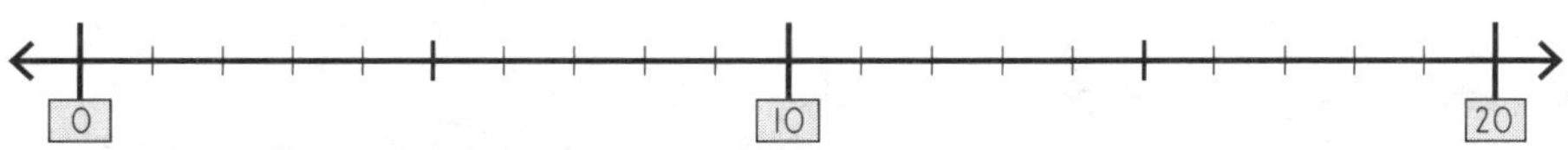

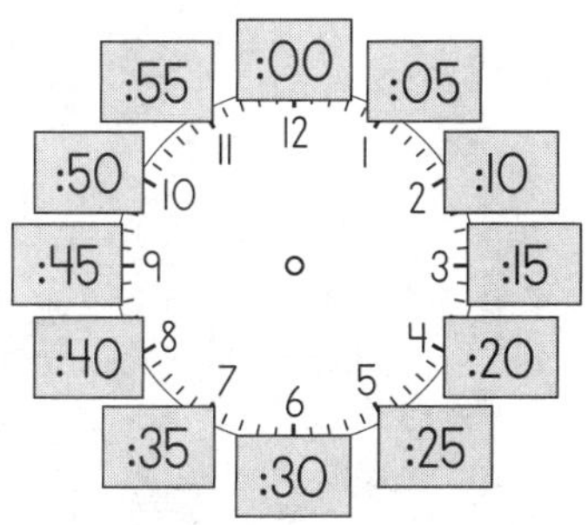

See the Week 17 **Teaching Math with Confidence** for more on the connection between the clock and number line.

What do the clock and number line have in common? *Sample answers: They both have tick marks and numbers. The tick marks are evenly spaced. Some tick marks are labeled and some aren't.*

How are the clock and number line different from each other? *Sample answers: The clock is round, but the number line is straight. The tick marks are numbered differently.*

Even though the clock is a different shape than the number line, you can tell the minutes the same way you tell numbers on the number line. Point to the tick mark for 19 on the number line. **Which tick mark is this?** *19.* **How do you know?** *Sample answers: It's 1 tick mark before 20. It's 4 tick marks after 15.*

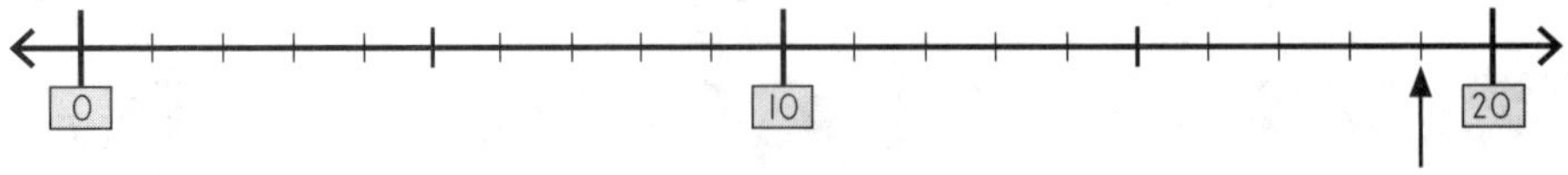

Point to the tick mark for 19 on the clock. Child points to the tick mark before the 4. **How do you know that it's 19?** *Sample answers: It's 1 tick mark before 20 minutes. It's 4 tick marks after 15 minutes.*

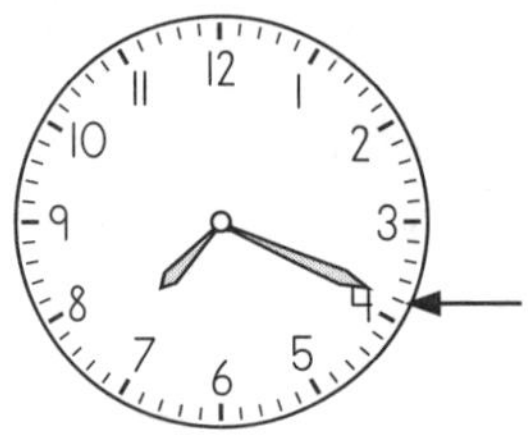

Have your child identify the tick marks for 4, 8, 10, 12, 14, and 17, first on the number line and then on the clock.

Activity: Identify Minutes on the Clock

Put away the number line and turn the Minute Labels face-down around the clock. Point to the following tick marks on the clock and have your child identify them.

32

29

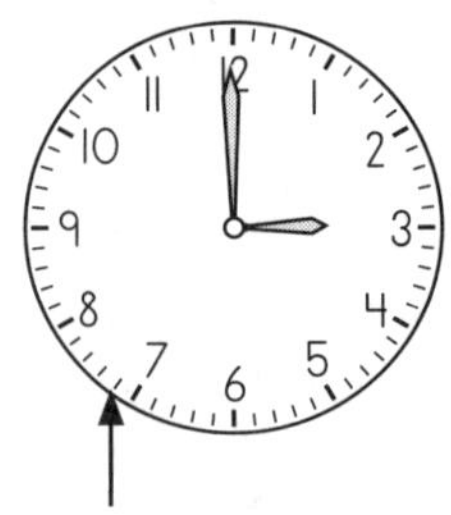

36

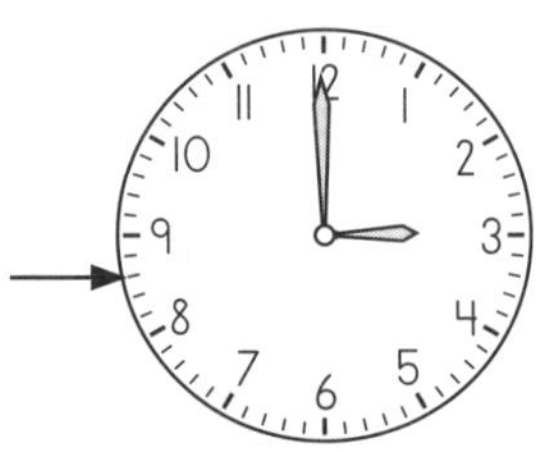

43

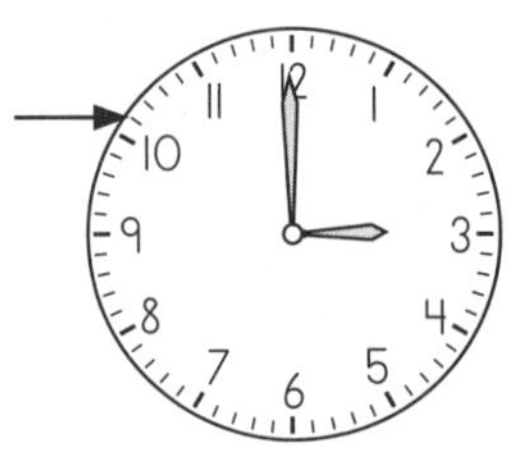

51

58

Encourage your child to recall the nearby 5-minute marks and use them to help identify the tick marks. For example, for 32: **30 minutes have passed since the start of the hour when the minute hand points to the 6. So, if the minute hand moves 2 more tick marks, it's at 32.** If she has trouble, allow her to turn over a nearby Minute Label to help.

Activity: Tell Time to the Minute

Now you're ready to tell the time with both hours and minutes! Set the clock to the following times and have your child tell each time. Have her identify the hour first and then the minutes.

4:36

7:21

8:59

9:04

If your child has trouble visually tracking where the minute hand is pointing, have her use her finger to trace a line from the end of the minute hand to the nearest tick mark.

Your child may have trouble telling the hour for 8:59 and 9:04, since the hour hand is very close to the 9. If so, encourage her to also consider the minute hand as she finds the hour. For example, for 8:59: **The minute hand isn't quite back to the top of the clock, so the new hour hasn't started yet. So, the hour hand must be just before the new hour, too.**

Workbook: Tell Time to the Minute and Assess Subtraction Fact Mastery

Have your child complete workbook pages 17.3A and 17.3B. Have her work horizontally across the rows of subtraction problems on 17.3B.

Save workbook page 17.3B so that you can look at it with workbook pages 17.1B, 17.2B, and 17.4B to assess your child's subtraction fact mastery.

Lesson 17.4
Practice Telling Time

	Purpose	Materials
Warm-up	• Count by 5-minute intervals • Practice memory work • Review mental subtraction	• Clock • Base-ten blocks, optional
Activities	• Practice telling time to the minute • Set a clock to match times	• Clock
Workbook	• Tell time to the minute • Assess subtraction fact mastery	• Workbook pages 17.4A and 17.4B

Warm-up: Counting, Memory Work, and Review

- Set the clock to 10:00. Have your child count by 5-minute intervals from 10:00 to 11:00: *10:00, 10:05, 10:10....* Have him turn the minute hand to match each time.
- **Are times in the morning a.m. or p.m.?** *A.m.* **Are times in the afternoon and evening a.m. or p.m.?** *P.m.*
- Write the following problems on paper and have your child solve them mentally. Allow him to use base-ten blocks as needed.
  - × 67 - 5 = *62*
  - × 50 - 20 = *30*
  - × 54 - 20 = *34*
  - × 80 - 40 = *40*
  - × 81 - 40 = *41*

Activity: Practice Telling Time to the Minute

In the last lesson, you learned how to tell time to the minute. Today, you'll practice telling time some more.

Set a clock to the following times and have your child tell each time.

2:09

3:41

6:16

7:49

10:56

12:01

Activity: Plan a Perfect Day with Times to the Minute

We're going to make a schedule for an imaginary perfect day. You get to choose whatever activities you want! The only rule is that none of the minutes in your schedule can be numbers we say when we count by 5s.

This "rule" ensures that your child gets lots of practice with setting times on the clock and telling time to the minute. Your child may feel that these times sound strange, since we usually round to the nearest 5 minutes in everyday conversation.

Start a simple chart like the following. **What time would you like to wake up?** *Answers will vary.* Have your child set the clock to the time he names.

Activity	Time
Wake up	8:32

Sample chart

What would you like to do next? At what time? *Answers will vary.* Have your child set the clock to the matching time. Continue in this way until your child has made a list of 8-10 activities.

Activity	Time
Wake up	8:32
Eat ice cream for breakfast	9:04
Go to the zoo	9:37
Have hot dogs for lunch	11:58
Come home and watch a movie	1:23
Make a huge fort outside	3:47
Go out for pizza	6:19
Play board games	7:33
Go to bed	9:59

Sample chart

Workbook: Tell Time to the Minute and Assess Subtraction Fact Mastery

Have your child complete workbook pages 17.4A and 17.4B. Have him work horizontally across the rows of subtraction problems on 17.4B.

Save workbook page 17.4B so that you can look at it with workbook pages 17.1B, 17.2B, and 17.3B to assess your child's subtraction fact mastery.

Lesson 17.5
Enrichment and Review (Optional)

	Purpose	Materials
Warm-up	• Count backward by 1s, 2s, 5s, or 10s • Review memory work • Review your child's favorite or most challenging activities from Week 17	• Varies, depending on the activities you choose
Picture Book	• Model elapsed time on a clock	• *Pigs on a Blanket,* written by Amy Axelrod and illustrated by Sharon McGinley-Nally
Enrichment Activity	• Understand minutes and seconds in the context of elapsed time in a video	• Online or streaming video with child-appropriate content, any length

Warm-up: Counting, Memory Work, and Review

- Have your child count backward from 200 to 100 by 1s, 2s, 5s, or 10s. (Choose whichever counting sequence your child needs to practice the most.)
- Quiz your child on the memory work through Week 16. See page 523 for the full list.
- If you have time, repeat one or two of the activities from this week's lessons. Choose activities your child especially enjoyed or found challenging.

Math Picture Book: *Pigs on a Blanket*

Read *Pigs on a Blanket,* written by Amy Axelrod and illustrated by Sharon McGinley-Nally. As you read, set a clock to 11:30 and then have your child turn the hands on a clock to match the time that passes in the book.

Help your child as needed to figure out how far to turn the clock hands each time. She will learn more about elapsed time in third grade.

Enrichment Activity: Minutes and Seconds in Videos

Begin playing an online or streaming video. (You don't need to actually watch the video, so any length and child-appropriate content is fine.) Pause the video and then discuss the way the progress bar represents time. Point out the following:

- The colon separating the minutes and seconds
- The current time that has elapsed in the video
- The total time left (or total length) of the video

Skip forward in the video several times and discuss how the times in the progress bar change.

If your child does not watch videos, use music instead.

Week 17 Answer Key

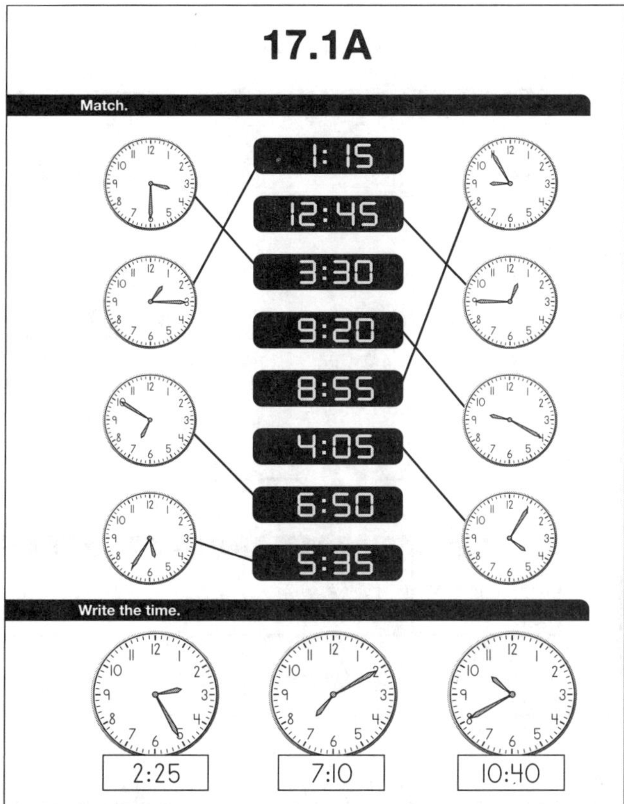

17.1A

Match.

1:15, 12:45, 3:30, 9:20, 8:55, 4:05, 6:50, 5:35

Write the time.

2:25 | 7:10 | 10:40

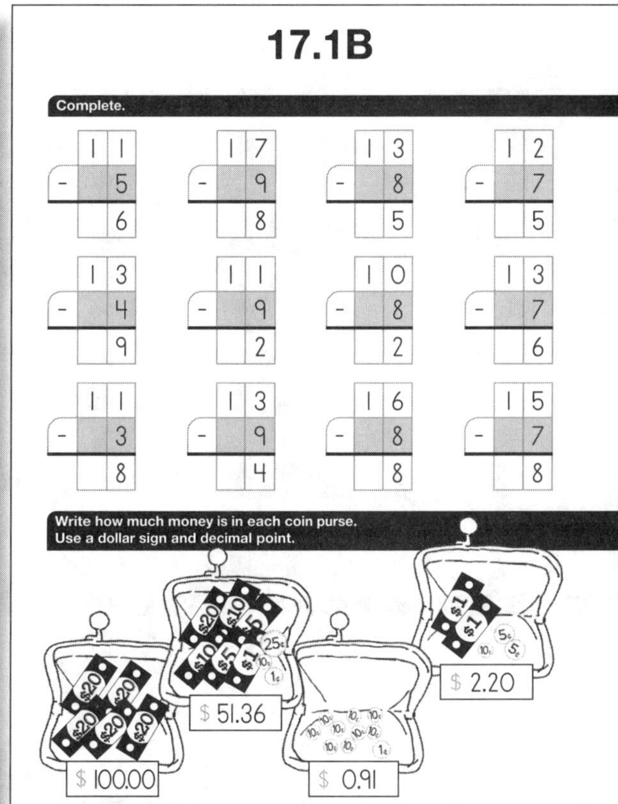

17.1B

Complete.

11 − 5 = 6 | 17 − 9 = 8 | 13 − 8 = 5 | 12 − 7 = 5

13 − 4 = 9 | 11 − 9 = 2 | 10 − 8 = 2 | 13 − 7 = 6

11 − 3 = 8 | 13 − 9 = 4 | 16 − 8 = 8 | 15 − 7 = 8

Write how much money is in each coin purse. Use a dollar sign and decimal point.

$ 100.00 | $ 51.36 | $ 0.91 | $ 2.20

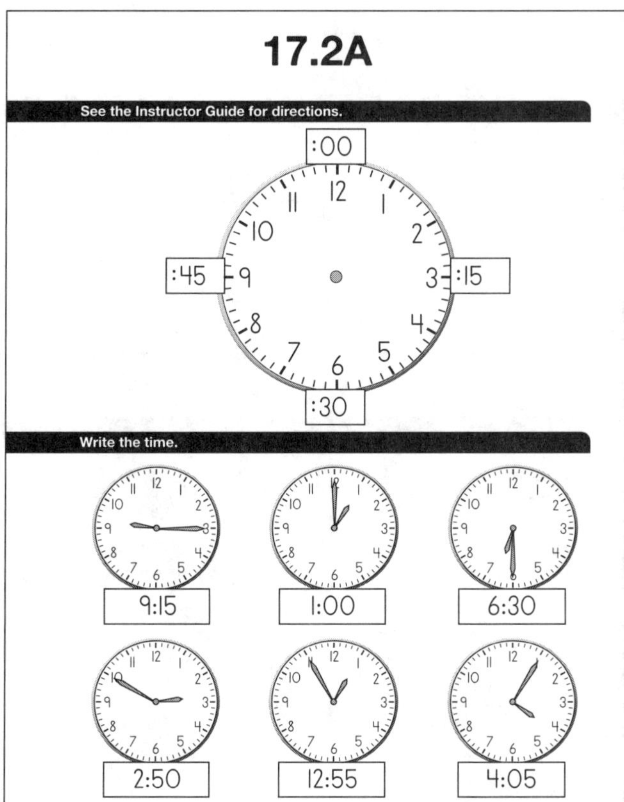

17.2A

See the Instructor Guide for directions.

:00 | :15 | :30 | :45

Write the time.

9:15 | 1:00 | 6:30

2:50 | 12:55 | 4:05

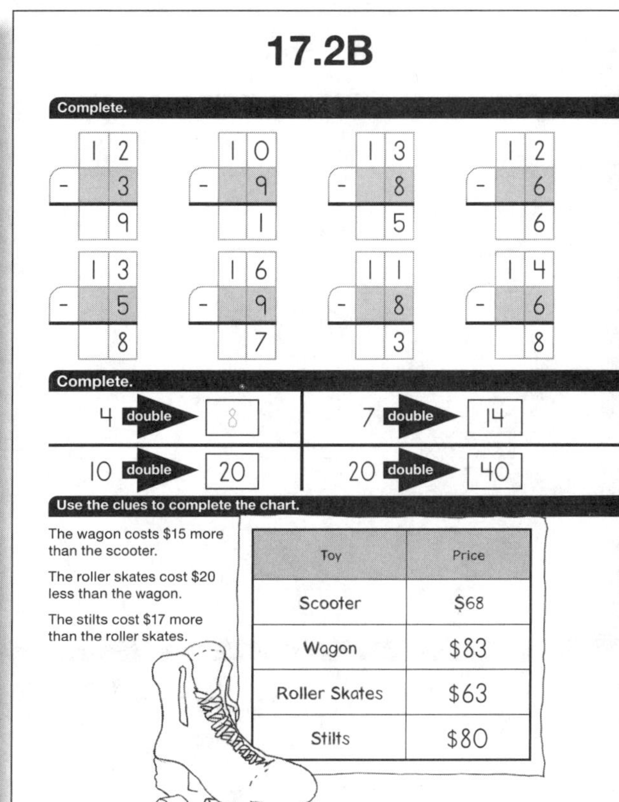

17.2B

Complete.

12 − 3 = 9 | 10 − 9 = 1 | 13 − 8 = 5 | 12 − 6 = 6

13 − 5 = 8 | 16 − 9 = 7 | 11 − 8 = 3 | 14 − 6 = 8

Complete.

4 double 8 | 7 double 14

10 double 20 | 20 double 40

Use the clues to complete the chart.

The wagon costs $15 more than the scooter.

The roller skates cost $20 less than the wagon.

The stilts cost $17 more than the roller skates.

Toy	Price
Scooter	$68
Wagon	$83
Roller Skates	$63
Stilts	$80

Week 17 Answer Key

17.3A

Match.

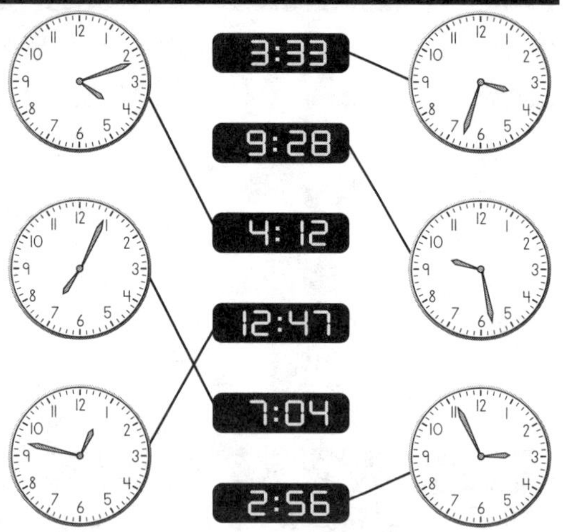

Write the time.

8:19	11:41	5:24

17.3B

Complete.

11 − 2 = 9	13 − 9 = 4	16 − 8 = 8	15 − 6 = 9
12 − 4 = 8	14 − 9 = 5	17 − 8 = 9	13 − 6 = 7
14 − 5 = 9	18 − 9 = 9	15 − 8 = 7	11 − 6 = 5

Complete the circles with <, >, or =.

40 (=) 40	17 (<) 71	76 (>) 75
40 (>) 4	104 (<) 140	98 (>) 89
148 (<) 184	150 (<) 160	200 (=) 200

17.4A

Write the time.

7:19	11:43	9:35

12:30	5:07	2:22

10:41	1:15	6:58

Complete the sequence.

17.4B

Complete.

12 − 5 = 7	15 − 9 = 6	12 − 8 = 4	14 − 7 = 7
11 − 4 = 7	12 − 9 = 3	17 − 8 = 9	16 − 7 = 9

Solve.

You have $45.
The toy costs $50.
How much more money do you need?

50 − 45 = 5

Your child may write 45+5=50. $ 5

You have $22.
The toy costs $30.
How much more money do you need?

30 − 22 = 8

$ 8

Unit 7 Checkpoint

What to Expect at the End of Unit 7

By the end of Unit 7, most children will be able to do the following:

- Identify a.m. or p.m. Many children will have trouble remembering the difference between the two abbreviations. You'll continue to review them as memory work to make sure your child learns them.
- Be familiar with half-hours and quarter-hours. Your child does not need to fully understand these terms, especially quarter-hour.
- Know which hour "owns" each part of the clock and identify the hour hand's position. Many children will need to be reminded to look closely at the hour hand's position and not just write the number closest to the hour hand.
- Count by 5s and use number-line thinking to tell time to the minute. Many children will have memorized the position for some of the minutes on the clock, but some will still need to count by 5s every time.

Is Your Child Ready to Move on?

Your child does not need to master telling time to the minute before moving on to Unit 8. Learning to tell time proficiently takes a lot of practice, and the warm-ups and review workbook pages will give your child plenty of opportunities to cement this challenging skill.

In Unit 8, your child will learn to subtract two-digit numbers mentally. Before moving on to Unit 8, your child should have already mastered the following skills:

- Solve simple mental subtraction problems with two-digit numbers (such as 45 – 2 or 60 - 40).
- Find answers to most of the subtraction facts to 20 mentally and in less than 3 seconds. (It's fine if your child is still working on getting faster at the harder facts.)

Use workbook pages 17.1B, 17.2B, 17.3B, and 17.4B to assess your child's progress with the subtraction facts. They're organized to make it easy for you to see which facts your child has mastered and which facts she still needs to practice. Each workbook page is organized in the same way:

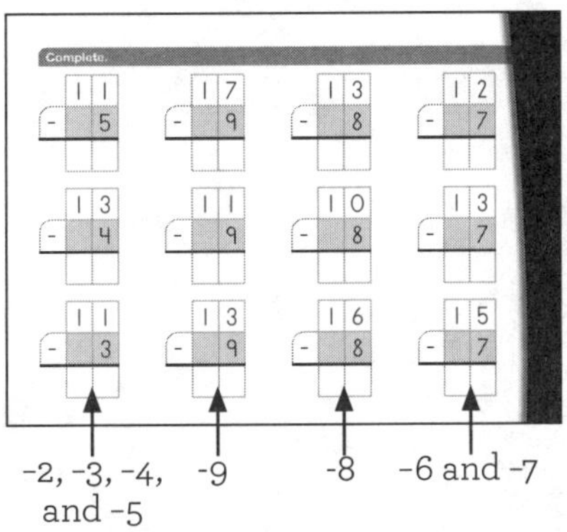

For example, if your child has several problems wrong in Column 3 on the pages (or took longer than 3 seconds to answer many of the problems), she needs more practice with the -8 facts.

What to Do If Your Child Needs More Practice

If your child needs more practice with mental subtraction or some of the subtraction facts, spend a few days practicing the corresponding activities or games before moving on to Unit 8.

Activities for solving simple mental subtraction problems

- Mental Math Magic with Subtraction (Lesson 3.3)
- Subtraction Mental Math Practice (Warm-up, Lessons 16.3 and 17.4)

Activities for practicing subtraction facts to 20

- Subtraction Climb and Slide (Lesson 1.3)
- Difference War (Lesson 9.1)
- Subtraction Race (-9 Version) (Lesson 9.2)
- Subtraction Race (-8 Version) (Lesson 9.4)
- Treasure Hunt (-6 and -7 facts, Lesson 10.2)
- Four in a Row (-2, -3, -4, and -5 facts, Lesson 11.1)

If you practice the subtraction facts for several days and find that your child does not have them fully mastered, move on to Unit 8 anyway. Children vary in how long it takes them to develop speed and fluency with the subtraction facts. Your child will continue to practice them in the context of mental subtraction in Unit 8.

Unit 8
Mental Subtraction to 100

Overview

In Unit 6, your child learned how to add one- and two-digit numbers in his head. In this unit, he'll use similar strategies to learn mental subtraction. First, he'll learn to subtract one-digit numbers from two-digit numbers. Then, he'll learn to subtract two-digit numbers from two-digit numbers.

$$42 - 4 = 38 \qquad 82 - 45 = 37$$

Your child will learn to solve subtraction problems like these in his head.

Many pilot testers reported that this unit looked too hard for their child at first glance. But, by the end, they were pleasantly surprised to find that their child could solve these difficult mental subtraction problems with confidence. The lessons include less independent practice than usual so that you can provide lots of support as your child tackles this challenging skill. As always, feel free to adjust your pace to your child and use base-ten blocks as often as needed to help him understand the strategies and concepts.

Week 18	Mental Subtraction, Part 1
Week 19	Mental Subtraction, Part 2

What Your Child Will Learn

In this unit your child will learn to:

- Mentally subtract one- or two-digit numbers from two-digit numbers

Recommended Math Picture Books (Optional)

These picture books are scheduled in the optional Enrichment and Review lessons at the end of each week.

- *Is a Blue Whale the Biggest Thing There Is?* by Robert E. Wells. Albert Whitman and Company, 1993.
- *Nothing Stopped Sophie: The Story of Unshakable Mathematician Sophie Germain,* written by Cheryl Bardoe and illustrated by Barbara McClintock. Little, Brown, and Company, 2018.

Week 18
Mental Subtraction, Part 1

Overview

Your child will learn how to mentally subtract one-digit numbers from two-digit numbers. You'll use base-ten blocks to help him master this foundational skill, just as you did with addition in Week 14.

Lesson 18.1	Subtract One-Digit Numbers from Multiples of 10
Lesson 18.2	Subtract One-Digit Numbers with Base-Ten Blocks
Lesson 18.3	Subtract One-Digit Numbers Mentally
Lesson 18.4	Practice Subtracting One-Digit Numbers
Lesson 18.5	Enrichment and Review (Optional)

Teaching Math with Confidence: How to Use Base-Ten Blocks without Them Becoming a Crutch

This week, you'll use base-ten blocks to teach your child how to subtract one-digit numbers from two-digit numbers. Manipulatives like counters and blocks are essential for helping children understand math, because they transform abstract ideas into things they can touch, see, and move around.

However, these materials can slow down children's mathematical growth if they're used too much. For example, if your child uses base-ten blocks to solve every single subtraction problem, he won't learn how to solve them mentally. Your goal as his teacher is to encourage him to use the manipulatives as much as he needs—but only as a stepping stone to solving problems without manipulatives.

This week's lessons provide suggestions for helping your child transition from blocks to mental computations, but feel free to adjust depending on your own child's needs.

- If your child is ever unsure or confused about how to solve a problem, use the base-ten blocks to clarify or demonstrate.
- If your child can confidently solve problems without counting one by one, don't slow him down by requiring him to use the base-ten blocks.
- If you're not sure whether your child understands a concept or strategy, have him pretend to be the teacher and demonstrate how to solve the problem with manipulatives.

Don't be surprised if your child sometimes relies on base-ten blocks and sometimes solves problems mentally. Children's math development does not always progress in a straight line, and they often need to consolidate learning with a step backward before they're ready to move forward.

Extra Materials Needed for Week 18

- For optional Enrichment and Review Lesson:
  - *Is a Blue Whale the Biggest Thing There Is?* by Robert E. Wells
  - Calculator (or calculator app)

Lesson 18.1
Subtract One-Digit Numbers from Multiples of 10

	Purpose	Materials
Warm-up	• Count by 10s • Practice memory work • Review identifying missing addends	• None
Activities	• Subtract one-digit numbers from multiples of 10 (like 30, 50, or 90)	• Base-ten blocks • Workbook page 18.1A • Four in a Row game board (from workbook page 18.1A) • Counters
Workbook	• Subtract one-digit numbers from multiples of 10	• Workbook page 18.1B

Warm-up: Counting, Memory Work, and Review

- Have your child count by 10s to 200.
- **What is another name for 12 a.m.?** *Midnight.*
  What is another name for 12 p.m.? *Noon.*
- Secretly write each of the following equations on a piece of paper and hide the addend indicated with a slip of paper. Have your child use her "x-ray vision" to identify the hidden number in each equation.

75 + [5] = 80 39 + [1] = 40 97 + [3] = 100

84 + [6] = 90 52 + [8] = 60

Activity: Subtract One-Digit Numbers from Multiples of 10

In Unit 5, you learned how to add numbers in your head. In this unit, you'll learn how to subtract numbers in your head. Today, you'll learn how to subtract one-digit numbers from the numbers you say when you count by 10s, like 50, 80, or 40.

Let's pretend the base-ten blocks are chocolate bars, and a hungry alligator is eating them up. Place 5 rods on the table. Cover 3 of the units on 1 rod with a slip of paper. **There are 50 pieces of chocolate. Then, the alligator eats 3.** Write 50 - 3 = on a piece of paper.

50 - 3 =

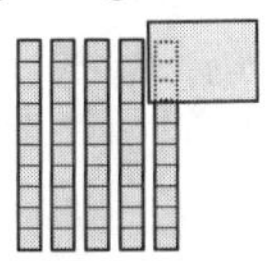

How many pieces of chocolate are left? *47.* If your child's not sure, ask: **How many tens are left?** *4.* **How many ones are left?** *7.* If she starts to count the visible units one by one, prompt her to think of the pairs that make 10: **3 and what make 10?** *7.* **I covered 3 units, so there must be 7 showing.** Have your child complete the written equation: 50 – 3= 47.

50 - 3 = 47

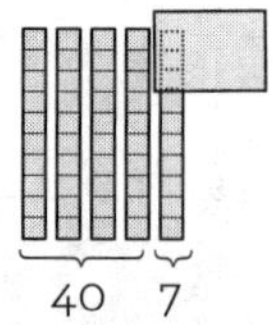

Have your child solve the following problems. Encourage her to use place-value thinking and the pairs that make 10 to find the answers.

40 - 5 = 35

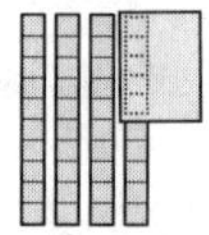

80 - 7 = 73

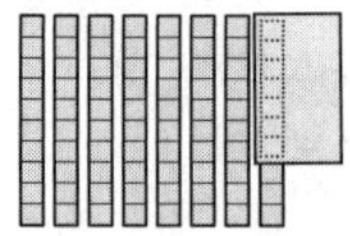

90 - 4 = 86

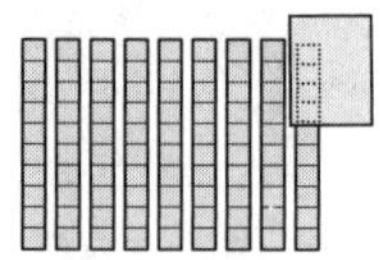

Activity: Four in a Row (Subtract from Multiples of 10)

Play Four in a Row. See Lesson 11.1 (page 176) for the general directions, and use the game board on workbook page 18.1. Keep base-ten blocks nearby to model the problems as needed.

Save this game board with your math materials so you can play again.

Workbook: Subtract One-Digit Numbers from Multiples of 10 and Review

Have your child complete workbook page 18.1B.

Lesson 18.2
Subtract One-Digit Numbers with Base-Ten Blocks

	Purpose	Materials
Warm-up	• Count by half-hour intervals • Practice memory work • Review subtracting one-digit numbers from multiples of 10	• Clock • Base-ten blocks, optional
Activities	• Subtract one-digit numbers from two-digit numbers in two steps	• Base-ten blocks • Workbook page 18.2A
Workbook	• Review previously-learned material	• Workbook page 18.2B

Warm-up: Counting, Memory Work, and Review

- Set the clock to 11:00. Have your child count by half-hour intervals from 11:00 to 2:00: *11:00, 11:30....* Have him turn the clock's hands to match each time.
- **What is another name for 12 a.m.?** *Midnight.*
  What is another name for 12 p.m.? *Noon.*
- Have your child solve the following mental subtraction problems. Use base-ten blocks as needed.
  - × 50 – 7 = *43*
  - × 40 – 5 = *35*
  - × 90 – 8 = *82*
  - × 80 – 6 = *74*
  - × 60 – 3 = *57*

Activity: Subtract One-Digit Numbers from Two-Digit Numbers

In Week 14, you learned how to add one-digit numbers to two-digit numbers by completing a 10 and adding in two steps. Today, you'll use the same strategy backward to subtract one-digit numbers from two-digit numbers. Instead of adding in two steps, we'll subtract in two steps.

Show your child the first problem at the top of workbook page 18.2A (53 – 4). Place 5 rods and 3 units on the table.

53 - 4 = ☐

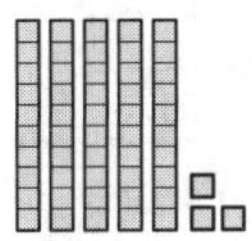

Let's pretend again the base-ten blocks are chocolate bars, and a hungry alligator is eating them up. There are 53 pieces of chocolate, and the alligator wants to eat 4.

First, the alligator eats the 3 units. Use a slip of paper to cover the 3 units. **53 minus 3 equals 50.**

53 - 4 = ☐

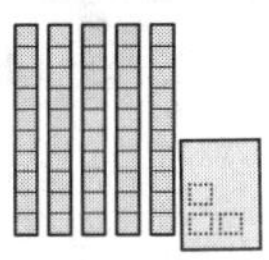

We want to subtract 4 ones, and we have already subtracted 3. How many more do we need to subtract? *1.* Use another slip of paper to cover 1 more unit. **50 minus 1 equals 49.** Have your child complete the written equation: 53 – 4 = 49.

53 - 4 = 49

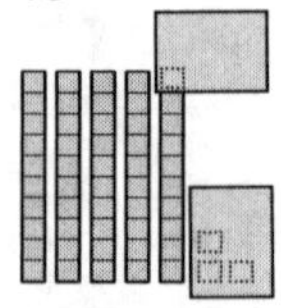

You may need to use more than one slip of paper to cover your base-ten blocks. Using sticky notes (or tape) also helps keep the paper from sliding.

Have your child use this method to solve the rest of the problems at the top of workbook page 18.2A.

42 - 6 = 36

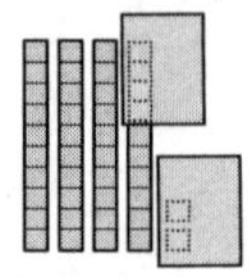

42 minus 2 equals 40. 40 minus 4 equals 36.

61 - 3 = 58

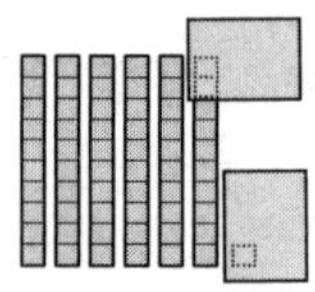

61 minus 1 equals 60. 60 minus 2 equals 58.

85 - 8 = 77

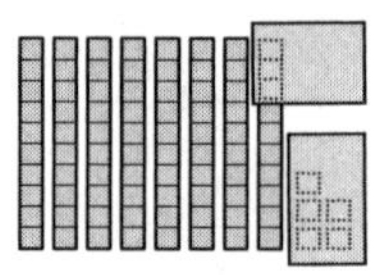

85 minus 5 equals 80. 80 minus 3 equals 77.

If your child has trouble keeping track of the numbers in his head, have him draw part-total lines below the one-digit number to show how he split it.

42 - 6 = 36

2 4

42 minus 2 equals 40. 40 minus 4 equals 36.

Activity: Play Roll and Subtract

Play Roll and Subtract. See Lesson 14.1 (page 225) for the general directions, and use the scorecards on workbook page 18.2A. Whoever has the greater difference in each round wins a point. For example, if Player 1 rolls a 4 and Player 2 rolls a 1 in Round 1:

Player 1	Player 2
41 - 4 = 37	41 - 1 = 40

If your child is still beginning to understand how to subtract these numbers, model the problems with base-ten blocks. If he is ready for more challenge, have him find the differences in the game mentally.

Workbook: Review

Have your child complete workbook page 18.2B.

Lesson 18.3
Subtract One-Digit Numbers Mentally

	Purpose	Materials
Warm-up	• Count by 20s • Practice memory work • Review telling time	• Clock
Activities	• Subtract one-digit numbers from two-digit numbers mentally	• Base-ten blocks • Playing cards
Workbook	• Subtract one-digit numbers from two-digit numbers mentally	• Workbook pages 18.3A and 18.3B

This lesson will help your child begin to subtract one-digit numbers from two-digit numbers mentally, without base-ten blocks. See the Week 18 **Teaching Math with Confidence** for more on preventing base-ten blocks from becoming a crutch.

Warm-up: Counting, Memory Work, and Review

- Count in unison with your child by 20s to 200.
- **What is another name for 12 a.m.?** *Midnight.*
  What is another name for 12 p.m.? *Noon.*
- Set the clock to the following times: 11:30, 11:39, 11:55, 12:00, 12:03, 12:16. Have your child tell each time.

Activity: Practice Subtracting One-Digit Numbers from Two-Digit Numbers

Today, you'll practice subtracting one-digit numbers from two-digit numbers in two steps more. You'll learn how to visualize these problems so you can solve them without base-ten blocks.

Let's warm up first by solving a problem with base-ten blocks. Show your child the first problem on workbook page 18.3A (62 – 5). Place 6 rods and 2 units on the table.

62 - 5 = ☐

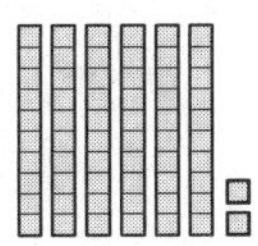

Have your child use the base-ten blocks to solve the problem (as in Lesson 18.2). Remind her to subtract in two steps.

62 - 5 = 57

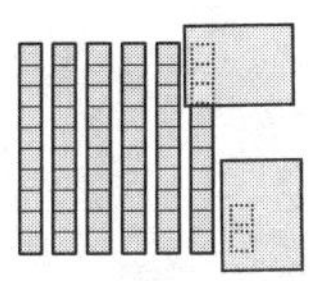

Show your child the second problem on workbook page 18.3A (51 – 3). Place 5 rods and 1 unit on the table. **This time, we won't use real slips of paper. Instead, imagine covering the blocks.** Have your child solve the problem. Encourage her to visualize subtracting the 1 loose unit first and then 2 more units.

51 - 3 = 48

If your child has trouble, allow her to use real slips of paper to cover the subtracted units.

For the third problem, try imagining base-ten blocks instead of using real base-ten blocks. Close your eyes and imagine 45 modeled with base-ten blocks. What do you see? *4 rods and 5 units.*

Now, close your eyes and imagine subtracting 6. How many would be left? *39*. Have her complete the written equation: 45 – 6 = 39.

45 - 6 = 39

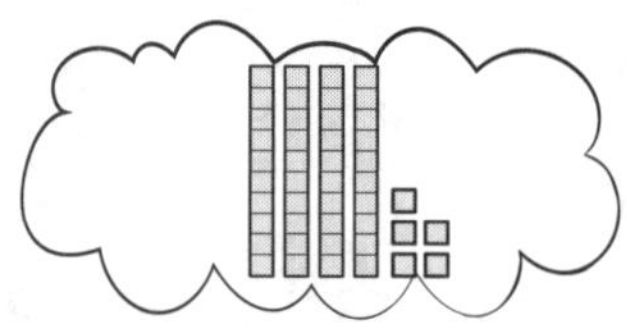

If your child isn't sure or makes a mistake, have her use base-ten blocks to find the answer.

Repeat with the final problem on the page: 84 – 9 = 75.

84 - 9 = 75

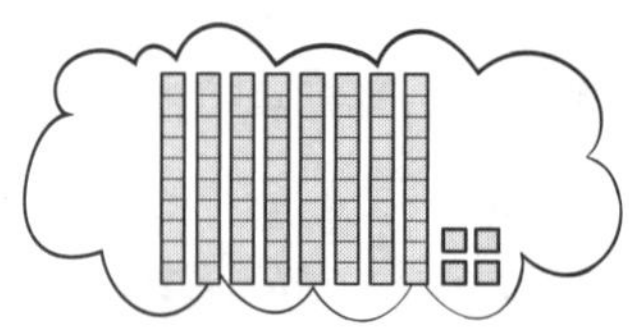

Activity: Play Race to Zero

Play Race to Zero.

If your child had trouble mentally subtracting one-digit numbers in the previous activity, modify this game to provide more support:

- Have each player take 5 rods at the beginning of the game.
- Cover the corresponding number of units with a slip of paper as you subtract.

Race to Zero

Materials: 4s, 5s, 6s, 7s, 8s, and 9s from a deck of playing cards (24 cards total)

Object of the Game: Be the first player to reach zero.

Shuffle the cards and place the stack face down on the table. Make a simple scorecard to record the score.

Sasha	Mom

On your turn, flip over the top card from the pile. Subtract the number shown from 50. Write a corresponding subtraction problem on your side of the score chart.

Sasha	Mom
50 - 6 = 44	

Sample first play

Play then passes to the other player. On your next turn, subtract the number on the card from your previous score.

Sasha	Mom
50 - 6 = 44	50 - 5 = 45
44 - 8 = 36	

Sample second play

Continue until one player reaches zero or flips over a card with a number greater than the previous score. The first player to do so wins.

Workbook: Subtract One-Digit Numbers from Two-Digit Numbers and Review

Have your child complete workbook pages 18.3A and 18.3B.

Lesson 18.4
Practice Subtracting One-Digit Numbers

	Purpose	Materials
Warm-up	• Count money • Practice memory work • Review identifying the total number of objects in an array	• Play money • Coins • Dot array and L-cover (Blackline Master 6)
Activities	• Solve subtraction word problems • Practice subtracting one-digit numbers from two-digit numbers	• Play money • Playing cards • Base-ten blocks, optional
Workbook	• Solve word problems • Subtract one-digit numbers from two-digit numbers	• Workbook pages 18.4A and 18.4B

Warm-up: Counting, Memory Work, and Review

- Place 1 twenty-dollar bill, 3 ten-dollar bills, 3 five-dollar bills, 3 quarters, 1 nickel, and 7 pennies on the table. **How much is this money worth?** *$65.87.*
- **What is another name for 12 a.m.?** *Midnight.*
  What is another name for 12 p.m.? *Noon.*
- Use the dot array and L-cover to show your child the following dot arrangements. Have her find the total number of dots in each array.

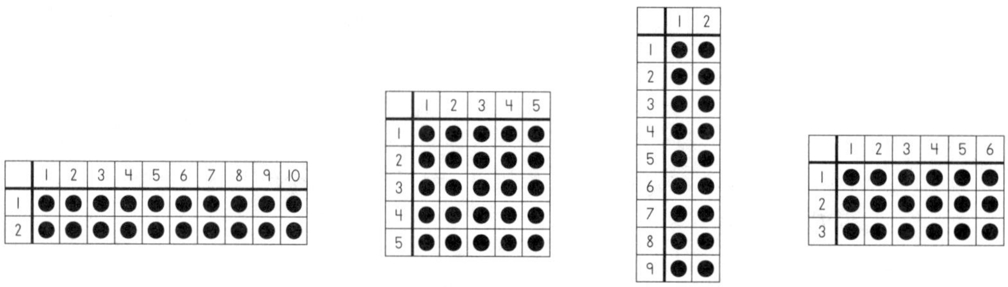

20 25 18 18

Activity: Solve Subtraction Word Problems

This week, you've learned how to subtract one-digit numbers from two-digit numbers. Today, you'll use what you've learned to solve word problems.

I'm going to read you a word problem. First, you'll write an equation to solve the problem. Then, we'll act out the problem with play money to check your answer.

> Completing the subtraction problem before acting it out with play money gives your child a chance to practice his mental subtraction skills and apply them to a real-life situation.

Here's the problem: You have $63. Then, you spend $7. How much money do you have now? Briefly discuss what your child might buy.

What subtraction problem matches the story? *63 – 7.* Have your child use mental subtraction to find the answer and complete the equation: 63 – 7 = 56.

Give your child 6 ten-dollar bills and 3 one-dollar bills. **May I have $7 please?** Have your child pretend to pay you. Give him a moment to realize that he needs to trade 1 ten-dollar bill for 10 one-dollar bills in order to have the correct bills.

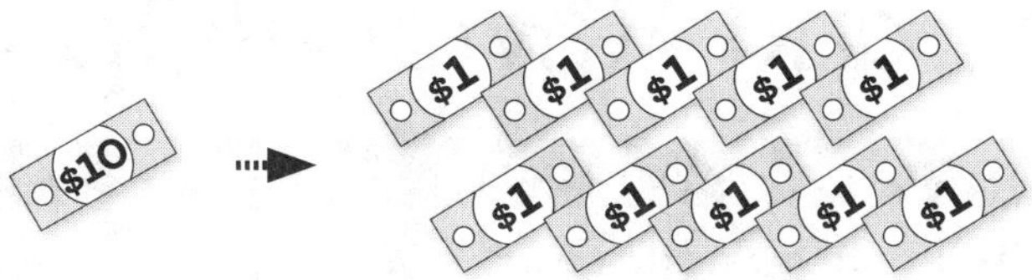

How much money do you have left? *$56.* **Just like you predicted when you solved the subtraction problem!**

Trading 1 ten-dollar bill for 10 one-dollar bills previews the trading that your child will do when he learns the traditional written subtraction process in Unit 12.

Have your child write and solve an equation for the following word problems. Then, act out each problem with play money.

- **You have $95. Then, you spend $8. How much do you have left?** *95 – 8 = 87. $87.*
- **You have $70. Then, you spend $6. How much do you have left?** *70 – 6 = 64. $64.*

Activity: Play Race to Zero

Play Race to Zero. This time, start at 100 and play until one of you reaches zero. See Lesson 18.3 (page 297) for directions. Allow your child to use base-ten blocks as needed.

Starting at 100 makes the game longer so that your child gets more practice. If you don't have time for the full game, start at 100 and play until one of you reaches 50.

Workbook: Subtract One-Digit Numbers from Two-Digit Numbers and Review

Have your child complete workbook pages 18.4A and 18.4B.

This workbook page provides an informal assessment of how well your child can mentally subtract one-digit numbers from two-digit numbers. If your child has trouble solving these problems without base-ten blocks, spend another day or two playing Race to Zero before moving on to Week 19.

Lesson 18.5
Enrichment and Review (Optional)

	Purpose	Materials
Warm-up	• Count backward from 200 to 100 by 1s, 2s, 5s, or 10s • Review memory work • Review your child's favorite or most challenging activities from Week 18	• Varies, depending on the activities you choose
Picture Book	• Explore large numbers	• *Is a Blue Whale the Biggest Thing There Is?*, by Robert E. Wells
Enrichment Activity	• Explore adding and subtracting on a calculator	• Calculator (or calculator app)

Warm-up: Counting, Memory Work, and Review

- Have your child count backward from 200 to 100 by 1s, 2s, 5s, or 10s. (Choose whichever counting sequence your child needs to practice the most.)
- Quiz your child on the memory work through Week 18. See page 523 for the full list.
- If you have time, repeat one or two of the activities from this week's lessons. Choose activities your child especially enjoyed or found challenging.

Math Picture Book: *Is a Blue Whale the Biggest Thing There Is?*

Read *Is a Blue Whale the Biggest Thing There Is?* by Robert E. Wells. As you read, marvel at the vast numbers and size of the universe.

Enrichment Activity: Explore a Calculator

Show your child how to add and subtract numbers on a calculator. Allow him to experiment with adding and subtracting large numbers, and give him time to explore the other buttons on the calculator.

Week 18 Answer Key

18.1A

See the Instructor Guide for how to play.
Save this game board for future lessons.

Four in a Row
Subtract from Multiples of 10

80 - 2	30 - 8	40 - 7	70 - 7	60 - 9
70 - 4	90 - 6	80 - 3	50 - 5	30 - 6
60 - 1	40 - 3	50 - 4	70 - 8	90 - 2
40 - 9	30 - 2	60 - 1	80 - 4	40 - 5
80 - 5	90 - 1	70 - 6	30 - 7	50 - 3

18.1B

Complete.

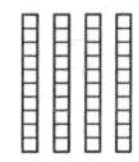

40 - 2 = 38

50 - 2 = 48
70 - 2 = 68
30 - 2 = 28

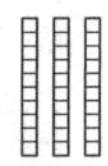

30 - 5 = 25

40 - 5 = 35
90 - 5 = 85
60 - 5 = 55

Label the numbers on the number line.

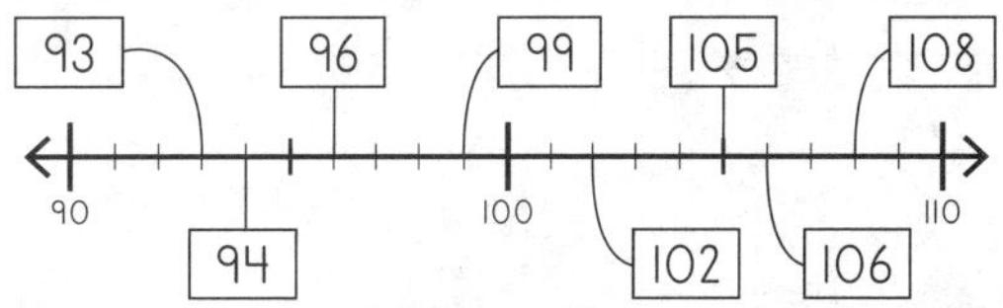

Write the time.

18.2A

See the instructor Guide for directions.

53 - 4 = 49

42 - 6 = 36

61 - 3 = 58

85 - 8 = 77

Roll and Subtract

Player 1	Player 2
41 - ☐ = ☐	41 - ☐ = ☐
32 - ☐ = ☐	32 - ☐ = ☐
50 - ☐ = ☐	50 - ☐ = ☐
71 - ☐ = ☐	71 - ☐ = ☐
82 - ☐ = ☐	82 - ☐ = ☐

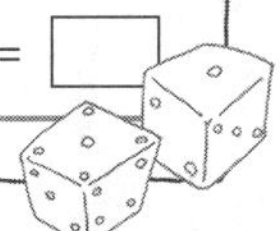

18.2B

Write the time.

Josh made a bar graph about the books he read.
Use the bar graph to complete the chart and answer the questions.

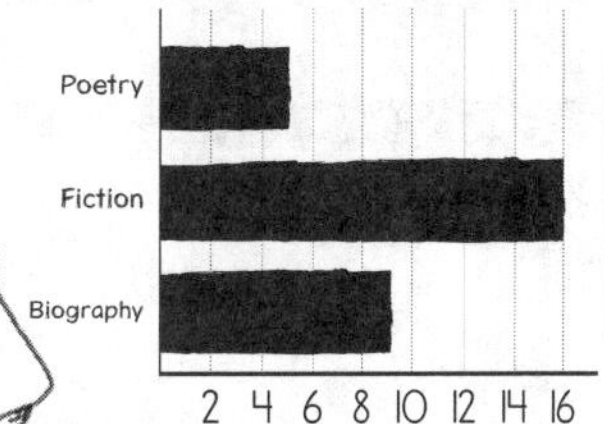

Poetry	5
Fiction	16
Biography	9

How many poetry books and biographies did he read?
14 books

How many more fiction books than biographies did he read?
7 books

How many more fiction books than poetry books did he read?
11 books

How many books did he read in all?
30 books

Week 18 Answer Key

18.3A

See the Instructor Guide for directions.

62 - 5 = 57	51 - 3 = 48
45 - 6 = 39	84 - 9 = 75

Write the answer to each subtraction problem. Use the key to color the quilt squares.

Key
Odd answers - Yellow
Even answers - Red

64 - 5 = 59	73 - 5 = 68	61 - 8 = 53
83 - 7 = 76	74 - 7 = 67	92 - 4 = 88
40 - 9 = 31	55 - 5 = 50	32 - 5 = 27

18.3B

Complete the sequences.

Count by hours: 10:00, 11:00, 12:00, 1:00, 2:00

Count by half hours: 5:30, 6:00, 6:30, 7:00, 7:30

Count by quarter hours: 12:15, 12:30, 12:45, 1:00, 1:15

Solve.

You have $40.
Then, you spend $6.
How much money do you have left?

$10 $10 $10 $10

40 − 6 = 34

$ 34

You have $40.
Then, you earn $6.
How much money do you have now?

$10 $10 $10 $10 $5 $1

40 + 6 = 46

$ 46

18.4A

Solve.

You have $36.
Then, you spend $9.
How much money do you have left?

$10 $10 $10 $5 $1

36 − 9 = 27

$ 27

You have $53.
Then, you spend $5.
How much money do you have left?

$20 $20 $10 $1 $1 $1

53 − 5 = 48

$ 48

Match.

73-4 — 69
71-6 — 65
84-7 — 77
73-7 — 66
80-5 — 75
85-9 — 76

18.4B

Write the time.

4:36 4:46 4:56

Complete each box with a number that makes the statement true.

20 > ☐	98 < ☐	146 > ☐
☐ = 80	☐ < 146	☐ > 150
0 < ☐	☐ = 32	156 < ☐

Many answers are possible.

Copy the shape.

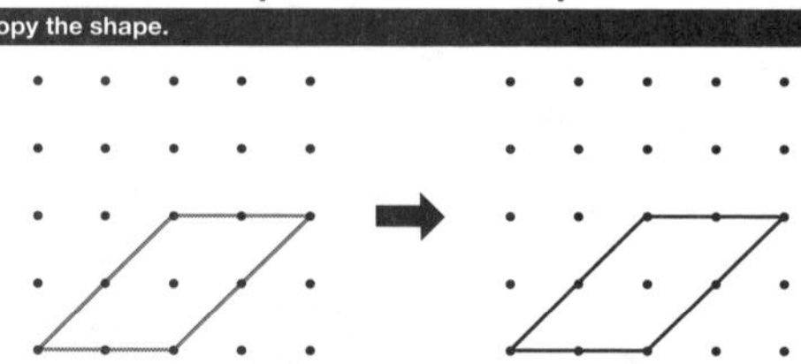

Week 19
Mental Subtraction, Part 2

Overview

Your child will learn how to subtract two-digit numbers from two-digit numbers. First, she will use base-ten blocks to solve the problems. Then, she'll progress to solving the problems mentally.

Lesson 19.1	Subtract Two-Digit Numbers from Multiples of 10
Lesson 19.2	Subtract Two-Digit Numbers with Base-Ten Blocks
Lesson 19.3	Subtract Two-Digit Numbers Mentally
Lesson 19.4	Subtract Two-Digit Numbers at the Pretend Store
Lesson 19.5	Enrichment and Review (Optional)

Teaching Math with Confidence: Why Mental Addition Strategies Don't Always Translate to Mental Subtraction

In Unit 6, you taught your child to use place-value thinking to solve two-digit mental addition problems in two steps. This week, you'll teach her a similar two-step strategy to subtract two-digit numbers. For example, to solve 45 – 26 mentally, your child will first subtract 20 from 45. Then, she'll subtract 6.

45 - 26 = 19
20 6

45 - 20 = 25
25 - 6 = 19

Your child will learn this two-step strategy for mental subtraction this week.

This strategy works well for all two-digit mental subtraction problems, which is why Unit 6 emphasized using a similar approach for addition. However, your child may be in the habit of breaking both addends into tens and ones when she adds mentally. For example, to add 45 and 26, some children prefer to add the tens and ones separately before combining them.

45 + 26 = 71
40 5 20 6

40 + 20 = 60
5 + 6 = 11
60 + 11 = 71

Breaking both numbers into tens and ones works for all two-digit mental addition problems.

This strategy works well for two-digit addition problems, but it doesn't work for all two-digit subtraction problems. For example, if you try to subtract the tens and ones separately for 45 – 26, you have to subtract 6 from 5. This isn't possible without negative numbers.

45 - 26 = 19
40 5 20 6

40 - 20 = 20
5 - 6 = ???

Your child may run into trouble if she tries to subtract the tens and ones separately.

If your child tries breaking both numbers into their expanded form to subtract this week, show her the above example. Remind her that we can add in any order, but we can't subtract in any order. (For example, 6 plus 7 equals 7 plus 6. But, 7 minus 6 does not equal 6 minus 7.) As a result, strategies that work for mental addition don't always work for mental subtraction.

Extra Materials Needed for Week 19

- 5 small toys
- 5 slips of paper
- For optional Enrichment and Review Lesson:
    - *Nothing Stopped Sophie: The Story of Unshakable Mathematician Sophie Germain,* written by Cheryl Bardoe and illustrated by Barbara McClintock

Lesson 19.1
Subtract Two-Digit Numbers from Multiples of 10

	Purpose	Materials
Warm-up	• Count by 20s to 200 • Practice memory work • Review mentally adding two-digit numbers	• None
Activities	• Subtract two-digit numbers from multiples of 10 (for example, 80 - 36), with base-ten blocks and mentally	• Base-ten blocks • Four in a Row game board (from workbook page 19.1A) • Counters
Workbook	• Review previously-learned material	• Workbook page 19.1B

Warm-up: Counting, Memory Work, and Review

- Have your child count by 20s to 200.
- **Are times in the afternoon and evening a.m. or p.m.?** *P.m.*
  Are times in the morning a.m. or p.m.? *A.m.*
- Write the following problems on paper and have your child solve them mentally. Allow her to use base-ten blocks as needed.
  - 52 + 37 = *89*
  - 24 + 36 = *60*
  - 58 + 23 = *81*

Activity: Subtract Two-Digit Numbers from Multiples of 10 with Base-Ten Blocks

In Week 16, you learned how to add two-digit numbers to two-digit numbers in two steps. This week, you'll learn how to subtract two-digit numbers from two-digit numbers in the same way. Today, we'll focus on subtracting two-digit numbers from numbers with zero in the ones-place, like 30, 80, or 60.

Write 60 - 25 = on a piece of paper. Have your child model 60 with base-ten blocks.

60 - 25 =

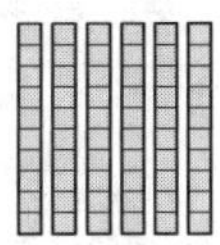

Before we subtract, let's split the second number into tens and ones. What's the expanded form of 25? *20 plus 5.* Draw part-total lines below 25 to split it into 20 and 5.

60 - 25 =

20 5

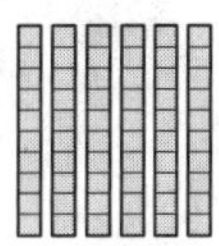

Cover 2 rods with a slip of paper. **What's 60 minus 20?** *40.*

60 - 25 =

→ 20 5

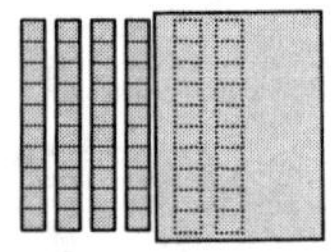

Cover 5 of the units on 1 rod with a slip of paper. **What's 40 minus 5?** *35.* **So, what's 60 minus 25?** *35.* Have your child complete the written equation: 60 – 25 = 35.

60 - 25 = 35

20 5 ←

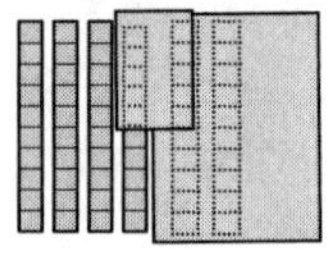

> The goal of mental math is to deepen your child's number sense and problem-solving ability, not test her memory, so it's fine to provide written support whenever needed. For example, for the above problem, write out each step if it helps to make the process clearer:
>
> 60 - 20 = 40   40 - 5 = 35

Have your child use this approach to solve the following problems.

40 - 12 = 28

10 2

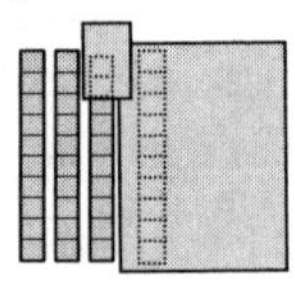

100 - 28 = 72

20 8

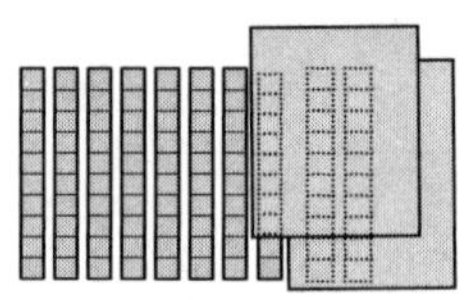

Activity: Subtract Two-Digit Numbers from Multiples of 10 Mentally

Let's try another one like this without base-ten blocks. Write 90 - 41 = on a piece of paper. Have your child show the expanded form of 41 with part-total lines.

90 - 41 = ☐

40 1

Point to the 90 and 40. **What's 90 minus 40?** *50.*

90 - 41 = ☐

↑

→40 1

Point to the 1. **What's 50 minus 1?** *49*. Have your child complete the written equation: 90 − 41 = 49.

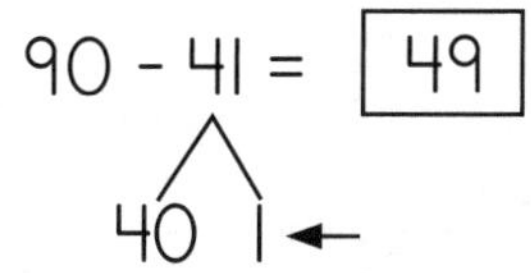

> If your child is confused, model the problem with base-ten blocks as in the previous activity.

Activity: Play Four in a Row (Two-Digit Subtraction)

Play Four in a Row with the game board on workbook page 19.1A. See Lesson 11.1 (page 176) for the general directions, and use the game board on workbook page 19.1.

> If your child had trouble mentally subtracting two-digit numbers in the previous activity, have her model the problems in the game with base-ten blocks.

Save this game board with your math materials so you can play again.

Workbook: Review

Have your child complete workbook page 19.1B.

Lesson 19.2
Subtract Two-Digit Numbers with Base-Ten Blocks

	Purpose	Materials
Warm-up	• Count by quarter-hour intervals • Practice memory work • Review subtracting two-digit numbers from multiples of 10	• Clock • Base-ten blocks, optional
Activities	• Subtract two-digit numbers with base-ten blocks	• Base-ten blocks • Workbook page 19.2A • Die
Workbook	• Review previously-learned material	• Workbook page 19.2B

Warm-up: Counting, Memory Work, and Review

- Set the clock to 5:00. Have your child count by quarter-hour intervals from 5:00 to 7:00: *5:00, 5:15....* Have him turn the clock's hands to match each time.
- **If a number has 1, 3, 5, 7, or 9 in the ones-place, is the number even or odd?** *Odd.* **If a number has 0, 2, 4, 6, or 8 in the ones-place, is the number even or odd?** *Even.*
- Write the following problems on paper and have your child solve them mentally. Allow him to use base-ten blocks as needed, and remind him to subtract in two steps (as in Lesson 19.1).
    - × 50 – 17 = *33*
    - × 40 – 25 = *15*
    - × 90 – 38 = *52*

Activity: Subtract Easier Two-Digit Numbers with Base-Ten Blocks

In the last lesson, you learned how to subtract two-digit numbers from numbers with zero in the ones-place. Today, you'll learn how to subtract two-digit numbers from other numbers. You'll subtract in two steps, just like the last lesson.

> The first two problems do not require breaking a 10 apart so that your child can learn the basic process before tackling more difficult numbers.

Show your child the first problem at the top of workbook page 19.2A (58 – 23). Place 5 rods and 8 units on the table. **What's the expanded form of 23?** *20 plus 3.* Have your child draw part-total lines to show the expanded form of 23.

58 - 23 = ☐
20 3

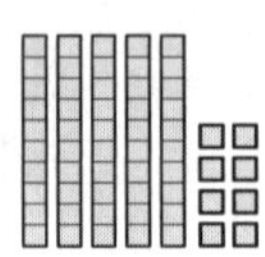

Now, we subtract 23 in two steps. First, we subtract the tens. Then, we subtract the ones.

What's 58 minus 20? *38.* Cover 2 rods.

58 - 23 =

20 3

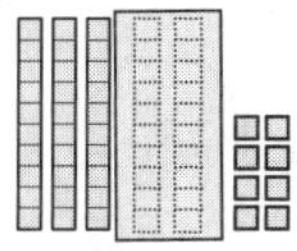

What's 38 minus 3? *35*. Cover 3 units. Have your child complete the written equation: 58 – 23 = 35.

58 - 23 = 35

20 3

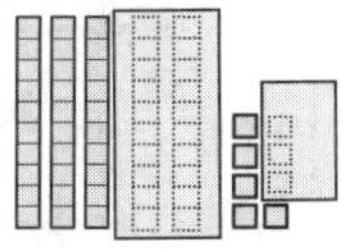

Have your child use the same process to complete the second problem (73 – 42).

73 - 42 = 31

40 2

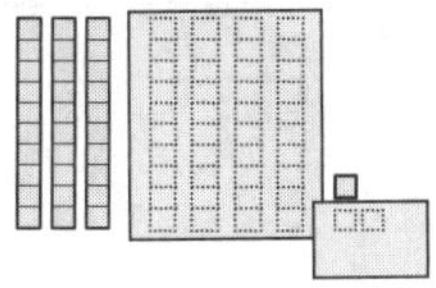

73 minus 40 equals 33. 33 minus 2 equals 31.

Activity: Subtract Harder Two-Digit Numbers with Base-Ten Blocks

Now, we'll try a problem with numbers that are a little bit harder. Show your child the next problem (63 – 24). Place 6 rods and 3 units on the table. **What's the expanded form of 24?** *20 plus 4*. Have your child draw part-total lines to match.

63 - 24 = ☐

20 4

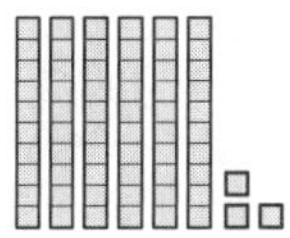

Now, we subtract 24 in two steps. What's 63 minus 20? *43*. Cover 2 rods.

63 - 24 = ☐

20 4

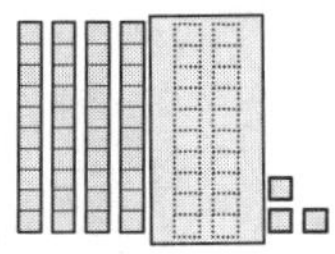

What's 43 minus 4? *39*. Cover 4 units and have him complete the written equation: 63 – 24 = 39.

63 - 24 = 39

20 4

Have your child use the same process to complete the final problem (81 – 47).

81 - 47 = 34

40 7

81 minus 40 equals 41. 41 minus 7 equals 34.

Activity: Play Roll and Subtract

Use the bottom of workbook page 19.2A to play Roll and Subtract. Play is the same as in Lesson 18.2, except that each player rolls the die two times per round. Write the first roll in the tens-place on your scorecard and the second roll in the ones-place. For example, if you roll a 4 and then a 6 in Round 1:

Player 1	Player 2
74 - [4 : 6] = [28]	74 - [:] = [ ]

First roll

Second roll

Workbook: Review

Have your child complete workbook page 19.2B.

Lesson 19.3
Subtract Two-Digit Numbers Mentally

	Purpose	Materials
Warm-up	• Count by ten-minute intervals • Practice memory work • Review reading and writing inequalities	• Clock
Activities	• Subtract two-digit numbers mentally	• Base-ten blocks, optional • Workbook page 19.3A
Workbook	• Subtract two-digit numbers mentally	• Workbook pages 19.3A and 19.3B

Warm-up: Counting, Memory Work, and Review

- Set the clock to 8:00. Have your child count by ten-minute intervals from 8:00 to 9:00: *8:00, 8:10....* Have her turn the clock's hands to match each time.
- **What do we call the result when we add numbers together?** *The sum.* **What do we call the result when we subtract a number from another number?** *The difference.*
- Write the following inequalities on a piece of paper and have your child read them. Also have your child make up a few inequalities and practice reading and writing them.
    - 126 < 154. *126 is less than 154.*
    - 110 > 103. *110 is greater than 103.*
    - 192 = 192. *192 equals 192.*

Activity: Subtract Two-Digit Numbers Mentally

In the last lesson, you learned how to subtract two-digit numbers with base-ten blocks. When I need to subtract in real life, I don't usually have base-ten blocks with me! Today, you'll learn how to subtract two-digit numbers mentally.

Show your child the first problem at the top of workbook page 19.3A (85 – 16). Have her draw part-total lines to show the expanded form of 16.

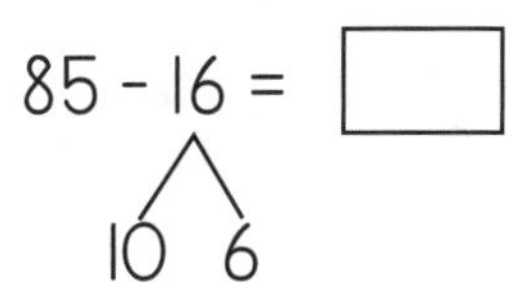

Now, we subtract 16 in two steps, just like in the last lesson. First, we subtract the tens. Then, we subtract the ones. Point to the 85 and 10. **What's 85 minus 10?** *75.*

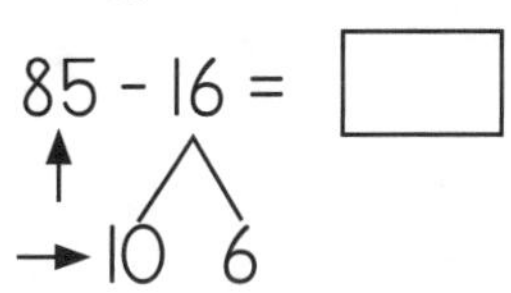

Point to the 6. **What's 75 minus 6?** *69.* Have your child complete the written equation: 85 – 16 = 69.

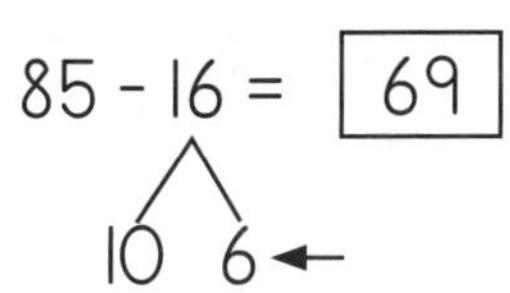

If your child isn't ready to subtract the numbers mentally (or feels overwhelmed), model the problems with base-ten blocks and have her imagine removing the blocks as she solves the problems (as in lesson 18.3). Gently nudge her towards visualizing base-ten blocks rather than modeling every problem concretely.

Have your child use the same process to complete the rest of the problems at the top of the page.

74 - 35 = [39]
30 5

74 - 30 = 44. 44 - 5 = 39.

95 - 47 = [48]
40 7

95 - 40 = 55. 55 - 7 = 48.

41 - 25 = [16]
20 5

41 - 20 = 21. 21 - 5 = 16.

Don't require your child to draw part-total lines if she doesn't need them. If your child needs the support of the part-total lines but resists drawing them, encourage her to point to the tens-place in the second number as she subtracts the tens, and the ones-place as she subtracts the ones. For example:

74 - 35 =
↑
74 - 30 = 44.

74 - 35 =
↑
44 - 5 = 39.

Workbook: Subtract Two-Digit Numbers and Review

Have your child complete workbook pages 19.3A and 19.3B.

On workbook page 19.3A, your child may draw part-total lines below the second number in each problem to help keep track of the numbers.

53 - 25 = [ ]
20 5

Lesson 19.4
Subtract Two-Digit Numbers at the Pretend Store

	Purpose	Materials
Warm-up	• Count by 2s, 5s, and 10s • Practice memory work • Review *more* and *less* with numbers on the number line	• Blank Number Line (Blackline Master 3)
Activities	• Solve money word problems • Practice subtracting two-digit numbers mentally	• 5 small toys • 5 slips of paper • Coins
Workbook	• Subtract two-digit numbers mentally	• Workbook pages 19.4A and 19.4B

Warm-up: Counting, Memory Work, and Review

- Label the Blank Number Line with 100, 110, and 120. Have your child count from 100 to 120 by 2s, 5s, and 10s. Have her point to each corresponding tick mark as she counts.

  Leave the number line out for the review activity below.

- **What is another name for 12 a.m.?** *Midnight.*
  What is another name for 12 p.m.? *Noon.*
- Ask your child the following number line riddles:
  - × **I'm thinking of a number that is 4 more than 100. What's my number?** *104.*
  - × **I'm thinking of a number that is 2 less than 110. What's my number?** *108.*
  - × **I'm thinking of a number that is 3 more than 110. What's my number?** *113.*
  - × **I'm thinking of a number that is 1 less than 120. What's my number?** *119.*
  - × **I'm thinking of a number that is 2 less than 115. What's my number?** *113.*

Activity: Subtract Two-Digit Numbers at the Pretend Store

This week, you have learned how to subtract two-digit numbers in your head. We often need to do mental math when we're shopping to compare prices or figure out how much money we have left. Today, you'll practice mental subtraction at the Pretend Store.

Write 25¢, 29¢, 65¢, 58¢, and 17¢ on slips of paper to make price tags. Lay 5 small toys in a row and have your child place a price tag next to each toy.

Have your child write and solve an equation to match each of the following problems.

- **How much more does the 29¢ item cost than the 25¢ item?** *4¢.*

  29¢ 25¢ $29 - 25 = 4$

If needed, remind your child to subtract the smaller number from the bigger number to find the difference.

- **How much more does the 65¢ item cost than the 25¢ item?** *40¢.*

  65¢ 25¢ $65 - 25 = 40$

- **How much less does the 58¢ item cost than the 65¢ item?** *7¢.*

  58¢ 65¢ $65 - 58 = 7$

- **How much does it cost to buy the item that costs 65¢ and the item that costs 17¢?** *82¢.*

  65¢ 17¢ $65 + 17 = 82$

- **I'm thinking of the item that costs 12¢ less than the 29¢ item. Which item am I thinking of?** *The item that costs 17¢.*

  $29 - 12 = 17$

Workbook: Mental Subtraction and Review

Have your child complete workbook pages 19.4A and 19.4B. Allow your child to use base-ten blocks as needed.

Show your child how to turn workbook page 19.4A as needed to make the problems easier to read.

Lesson 19.5
Enrichment and Review (Optional)

	Purpose	Materials
Warm-up	• Count backward from 200 to 100 by 1s, 2s, 5s, or 10s • Review memory work • Review your child's favorite or most challenging activities from Week 19	• Varies, depending on the activities you choose
Picture Book	• Learn about the life of a famous mathematician and the kinds of questions that mathematicians study	• *Nothing Stopped Sophie: The Story of Unshakable Mathematician Sophie Germain,* written by Cheryl Bardoe and illustrated by Barbara McClintock
Enrichment Activity	• Practice mental arithmetic with a guess-my-number trick	• None

Warm-up: Counting, Memory Work, and Review

- Have your child count backward from 200 to 100 by 1s, 2s, 5s, or 10s. (Choose whichever counting sequence your child needs to practice the most.)
- Quiz your child on the memory work through Week 18. See page 523 for the full list.
- If you have time, repeat one or two of the activities from this week's lessons. Choose activities your child especially enjoyed or found challenging.

Math Picture Book: *Nothing Stopped Sophie: The Story of Unshakable Mathematician Sophie Germain*

Read *Nothing Stopped Sophie: The Story of Unshakable Mathematician Sophie Germain,* written by Cheryl Bardoe and illustrated by Barbara McClintock. After you read, look together at the different equations that mathematicians solve on the endpapers.

Enrichment Activity: Learn a Guess-My-Number Trick

I have a guess-my-number trick to show you today! Have your child secretly choose a number between 0 and 25 and write the number on a piece of paper. Give your child the following instructions (in order). After each instruction, have your child secretly write down her response.

- **Choose a number greater than 0 and less than 25.** *Sample response: Child chooses 13.*
- **Double your number.** *Sample: Double 13 is 26.*
- **Add 20 to your new number.** *Sample: 26 + 20 = 46.*
- **Subtract 6 from your new number.** *Sample: 46 – 6 = 40.*
- **Find half of your new number.** *Sample: Half of 40 is 20.*
- **Add 4 to your new number.** *Sample: 20 + 4 = 24.*
- **Tell me this number.** *Sample: 24.*

Subtract 11 from your child's final number to find her secret number. For example, if her final number is 24, subtract 11 from 24 to find that her secret number is 13. **Your secret number is 13!** Repeat with several other secret numbers. Then, reverse roles: choose your own secret number, and have your child read the directions to you. Have her subtract 11 from your final result to find your secret number.

Week 19 Answer Key

19.1A

See the Instructor Guide for how to play.
Save this game board for future lessons.

Four in a Row
Two-Digit Subtraction

80 - 12	30 - 18	40 - 27	70 - 37	60 - 29
70 - 54	90 - 26	80 - 33	50 - 35	30 - 16
60 - 31	40 - 23	50 - 24	70 - 28	90 - 42
40 - 19	30 - 12	60 - 51	80 - 54	40 - 25
80 - 35	90 - 61	70 - 46	30 - 17	50 - 33

19.1B

Complete the sequences.

Count by 5 minutes	8:40	8:45	8:50	8:55	9:00
Count by 10 minutes	8:40	8:50	9:00	9:10	9:20
Count by 1 minute	8:40	8:41	8:42	8:43	8:44

Laura counted the children in each swim class.
Use her chart to make a bar graph.

Class	Number of Children
Minnows	10
Fish	5
Dolphins	12

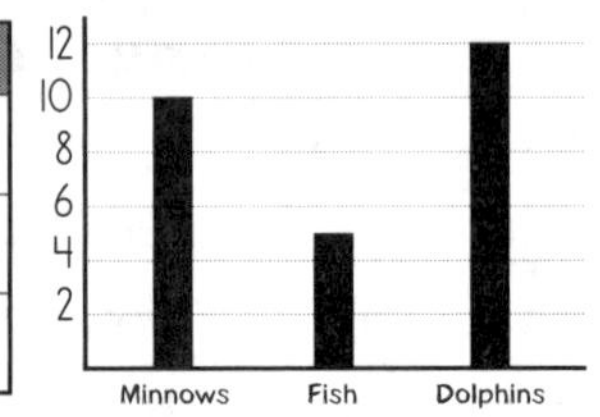

19.2A

See the Instructor Guide for directions.

58 - 23 = 35

73 - 42 = 31

63 - 24 = 39

81 - 47 = 34

Roll and Subtract

Player 1	Player 2
74 - ___ = ___	74 - ___ = ___
93 - ___ = ___	93 - ___ = ___
81 - ___ = ___	81 - ___ = ___
70 - ___ = ___	70 - ___ = ___
92 - ___ = ___	92 - ___ = ___

19.2B

Solve. Write your own equation to match each word problem.

Eden does 35 jumping jacks and 20 sit-ups.
How many exercises does she do?

35 + 20 = 55

55 exercises

Eden does 35 jumping jacks and 20 sit-ups.
How many more jumping jacks than sit-ups does she do?

35 - 20 = 15

15 more

Complete.

72 ¢

68 ¢

Write the time.

8:28

8:30

8:32

Week 19 Answer Key

19.3A

See the Instructor Guide for directions.

85 - 16 = 69

74 - 35 = 39

95 - 47 = 48

41 - 25 = 16

Match.

- 53 - 25 → 28
- 85 - 46 → 39
- 81 - 33 → 48
- 93 - 64 → 29
- 87 - 58 → 29
- 91 - 53 → 38
- 80 - 32 → 48
- 66 - 27 → 39

19.3B

Write the time.

11:55 | 12:00 | 6:00

Ian made a pictograph about how much time he spent playing outside. Use the pictograph to complete the chart and answer the questions.

Winter Activities

Skating	○○○○○○
Sledding	○○○○○○○
Building Snowmen	○○○

○ = 5 minutes

Activity	Minutes
Skating	30
Sledding	35
Building Snowmen	15

Which activity did he do the longest? Sledding

Which activity did he do the shortest? Building Snowmen

How much more time did he spend sledding than skating? 5 minutes

How much less time did he spend making snowmen than sledding? 20 minutes

19.4A

Write the answer to each problem. Then, use the key to color the pinwheel.

Key
16 - red
35 - orange
48 - yellow
66 - green
88 - blue

19.4B

Complete.

1 year = 12 months

1 week = 7 days

1 day = 24 hours

1 hour = 60 minutes

1 minute = 60 seconds

Color the even numbers yellow. Color the odd numbers red.

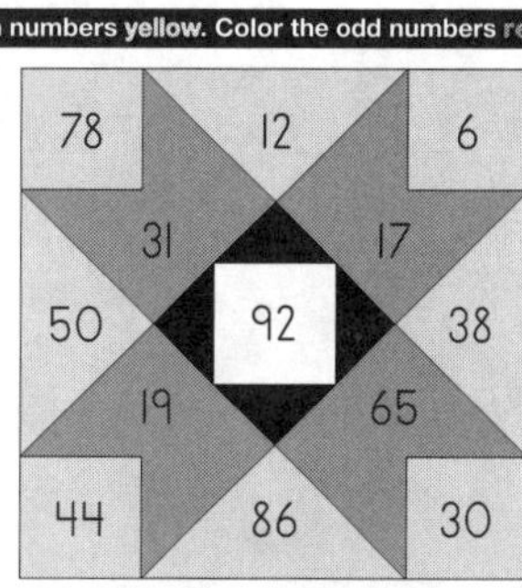

Write the time.

6:30 | 1:47 | 10:08

Unit 8 Checkpoint

What to Expect at the End of Unit 8

By the end of Unit 8, most children will be able to do the following:

- Subtract one-digit numbers and two-digit numbers from two-digit numbers. Some children will be able to solve these problems completely mentally, but many will still need to use base-ten blocks in order to find the answers.

Is Your Child Ready to Move on?

In Unit 9, your child will learn how to measure length. She will practice mental subtraction more during the review activities and workbook pages in Unit 9. She does not need to have mastered mental subtraction before moving on to this unit.

Unit 9
Length

Overview

Your child will learn how to measure length with both U.S. customary units (inches/feet/yards) and metric units (centimeters/meters). You'll also introduce her to miles and kilometers and teach her to solve word problems that involve length.

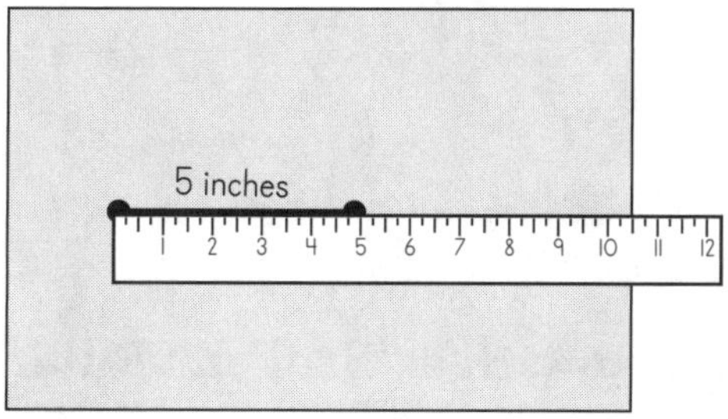

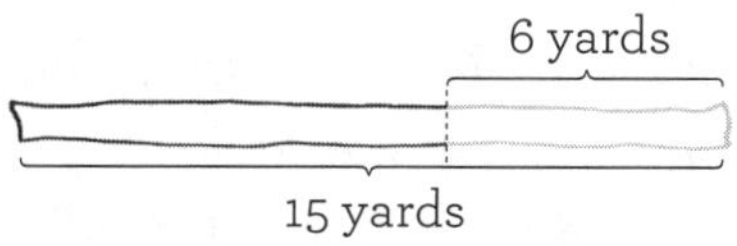

Sarah has 15 yards of ribbon. Then, she uses 6 yards to make a craft. How much does she have left?

Many families find this unit a fun break after the intense focus on mental subtraction in Unit 8. Your child will continue to practice mental addition and subtraction in the review activities and worksheets to consolidate these important skills.

Week 20	Inches, Feet, Yards, and Miles
Week 21	Centimeters, Meters, and Kilometers

What Your Child Will Learn

In this unit your child will learn to:

- Approximate the length of an inch, foot, yard, centimeter, and meter
- Estimate and measure length in inches, feet, yards, centimeters, and meters
- Measure an object's length when the object is not aligned with the ruler's endpoint
- Choose appropriate units for measuring in real-life situations

Recommended Math Picture Books (Optional)

These picture books are scheduled in the optional Enrichment and Review lessons at the end of each week.

- *Actual Size,* by Steve Jenkins. HMH Books for Young Readers, 2009.
- *Polly's Pen Pal,* written by Stuart J. Murphy and illustrated by Rémy Simard. HarperCollins, 2005.

Week 20
Inches, Feet, Yards, and Miles

Overview

Your child will learn how to estimate and measure length in inches, feet, and yards. You'll also introduce him to miles and teach him how to measure objects that aren't aligned with the ruler's endpoint.

Lesson 20.1	Measure in Inches
Lesson 20.2	Measure with a "Broken" Ruler
Lesson 20.3	Measure in Feet and Inches
Lesson 20.4	Yards and Miles
Lesson 20.5	Enrichment and Review (Optional)

Teaching Math with Confidence: Measuring with a "Broken" Ruler

In first grade, your child learned how to measure length with repeated units. You taught him to align 1-inch (or 1-centimeter) squares along an object to find its length, and you also introduced him to measuring with a ruler.

As children begin to use rulers, they often concentrate so intently on the ruler's markings that they temporarily ignore their common sense. For example, many second-graders would say that all of these objects are 9 inches long, since the 9-inch mark is aligned with the right edge of each object. Without parental support, they focus so tightly on the ruler's tick marks that they forget to consider whether their measurements are logical.

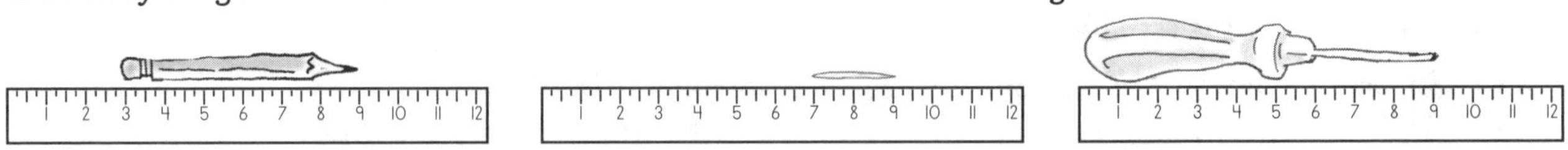

You'll help your child avoid this mistake by challenging him to measure with a "broken" ruler this week. You'll cover the ruler's left edge with paper and then ask your child to use the covered ruler to measure length. This activity nudges your child to think about measurement in a deeper way. He can't just look at the rightmost number on the ruler but instead must focus on how many 1-inch spaces equal the length.

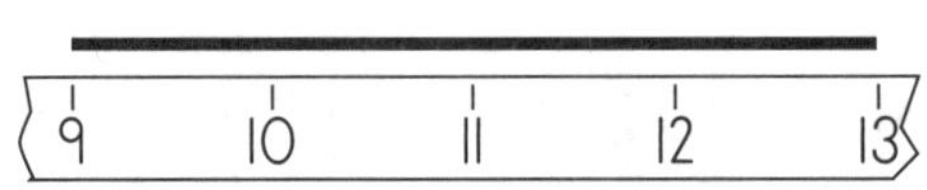

Using a "broken" ruler to measure a line.

Extra Materials Needed for Week 20

- Scissors
- Paper
- Tape
- For optional Enrichment and Review Lesson:
    - *Actual Size*, by Steve Jenkins
    - Map of your local area (or map app)

You will also need a 1-foot ruler, marked in inches, for this week's lessons.

Lesson 20.1
Measure in Inches

	Purpose	Materials
Warm-up	• Count by 2s on the dot array • Practice memory work • Review mental subtraction	• Dot array and L-cover (Blackline Master 6) • Base-ten blocks, optional
Activities	• Review measuring in inches • Draw lines of a given length in inches	• 1-foot ruler • Playing cards • Counters
Workbook	• Measure in inches with a ruler	• Workbook pages 20.1A and 20.1B • 1-foot ruler

Warm-up: Counting, Memory Work, and Review

- Slide the L-cover on the dot array to reveal 2 dots at a time. Have your child count by 2s to tell how many dots are visible in each array. Continue to 20.

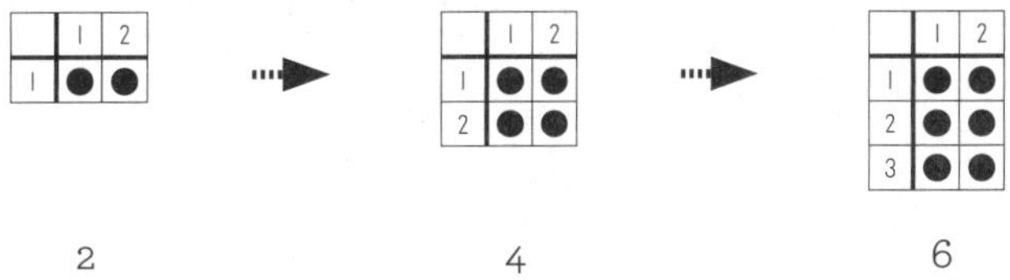

- **How many minutes equal a half-hour?** *30.*
  How many minutes equal a quarter-hour? *15.*
- Write the following problems on paper and have your child solve them mentally. Allow her to use base-ten blocks as needed.
  - 45 − 3 = *42*
  - 45 − 6 = *39*
  - 45 − 16 = *29*
  - 45 − 25 = *20*
  - 45 − 28 = *17*

Activity: Review Inches

We are starting a new unit on measuring length. Today, we'll review how to measure in inches with a ruler. Briefly discuss your child's experiences with measuring length. For example: **You helped measure the wood for the new shelf. The doctor measures your height at every visit.**

Show your child a 1-foot ruler. **This ruler measures in inches.** Point to the leftmost tick mark on the ruler with one hand, and point to the 1-inch mark with the other hand. **From here to here is 1 inch.**

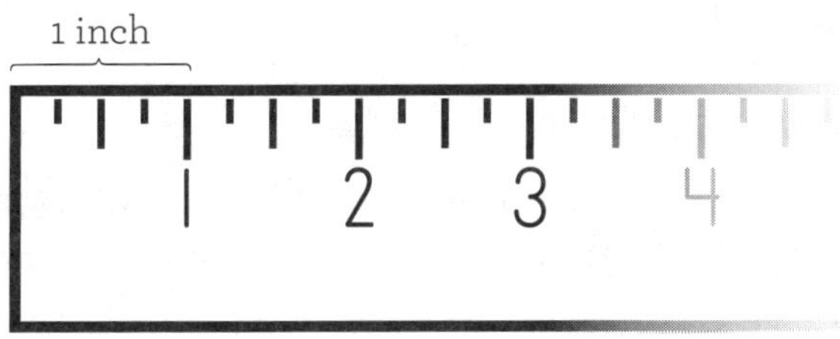

Try to hold your thumb and first finger one inch apart. *Child holds thumb and forefinger about one inch apart.* Use the ruler to check her estimate.

If your family uses the metric system, explain that inches are like centimeters and used in the U.S. to measure small items. Your child will study metric measurement in Week 21.

Activity: Measure Lines in Inches

Place the ruler on a piece of paper as shown and draw a dot above the tick mark for zero. **Let's pretend that a ladybug is crawling on the paper. I'll draw the path that she takes.** Draw a line from the dot to the 5-inch mark. Make another dot at the 5-inch mark. **How far did the ladybug crawl?** *5 inches.* Label the line as shown.

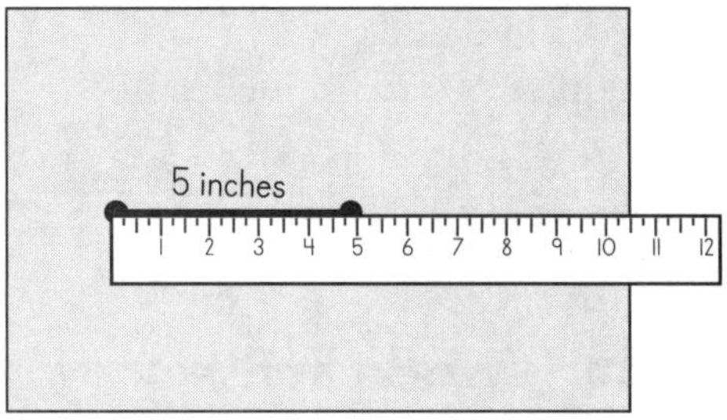

Then, she turns. Have your child close her eyes while you secretly rotate the paper and ruler and draw a 3-inch line as shown. Take the ruler off the paper before she opens her eyes. Have your child measure and label the new path.

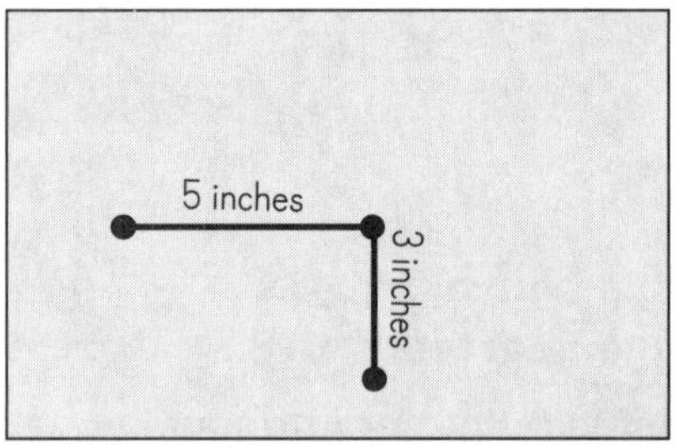

Lining up the ruler with the object to be measured is often the most difficult aspect of measuring length. Taking the ruler off the paper before your child opens her eyes ensures that she practices this skill.

If your ruler has the tick mark for zero indented from the end, show your child how to align the edge of the workbook with the tick mark rather than the end of the ruler.

Secretly draw 4-inch, 2-inch, 8-inch, and 3-inch lines as shown. After you draw each line, remove the ruler from the page and have your child measure and label the distance.

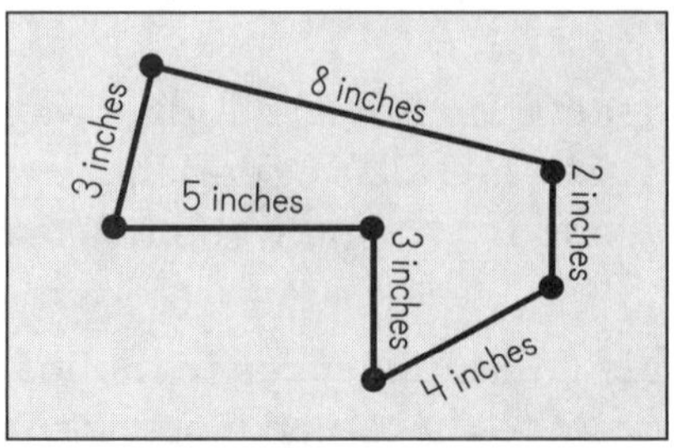

Where did the ladybug end up? *Back where she started!* **How far did she travel?** *25 inches.* If your child's not sure, point out that she can add the lengths of the lines.

Activity: Play Measurement Tag

Play one round of Measurement Tag. **This game is like Tag, but on paper! One of us will be "it." The other person will be the tagger and try to catch the person who's "it."**

Measurement Tag

Materials: Paper; playing cards with face cards removed (40 cards total); ruler; counters of two different colors to use as playing pieces

Object of the Game: If you are the tagger (or "it"), your goal is to tag your opponent by landing within 1 inch of their playing piece. If you are not the tagger, your goal is to avoid getting tagged for as long as possible.

Shuffle the cards and place the stack face down on the table. Each player chooses a marker or colored pencil and draws a starting dot on opposite corners of a piece of paper. Each player also chooses a counter to use as their playing piece and places it on top of the starting dot.

Decide which player will be the tagger. The tagger goes first.

On your turn, flip over a card. Use the ruler to draw a straight line of that length from your starting dot across the paper. For example, if you turn over a 6, draw a 6-inch line from your starting dot across the paper. Draw a dot at the other end and move your playing piece to this end dot. The line may go in any direction, and it may cross any previously-drawn lines.

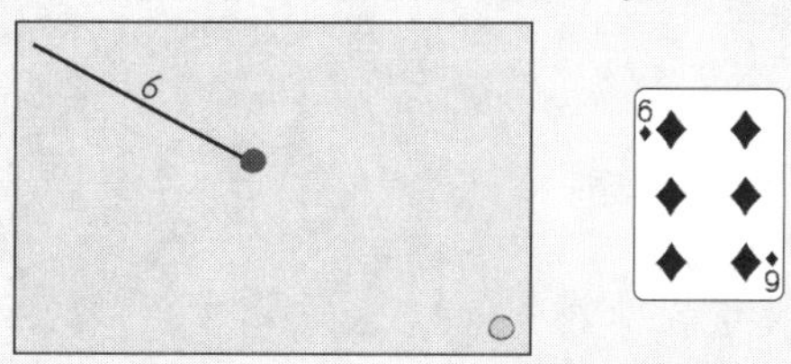

Sample first move by tagger. The tagger should try to draw a line that moves her playing piece towards the other player's playing piece.

Then the other player takes a turn in the same way.

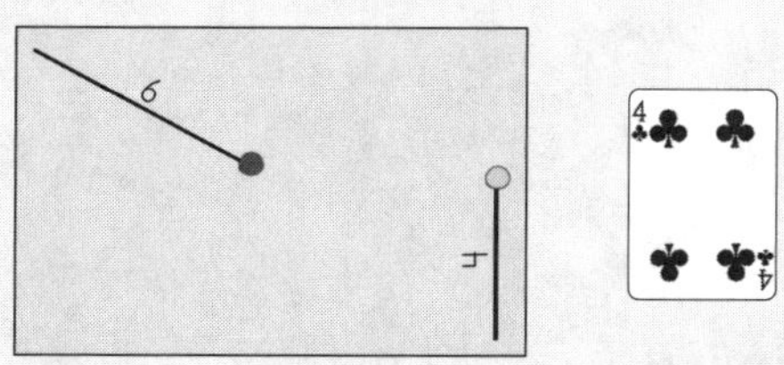

Sample first move by the player who is "it." This player should draw a line that moves his playing piece away from the tagger's playing piece.

Take turns flipping over cards and drawing lines. If you flip over a card and the matching line does not fit on the paper, take a different card. The game ends when the tagger moves her playing piece within 1 inch of the other player's playing piece.

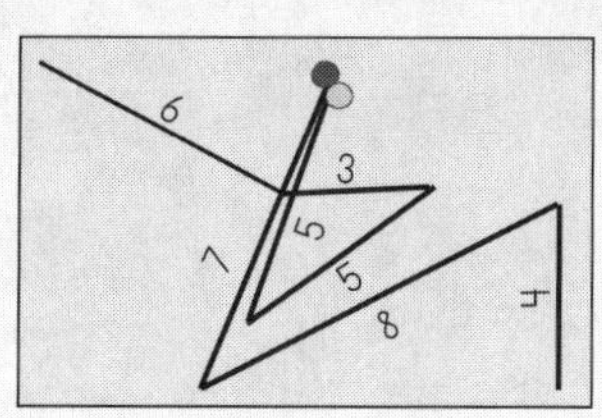

Sample final paper

Workbook: Measure in Inches and Review

Have your child complete workbook pages 20.1A and 20.1B.

Lesson 20.2
Measure with a "Broken" Ruler

	Purpose	Materials
Warm-up	• Count twenty-dollar bills by 20 • Practice memory work • Review counting out paper bills	• Play money • 3 small school items (i.e., pencil, ruler, eraser)
Activities	• Compare the number line and ruler • Deepen understanding of length by measuring with a ruler that does not begin at zero	• 1-foot ruler • Blank Number Line (Blackline Master 3) • Tape • Playing cards • Counters
Workbook	• Use a "broken" ruler to measure in inches	• Workbook pages 20.2A and 20.2B

See the Week 20 **Teaching Math with Confidence** for the benefits of measuring length with a "broken" ruler.

Warm-up: Counting, Memory Work, and Review

- Place about 5-10 twenty-dollar bills on the table. **About how much do you think these bills are worth?** *Answers will vary.* Have your child count by 20s to find their value.
- **How many minutes equal a half-hour?** *30.*
  How many minutes equal a quarter-hour? *15.*
- Write $107, $160, and $138 on separate slips of paper. **The Pretend Store is expensive today!** Place each next to a small school item (like a pencil, ruler, and eraser). Give your child paper bills and have him pretend to buy the items.

Activity: Compare a Ruler with the Number Line

In the last lesson, we reviewed inches. Today, you'll learn more about measuring in inches. Try to hold your thumb and first finger one inch apart. *Child holds thumb and forefinger about one inch apart.* Use the ruler to check his estimate.

Show your child a 1-foot ruler and the Blank Number Line (labeled with 0, 10, and 20). **The ruler looks a lot like the number line!**

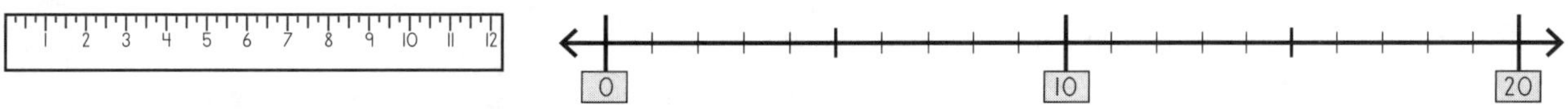

What do the ruler and number line have in common? *Sample answers: They both have tick marks and numbers. The tick marks are evenly spaced. The numbers increase from left to right.*

How are the ruler and number line different from each other? *Sample answers: The ruler has more tick marks and numbers. The ruler is made from wood. The ruler doesn't have zero on it.*

One big difference is that most rulers don't have zero printed on them. Where do you think zero belongs on the ruler? *Possible answers: At the end of the ruler. At the first tick mark.*

The very first tick mark on the ruler is 0, because the numbers count inches starting from that tick mark. Show your child the leftmost tick mark on the ruler. It may be on the very edge of the ruler or indented slightly.

Activity: Measure Lines with a "Broken" Ruler

Have your child close his eyes while you secretly draw a 4-inch line on a piece of paper. Take the ruler off the paper before he opens his eyes. Wrap a slip of paper around the ruler so that the 1-inch mark is hidden.

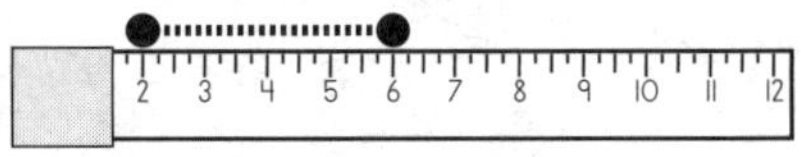

Let's pretend the covered part of the ruler broke off. How could you still use the ruler to measure the line? *Answers will vary.* Give your child a few moments to experiment with using the ruler to measure the line.

Here's one way. Align the ruler under the line as shown. **Now, I can use the tick marks on the ruler to see how many inches long the line is.** Slide your finger along the line and count the inches: **1, 2, 3, 4. So, the line is 4 inches long.**

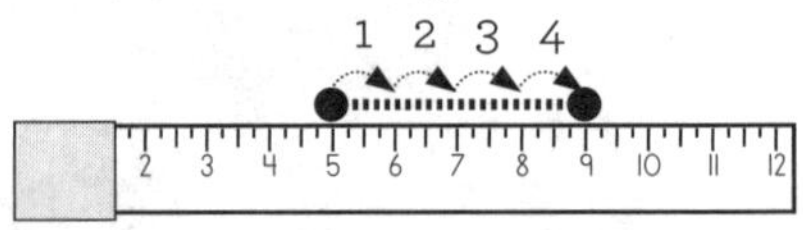

I could line up the ruler other ways, too. Align the ruler so that the 3-inch mark is directly below the left end of the line. Again, slide your finger along the line and count the inches: **1, 2, 3, 4. No matter how I line up the ruler, the line is 4 inches long.**

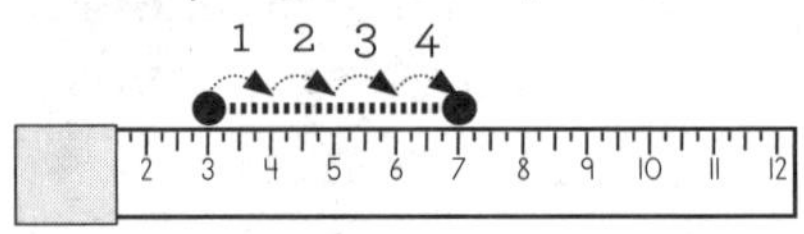

Have your child close his eyes while you draw a 2-inch line, a 5-inch line, and an 8-inch line. Then, have him measure each line with the "broken" ruler and label its length.

Activity: Play Measurement Tag with a "Broken" Ruler

Play 1 round of Measurement Tag, but use the "broken" ruler to draw the lines. See Lesson 20.1 (page 323) for directions.

> Encourage your child to use addition to draw the lines. For example, if he flips over a 6, he might align the 2-inch mark on the ruler with his starting dot. Then, he can add 2 + 6 to find that his line should stop at the 8-inch mark on the ruler.

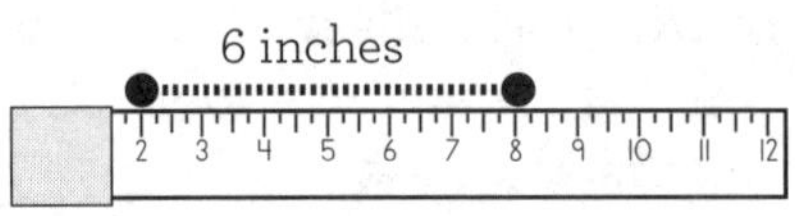

$2 + 6 = 8$

Workbook: Measure with a "Broken" Ruler and Review

Have your child complete workbook pages 20.2A and 20.2B.

Lesson 20.3
Measure in Feet and Inches

	Purpose	Materials
Warm-up	• Count by 5s on the dot array • Practice memory work • Review addition facts	• Dot array and L-cover (Blackline Master 6) • Addition Crash game boards (from workbook page 4.1A) • Counters • Playing cards
Activities	• Review feet • Measure length in feet and inches	• 1-foot ruler
Workbook	• Measure length in feet and inches	• Workbook pages 20.3A and 20.3B

In real life, we often use a combination of units to accurately describe lengths. For example, in the U.S. customary system, we typically use both feet and inches to measure our height. This lesson introduces your child to using these compound units. Note that she is not expected to be able to convert feet to inches or inches to feet in second grade.

Warm-up: Counting, Memory Work, and Review

- Slide the L-cover on the dot array to reveal 5 dots at a time. Have your child count by 5s to tell how many dots are visible in each array. Continue to 50.

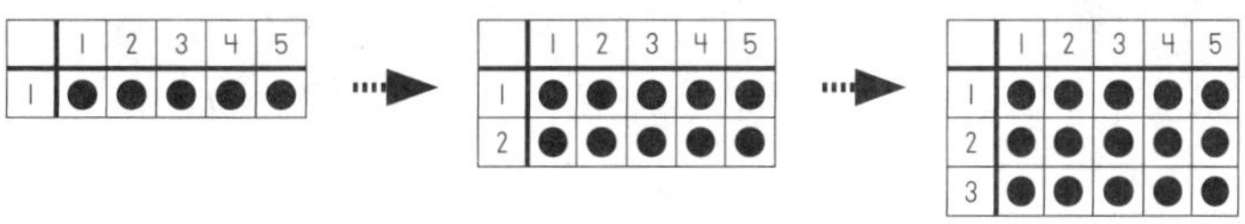

5 10 15

- **How many minutes equal a half-hour?** *30.*
  How many minutes equal a quarter-hour? *15.*
- Play Addition Crash, +8 Version. See Lesson 4.3 (page 67) for directions.

  If your child knows the +8 facts well, play a different addition fact game instead, such as Addition Bingo (+6 or +7 Version) or Addition Crash (+9 Version).

Activity: Measure a Table in Feet and Inches

In the last two lessons, you reviewed measuring in inches. Today, you'll learn how to measure with feet and inches. 12 inches equal 1 foot. This ruler is one foot long.

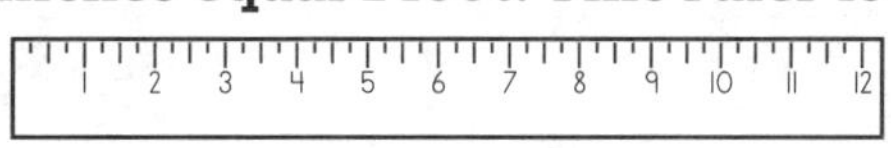

Try to hold your hands about one foot apart. *Child holds hands about one foot apart.* Place the ruler between her hands to check her estimate.

Show your child a table that's about 4-6 feet long. **About how many feet long do you think this table is?** *Answers will vary.* Encourage your child to imagine placing the ruler along the table to find a reasonable estimate (but don't allow her to actually measure it yet).

Begin a simple chart and record her estimate.

Household Object	Estimate	Actual Length
Table	4 feet	

Let's use both feet and inches to measure the table. First, we measure as many whole feet as possible. Then, we measure the rest in inches.

Show your child how to use the one-foot ruler to measure the table in feet and inches. Align the ruler with one edge of the table. Then, place your finger at the end of the ruler and slide the ruler to the other side of your finger.

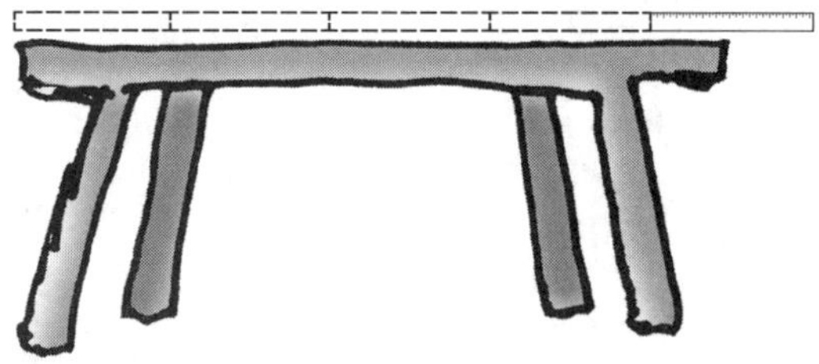

"The table is 4 feet and 5 inches long."

Record the result in your chart.

Household Object	Estimate	Actual Length
Table	4 feet	4 feet, 5 inches

Sliding the ruler in this way helps children understand concretely what it means to measure in both feet and inches, but it does tend to make the measurements less accurate. If you'd like to measure these lengths more precisely, use a tape measure marked in feet and inches.

Activity: Measure Household Objects in Feet and Inches

Begin a simple chart as shown. Have your child choose several household objects that are more than 1 foot long.

Have her first estimate the length of each object in feet. Then, have her measure each object in feet and inches with the ruler. Record the results in the chart.

Household Object	Estimate	Actual Length
Table	4 feet	4 feet, 5 inches
Bookshelf	3 feet	2 feet, 10 inches
Counter	9 feet	7 feet, 8 inches
Piano	4 feet	4 feet, 7 inches
Bed	7 feet	6 feet, 3 inches
Rug	8 feet	7 feet, 6 inches

Workbook: Measure in Feet and Inches and Review

Have your child complete workbook pages 20.3A and 20.3B. Point out that the 1-foot rulers on the page are pictures of rulers, and that the printed pictures are not actually 1 foot long.

Lesson 20.4
Yards and Miles

	Purpose	Materials
Warm-up	• Count by quarter-hour intervals • Practice memory work • Review mental subtraction	• Clock • Base-ten blocks, optional
Activities	• Introduce yards and miles • Learn that 3 feet (or 36 inches) equal 1 yard • Identify whether objects are shorter, longer, or equal to a yard	• Paper • Scissors • Tape • 1-foot ruler
Workbook	• Choose a sensible unit for a given length	• Workbook pages 20.4A and 20.4B

Warm-up: Counting, Memory Work, and Review

- Set the clock to 11:00. Have your child count by quarter-hour intervals from 11:00 to 1:00. Have him turn the clock's hands to match each time.
- **How many minutes equal a half-hour?** *30.*
  How many minutes equal a quarter-hour? *15.*
- Write the following problems on paper and have your child solve them mentally. Allow him to use base-ten blocks as needed.
  - 32 − 6 = *26*
  - 45 − 8 = *37*
  - 70 − 9 = *61*
  - 43 − 25 = *18*
  - 94 − 36 = *58*

Activity: Make a Paper Yardstick

This week, you have learned about inches and feet. Today, you will learn about yards and miles.

We're going to make a paper strip that's 1 yard long. First, we need a long strip of paper to measure. Help your child fold a piece of copy paper into fourths, cut the paper along the fold lines, and tape the strips together.

3 feet equal 1 yard. Let's measure to make the paper strip 3 feet long. Help your child use the 1-foot ruler to mark 1-foot increments along the edge of the strip. Number each mark and continue until he's measured out 3 feet.

Have your child draw a line at the 3-foot mark and cut along the line. Have him write "1 yard" on the back of the strip.

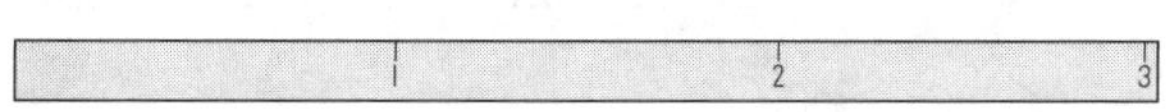

Discuss your child's experiences with yards. For example: **The lanes at the swimming pool are 25 yards long. A football field is 100 yards long.**

If your family uses the metric system, explain that a yard is a little shorter than a meter. Your child will learn about meters in Week 21.

Do you think you're taller or shorter than 1 yard? *Answers will vary.* Hold the paper yardstick vertically and compare it to your child's height.

Try to hold your hands about one yard apart. Child holds hands about one yard apart. Place the paper yardstick between his hands to check his estimate.

3 feet equal 1 yard. How many inches are in 1 foot? *12.* **So, how can we find how many inches are in a yard?** *Add 12 plus 12 plus 12.* Write 12 + 12 + 12 = on a piece of paper and have your child find the sum mentally.

$$12 + 12 + 12 = 36$$

Your child will memorize the number of inches and feet that equal a yard in the memory work in Week 22.

Activity: 1 Yard Scavenger Hunt

Now, we're going to go on a scavenger hunt. This scavenger hunt has 3 parts.

First, find 3 pieces of furniture shorter than a yard. *Sample answers: stepstool, lamp, bench.* Have your child compare each object with the paper yardstick to check.

Next, find 3 pieces of furniture taller than a yard. *Sample answers: refrigerator, large bookcase, coat rack.* Have your child compare each object with the paper yardstick.

Last, find 3 pieces of furniture about a yard tall. *Sample answers: couch, kitchen counter, small bookcase.* Again, have your child compare each object with the paper yardstick.

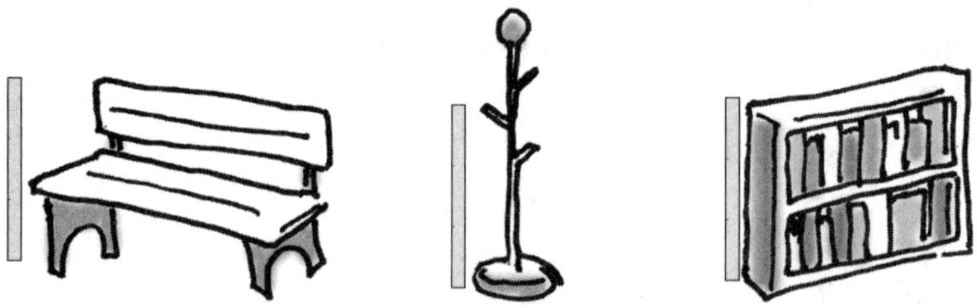

Finding objects that exactly equal a yard may be difficult. It's fine if these objects are several inches longer or shorter than a yard.

Save this paper yardstick to compare with a paper meterstick in Lesson 21.3.

Activity: Introduce Miles

Now you've learned about inches, feet, and yards. We use these units for measuring objects and short distances. But when we need to measure longer distances, we use miles. 1 mile is 5,280 feet long!

Your child does not need to memorize how many feet equal a mile.

Discuss your child's experiences with miles, and tell him the length of some familiar trips in miles. For example: **The walk to the library is about 1 mile. Our bike ride last week was 6 miles long. Grandma and Grandpa's house is about 20 miles away.**

See Lesson 20.5 for an enrichment activity to help make this abstract idea of miles more concrete.

Workbook: Choose a Sensible Unit and Review

Have your child complete workbook pages 20.4A and 20.4B.

Lesson 20.5
Enrichment and Review (Optional)

	Purpose	Materials
Warm-up	• Count backward from 200 to 100 by 1s, 2s, 5s, or 10s • Review memory work • Review your child's favorite or most challenging activities from Week 20	• Varies, depending on the activities you choose
Picture Book	• Understand U.S. customary units in the context of close-up views of animals	• *Actual Size,* by Steve Jenkins
Enrichment Activity	• Experience the length of a mile	• Map of your local area (or map app)

Warm-up: Counting, Memory Work, and Review

- Have your child count backward from 200 to 100 by 1s, 2s, 5s, or 10s. (Choose whichever counting sequence your child needs to practice the most.)
- Quiz your child on the memory work through Week 20. See page 523 for the full list.
- If you have time, repeat one or two of the activities from this week's lessons. Choose activities your child especially enjoyed or found challenging.

Math Picture Book: *Actual Size*

Read *Actual Size,* by Steve Jenkins. As you read, make sure to read the measurements listed in the captions.

Enrichment Activity: Walk (or Bike, or Drive) a Mile

Use a map or map app to plot a 1-mile route around your neighborhood or at a nearby park. Walk (or bike or drive) the route with your child so he can physically experience the length of a mile.

If your family uses the metric system, plot a 1-kilometer route instead. You will teach your child more about kilometers in Week 21.

Week 20 Answer Key

20.1A

Use a ruler to measure the ribbons in inches.

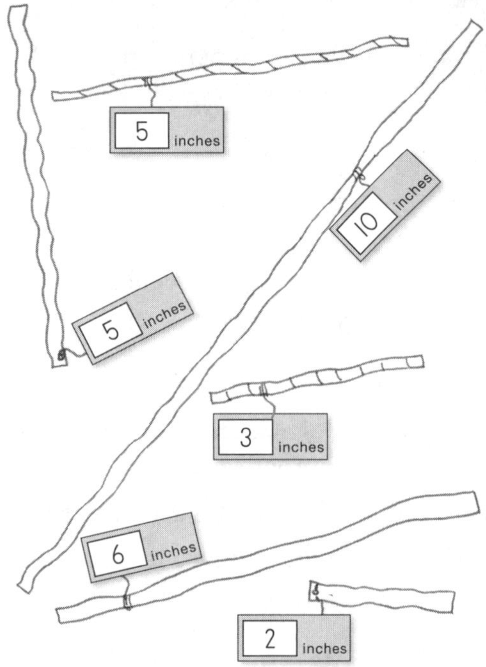

20.1B

Complete.

100 → -5 → 95 → -10 → 85 → -15 → 70 → -8 → 62

82 → -24 → 58 → -15 → 43 → -26 → 17 → -17 → 0

51 → -4 → 47 → -6 → 41 → -4 → 37 → -7 → 30

Complete the equations to match.

100: 80, 20

80 + 20 = 100
20 + 80 = 100
100 - 80 = 20
100 - 20 = 80

Write the time.

5:55 | 12:30 | 7:16

20.2A

Use the "broken" rulers to measure the leaves.

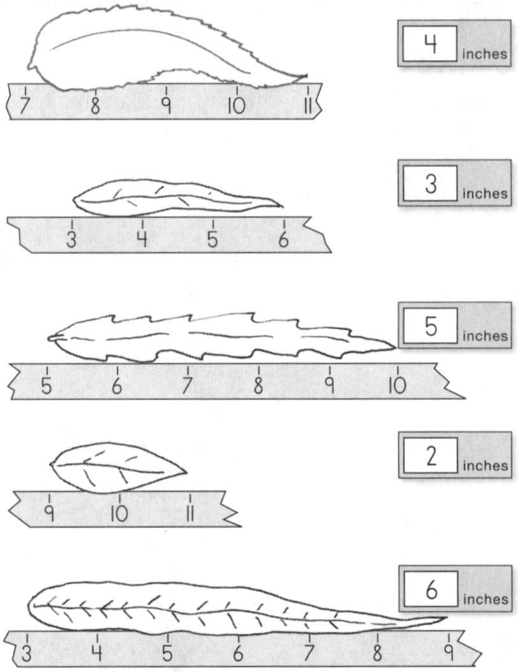

20.2B

Complete.

45 - 32 = 13
56 - 27 = 29
80 - 76 = 4
90 - 23 = 67
62 - 16 = 46
41 - 25 = 16

Complete the missing numbers in the sequences.

Week 20 Answer Key

20.3A

Match. Each ruler is 1 foot long.

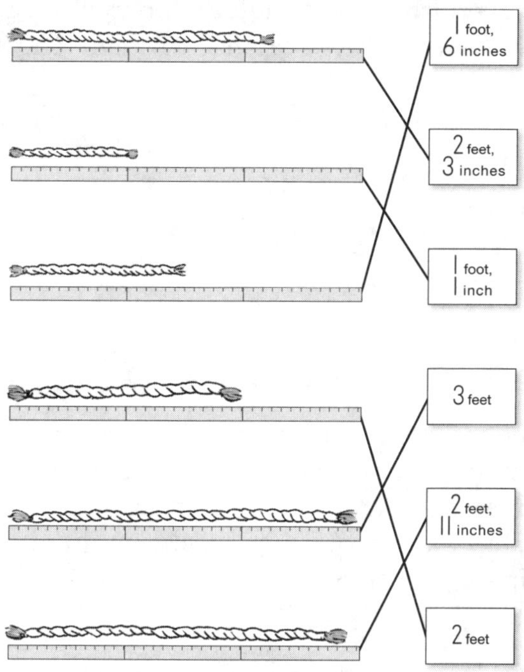

20.3B

Complete.

43 - 9 =	34	43 + 9 =	52
62 - 8 =	54	62 + 8 =	70
91 - 3 =	88	91 + 3 =	94
76 - 7 =	69	76 + 7 =	83
84 - 6 =	78	84 + 6 =	90
55 - 9 =	46	55 + 9 =	64

Use the key to color the hearts.

Complete.

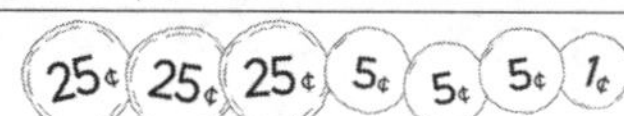

91 ¢

20.4A

Circle the more sensible measurement for each item.

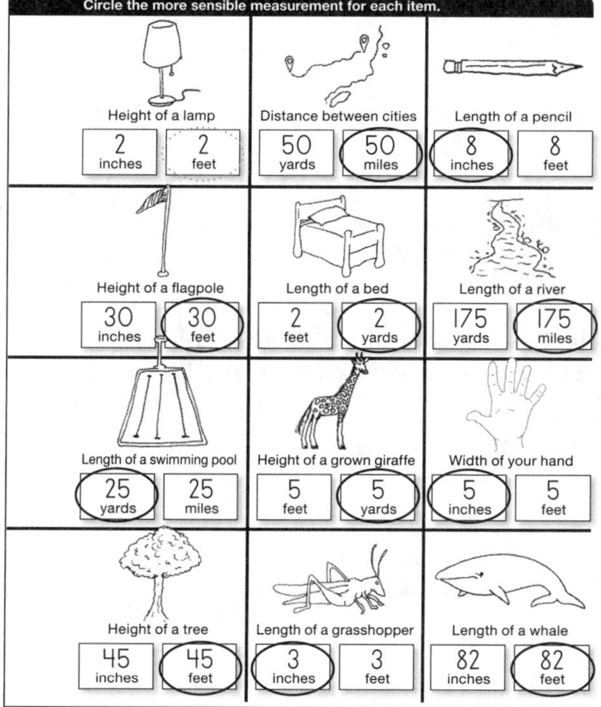

Height of a lamp	2 inches	**2 feet**
Distance between cities	50 yards	**50 miles**
Length of a pencil	**8 inches**	8 feet
Height of a flagpole	30 inches	**30 feet**
Length of a bed	2 feet	**2 yards**
Length of a river	175 yards	**175 miles**
Length of a swimming pool	**25 yards**	25 miles
Height of a grown giraffe	5 feet	**5 yards**
Width of your hand	**5 inches**	5 feet
Height of a tree	45 inches	**45 feet**
Length of a grasshopper	**3 inches**	3 feet
Length of a whale	82 inches	**82 feet**

20.4B

Complete.

70 - 5 =	65	71 - 5 =	66
80 - 3 =	77	81 - 3 =	78
30 - 8 =	22	31 - 8 =	23
50 - 4 =	46	51 - 4 =	47
60 - 9 =	51	61 - 9 =	52
40 - 7 =	33	41 - 7 =	34

Cooper made a line graph of the high temperature each day. Use the graph to complete the chart.

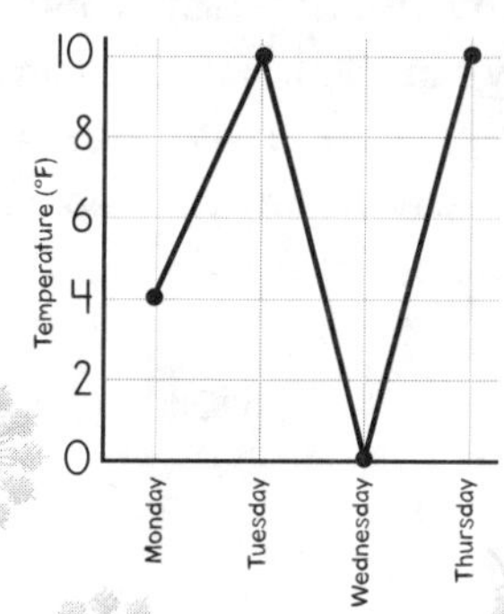

Day	High Temperature
Monday	4
Tuesday	10
Wednesday	0
Thursday	10

Week 21
Centimeters, Meters, and Kilometers

Overview

Your child will learn how to estimate and measure length in centimeters and meters. You will also introduce her to kilometers and teach her how to draw sketches to solve length word problems.

Lesson 21.1	Measure in Centimeters
Lesson 21.2	Centimeter Word Problems
Lesson 21.3	Meters and Kilometers
Lesson 21.4	Length Word Problems
Lesson 21.5	Enrichment and Review (Optional)

Teaching Math with Confidence: Adding and Subtracting Measured Quantities Instead of Countable Objects

In kindergarten and first grade, your child learned to solve word problems about individual, countable objects, like stickers, apples, or lollipops. She used counters to represent the objects, and then she joined or separated the counters to model addition or subtraction. Whether the problem was about chocolate chips, toy planes, or puppies, she could model 2 + 3 by joining a group of 2 counters with a group of 3 counters.

Using counters to model 2 + 3. These counters could stand for any individual, countable object.

Throughout second grade, your child has begun to work with quantities that are measured rather than counted. She has learned how to use labels on a bar graph to compare the bars, how to use a clock's tick marks to measure time, and how to use a ruler's tick marks to measure length. The subdivisions in these models helped your child transition from thinking about countable objects to measurable lengths.

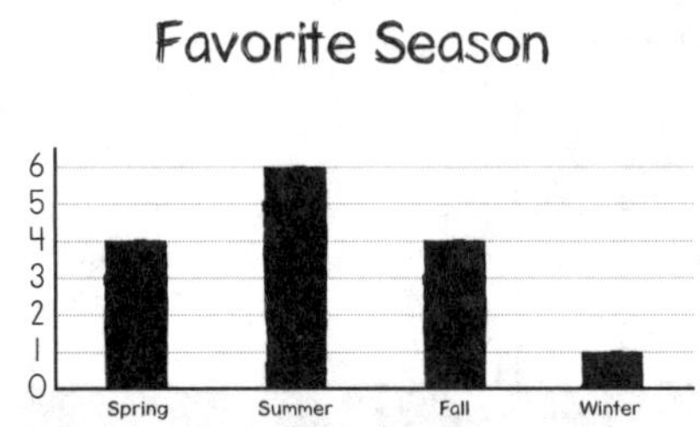

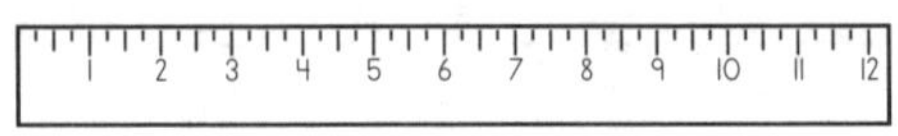

This week, your child will learn how to solve length word problems. For example, you'll pose this problem to your child in Lesson 21.4: **Sarah has 15 yards of ribbon. Then, she uses 6 yards to make a craft. How much does she have left?** Children often find these problems more challenging than the earlier problems, because there are no individual objects to visualize or count.

Instead of modeling these problems with counters, you'll teach your child to represent them with simple line drawings. These sketches will help make the problems more concrete so that your child can visualize them, identify the correct operation, and solve. For example, for the above problem, you'll draw a sketch like the following to help your child see that she should subtract 15 – 6 to find that there are 9 yards of ribbon left.

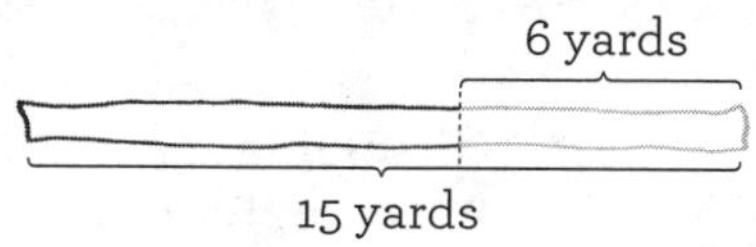

Sarah has 15 yards of ribbon. Then, she uses 6 yards to make a craft. How much does she have left?

Extra Materials Needed for Week 21

- 6 narrow paper strips, about 11 inches long and ½-inch wide (or 28 cm long and 1-centimeter wide)
- Markers or colored pencils
- Scissors
- Stapler
- Paper
- Tape
- 7 slips of paper or sticky notes
- For optional Enrichment and Review Lesson:
    - *Polly's Pen Pal,* written by Stuart J. Murphy and illustrated by Rémy Simard
    - 1-cup measuring cup or 1-liter measuring cup
    - Ingredients for your choice of recipe involving cups or liters. (See Lesson 21.5 (page 345) for sample recipes.)

You will also need a 30-centimeter ruler, marked in centimeters, for this week's lessons. Many 1-foot rulers are marked on the other edge or side in centimeters.

Lesson 21.1
Measure in Centimeters

	Purpose	Materials
Warm-up	• Count by 3s on the dot array • Practice memory work • Review mental subtraction	• Dot array and L-cover (Blackline Master 6) • Base-ten blocks, optional
Activities	• Introduce the metric system and centimeters • Measure lengths in centimeters	• 30-centimeter (or 1-foot) ruler marked in centimeters and inches • 6 narrow paper strips, about 11 inches long and ½-inch wide (or 28 centimeters long and 1 centimeter wide) • Markers or colored pencils • Scissors
Workbook	• Measure lines in centimeters	• Workbook pages 21.1A and 21.1B • 30-centimeter ruler

Warm-up: Counting, Memory Work, and Review

- Slide the L-cover on the dot array to reveal 3 dots at a time. Have your child count by 3s to tell how many dots are visible in each array. Continue to 30.

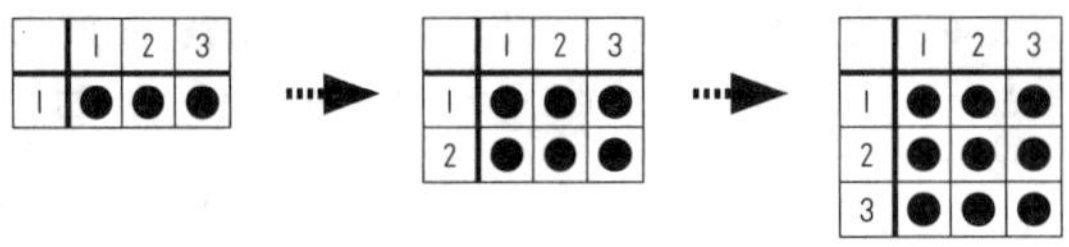

3 6 9

> Encourage your child to add 3 to the previous total to find each new total. She will gradually learn to count by 3s over the next few weeks of lessons.

- **How many cents equal 1 dollar?** *100.*
- Write the following problems on paper and have your child solve them mentally. Allow her to use base-ten blocks as needed.
  - × 80 − 3 = *77*
  - × 80 − 7 = *73*
  - × 80 − 11 = *69*
  - × 80 − 25 = *55*
  - × 80 − 79 = *1*

Activity: Introduce Centimeters

People in different countries often do things differently from each other. They eat different food, speak different languages, and follow different customs. Briefly discuss your child's experience of different countries and cultures.

People even use different measurement systems in different countries! Last week, you learned about inches, feet, yards, and miles. These units are used in the United States, and sometimes in the United Kingdom and Canada. But people in most of the other countries of

the world use a measurement system called the metric system. This week, you'll learn about the metric system and how to measure length with centimeters, meters, and kilometers.

Polly's Pen Pal, the optional picture book suggested for this week, provides a fun introduction to the two measurement systems. Feel free to read the book during this lesson to introduce the differences between the metric and U.S. customary systems.

Show your child a 30-centimeter ruler. Point to the leftmost tick mark on the ruler with one hand, and point to the 1-centimeter mark with the other hand. **From here to here is 1 centimeter.**

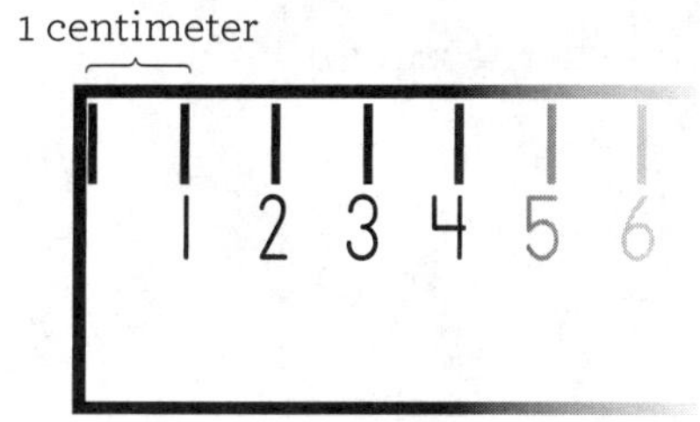

Try to hold your thumb and first finger one centimeter apart. *Child holds thumb and forefinger about one centimeter apart.* Use the ruler to check her estimate.

If your ruler is marked in both inches and centimeters, point out the two sides of the ruler to your child.

Activity: Measure Paper Strips in Centimeters

We'll cut paper strips to different lengths and color them to make a rainbow craft in the next lesson. The first strip should be 27 centimeters long and red. Show your child how to align a paper strip above the ruler and draw a line at the 27-centimeter mark. Then, have her cut along the line and color the strip red. Lightly write "27 cm" on the strip.

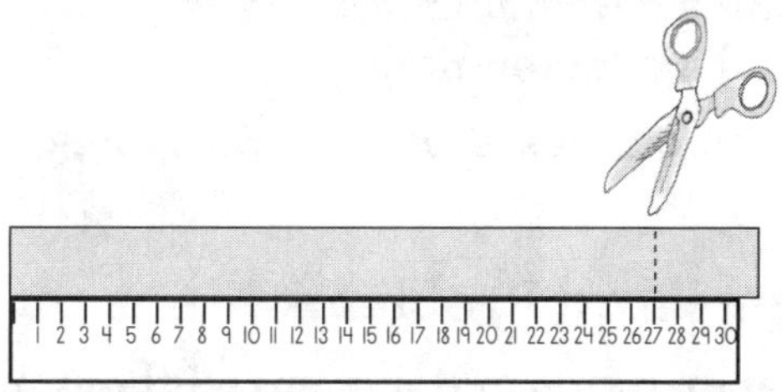

Labeling the strips with their lengths makes them easier to use to solve word problems in Lesson 21.2. Use pencil so your child can erase the labels before constructing the craft.

Have your child measure, cut, color, and label the following paper strips:

- Orange: 24 centimeters
- Yellow: 21 centimeters
- Green: 18 centimeters
- Blue: 15 centimeters
- Purple: 12 centimeters

Activity: Play Measurement Tag

Play one round of Measurement Tag, but use centimeters instead of inches. For example, if you flip over a 5, draw a 5-centimeter line. See Lesson 20.1 (page 323) for full directions.

Workbook: Measure in Centimeters and Review

Have your child complete workbook pages 21.1A and 21.1B.

Lesson 21.2
Centimeter Word Problems

	Purpose	Materials
Warm-up	• Count backward • Practice memory work • Review telling time to the minute	• Clock
Activities	• Solve word problems involving centimeters	• 30-centimeter (or 1-foot) ruler marked in centimeters • Stapler • paper strips from previous lesson
Workbook	• Measure length in centimeters • Solve word problems involving centimeters	• Workbook pages 21.2A and 21.2B

Warm-up: Counting, Memory Work, and Review

- Have your child count backward from the following numbers. Prompt him as needed, and stop him after he reaches the last number listed.
    - **Count backward from 172:** *172, 171, 170, 169, 168.*
    - **Count backward from 130:** *130, 129, 128, 127, 126.*
    - **Count backward from 101:** *101, 100, 99, 98, 97.*
- **How many minutes equal a half-hour?** *30.*
  How many minutes equal a quarter-hour? *15.*
- Set the clock to the following times: 6:00, 6:17, 6:30, 6:45, 6:46, 6:57, 7:07, 7:20. Have your child tell each time.

Activity: Solve Centimeter Word Problems

In the last lesson, you made paper strips and measured them in centimeters. Before we make the strips into a craft, we'll use them to solve some word problems.

Place the yellow and green strips end to end. **Let's pretend I wanted to connect the yellow and green strips to make a craft. The yellow strip is 21 centimeters long, and the green strip is 18 centimeters long. So, I can add 21 plus 18 to find the total length.** Write "21 + 18 =" on a piece of paper. Have your child use mental math to complete the equation: 21 + 18 = 39.

21 + 18 = 39 

Have your child write equations to find the total length of the following paper-strip combinations:

- Blue and purple. *15 + 12 = 27. 27 centimeters.*
- Orange and green. *24 + 18 = 42. 42 centimeters.*
- Red, orange, and yellow. *27 + 24 + 21 = 72. 72 centimeters.*

I wonder how much longer the red strip is than the orange strip. Line up the red strip and orange strip as shown. **The red strip is 27 centimeters long, and the orange strip is 24 centimeters long. So, I can subtract the bigger number minus the smaller number to find the difference.** Write "27 – 24 =" on a piece of paper. Have your child use mental math to complete the equation: 27 – 24 = 3.

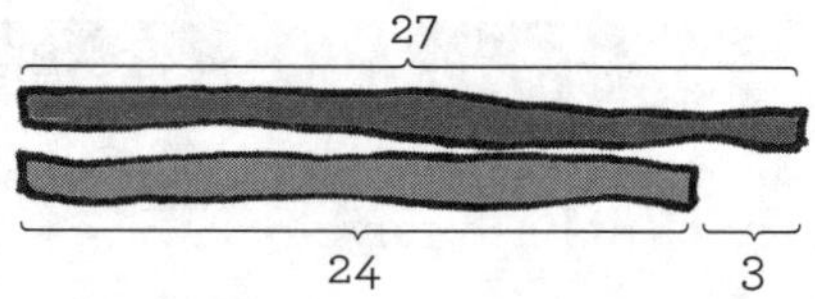

Have your child use the ruler to check that the red strip is 3 centimeters longer than the orange strip.

We can say the red strip is 3 centimeters longer than the orange strip. Or, we can say the orange strip is 3 centimeters shorter than the red strip. Either way, they have a difference of 3 centimeters.

Have your child write equations to find the difference in lengths for the following pairs of paper strips:

- Orange and green. *24 – 18 = 6. 6 centimeters.*
- Red and blue. *27 – 15 = 12. 12 centimeters.*
- Red and purple. *27 – 12 = 15. 15 centimeters.*

Activity: Make a Rainbow Craft

Now let's make the strips into a rainbow craft. Stack the colored strips in order, with the longest strip at the bottom and the shortest strip at the top. Align the left edges of all the strips and staple the left edges together.

Align the right edges of all the strips and staple again to create the rainbow.

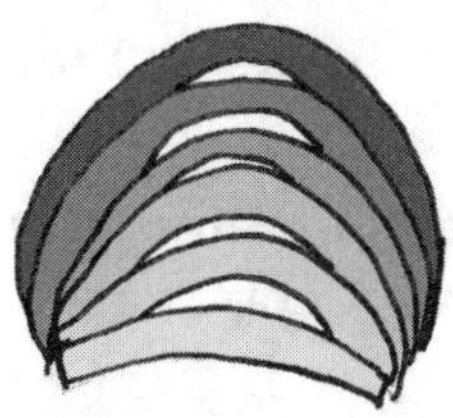

Workbook: Solve Centimeter Word Problems and Review

Have your child complete workbook pages 21.2A and 21.2B.

Lesson 21.3
Meters and Kilometers

	Purpose	Materials
Warm-up	• Count combinations of base-ten blocks • Practice memory work • Review addition facts	• Base-ten blocks • Addition Bingo game boards (from workbook page 5.1A) • Counters • Playing cards
Activities	• Introduce meters and kilometers • Learn that 100 centimeters equal 1 meter • Estimate and measure length in meters	• Paper • Scissors • Tape • 30-centimeter (or 1-foot) ruler marked in centimeters • Paper yardstick (from Lesson 20.4)
Workbook	• Choose a sensible unit for a given length	• Workbook pages 21.3A and 21.3B

Warm-up: Counting, Memory Work, and Review

- Place 12 rods and 5 units on the table. **What is the value of these blocks?** *125.*
- **What is another name for 12 a.m.?** *Midnight.*
  What is another name for 12 p.m.? *Noon.*
- Play Addition Bingo, +7 Version. See Lesson 5.1 (page 76) for directions.
-
-

Activity: Make a Paper Meterstick

This week, you have learned about centimeters. Today, you will learn about two more metric units: meters and kilometers.

We're going to make a paper strip that's 1 meter long. First, we need a long strip of paper to measure. Help your child fold a piece of copy paper into fourths, cut the paper along the fold lines, and tape the strips together.

100 centimeters equal 1 meter. Let's measure to make the paper strip 100 centimeters long. Help your child use the 30-centimeter ruler to mark increments of 10 centimeters along the edge of the paper strip. Number each mark and continue until she's measured out 100 centimeters.

Have your child draw a line at the 100-centimeter mark and cut along the line. Have her write "1 meter" on the back of the strip.

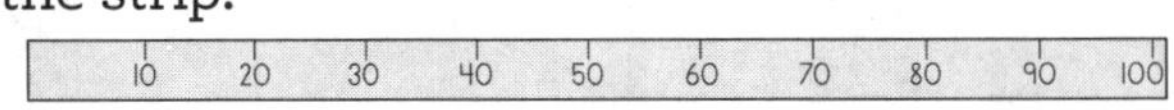

Discuss your child's experiences with meters. For example: **The runners at the Olympics sprint 100 meters.**

Have your child compare the paper meterstick with the paper yardstick you made in Lesson 20.4. **Which is longer: a yard or a meter?** *A meter.*

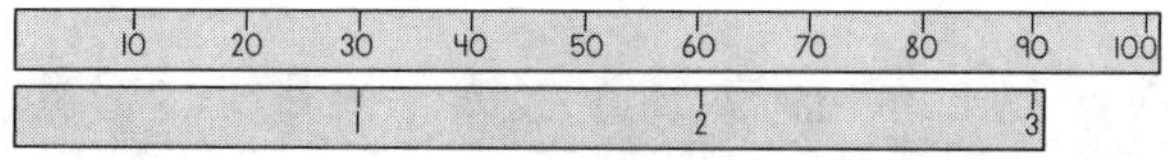

Activity: Measure in Meters

About how many meters long do you think this room is? *Answers will vary.* Encourage your child to find a reasonable estimate by imagining placing the paper meterstick in a line across the room.

Help your child measure the length of the room with the paper meterstick. Place the meterstick against one wall. Then, have her place her finger at the end of the meterstick and slide it to the other side of her finger.

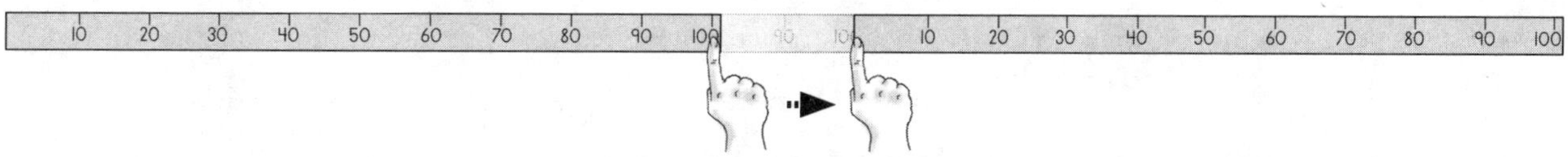

So, how many meters long is the room? *Answers will vary.*

Have your child estimate and measure the length of several other rooms in your home.

> Encourage your child to use phrases like "a little longer" or "a little shorter" to describe the length if it is not a whole number of meters. For example: *The kitchen is a little longer than 4 meters. The bathroom is a little narrower than 2 meters.*

Save the paper meterstick for future lessons.

Activity: Introduce Kilometers

In the metric system, we use centimeters and meters for measuring objects and short distances. But when we need to measure longer distances, we use kilometers. 1 kilometer is 1,000 meters long!

Discuss your child's experiences with kilometers, and tell him the length of some familiar trips in kilometers. For example: **The fun run that we did was 5 kilometers long. Uncle Joe and Aunt Susie live about 50 kilometers away.**

> If you use U.S. customary units and don't know off-hand any distances in kilometers, use a map app set to kilometers to find the length of a few familiar trips.

Workbook: Choose a Sensible Unit and Review

Have your child complete workbook pages 21.3A and 21.3B.

Lesson 21.4
Length Word Problems

	Purpose	Materials
Warm-up	• Count money • Practice memory work • Review mental addition	• Play money • Base-ten blocks, optional
Activities	• Review units for length • Solve length word problems	• 7 slips of paper or sticky notes
Workbook	• Solve length word problems	• Workbook pages 21.4A and 21.4B

See the Week 21 **Teaching Math with Confidence** for how these length word problems differ from the word problems your child has solved up to this point.

Warm-up: Counting, Memory Work, and Review

- Place 6 twenty-dollar bills, 4 ten-dollar bills, and 5 five-dollar bills on the table. **How much is this money worth?** *$185.*
- **Are times in the afternoon and evening a.m. or p.m.?** *P.m.*
  Are times in the morning a.m. or p.m.? *A.m.*
- Write the following problems on paper and have your child solve them mentally. Allow him to use base-ten blocks as needed.
  - 36 + 5 = *41*
  - 36 + 10 = *46*
  - 36 + 15 = *51*
  - 36 + 20 = *56*
  - 36 + 25 = *61*

Activity: Make a Measurement Chart

You have learned a lot about measuring length! Today, we'll make a poster to summarize what you've learned. You'll also solve length word problems.

Write the following units on sticky notes or slips of paper: yard, centimeter, mile, meter, inch, kilometer, foot. Also begin a simple chart.

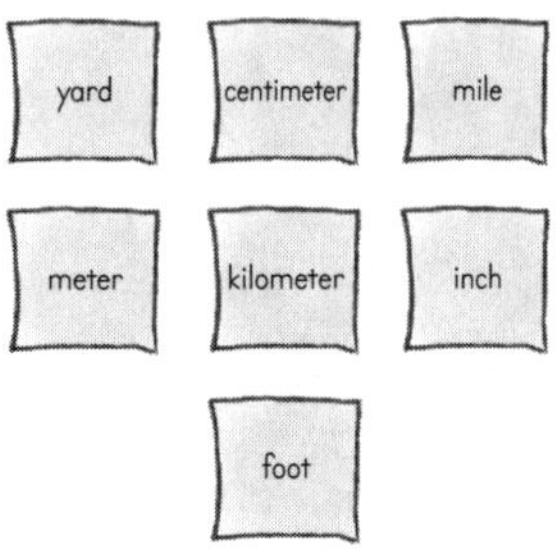

U.S. Customary Units	Metric Units

Have your child sort the sticky notes into the correct columns on the chart. Then, have him arrange the units in order from shortest to longest within each column.

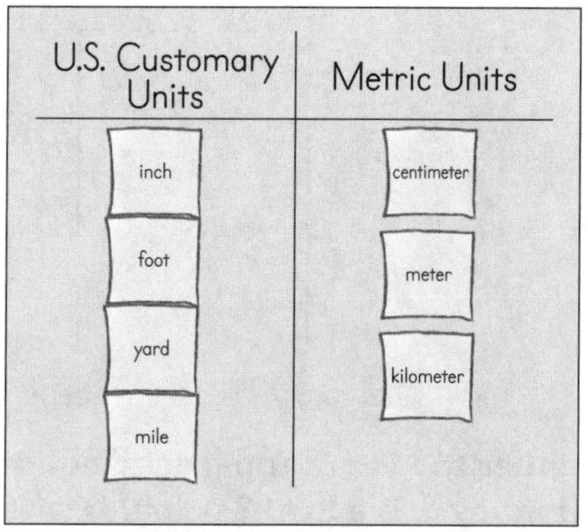

Name each unit in order and have your child approximate its length with his hands (except for mile and kilometer!)

> This activity provides an informal assessment of how well your child can approximate these units of length.

Activity: Draw Sketches to Solve Length Word Problems

Now, we'll use these units to solve word problems. I'll show you how to draw sketches to help solve the problems. When we draw a sketch in math, we keep it very simple. We only include the information we need to help understand and solve the problem.

Here's the first problem: Sarah has 15 yards of ribbon. Then, she uses 6 yards to make a craft. How much does she have left?

Here's how I draw a sketch to help solve the problem. First, I'll draw the line to stand for the ribbon that she started with. Draw a line and label it "15 yards." **Now, I'll cross out the part that she used.** Shade a portion of the line (as shown below) and label this part 6 yards.

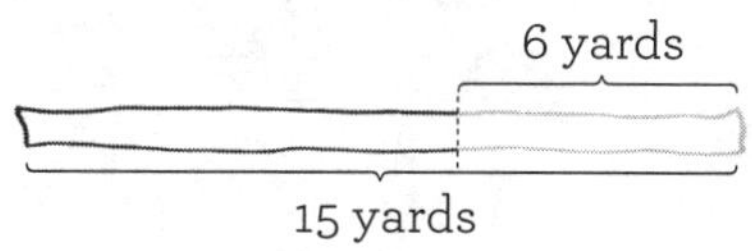

The sketch helps me see that I can subtract 15 minus 6 to find how much ribbon is left. Write 15 – 6 = next to the drawing. Have your child complete the equation: 15 – 6 = 9. **So, how much ribbon does she have left?** *9 yards.*

> Make sure your child includes the correct units in his answer.

Have your child solve the following word problems. For each problem, help him draw a simple sketch and write an equation to match before finding the answer.

- **Jonathan swam 50 meters in the pool on Monday. On Tuesday, he swam 25 meters further than he swam on Monday. How far did he swim on Tuesday?** *75 meters.*

$$50 + 25 = 75$$

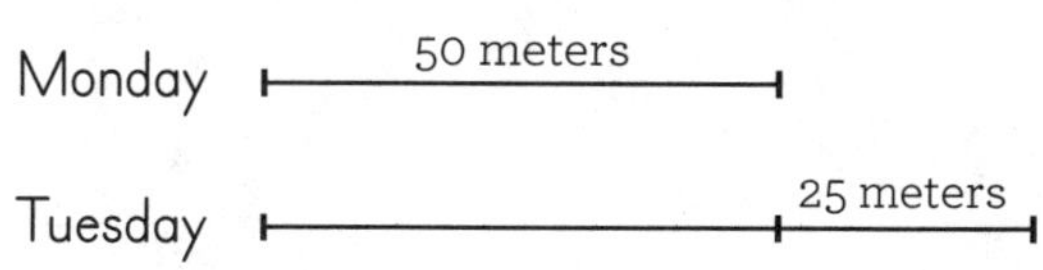

- **Sara is 50 inches tall. Her little sister Phoebe is 2 inches shorter than Sara. How many inches tall is Phoebe?** *48 inches.*

$50 - 2 = 48$

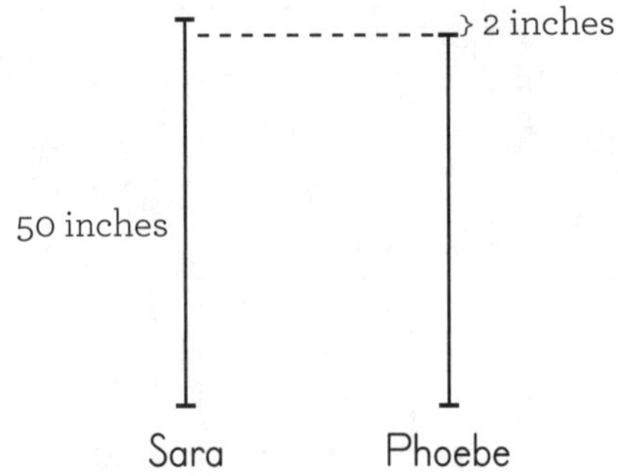

- **Sam's family drove 47 miles to his grandparents' house. Then, they drove 47 miles home again. How far did they drive in all?** *94 miles.*

$47 + 47 = 94$

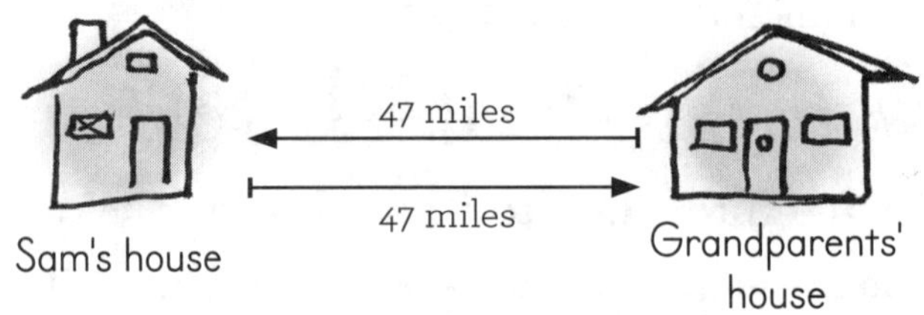

Workbook: Solve Length Word Problems and Review

Have your child complete workbook pages 21.4A and 21.4B.

Lesson 21.5
Enrichment and Review (Optional)

	Purpose	Materials
Warm-up	• Count backward from 200 to 100 by 1s, 2s, 5s, or 10s • Review memory work • Review your child's favorite or most challenging activities from Week 21	• Varies, depending on the activities you choose
Picture Book	• Understand the difference between metric and U.S. customary units	• *Polly's Pen Pal,* written by Stuart J. Murphy and illustrated by Rémy Simard
Enrichment Activity	• Introduce cups or liters • Use cups or liters to make a recipe	• 1-cup measuring cup or 1-liter measuring cup • Ingredients for your choice of recipe involving cups or liters (See below for sample recipes.)

Warm-up: Counting, Memory Work, and Review

- Have your child count backward from 200 to 100 by 1s, 2s, 5s, or 10s. (Choose whichever counting sequence your child needs to practice the most.)
- Quiz your child on the memory work through Week 20. See page 523 for the full list.
- If you have time, repeat one or two of the activities from this week's lessons. Choose activities your child especially enjoyed or found challenging.

Math Picture Book: *Polly's Pen Pal*

Read *Polly's Pen Pal,* written by Stuart J. Murphy and illustrated by Rémy Simard. As you read, discuss the different units that Polly and her pen pal use in the book.

Enrichment Activity: Follow a Recipe with Cups or Liters

Show your child a measuring cup for your family's measurement system (either 1-cup or 1-liter). Discuss how measuring cups are used to measure how much space things take up. Then, use the measuring cup to follow a recipe of your choice that involves measuring ingredients in either cups or liters. Or, use one of the recipes below.

Salt Dough

Mix together 2 cups of flour and 1 cup of salt. Stir in a total of 1 cup of cold water, a few tablespoons at a time. Once all the water is mixed in, knead the dough for about 10 minutes. Let the dough rest for 20 minutes, then sculpt and mold like modeling clay.

If you'd like to harden your child's creations, you can bake them at 250° F until dry, about 2 hours.

Liter Punch

Mix together in a large pitcher:

- **1 liter pineapple juice**
- **1 liter orange juice**
- **1 liter lemon-lime soda**

Add ice and berries or fruit slices.

Feel free to modify the recipe to match whatever juice or soda you have on hand.

Week 21 Answer Key

21.1A

Use a ruler to measure the sticks in centimeters.

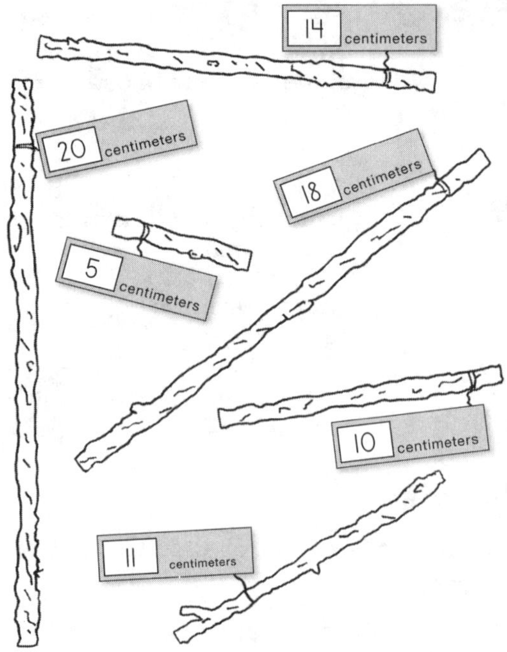

21.1B

Match.

Problem	Answer	Problem
95 - 41	54	74 - 20
68 - 19	49	90 - 41
80 - 58	22	87 - 65
73 - 36	37	61 - 24

Solve.

Alice has $24. The skates cost $30. How much more money does she need to buy them?

30 − 24 = 6

$6

Your child may write 24 + 6 = 30.

Simon has $9. The sled costs $23. How much more money does he need to buy it?

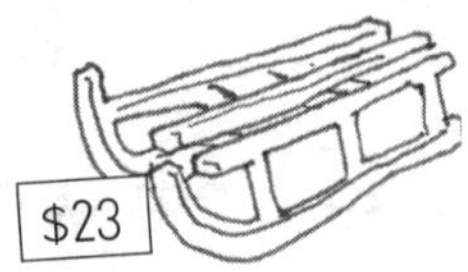

23 − 9 = 14

$14

Your child may write 14 + 9 = 23.

21.2A

Use a ruler to measure the school supplies in centimeters.

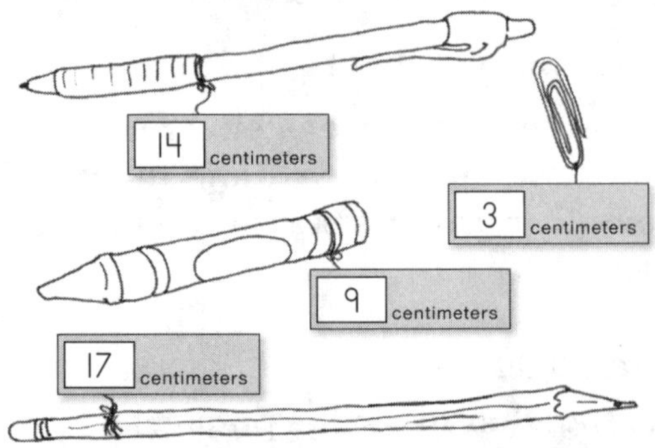

Use the measurements to complete the equations and answer the questions.

How much longer is the crayon than the paper clip?

9 − 3 = 6

6 centimeters

How much longer is the pen than the paper clip?

14 − 3 = 11

11 centimeters

How much shorter is the crayon than the pencil?

17 − 9 = 8

8 centimeters

How much shorter is the pen than the pencil?

17 − 14 = 3

3 centimeters

21.2B

Complete.

73 - 23 = 50
72 - 23 = 49
71 - 23 = 48

83 - 23 = 60
83 - 22 = 61
83 - 21 = 62

63 - 23 = 40
53 - 23 = 30
43 - 23 = 20

93 - 23 = 70
93 - 33 = 60
93 - 43 = 50

Write the value of the base-ten blocks.

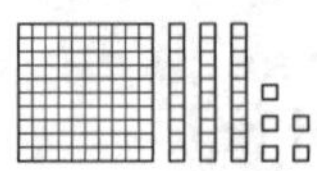

135

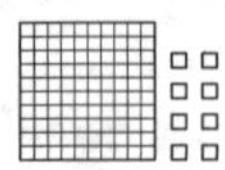

108

Complete. Use a decimal point and a dollar sign.

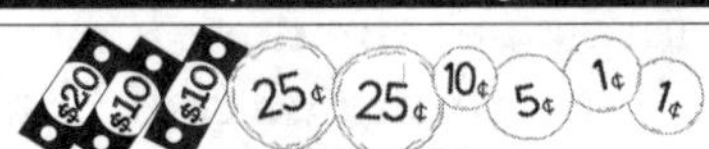

$40.67

$80.80

Week 21 Answer Key

21.3A

Circle the more sensible measurement for each item. (circled answers shown in bold)

Height of a chair	1 centimeter	**1 meter**
length of a hike	5 meters	**5 kilometers**
Length of a crayon	**7 centimeters**	7 meters
Height of a house	**6 meters**	6 kilometers
Length of a bathtub	**150 centimeters**	150 meters
Height of a book	**20 centimeters**	20 meters
Length of a worm	**12 centimeters**	12 meters
Length of a swimming pool	**25 meters**	25 kilometers
Height of an elephant	2 centimeters	**2 meters**
Length of a bus	12 centimeters	**12 meters**
Length of your foot	**18 centimeters**	18 meters
Distance between cities	40 meters	**40 kilometers**

21.3B

Complete.

29 → +6 → 35 → +8 → 43 → +8 → 51 → +9 → 60

74 → -12 → 62 → -12 → 50 → -12 → 38 → -12 → 26

85 → +4 → 89 → +5 → 94 → +5 → 99 → +1 → 100

Connor, Santiago and Caroline played a game. Use their scorecard to answer the questions.

Scorecard

Name	Score
Connor	36
Santiago	38
Caroline	43

Who scored the most points? Caroline

Who scored the fewest points? Connor

How many more points did Santiago score than Connor?
38 − 36 = 2
2 points

How many more points did Caroline score than Santiago?
43 − 38 = 5
5 points

21.4A

Solve. Write your own equation to match each word problem.

Claire was 29 inches tall. Then, she grew 3 inches. How tall is she now?

3 inches / 29 inches

29 + 3 = 32
32 inches

James has a ribbon 34 centimeters long. He uses 12 centimeters for a craft project. How many centimeters are left?

12 centimeters / 34 centimeters

34 − 12 = 22
22 centimeters

Caden's plant is 13 inches tall. Olivia's plant is 17 inches tall. How much taller is Olivia's plant than Caden's?

13 inches / 17 inches

17 − 13 = 4
4 inches

Amir's family hiked 2 kilometers on the red trail, 3 kilometers on the green trail, and 1 kilometer on the blue trail. How far did they hike in all?

1 kilometer / 2 kilometers / 3 kilometers

2 + 3 + 1 = 6
6 kilometers

21.4B

Complete.

42 - 26 = 16	54 - 17 = 37
60 - 45 = 15	81 - 63 = 18
93 - 34 = 59	72 - 52 = 20

Write the time.

1:45 | 3:20 | 12:07

Write the expanded form for each number.

87 = 80 + 7	134 = 100 + 30 + 4
162 = 100 + 60 + 2	151 = 100 + 50 + 1
199 = 100 + 90 + 9	109 = 100 + 9

Unit 9 Checkpoint

What to Expect at the End of Unit 9

By the end of Unit 9, most children will be able to do the following:

- Approximate the length of an inch, foot, yard, centimeter, and meter with their hands and choose appropriate units for measuring in real-life situations. Most second-graders will be quite comfortable with these skills when using their family's measurement system but will still be working on these skills with the other measurement system.
- Estimate length in inches, feet, yards, centimeters, or meters. Most second-graders will be somewhat close when using their family's measurement system and much less accurate with the other measurement system.
- Measure length with a ruler to the nearest inch or centimeter, even if the object is not aligned with the end of the ruler. Some children will still need coaching when the object is not aligned with the end of the ruler.
- Place a 1-foot ruler, yardstick, or meterstick end to end to measure length.

Is Your Child Ready to Move on?

In Unit 10, your child will learn to add two-digit numbers with the standard written process. He will continue to build on the mental math and addition facts skills that he has been developing all year long, but he does not need to master any other specific skills before moving on to Unit 10.

Unit 10
Written Addition to 200

Overview

In Unit 6, your child deepened his number sense and place-value knowledge as he learned how to add two-digit numbers mentally. In this unit, he'll apply that knowledge as he learns the standard algorithm for written vertical addition. (You may know this process as "carrying the 1" or "stack math.")

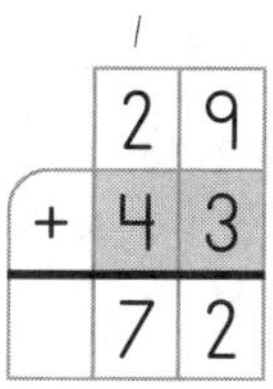

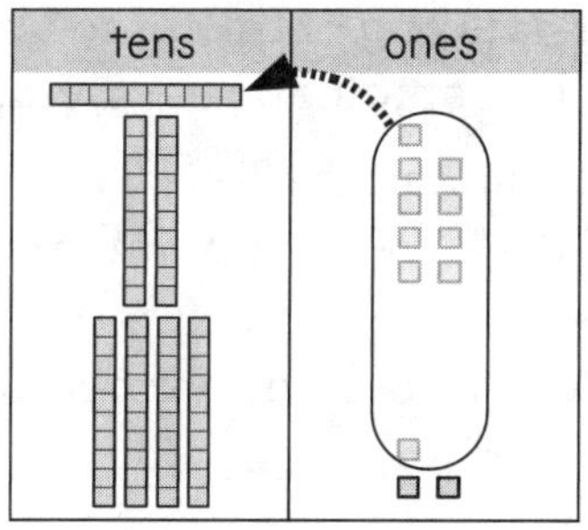

First, you'll use base-ten blocks to help your child develop conceptual understanding of the process. Then, he'll solve problems without base-ten blocks so he builds fluency. That way, he'll not only understand how to add multi-digit numbers, but he'll also understand why this process works. You'll use a similar approach to teach him the standard subtraction algorithm in Unit 12.

Week 22	Understand the Steps in Written Addition
Week 23	Build Fluency with Written Addition

What Your Child Will Learn

In this unit your child will learn to:

- Understand the steps in the written addition algorithm and model them with base-ten blocks
- Fluently add two-digit numbers, with a sum up to 200

Recommended Math Picture Books (Optional)

These picture books are scheduled in the optional Enrichment and Review lessons at the end of each week.

- *Blockhead: The Life of Fibonacci,* written by Joseph D'Agnese and illustrated by John O'Brien. Henry Holt and Company, 2010.
- *Dozens of Doughnuts,* written by Carrie Finison and illustrated by Brianne Farley. G.P. Putnam, 2020.

Week 22
Understand the Steps in Written Addition

Overview

Your child will learn how to use the written addition process to add two-digit numbers. You'll use base-ten blocks to help your child build on his place-value knowledge and develop a thorough conceptual understanding of this process. Next week, your child will practice more so that he becomes fluent and automatic at solving written two-digit addition problems.

Lesson 22.1	Demonstrate Two-Digit Written Addition
Lesson 22.2	Add Two-Digit Numbers with Base-Ten Blocks
Lesson 22.3	Add Two-Digit Numbers with Sums Greater Than 100
Lesson 22.4	Add Two-Digit Numbers
Lesson 22.5	Enrichment and Review (Optional)

Teaching Math with Confidence: Developing Conceptual Understanding of the Written Addition Algorithm

This week, your child reaches an important milestone in his math education: his first algorithm. An algorithm is an efficient, reliable, step-by-step method for solving a problem. This week, he'll learn the multi-digit addition algorithm. Later in his math education, he'll learn algorithms for multi-digit subtraction, multiplication, division, and more.

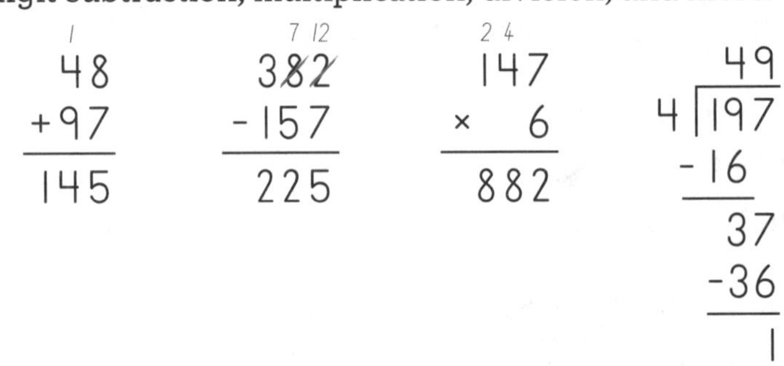

Sample problems solved with algorithms.

There are two essential stages in teaching algorithms:

- **Stage 1:** Help your child understand the steps in the algorithm.
- **Stage 2:** Give your child plenty of practice so that he becomes fluent and automatic at carrying out the steps.

These two stages complement each other. When children understand the steps in the process, they memorize them more quickly, make fewer mistakes, and find and correct their mistakes more easily. They also develop the important attitude that math makes sense! This conceptual understanding then serves as a base for developing full fluency and confidence with using the algorithm to solve problems.

This week, you'll focus on conceptual understanding of the addition algorithm. You'll use base-ten blocks to make the steps concrete, and you'll use familiar place-value language (such as "trading") to help your child connect the steps to what he already knows about place value. The lessons include a mix of problems—some that involve no trading, some that involve trading ones, some that involve trading tens, and some that involve trading both ones and tens—so that your child actively thinks about the steps in solving the problems.

$$\begin{array}{r} \\ 23 \\ +34 \\ \hline 57 \end{array} \qquad \begin{array}{r} {\scriptstyle 1} \\ 29 \\ +43 \\ \hline 72 \end{array} \qquad \begin{array}{r} \\ 71 \\ +53 \\ \hline 124 \end{array} \qquad \begin{array}{r} {\scriptstyle 1} \\ 68 \\ +42 \\ \hline 110 \end{array}$$

This week's lessons do not include independent practice of the addition algorithm. Instead, you'll work with your child on side A of the worksheets during the lesson activities to ensure that he fully understands the process. (He'll continue to complete side B independently.) Once your child has this thorough conceptual understanding, he'll be ready to develop more independence and fluency next week.

Extra Materials Needed for Week 22

- Paper clip
- For optional Enrichment and Review Lesson:
    - *Blockhead: The Life of Fibonacci*, written by Joseph D'Agnese and illustrated by John O'Brien

Lesson 22.1
Demonstrate Two-Digit Written Addition

	Purpose	Materials
Warm-up	• Count combinations of base-ten blocks • Practice memory work • Review place-value vocabulary	• Base-ten blocks
Activities	• Use base-ten blocks to act out the steps in a two-digit addition algorithm • Demonstrate how to record the steps in the addition algorithm	• Workbook page 22.1A • Base-ten blocks • Place-Value Chart (Blackline Master 5)
Workbook	• Review previously-learned material	• Workbook page 22.1B

In this lesson, your child will model addition problems with base-ten blocks while you record the written numbers. Dividing up the responsibility in this way helps your child focus on the meaning of each step in the process without getting bogged down by writing. She'll learn how to record the steps herself in Lesson 22.2.

This lesson involves pretending to work at a chocolate shop. To make the lesson more fun, you may want to have some chocolate chips or candy for your child to snack on while she works.

Warm-up: Counting, Memory Work, and Review

- Place 11 rods and 17 units on the table. **What is the value of these blocks?** *127.*
- **How many inches equal 1 foot?** *12.* **How many feet equal 1 yard?** *3.* **How many inches equal 1 yard?** *36.*
- Write the number 170 on a piece of paper. **How many digits does this number have?** *3.* **Which digit is in the ones-place?** *0.* **The tens-place?** *7.* **The hundreds-place?** *1.*

Activity: Add Two-Digit Numbers at the Chocolate Shop

In Unit 6, you learned how to add two-digit numbers in your head. Mental math can be really helpful, but some real-life math problems are too complicated to solve mentally. Mathematicians have created step-by-step methods to make it easier to solve problems. These methods are called algorithms. They're like recipes for math. When you follow the directions correctly, you always get the right answer.

See the Week 22 **Teaching Math with Confidence** for the two key stages of teaching algorithms.

In this unit, you'll learn how to use the addition algorithm to add two-digit numbers.

Today, we'll pretend we work at a chocolate shop. Let's pretend the base-ten blocks are chocolate. Each unit block is 1 square of chocolate, and each rod is a bar with 10 squares.

Show your child workbook page 22.1A. **This page has 6 packing slips, with 2 orders on each packing slip. Our job is to combine the 2 orders on each packing slip and find their total.**

The packing directions at the top mimic the standard written addition algorithm. Introducing them in the context of a chocolate shop helps your child concretely understand the meaning of each step. She'll learn a more general version of the addition algorithm in Lesson 22.2.

Point to the first packing slip on the page. **Order 1 has 4 bars and 8 squares. Order 2 has 3 bars and 4 squares.** Have your child place 4 rods and 8 units in the top part of the Place-Value Chart and 3 rods and 4 units in the bottom part.

	Bars	Squares
Order 1	4	8
Order 2	3	4
Total		

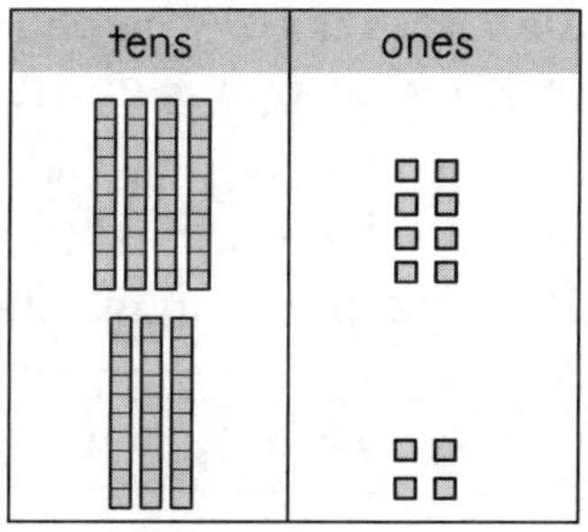

Read the first step in the "Chocolate Shop Packing Directions" at the top of the page: ***Add the squares.* How many squares are there?** *12.*

	Bars	Squares
Order 1	4	8
Order 2	3	4
Total		

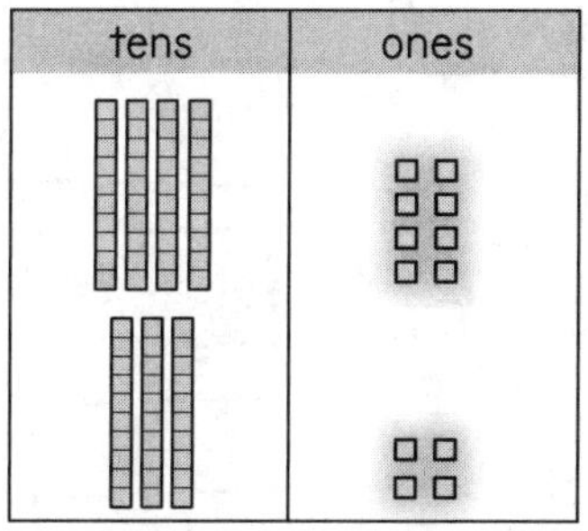

Do not write anything on the workbook page at this point.

Read the next step: ***If there are more than 9 squares, trade 10 squares for 1 bar.* Are there more than 9 squares?** *Yes.* Have your child trade 10 unit blocks for 1 rod. Place the rod horizontally in the tens-column. **We added 1 more bar, so I'll record that on the packing slip. That leaves 2 squares.** Write 1 and 2 as shown.

	Bars	Squares
	1	
Order 1	4	8
Order 2	3	4
Total		2

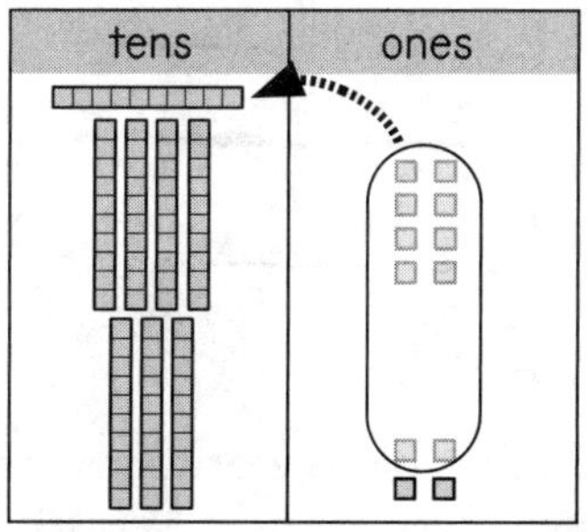

Placing the new rod horizontally makes it visually distinct from the other rods.

Be sure to write the 1 in the tens-place first and the 2 in the ones-place second. Writing them in this order mimics the way you normally write 12, and so it will help your child understand what she is doing when she begins to record the steps herself.

Read the last step: ***Add the bars.* How many bars are there?** *8.* Write 8 as shown. **So, how many total squares of chocolate are in this order?** *82.* **Yum!**

	Bars	Squares
	1	
Order 1	4	8
Order 2	3	4
Total	8	2

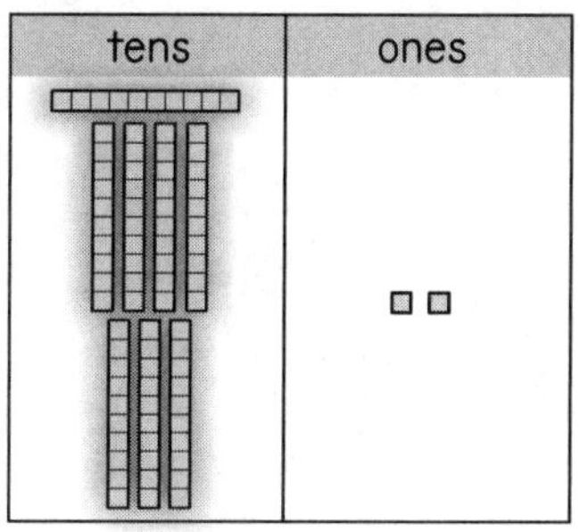

Asking this question ensures that your child pays attention to the underlying meaning of the answer.

Looks like we have some more orders to pack! You create each order with base-ten blocks, and I'll write the numbers on the packing slips. Continue in the same way with the rest of the problems on workbook page 22.1A. For each problem:

- Have your child model the two orders with base-ten blocks.
- Have your child follow the "Packing Directions" for each packing slip.
- Write the corresponding numbers on the packing slip.

	Bars	Squares
	1	
Order 1	4	8
Order 2	3	4
Total	8	2

	Bars	Squares
	1	
Order 1	2	6
Order 2	6	7
Total	9	3

	Bars	Squares
	1	
Order 1	5	9
Order 2	2	1
Total	8	0

	Bars	Squares
Order 1	3	3
Order 2	6	6
Total	9	9

	Bars	Squares
	1	
Order 1	8	2
Order 2		9
Total	9	1

	Bars	Squares
	1	
Order 1	3	5
Order 2	5	9
Total	9	4

Workbook: Review

Have your child complete workbook page 22.1B.

Lesson 22.2
Add Two-Digit Numbers with Base-Ten Blocks

	Purpose	Materials
Warm-up	• Count base-ten blocks • Practice memory work • Review approximating the length of an inch, foot, and yard	• Base-ten blocks • 1-foot ruler • Paper yardstick (from Lesson 20.4) or real yardstick
Activities	• Model the addition algorithm with base-ten blocks • Use the addition algorithm to add two-digit numbers with a sum less than 100 • Trade 10 ones for 1 ten when adding	• Workbook page 22.2A • Base-ten blocks • Place-Value Chart (Blackline Master 5)
Workbook	• Review previously-learned material	• Workbook page 22.2B

Warm-up: Counting, Memory Work, and Review

- Place 13 rods and 15 units on the table. **What is the value of these blocks?** *145.*
- **How many inches equal 1 foot?** *12.* **How many feet equal 1 yard?** *3.* **How many inches equal 1 yard?** *36.*
- Have your child hold his hands one inch apart. Use a ruler to check how accurate his approximation is. Then, repeat with one foot and one yard.

Activity: Add Two-Digit Numbers without Trading

In the last lesson, you learned that an algorithm is like a recipe for solving problems. Today, we'll use the addition algorithm and base-ten blocks to add two-digit numbers. You'll see that the algorithm is a lot like the packing directions that we used to pack orders at the chocolate shop!

Show your child the diagram at the top of workbook page 22.2A. **Computer programmers write algorithms to tell computers and robots how to work. They make diagrams like this to show the steps in their algorithms.**

Let's pretend that you're a robot. You're programmed to follow this Addition Algorithm program. Point to the first exercise (23 + 34). Have your child model 23 and 34 with base-ten blocks on the Place-Value Chart.

The program says: *Start with the ones-place.* The first step says: *Add the digits.* Point to the digits in the ones-place. **What's 3 plus 4?** *7.*

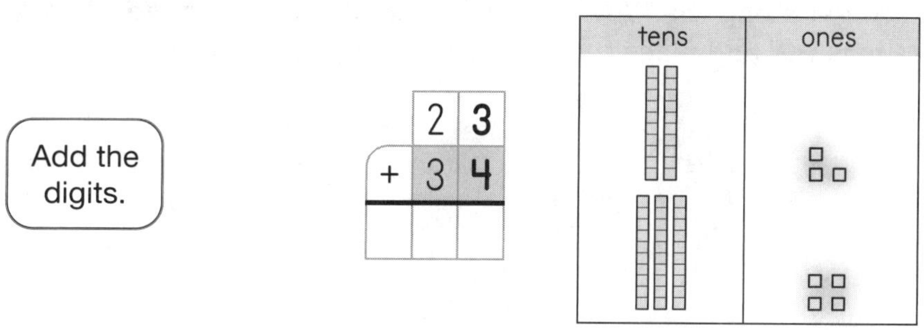

Do not write anything on the workbook page yet.

Point to the next step in the diagram. **Is the sum greater than 9?** *No.* **So, we follow the path labeled "No."** Trace your finger along the "No" arrow. **The last step is: *Record your work.* The sum of the digits in the ones-place is 7. So, write 7 in the answer's ones-place.** Have your child write 7 in the sum's ones-place.

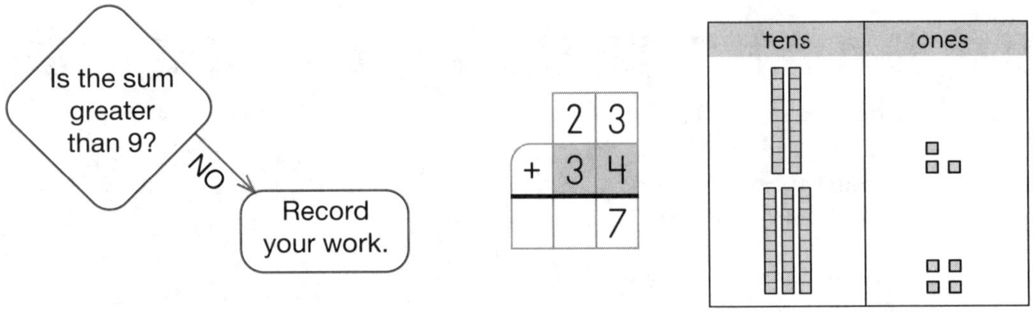

The program says: *Follow the steps for all the places.* So, we go back to the beginning and follow the steps for the tens-place. Follow the steps in the diagram (using similar dialogue as above) to add the tens. **So, what's 23 + 34?** *57.* **Great job, robot!**

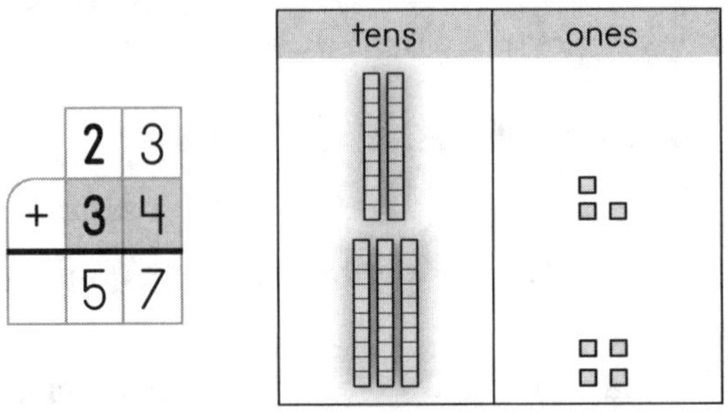

Activity: Two-Digit Addition with Trading

Point to the second exercise (29 + 43). Have your child model 29 and 43 with base-ten blocks on the Place-Value Chart.

Which place do we start with? *The ones-place.* **What's the first step?** *Add the digits.* Point to the digits in the ones-place. **What's 9 plus 3?** *12.*

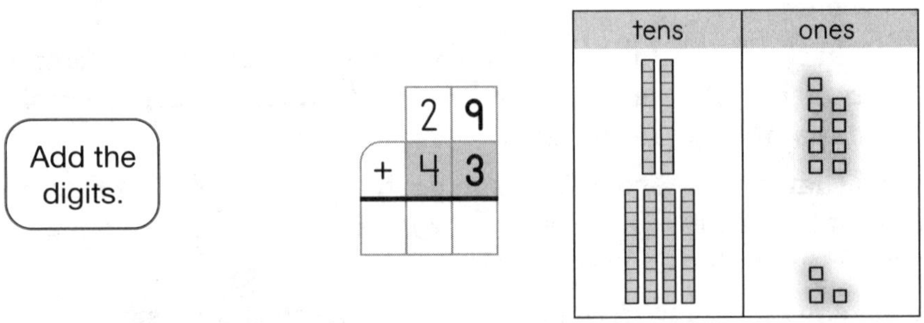

Point to the next step. **Is the sum greater than 9?** *Yes.* **So, we follow the path labeled "Yes."** Trace your finger along the "Yes" arrow. **The next step is: *Trade.*** Have your child trade the 10 unit blocks for 1 rod and place the rod horizontally in the tens-column.

What's the last step? *Record.* **You added 1 more rod to the tens-place, so write a 1 above the tens-place.** Have your child write a 1 above the tens-place. **There are 2 units left in the ones-place, so write a 2 in the ones-place.** Have your child write a 2 in the answer's ones-place.

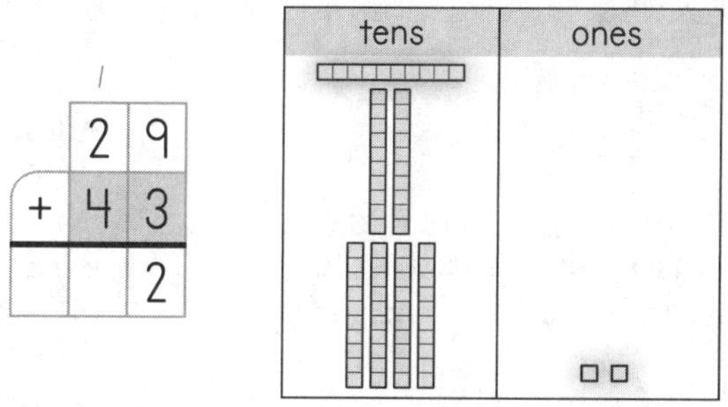

Now, we go back to the beginning and follow the steps for the tens-place. Help your child follow the steps to add the tens. **Make sure to add together all 3 of the digits in the tens-place.**

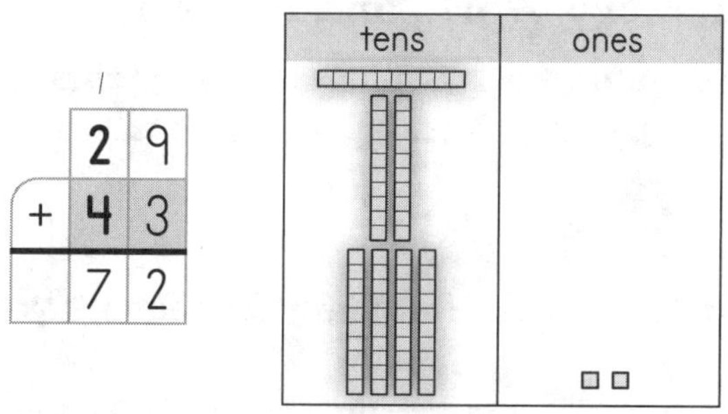

Activity: Add Two-Digit Numbers Like a Robot

Continue in the same way with the rest of the problems on the workbook page. Have your child model each problem with base-ten blocks, follow the steps in the addition algorithm, and record his work in writing.

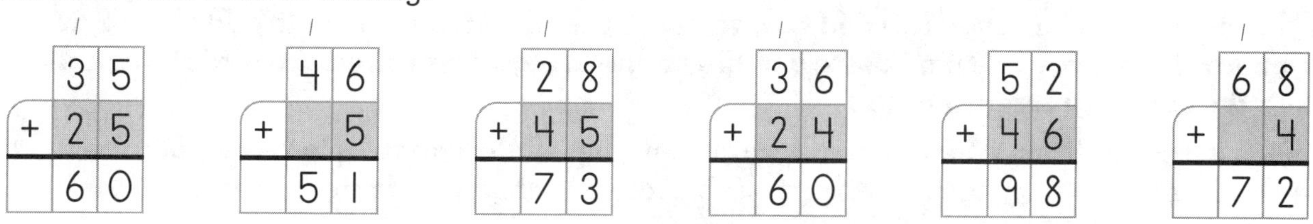

Save workbook page 22.2A so your child can refer to the Addition Algorithm diagram.

Workbook: Review

Have your child complete workbook page 22.2B.

Lesson 22.3
Add Two-Digit Numbers with Sums Greater than 100

	Purpose	Materials
Warm-up	• Count by 3s • Practice memory work • Review measuring in centimeters	• Counters • 30-centimeter (or 1-foot) ruler, marked in centimeters • Several writing utensils of different lengths
Activities	• Use the addition algorithm to add two-digit numbers with a sum greater than 100 • Trade 10 tens for 1 hundred when adding	• Addition Algorithm diagram (from workbook page 22.2A) • Workbook pages 22.3A • Base-ten blocks • Place-Value Chart (Blackline Master 5) • Paper clip
Workbook	• Review previously-learned material	• Workbook page 22.3B

Warm-up: Counting, Memory Work, and Review

- Arrange 7 groups of 3 counters on the table. Have your child count by 3s to find the total number of counters: *3, 6, 9, 12, 15, 18, 21.* If she has trouble, encourage her to add 3 to her previous number.

- **How many inches equal 1 foot?** *12.* **How many feet equal 1 yard?** *3.* **How many inches equal 1 yard?** *36.*
- Place several writing utensils of different lengths on the table, such as crayons, pencils, or markers. Have your child estimate the length of each object in centimeters and then use a ruler to measure its actual length.

Activity: Add Two-Digit Numbers with a Sum Greater Than 100

In the last two lessons, you learned how to use the addition algorithm to add two-digit numbers. Today, you'll learn how to use the addition algorithm to add two-digit numbers when the sum is greater than 100.

We'll use the Addition Algorithm diagram from the last lesson to help remember the steps. Place workbook page 22.2A on the table for your child to refer to as needed.

Point to the first exercise on workbook page 22.3A (71 + 53). Have your child model 71 and 53 with base-ten blocks on the Place-Value Chart. Use both pages of the Place-Value Chart.

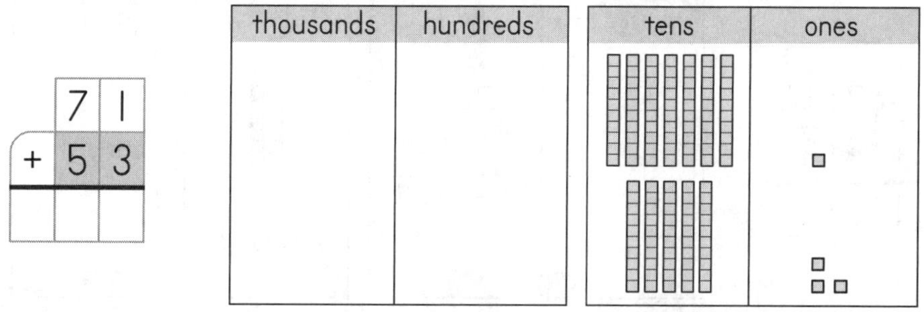

Which place do we start with? *The ones-place.* Have your child add the digits in the ones-place and record their sum. If she has trouble remembering the steps, have her refer to the Addition Algorithm diagram (from workbook page 22.2A).

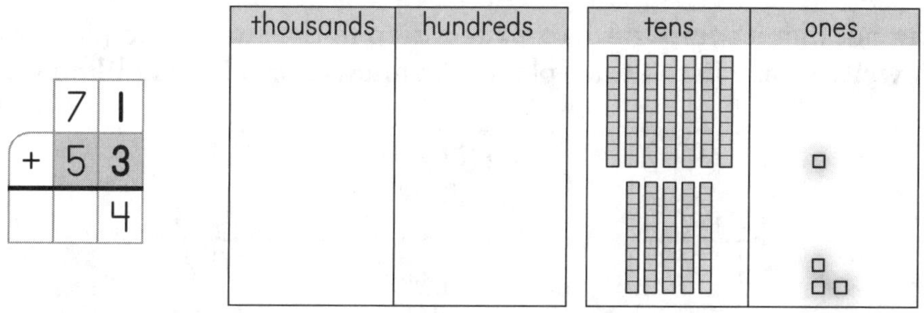

What do we do next? *Follow the steps for the tens-place.* Have your child follow the steps to add the digits in the tens-place and trade 10 rods for 1 flat.

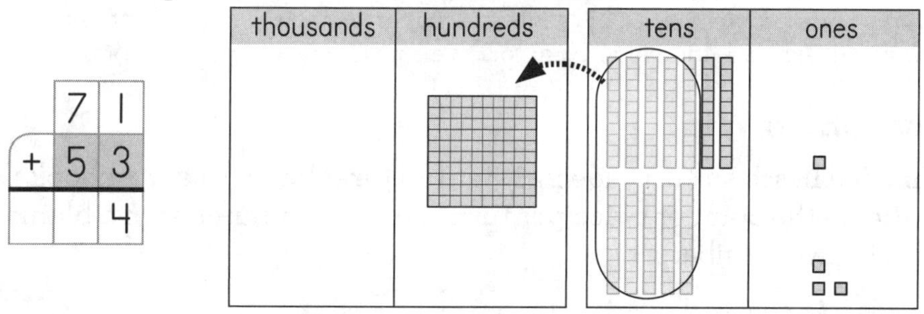

What's the last step? *Record.* **You added 1 hundred to the hundreds-place.** Have your child write a 1 above the hundreds-place as shown. **That leaves 2 tens in the tens-place, so write a 2 in the tens-place.** Have your child write 2 in the answer's tens-place.

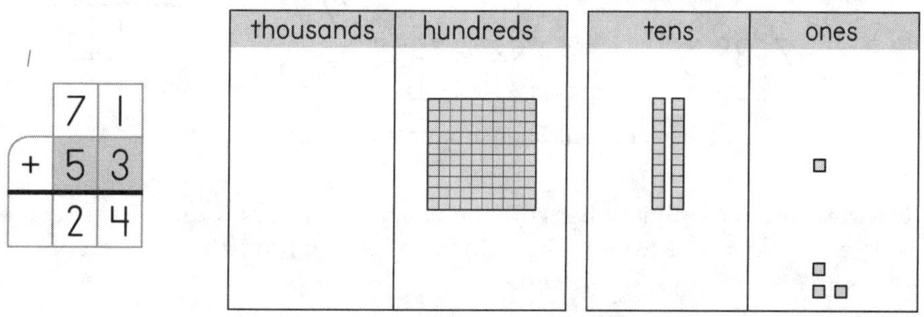

Writing 1 above the hundreds-place makes clear that your child traded 10 tens for 1 hundred. It also previews the trading and recording that your child will do when she adds 3-digit numbers in Unit 14. If your child comments that this step is unnecessary, she may write the 1 directly in the answer's hundreds-place instead.

The only digit in the hundreds-place is 1, so the sum of the digits in the hundreds-place is 1. Have your child write 1 in the answer's hundreds-place. **So, what's 71 plus 53?** *124.*

		7	1
+		5	3
	1	2	4

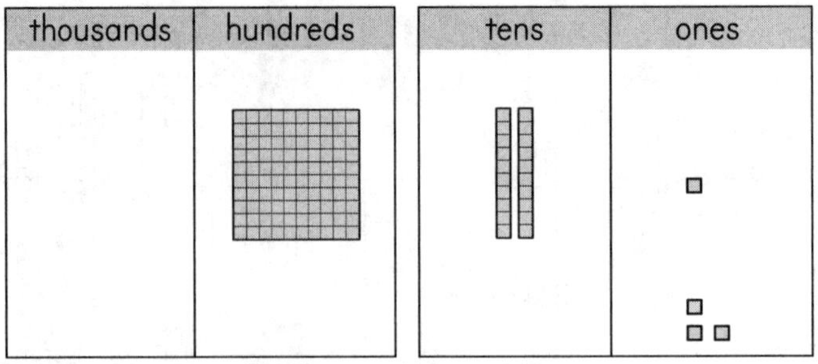

Continue in the same way with the other 3 problems in the top row of the workbook page.

For 37 + 95, point out that you trade both the ones and the tens: **In two-digit addition problems, we can trade the ones, or the tens, or both.**

For 64 + 43, point out that it's important to write a zero in the sum's tens-place as a placeholder: **If you didn't write a zero in the tens-place, the answer would look like 17 instead of 107!**

		9	2
+		3	5
	1	2	7

		3	7
+		9	5
	1	3	2

		6	4
+		4	3
	1	0	7

Some children resist using the addition algorithm because they prefer to use mental math. If your child does this, praise his mental math skills. Explain that practicing the addition algorithm with two-digit numbers prepares him to solve problems with big numbers that are difficult to add mentally. If he's interested, demonstrate how you use the addition algorithm to solve a problem with many digits.

Activity: Play Spin to Win

Play Spin to Win. See Lesson 14.2 (page 228) for full directions. Use workbook page 22.3A. Spin the paper clip on the spinner twice per turn. Write each number in a blank grid and then find the sum of your two numbers.

		9	4
+		5	7
	1	5	1

Spin twice each turn. Then, find the sum of the two spins.

Alternating plays with your child provides her with many examples of how to correctly solve the problems. Keep a close eye on your child as she records the written steps, and immediately correct any mistakes. Model the problems with base-ten blocks as needed.

Workbook: Review

Have your child complete workbook pages 22.3B.

Lesson 22.4
Add Two-Digit Numbers

	Purpose	Materials
Warm-up	• Count by 3s on the dot array • Practice memory work • Review identifying the total number of objects in an array	• Dot array and L-cover (Blackline Master 6)
Activities	• Assess how well your child knows and understands the steps in the addition algorithm • Practice adding two-digit numbers	• Workbook page 22.4A • Base-ten blocks • Playing cards
Workbook	• Review previously-learned material	• Workbook page 22.4B

Warm-up: Counting, Memory Work, and Review

- Slide the L-cover on the dot array to reveal 1 row of 3 dots. **How many dots are showing?** *3.* Continue revealing one row at a time and having your child name the total number of dots until you reach 30.
- **How many inches equal 1 foot?** *12.* **How many feet equal 1 yard?** *3.* **How many inches equal 1 yard?** *36.*
- Use the dot array and L-cover to show your child the following dot arrangements. Have him find the total number of dots in each array.

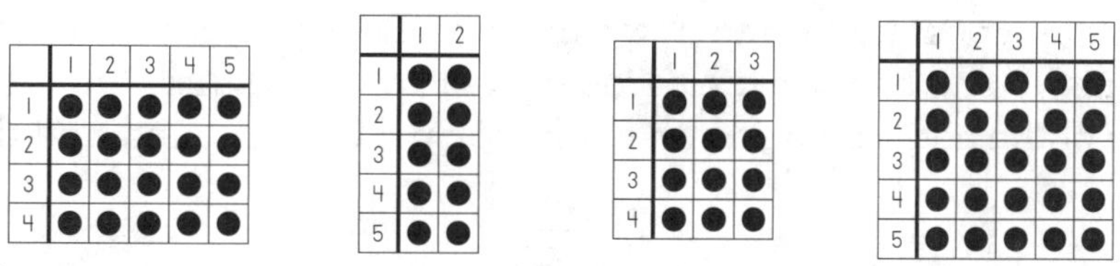

20 10 12 25

Activity: Have Your Child "Be the Teacher"

In the last lesson, you learned how to use the addition algorithm to add two-digit numbers when the sum is greater than 100. Today, we'll practice the addition algorithm some more.

Show your child the two problems at the top of workbook page 22.4A, and place base-ten blocks on the table. **Let's pretend that you're the teacher and I'm the student. Show me how to solve these problems with the base-ten blocks and the addition algorithm.**

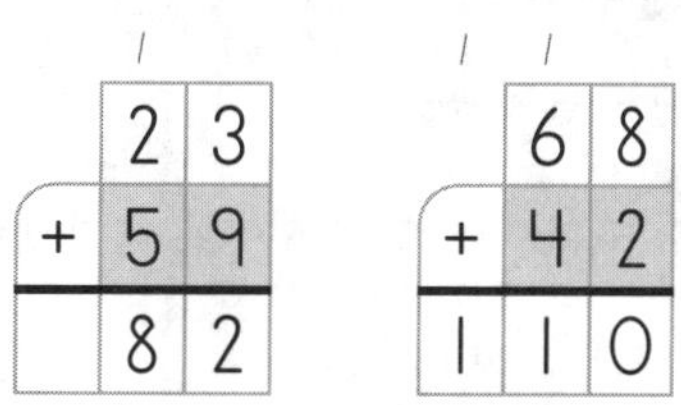

Have your child demonstrate how to solve the problem. As he works, occasionally pretend to be confused and ask him to explain what he's doing. For example:

- For 23 + 59: **Why did you write a 1 above the tens-place?** *I traded 10 ones for 1 ten.*
- For 23 + 59: **Which blocks match the 2 in the ones-place?** *The 2 unit blocks left after I traded 10 ones for 1 ten.*
- For 23 + 59: **Which blocks match the 8 in the tens-place?** *The 8 rods.*
- For 68 + 42: **Why is there a zero in the ones-place?** *I traded all 10 ones for 1 ten, and there are zero ones left.*
- For 68 + 42: **Why do you write a 1 in the hundreds-place?** *I traded 10 tens for 1 hundred.*

Prompt him as needed, and allow him to refer to the Addition Algorithm diagram (from workbook page 22.2A) if he forgets any of the steps.

> This activity serves as an informal assessment of how well your child knows and understands the steps in the addition algorithm. He will continue to build fluency and proficiency with the algorithm this week.

Activity: Play Two-Digit Plus Two-Digit War

Play Two-Digit Plus Two-Digit War. Have your child use base-ten blocks to model the problems only if needed.

Two-Digit Plus Two-Digit War

Materials: 4s, 5s, 6s, 7s, 8s, and 9s from 2 decks of playing cards (48 cards total); workbook page 22.4A

Object of the Game: Win the most points by creating the greater sum.

Shuffle the cards and deal them face down in a pile. Each player flips over 4 cards from the top of the pile. Then, they use the cards to create 2 two-digit numbers, write the numbers in one of the addition grids on workbook page 22.4A, and find their sum.

Sample play

Whoever has the greater sum wins a point. If the sums are equal, both players win a point.

Continue until you have filled in all of the blank grids on the page. Whoever has won more points wins the game.

> Arranging the cards to create the numbers with the greatest possible sum helps your child focus on the place value and meaning of each digit in each number. This game uses only 4s, 5s, 6s, 7s, 8s, and 9s to ensure that many of the sums are greater than 100.

Workbook: Review

Have your child complete workbook page 22.4B.

Lesson 22.5
Enrichment and Review (Optional)

	Purpose	Materials
Warm-up	• Count backward from 200 to 100 by 1s, 2s, 5s, or 10s • Review memory work • Review your child's favorite or most challenging activities from Week 22	• Varies, depending on the activities you choose
Picture Book	• Enjoy a famous number pattern • Learn about the life of a famous mathematician	• *Blockhead: The Life of Fibonacci,* written by Joseph D'Agnese and illustrated by John O'Brien
Enrichment Activity	• Find numbers in the Fibonacci number sequence	• None

Warm-up: Counting, Memory Work, and Review

- Have your child count backward from 200 to 100 by 1s, 2s, 5s, or 10s. (Choose whichever counting sequence your child needs to practice the most.)
- Quiz your child on the memory work through Week 22. See page 523 for the full list.
- If you have time, repeat one or two of the activities from this week's lessons. Choose activities your child especially enjoyed or found challenging.

Math Picture Book: *Blockhead: The Life of Fibonacci*

Read *Blockhead: The Life of Fibonacci,* written by Joseph D'Agnese and illustrated by John O'Brien. After you read, look at the final page in the book for discussion questions and a list of items to find in the illustrations.

> If your child is intrigued by Fibonacci numbers, look online for pictures and videos that demonstrate the Fibonacci sequence in nature. Your child may also enjoy *Growing Patterns: Fibonacci Numbers in Nature,* written by Sarah C. Campbell and photographed by Sarah C. Campbell and Richard P. Campbell.

Enrichment Activity: Explore Fibonacci Numbers

Write the first few numbers of the Fibonacci sequence on a piece of paper: 1, 1, 2, 3, 5, 8. Explain that a famous mathematician named Fibonacci discovered this number sequence. Show your child how each number in the series is the sum of the two numbers before it.

1 1 2 3 5 8

Each number is the sum of the two numbers before it. 1 + 1 = 2, 1 + 2 = 3, 2 + 3 = 5, 3 + 5 = 8.

Have your child add 5 and 8 to find that the next number in the sequence is 13. Have him continue the sequence until he reaches 144. (He can use either mental math or the written addition algorithm as he adds the numbers.)

1 1 2 3 5 8 13 21 34 55 89 144

The Fibonacci sequence up to 144.

Week 22 Answer Key

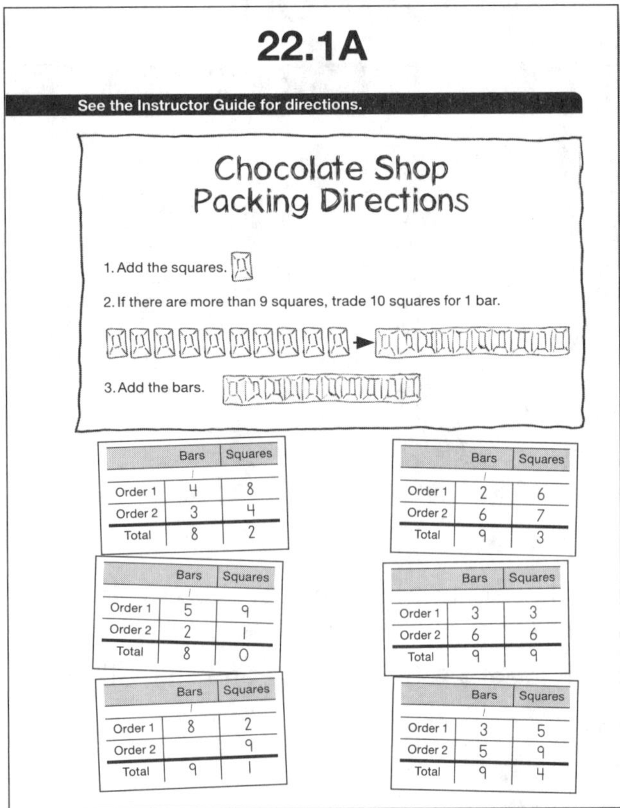

22.1A

See the Instructor Guide for directions.

Chocolate Shop Packing Directions

1. Add the squares.
2. If there are more than 9 squares, trade 10 squares for 1 bar.
3. Add the bars.

	Bars	Squares
Order 1	4	8
Order 2	3	4
Total	8	2

	Bars	Squares
Order 1	2	6
Order 2	6	7
Total	9	3

	Bars	Squares
Order 1	5	9
Order 2	2	1
Total	8	0

	Bars	Squares
Order 1	3	3
Order 2	6	6
Total	9	9

	Bars	Squares
Order 1	8	2
Order 2		9
Total	9	1

	Bars	Squares
Order 1	3	5
Order 2	5	9
Total	9	4

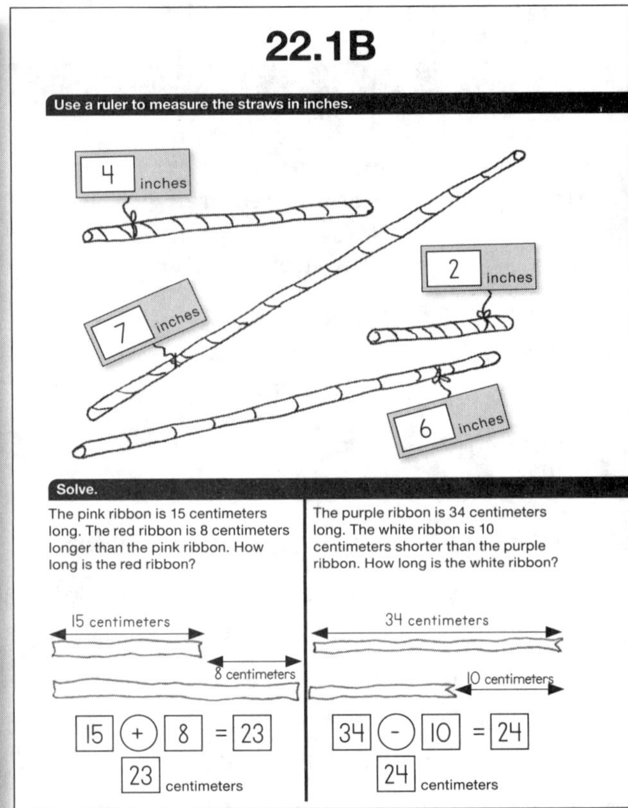

22.1B

Use a ruler to measure the straws in inches.

4 inches

7 inches

2 inches

6 inches

Solve.

The pink ribbon is 15 centimeters long. The red ribbon is 8 centimeters longer than the pink ribbon. How long is the red ribbon?

15 centimeters, 8 centimeters

15 + 8 = 23

23 centimeters

The purple ribbon is 34 centimeters long. The white ribbon is 10 centimeters shorter than the purple ribbon. How long is the white ribbon?

34 centimeters, 10 centimeters

34 − 10 = 24

24 centimeters

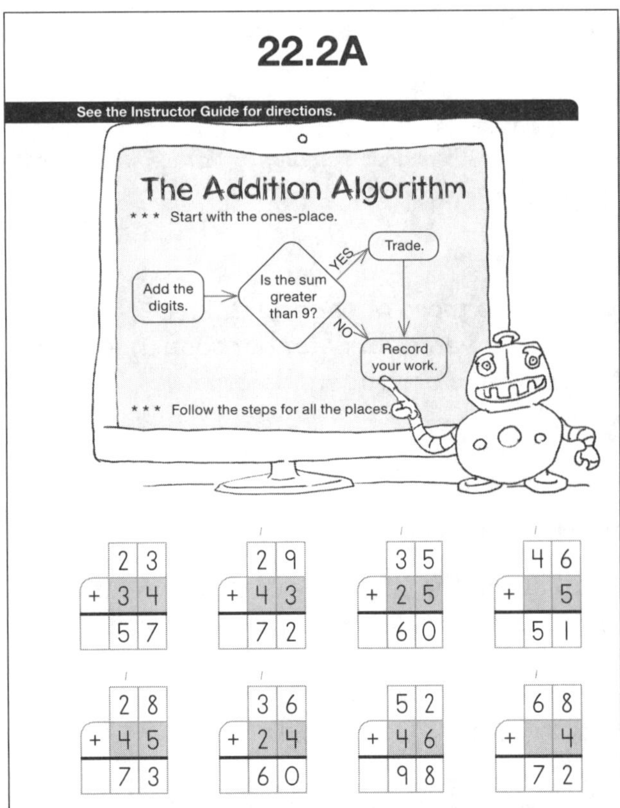

22.2A

See the Instructor Guide for directions.

The Addition Algorithm

*** Start with the ones-place.

Add the digits. → Is the sum greater than 9? YES → Trade. → Record your work. NO → Record your work.

*** Follow the steps for all the places.

23 + 34 = 57

29 + 43 = 72

35 + 25 = 60

46 + 5 = 51

28 + 45 = 73

36 + 24 = 60

52 + 46 = 98

68 + 4 = 72

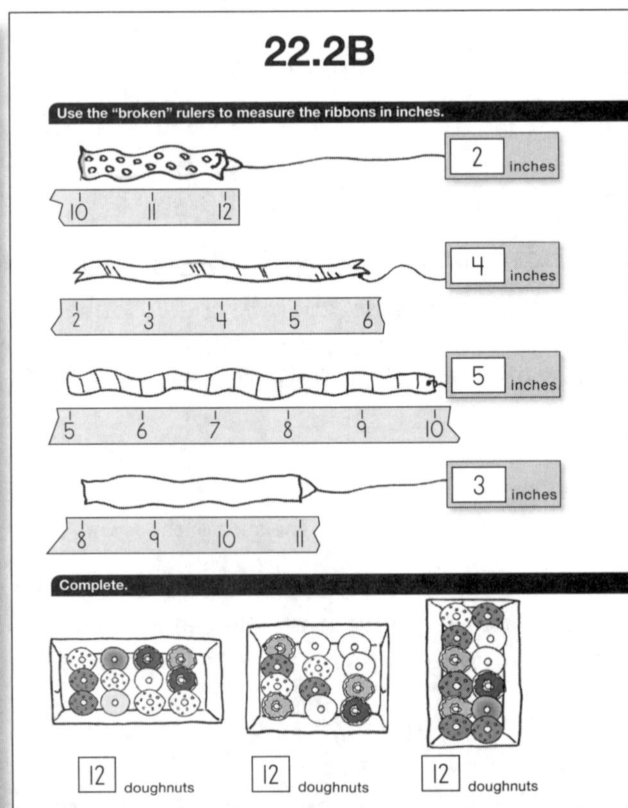

22.2B

Use the "broken" rulers to measure the ribbons in inches.

10 11 12 — 2 inches

2 3 4 5 6 — 4 inches

5 6 7 8 9 10 — 5 inches

8 9 10 11 — 3 inches

Complete.

12 doughnuts

12 doughnuts

12 doughnuts

Week 22 Answer Key

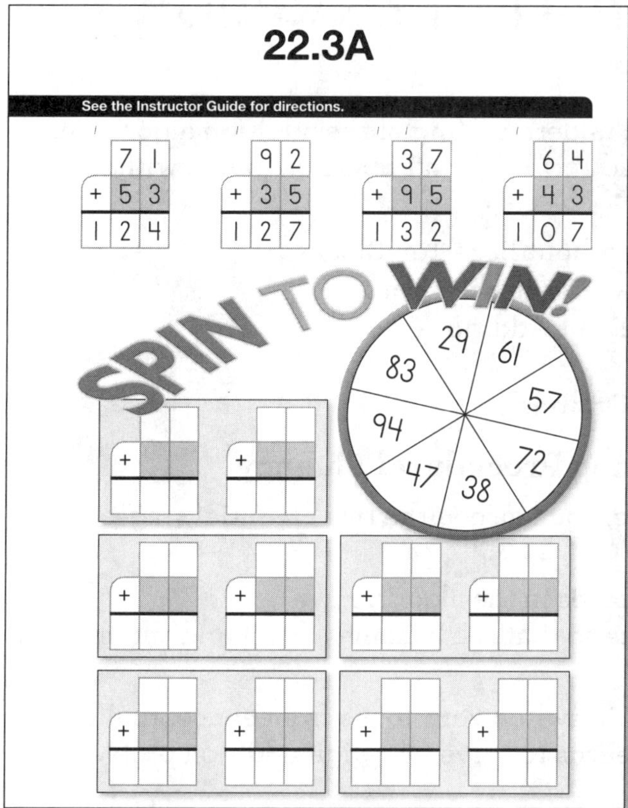

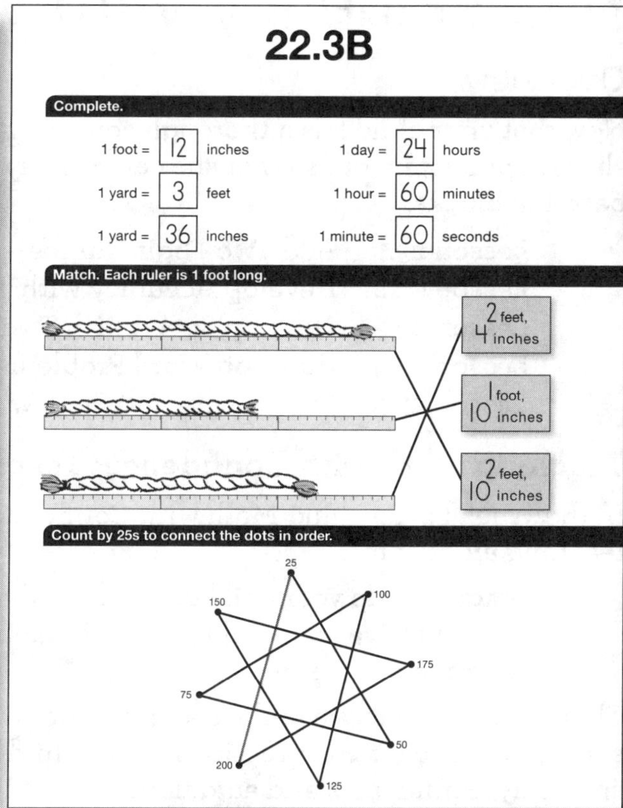

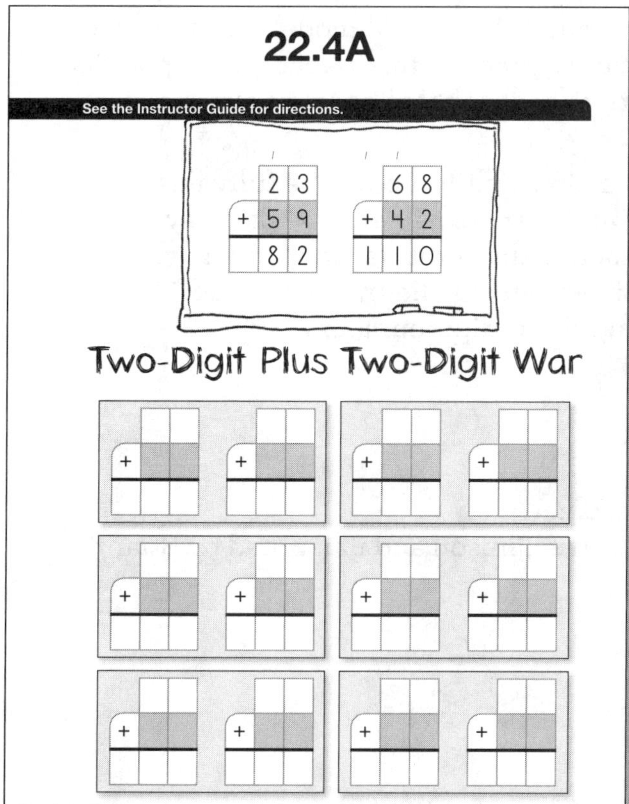

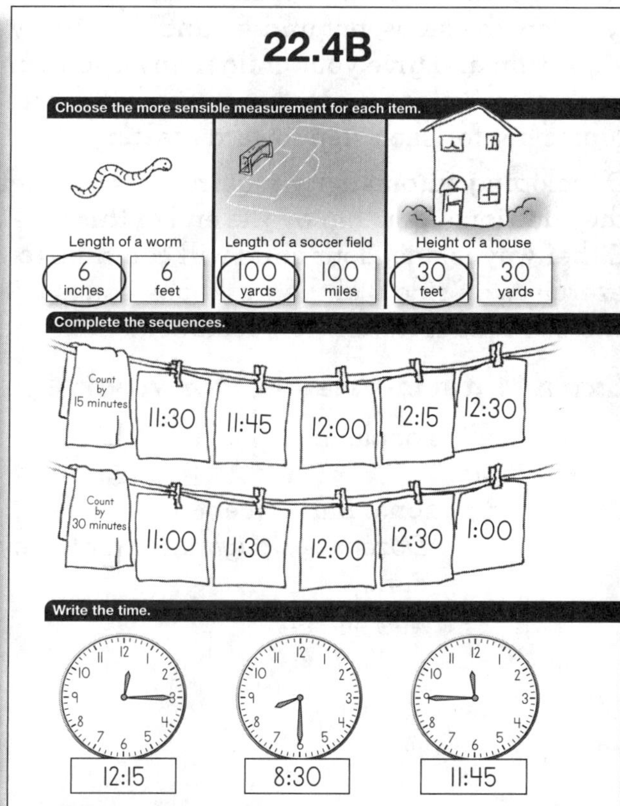

Week 23
Build Fluency with Written Addition

Overview

Now that your child has a thorough conceptual understanding of the addition algorithm, she will practice more so that she can fluently add two-digit numbers on paper, without base-ten blocks.

Lesson 23.1	Add Two-Digit Numbers without Base-Ten Blocks
Lesson 23.2	Develop Accuracy with Two-Digit Addition
Lesson 23.3	Develop Speed with Two-Digit Addition
Lesson 23.4	Addition Word Problems
Lesson 23.5	Enrichment and Review (Optional)

Teaching Math with Confidence: Teaching Procedural Fluency

In the Week 22 Teaching Math with Confidence, you learned the two essential stages in teaching algorithms:

- **Stage 1:** Help your child understand the steps in the algorithm.
- **Stage 2:** Give your child plenty of practice so that she becomes fluent and automatic at carrying out the steps.

This week, you'll move to the second stage. You'll switch your focus from conceptual understanding to procedural practice so your child learns to solve two-digit addition problems smoothly, confidently, and automatically.

Teaching procedural fluency is very different from teaching for conceptual understanding. It's more like teaching a child to tie her shoes: your goal is to teach your child to correctly follow the steps, not understand the theory of shoe-tying! You'll model the steps in the algorithm and give your child many opportunities to practice this week. As she practices, you'll watch closely, give her immediate corrective feedback if she makes a mistake, and praise her for each step toward mastery.

Developing automaticity requires lots of practice. Some children will be fully fluent with the addition algorithm by the end of this week, while others will only be partway there. Either way is fine. Your child will continue to practice the addition algorithm in the review exercises on side B of the workbook pages to further develop her fluency. Then, in Unit 14, she'll extend it further to become fluent at adding three-digit numbers.

Extra Materials Needed for Week 23

- 12 slips of paper
- Timer
- For optional Enrichment and Review Lesson:
    - × *Dozens of Doughnuts,* written by Carrie Finison and illustrated by Brianne Farley
    - × Egg carton

Lesson 23.1
Add Two-Digit Numbers without Base-Ten Blocks

	Purpose	Materials
Warm-up	• Count by 3s on the dot array • Practice memory work • Review a.m. and p.m.	• Dot array and L-cover (Blackline Master 6)
Activities	• Add two-digit numbers on paper, without base-ten blocks	• Base-ten blocks • Place-Value Chart (Blackline Master 5) • Workbook page 23.1A • 12 slips of paper
Workbook	• Review previously-learned material	• Workbook page 23.1B

Warm-up: Counting, Memory Work, and Review

- Slide the L-cover on the dot array to reveal one row of 3 dots. **How many dots are showing?** *3.* Continue revealing one row at a time and having your child name the total number of dots until you reach 30.
- **What is another name for 12 a.m.?** *Midnight.* **What is another name for 12 p.m.?** *Noon.*
- Name several events and times in your daily schedule. Have your child identify each time as a.m. or p.m. For example:
  - × **We're going to gymnastics class at 3:30 this afternoon. Is that a.m. or p.m.?** *P.m.*
  - × **We usually eat a snack around 10 in the morning. Is that a.m. or p.m.?** *A.m.*
  - × **We usually eat lunch around noon. Is that 12 o'clock a.m. or 12 o'clock p.m.?** *P.m.*

Activity: Add Two-Digit Numbers without Base-Ten Blocks

Last week, you learned how to use the addition algorithm to add two-digit numbers. This week, you'll practice more so you can add two-digit numbers fluently, without needing base-ten blocks. When you can do something fluently, you can do it confidently and automatically, without having to think about it very much. What are some things that you can do fluently? *Sample answers: Tie my shoes. Write my name. Ride a bike. Play "Twinkle, Twinkle" on the piano.*

Becoming fluent at a new skill takes a lot of practice! When you first learned how to write your name, you had to think hard about every single letter. You practiced writing your name over and over, and now you can write your name without even thinking about it.

> See the Week 23 **Teaching Math with Confidence** for more on helping your child develop fluency with the addition algorithm.

Today, you'll first try solving written addition problems without base-ten blocks. Then, we'll play a game for more practice.

Point to the first exercise on workbook page 23.1A (76 + 19). **Try solving this problem with the addition algorithm. While you work, I'll model the problem with base-ten blocks. Once we finish, we'll compare our answers and make sure they match.**

Have your child solve the problem. While she works, model the two addends with base-ten blocks on the Place-Value Chart and trade 10 of the units for 1 rod. Cover the blocks with a piece of paper.

$$\begin{array}{rrr} & \scriptstyle 1 & \\ & 7 & 6 \\ + & 1 & 9 \\ \hline & 9 & 5 \end{array}$$

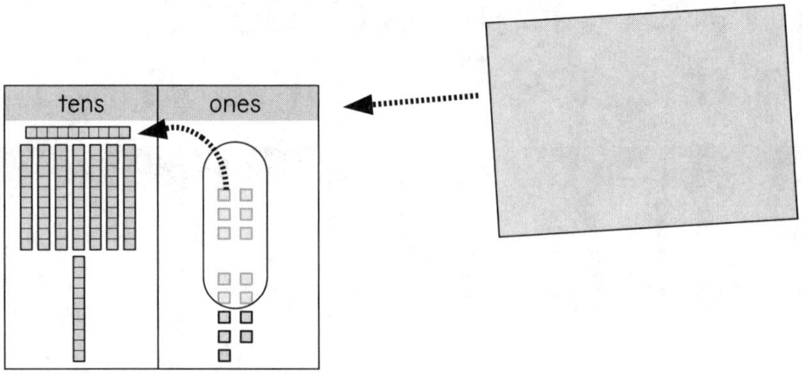

So, what's 76 plus 19? *95.* Remove the cover from the blocks so your child can check whether her answer matches the blocks. If her answer does not match, have her use the blocks to find the correct sum.

Continue in the same way with the rest of the problems in the row.

$$\begin{array}{rrr} \scriptstyle 1 & & \\ & 3 & 5 \\ + & 8 & 1 \\ \hline 1 & 1 & 6 \end{array} \qquad \begin{array}{rrr} \scriptstyle 1 & & \\ & 6 & 2 \\ + & 5 & 3 \\ \hline 1 & 1 & 5 \end{array} \qquad \begin{array}{rrr} & \scriptstyle 1 & \\ & 8 & 5 \\ + & & 7 \\ \hline & 9 & 2 \end{array}$$

Activity: Play Snowball Fight

Play Snowball Fight. See Lesson 15.3 (page 246) for general directions. Write the following numbers on slips of paper: 46, 48, 53, 59, 64, 67, 75, 76, 82, 88, 95, 99. Use these slips of paper as your "snowballs" and record the sums in the blank grids on workbook page 23.1A.

Workbook: Review

Have your child complete workbook page 23.1B.

Lesson 23.2
Develop Accuracy with Two-Digit Addition

	Purpose	Materials
Warm-up	• Count by ten-minute intervals • Practice memory work • Review approximating the length of an inch and centimeter	• Clock • 30-centimeter ruler • Paper meterstick (from lesson 21.3) or real meterstick
Activities	• Develop greater accuracy with the addition algorithm • Practice written two-digit addition	• Workbook page 23.2A • Counters
Workbook	• Review previously-learned material	• Workbook page 23.2B

In this lesson, you'll give your child feedback on every single digit he writes so that he becomes even more automatic and accurate at following the steps in the addition algorithm.

Warm-up: Counting, Memory Work, and Review

- Set the clock to 2:00. Have your child count by ten-minute intervals from 2:00 to 4:00. Have him turn the clock's hands to match each time.
- **How many inches equal 1 foot?** *12.* **How many feet equal 1 yard?** *3.* **How many inches equal 1 yard?** *36.*
- Have your child hold his hands 1 centimeter apart. Use a ruler to check how accurate his approximation is. Then, repeat with 1 meter.

Activity: Practice the Steps in Two-Digit Addition

In the last lesson, you practiced solving two-digit addition problems without base-ten blocks. Today, you'll practice some more with a silent activity and game.

Show your child the first exercise on workbook page 23.2A (56 + 68). **Watch as I solve this problem. Tap your pencil on the table each time I write a correct number. We'll do this completely silently so we can both concentrate.**

Silent teaching may feel strange, but children often enjoy the change of pace (and concentrate more intently, too). Having your child tap his pencil after you write each number ensures that he carefully observes how you solve the problem.

Slowly and deliberately solve the problem. Your child should tap his pencil on the table after you write each number.

	1	
	5	6
+	6	8
1	2	4

For the second exercise, reverse roles: have your child solve the problem, while you tap your pencil on the table every time he writes a correct number. If he makes a mistake, do not tap the table. Instead, give him a puzzled look to prompt him to check his work. Alternate roles for the third and fourth exercises as well.

	9	4
+	5	7
1	5	1

	4	9
+	5	1
1	0	0

	7	7
+	4	1
1	1	8

Providing feedback through tapping and silence allows you to correct your child's mistakes in a neutral and non-emotional way. This approach can be especially helpful if your child tends to lash out or show frustration when corrected.

Activity: Play Connect the Boxes

Play Connect the Boxes. Play silently so that both you and your child can concentrate on solving the problems correctly and providing feedback to each other through tapping the table.

Connect the Boxes

Materials: Connect the Boxes game board (from workbook page 23.2A); 8 counters of 2 different colors

Object of the Game: Cover more boxes in a straight line than the other player.

Each player takes 8 counters of a different color.

On your turn, choose an addition problem and solve the problem. While you solve the problem, your opponent should tap the table each time you write the next correct number in the problem. Once you finish, cover the box with your one of your counters.

Take turns until all the boxes are covered. Count how many boxes in a row each player has covered, either horizontally, vertically, or diagonally. Whoever has the longer straight line of boxes wins the game.

Workbook: Review

Have your child complete workbook page 23.2B.

Lesson 23.3
Develop Speed with Two-Digit Addition

	Purpose	Materials
Warm-up	• Count by 3s • Practice memory work • Review the relationship between addition and subtraction	• Counters
Activities	• Develop speed at adding two-digit numbers	• Workbook page 23.3A • Timer
Workbook	• Review previously-learned material	• Workbook page 23.3B

In this lesson, you'll time your child as she completes a column of two-digit addition problems. The goal of this activity is simply to help your child develop greater automaticity, no matter how fast her "normal" speed is. If time pressure makes her become anxious or freeze up, skip timing her and instead simply have her solve the problems at her own pace.

Children vary tremendously in their processing speed. Some children can whip through arithmetic problems, while others will always need a little longer to think through each step, write the digits, and move on to the next step. Don't worry if your child is still quite slow at two-digit addition and needs a lot of time to solve the problems.

Warm-up: Counting, Memory Work, and Review

- Arrange 9 groups of 3 counters on the table. Have your child count by 3s to find the total number of counters: *3, 6, 9, 12, 15, 18, 21, 24, 27.* If she has trouble, encourage her to add 3 to her previous number.
- Write the numbers 43, 7, and 50 on a piece of paper. Have your child write the matching family of addition and subtraction equations.

$$43 + 7 = 50$$
$$7 + 43 = 50$$
$$50 - 43 = 7$$
$$50 - 7 = 43$$

- **How many minutes equal a half-hour?** *30.* **How many minutes equal a quarter-hour?** *15.* **What do we call the answer to an addition problem?** *The sum.* **What do we call the answer to a subtraction problem?** *The difference.*

Activity: Two-Digit Addition Sprints

In the last lesson, you practiced adding two-digit numbers with the addition algorithm. Today, you'll practice more so that you become even more fluent and automatic at solving them.

When runners want to become faster at running, they practice sprinting short distances as fast as they possibly can. Today, you're going to do addition sprints! You'll solve just 4 problems at a time, but you'll see if you can push yourself to work just a little faster each time.

Show your child workbook page 23.3A. **Today, you're going to solve the problems on all 3 race courses. Go as fast as you can without making mistakes. I'll time you on each race course, and you can try to go just a little faster each time.**

Use a piece of paper to cover all but the leftmost column.

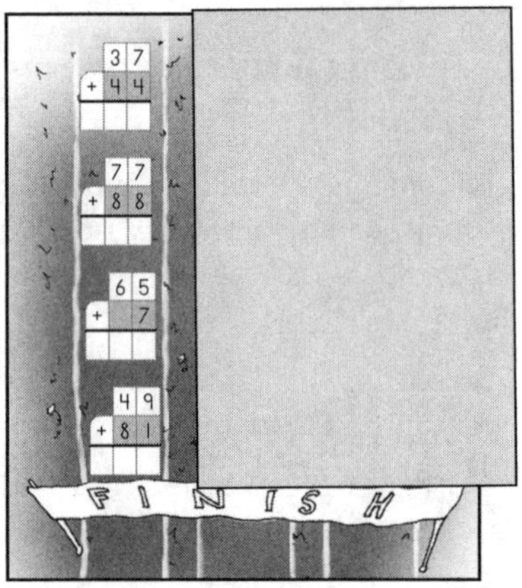

I'll time you while you solve these 4 problems. How long do you think it will take you to solve them? *Answers will vary.* Use a timer to time how long it takes your child to complete the problems. Check each problem as she solves it, and have her fix any mistakes immediately.

Once she finishes, announce her time and write it at the bottom of the page below the column. For example: **Way to go! You solved all those problems in 57 seconds.**

Next, you'll solve the 4 problems in the middle column. I wonder if you can beat your first time! Again, time your child as she solves the problems in the middle columns. Announce her new time and write it at the bottom of the page. Discuss whether she took a shorter or longer time to finish the column. For example: **Wow, you solved all the problems in 52 seconds this time! That's 5 seconds faster than the first column.**

Repeat this process with the last column. Encourage your child to stay focused and solve the final 4 problems as quickly as possible. When she finishes, look at the times you wrote down and praise any improvement.

See page 377 for answers to these problems.

Workbook: Review

Have your child complete workbook page 23.3B.

Lesson 23.4
Addition Word Problems

	Purpose	Materials
Warm-up	• Count coins • Practice memory work • Review comparing numbers	• Coins
Activities	• Solve two-digit addition word problems • Correctly align the digits in two-digit addition problems	• Workbook page 23.4A
Workbook	• Add two-digit numbers with the addition algorithm	• Workbook pages 23.4A and 23.4B

Warm-up: Counting, Memory Work, and Review

- Place 4 quarters, 3 dimes, 1 nickel, and 2 pennies on the table. **How many cents is this money worth?** *137¢.*
- **Are times in the afternoon and evening a.m. or p.m.?** *P.m.*
  Are times in the morning a.m. or p.m.? *A.m.*
- Secretly choose a number between 100 and 200. **I'm thinking of a number that's greater than 100 and less than 200.** Have your child guess your number. After each guess, tell whether your secret number is more or less than his guess. Continue until he figures out your secret number.

Activity: Solve Two-Digit Addition Word Problems

In this unit, you have learned how to use the addition algorithm to add two-digit numbers. Today, you'll use the addition algorithm to solve word problems.

Show your child workbook page 23.4A and read aloud the first problem: ***How many sugar cookies and peanut butter cookies were sold?*** **How will you solve this problem?** *Add the number of sugar cookies to the number of peanut butter cookies.*

How many sugar cookies were sold? *38.* **How many peanut butter cookies were sold?** *43.* Have your child write both numbers in the blank grid and find their sum. Check that he writes the digits in the correct spots in the grid.

	1	
	3	8
+	4	3
	8	1

Repeat with the other word problems.

	1	
	3	8
+	5	9
	9	7

1	1	
	4	3
+	5	9
1	0	2

Activity: Compare and Contrast Mental Math and the Addition Algorithm

You now know how to solve two-digit addition problems both in your head and with the addition algorithm.

Write "38 + 43 =" horizontally on a piece of paper. **This problem has the same numbers as one of the problems you just showed me.** Have your child solve the problem mentally: *38 plus 40 equals 78. 78 plus 3 equals 81.*

$$38 + 43 = 81$$

$$\begin{array}{rr} & 1 \\ & 3\,8 \\ + & 4\,3 \\ \hline & 8\,1 \end{array}$$

Use the following questions to compare and contrast the two different methods.

- **How are these two ways of solving the problem different from each other?** *Sample answers: One is written down and one is in your head. You start with the tens-place in mental addition, but you start with the ones-place for the addition algorithm. In the addition algorithm, you trade 10 ones for 1 ten.*
- **What do the two ways of solving the problem have in common?** *Sample answers: Both give the same answer. Both involve using place value to break the numbers apart.*
- **Which way do you like better for solving this problem?** *Answers will vary.*

This math book will give you lots of practice with both mental math and the addition algorithm, because it's important to know both ways to solve problems. In your workbook, solve horizontal problems mentally. Solve vertical problems with the algorithm. But when you solve addition problems in real life, you can use whichever way you prefer.

Workbook: Add Two-Digit Numbers and Review

Have your child complete workbook pages 23.4A and 23.4B.

> The bottom part of workbook page 23.4A serves as an assessment of your child's fluency and accuracy with two-digit addition. See the Unit 10 Checkpoint for more on assessing your child's progress.

Lesson 23.5
Enrichment and Review (Optional)

	Purpose	Materials
Warm-up	• Count backward from 200 to 100 by 1s, 2s, 5s, or 10s • Review memory work • Review your child's favorite or most challenging activities from Week 23	• Varies, depending on the activities you choose
Picture Book	• Learn that 1 dozen equals 12 items • Explore division	• *Dozens of Doughnuts*, written by Carrie Finison and illustrated by Brianne Farley
Enrichment Activity	• Understand that 1 dozen equals 12 items • Make a chart showing how many items are in different numbers of dozens	• Egg carton

Warm-up: Counting, Memory Work, and Review

- Have your child count backwards from 200 to 100 by 1s, 2s, 5s, or 10s. (Choose whichever counting sequence your child needs to practice the most.)
- Quiz your child on the memory work through Week 22. See page 523 for the full list.
- If you have time, repeat one or two of the activities from this week's lessons. Choose activities your child especially enjoyed or found challenging.

Math Picture Book: *Dozens of Doughnuts*

Read *Dozens of Doughnuts*, written by Carrie Finison and illustrated by Brianne Farley. As you read, discuss how many doughnuts each friend eats and how the number decreases as more friends arrive.

Enrichment Activity: Explore Dozens

Show your child an egg carton and explain that 1 dozen eggs equals 12 eggs. Discuss any other items you buy in sets of a dozen, such as doughnuts or rolls.

How many eggs are in 2 dozen? *24.* **How do you know?** *Sample answer: 12 plus 12 equals 24.* Start a chart, and have your child use addition to find how many eggs are in each number of dozens, up to 10 dozen.

Dozens	Number of Eggs
1	12
2	24
3	36
4	48
5	60
6	72
7	84
8	96
9	108
10	120

Week 23 Answer Key

23.1A

See the Instructor Guide for directions.

76 + 19 = 95	35 + 81 = 116	62 + 53 = 115	85 + 7 = 92

Snowball Fight

46, 48, 53, 59, 64, 67, 75, 76, 82, 88, 95, 99

23.1B

Use a ruler to measure the sticks in centimeters.

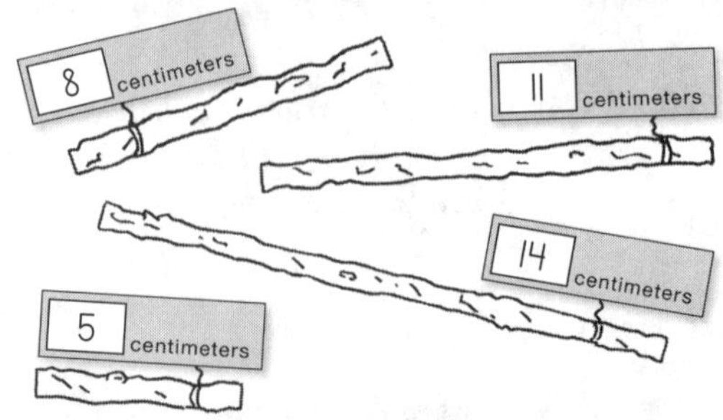

Write how much money is in each coin purse. Use a dollar sign and decimal point.

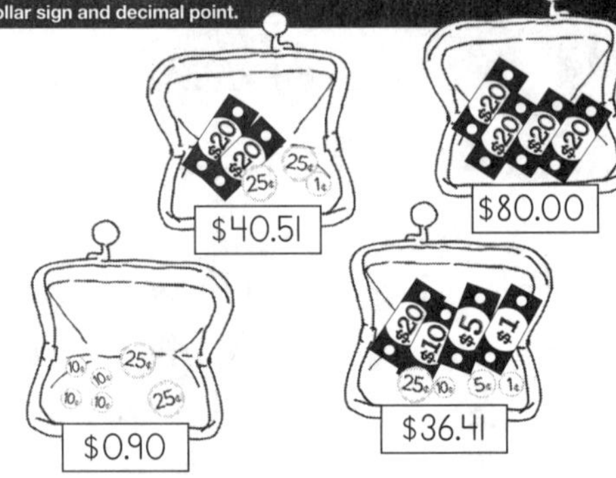

23.2A

See the Instructor Guide for directions.

56 + 68 = 124	94 + 57 = 151	49 + 51 = 100	77 + 41 = 118

Connect the Boxes

73 + 34 = 107	98 + 40 = 138	89 + 61 = 150	96 + 17 = 113
66 + 78 = 144	93 + 41 = 134	81 + 63 = 144	74 + 69 = 143
80 + 56 = 136	97 + 32 = 129	99 + 8 = 107	31 + 70 = 101
22 + 58 = 80	55 + 84 = 139	88 + 62 = 150	65 + 91 = 156

23.2B

Choose the more sensible measurement for each item.

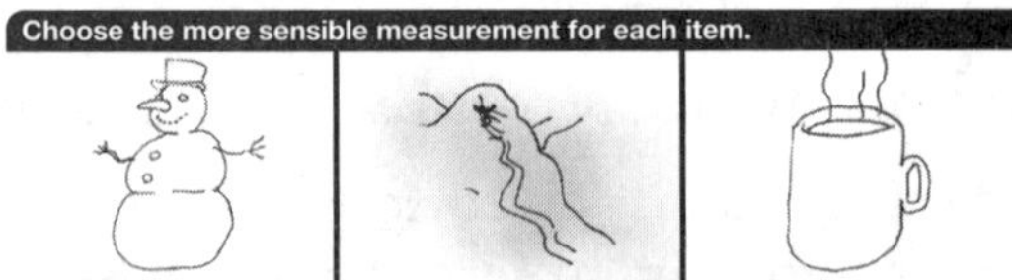

Height of a snowman	Length of a sledding hill	Height of a mug
1 centimeter / **1 meter** (circled)	**100 meters** (circled) / 100 kilometers	9 meters / **9 centimeters** (circled)

Label the numbers on the number line.

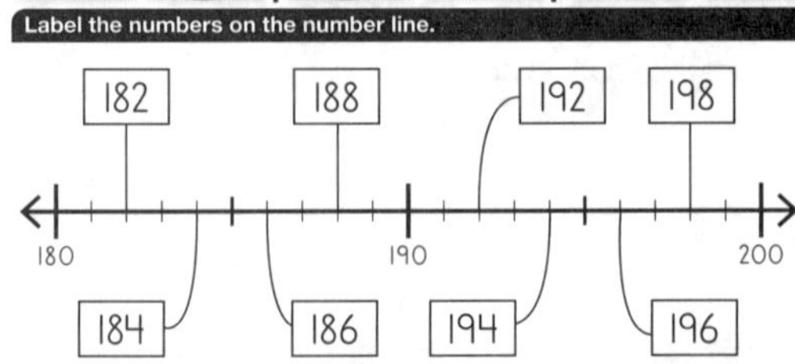

Complete.

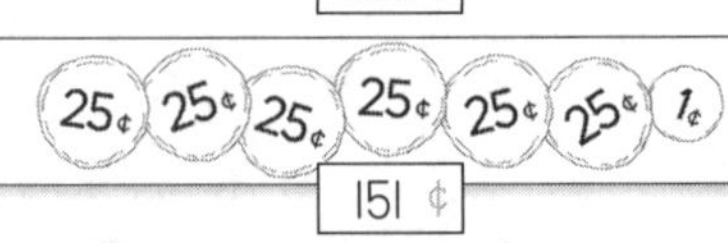

Week 23 Answer Key

23.3A

See the Instructor Guide for directions.

37 + 44 = 81	57 + 47 = 104	38 + 95 = 133
77 + 88 = 165	55 + 25 = 80	43 + 52 = 95
65 + 7 = 72	46 + 89 = 135	16 + 86 = 102
49 + 81 = 130	79 + 8 = 87	62 + 38 = 100

FINISH

23.3B

Write an equation to match. Then, solve.

Roberto's foot is 8 inches long.
Mom's foot is 10 inches long.
How much longer is Mom's foot than Roberto's?

Charlotte's foot is 7 inches long.
Dad's foot is 12 inches long.
How much shorter is Charlotte's foot than Dad's?

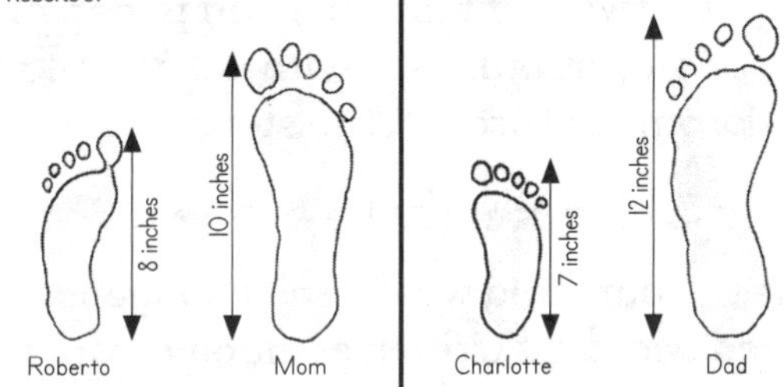

10 − 8 = 2 — 2 inches

12 − 7 = 5 — 5 inches

Complete each box with a number that makes the statement true.

1 > ☐	☐ < 109
178 = ☐	46 > ☐
100 < ☐	☐ < 200

Many answers are possible.

23.4A

Lincoln helped at the bake sale. He made a chart of how many cookies were sold. Use the chart to answer the questions.

Type	Number Sold
Sugar	38
Peanut butter	43
Chocolate	59

How many sugar cookies and peanut butter cookies were sold?

38 + 43 = 81 — 81 cookies

How many sugar cookies and chocolate cookies were sold?

38 + 59 = 97 — 97 cookies

How many peanut butter cookies and chocolate cookies were sold?

43 + 59 = 102 — 102 cookies

Complete.

88 + 46 = 134	49 + 36 = 85	74 + 94 = 168	56 + 8 = 64
24 + 67 = 91	74 + 76 = 150	58 + 80 = 138	42 + 93 = 135

23.4B

Write the time.

1:45   3:20   12:07

Complete the missing numbers in the sequences.

Count by 25s: 25, 50, 75, 100, 125, 150

Count by 5s: 85, 90, 95, 100, 105, 110

Copy the shape.

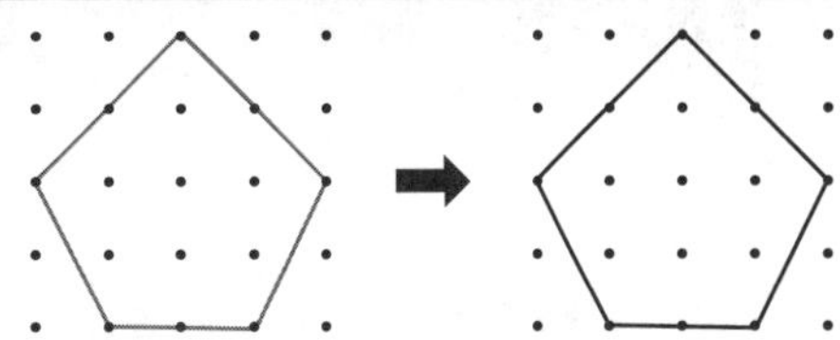

Unit 10 Checkpoint

What to Expect at the End of Unit 10

By the end of Unit 10, most children will be able to do the following:

- Model the steps in the addition algorithm with base-ten blocks and explain how the blocks correspond to the written digits.
- Add two-digit numbers on paper, mostly fluently. Some children will be able to add two-digit numbers with ease, while others will still need to stop and think as they progress through the steps.

Is Your Child Ready to Move on?

In Unit 11, your child will learn about geometry and fractions. She does not need to have fully mastered two-digit written addition before moving on to Unit 11. She'll continue to practice the addition algorithm in the review portions of the workbook pages.

Unit 11
Geometry and Fractions

Overview

Your child will learn how to identify and describe polygons and three-dimensional solids. She'll develop her spatial skills as she completes shape puzzles and draws lines to cut shapes into equal parts. She'll also learn how to read, write, and compare simple fractions.

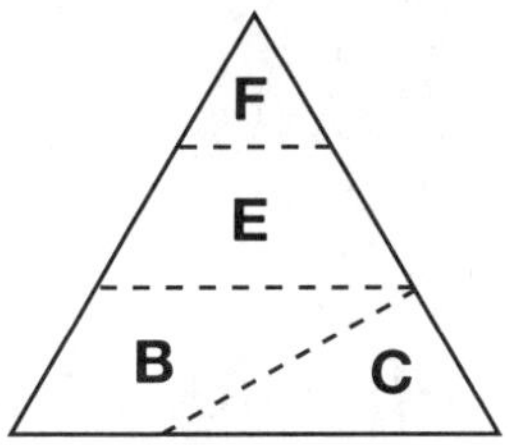

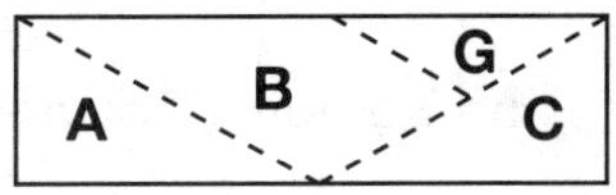

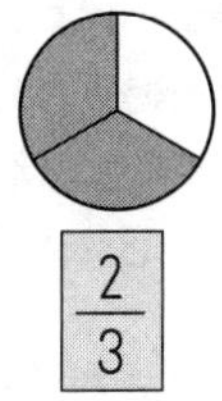

Week 24	Polygons and 3-D Solids
Week 25	Fractions

Many children find this unit a pleasant change of pace after working hard to learn the steps in the addition algorithm. Your child will practice the addition algorithm in the review exercises to continue to build fluency and automaticity. She'll also review the subtraction facts with games and workbook exercises so that she's ready to tackle the subtraction algorithm in Unit 12.

What Your Child Will Learn

In this unit your child will learn to:

- Name, describe, and draw polygons with different numbers of sides (triangles, quadrilaterals, pentagons, hexagons, and octagons)
- Name three-dimensional solids (spheres, cones, cubes, cylinders, and rectangular prisms)
- Reason about polygons and use spatial skills to complete puzzles
- Split shapes into halves, thirds, fourths, sixths, and eighths, and read and write fractions to describe fractional parts
- Use hands-on materials to compare fractions

Recommended Math Picture Books (Optional)

These picture books are scheduled in the optional Enrichment and Review lessons at the end of each week.

- *Perfect Square,* by Michael Hall. Greenwillow Books, 2011.
- *If You Were a Fraction,* written by Trisha Speed Shaskan and illustrated by Francesca Carabelli. Picture Window Books, 2008.

Week 24
Polygons and 3-D Solids

Overview

Your child will learn how to identify different types of polygons. He'll develop his spatial skills with a polygon puzzle and also learn the names of three-dimensional solids.

Lesson 24.1	Introduce Polygons
Lesson 24.2	Polygon Puzzles
Lesson 24.3	Identify Polygons
Lesson 24.4	3-D Solids
Lesson 24.5	Enrichment and Review (Optional)

Teaching Math with Confidence: Developing Spatial Skills with a Puzzle

In Lessons 24.2 and 24.3, your child will develop his spatial skills as he puts together mosaic puzzle pieces to create more complex shapes. (This special set of puzzle pieces has been popularized by a Dutch math educator named Pierre Van Hiele.) It's similar to the tangram used in *First Grade Math with Confidence*, but it includes a wider variety of shapes and angles for more variety and challenge.

Your child will discover how to flip, slide, and turn the pieces to make them fit together to create larger shapes.

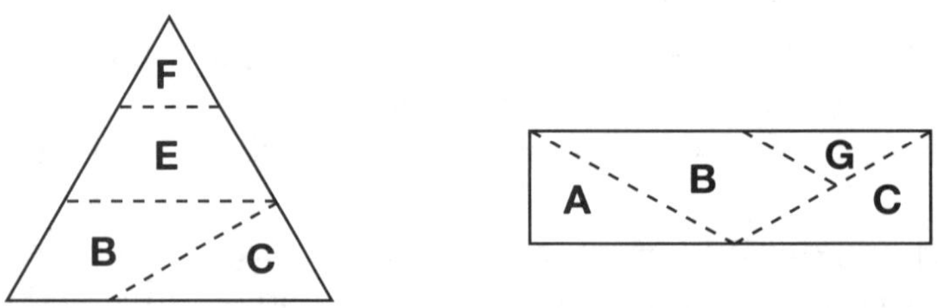

He'll also explore how to make many different shapes out of just a few pieces. For example, in Lesson 24.3, he'll find that he can make 6 different shapes from just 2 triangles.

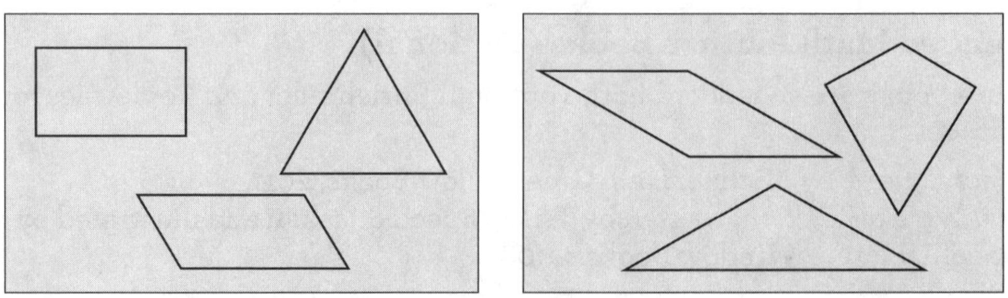

These hands-on experiences with different types of shapes and angles build your child's spatial skills and prepare him for more formal geometry work in future years.

Extra Materials Needed for Week 24

- Markers or colored pencils
- 8 toothpicks, popsicle sticks, straws, or other long, narrow objects
- Household items in the shape of a sphere, cone, cylinder, cube, and rectangular prism. Suggested items:
    - Sphere: basketball, baseball, globe
    - Cone: party hat, sports cone, ice cream cone
    - Cylinder: can, oatmeal canister, toy drum
    - Cube: Rubik's cube, dice, sugar cube
    - Rectangular prism: cereal box, shipping box, stick of butter
- Empty cardboard box
- For optional Enrichment and Review Lesson:
    - *Perfect Square*, by Michael Hall
    - Several sheets of construction paper, origami paper, or copy paper
    - Glue, optional
    - Large sheets of paper, optional

You will also need the mosaic puzzle pieces from Blackline Master 8, cut apart.

Lesson 24.1
Introduce Polygons

	Purpose	Materials
Warm-up	• Count by 100s to 1000 • Practice memory work • Review subtraction facts	• Base-ten blocks • Subtraction Race game board (from workbook page 9.2A) • Coin • Counters
Activities	• Introduce polygons • Identify and create polygons with different numbers of sides • Find real-life examples of pentagons, hexagons, and octagons	• Workbook page 24.1A • 8 toothpicks, popsicle sticks, straws, or other long, narrow objects
Workbook	• Identify polygons	• Workbook pages 24.1A and 24.1B

If you use toothpicks or straws to make the shapes in this lesson, you may want to place them on a towel to prevent rolling.

Warm-up: Counting, Memory Work, and Review

- Place 10 flats on the table. Demonstrate how to count them by 100s: **100, 200, 300, 400, 500, 600, 700, 800, 900, 1000.** Encourage your child to listen for familiar patterns and join you as much as she can.

  You will gradually introduce your child to the counting sequence to 1000 during Units 11 and 12. She will learn more about the numbers to 1000 in Unit 13.

- **How many centimeters equal 1 meter?** *100.*
- Play Subtraction Race (-9 Version). See Lesson 9.2 (page 149) for directions.

Activity: Introduce Polygons

In first grade, you learned about circles, triangles, rectangles, and squares. Have your child draw an example of each shape.

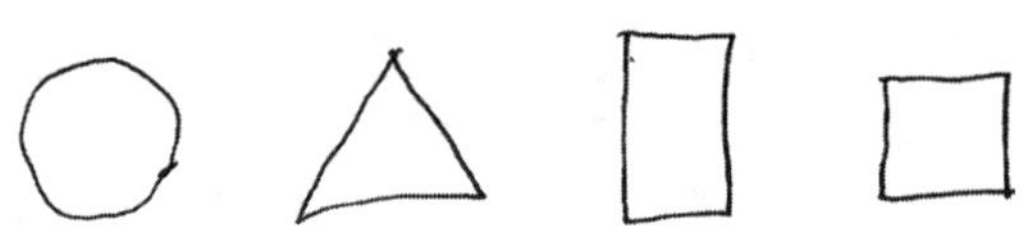

This year, you'll learn about polygons. Polygons are flat, closed shapes with straight sides. Triangles, rectangles, and squares are polygons. Circle the triangle, rectangle, and square your child drew. **Circles are not polygons, because they don't have straight sides.** Draw an X through the circle your child drew.

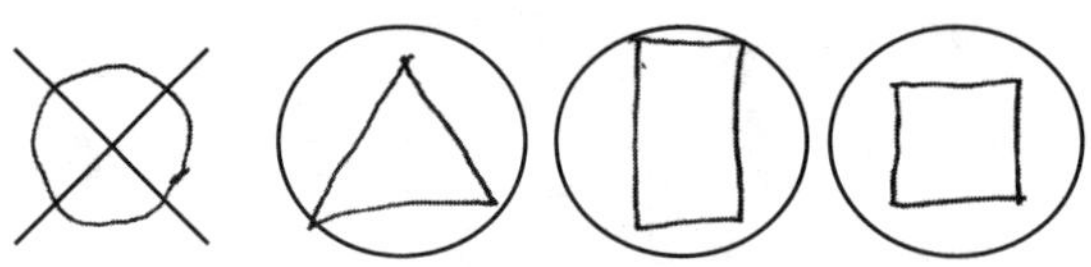

Show your child the shapes at the top of workbook page 24.1A. Have her circle each polygon and X each shape that is not a polygon. Remind her as needed that polygons must be closed with straight sides.

Activity: Make a Polygon Chart

Today, we'll make a Polygon Chart with names and numbers of sides for some everyday polygons. We'll make an example of each kind of polygon, too. Place toothpicks on the table, and begin a chart like the following:

Name of Shape	Number of Sides	Number of Angles

Use 3 toothpicks to make a triangle. **In first grade, you learned that triangles have 3 sides and 3 angles. We call the outside edges of a polygon its sides.** Use your finger to trace the edges of the triangle. Count each side as you trace it: **1, 2, 3.**

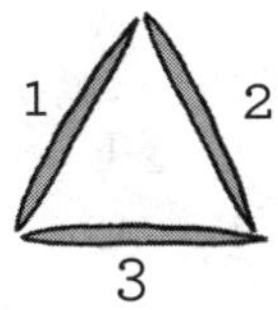

The sides meet to form angles. Use your finger to point to each angle in the triangle: **1, 2, 3.** Complete the first line of the chart as shown.

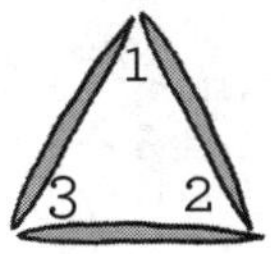

Name of Shape	Number of Sides	Number of Angles
Triangle	3	3

Shapes with 4 sides are called quadrilaterals. Squares and rectangles have 4 sides, so they are types of quadrilaterals. Have your child make a quadrilateral out of the toothpicks and complete the next line of the chart.

Examples of possible quadrilaterals

Name of Shape	Number of Sides	Number of Angles
Triangle	3	3
Quadrilateral	4	4

There are many different quadrilaterals your child can make. Accept any shape with 4 connected, straight sides.

Continue in the same way with pentagons, hexagons, heptagons, and octagons. Add each polygon to the chart and have your child construct the polygon with the corresponding number of toothpicks.

Name of Shape	Number of Sides	Number of Angles
Triangle	3	3
Quadrilateral	4	4
Pentagon	5	5
Hexagon	6	6
Heptagon	7	7
Octagon	8	8

Your child will memorize the definition of these polygons in the Week 26 memory work. The term *heptagon* is not commonly used, so your child does not need to memorize it.

Activity: Polygon Scavenger Hunt

Walk around your home with your child and look for pentagons, hexagons, and octagons. You might find pentagons and hexagons on a soccer ball, a hexagon at the end of a pencil, or octagons in your floor tiles. You may also find them in toys (such as wooden puzzles, magnet tiles, or baby toys) and home décor items (such as fabric patterns, mirrors, or clocks).

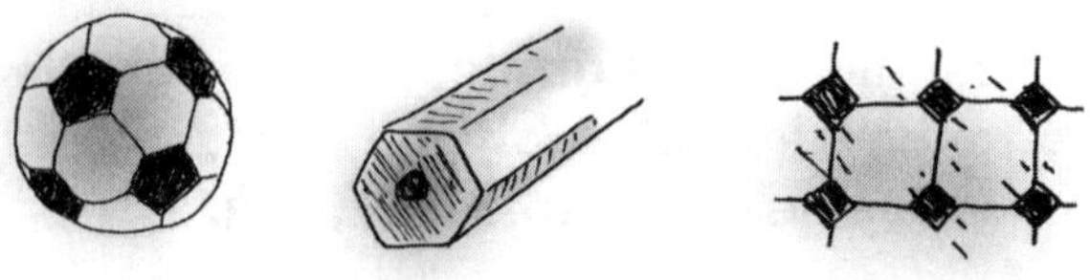

Most second-graders have less experience with pentagons, hexagons, and octagons than triangles and quadrilaterals, so the scavenger hunt focuses on just these types of polygons.

Workbook: Identify and Draw Polygons and Review

Have your child complete workbook pages 24.1A and 24.1B.

If your child loses track while counting the polygons' sides, have her trace the sides with her pencil and count each side as she traces it.

Lesson 24.2
Polygon Puzzles

	Purpose	Materials
Warm-up	• Count by 3s • Practice memory work • Review subtraction facts	• Base-ten blocks • Four in a Row game board (from workbook page 11.1A) • Counters
Activities	• Identify attributes of triangles and quadrilaterals • Identify right angles • Develop spatial skills by creating polygons with geometric puzzle pieces	• Mosaic puzzle pieces (Blackline Master 8), cut apart
Workbook	• Develop spatial skills by filling in outlines with puzzle pieces	• Workbook pages 24.2A and 24.2B • Mosaic puzzle pieces (Blackline Master 8), cut apart

Warm-up: Counting, Memory Work, and Review

- Have your child count by 3s to 30.
- **How many centimeters equal 1 meter?** *100.*
- Play Four in a Row. See Lesson 11.1 (page 176) for directions,

Activity: Sort and Discuss Triangles and Quadrilaterals

In the last lesson, you learned that polygons are flat, closed shapes with straight sides.

We'll use special puzzle pieces to make polygons today. Show your child the cut-apart mosaic puzzle pieces from Blackline Master 8. Give him a few minutes to experiment with the pieces and create designs with them. Allow him to flip the pieces over as needed to make them fit together.

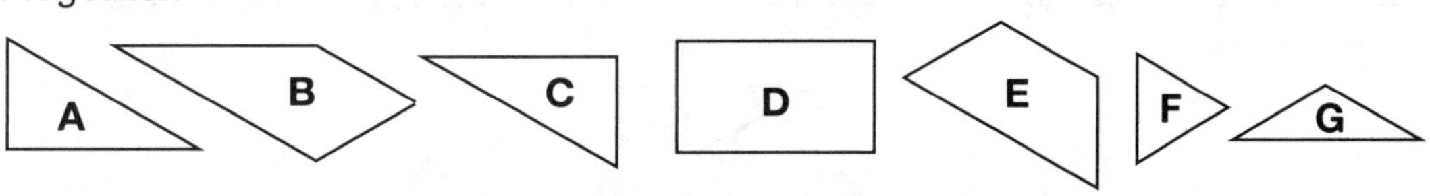

See the Week 24 **Teaching Math with Confidence** for how these puzzle pieces help your child develop spatial skills.

What do we call polygons with 3 sides? *Triangles.* **What do we call polygons with 4 sides?** *Quadrilaterals.* Have your child sort the mosaic puzzle pieces based on whether they are triangles or quadrilaterals.

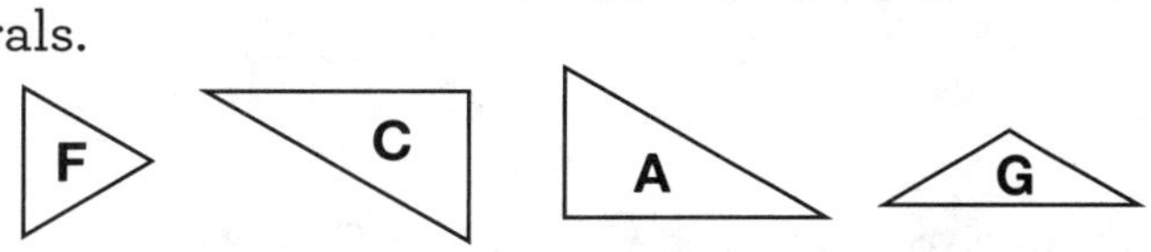

Triangles

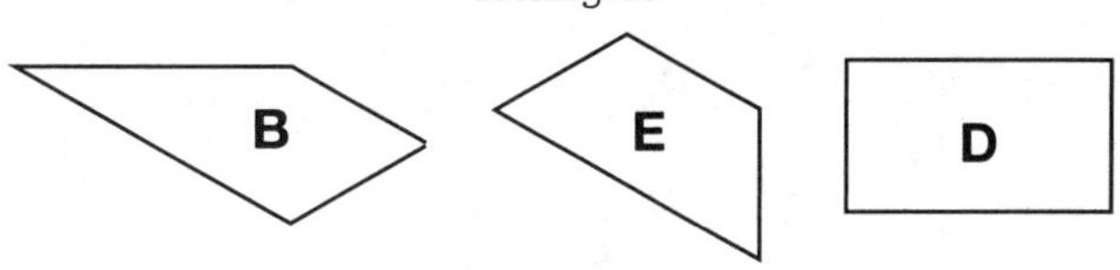

Quadrilaterals

Discuss the triangles with the following questions:

- **What do the triangles have in common?** *They all have 3 sides and 3 angles.*
- **How are the triangles different from each other?** *Sample answers: G looks more squished than the others. A and C have corners like a piece of paper, but G and F don't. F has all equal sides.*
- **Which triangle has all equal sides?** *F.*
- **Which triangle has two equal sides?** *G.*
- **Which two triangles are congruent to each other and have the same shape and size?** *A and C.* Place A on top of C to show that the triangles are congruent to each other.

Discuss the quadrilaterals with the following questions.

- **What do all these quadrilaterals have in common?** *They all have 4 sides and 4 angles.*
- **How are these quadrilaterals different from each other?** *Sample answers: D is a rectangle, but B and E aren't. B looks very pointy! E is a trapezoid.*

Activity: Review Right Angles

In first grade, you learned that a right angle is an angle that looks like the corner on a piece of paper. Which of the triangle puzzle pieces have a right angle? *A and C.* Tear off the corner of a piece of paper. Place the corner inside the right angle on each puzzle piece to demonstrate.

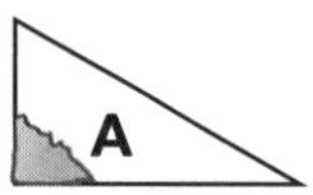

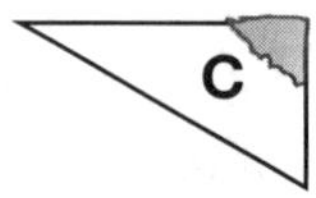

Which of the quadrilateral puzzle pieces has a right angle? *D.* **How many right angles does puzzle piece D have?** *4.* Place the corner inside each angle to demonstrate. **Rectangles and squares must always have 4 right angles.**

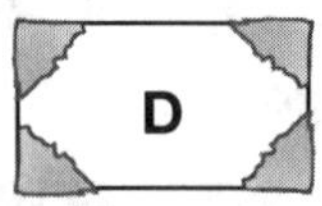

Activity: Develop Spatial Skills with a Shape Puzzle

Some of the puzzle pieces can be put together to cover other pieces. Place A and C on top of D to demonstrate.

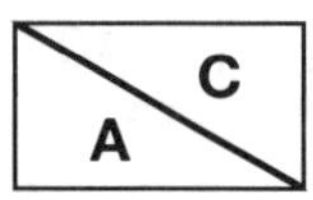

Which two pieces can you use to cover C? *F and G.*

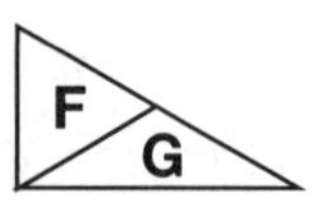

Which two pieces can you use to cover B? *F and A.*

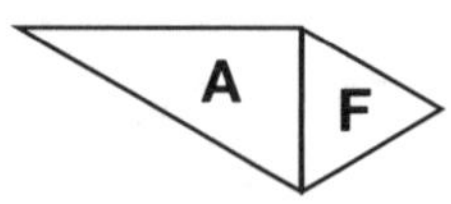

Which two pieces can you use to cover E? *A and G, or C and G.*

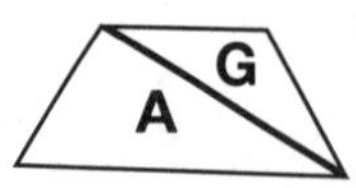

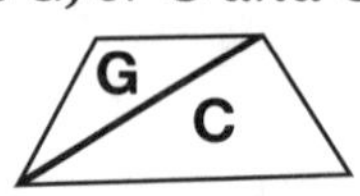

Which 3 pieces can you use to cover D? *C, F, and G, or A, F, and G.*

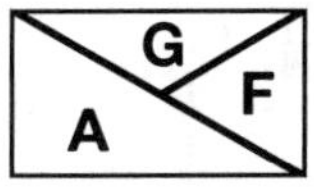

Workbook: Practice Spatial Skills and Review

Have your child complete workbook pages 24.2A and 24.2B.

If your child struggles to draw lines to show where he put each piece, have him show you how he completed the outlines instead.

Lesson 24.3
Identify Polygons

	Purpose	Materials
Warm-up	• Count by 100s • Practice memory work • Review telling time	• Base-ten blocks • Clock
Activities	• Develop spatial skills • Practice identifying polygons	• Mosaic puzzle pieces (Blackline Master 8), cut apart • Polygon Four in a Row game board (from workbook page 24.3A) • Die • Counters
Workbook	• Review previously-learned material	• Workbook page 24.3B

Warm-up: Counting, Memory Work, and Review

- Place 10 flats on the table. Count them by 100s in unison with your child.
- **How many centimeters equal 1 meter?** *100.*
- Set the clock to the following times: 10:00, 10:08, 10:23, 10:39, 10:50, 10:58, 11:00. Have your child tell each time.

Activity: Develop Spatial Skills with a Polygon Challenge

Give your child puzzle pieces A and C, and put the rest of the pieces aside. Place a few sheets of paper on the table. **I have a polygon challenge for you today! How many different polygons you can make by putting these two pieces together? The only rule is that any sides that touch must be the same length. So, shapes like this don't count.** Place the pieces together as shown to demonstrate.

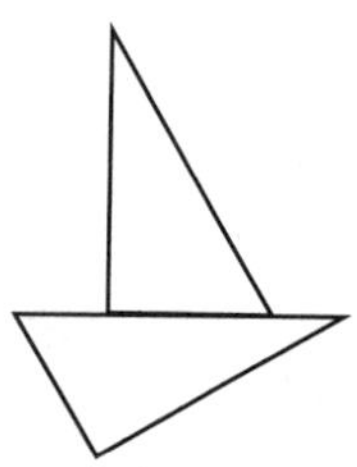

I'll trace each polygon after you make it. Have your child turn and flip the pieces to create polygons. Trace each polygon after she makes it.

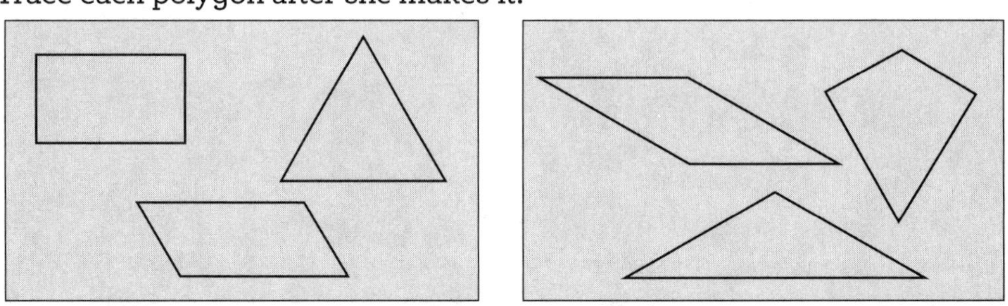

If your child doesn't find all 6 different ways to put the pieces together, demonstrate the missing ways for him. Look at the traced outlines, and have your child tell whether each polygon is a triangle or quadrilateral. Label each polygon as shown.

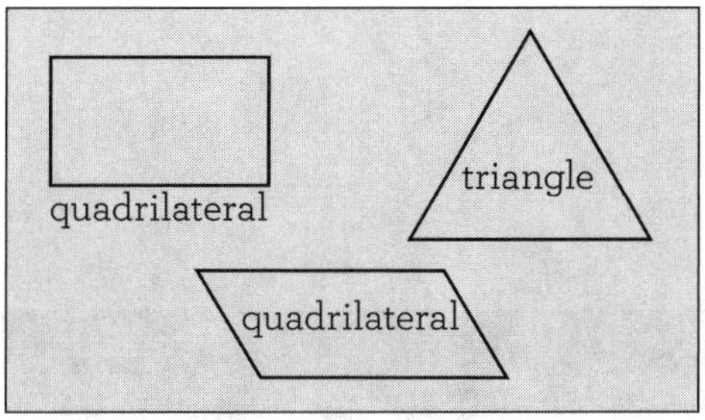

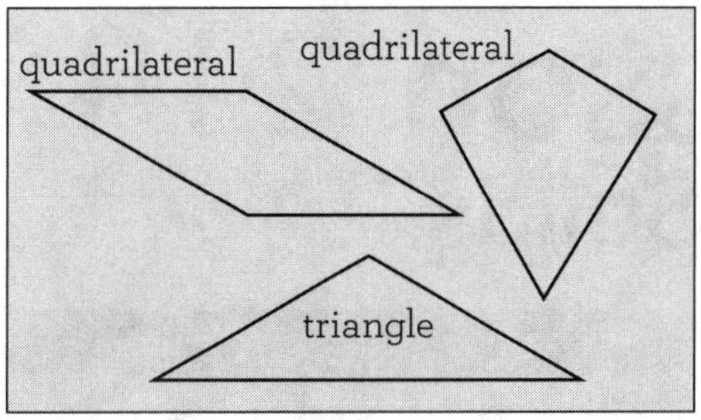

Activity: Practice Identifying Polygons and Right Angles

Play Polygon Four in a Row.

This game includes many "weird-looking" polygons so that your child gets lots of practice counting the polygons' sides and identifying right angles. Remind her as needed of the definition of each type of polygon. Encourage her to trace the polygons with her finger to help keep track as she counts their sides.

Polygon Four in a Row

Materials: Polygon Four in a Row game board (from workbook page 24.3A); 15 counters per player, with a different color for each player; die

Object of the Game: Be the first player to place counters in 4 squares in a row, either horizontally, vertically, or diagonally.

On your turn, roll the die. Use the key at the bottom of the page to see what type of polygon you can cover. For example, if you roll a 5, you can cover any pentagon on the game board. Cover that type of polygon with one of your counters.

Key

wild	triangle	pentagon
Any polygon with a right angle	quadrilateral	hexagon

If you roll a 5, cover any pentagon.

If you roll a 1, you may cover any polygon on the board.

Play then passes to the other player. Continue until one player covers 4 boxes in a row, either horizontally, vertically, or diagonally.

Save this game board with your math materials so you can play again.

Workbook: Review

Have your child complete workbook page 24.3B.

Lesson 24.4
3-D Solids

	Purpose	Materials
Warm-up	• Count by 4s on the dot array • Practice memory work • Review subtraction facts	• Dot array and L-cover (Blackline Master 6) • Counters • Treasure Hunt game board (from workbook page 10.2A) • Die
Activities	• Identify common three-dimensional solids • Recognize two-dimensional shapes as the faces of three-dimensional solids	• Household items in the shape of a rectangular prism, cube, cylinder, cone, and sphere. (See Extra Materials on page 381 for suggestions.) • Empty cardboard box
Workbook	• Identify three-dimensional solids	• Workbook pages 24.4A and 24.4B

Warm-up: Counting, Memory Work, and Review

- Slide the L-cover on the dot array to reveal 4 dots at a time. Have your child count by 4s to tell how many dots are visible in each array. Continue until you reach 40.

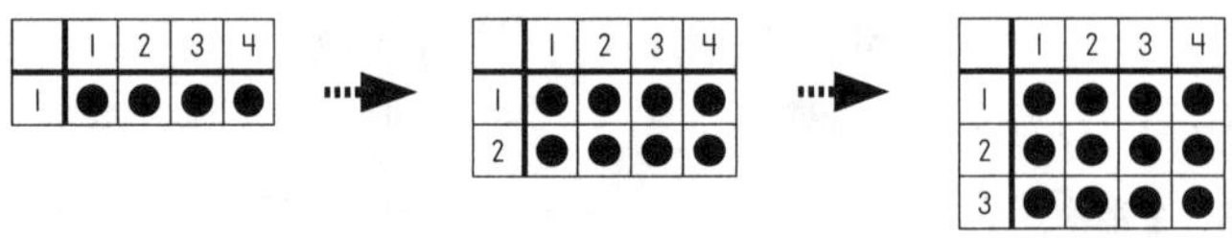

4 8 12

- **How many centimeters equal 1 meter?** *100.*
- Play Treasure Hunt. See Lesson 10.2 (page 165) for directions.

Activity: Introduce 3-D Shapes

This week, you've learned about many different types of polygons. Polygons are flat, like a piece of paper. Show your child a piece of paper. **We call flat shapes two-dimensional.**

Crumple the piece of paper into a ball. **The piece of paper isn't flat any more. Now, it takes up space! Shapes that take up space are called three-dimensional solids. We'll explore three-dimensional solids today.**

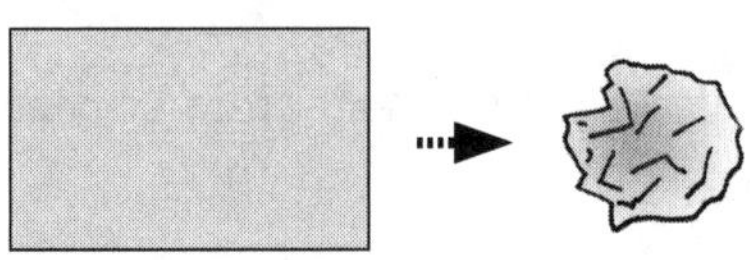

If your child is familiar with the term 3-D, explain that it's an abbreviation of 3-dimensional.

Show your child household items in the shape of a rectangular prism, cube, cylinder, cone and sphere.

rectangular prism

cube

cylinder

cone

sphere

Tell your child the name of each solid, and discuss each solid with the following questions:

- **Boxes are rectangular prisms. Each flat side is called a face. How many faces does this rectangular prism have?** *6.* Help your child count the faces. **What shape is each face?** *A rectangle.*

Rectangular prisms have 6 faces: the bottom, top, and 4 vertical sides. Each face is a rectangle.

- **Cubes are a special kind of rectangular prism. How many faces do they have?** *6.* **What shape is each face?** *A square.*

Cubes have 6 faces: the bottom, top, and 4 vertical sides. Each face is a square.

- **Cans and round canisters are cylinders. They have one curved surface and two flat faces.** Show your child the flat faces at the top and bottom of the cylinder. **What shape is each flat face?** *A circle.*

Cylinders have 1 curved surface and 2 flat faces.
In an oatmeal container, the vertical part is the curved surface, and the top and bottom are the flat faces.

- **Ice cream cones and party hats are cones. They have 1 curved surface and 1 flat face.** Show your child the curved surface and the flat face on the cone. **What shape is the flat face?** *A circle.*

Cones have 1 curved surface and 2 flat faces. In a party hat, the curved surface is the paper that makes up the hat. If you were to close the hat at the bottom with a round piece of paper, that circle would be the flat face.

Technically, a true cone must be fully closed. Most household cones are open, though, so simply have your child imagine a flat face on your cone.

- **Balls are examples of spheres. They have 1 curved surface that covers the entire solid. Spheres must be fully round. If I squish a ball, it's no longer a sphere.**

Spheres have 1 curved face and are fully round.

Activity: Unfold Boxes

Show your child an empty cardboard box. **What three-dimensional solid is this box?** *A rectangular prism.* **It's three-dimensional, but it's made out of a two-dimensional piece of cardboard.** Help your child unfold the box until it is completely flat.

> You may need to tear open flaps, peel off tape, or cut along an edge to make the box completely open.

Examine the unfolded box with your child. Have him identify the top, bottom, and sides of the box. Then, have him try to re-fold the box back into its original shape.

> If you have time, have your child cut a vertical line through an empty paper towel or toilet paper tube. He may be surprised to find that it unfolds to become a rectangle!

Workbook: Identify 3-D Shapes and Review

Have your child complete workbook pages 24.4A and 24.4B.

Lesson 24.5
Enrichment and Review (Optional)

	Purpose	Materials
Warm-up	• Count backward from 200 to 100 by 1s, 2s, 5s, or 10s • Review memory work • Review your child's favorite or most challenging activities from Week 24	• Varies, depending on the activities you choose
Picture Book	• Develop spatial skills by mentally flipping and turning shapes	• *Perfect Square,* by Michael Hall
Enrichment Activity	• Develop spatial skills by cutting paper into shapes and arranging the shapes	• Several sheets of construction paper, origami paper, or copy paper • Glue, optional • Large sheets of paper, optional

Warm-up: Counting, Memory Work, and Review

- Have your child count backward from 200 to 100 by 1s, 2s, 5s, or 10s. (Choose whichever counting sequence your child needs to practice the most.)
- Quiz your child on the memory work through Week 24. See page 523 for the full list.
- If you have time, repeat one or two of the activities from this week's lessons. Choose activities your child especially enjoyed or found challenging.

Math Picture Book: *Perfect Square*

Read *Perfect Square*, by Michael Hall. As you read, choose a few pieces in each finished design and see if you can find them in the original cut-apart square on the previous page.

Enrichment Activity: Make One-Sheet Paper Collages

Have your child cut a sheet of paper into shapes and then arrange the shapes to make a design. Encourage him to use every part of the paper, so that the whole piece of paper is used in the design. If he'd like, he can glue his design onto a larger piece of paper.

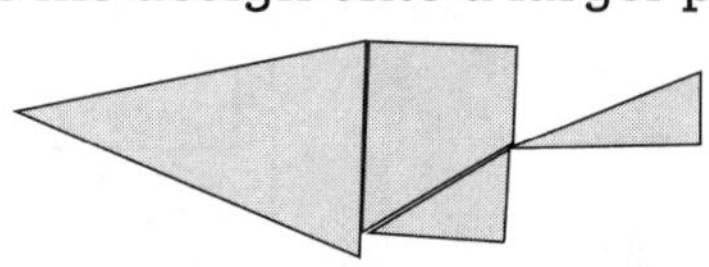

If your child isn't sure how to start, suggest he cut the paper into squares and then experiment with arranging the squares.

Have your child make several designs in this way. Discuss the similarities and differences between the designs. Marvel at how different the designs can look from each other even though they're all made from one sheet of paper.

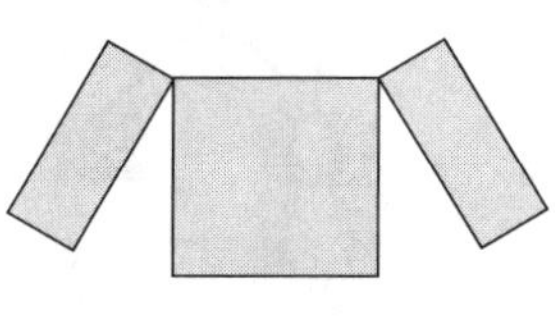
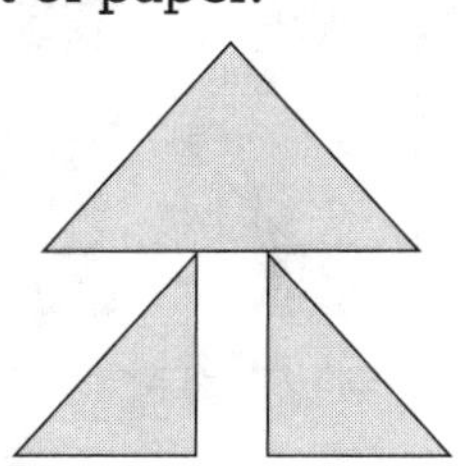
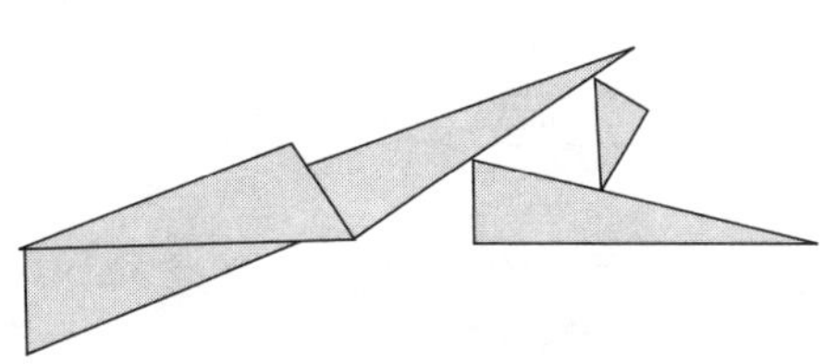

Week 24 Answer Key

24.1A

Circle the polygons. X the shapes that are not polygons.

Match each polygon to its name.

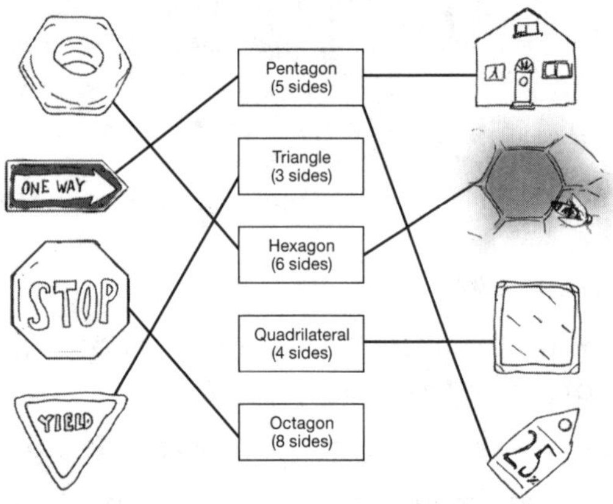

24.1B

Complete.

$38 + 54 = 92$

$76 + 41 = 117$

$49 + 8 = 57$

$99 + 32 = 131$

Use the key to color the blocks.

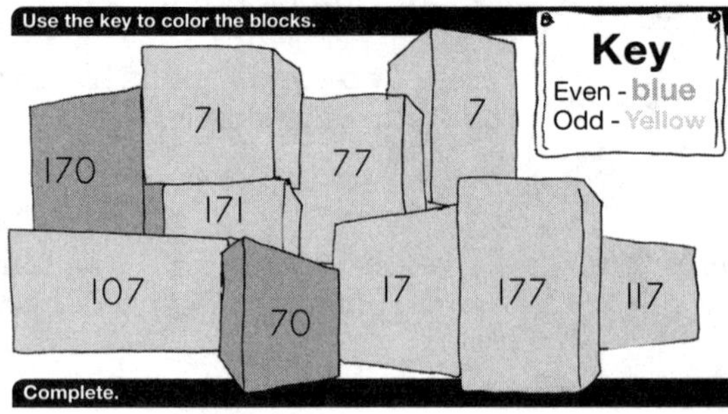

Complete.

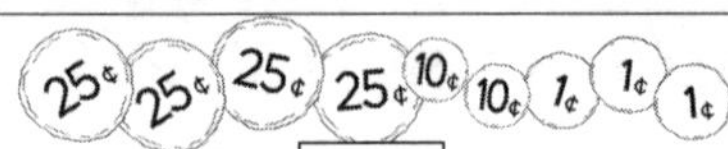

123 ¢

106 ¢

24.2A

Use the puzzle pieces to cover the polygons. Draw lines to show where you put each piece.

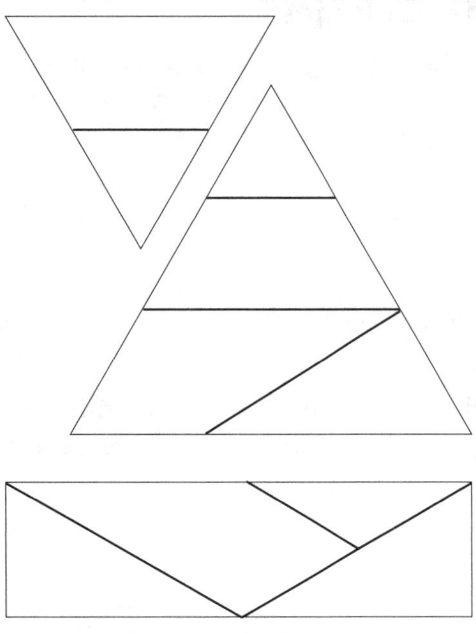

24.2B

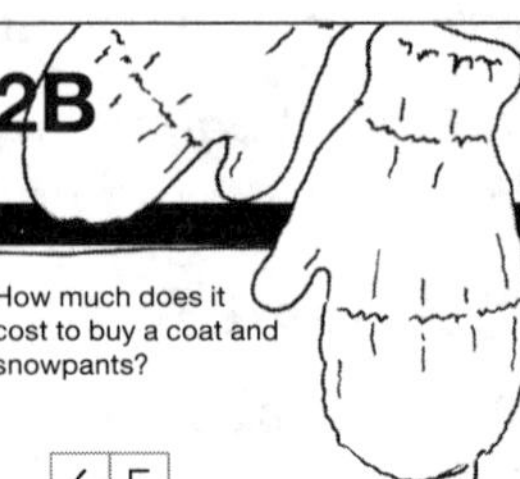

Use the chart to answer the questions.

Snowpants	$56
Coat	$65
Boots	$38
Gloves	$17
Hat	$12

How much does it cost to buy a coat and snowpants?

$65 + 56 = 121$ — $ 121

How much does it cost to buy boots and gloves?

$38 + 17 = 55$ — $ 55

How much does it cost to buy boots and a hat?

$38 + 12 = 50$ — $ 50

Match the pairs that equal 100.

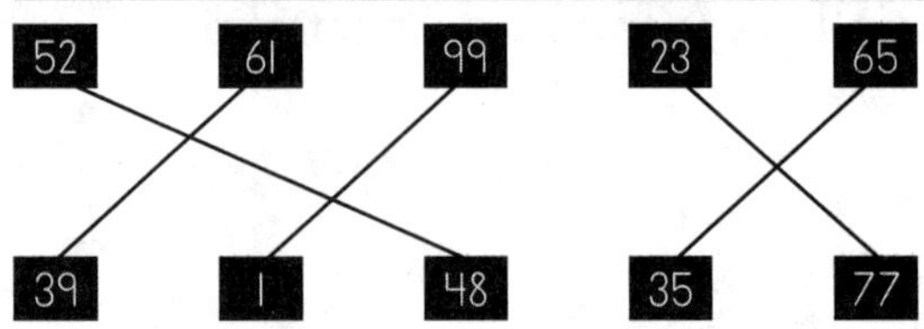

Week 24 Answer Key

24.3A

See Instructor Guide for directions. Save this game board for future lessons.

Polygon Four in a Row

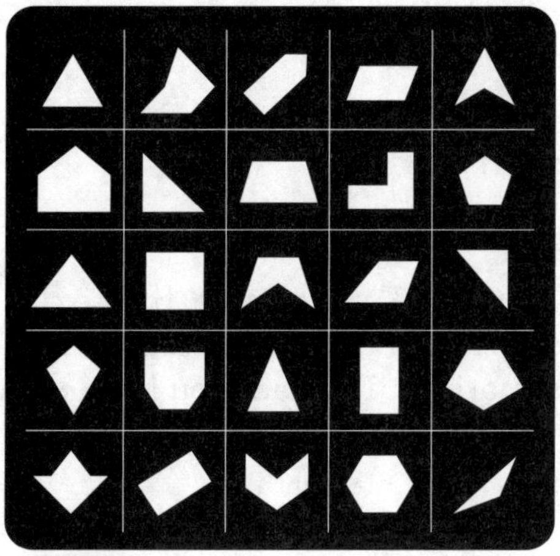

Key

Wild	Triangle	Pentagon
Any polygon with a right angle	Quadrilateral	Hexagon

24.3B

Complete.

29 + 35 = 64

85 + 72 = 157

42 + 58 = 100

79 + 53 = 132

Harper made a graph about how much snow fell each month. Use the graph to complete the chart and answer the questions. Write your own equation for each question.

Total Snowfall

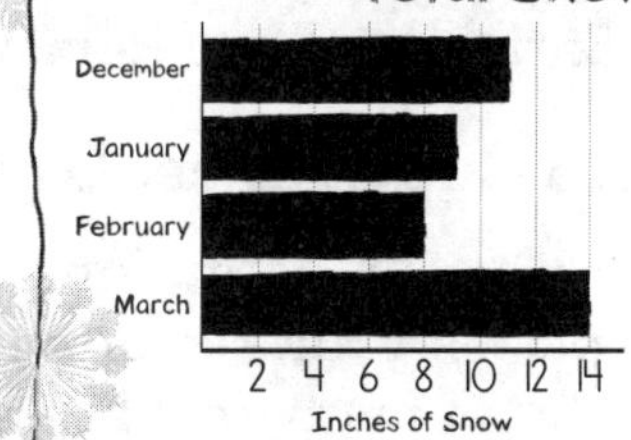

Month	Inches of Snow
December	11
January	9
February	8
March	14

How much snow fell in December and January?
11 + 9 = 20
20 inches

How much more snow fell in March than February?
14 - 8 = 6
6 inches

How much less snow fell in January than March?
14 - 9 = 5
5 inches

How much snow fell in all 4 months?
11 + 9 + 8 + 14 = 42
42 inches

24.4A

Match each shape to its name.

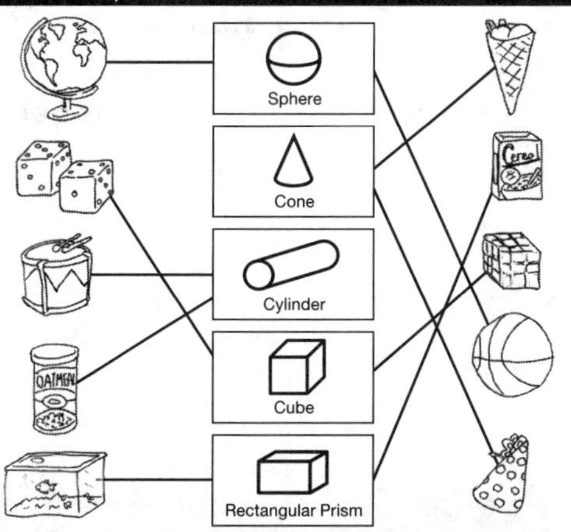

Draw a shape that matches each description.

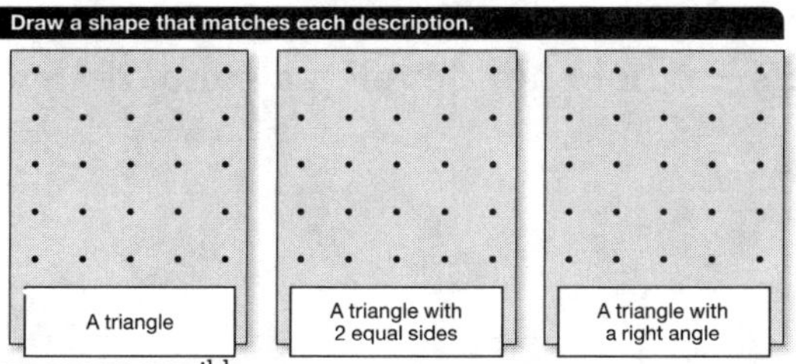

Many answers are possible.

24.4B

Complete.

58 + 27 = 85

70 + 82 = 152

57 + 64 = 121

75 + 63 = 138

Color the triangles blue. Color the quadrilaterals green.

Complete.

11 - 5 = 6	17 - 9 = 8	13 - 8 = 5
12 - 7 = 5	13 - 4 = 9	11 - 9 = 2
10 - 8 = 2	13 - 7 = 6	11 - 3 = 8
13 - 9 = 4	16 - 8 = 8	15 - 7 = 8

Week 25
Fractions

Overview

Your child will learn how to split shapes into fractional parts and write fractions to describe the parts. She'll also use hands-on materials to compare fractions.

Lesson 25.1 Halves, Thirds, and Fourths
Lesson 25.2 Read and Write Fractions
Lesson 25.3 Sixths and Eighths
Lesson 25.4 Compare Fractions
Lesson 25.5 Enrichment and Review (Optional)

Teaching Math with Confidence: Using Counting to Understand Fractions

Many math books use a "parts" definition to teach fractions. For example, they explain that 3/8 means "3 out of 8 parts." Children often have trouble with this definition, because you cannot see all the "parts" in many real-life fraction situations. Instead, you'll teach your child to count fractional parts just as she counts apples or pencils.

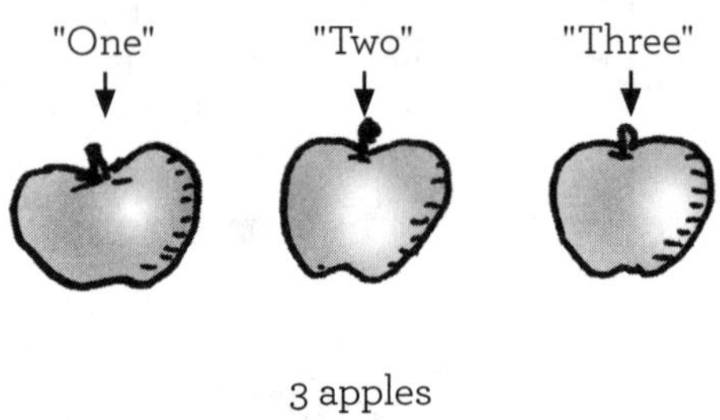

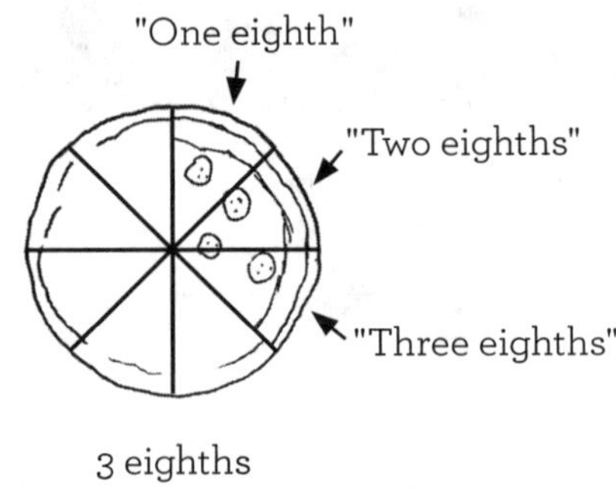

Once your child is comfortable with naming and counting fractional parts, you'll show her that written fractions are simply a way to record these counts. The top number in a fraction tells how many fractional parts there are, while the bottom number tells what kind of fractional parts you're counting. For example, the 3 in 3/8 tells that there are 3 fractional parts. The 8 tells that these fractional parts are eighths.

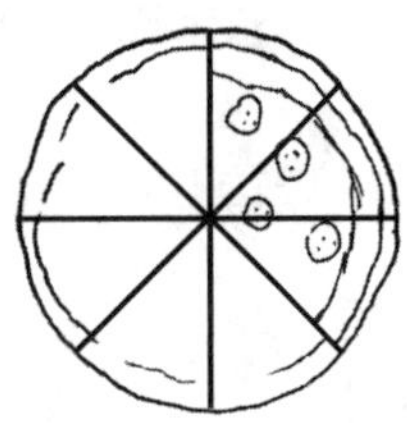

$\frac{3}{8}$ ← Number of fractional parts (3); Type of fractional part (8)

In future years, your child will learn that fractions are a type of number and that the fraction bar means the top number is divided by the bottom number. For now, you'll use this counting definition—along with hands-on materials—to help her develop a solid, real-world understanding of written fractions.

Extra Materials Needed for Week 25

- Crayons or colored pencils
- Scissors
- 26 index cards or slips of paper
- Several writing utensils of different lengths
- For optional Enrichment and Review Lesson:
    - *If You Were a Fraction,* written by Trisha Speed Shaskan and illustrated by Francesca Carabelli
    - Measuring cups (1/4-cup, 1/3-cup, ½-cup, and 1-cup)
    - Trail mix ingredients (See the recipe in Lesson 25.5 (page 411) for suggested ingredients.)

You will also need the Fraction Bars from Blackline Master 9, cut apart on the solid lines.

Lesson 25.1
Halves, Thirds, and Fourths

	Purpose	Materials
Warm-up	• Count by 100s to 1000 • Practice memory work • Review subtraction facts	• Base-ten blocks • Subtraction Race game board (from workbook page 9.2A) • Coin • Counters
Activities	• Use hands-on materials to represent fractional amounts with halves, thirds, or fourths • Compare simple fractions with hands-on models	• Fraction Bars (Blackline Master 9), cut apart on the solid lines • Crayons or colored pencils • Scissors • 9 blank index cards or slips of paper
Workbook	• Color fractional parts	• Workbook pages 25.1A and 25.1B

Warm-up: Counting, Memory Work, and Review

- Place 10 flats on the table. Have your child count them by 100s.
- **How many inches equal 1 foot?** *12.* **How many feet equal 1 yard?** *3.* **How many inches equal 1 yard?** *36.*
- Play Subtraction Race (-8 Version). See Lesson 9.4 (page 154) for directions.

Activity: Make Fraction Bars for Halves, Fourths, and Thirds

This week, you'll learn about fractions. A fraction is a number that represents part of a whole. Today, we'll make Fraction Bars to model fractions with halves, thirds, and fourths.

When we divide something into 2 equal pieces, the parts are called *halves*. How do you use halves in real life? *Sample answers: I cut my sandwich in half. My basketball games have a halftime in the middle. My favorite show is half an hour long. I'm 7 and a half!*

Show your child the Fraction Bars from Blackline Master 9, cut apart on the solid lines. **This week, we'll pretend each of these paper strips is a granola bar. We'll cut them up to show fractional parts.**

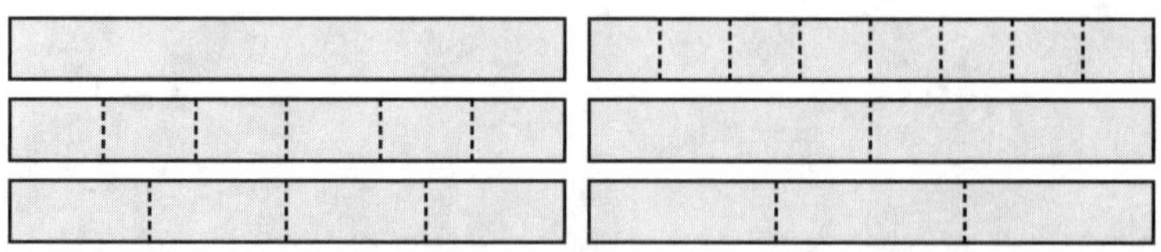

We'll pretend that one whole strip is a whole granola bar. Write "whole" on the paper strip with no dotted lines. Have your child lightly color the strip red with a crayon or colored pencil.

Coloring the Fraction Bars makes it easier to sort them and use them in this week's lesson activities. Your child does not need to color the bars perfectly. If you're short on time, she can even just draw a red line across the middle of the bar.

Which strip has a dotted line that splits it in half? *Child points to strip shown below.* **Let's pretend we want to share this granola bar.** Have your child cut the strip on the dotted line. Write "half" on each piece and have your child lightly color the pieces orange.

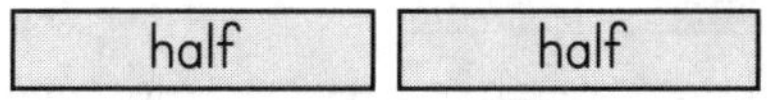

When we cut something into 4 equal pieces, the parts are called *fourths*. Fourths can also be called *quarters*. How do you use fourths or quarters in real life? *Sample answers: We use a one-fourth measuring cup when we bake. My soccer games are divided into 4 quarters. I have 6 quarters in my piggy bank.*

Which strip has dotted lines that split it into fourths? *Child points to strip shown below.* **Let's pretend 4 people want to equally split this granola bar.** Have your child cut the strip on the dotted lines. Write "fourth" on each piece and have your child lightly color the pieces green.

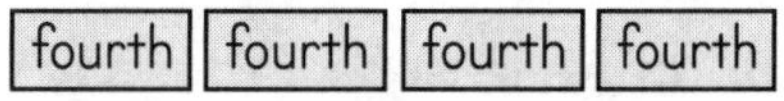

Let's pretend 3 people want to share a granola bar. When we cut something into 3 equal pieces, the parts are called *thirds*. Can you find the paper strip with dotted lines that split it into thirds? Child points to strip shown below. Have your child cut the strip on the dotted lines. Write "third" on each piece and have your child lightly color the pieces yellow.

Set aside the other two Fraction Bars. You will use them in Lesson 25.4.

Activity: Compare Fractions Orally

The purpose of this activity is to help your child concretely understand what fractional amounts like "two-thirds" or "one-fourth" mean. Focus on helping her connect the oral names to the Fraction Bars. She will learn how to write fractions in Lesson 25.2, and she will learn more about comparing fractions in Lesson 25.4.

Organize the Fraction Bars as shown.

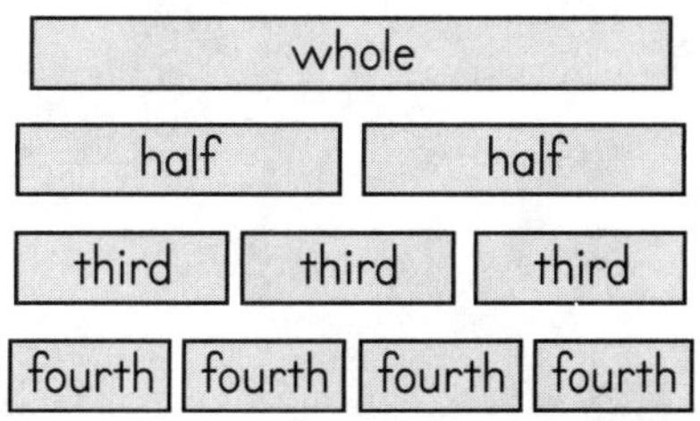

Organizing the Fraction Bars makes it easier to find the pieces as you discuss them.

Ask your child the following questions about the Fraction Bars. Use the Fraction Bars to model each question.

- **Which is more: 1 third of a granola bar or 1 fourth of a granola bar?** *1 third.*

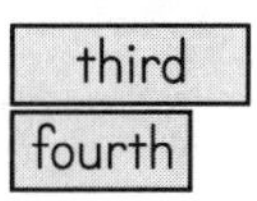

- **Which is less: 1 third of a granola bar or 2 thirds of a granola bar?** *1 third.*

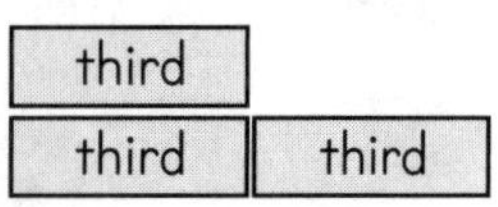

- **Which is more: 1 third of a granola bar or 2 fourths of a granola bar?** *2 fourths.*

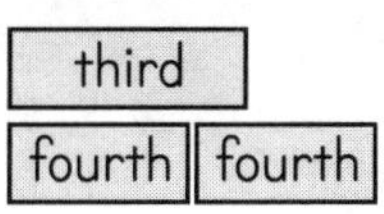

- **Which is less: 1 half of a granola bar or 2 fourths of a granola bar?** *They're equal.*

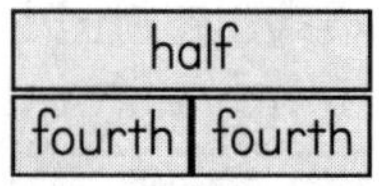

- **Which is more: 3 fourths of a granola bar or 1 whole granola bar?** *1 whole.*

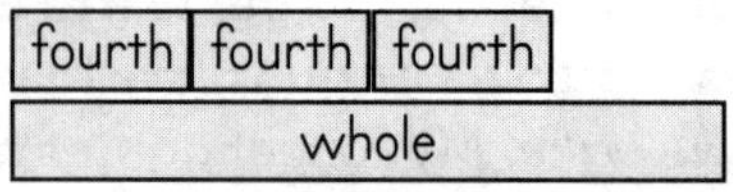

- **Which is less: 3 thirds of a granola bar or 1 whole granola bar?** *They're equal.*

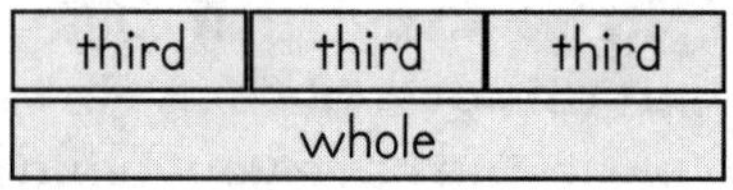

Save these Fraction Bars for future lessons. (You may want to put them in an envelope or zip-top bag for safekeeping.)

Workbook: Color Fractional Parts and Review

Have your child complete workbook pages 25.1A and 25.1B.

Lesson 25.2
Read and Write Fractions

	Purpose	Materials
Warm-up	• Count by 4s on the dot array • Practice memory work • Review finding half	• Dot array and L-cover (Blackline Master 6)
Activities	• Read and write fractions with halves, thirds, or fourths • Identify the fractional amount shaded in a variety of shapes	• Fraction Bars (from Lesson 25.1) • 9 blank index cards or slips of paper • Fraction Bump game board (from workbook page 25.2A) • Counters • Die
Workbook	• Read and write fractions with halves, thirds, or fourths	• Workbook page 25.2B

Warm-up: Counting, Memory Work, and Review

- Slide the L-cover on the dot array to reveal 4 dots at a time. Have your child count by 4s to tell how many dots are visible in each array. Continue to 40.
- **How many centimeters equal 1 meter?** *100.*
- Have your child find half of the following numbers.
  - **What's half of 4?** *2.*
  - **What's half of 40?** *20.*
  - **What's half of 6?** *3.*
  - **What's half of 60?** *30.*
  - **What's half of 8?** *4.*
  - **What's half of 80?** *40.*

Activity: Write Fractions for Halves, Thirds, and Fourths

In the last lesson, we modeled halves, thirds, and fourths with Fraction Bars. Today, you'll learn how to write fractions. A fraction is a number that represents part of a whole. Organize the Fraction Bars as shown.

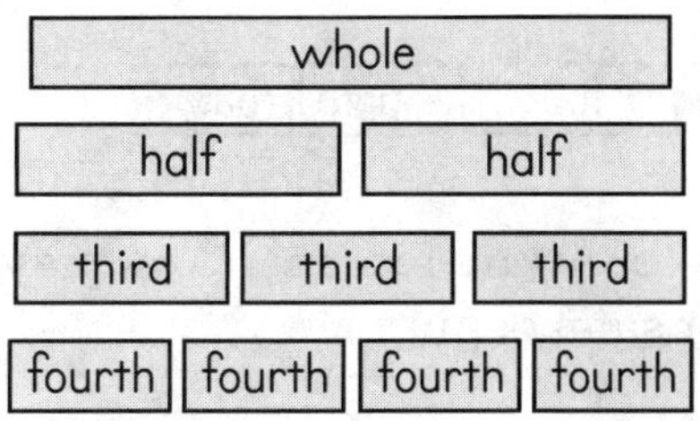

May I have 3 fourths please? *Child gives you 3 fourths.* Write 3/4 on an index card, with a horizontal line between the 3 and 4. **Here's how we write three-fourths.** Point to the 3 as you say "three" and the 4 as you say "fourths."

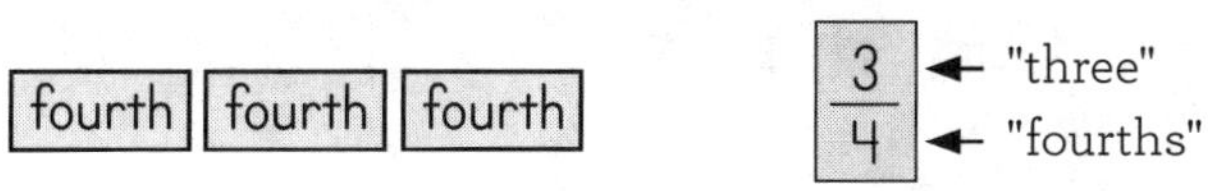

Always write fractions with a horizontal line (and not a diagonal one) so your child can easily see which number is on the top and which number is on the bottom.

The top number tells how many parts we have. We have 3 parts. The bottom number tells what kind of parts we have. The 4 means that we split the whole into 4 parts, or fourths.

| fourth | fourth | fourth |

$\frac{3}{4}$ — 3 ← Number of fractional parts; 4 ← Type of fractional part

See the Week 25 **Teaching Math with Confidence** for more on this definition of fractions. In future grades, your child will learn that the top number is called the numerator, and the bottom number is called the denominator.

May I have 1 third please? *Child gives you 1 third.* Draw a horizontal line on a new index card. **How many parts do I have?** *1.* Write 1 above the line. **What kind of parts do I have?** *Thirds.* Write 3 below the fraction bar. **So, this is how we write one-third.**

| third | → $\frac{1}{3}$

May I have 2 halves please? *Child gives you 2 halves.* Draw a horizontal line on a new index card. **How many parts do I have?** *2.* Write 2 above the line. **What kind of parts do I have?** *Halves.* Write 2 below the line. **We split the whole into 2 parts, or halves.**

| half | half | → $\frac{2}{2}$

Have your child help you make Fraction Cards for the following fractional amounts.

| half | → $\frac{1}{2}$

| third | third | → $\frac{2}{3}$

| third | third | third | → $\frac{3}{3}$

| fourth | → $\frac{1}{4}$

| fourth | fourth | → $\frac{2}{4}$

| fourth | fourth | fourth | fourth | → $\frac{4}{4}$

Save these Fraction Cards for future lessons. (You may want to put them in an envelope or zip-top bag for safekeeping.)

Activity: Play Fraction Bump

Play Fraction Bump.

This game gives your child practice at identifying fractional parts in a variety of shapes. Encourage your child to think about how many parts are shaded and what kind of parts they are as he identifies the fractions. For example: **How many parts are colored in?** *2.* **What kind of parts are they?** *Thirds.* **So, look for the fraction with a 2 on top and 3 on the bottom.**

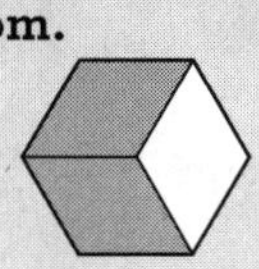

Fraction Bump

Materials: Fraction Bump game board (from workbook page 25.2A); 10 counters per player, with a different color for each player; die

Object of the Game: Place the most counters in the boxes in the middle of the game board.

Have each player choose a different-colored counter to use as a game token and place it on one of the Start squares.

On your turn, roll the die and advance your token the corresponding number of squares clockwise around the path. Name the fraction that matches the picture on the square you landed on. Cover the matching fraction in the middle of the game board with one of your counters.

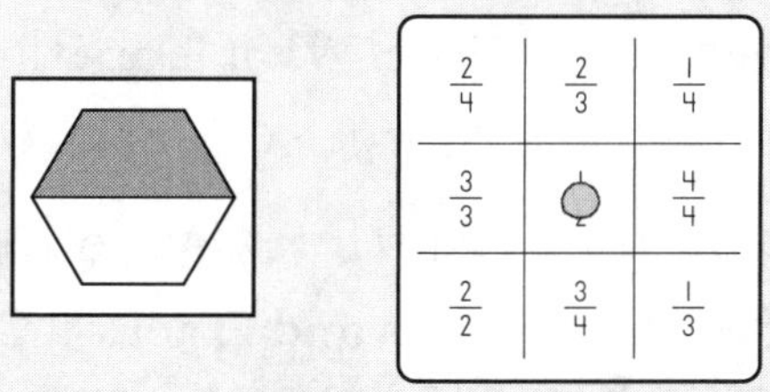

If you land on this shape, put a counter on the box labeled 1/2.

If your opponent already has a counter on the matching fraction, "bump" his counter off the game board and replace it with one of your counters.

Play then passes to the other player. Continue until there is a counter on every large fraction in the middle of the game board. The player with the most counters on the game board wins.

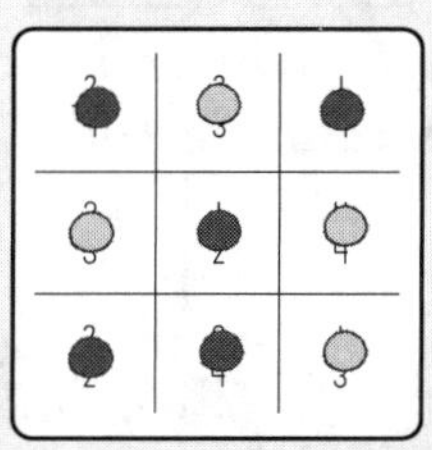

Sample final game board. The player with black counters wins, because he has more counters on the game board.

Workbook: Read and Write Fractions and Review

Have your child complete workbook pages 25.2A and 25.2B.

Lesson 25.3
Sixths and Eighths

	Purpose	Materials
Warm-up	• Count by 10s from 200 to 300 • Practice memory work • Review reading fractions	• Base-ten blocks • Fraction Bump game board (from workbook page 25.2A) • Counters • Die
Activities	• Write fractions with sixths and eighths • Find pairs of fractions that make one whole	• Fraction Bars for sixths and eighths (from Blackline Master 9), cut apart on the solid lines • Crayons or colored pencils • Scissors • 14 blank index cards or slips of paper
Workbook	• Write fractions	• Workbook pages 25.3A and 25.3B

Warm-up: Counting, Memory Work, and Review

- **Count with me by 10s starting at 200. We'll model the numbers with base-ten blocks as we count: 210, 220, 230...** Add a rod as you say each new number, and continue until you reach 300. When you reach 300, trade the 10 rods for 1 flat.
- **What is another name for 12 p.m.?** *Noon.* **What is another name for 12 a.m.?** *Midnight.*
- Play Fraction Bump. See Lesson 25.2 (page 403) for directions.

Activity: Make Fraction Bars and Fraction Cards for Sixths and Eighths

In the last two lessons, we made Fraction Bars and Fraction Cards for halves, thirds, and fourths. Today, we'll make Fraction Bars and Fraction Cards for sixths and eighths. Place the two remaining Fraction Bars left to cut apart on the table.

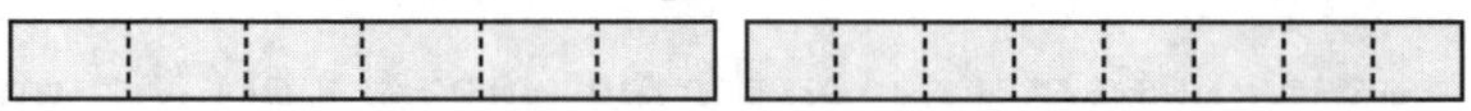

Let's pretend 6 people want to share a granola bar. When we cut something into 6 equal pieces, the parts are called *sixths*. Have your child cut the matching strip apart on the dotted lines. Write "sixth" on each piece and have your child lightly color the pieces blue.

sixth | sixth | sixth | sixth | sixth | sixth

Here's how we write one-sixth. Write 1/6 on an index card. **What does the top number tell?** *How many parts.* **What does the bottom number tell?** *What kind of parts.*

sixth $\frac{1}{6}$ ← "one" ← "sixth"

Help your child make Fraction Cards for 2/6, 3/6, 4/6, 5/6, and 6/6.

$\frac{2}{6}$ $\frac{3}{6}$ $\frac{4}{6}$ $\frac{5}{6}$ $\frac{6}{6}$

Let's pretend 8 people want to share a granola bar. When we cut something into 8 equal pieces, the parts are called *eighths*. Have your child cut the matching strip apart on the dotted lines. Write "eighth" on each piece and have your child lightly color the pieces purple.

Help your child make Fraction Cards for 1/8, 2/8, 3/8, 4/8, 5/8, 6/8, 7/8, and 8/8.

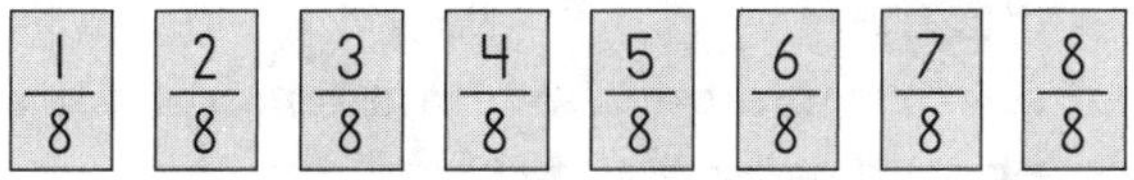

Activity: Identify Pairs of Fractions That Equal One Whole

Organize the Fraction Bars and Fraction Cards for sixths as shown. **How many sixths equal the whole granola bar?** *6.*

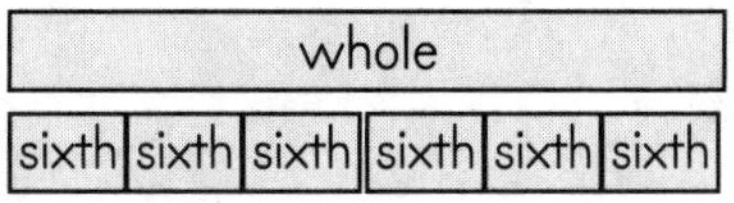

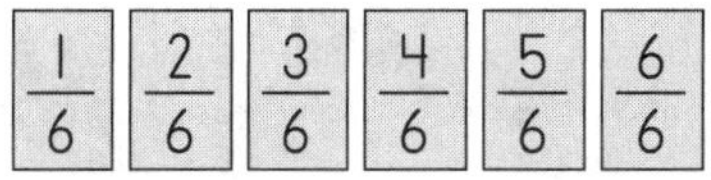

Let's pretend we both want some of this granola bar that's cut into sixths. Let's pretend I eat two-sixths of it. Separate the sixths into a group of 2 and a group of 4. Place the Fraction Card with 2/6 below the Fraction Bars. **What fraction of the granola bar is left for you to eat?** *Four-sixths.* Have your child place the matching Fraction Card below the Fraction Bars.

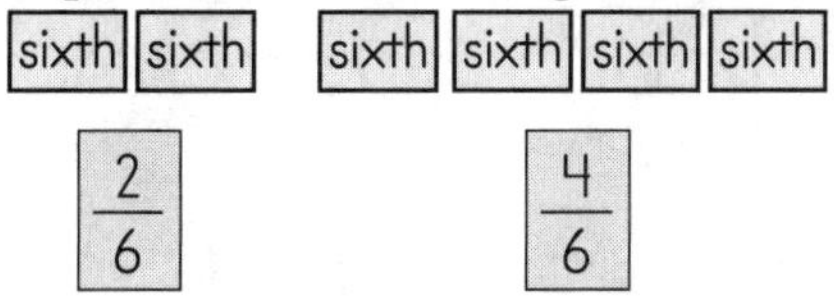

If I eat five-sixths of the granola bar, how much is left for you? *One-sixth.* Arrange the Fraction Bars and Cards to match.

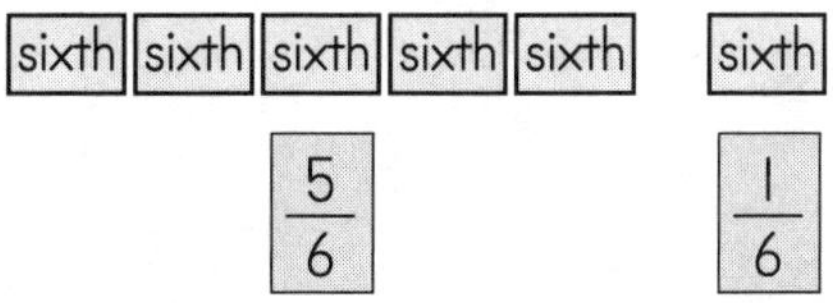

If I eat three-sixths of the granola bar, how much is left for you? *Three-sixths.* **We'd both get the same amount!** Have your child find the Fraction Card with 3/6 and place it next to the Fraction Bars (since you only have one 3/6 card).

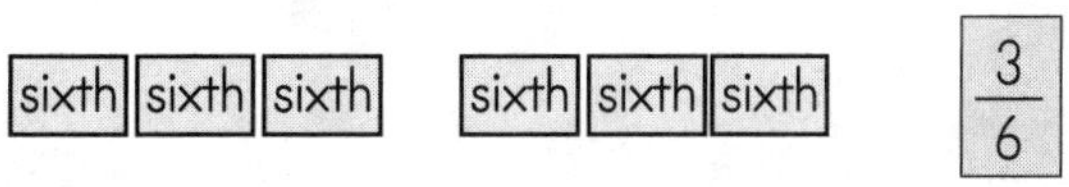

Organize the Fraction Bars and Fraction Cards for eighths as shown. **How many eighths equal the whole granola bar?** *8.*

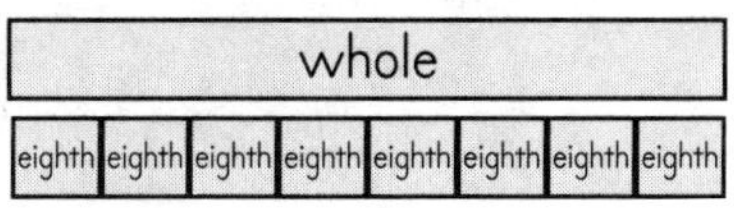

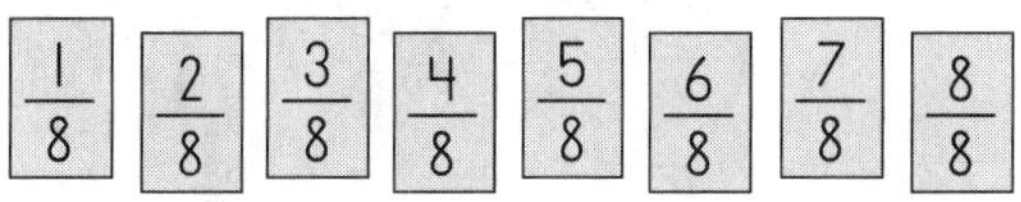

Use the Fraction Bars and Fraction Cards to model the following questions:

- **If I eat one-eighth of the granola bar, how much is left for you?** *Seven-eighths.*

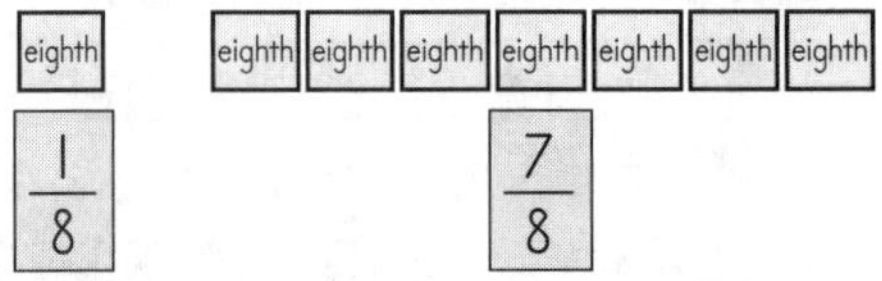

- **If I eat six-eighths of the granola bar, how much is left for you?** *Two-eighths.*

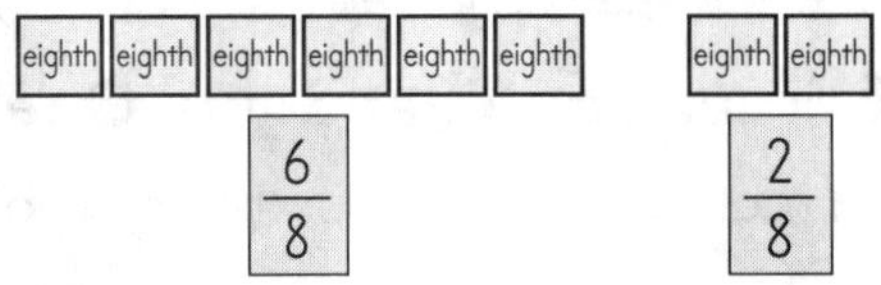

- **If I eat five-eighths of the granola bar, how much is left for you?** *Three-eighths.*

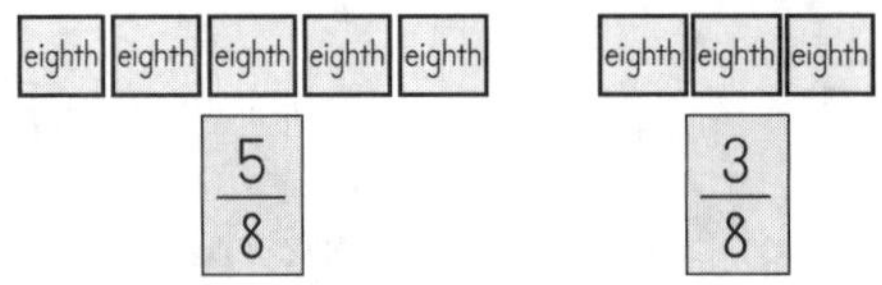

- **If we share the granola bar equally, how many eighths do each of us get?** *Four-eighths.*

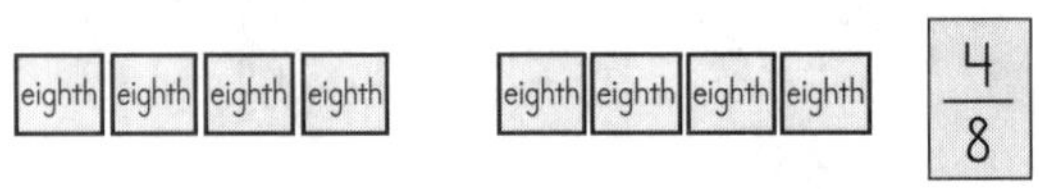

Save the new Fraction Bars and Cards for future lessons.

Workbook: Find Pairs of Fractions That Equal One Whole and Review

Have your child complete workbook pages 25.3A and 25.3B.

Lesson 25.4
Compare Fractions

	Purpose	Materials
Warm-up	• Count by 4s • Practice memory work • Review reading inequalities	• Counters
Activities	• Compare fractions with hands-on materials	• Fraction Bars (Blackline Master 9), cut apart and labeled • Fraction Cards (from Lesson 25.2 and 25.3)
Workbook	• Color pictures to compare fractions	• Workbook pages 25.4A and 25.4B

Warm-up: Counting, Memory Work, and Review

- Arrange 8 groups of 4 counters on the table. Have your child count by 4s to find the total number of counters: *4, 8, 12, 16, 20, 24, 28, 32.* If he has trouble, encourage him to add 4 to the previous number.

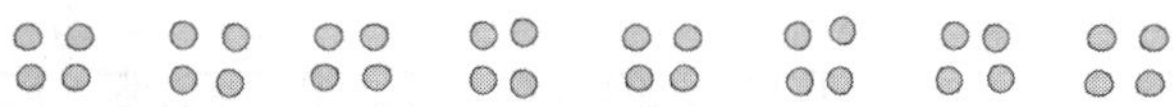

- **How many minutes equal a half-hour?** *30.*
  How many minutes equal a quarter-hour? *15.*
- Write the following inequalities on a piece of paper and have your child read them. Also have your child make up a few inequalities and practice reading and writing them.
  - 38 = 38. *38 equals 38.*
  - 90 < 109. *90 is less than 109.*
  - 200 > 20. *200 is greater than 20.*

Activity: Compare Fractions

In the last lesson, you learned about sixths and eighths. Today, you'll learn how to compare fractions. Organize the Fraction Bars as shown.

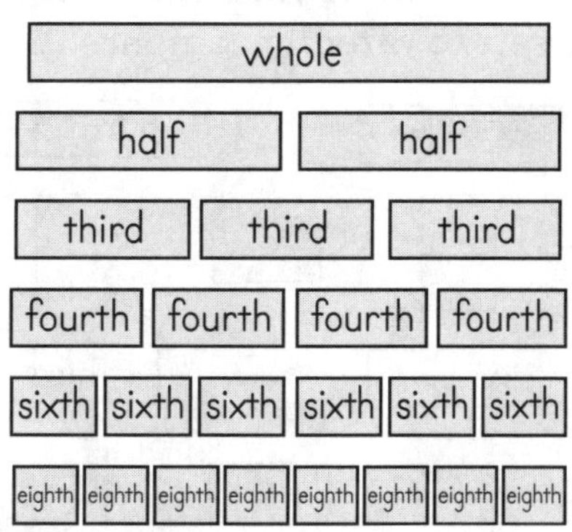

We can compare fractions just like we compare whole numbers. What are the 3 signs we use to compare numbers? *The greater-than sign, the less-than sign, and the equals sign.* Have your child write each sign on a slip of paper.

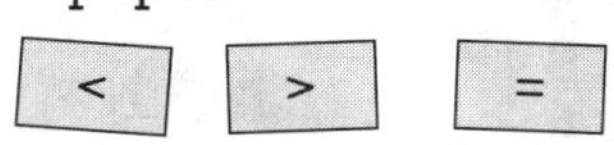

Place the 1/2 and 1/4 Fraction Cards on the table. Have your child place the corresponding Fraction Bar above each card.

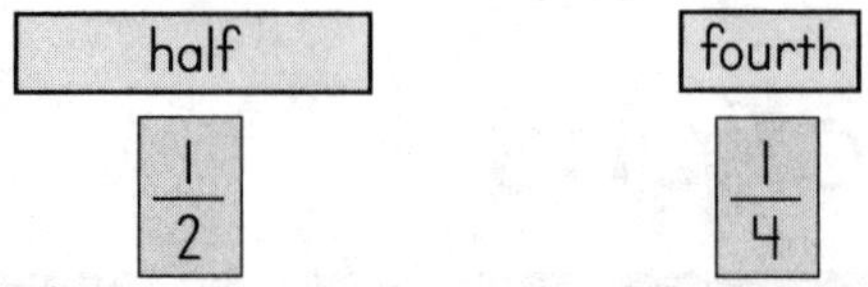

Which is more: one-half of a granola bar or one-fourth of a granola bar? *One-half.* **So, one-half is greater than one-fourth.** Have your child place the > sign between the Fraction Cards.

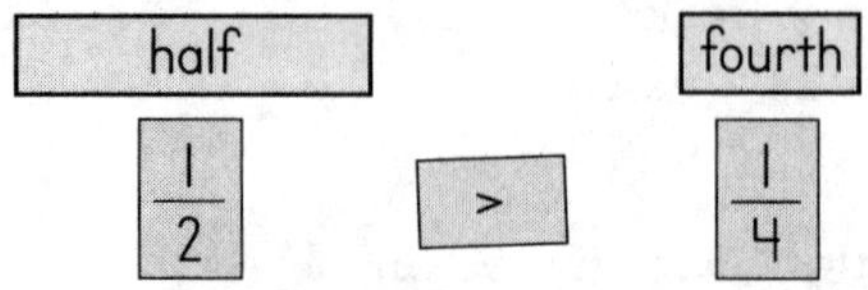

If your child isn't sure, have him line up the Fraction Bars to see that one-half is greater than one-fourth.

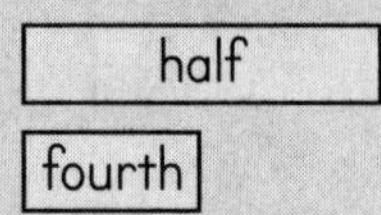

Place the 2/8 and 5/8 Fraction Cards on the table. Have your child place the corresponding Fraction Bars above each card. **Which is more: two-eighths of a granola bar or five-eighths of a granola bar?** *Five-eighths.* **So, two-eighths is less than five-eighths.** Have your child place the < sign between the Fraction Cards.

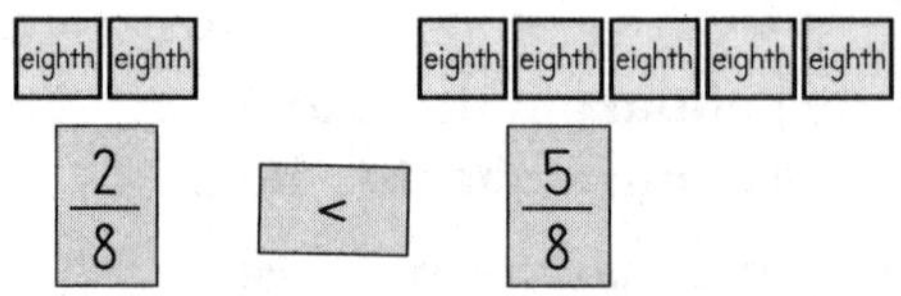

Place the 1/2 and 2/4 Fraction Cards on the table. Have your child place the corresponding Fraction Bars above each card. **Which is more: one-half of a granola bar or two-fourths of a granola bar?** *They're the same!* Encourage your child to line up the Fraction Bars to verify that one-half equals two-fourths. Have your child place the = sign between the Fraction Cards.

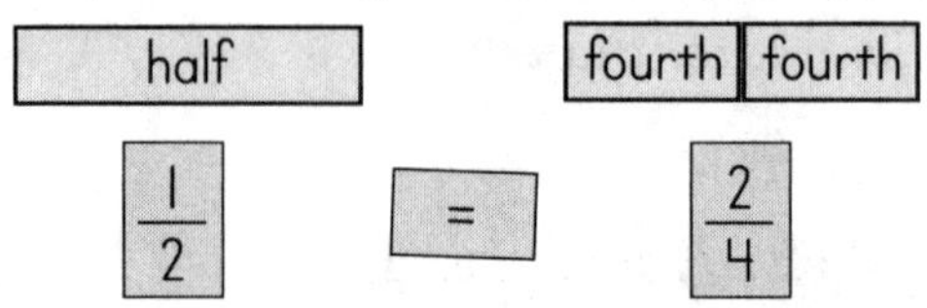

Repeat with the following pairs of fractions. If your child isn't sure which fraction is greater, have him line up the Fraction Bar sets to directly compare their lengths.

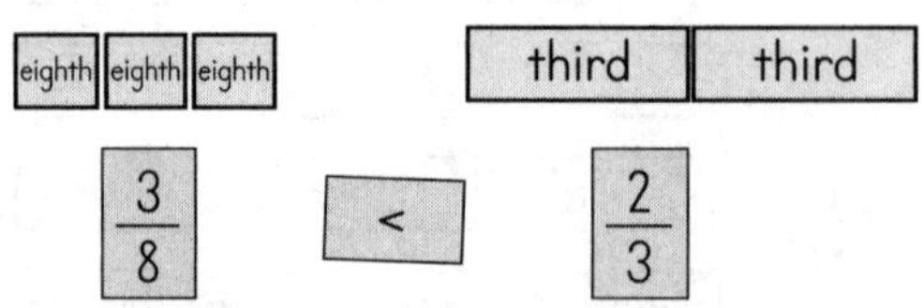

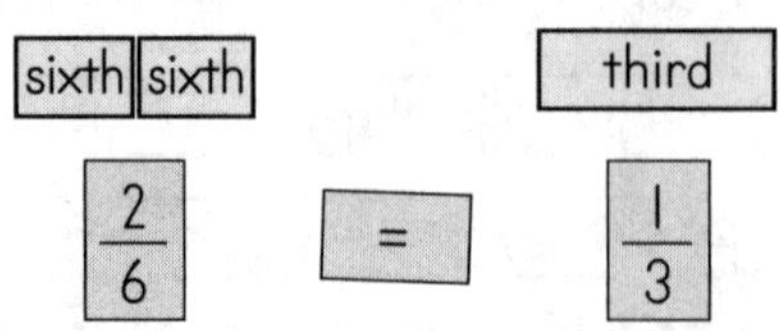

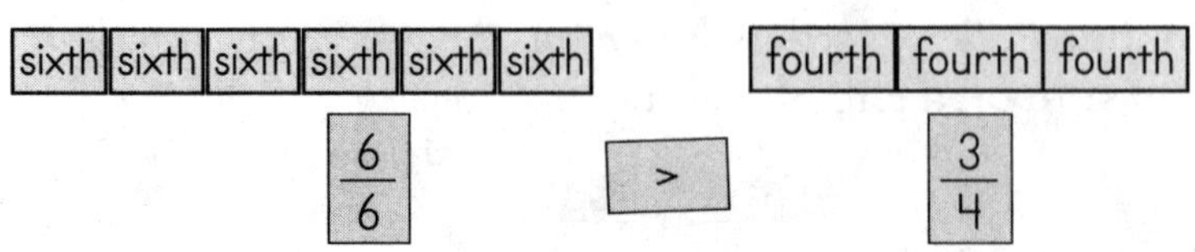

Activity: Play Fraction War

Play Fraction War.

Fraction War

Materials: Fraction Cards; Fraction Bars

Object of the Game: Win the most cards.

Shuffle the Fraction Cards and deal the cards face down in two equal piles. Set aside the one leftover card.

Both players flip over their top card and model the fraction on the card with Fraction Bars. Whoever has the greater fraction wins both cards.

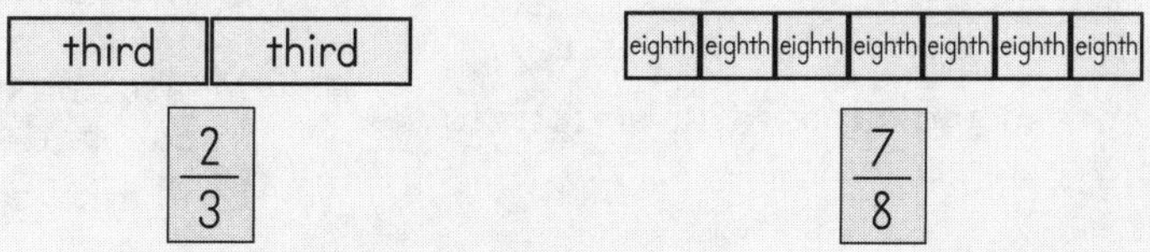

Sample play. The player with 7/8 wins, since 7/8 is greater than 2/3.

If the fractions are equal, leave the cards face-up on the table and have both players flip over their next card. Whoever has the greater fraction wins all the face-up cards.

Play until the piles run out. Whoever has won more cards wins the game.

Workbook: Compare Fractions and Review

Have your child complete workbook pages 25.4A and 25.4B.

Lesson 25.5
Enrichment and Review (Optional)

	Purpose	Materials
Warm-up	• Count by 3s and 4s • Review memory work • Review your child's favorite or most challenging activities from Week 25	• Varies, depending on the activities you choose
Picture Book	• Understand fractions in many real-life contexts	• *If You Were a Fraction,* written by Trisha Speed Shaskan and illustrated by Francesca Carabelli
Enrichment Activity	• Use measuring cups with fractions to measure ingredients	• Measuring cups (1/4-cup, 1/3-cup, ½-cup, and 1-cup) • Trail mix ingredients

Warm-up: Counting, Memory Work, and Review

- Have your child count by 3s to 30 and by 4s to 40.
- Quiz your child on the memory work through Week 24. See page 523 for the full list.
- If you have time, repeat one or two of the activities from this week's lessons. Choose activities your child especially enjoyed or found challenging.

Math Picture Book: *If You Were a Fraction*

Read *If You Were a Fraction,* written by Trisha Speed Shaskan and illustrated by Francesca Carabelli. As you read, point out the written fractions and discuss how the fractions match the illustrations.

Enrichment Activity: Make Fraction Trail Mix

Show your child a set of measuring cups. Have him read the fraction printed on each cup.

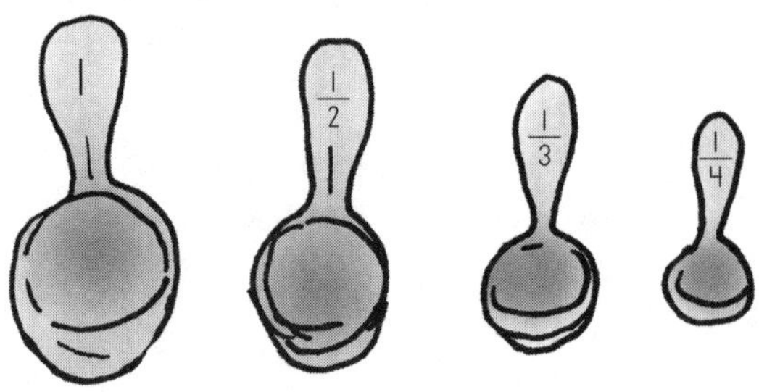

How many halves make 1 whole? *2.* **So, 2 half-cups equal 1 whole cup.** Have your child pour 2 half-cups of water into the 1 cup measure to check that this is true. Repeat with 3 third-cups and 4 fourth-cups.

Then, help your child use the measuring cups to make the following trail mix recipe. For ⅔ and ¾, encourage her to think about how to use the ⅓ cup and ¼ cup to measure out the correct amounts. For example: **The recipe says that we need two-thirds of a cup of small crackers, but we don't have a ⅔ cup measure. How could we use the ⅓ cup to help?** *We can use the ⅓ cup twice!*

Fraction Trail Mix Recipe

Mix together in a large bowl:

- ¼ cup of something sweet, like chocolate chips or mini marshmallows
- ⅓ cup of dried fruit
- ½ cup of nuts
- ⅔ cup of small crackers
- ¾ cup of small pretzels
- 1 cup of cereal pieces

Feel free to modify the recipe to match the ingredients you have on hand.

Week 25 Answer Key

25.1A

Draw lines to cut each cake to match the label.

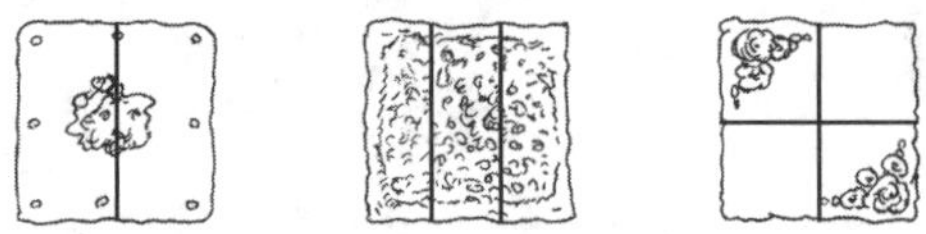

Halves | Thirds | Fourths

Sample answers. Many answers are possible.

Follow the directions to color the shapes in each row.

Color 1 half.

Color 1 third.

Color 3 fourths.

Color 4 fourths.

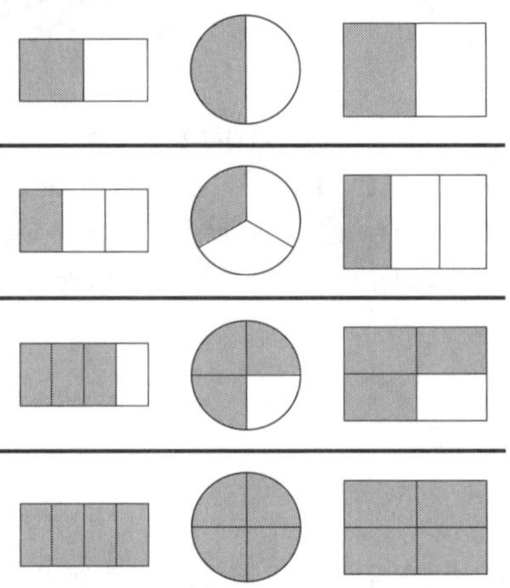

Sample answers. Many answers are possible.

25.1B

Complete.

66	24	39	26
+ 77	+ 52	+ 45	+ 83
143	76	84	109

Complete the missing numbers in the sequence.

Count by 3s: 3, 6, 9, 12, 15, 18

Count by 10s: 83, 93, 103, 113, 123, 133

Count by 5s: 155, 160, 165, 170, 175, 180

Match each shape to its name.

Quadrilateral | Hexagon | Octagon | Pentagon

25.2A

See Instructor Guide for directions.
Save this game board for future lessons.

Fraction Bump

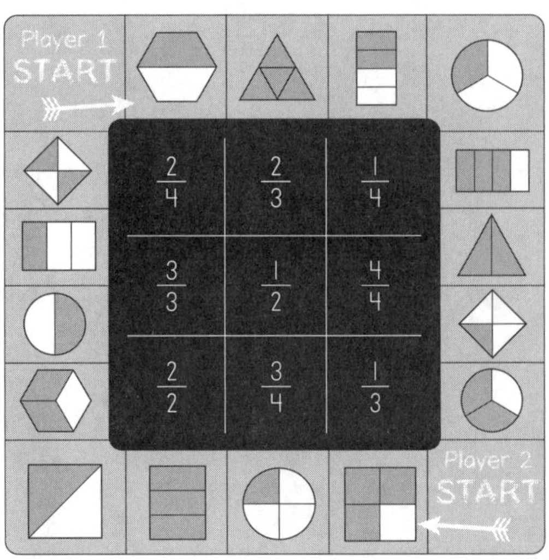

25.2B

How much pizza is left? Match.

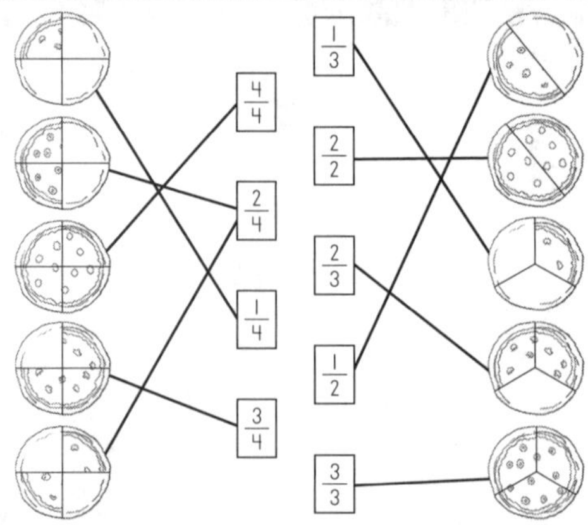

Complete.

11 - 2 = 9	13 - 9 = 4	15 - 6 = 9
16 - 8 = 8	12 - 4 = 8	14 - 9 = 5
17 - 8 = 9	13 - 6 = 7	18 - 9 = 9
14 - 5 = 9	15 - 8 = 7	11 - 6 = 5

Week 25 Answer Key

25.3A

Write a fraction for the purple part of each shape.

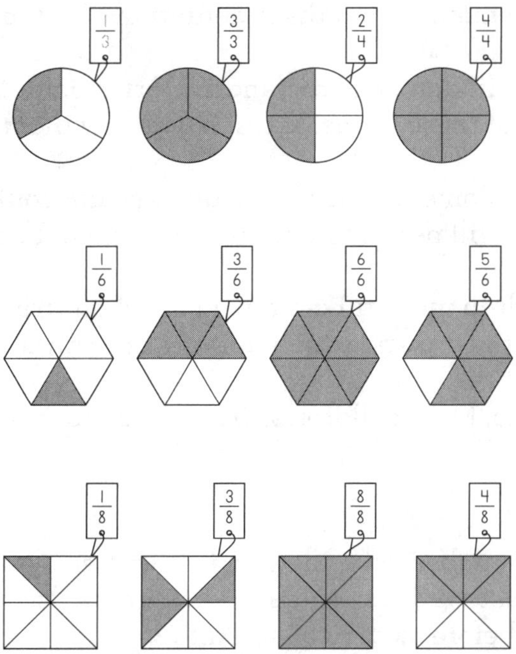

25.3B

Complete.

86 + 4 = 90 | 68 + 34 = 102 | 60 + 80 = 140 | 95 + 65 = 160

Emma made a pictograph about her stuffed animals. Use the pictograph to complete the chart.

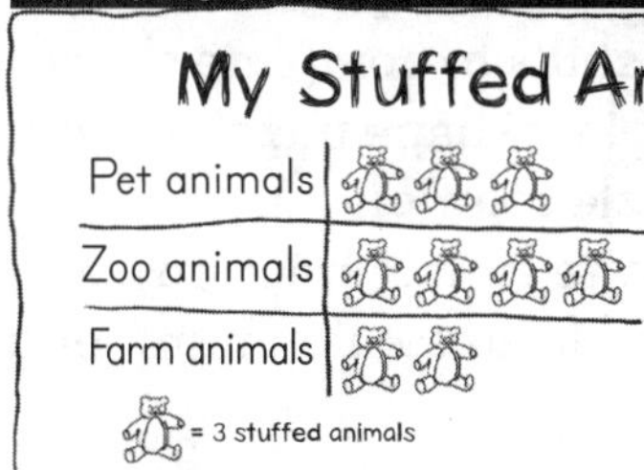

Type of Animal	Number
Pet	9
Zoo	12
Farm	6

Complete.

12 - 3 = 9 | 10 - 9 = 1 | 13 - 8 = 5

12 - 6 = 6 | 13 - 5 = 8 | 16 - 9 = 7

11 - 8 = 3 | 14 - 6 = 8 | 10 - 5 = 5

25.4A

Color the shapes to match the fractions. Then, complete each circle with <, >, or =.

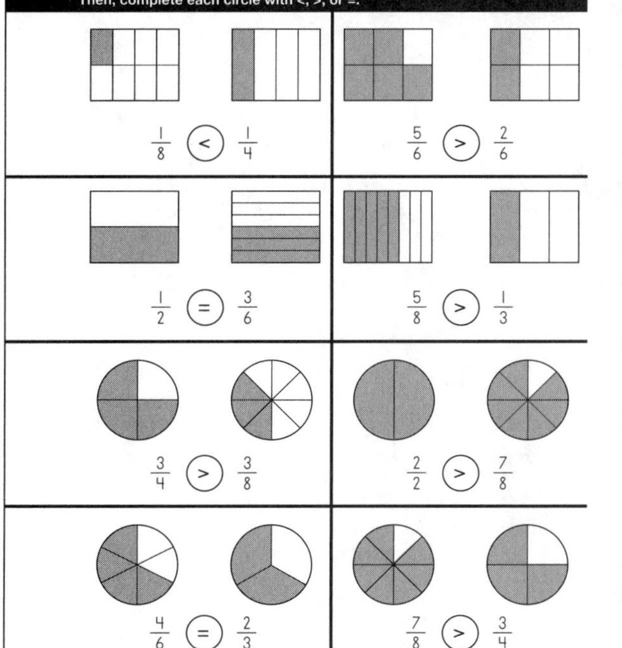

Sample answers. Other ways to color shapes are possible.

25.4B

Complete.

55 + 9 = 64 | 62 + 37 = 99 | 59 + 74 = 133 | 56 + 81 = 137

Complete.

12 - 5 = 7 | 15 - 9 = 6 | 12 - 8 = 4

14 - 7 = 7 | 11 - 4 = 7 | 17 - 8 = 9

12 - 9 = 3 | 16 - 7 = 9 | 13 - 5 = 8

Match each shape to its name.

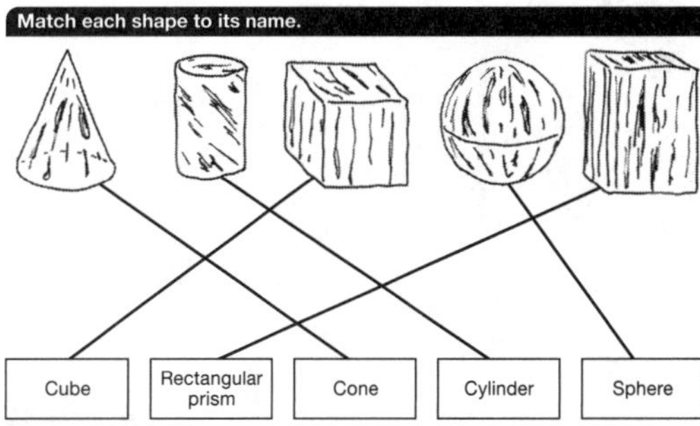

Unit 11 Checkpoint

What to Expect at the End of Unit 11

By the end of Unit 11, most children will be able to do the following:

- Name, describe, and draw triangles, quadrilaterals, pentagons, hexagons, and octagons. Many children will still be working on memorizing these definitions. Your child will practice them in the memory work in Week 26.
- Name and describe spheres, cones, cubes, cylinders, and rectangular prisms. It's fine if your child has not already memorized all of these terms, and she'll review them in the review workbook pages.
- Use spatial skills to complete shape puzzles. Some will be able to quickly and confidently complete shape puzzles, while others will need more time to experiment before finding puzzle solutions.
- Read and write simple fractions. Some children may still get mixed up when writing fractions and forget which number goes on the top and which number goes on the bottom.
- Use hands-on materials to compare fractions. Most children will still need to model each fraction before comparing.

Is Your Child Ready to Move on?

In Unit 12, your child will learn to subtract two-digit numbers with the standard written algorithm. She will continue to build on the subtraction facts and his mental subtraction skills, but she does not need to master any other specific skills before moving on to Unit 12.

Unit 12
Written Subtraction to 200

Overview

Your child will learn the standard algorithm for written vertical subtraction. (You may know this process as "borrowing the 1" or "stack math.") You'll use the same approach that you used to teach him the addition algorithm in Unit 10. First, you'll use base-ten blocks to help your child develop conceptual understanding of the process. Then, he'll solve problems without base-ten blocks so he builds fluency.

$$\begin{array}{r} {\scriptstyle 5\ 15} \\ 1\cancel{6}\cancel{5} \\ -\ 38 \\ \hline 127 \end{array}$$

In Unit 14, he'll then learn how to apply the subtraction algorithm to three-digit numbers.

Week 26	Understand the Steps in Written Subtraction
Week 27	Build Fluency with Written Subtraction

What Your Child Will Learn

In this unit your child will learn to:

- Understand the steps in the written subtraction algorithm and model them with base-ten blocks
- Fluently subtract two-digit numbers from numbers up to 200

Recommended Math Picture Books (Optional)

These picture books are scheduled in the optional Enrichment and Review lessons at the end of each week.

- *Shark Swimathon,* written by Stuart J. Murphy and illustrated by Lynne Cravath. HarperCollins, 2001.
- *Infinity and Me,* written by Kate Hosford and illustrated by Gabi Swiatkowska. Carolrhoda Books, 2012.

Week 26
Understand the Steps in Written Subtraction

Overview

Your child will learn how to use the subtraction algorithm to subtract two-digit numbers from the numbers to 200. He'll solve a mix of problems, including problems that do not involve trading and problems that do.

As in Unit 10, you'll first use base-ten blocks to help your child develop a thorough conceptual understanding of this process. Next week, you'll focus on helping him develop greater fluency and automaticity.

Lesson 26.1	Demonstrate Two-Digit Written Subtraction
Lesson 26.2	Subtract Two-Digit Numbers with Base-Ten Blocks
Lesson 26.3	Trade Once to Subtract Two-Digit Numbers from Numbers Greater Than 100
Lesson 26.4	Trade Twice to Subtract Two-Digit Numbers from Numbers Greater Than 100
Lesson 26.5	Enrichment and Review (Optional)

Teaching Math with Confidence: Developing Conceptual Understanding of the Written Subtraction Algorithm

In this unit, your child will learn the step-by-step process for subtracting multi-digit numbers. This unit's structure and flow is very similar to Unit 10, where you taught your child the multi-digit addition algorithm. Just as in that unit, you'll first help your child understand the steps in the algorithm. Then, you'll provide plenty of practice so that he becomes fluent and automatic at carrying out the steps.

If you're like most adults, you probably learned to "borrow" a ten from the tens-place and record your work with a teeny 1 squished between the tens-place and ones-place.

$$\begin{array}{r} {\scriptstyle 6} \\ \not{7}{\scriptstyle 1}2 \\ -\ 45 \\ \hline 27 \end{array}$$

Traditional method. "I borrowed a ten."

Children often feel confused by this use of the word "borrow." They know that if you "borrow" something, you should return it—and the tens-place never seems to get its ten back! They also find it hard to remember what the small 1 means when it's crunched between the ones-place and tens-place.

Math with Confidence uses two specific wording and record-keeping techniques to help your child learn the subtraction algorithm more easily. First, you'll use the word "trading" instead of "borrowing." You and your child have been "trading" 1 ten for 10 ones all year long, so this language will reassure him that the subtraction algorithm is simply an extension of what he already knows.

Second, you'll cross out the digit in the ones-place and write the new number of ones above the crossed-out digit (instead of squishing that teeny 1 between the ones-place and tens-place). That way, it's clear how many ones are in the ones-place.

$$\begin{array}{r} {\scriptstyle 6\ 12} \\ \not{7}\not{2} \\ -\ 45 \\ \hline 27 \end{array}$$

Math with Confidence method. "I traded 1 ten for 10 ones."

These may feel like minor details, but they make a huge difference in helping children master the subtraction algorithm.

Extra Materials Needed for Week 26

- Several writing utensils of different lengths
- Paper clip
- For optional Enrichment and Review Lesson:
    - *Shark Swimathon,* written by Stuart J. Murphy and illustrated by Lynne Cravath
    - Children's book with more than 100 pages and fewer than 200 pages

Lesson 26.1
Demonstrate Two-Digit Written Subtraction

	Purpose	Materials
Warm-up	• Count by 10s from 300 to 400 • Practice memory work • Review doubling	• Base-ten blocks
Activities	• Use base-ten blocks to act out the steps in the subtraction algorithm • Demonstrate how to record the steps in the subtraction algorithm	• Workbook page 26.1A • Base-ten blocks • Place-Value Chart (Blackline Master 5)
Workbook	• Review previously-learned material	• Workbook page 26.1B

In this lesson, your child will model subtraction problems with base-ten blocks while you record the written numbers. She'll learn how to record the steps herself in Lesson 26.2.

Warm-up: Counting, Memory Work, and Review

- **Count with me by 10s starting at 300. We'll model the numbers with base-ten blocks as we count: 310, 320, 330...** Add a rod as you say each new number, and continue until you reach 400. When you reach 400, trade the 10 rods for 1 flat.
- **How many sides does a triangle have?** *3.* **A quadrilateral?** *4.* **A pentagon?** *5.* **A hexagon?** *6.* **An octagon?** *8.*
- Have your child double the following numbers. Encourage her to use mental addition to find the answers. For example: 42 plus 42 equals 84.
    - **Double 42.** *84.*
    - **Double 23.** *46.*
    - **Double 35.** *70.*
    - **Double 36.** *72.*
    - **Double 39.** *78.*

Activity: Subtract Two-Digit Numbers at the Chocolate Shop

In Unit 10, you learned how to use the addition algorithm to add two-digit numbers. In this unit, you'll learn how to use the subtraction algorithm to subtract two-digit numbers. Today, we'll pretend again that we work at a chocolate shop. Each unit block is 1 square of chocolate, and each rod is a bar with 10 squares.

Show your child workbook page 26.1A. **One day, we open the shop and start the day with 9 bars and 5 squares of chocolate.** Place 9 rods and 5 units on the Place-Value Chart. **How many total squares of chocolate is that?** *95.*

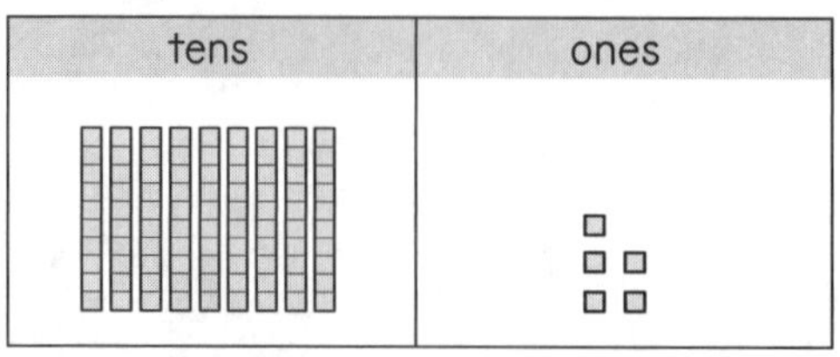

> The steps in the packing directions mimic the standard written subtraction algorithm. She'll learn a more general form of the subtraction algorithm in Lesson 26.2.

Point to the first inventory slip on the page. **Order 1 is for 1 bar and 7 squares. We'll follow the packing directions to pack the order and figure out how much chocolate we have left in the shop.** Point to the "Chocolate Shop Packing Directions" at the top of the page. **What's the first step?** *Check whether you have enough squares for the order.* **Do we have enough loose squares to pack 7 squares in the order?** *No.*

	Bars	Squares
Total	9	5
Order 1	1	7
New Total		

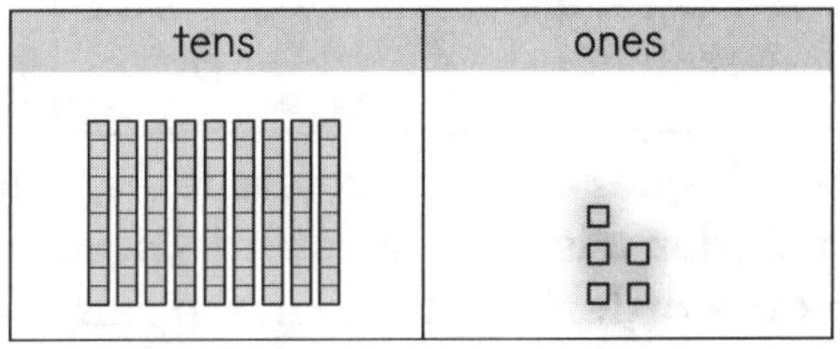

Since there are only 5 loose squares, you do not have enough to pack 7 squares.

What's the next step? *If you don't have enough squares, trade 1 bar for 10 squares.* Have your child trade 1 rod for 10 unit blocks. Place the unit blocks in the ones-column.

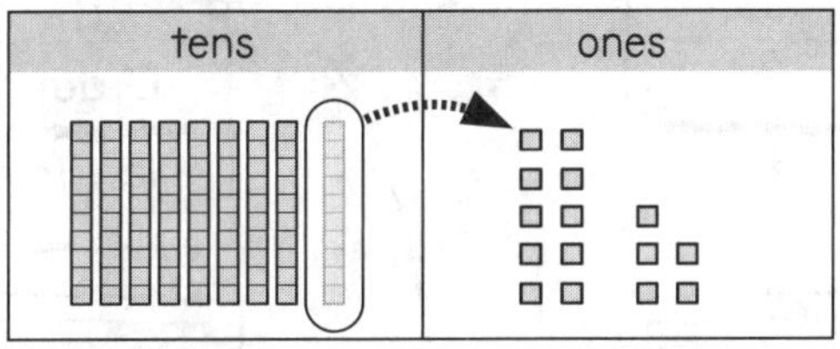

We traded 1 bar, so we have 8 bars now. Cross out the 9 and write 8 above it. **Now we have 15 squares.** Cross out the 5 and write 15 above it.

	Bars	Squares
	8	15
Total	~~9~~	~~5~~
Order 1	1	7
New Total		

What's the next step? *Subtract the squares.* Have your child remove 7 unit blocks from the ones-column. **How many squares are left?** *8.* Write 8 as shown.

	Bars	Squares
	8	15
Total	~~9~~	~~5~~
Order 1	1	7
New Total		8

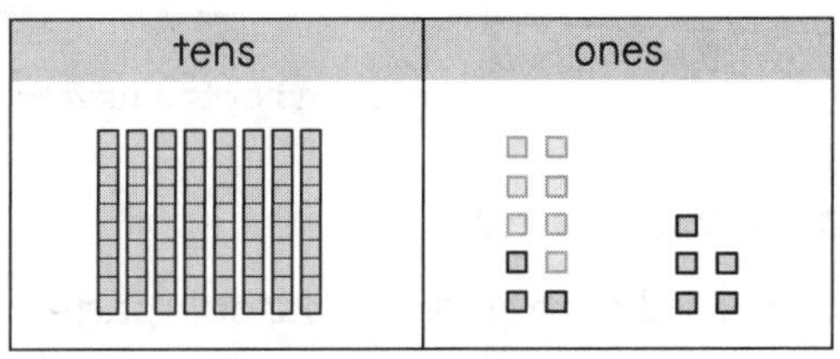

What's the last step? *Subtract the bars.* Have your child remove 1 rod from the tens-column. **How many bars are left?** *7.* Write 7 as shown. Have your child pretend to put the 1 rod and 7 squares in a box and mail it to a pretend customer. **How many squares of chocolate are left at our shop?** *78.*

	Bars	Squares
	8	15
Total	~~9~~	~~5~~
Order 1	1	7
New Total	7	8

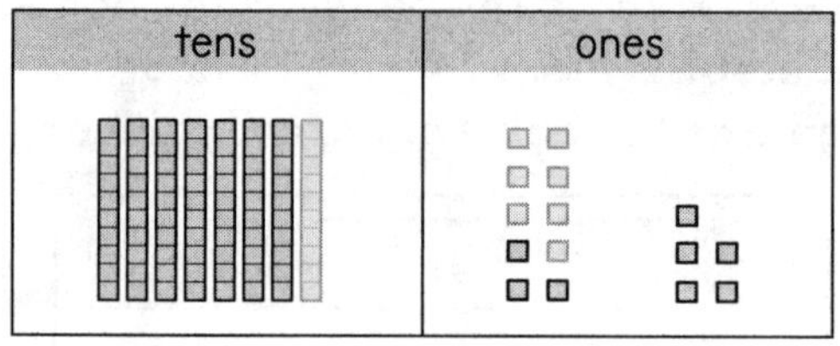

We have 78 squares of chocolate left at the store. Write 78 on the top line of the next inventory slip. **Order 2 is for 2 bars and 3 squares. I wonder how much chocolate will be left after you pack the order!** Continue in the same way with the rest of the problems on workbook page 26.1A.

	Bars	Squares
	8	15
Total	~~9~~	~~5~~
Order 1	1	7
New Total	7	8

	Bars	Squares
Total	7	8
Order 2	2	3
New Total	5	5

	Bars	Squares
	4	15
Total	~~5~~	~~5~~
Order 3		9
New Total	4	6

	Bars	Squares
Total	4	6
Order 4		6
New Total	4	0

	Bars	Squares
	3	10
Total	~~4~~	~~0~~
Order 5	1	8
New Total	2	2

	Bars	Squares
	1	12
Total	~~2~~	~~2~~
Order 6	1	4
New Total		8

Transfer the new total to the next inventory slip.

Workbook: Review

Have your child complete workbook page 26.1B.

Lesson 26.2
Subtract Two-Digit Numbers with Base-Ten Blocks

	Purpose	Materials
Warm-up	• Count by 4s to 40 • Practice memory work • Review finding more and less on the number line	• Blank Number Line (Blackline Master 3)
Activities	• Model the subtraction algorithm with base-ten blocks • Use the subtraction algorithm to add two-digit numbers from numbers less than 100	• Workbook page 26.2A • Base-ten blocks • Place-Value Chart (Blackline Master 5)
Workbook	• Review previously-learned material	• Workbook page 26.2B

Warm-up: Counting, Memory Work, and Review

- Have your child count by 4s to 40.
- **How many sides does a triangle have?** *3.* **A quadrilateral?** *4.* **A pentagon?** *5.* **A hexagon?** *6.* **An octagon?** *8.*
- Label the Blank Number Line with 140, 150, and 160. Ask your child the following number line riddles.
    - **This number is 4 more than 149.** *153.*
    - **This number is 2 less than 160.** *158.*
    - **This number is 7 more than 141.** *148.*
    - **This number is 1 more than 150.** *151.*
    - **This number is halfway between 140 and 150.** *145.*

Activity: Subtract Two-Digit Numbers without Trading

In Unit 10, you learned the addition algorithm. Remember, an algorithm is like a recipe for solving problems. Today, we'll use the subtraction algorithm and base-ten blocks to subtract two-digit numbers. It's a lot like the packing directions from the chocolate shop!

Show your child the diagram at the top of workbook page 26.2A. **Let's pretend that you're a robot. You're programmed to follow this Subtraction Algorithm program.** Point to the first exercise (76 – 24). Have your child model 76 with base-ten blocks on the Place-Value Chart.

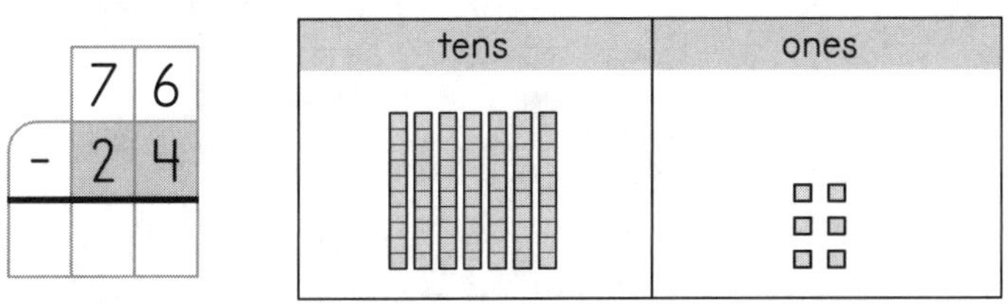

The program says: ***Start with the ones-place.*** **The first step is a question:** ***Is the top digit greater than or equal to the bottom digit?*** Point to the digits in the ones-place. **Is the top digit greater than or equal to the bottom digit?** *Yes.*

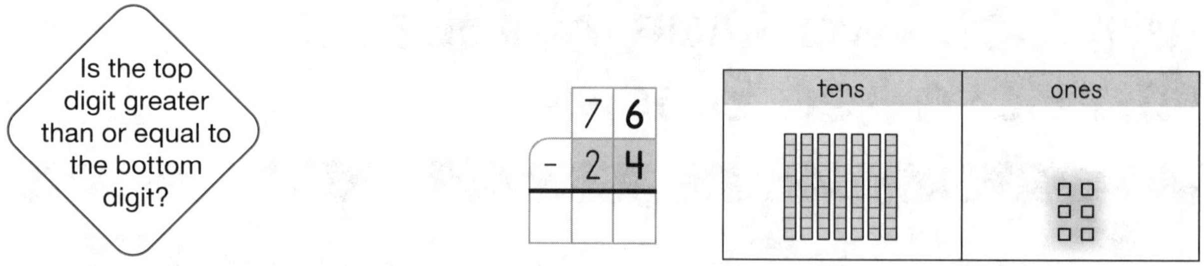

So, we follow the path labeled "Yes." Trace your finger along the "Yes" arrow until you reach the next step. **This step says:** ***Subtract.*** Have your child remove 2 unit blocks from the ones-column. **What is 6 minus 4?** *2.* Have your child write 2 in the answer's ones-place.

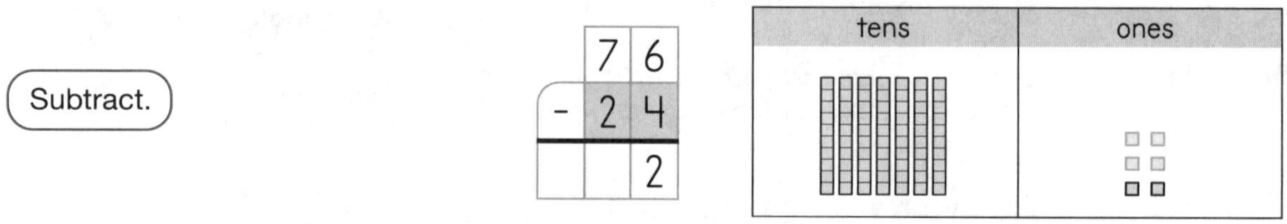

The program says: ***Follow the steps for all the places.*** **So, we go back to the beginning and follow the steps for the tens-place.** Help your child follow the steps to subtract the tens. **So, what's 76 – 24?** *52.* **Great job, robot!**

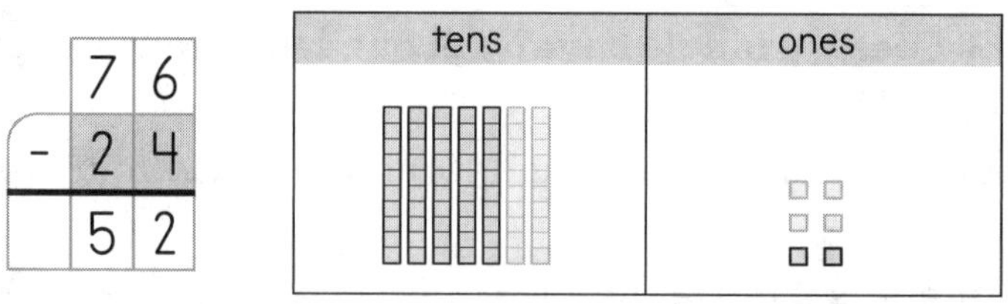

Activity: Two-Digit Subtraction with Trading

Point to the second exercise (61 – 19). Have your child model 61 with base-ten blocks on the Place-Value Chart.

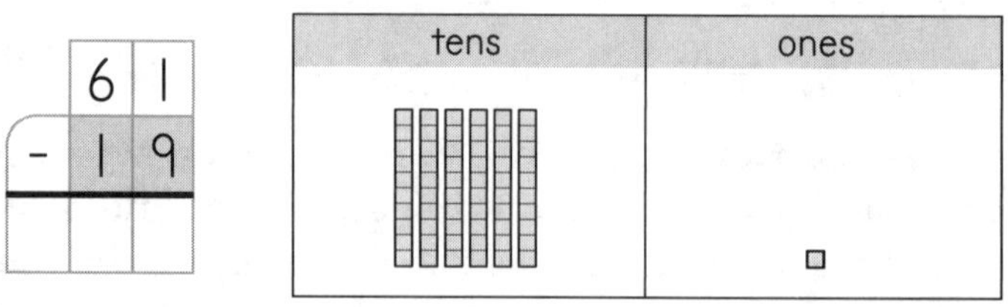

Which place do we start with? *The ones-place.* **The first step says:** ***Is the top digit greater than or equal to the bottom digit?*** Point to the digits in the ones-place. **Is 1 greater than or equal to 9?** *No.*

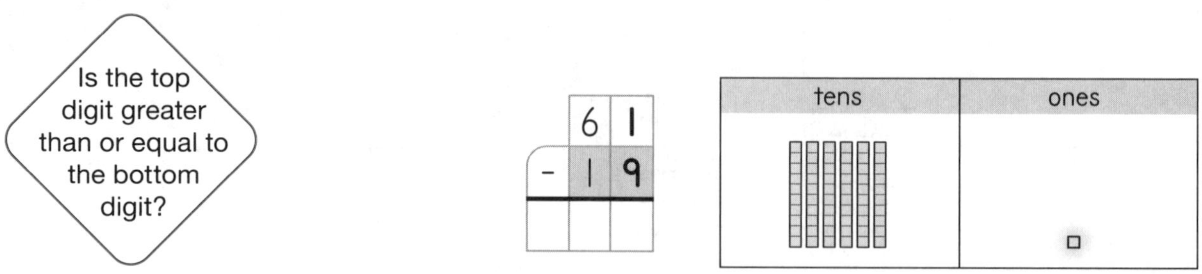

So, we follow the path labeled "No." Trace your finger along the "No" arrow. **The next step is: *Trade*. Trade 1 ten for 10 ones.** Have your child trade 1 rod for 10 unit blocks and place the 10 unit blocks in the ones-column.

Trade.

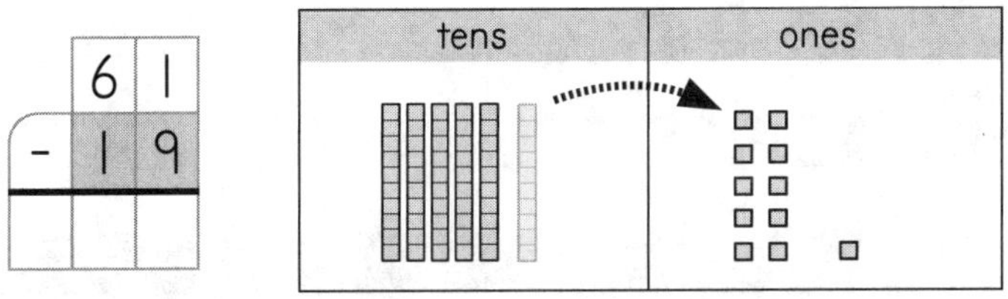

Now, you have 5 tens. Have your child cross out the 6 and write 5 above it. **You have 11 ones.** Have your child cross out the 1 and write 11 above it.

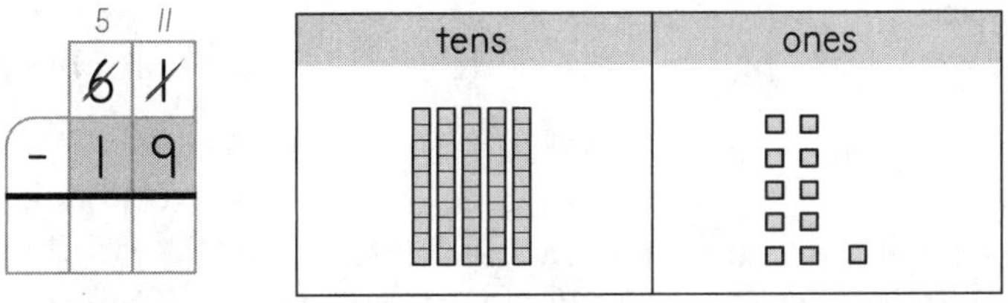

You may have learned to write a small 1 next to the 5 when trading 1 ten for 10 ones. See the Week 26 **Teaching Math with Confidence** for more on why this program has your child use this different recording method.

What's the next step? *Subtract.* Have your child remove 9 unit blocks from the ones-column. **What's 11 minus 9?** 2. Have your child write 2 in the answer's ones-place.

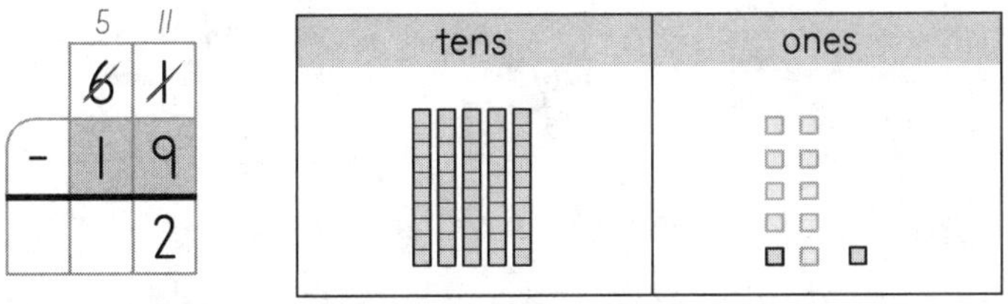

Now, we go back to the beginning and follow the steps for the tens-place. Help your child follow the steps to subtract the tens.

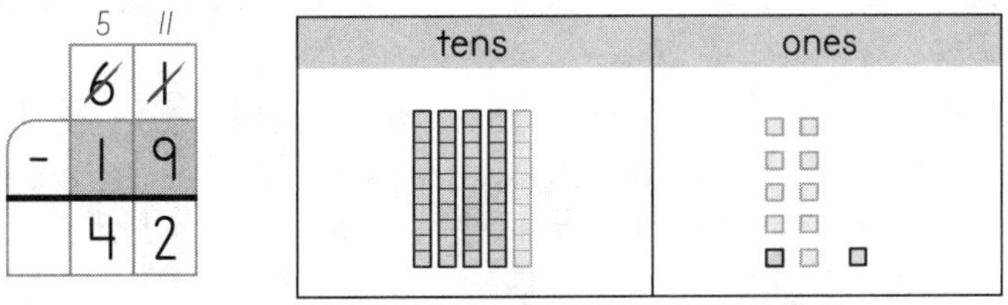

Activity: Subtract Two-Digit Numbers Like a Robot

Continue in the same way with the rest of the problems on the workbook page. Model each problem with base-ten blocks so your child concretely understands the steps.

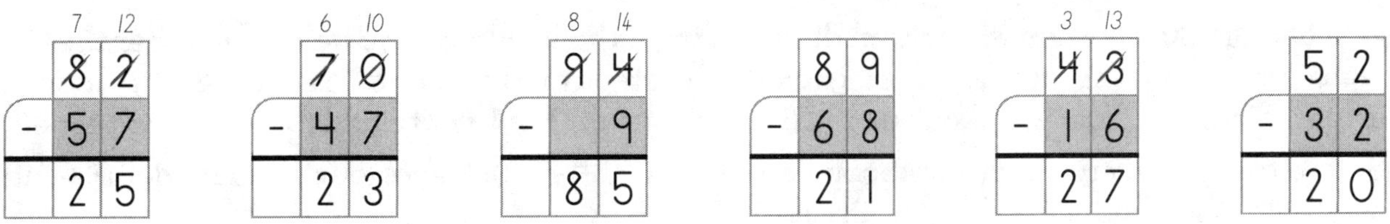

Save workbook page 26.2A so your child can refer to the Subtraction Algorithm diagram.

Workbook: Review

Have your child complete workbook page 26.2B.

Lesson 26.3
Trade Once to Subtract Two-Digit Numbers from Numbers Greater than 100

	Purpose	Materials
Warm-up	• Count by 100s • Practice memory work • Review measuring in centimeters	• Play money • 30-centimeter (or 1-foot) ruler, marked in centimeters • Several writing utensils of different lengths
Activities	• Use the subtraction algorithm to subtract two-digit numbers from numbers greater than 100 • Trade 1 hundred for 10 tens when subtracting	• Workbook page 26.3A • Subtraction Algorithm diagram (from workbook page 26.2A) • Base-ten blocks • Place-Value Chart (Blackline Master 5) • Paper clip
Workbook	• Review previously-learned material	• Workbook page 26.3B

The exercises in this lesson involve trading 1 ten for 10 ones, or 1 hundred for 10 tens, but not both. Your child will work on problems that require two trades in Lesson 26.4.

Warm-up: Counting, Memory Work, and Review

- Place 8-10 hundred-dollar bills on the table. Have your child count by 100s to find their value.
- **How many sides does a triangle have?** *3.* **A quadrilateral?** *4.* **A pentagon?** *5.* **A hexagon?** *6.* **An octagon?** *8.*
- Place several writing utensils of different lengths on the table, such as crayons, pencils, or markers. Have your child choose a writing utensil, estimate its length in centimeters, and then use a ruler to measure its actual length. Repeat with all of the writing utensils.

Activity: Review Trading 1 Ten to Subtract

In the last lesson, you learned how to use the subtraction algorithm to subtract two-digit numbers from numbers up to 100. Today, you'll learn how to use the subtraction algorithm to subtract two-digit numbers from numbers greater than 100.

We'll use the Subtraction Algorithm diagram from the last lesson to help remember the steps. Even though the numbers are greater, the steps are the same. Place the Subtraction Algorithm diagram (from workbook page 26.2A) on the table for your child to refer to as needed.

Point to the first exercise on workbook page 26.3A (165 – 38). Have your child model 165 with base-ten blocks on the Place-Value Chart.

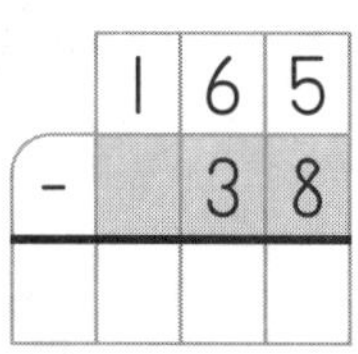

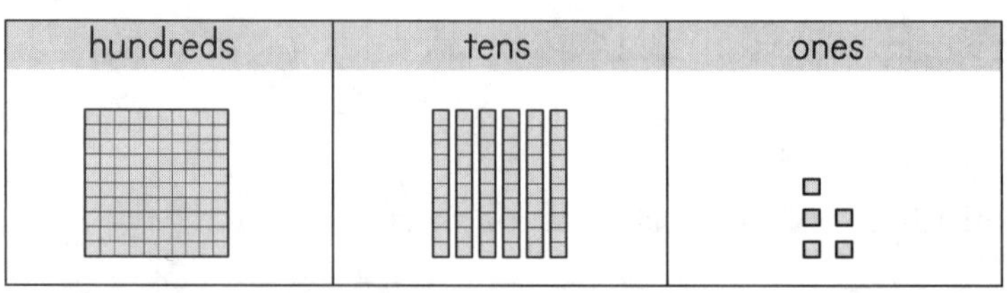

Help your child follow the steps in the subtraction algorithm to subtract the ones and tens.

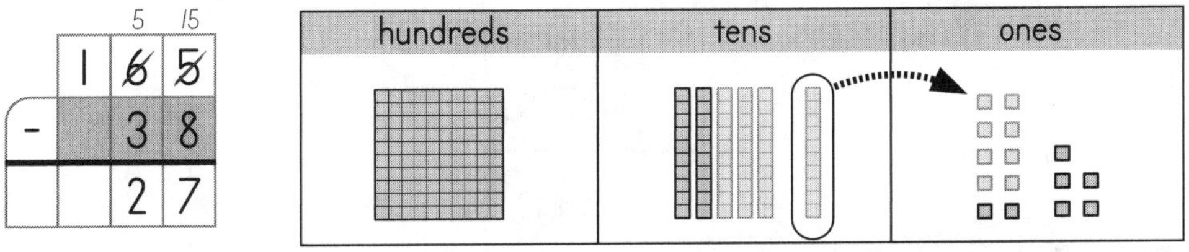

When you get to the hundreds-place, say: **Now, we go back to the beginning and follow the steps for the hundreds-place. We have 1 hundred. We don't subtract any hundreds from it, so there is 1 hundred left.** Have your child write a 1 in the answer's hundreds-place. **So, what's 165 minus 38?** *127.*

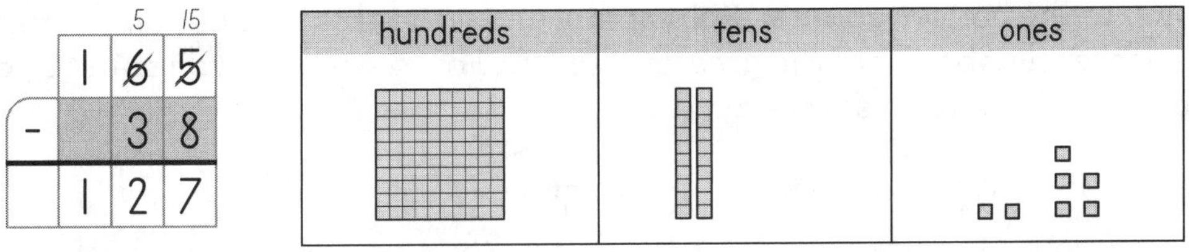

Activity: Trade 1 Hundred to Subtract

Point to the second exercise on workbook page 26.3A (129 – 67). Have your child model 129 with base-ten blocks on the Place-Value Chart and subtract the ones.

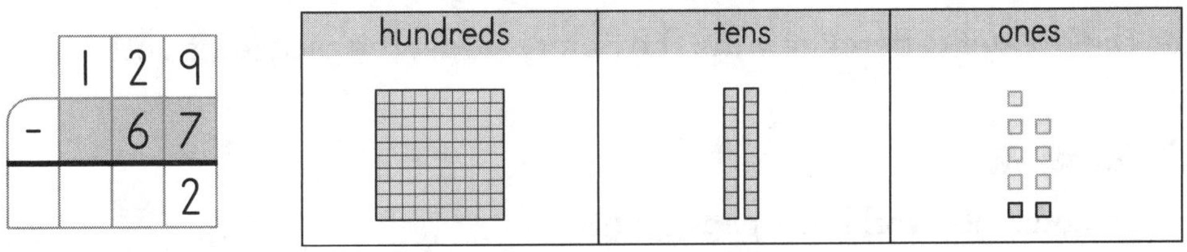

Now, we follow the steps for the tens-place. Is the top digit greater than or equal to the bottom digit? *No.* **So, the next step is to trade. We need more tens, so we trade 1 hundred for 10 tens.** Have your child trade 1 flat for 10 rods and place the rods in the tens-column.

You traded the hundred for 10 tens, so you need to record that you don't have any hundreds. Have your child cross out the 1. You have 12 tens. Have your child cross out the 2 and write 12 above it.

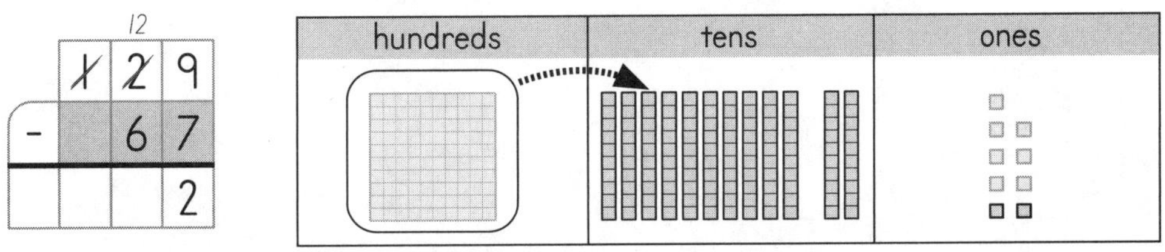

Now you're ready to subtract the tens. Have your child remove 6 rods, subtract 12 – 6, and record the difference. **There aren't any hundreds, so we don't need to subtract or record anything in the hundreds-place.**

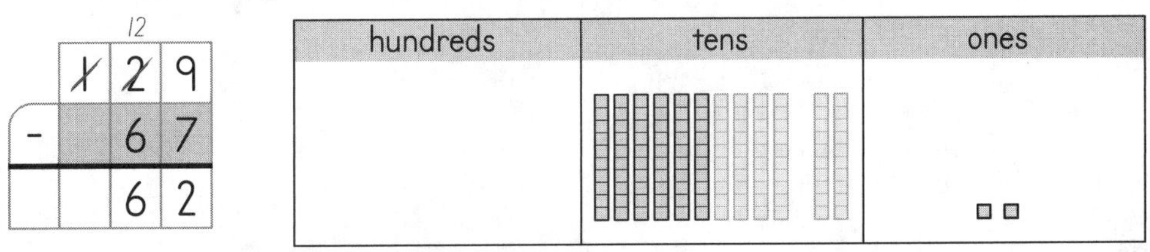

If your child wonders if she should write a zero in the hundreds-place, remind her that we only include zeros when they're needed as place-holders.

Have your child solve 137 – 54 in the same way.

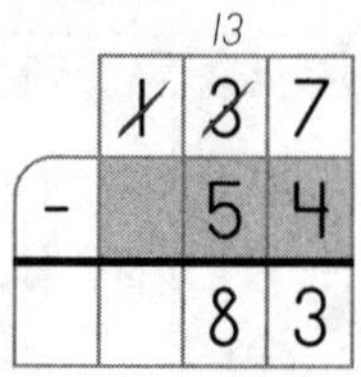

Activity: Play Spin to Win

Play Spin to Win. See Lesson 14.2 (page 228) for full directions. Use workbook page 26.3A. On your turn, hold the pencil upright and spin the paper clip so that it spins freely around the top spinner. Write this number on the top line of the first blank grid. Then, move the paper clip and pencil to the bottom spinner. Spin again, and write this number on the next line. Subtract the lesser number from the greater number. For example, if you spin 184 on the top spinner and 48 on the bottom spinner:

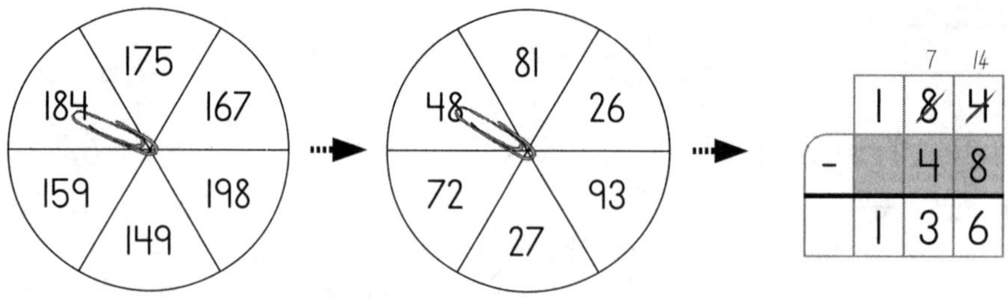

Whoever has the greater difference wins the point. Model the problems with base-ten blocks as needed.

Workbook: Review

Have your child complete workbook page 26.3B.

Lesson 26.4
Trade Twice to Subtract Two-Digit Numbers from Numbers Greater Than 100

	Purpose	Materials
Warm-up	• Count coins • Practice memory work • Review writing money amounts with a dollar sign and decimal point	• Coins
Activities	• Trade twice to subtract two-digit numbers from numbers greater than 100	• Workbook page 26.4A • Base-ten blocks • Place-Value Chart (Blackline Master 5) • Subtraction Algorithm diagram (from workbook page 26.2A), optional • Paper clip
Workbook	• Review previously-learned material	• Workbook page 26.4B

Warm-up: Counting, Memory Work, and Review

- Place 3 quarters, 5 dimes, 2 nickels, and 3 pennies on the table. **How many cents is this money worth?** *138¢.*
- **How many sides does a triangle have?** *3.* **A quadrilateral?** *4.* **A pentagon?** *5.* **A hexagon?** *6.* **An octagon?** *8.*
- Name the following amounts of money. Have your child write each amount with a dollar sign and decimal point.
    - × **One dollar and thirty-four cents.** *$1.34.*
    - × **Thirty-four cents.** *$0.34.*
    - × **Thirty-four dollars.** *$34.00.*
    - × **Six dollars and eight cents.** *$6.08.*
    - × **Eighty cents.** *$0.80.*

Activity: Trade Twice to Subtract

In the last lesson, you learned how to use the subtraction algorithm to subtract two-digit numbers from numbers greater than 100.

You had to trade 1 ten or 1 hundred to solve some of the problems. Today, you'll solve subtraction problems where you have to trade both 1 ten and 1 hundred.

Point to the first exercise on workbook page 26.4A (134 – 56). Have your child model 134 with base-ten blocks on the Place-Value Chart.

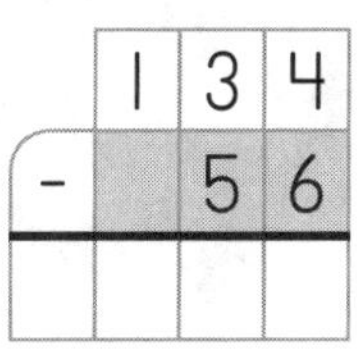

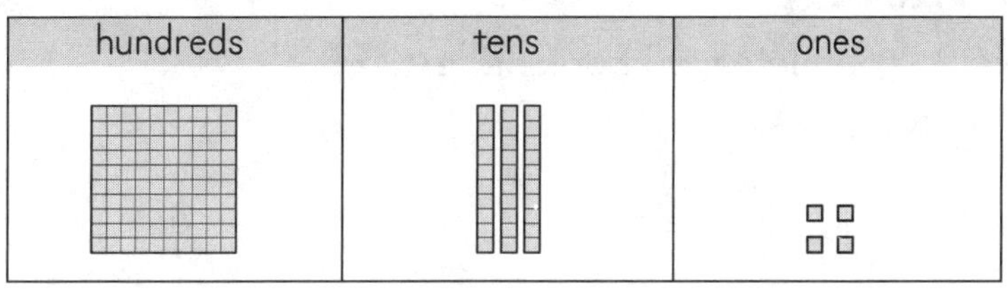

Which place do we start with? *The ones-place.* Have your child trade 1 rod for 10 units, record the trade, and then subtract. If he has trouble remembering the steps, have him refer to the Subtraction Algorithm diagram (from workbook page 26.2A).

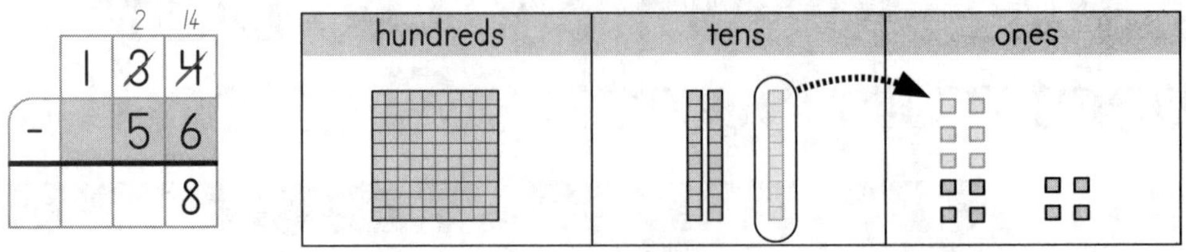

What do we do next? *Follow the steps for the tens-place.* Have your child trade 1 flat for 10 rods and place the rods in the tens-column. **Now you have 12 tens instead of 2 tens.** Have your child cross out the 1 in the hundreds-place. Show your child how to write a 1 next to the 2 in the tens-place, so that it's clear there are 12 tens.

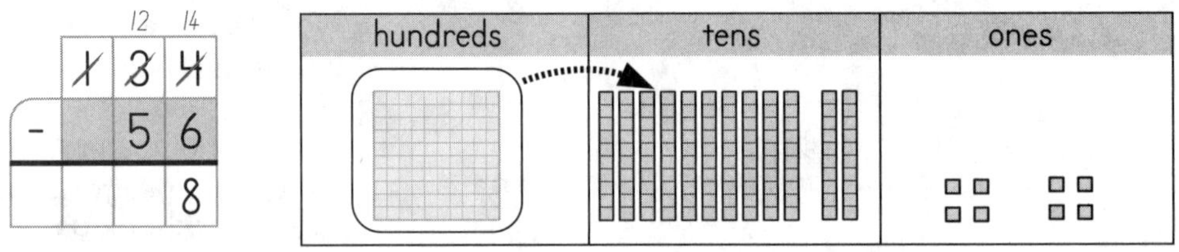

If your child finds this confusing, he can cross out the 2 and write 12 above it instead.

Now you're ready to subtract the tens. Have your child remove 5 rods, subtract 12 – 5, and record the difference.

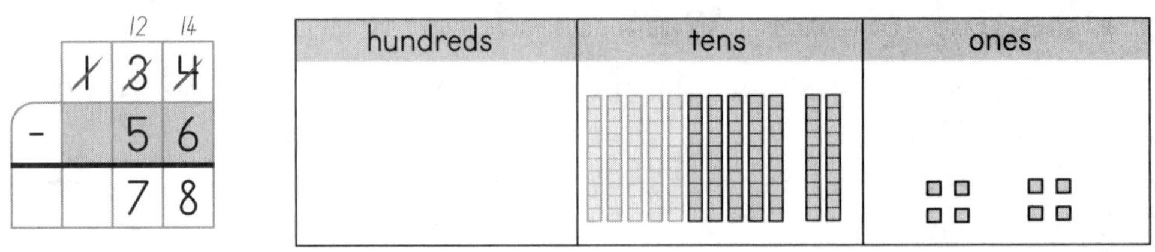

Have your child solve 152 – 79 and 140 – 85 in the same way. Guide him as he records his trades. Use base-ten blocks as needed.

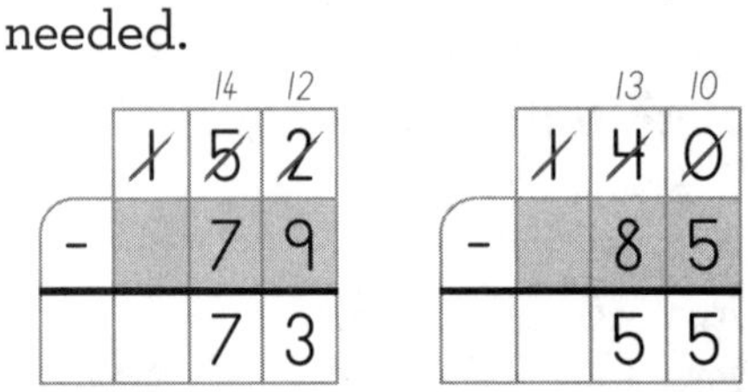

None of these problems require trading across a zero, as in 104 – 76. Your child will learn how to solve these more-challenging problems in Week 31 after he has already mastered the basic subtraction algorithm.

Activity: Play Spin to Win

Play Spin to Win with the game board on 26.4A. See Lesson 26.3 (page 426) for directions.

The numbers on the spinners ensure that your child practices trading twice as he solves the problems.

Workbook: Review

Have your child complete workbook page 26.4B.

Lesson 26.5
Enrichment and Review (Optional)

	Purpose	Materials
Warm-up	• Count by 3s and 4s • Review memory work • Review your child's favorite or most challenging activities from Week 26	• Varies, depending on the activities you choose
Picture Book	• Understand how the subtraction algorithm helps solve real-life problems	• *Shark Swimathon,* written by Stuart J. Murphy and illustrated by Lynne Cravath
Enrichment Activity	• Use subtraction to figure out how many pages are left to read in a book	• Children's book with more than 100 pages and fewer than 200 pages

In the enrichment activity, your child will use his subtraction skills to figure out how many pages are left in a book. This activity is especially fun if you use a book that you're currently reading aloud to your child (or that he is reading independently). Try to use a book with more than 100 pages and fewer than 200 pages so that the subtraction problems are appropriately challenging.

Warm-up: Counting, Memory Work, and Review

- Have your child count by 3s to 30 and by 4s to 40.
- Quiz your child on the memory work through Week 26. See page 523 for the full list.
- If you have time, repeat one or two of the activities from this week's lessons. Choose activities your child especially enjoyed or found challenging.

Math Picture Book: *Shark Swimathon*

Read *Shark Swimathon,* written by Stuart J. Murphy and illustrated by Lynne Cravath. As you read, pay special attention to how the sharks use the subtraction algorithm to figure out how many laps they have left to swim.

Enrichment Activity: How Many Pages are Left?

Show your child a book with more than 100 pages and fewer than 200 pages. Have your child find the total number of pages in the book. Also have him find the page number for the last page of the first chapter. (If the book doesn't have chapters, choose another logical division in the book.)

Let's pretend you just finished reading the first chapter. We can subtract to find how many pages you have left to read. Use the page numbers to write a corresponding subtraction problem and have your child subtract to find the number of pages left. For example:

143 ← Total number of pages in the book
− 29 ← Number of pages in the first chapter
114 ← Number of pages left to read

I've read 29 pages, so I have 114 pages to go!

Repeat with several other places in the book. For each, write a subtraction problem and have your child subtract to find out how many pages are left after that point in the book.

Week 26 Answer Key

26.1A

See the Instructor Guide for directions.

Chocolate Shop Packing Directions

1. Check whether you have enough squares for the order.
2. If you don't have enough squares, trade one bar for 10 squares.

3. Subtract the squares.
4. Subtract the bars.

	Bars	Squares
	8	15
Total	~~9~~	~~5~~
Order 1	1	7
New Total	7	8

	Bars	Squares
Total	7	8
Order 2	2	3
New Total	5	5

	Bars	Squares
	4	15
Total	~~5~~	~~5~~
Order 3		9
New Total	4	6

	Bars	Squares
Total	4	6
Order 4		6
New Total	4	0

	Bars	Squares
	3	10
Total	~~4~~	~~0~~
Order 5	1	8
New Total	2	2

	Bars	Squares
	1	12
Total	~~2~~	~~2~~
Order 6	1	4
New Total		8

26.1B

Solve.

Rodrigo's family drove 36 kilometers to his soccer game. Then, they drove 36 kilometers back. How far did they drive in all?

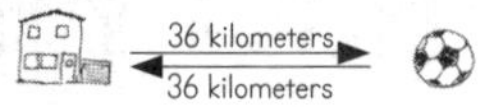

36 + 36 = 72

72 kilometers

Kaylee's family drove 79 miles to her cousin's house. Then, they drove 79 miles back. How far did they drive in all?

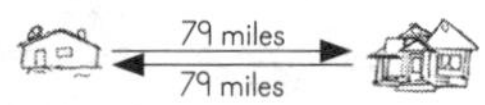

79 + 79 = 158

158 miles

Complete the missing numbers in the sequences.

Count by 3s: 3, 6, 9, 12, 15, 18

Count by 4s: 4, 8, 12, 16, 20, 24

Count by 2s: 166, 168, 170, 172, 174, 176

26.2A

See the Instructor Guide for directions.

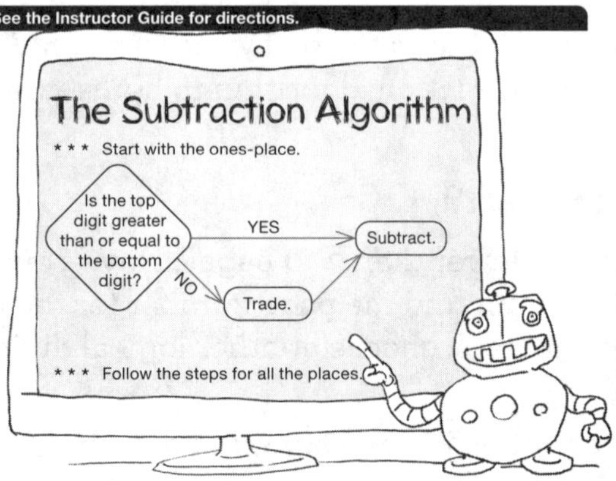

76 − 24 = 52

~~6~~ ~~1~~ (5, 11) 61 − 19 = 42

~~8~~ 2 (7, 12) 82 − 57 = 25

~~7~~ ~~0~~ (6, 10) 70 − 47 = 23

~~9~~ ~~4~~ (8, 14) 94 − 9 = 85

89 − 68 = 21

~~4~~ ~~3~~ (3, 13) 43 − 16 = 27

52 − 32 = 20

26.2B

Choose the more sensible measurement for each item.

Length of a baby: **2 feet** (circled) / 2 yards

Length of a fork: 8 feet / **8 inches** (circled)

Length of a playground: 50 miles / **50 yards** (circled)

Label each spot on the number line.

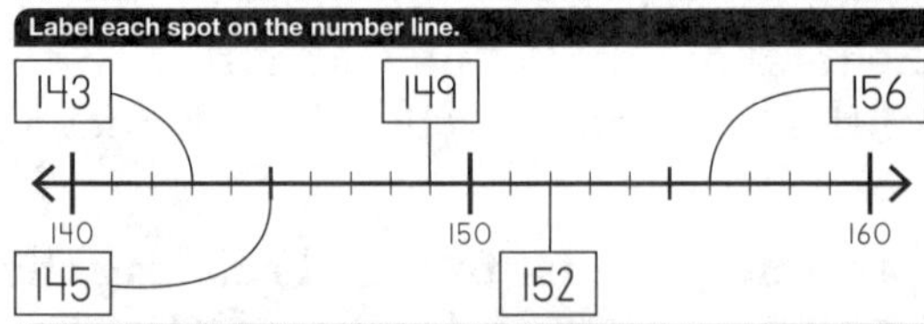

Color the shapes to match the fractions.

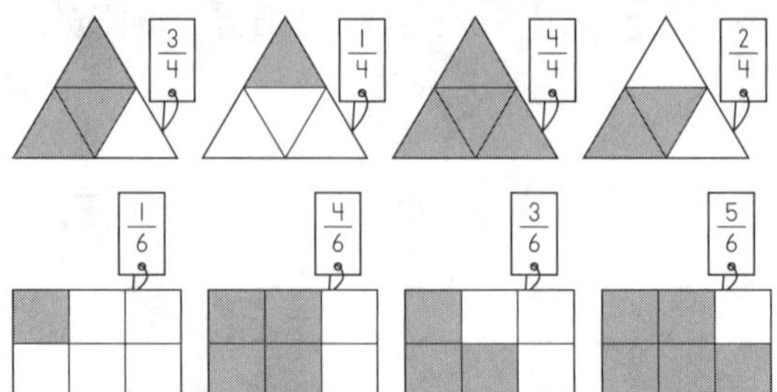

Sample answers. Other ways to color the shapes are possible.

Week 26 Answer Key

26.3A

See the Instructor Guide for directions.

1 6 5 − 3 8 = 1 2 7 (regrouping: 5, 15)	1 2 9 − 6 7 = 6 2 (regrouping: 12)	1 3 7 − 5 4 = 8 3 (regrouping: 13)

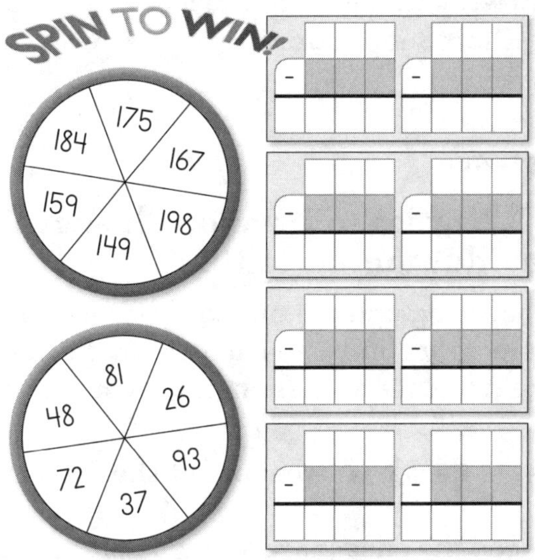

26.3B

Complete.

1 week = 7 days
1 day = 24 hours
1 hour = 60 minutes
1 minute = 60 seconds
1 yard = 3 feet
1 yard = 36 inches
1 foot = 12 inches
1 meter = 100 centimeters

Complete the missing numbers in the 200 chart.

151	152	153	154	155	156	157	158	159	160
161	162	163	164	165	166	167	168	169	170
171	172	173	174	175	176	177	178	179	180
181	182	183	184	185	186	187	188	189	190
191	192	193	194	195	196	197	198	199	200

Write how many.

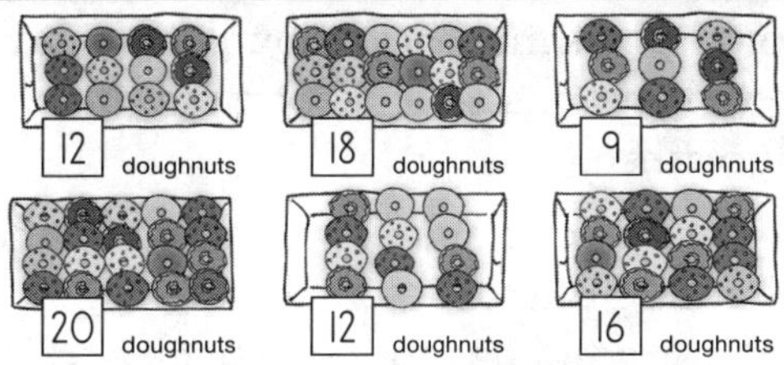

12 doughnuts
18 doughnuts
9 doughnuts
20 doughnuts
12 doughnuts
16 doughnuts

26.4A

See the Instructor Guide for directions.

1 3 4 − 5 6 = 7 8 (regrouping: 12, 14)	1 5 2 − 7 9 = 7 3 (regrouping: 14, 12)	1 4 0 − 8 5 = 5 5 (regrouping: 13, 10)

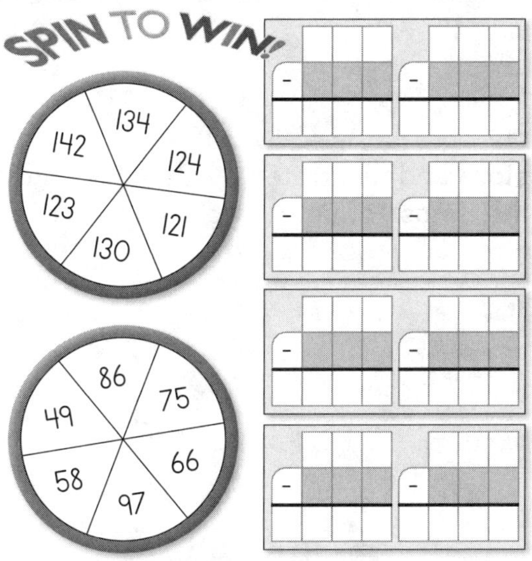

26.4B

Complete.

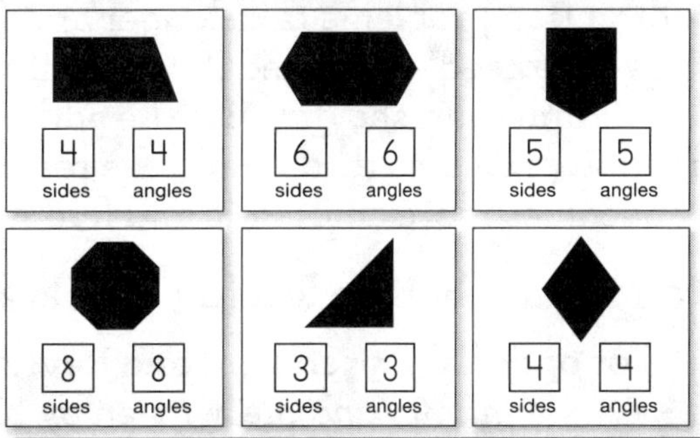

4 sides, 4 angles
6 sides, 6 angles
5 sides, 5 angles
8 sides, 8 angles
3 sides, 3 angles
4 sides, 4 angles

Write a fraction for the pink part of each shape.

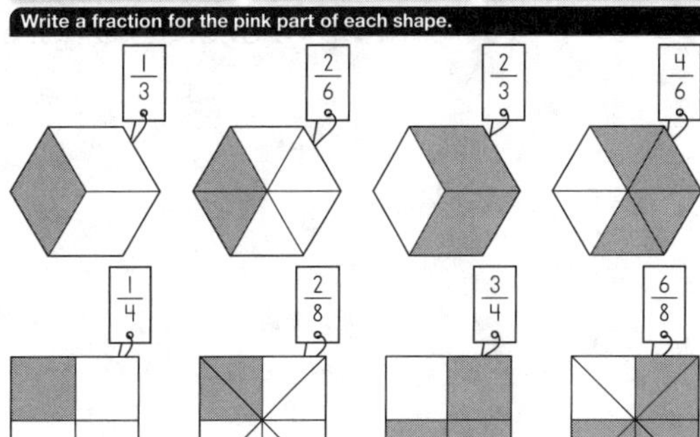

$\frac{1}{3}$ $\frac{2}{6}$ $\frac{2}{3}$ $\frac{4}{6}$

$\frac{1}{4}$ $\frac{2}{8}$ $\frac{3}{4}$ $\frac{6}{8}$

Week 27
Build Fluency with Written Subtraction

Overview

Now that your child has a thorough conceptual understanding of the subtraction algorithm, she will practice more so that can fluently subtract two-digit numbers on paper, without base-ten blocks.

Lesson 27.1	Subtract Two-Digit Numbers without Base-Ten Blocks
Lesson 27.2	Develop Accuracy with Two-Digit Subtraction
Lesson 27.3	Use Addition to Check Subtraction
Lesson 27.4	Subtraction Word Problems
Lesson 27.5	Enrichment and Review (Optional)

Teaching Math with Confidence: Why Is It Harder to Develop Fluency with the Subtraction Algorithm than the Addition Algorithm?

Multi-digit subtraction often feels much more exhausting and tedious to children than the addition algorithm. Even though the algorithms are very similar to each other, the subtraction algorithm has several complexities that make it feel more challenging than the addition algorithm.

- Before your child starts subtracting, she has to decide whether or not she needs to trade 1 ten for 10 ones.
- Your child has to move back and forth between the ones-place and tens-place as she solves the problems. With addition, she can flow directly from the ones-place to the tens-place.
- Your child is likely slightly slower at recalling the subtraction facts than the addition facts, even if she has a solid mastery of both sets of facts.

Individually, each of these is a minor issue. But when they're combined, they make written subtraction problems take longer and feel more tiring than written addition problems. Don't be surprised or worried if your child takes longer to become fluent with the subtraction algorithm than she did with the addition algorithm. She'll continue to practice written subtraction problems throughout the rest of the year (and in third grade) so that she eventually becomes more automatic and fluent.

Extra Materials Needed for Week 27

- For optional Enrichment and Review Lesson:
  - *Infinity and Me,* written by Kate Hosford and illustrated by Gabi Swiatkowska
  - Toy catalog or access to a website with items your child would like to buy

Lesson 27.1
Subtract Two-Digit Numbers without Base-Ten Blocks

	Purpose	Materials
Warm-up	• Count by 1s • Practice memory work • Review measuring in feet and inches	• Play money • 1-foot ruler
Activities	• Subtract two-digit numbers on paper, without base-ten blocks	• Workbook page 27.1A • Base-ten blocks • Place-Value Chart (Blackline Master 5)
Workbook	• Review previously-learned material	• Workbook page 27.1B

Warm-up: Counting, Memory Work, and Review

- Place 5 hundred-dollar bills and 15-20 one-dollar bills on the table. **Let's count this money by 1s, starting at 500.** Count the money in unison with your child: **500, 501, 502....**
- **How many minutes equal a half-hour?** *30.*
  How many minutes equal a quarter-hour? *15.*
- Choose an object in the room about 5 feet long. Have your child measure it in feet and inches with a 1-foot ruler (as in Lesson 20.3). For example: *The bookshelf is 4 feet and 10 inches.*

Activity: Subtract Two-Digit Numbers without Base-Ten Blocks

You have learned how to subtract two-digit numbers with the subtraction algorithm. For the rest of this week, you'll practice more so you can subtract two-digit numbers fluently, without needing base-ten blocks. Today, you'll first try solving written subtraction problems without base-ten blocks. Then, we'll play a game.

Point to the first exercise on workbook page 27.1A (118 – 62). **Try solving this problem with the subtraction algorithm. While you work, I'll model the problem with base-ten blocks. Once we finish, we'll compare our answers and make sure they match.**

Have your child solve the problem. While she works, model 118 with base-ten blocks on the Place-Value Chart. Trade 1 flat for 10 rods, and then subtract 6 rods and 2 units. Cover your final block arrangement with a piece of paper.

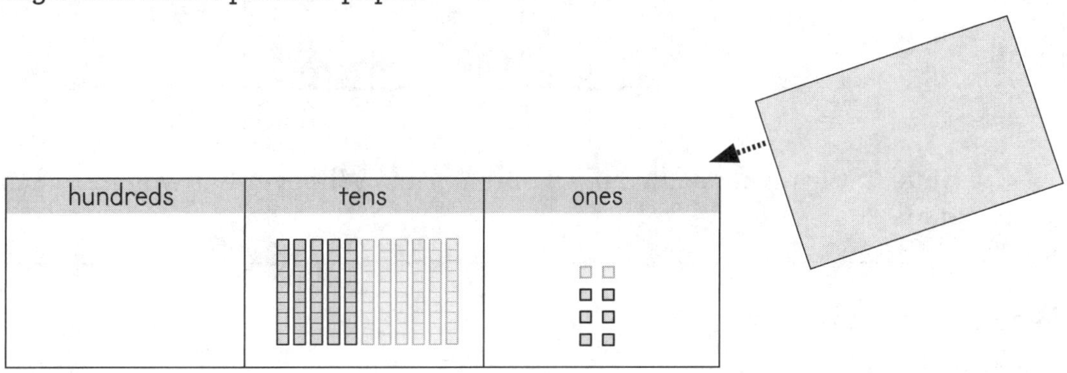

So, what's 118 minus 62? *56.* Remove the cover from the blocks so your child can check whether her answer matches the blocks. If her answer does not match, have her use the blocks to find the correct answer.

Continue in the same way with the rest of the problems in the row.

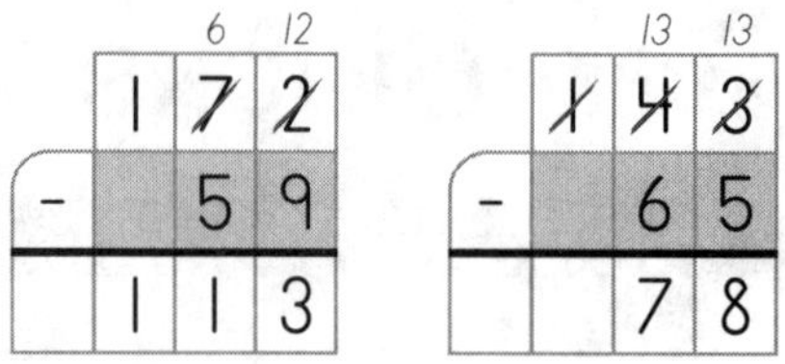

Activity: Play What's the Difference?

We're going to play a game called What's the Difference? In this game, the player who goes first can always win if she chooses her numbers well. I'll let you go first. See if you can figure out the winning strategy! Play What's the Difference?

In this game, your score is the difference between the two numbers that you pick. To maximize the difference, the best strategy is to pick the greatest tan number available and the lowest pink number available. Telling your child to look for the winning strategy before you play helps her develop a more sophisticated and abstract understanding of subtraction—even if that means you don't have a chance of beating her!

What's the Difference?

Materials: Workbook page 27.1A

Object of the Game: Win the most points.

On your turn, choose 1 tan number and 1 pink number from the printed number bank on the workbook page. (The tan numbers are all greater than 100, while the pink numbers are less than 100.)

Cross out each number you choose. Write the tan number on the top line of the first blank grid, and the pink number on the next line of the grid. Subtract to find their difference.

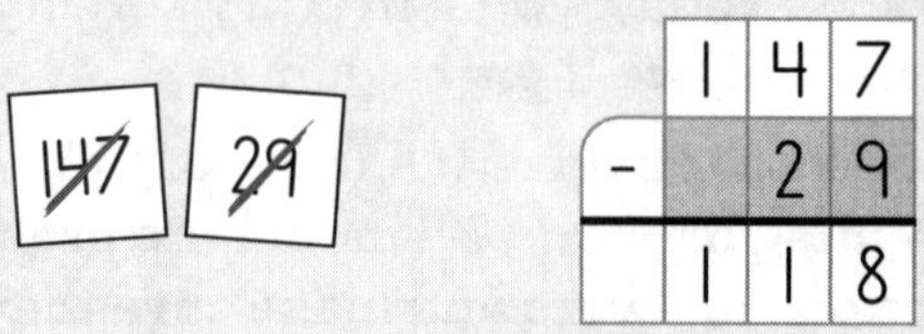

Then, have the other player choose two numbers, write the numbers in the neighboring blank grid, and find their difference. Whoever has the greater difference wins a point.

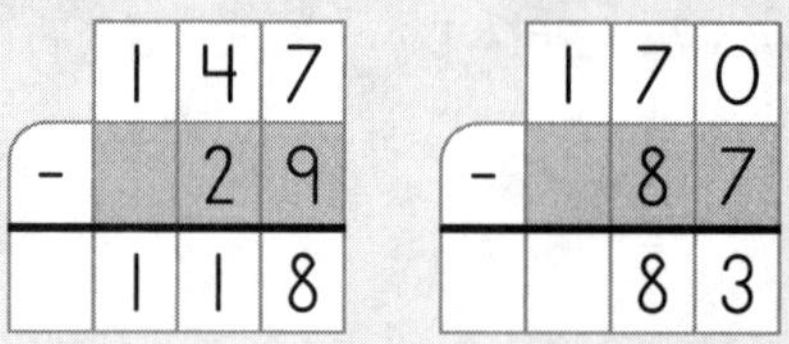

Continue until you have filled in all of the grids. Whoever has won more points wins the game.

Workbook: Review

Have your child complete workbook page 27.1B.

Lesson 27.2
Develop Accuracy with Two-Digit Subtraction

	Purpose	Materials
Warm-up	• Count by 4s to 40 • Practice memory work • Review pairs that make 100	• None
Activities	• Develop greater accuracy with the subtraction algorithm	• Workbook page 27.2A • Counters
Workbook	• Review previously-learned material	• Workbook page 27.2B

Warm-up: Counting, Memory Work, and Review

- Have your child count by 4s to 40.
- **Are times in the afternoon and evening a.m. or p.m.?** *P.m.*
  Are times in the morning a.m. or p.m.? *A.m.*
- Secretly write each of the following equations on a piece of paper and hide the addend indicated with a slip of paper. Have your child use his "x-ray vision" to identify the hidden numbers.

50 + [50] = 100 51 + [49] = 100 55 + [45] = 100

52 + [48] = 100 59 + [41] = 100

Activity: Practice the Steps in Two-Digit Subtraction

In the last lesson, you solved two-digit subtraction problems without base-ten blocks. Today, you'll practice some more with a silent activity and game.

Show your child the first exercise on workbook page 27.2A (126 – 78). **Watch as I solve this problem. Tap your pencil on the table each time I write a correct number. We'll do this completely silently so we can both concentrate.**

Slowly and deliberately solve the problem. Your child should tap his pencil on the table after you write each number.

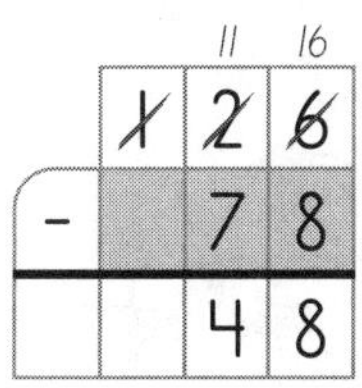

For the second exercise, reverse roles: have your child solve the problem while you tap your pencil every time he writes a correct number. If he makes a mistake, do not tap the table. Instead, give him a puzzled look to prompt him to check his work. Have him solve the third exercise in this way as well.

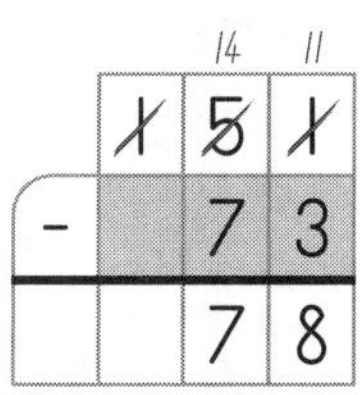

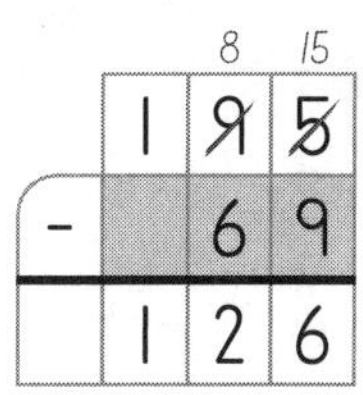

Most children find mastering the subtraction algorithm more difficult than mastering the addition algorithm. It's fine if your child isn't completely fluent with the subtraction algorithm yet. See the Week 27 **Teaching Math with Confidence** for more on why children often take longer to develop fluency with the subtraction algorithm than the addition algorithm.

Activity: Play Connect the Boxes

Play Connect the Boxes. See Lesson 23.2 (page 370) for directions. Play silently so that both you and your child can concentrate on solving the problems correctly and providing feedback to each other by tapping the table.

Workbook: Review

Have your child complete workbook page 27.2B.

Lesson 27.3
Use Addition to Check Subtraction

	Purpose	Materials
Warm-up	• Count by 3s to 30 • Practice memory work • Review identifying polygons	• Polygon Four in a Row game board (from workbook page 24.3A) • Die • Counters
Activities	• Review the relationship between addition and subtraction • Learn how to use addition to check subtraction	• Workbook page 27.3A • Part-Total Mat (Blackline Master 2) • Base-ten blocks, optional
Workbook	• Review previously-learned material	• Workbook page 27.3B

Warm-up: Counting, Memory Work, and Review

- Have your child count by 3s to 30.
- **How many centimeters equal 1 meter?** *100.*
- Play Polygon Four in a Row. See Lesson 24.3 (page 389) for directions.

Activity: Review the Relationship Between Addition and Subtraction

You have worked hard to learn the subtraction algorithm in this unit! Today, you'll learn how you can use addition to check the answers to subtraction problems.

First, let's review how addition and subtraction are related to each other. Show your child the Part-Total Diagrams at the top of workbook page 27.3A. Have your child write 4 related addition and subtraction equations to match each Part-Total Diagram.

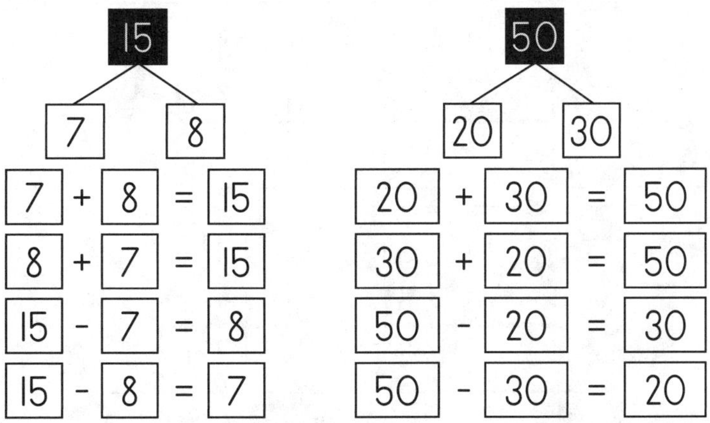

Remember, addition is the opposite of subtraction. When we subtract, we separate a total into parts. Pantomime separating a group of objects into two groups. **If we add those parts back together, we get the original total.** Pantomime pushing two groups of objects together to make one group.

Activity: Use Addition to Check Subtraction

Have your child solve the first subtraction problem at the bottom of 27.3A (95 – 28). Allow her to use base-ten blocks to model the problem if needed, but do not require her to use them.

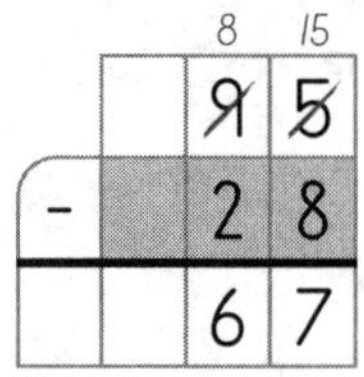

After you solve a subtraction problem, you can add to check that your answer is correct. Have your child write the numbers from the problem in the correct spots on the Part-Total Mat.

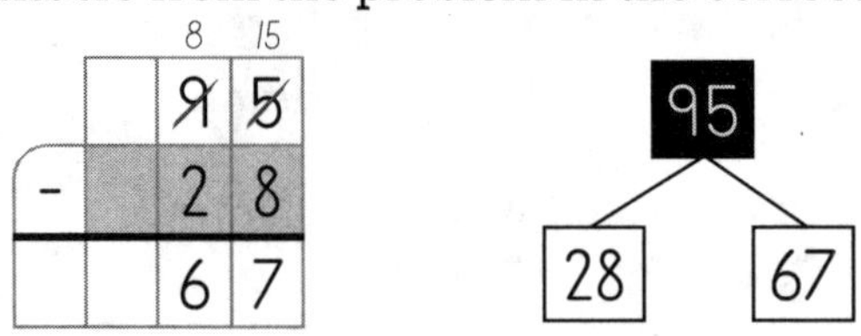

The total is 95. The parts are 28 and 67. So, what answer should I get if I add 28 and 67? *95.* Write 67 and 28 in the neighboring blank grid. Have your child solve the problem with the addition algorithm.

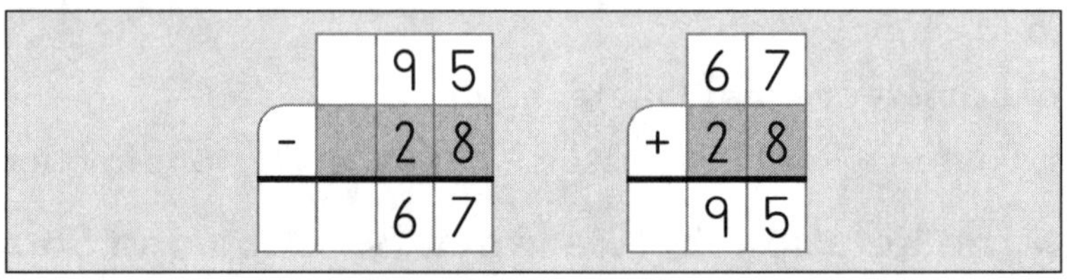

If you didn't get a sum of 95, then you would know you made a mistake and need to check your work.

Have your child solve the other two subtraction problems on the page in the same way. After she solves each subtraction problem, have her write and solve an addition problem to check her work.

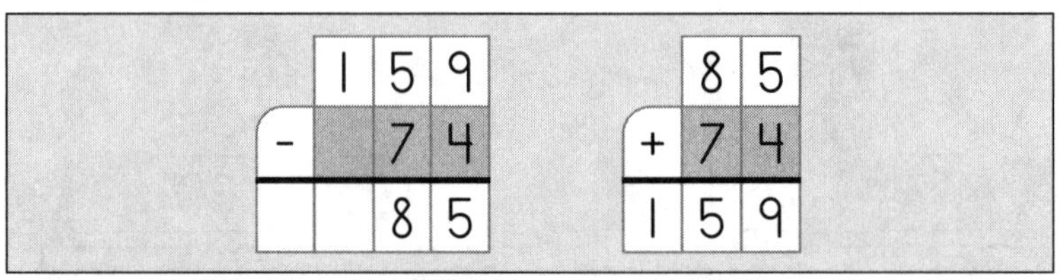

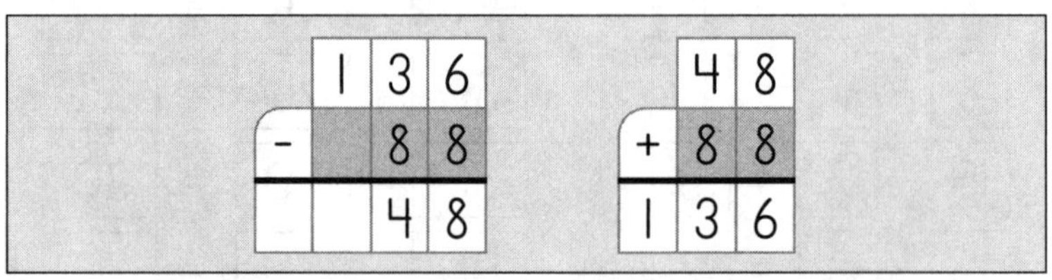

Your child can write the addends in the addition problems in any order.

Workbook: Review

Have your child complete workbook page 27.3B.

Lesson 27.4
Subtraction Word Problems

	Purpose	Materials
Warm-up	• Count by 5s • Practice memory work • Review comparing fractions	• Play money • Fraction Bars (Blackline Master 9), cut apart and labeled • Fraction Cards (from Lesson 25.2 and 25.3)
Activities	• Solve two-digit subtraction word problems	• Workbook page 27.4A
Workbook	• Subtract two-digit numbers with the subtraction algorithm	• Workbook pages 27.4A and 27.4B

Warm-up: Counting, Memory Work, and Review

- Place 4 hundred-dollar bills and 10-15 five-dollar bills on the table. **Let's count this money by 5s, starting at 400.** Count the bills by 5s in unison with your child: **400, 405, 410...**
- **What is another name for 12 p.m.?** *Noon.* **What is another name for 12 a.m.?** *Midnight.*
- Play Fraction War. See Lesson 25.4 (page 409) for directions.

Activity: Solve Two-Digit Subtraction Word Problems

In this unit, you have learned how to use the subtraction algorithm to subtract two-digit numbers. Today, you'll use the subtraction algorithm to solve word problems.

Show your child workbook page 27.4A and read aloud the first problem: ***How many more oatmeal raisin cookies than lemon cookies were sold?*** **How will you solve this problem?** *Subtract the number of lemon cookies sold from the number of oatmeal raisin cookies sold.* If needed, remind your child that he can subtract the lesser number from the greater number to find the difference.

How many oatmeal raisin cookies were sold? *123.* **How many lemon cookies were sold?** *49.* Have your child write the numbers in the blank grid and find their difference. Check that he writes the digits in the correct spots in the grid.

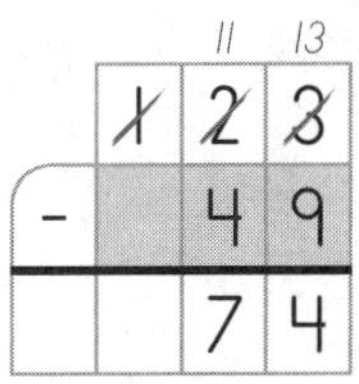

Repeat with the other word problems on the page.

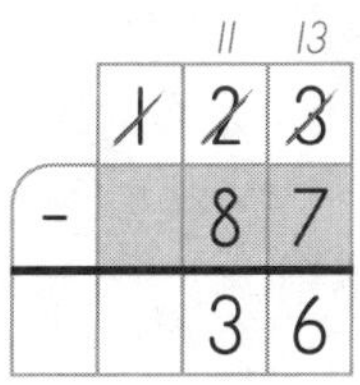

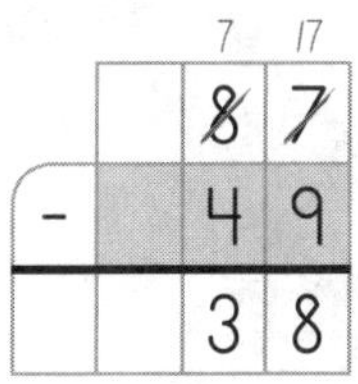

Workbook: Subtract Two-Digit Numbers and Review

Have your child complete workbook pages 27.4A and 27.4B.

The bottom part of workbook page 27.4A serves as an assessment of your child's fluency and accuracy with two-digit subtraction. See the Unit 12 Checkpoint for more on assessing your child's progress with this skill.

If your child has trouble counting by half-hours and quarter-hours to complete the time sequences on workbook page 27.4B, have him use a real clock to show the times. For example, for the first exercise, have him set a clock to 7:00. Then, he can move the hands a half-hour backward to see that 6:30 comes before 7:00 in the sequence.

Lesson 27.5
Enrichment and Review (Optional)

	Purpose	Materials
Warm-up	• Count by 3s and 4s • Review memory work • Review your child's favorite or most challenging activities from Week 27	• Varies, depending on the activities you choose
Picture Book	• Explore the concept of infinity	• *Infinity and Me,* written by Kate Hosford and illustrated by Gabi Swiatkowska
Enrichment Activity	• Practice two-digit subtraction in the context of money	• Toy catalog or access to a website with items your child would like to buy • Play money

Warm-up: Counting, Memory Work, and Review

- Have your child count by 3s to 30 and by 4s to 40.
- Quiz your child on the memory work through Week 26. See page 523 for the full list.
- If you have time, repeat one or two of the activities from this week's lessons. Choose activities your child especially enjoyed or found challenging.

Math Picture Book: *Infinity and Me*

Read *Infinity and Me,* written by Kate Hosford and illustrated by Gabi Swiatkowska. As you read, enjoy the poetic descriptions of infinity and encourage your child to make up her own imaginative descriptions.

Enrichment Activity: Shopping Spree

Give your child \$150 in play money (1 hundred-dollar bill and 5 ten-dollar bills). Have her choose an item she would like to pretend to buy from a toy catalog or website and use the subtraction algorithm to figure out how much money she has left. For example, if she chooses an item that costs \$37:

$$\begin{array}{r} {\scriptstyle 4\ 10} \\ 1\not{5}\not{0} \\ -\ 37 \\ \hline 113 \end{array}$$

Then, have her pretend to pay for the item with the play money and check that she has the correct amount of money left.

If the price includes cents, round the price to the nearest dollar. Your child may need to trade bills in order to pay with the correct bills. As she trades the bills, discuss how the bills match the subtraction algorithm. For example: You had 5 tens. You traded 1 ten for 10 ones, so now you have 4 tens left.

Repeat with other items. Each time, have her subtract to find out how much money she has left. Continue until she has pretended to spend all the money.

Week 27 Answer Key

27.1A

See the Instructor Guide for directions.

	1	1	8
-		6	2
		5	6

	1	7	2
-		5	9
	1	1	3

	1	4	3
-		6	5
		7	8

What's the Difference?

147	155	87	58
169	138	99	46
181	170	63	90
163	131	55	83

27.1B

Match.

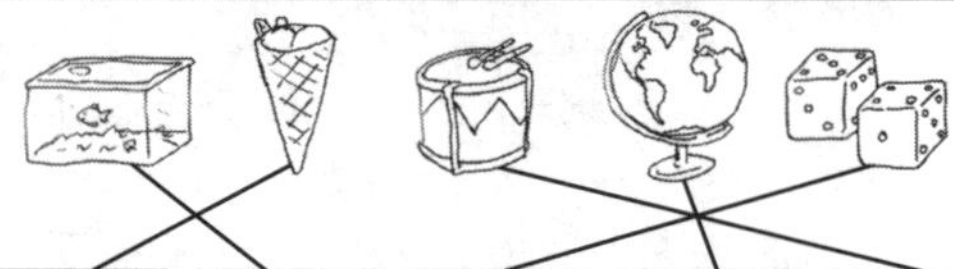

Cone | Rectangular prism | Cube | Sphere | Cylinder

Use a ruler to measure the ribbons in inches.

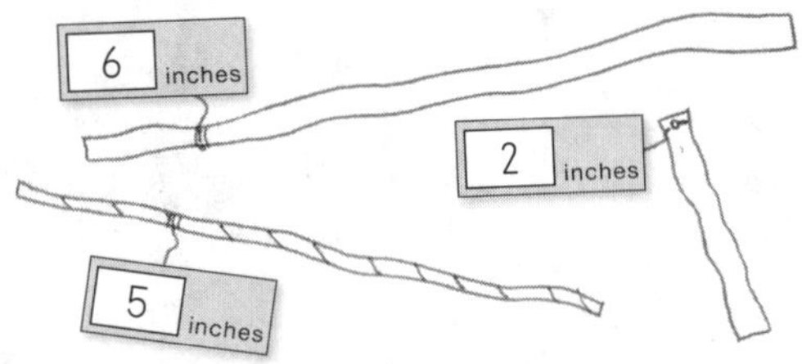

Write the expanded form for each number.

41 = 40 + 1	140 = 100 + 40
141 = 100 + 40 + 1	104 = 100 + 4
144 = 100 + 40 + 4	114 = 100 + 10 + 4

27.2A

See the Instructor Guide for directions.

	1	2	6
-		7	8
		4	8

	1	5	1
-		7	3
		7	8

	1	9	5
-		6	9
	1	2	6

Connect the Boxes

171 − 54 = 117	71 − 36 = 35	84 − 69 = 15	91 − 35 = 56
146 − 68 = 78	92 − 56 = 36	63 − 28 = 35	51 − 37 = 14
182 − 57 = 125	97 − 54 = 43	80 − 47 = 33	65 − 9 = 56
125 − 92 = 33	98 − 52 = 46	55 − 36 = 19	93 − 64 = 29

27.2B

Choose the more sensible measurement for each item.

Length of a baby	Length of a fork	Length of a playground
(50 centimeters) / 50 meters	20 meters / (20 centimeters)	45 kilometers / (45 meters)

Write the time.

11:05 | 10:57 | 12:12

Color the shapes to match the fractions. Then, complete each circle with <, >, or =.

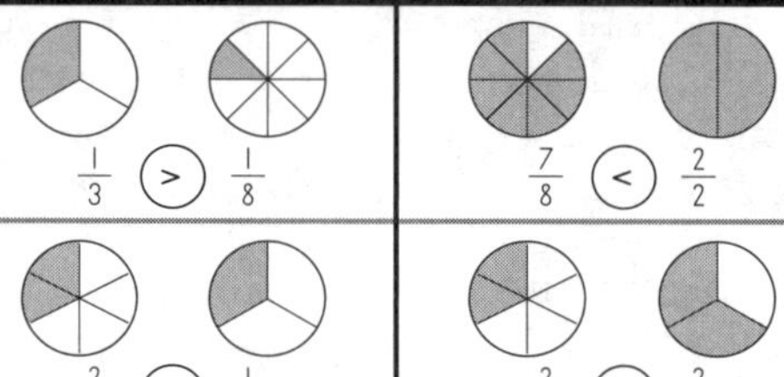

$\frac{1}{3} > \frac{1}{8}$ | $\frac{7}{8} < \frac{2}{2}$

$\frac{2}{6} = \frac{1}{3}$ | $\frac{2}{6} < \frac{2}{3}$

Week 27 Answer Key

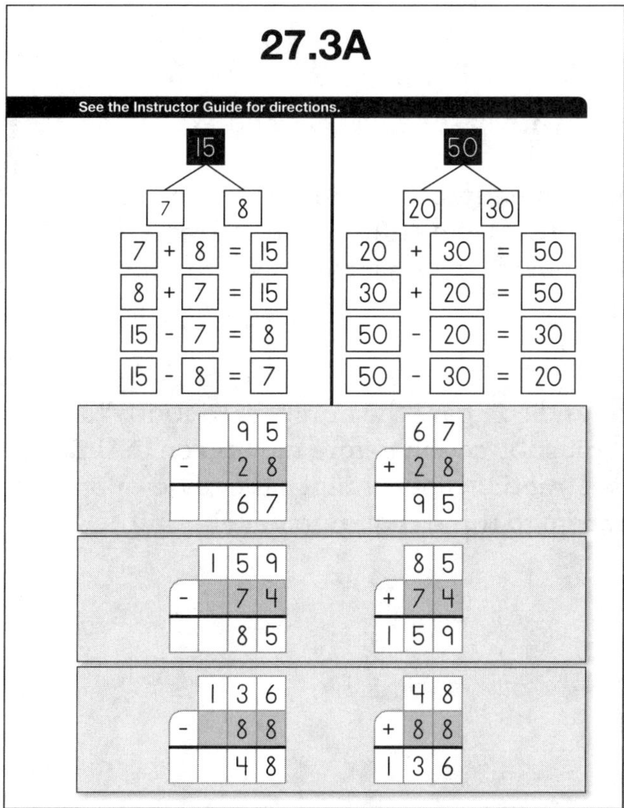

27.3A

See the Instructor Guide for directions.

15 → 7, 8

7 + 8 = 15
8 + 7 = 15
15 - 7 = 8
15 - 8 = 7

50 → 20, 30

20 + 30 = 50
30 + 20 = 50
50 - 20 = 30
50 - 30 = 20

95 - 28 = 67; 67 + 28 = 95

159 - 74 = 85; 85 + 74 = 159

136 - 88 = 48; 48 + 88 = 136

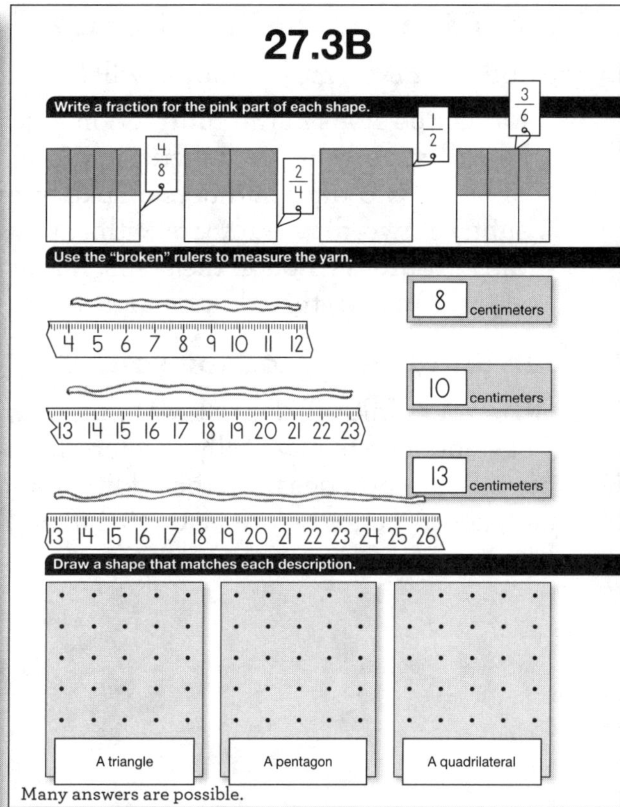

27.3B

Write a fraction for the pink part of each shape.

4/8, 2/4, 1/2, 3/6

Use the "broken" rulers to measure the yarn.

8 centimeters

10 centimeters

13 centimeters

Draw a shape that matches each description.

A triangle | A pentagon | A quadrilateral

Many answers are possible.

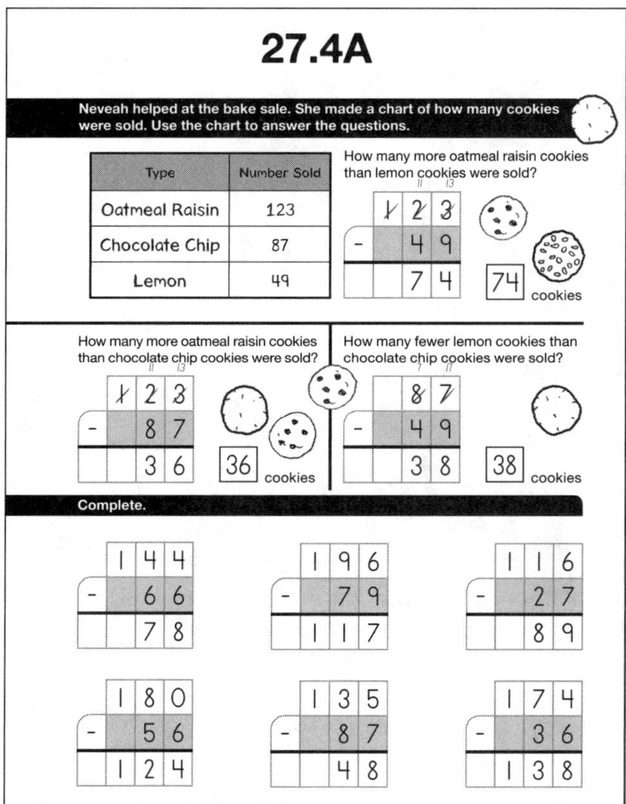

27.4A

Neveah helped at the bake sale. She made a chart of how many cookies were sold. Use the chart to answer the questions.

Type	Number Sold
Oatmeal Raisin	123
Chocolate Chip	87
Lemon	49

How many more oatmeal raisin cookies than lemon cookies were sold?

123 - 49 = 74 — 74 cookies

How many more oatmeal raisin cookies than chocolate chip cookies were sold?

123 - 87 = 36 — 36 cookies

How many fewer lemon cookies than chocolate chip cookies were sold?

87 - 49 = 38 — 38 cookies

Complete.

144 - 66 = 78
196 - 79 = 117
116 - 27 = 89
180 - 56 = 124
135 - 87 = 48
174 - 36 = 138

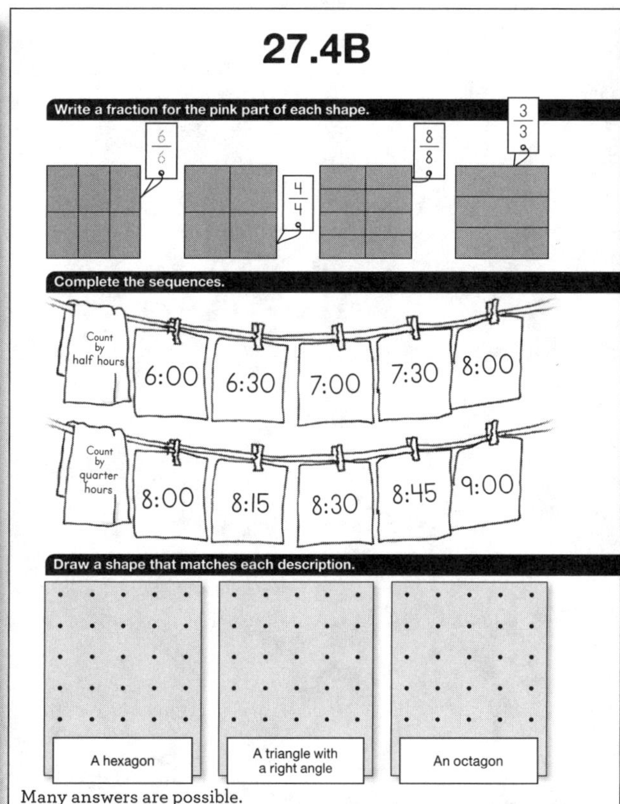

27.4B

Write a fraction for the pink part of each shape.

6/6, 4/4, 8/8, 3/3

Complete the sequences.

Count by half hours: 6:00, 6:30, 7:00, 7:30, 8:00

Count by quarter hours: 8:00, 8:15, 8:30, 8:45, 9:00

Draw a shape that matches each description.

A hexagon | A triangle with a right angle | An octagon

Many answers are possible.

Unit 12 Checkpoint

What to Expect at the End of Unit 12

By the end of Unit 12, most children will be able to do the following:

- Model the steps in the subtraction algorithm with base-ten blocks and explain how the blocks correspond to the written digits.
- Subtract two-digit numbers on paper, mostly fluently. Some children will be able to subtract two-digit numbers with ease, while others will still need to stop and think as they progress through the steps. Many children will be less fluent with the subtraction algorithm than the addition algorithm.

Is Your Child Ready to Move on?

In Unit 13, your child will learn how to read, write, and compare the numbers to 1000. Your child does not need to have fully mastered two-digit subtraction before moving on to Unit 13. He'll continue to practice both the addition and subtraction algorithms in the review portions of the workbook pages before he begins to apply them to three-digit numbers in Unit 14.

Unit 13
Numbers to 1000

Overview

Your child will build on what she knows about the numbers to 200 as she learns to read, write, and compare numbers to 1000. She'll also learn how to perform simple mental math with three-digit numbers, find pairs that make 1000, and count larger money amounts. As in the previous units, you'll use base-ten blocks, play money, and the number line to help her develop deep number sense with the numbers to 1000.

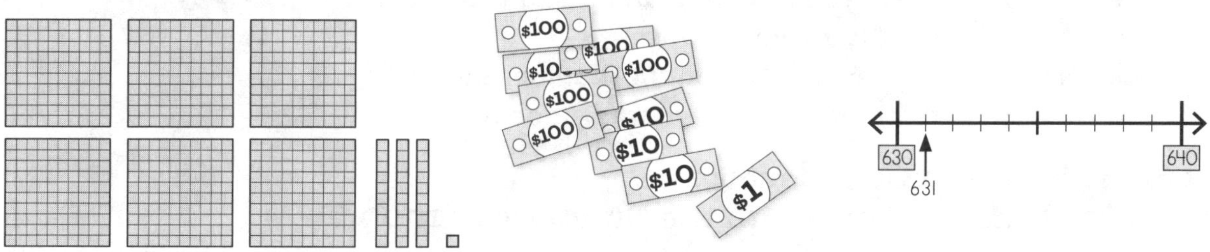

3 different ways to represent 631.

Your child may find this unit a welcome break after the challenge of mastering the subtraction algorithm! She'll continue to build fluency and automaticity with the addition and subtraction algorithms in the review exercises. In Unit 14, she'll integrate all these skills as she learns to add and subtract three-digit numbers with the written processes.

Week 28	Numbers to 1000
Week 29	Mental Math with Numbers to 1000

What Your Child Will Learn

In this unit your child will learn to:

- Read, write, and compare numbers to 1000
- Write numbers to 1000 in expanded form
- Identify even and odd numbers to 1000
- Count by 1s, 2s, 5s, or 10s to 1000
- Solve simple mental addition and subtraction problems with the numbers to 1000
- Identify pairs that make 1000
- Count money amounts up to $1000

Recommended Math Picture Books (Optional)

These picture books are scheduled in the optional Enrichment and Review lessons at the end of each week.

- *How Much is a Million?*, written by David M. Schwartz and illustrated by Steven Kellogg. Mulberry Books, 1985.
- *Sir Cumference and All the King's Tens: A Math Adventure*, written by Cindy Neuschwander and illustrated by Wayne Geehan. Charlesbridge, 2009.

Week 28
Numbers to 1000

Overview

Your child will extend his knowledge of place value and the counting sequence to read, write, and compare numbers to 1000. He'll also learn how to write numbers to 1000 in expanded form, identify evens and odds, and count by 2s.

Lesson 28.1 Compare Numbers to 1000
Lesson 28.2 Expanded Form for Numbers to 1000
Lesson 28.3 Page Numbers to 1000
Lesson 28.4 Numbers to 1000 on the Number Line
Lesson 28.5 Enrichment and Review (Optional)

Teaching Math with Confidence: Developing Number Sense with the Numbers to 1000

This week, you'll teach your child how to read, write, and compare numbers to 1000. Children are sometimes intimidated by these larger numbers. To prevent this, you'll show him how to build on what he already knows about place value and counting to make sense of them.

First, you'll teach him to read and write numbers to 1000. Just as with the numbers to 200, we read and write these numbers from left to right, according to each digit's place value. You'll also teach him how to use place value to write these numbers in expanded form.

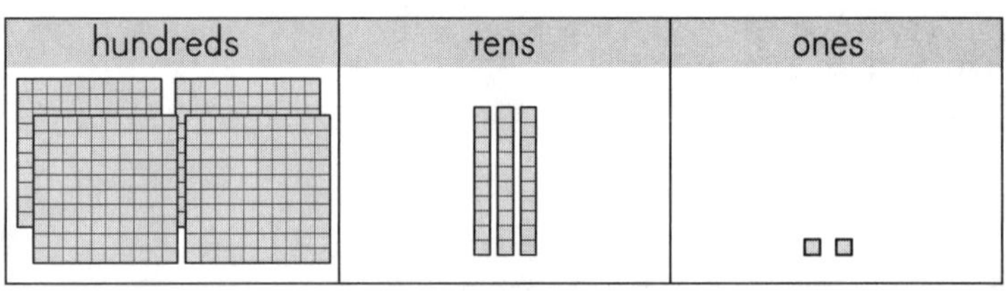

432 = 400 + 30 + 2

You'll also teach him to identify numbers on the number line, using the same reasoning that he used for the numbers to 200. He'll see that he can follow familiar patterns to identify the numbers. For example, he already knows that the tick mark after 160 is 161. By the same logic, the tick mark after 460 is 461.

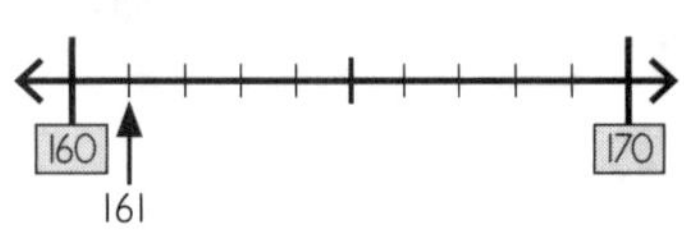

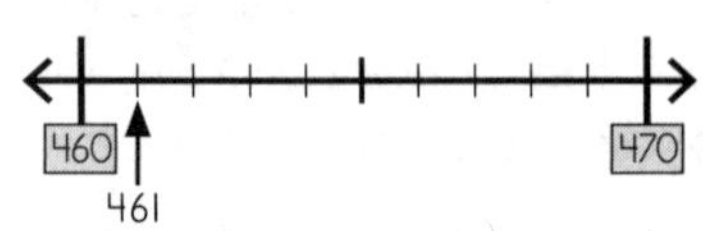

As you teach your child this week, constantly encourage him to use what he already knows about the numbers to 200 to make sense of the numbers to 1000. This will help demystify these numbers and help him feel more comfortable with them. He'll learn to perform mental addition and subtraction with the numbers to 1000 in Week 29.

Extra Materials Needed for Week 28

- 6 slips of paper
- Book with over 1000 pages
- For optional Enrichment and Review Lesson:
    - *How Much is a Million?*, written by David M. Schwartz and illustrated by Steven Kellogg
    - Felt-tip marker or bingo dotter, optional
    - Posterboard or construction paper, optional
    - Small food items, such as popcorn, dried beans, or macaroni, optional

Lesson 28.1
Compare Numbers to 1000

	Purpose	Materials
Warm-up	• Count by 100s • Practice memory work • Review place-value vocabulary	• Play money
Activities	• Read numbers to 1000 • Compare numbers to 1000	• Base-ten blocks • Place-Value Chart (Blackline Master 5) • Playing cards
Workbook	• Write numbers to 1000 • Compare numbers to 1000	• Workbook pages 28.1A and 28.1B

Warm-up: Counting, Memory Work, and Review

- Place 6-8 hundred-dollar bills on the table. Have your child count by 100s to find their value.
- **How many sides does a triangle have?** *3.* **A quadrilateral?** *4.* **A pentagon?** *5.* **A hexagon?** *6.* **An octagon?** *8.*
- Write the number 198 on a piece of paper. **How many digits does this number have?** *3.* **Which digit is in the ones-place?** *8.* **The tens-place?** *9.* **The hundreds-place?** *1.* Also have your child write 198 in expanded form.

$$198 = 100 + 90 + 8$$

Activity: Read and Compare Numbers to 1000

This year, you have learned about place value with the numbers to 200. Today, you'll use what you know about place value to read and compare numbers to 1000.

Write 638 on a piece of paper. Draw a horizontal line across the Place-Value Chart. Have your child place blocks on the top of the chart to match each digit in 638, as shown. (He can stack the flats as needed.)

638

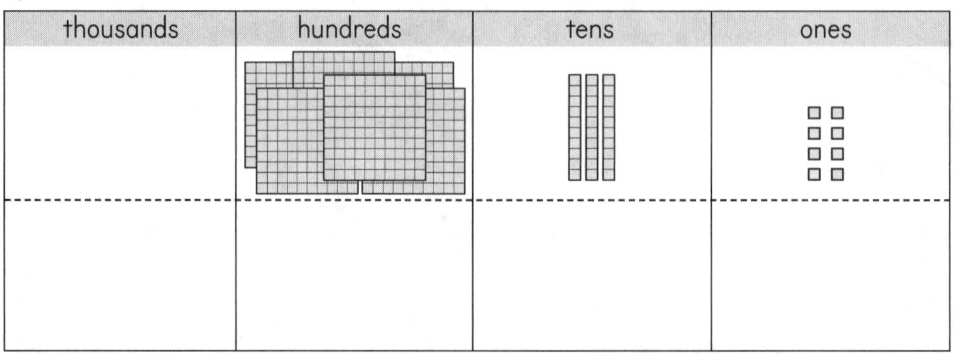

How do you think we read this number? *Six hundred thirty-eight.* If your child is not sure, point to each column as you name the value of the blocks in it: **600...30...8. So, the number is six hundred thirty-eight.**

> In American English, the number 638 is usually read as "six hundred thirty-eight." In British English, it is typically read as "six hundred and thirty-eight." Either way is fine, but make sure not to read it as "six-three-eight" so your spoken words reinforce the digits' place-value meaning.

Write 386 on a piece of paper, below 638. Have your child place blocks on the bottom of the Place-Value Chart to match.

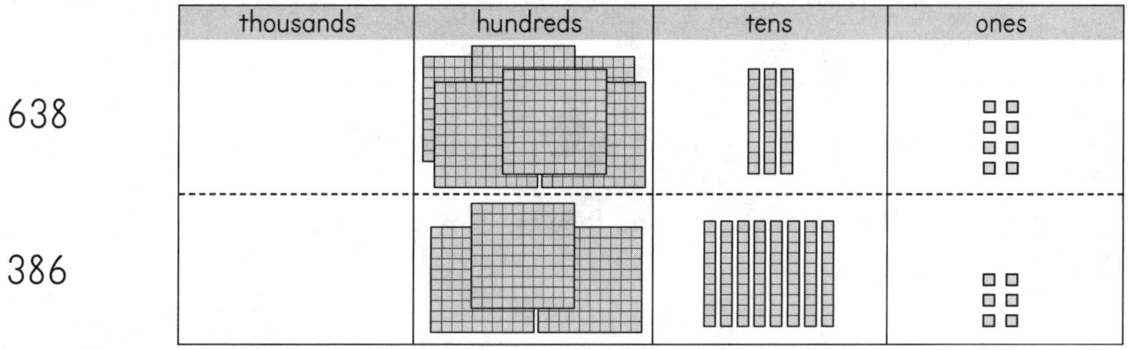

How do you think we read this number? *Three hundred eighty-six.* If your child is not sure, point to each column as you name the value of the blocks in it: **300...80...6. So, the number is three hundred eighty-six.**

Which number is greater, 638 or 386? *638.* **How do you know?** *Sample answer: 638 has more hundreds than 386.*

Repeat with the following pairs of numbers. Have your child model each number with base-ten blocks.

- 545 and 546. *546 is greater than 545.*
- 832 and 799. *832 is greater than 799.*
- 406 and 460. *460 is greater than 406.*

Activity: Prepare to Play Three-Digit War

We're going to play War to practice comparing three-digit numbers. In this version of the game, you get 3 cards and use them to make a three-digit number. Whoever has the greater number wins all the cards.

Before we play, we'll first investigate how to arrange the cards to make the greatest number possible. Place a 2, 5, and 8 from a deck of playing cards on the table. (Any suit is fine.) **Here's one way to arrange the cards.** Make the number 528 from the cards. Write 528 on a piece of paper.

528

There are 5 more ways to arrange the cards. I wonder how many of them you can find! Have your child find as many different ways as she can to arrange the cards. Record each number that she makes.

Below are all possible three-digit numbers. If your child misses any, demonstrate the arrangement and add the matching numbers to the list.

528 258
582 825
285 852

Which number is greatest? *852.* **Which number is least?** *258.* **What do you think is the best strategy for arranging your cards in Three-Digit War?** *Sample answer: Put the greatest digit in the hundreds-place and the next-greatest digit in the tens-place.*

Activity: Play Three-Digit War

Play Three-Digit War. Have your child say the numbers aloud as she plays to practice reading three-digit numbers.

Three-Digit War

Materials: 1 deck of cards, 10s and face cards removed (36 cards total)

Object of the Game: Win the most cards.

Shuffle the cards and deal them face down in two piles. Both players flip over the top 3 cards in their pile and use the digits to make the greatest possible three-digit number. (For example, if you turn over a 5, 9, and 1, you can make 159, 195, 519, 591, 915, or 951. Choose 951, since it is greatest.)

Make the greatest possible three-digit number from your cards.

Whoever has the greater number wins all 6 cards.

If the numbers are equal, leave the cards face-up on the table and have both players make a new three-digit number with the next 3 cards in their piles. Whoever creates the greater number wins all the face-up cards.

Play until the piles run out. Whoever has won more cards wins the game.

Workbook: Write and Compare Numbers to 1000 and Review

Have your child complete workbook pages 28.1A and 28.1B.

Lesson 28.2
Expanded Form for Numbers to 1000

	Purpose	Materials
Warm-up	• Count by 1s • Practice memory work • Review comparing three-digit numbers	• Play money • Playing cards
Activities	• Understand that 10 hundreds equal 1 thousand • Write three-digit numbers in expanded form	• Base-ten blocks • Place-Value Chart (Blackline Master 5) • Number Machine (from Lesson 6.1) • 6 slips of paper
Workbook	• Read numbers to 1000 • Write three-digit numbers in expanded form	• Workbook pages 28.2A and 28.2B

Warm-up: Counting, Memory Work, and Review

- Place 7 hundred-dollar bills and 15-20 one-dollar bills on the table. Have your child count by 1s, starting at 700, to find the money's value.
- **What do we call the result when we add numbers together?** *The sum.* **What do we call the result when we subtract a number from another number?** *The difference.*
- Play Three-Digit War. See Lesson 28.1 (page 450) for directions.

Activity: Introduce the Thousands-Place

Today, you'll learn about the number 1000. We'll also use the Number Machine! Place the Place-Value Chart and base-ten blocks on the table. Put 1 unit block in the ones-place, 1 rod in the tens-place, and 1 flat in the hundreds-place.

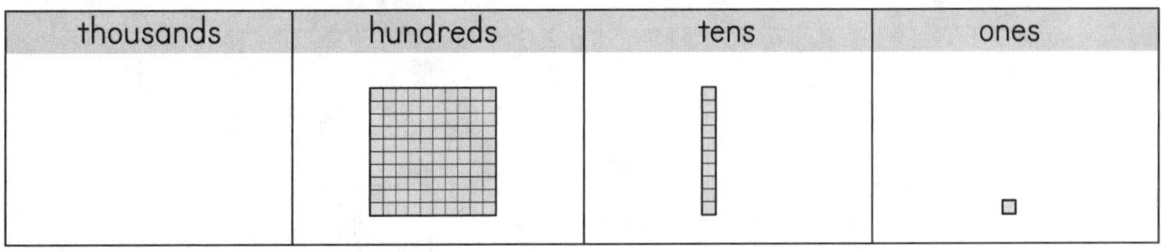

How many ones equal 1 ten? *10.* **How many tens equal 1 hundred?** *10.* **So, how many hundreds do you think equal 1 thousand?** *10.* Show your child the thousand-cube and place it in the thousands-place.

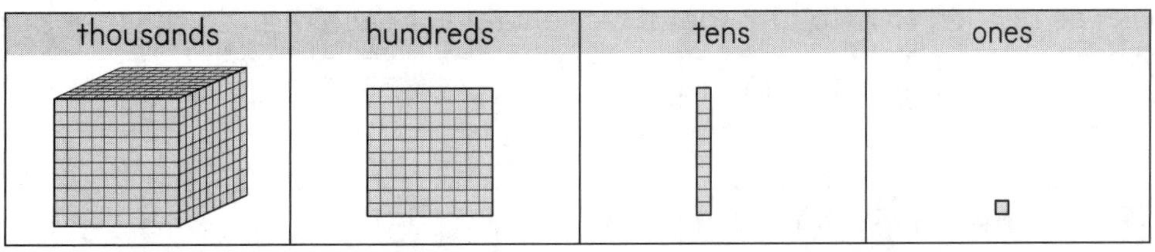

This pattern continues for larger numbers, too! You'll learn about numbers greater than 1000 next year.

Let's check that the thousand-cube is really the same size as 10 flats. Stack 10 flats and compare them to the thousand-cube. **Here's how we write 1000.** Write 1000 on a piece of paper.

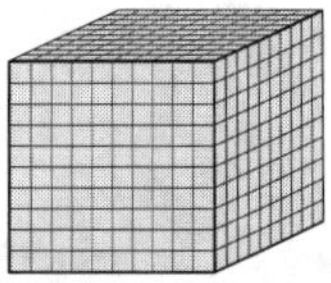
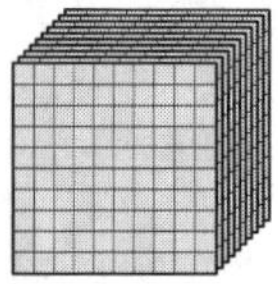

1000

Activity: Write Numbers in Expanded Form with the Number Machine

Stand the Number Machine on the table between you and your child. Pretend to turn a knob on the front of the machine to set it. **Let's see what happens when I put 482 into the Number Machine on this setting.** Write 482 on a slip of paper and slide it behind the Number Machine screen. Secretly write "400 + 80 + 2" on the back of the slip and slide it out from behind the other side.

Hmm, what do you think the Number Machine is doing to the number on this setting? *Writing the expanded form of the number.*

The Number Machine is on the expanded form setting. Remember, the expanded form of a number shows the value of each digit. Write 395 on a piece of paper. **What do you think will come out of the Number Machine for this number?** *300 + 90 + 5.*

Slide the slip of paper with 395 behind the Number Machine. Secretly write "300 + 90 + 5" on the back of the slip and slide it out from behind the other side.

395 → 300+90+5

If your child is uncertain, have him write the digits on the Place-Value Chart and model them with base-ten blocks. **What's the value of the 3?** *300.* **What's the value of the 9?** *90.* **What's the value of the 5?** *5.* **So, the expanded form of 395 is 300 plus 90 plus 5.**

	thousands	hundreds	tens	ones
395		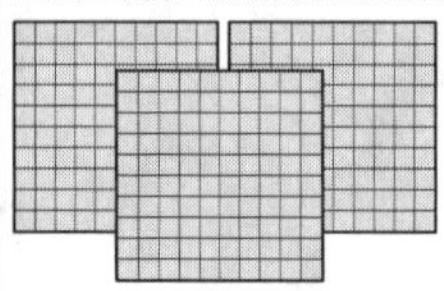	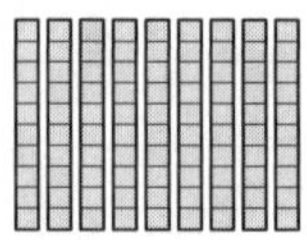	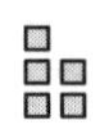

Let's leave the Number Machine on the expanded form setting and put some more numbers into it. Have your child predict the Number Machine's results for the following numbers. Use base-ten blocks as needed to help him identify the value of each digit in the numbers.

581 → 500+80+1

777 → 700+70+7

409 → 400+9

650 → 600+50

Your child does not need to write the value of any placeholder zeros in the number.

Workbook: Write Numbers in Expanded Form and Review

Have your child complete workbook pages 28.2A and 28.2B.

Lesson 28.3
Page Numbers to 1000

	Purpose	Materials
Warm-up	• Count by 1s from any number to 1000 • Practice memory work • Review comparing numbers to 1000	• None
Activities	• Identify the numbers that come before and after a given number	• Book with over 1000 pages
Workbook	• Count forward and backward from numbers to 1000 • Identify the numbers that come before and after a given number	• Workbook pages 28.3A and 28.3B

Children often have trouble locating pages in large books, so this lesson provides practice with this very useful skill. You will need a book with over 1000 pages. You'll only look at the page numbers, so choose any book with child-appropriate content, such as a dictionary, Bible, textbook, or cookbook.

Warm-up: Counting, Memory Work, and Review

- Have your child count forward from the following numbers. Prompt her as needed, and stop her after she reaches the last number listed.
    - **Count forward from 632:** *632, 633, 634, 635, 636.*
    - **Count forward from 586:** *586, 587, 588, 589, 590.*
    - **Count forward from 949:** *949, 950, 951, 952, 953.*
- **How many hundreds equal 1 thousand?** *10.*
- Secretly choose a number between 1 and 1000. **I'm thinking of a number that's greater than 1 and less than 1000.** Have your child guess your number. After each guess, tell whether your secret number is more or less than her guess. Continue until she figures out your secret number.

    If your child has trouble remembering the numbers she has already guessed, write the guesses on a piece of paper.

Activity: Identify the Next Page Number

In the last two lessons, you have learned about the numbers to 1000. Knowing about the numbers to 1000 is very helpful when you want to find a page in a long book. Show your child a book with over 1000 pages. Open the book to several different pages and have her read the page number. Include page 1000.

Open the book to page 137. **What page comes after page 137?** *138.* Turn the page so your child can check.

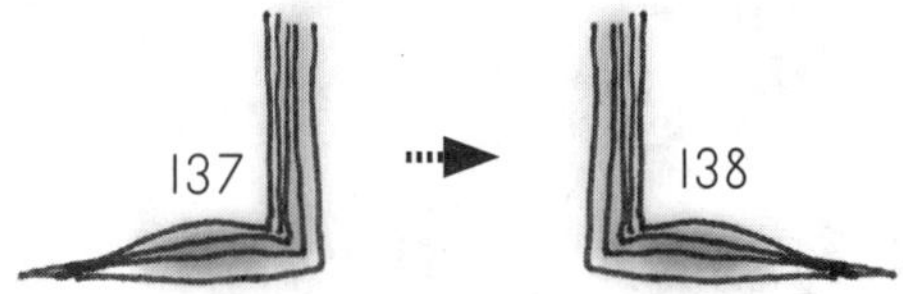

Page 138 comes after page 137, just like page 38 comes after page 37. The numbers after 200 follow this pattern, too. Open the book to page 237. **What page comes after page 237?** *238.* Turn the page so your child can check.

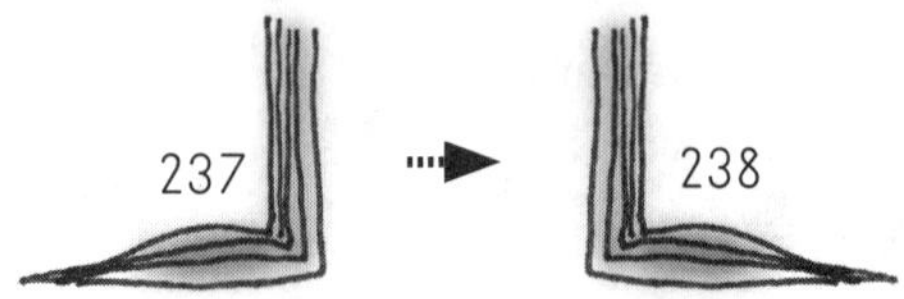

Repeat with pages 865 and 319. For each, have your child predict the page number for the next page and then turn the page to check.

See the Week 28 **Teaching Math with Confidence** for more on helping your child develop number sense with the numbers to 1000.

Activity: Identify the Previous Page Number

Open the book to page 162. **What page comes before page 162?** *161.* Turn the page to check.

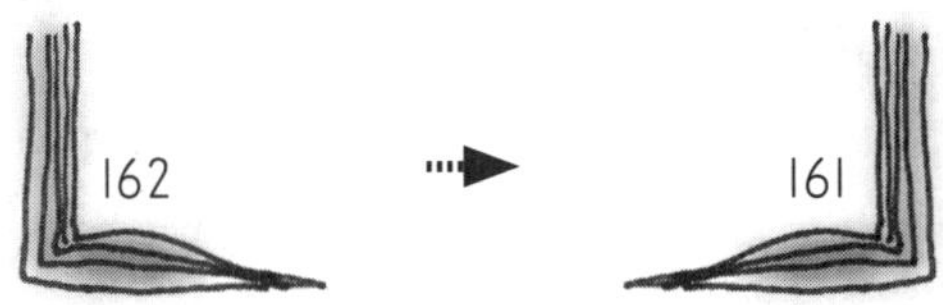

Open the book to page 562. **What page comes before page 562?** *561.*

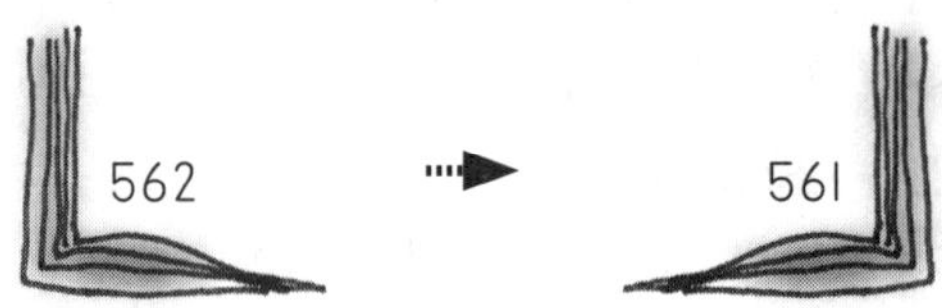

Repeat with pages 348 and 990. For each, have your child predict the page number for the previous page and turn the page to check.

Activity: Find Specific Pages in a Book

Show your child the book's Table of Contents. Choose a chapter in the middle of the book and show your child the page number where the chapter begins. **Let's pretend I wanted to start reading at this page. Can you open the book to that page for me?** *Child opens the book to the correct page number.*

Finding the page helps your child develop a deeper understanding of the number sequence to 1000, but it may take some trial and error. If she starts turning over one page at a time, encourage her to flip many pages at once instead.

Repeat with several other chapters in the book. Include chapters from the beginning, middle, and end of the book to give her practice with a range of numbers.

You will need this book again for the warm-up activity for Lesson 30.2.

Workbook: Count Forward and Backward and Review

Have your child complete workbook pages 28.3A and 28.3B.

Lesson 28.4
Numbers to 1000 on the Number Line

	Purpose	Materials
Warm-up	• Count backward • Practice memory work • Review identifying numbers on the number line	• Blank Number Line (Blackline Master 3)
Activities	• Identify numbers to 1000 on the number line • Count by 2s from numbers to 1000 • Identify even and odd numbers to 1000	• Blank Number Line (Blackline Master 3)
Workbook	• Identify numbers to 1000 on the number line • Identify even and odd numbers to 1000	• Workbook pages 28.4A and 28.4B

Warm-up: Counting, Memory Work, and Review

- Have your child count backward from the following numbers. Prompt him as needed, and stop him after he reaches the last number listed.
  - **Count backward from 949:** *949, 948, 947, 946, 945.*
  - **Count backward from 412:** *412, 411, 410, 409, 408.*
  - **Count backward from 632:** *632, 631, 630, 629, 628.*
- **How many hundreds equal 1 thousand?** *10.*
- Label the Blank Number Line with 150, 160, and 170. Have your child point to the tick mark for each of the following numbers: 161, 152, 157, 164, and 168.

Activity: Identify Numbers to 1000 on the Number Line

You have already learned how to find the numbers to 200 on the number line. You can use the same kind of thinking to find the numbers to 1000 on the number line.

Label the blank number line with 450, 460, and 470. Point to 460. **If this mark is 460, where is 461?** *Child points to next tick mark.*

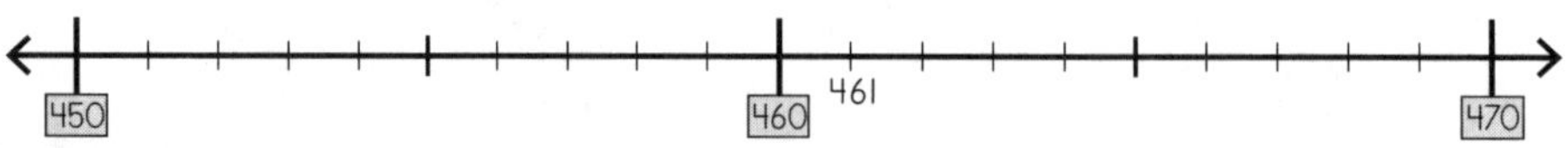

Where is 459? *Child points to tick mark before 460.* Have your child point to 452, 457, 464, and 468 (one at a time).

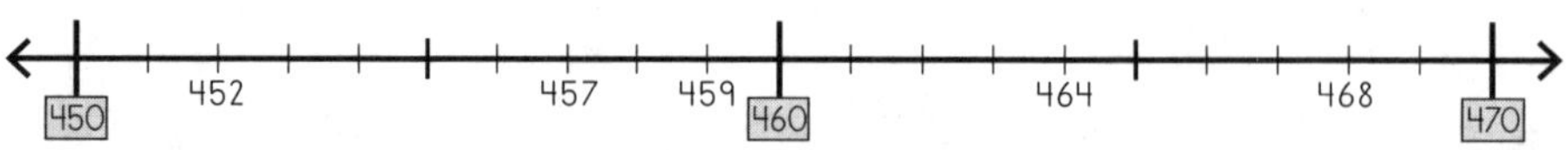

Then, reverse the process. Point to 463. **What number is this?** *463.* **How do you know?** *Possible answer: It's 3 tick marks after 460.*

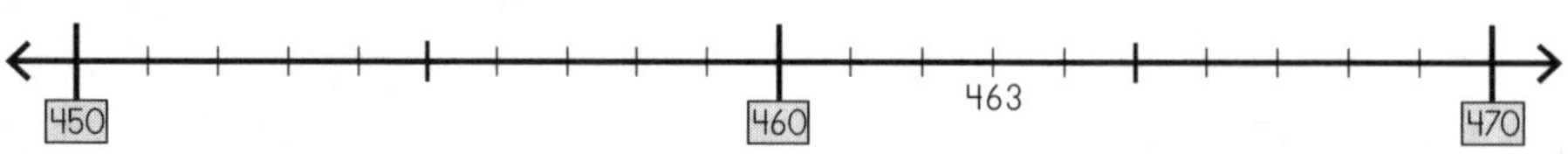

Point to 456, 459, 462, and 469 (one at a time) and have your child identify them.

What number is halfway between 450 and 460? *455.* **What number is halfway between 460 and 470?** *465.*

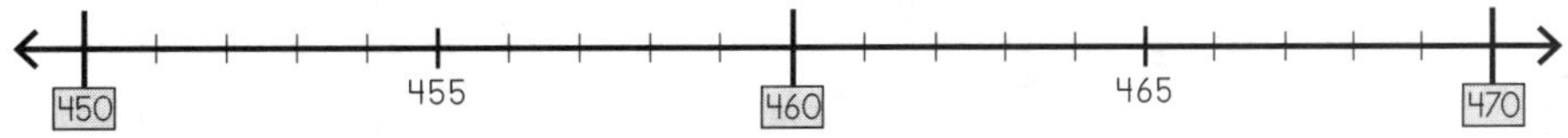

Count by 2s from 50 to 70. *50, 52, 54...* **You can use the same pattern to count from 450 to 470 on the number line.** Have your child count by 2s from 450 to 470: *450, 452, 454...* Have him point to the corresponding tick marks on the number line as he says each number. Prompt him as needed.

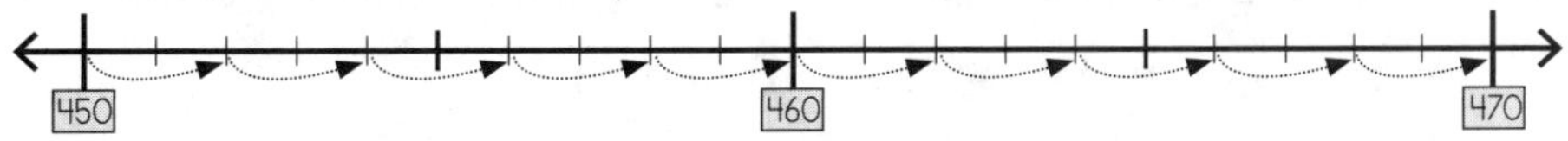

Activity: Cross the Century on the Number Line

Secretly label the number line with 790, 800, and 810. Cover the number line so that only the tick marks from 790 to 799 are showing. Have your child point to the following numbers: 791, 795, 796, 799.

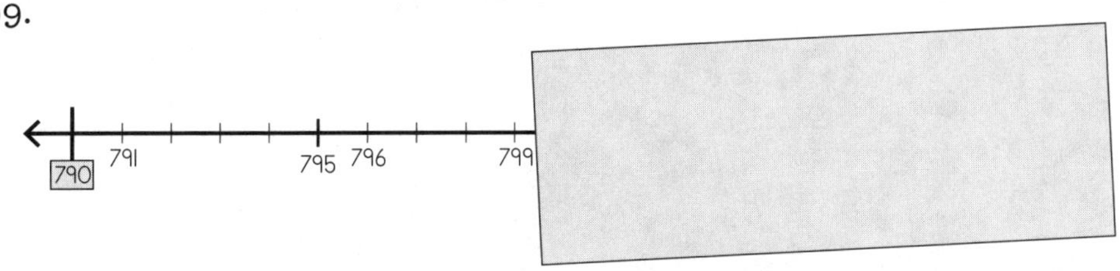

What number comes after 799? *800.* **How do you know?** *Answers will vary.* Remove the paper so your child can see the rest of the number line. Have him point to 804, 805, and 807.

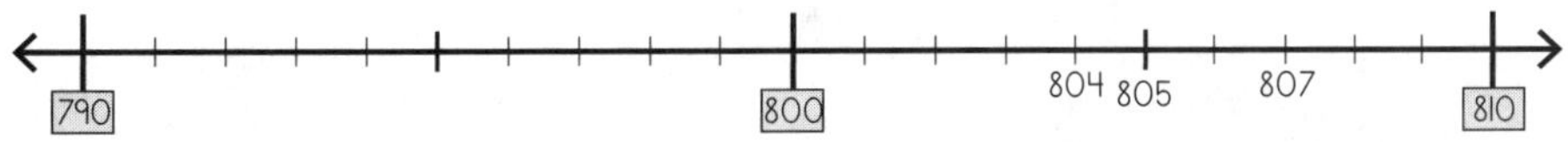

Sometimes children have trouble remembering what number comes next when they get to a new hundred. Just think: What's the next hundred? If you're counting in the 700s, the next hundred is 800. Have your child identify what number comes after each of the following numbers.

- **What number comes after 299?** *300.*
- **What number comes after 699?** *700.*
- **What number comes after 599?** *600.*
- **What number comes after 999?** *1000.*

Your child will practice crossing the century more in Week 29.

Activity: Even and Odd Numbers to 1000

You can also use the patterns you already know to identify even and odd numbers to 1000. If a number has 1, 3, 5, 7, or 9 in the ones-place, is the number even or odd? *Odd.* **If a number has 0, 2, 4, 6, or 8 in the ones-place, is the number even or odd?** *Even.*

You can use those rules to look at any number's ones-place and tell whether the number is even or odd. Write 398 on a piece of paper. **Underline the digit in the ones-place.** *Child underlines the 8.* **398 has an 8 in the ones-place. So, is it even or odd?** *Even.*

39<u>8</u>

Underlining the digit in the ones-place ensures that your child looks at the correct digit.

Write the following numbers on a piece of paper. Have your child underline the digit in the ones-place and tell whether the number is even or odd.

- **131.** *Odd.*
- **650.** *Even.*
- **847.** *Odd.*
- **509.** *Odd.*
- **800.** *Even.*

Workbook: Identify Numbers on the Number Line and Review

Have your child complete workbook pages 28.4A and 28.4B.

Lesson 28.5
Enrichment and Review (Optional)

	Purpose	Materials
Warm-up	• Count from 200 to 300 by 1s or 2s • Review memory work • Review your child's favorite or most challenging activities from Week 28	• Varies, depending on the activities you choose
Picture Book	• Understand the magnitude of one million	• *How Much is a Million?,* written by David M. Schwartz and illustrated by Steven Kellogg
Enrichment Activity	• Count to 1000 • Physically experience the magnitude of the number 1000	• Felt-tip marker or bingo dotter, optional • Posterboard or construction paper, optional • Small food items, such as popcorn kernels, dried beans, or grains of rice, optional

Warm-up: Counting, Memory Work, and Review

- Have your child count from 200 to 300 by 1s or 2s. (Choose whichever counting sequence your child needs to practice the most.)
- Quiz your child on the memory work through Week 28. See page 523 for the full list.
- If you have time, repeat one or two of the activities from this week's lessons. Choose activities your child especially enjoyed or found challenging.

Math Picture Book: *How Much is a Million?*

Read *How Much is a Million?,* written by David M. Schwartz and illustrated by Steven Kellogg. As you read, marvel with your child at the many different ways the book illustrates the enormity of the number.

Enrichment Activity: How Much is 1000?

Choose from one of the following activities to give your child the opportunity to count to 1000. You may want to split the activity over several days if your child tires of counting.

- **Craft project:** Have your child use a felt-tip marker or bingo dotter to make 1000 dots on a piece of posterboard or several sheets of paper. Have him count as he makes each dot.
- **Walk 1000 steps:** Have your child count 1000 steps on a walk around your neighborhood or at a park. Before he starts counting, ask him to predict how far he will get. Afterward, discuss how close his estimate was to the actual distance.
- **Estimate and count objects:** Show your child a small food item, like popcorn kernels, dried beans, or grains of rice. Ask him to pour out about 1000 pieces of the food. Then, have him count to find the actual number that he poured out. (Stop if he reaches 1000.) Discuss how his estimate compares to the actual number.

Week 28 Answer Key

28.1A

Write the value of each set of base-ten blocks.

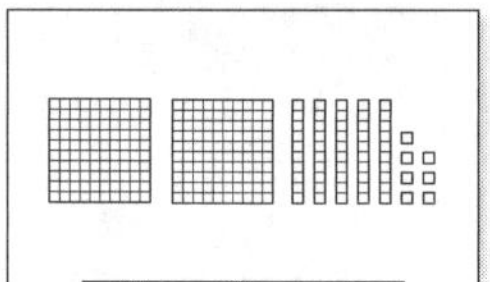

100s	10s	1s
2	5	7

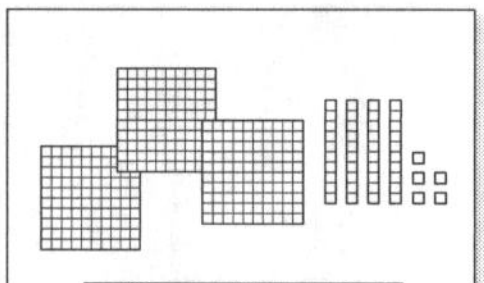

100s	10s	1s
3	4	5

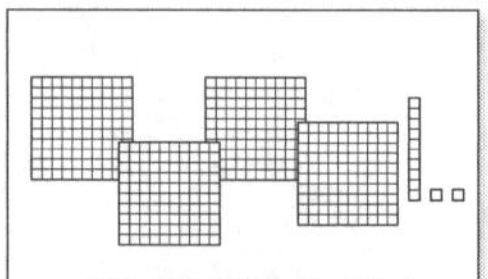

100s	10s	1s
4	1	2

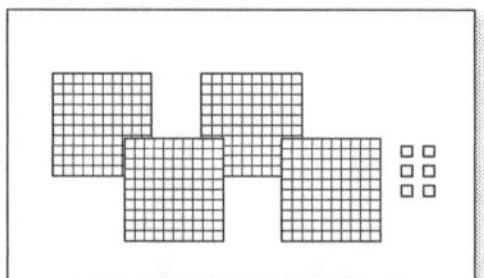

100s	10s	1s
4	0	6

Complete the circles with <, >, or =.

425 (<) 525	628 (>) 618	923 (<) 924
847 (>) 609	352 (=) 352	714 (<) 900
700 (>) 450	809 (<) 890	600 (>) 599

28.1B

Complete.

154 − 81 = 73

136 − 99 = 37

99 − 37 = 62

Elena made a graph about the spring flowers at the park. Use the graph to complete the chart and answer the questions.

Spring Flowers

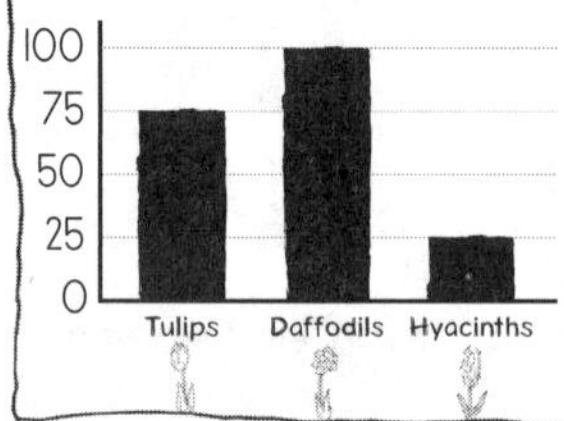

Flower	Number
Tulips	75
Daffodils	100
Hyacinths	25

How many more daffodils than tulips are there?
100 − 75 = 25
25 more

How many fewer hyacinths than tulips are there?
75 − 25 = 50
50 fewer

How many more daffodils than hyacinths are there?
100 − 25 = 75
75 more

How many flowers are there in all?
75 + 100 + 25 = 200
200 flowers

28.2A

Match.

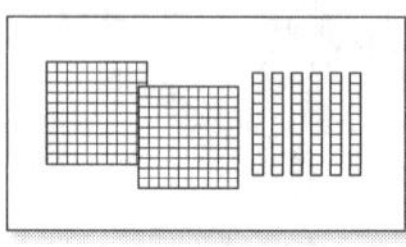 — 260

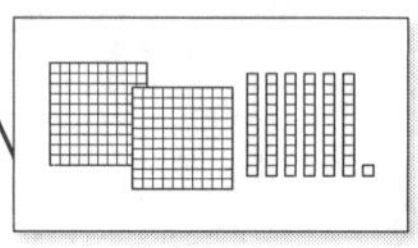 — 261

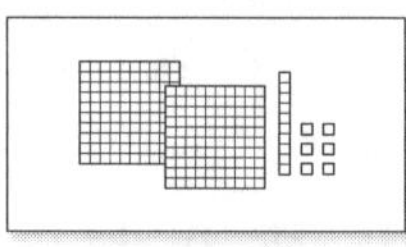 — 216

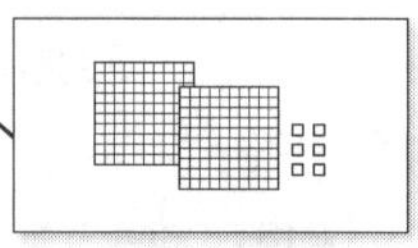 — 206

Write the expanded form for each number.

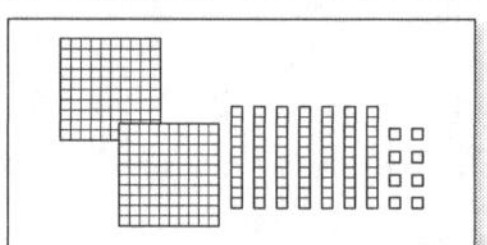

278 = 200 + 70 + 8

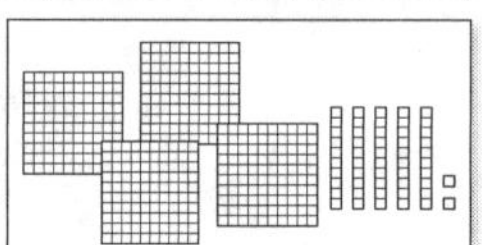

452 = 400 + 50 + 2

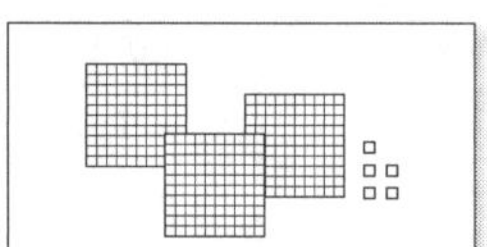

305 = 300 + 5

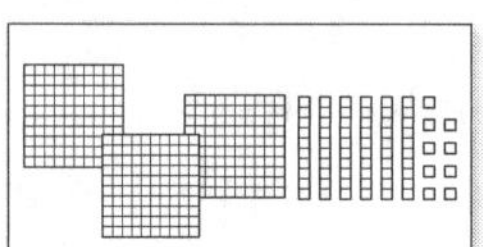

369 = 300 + 60 + 9

28.2B

Complete.

82 − 56 = 26

157 − 74 = 83

132 − 85 = 47

Complete.

1 week = 7 days	1 yard = 3 feet
1 day = 24 hours	1 yard = 36 inches
1 hour = 60 minutes	1 foot = 12 inches
1 minute = 60 seconds	1 meter = 100 centimeters

Match. Each ruler is 1 foot long.

 — 1 foot, 2 inches

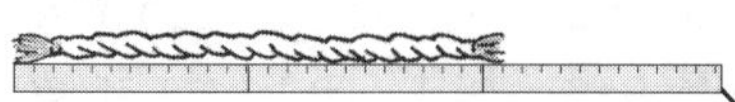 — 2 feet, 1 inches

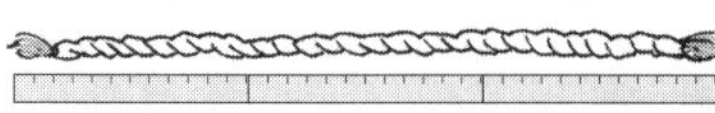 — 3 feet

Week 28 Answer Key

28.3A

Complete the missing numbers in the sequences.

Count by 1s: 375, 376, 377, 378, 379

Count by 1s: 609, 610, 611, 612, 613

Count by 1s: 724, 725, 726, 727, 728

Write the numbers that come before and after.

Before	Number	After
373	374	375
246	247	248
931	932	933
485	486	487
564	565	566
798	799	800
607	608	609
852	853	854

28.3B

Complete.

$90 - 39 = 51$

$125 - 68 = 57$

$199 - 76 = 123$

Shade the shapes to match the fractions. Then, complete each circle with <, >, or =.

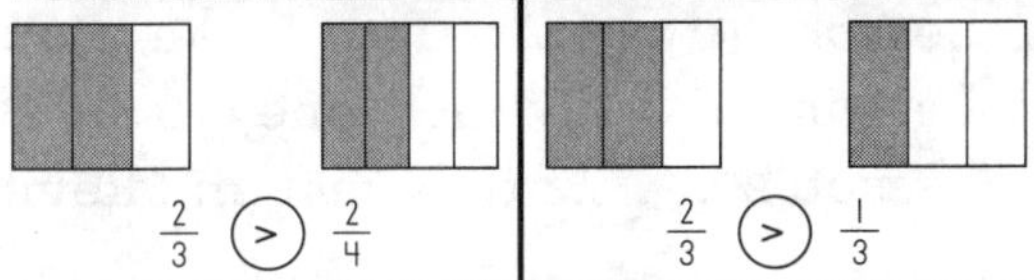

$\frac{2}{3} > \frac{2}{4}$

$\frac{2}{3} > \frac{1}{3}$

$\frac{2}{3} > \frac{2}{6}$

$\frac{2}{3} = \frac{4}{6}$

Other ways to color the shapes are possible.

Complete. Use a decimal point.

$ 135.60

28.4A

Connect each number to its spot on the number lines.

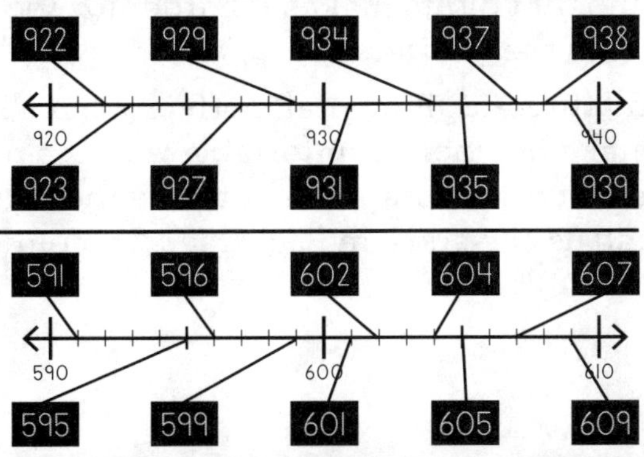

Color the even numbers blue. Color the odd numbers yellow.

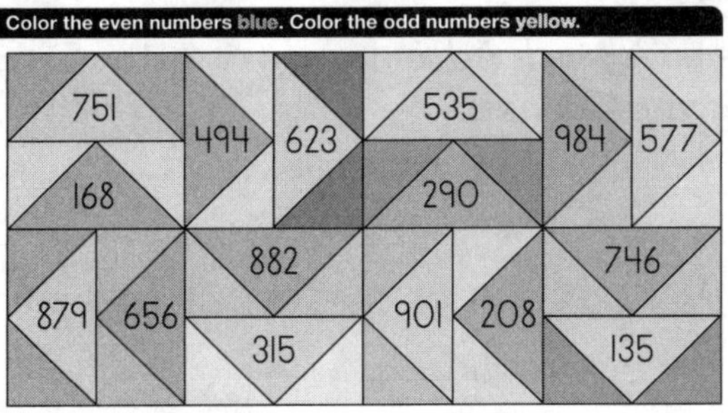

28.4B

Use the pictures to answer the questions.

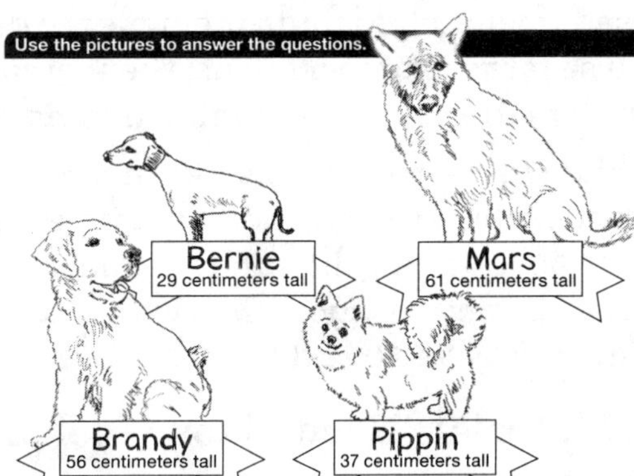

How much taller is Brandy than Bernie?

$56 - 29 = 27$ — 27 centimeters

How much shorter is Pippin than Mars?

$61 - 37 = 24$ — 24 centimeters

How much taller is Mars than Brandy?

$61 - 56 = 5$ — 5 centimeters

How much shorter is Bernie than Pippin?

$37 - 29 = 8$ — 8 centimeters

Week 29
Mental Math with Numbers to 1000

Overview

Your child will build on her understanding of place value to add ones, tens, or hundreds to numbers to 1000. She'll also learn how to find pairs that equal 1000 and count larger money combinations.

Teaching Math with Confidence: Preparing to Use the Addition and Subtraction Algorithms with Three-Digit Numbers

In Weeks 30 and 31, your child will learn how to use the written algorithms to add and subtract three-digit numbers. This week, she will learn to mentally add and subtract three-digit numbers so that she's more comfortable with these numbers before she tackles written addition and subtraction.

Throughout the week, you'll use base-ten blocks and play money to help your child concretely understand place value in three-digit numbers. You'll teach her how to add and subtract ones, tens, or hundreds separately. For example, she'll solve problems like 300 + 500, 800 – 200, 342 + 300, or 654 – 4. You'll also briefly introduce her to problems that involve crossing a century, like 699 + 2 or 700 – 5.

These simple problems may feel like a step backward after the challenging two-digit mental addition and subtraction problems that your child solved in Units 6 and 8. But don't be surprised if your child finds them plenty difficult! Children need time to get comfortable with these larger numbers. Plus, the increased number of digits makes it harder for second-graders to keep all the digits in mind as they find the answers.

Your child will learn how to solve more challenging three-digit mental math problems in third grade. For now, this mental math work will make her more comfortable with the numbers to 1000, reinforce her understanding of place value, and prepare her to use the addition and subtraction algorithms with understanding as she adds and subtracts three-digit numbers in Weeks 30 and 31.

Extra Materials Needed for Week 29

- 5 slips of paper
- For optional Enrichment and Review Lesson:
    - *Sir Cumference and All the King's Tens: A Math Adventure,* written by Cindy Neuschwander and illustrated by Wayne Geehan
    - Paper
    - Tape

Lesson 29.1
Mental Addition with Numbers to 1000

	Purpose	Materials
Warm-up	• Count by 2s • Practice memory work • Review expanded form	• None
Activities	• Use place-value thinking to add ones, tens, or hundreds to three-digit numbers • Complete a hundred to add a one-digit number to a three-digit number	• Base-ten blocks • Place-Value Chart (Blackline Master 5) • Playing cards
Workbook	• Practice mental addition with numbers to 1000	• Workbook pages 29.1A and 29.1B

See the Week 29 **Teaching Math with Confidence** to learn how the simple mental math problems in this lesson and Lesson 29.2 prepare your child to apply the addition and subtraction algorithms to three-digit numbers.

Warm-up: Counting, Memory Work, and Review

- Have your child count forward by 2s from the following numbers. Prompt her as needed, and stop her after she reaches the last number listed.
    - **Count by 2s from 436:** *436, 438, 440, 442, 444.*
    - **Count by 2s from 860:** *860, 862, 864, 866, 868.*
    - **Count by 2s from 594:** *594, 596, 598, 600, 602.*
- **How many hundreds equal 1 thousand?** *10.*
- Have your child tell the expanded form of the following numbers.
    - 974. *900 + 70 + 4.*
    - 439. *400 + 30 + 9.*
    - 610. *600 + 10.*
    - 804. *800 + 4.*

Activity: Use Place-Value Thinking to Add Ones, Tens, or Hundreds

This year, you've learned how to use place-value thinking to solve mental math problems with two-digit numbers. Today, you'll use place-value thinking to solve mental addition problems.

Write "342 + 3 =" on a piece of paper. Model 342 with base-ten blocks on the Place-Value Chart.

342 + 3 =

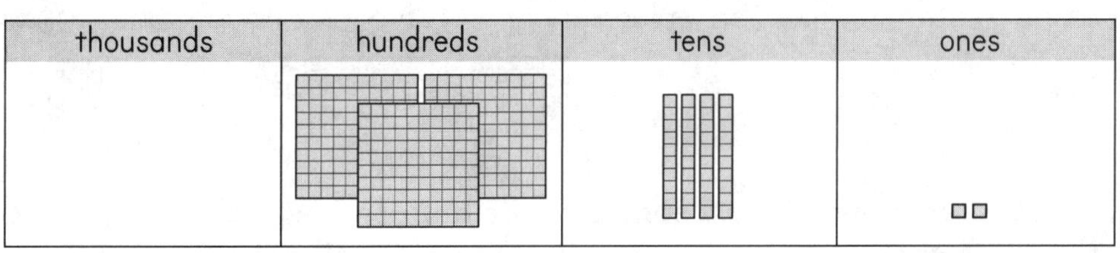

Imagine adding 3 ones to the Place-Value Chart. What would the total be? *345*. If your child is not sure, have her add 3 units to the Place-Value Chart. Have her complete the written equation: 342 + 3 = 345.

342 + 3 = 345

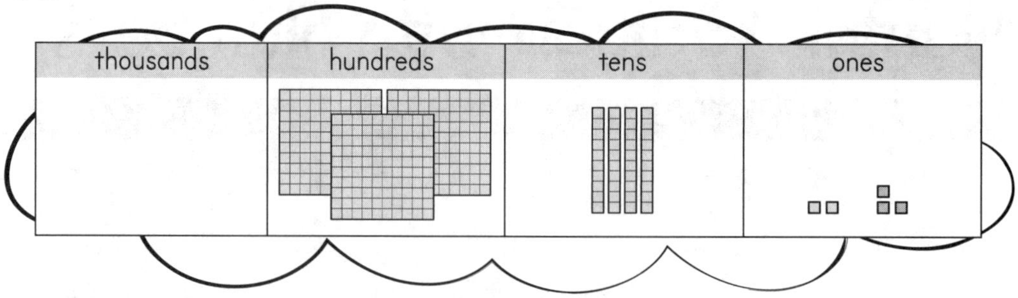

Write "342 + 30 =" on a piece of paper. **This time, imagine adding 3 tens to the Place-Value Chart. What would the total be?** *372*. If your child is not sure, have her add 3 rods to the Place-Value Chart. Have her complete the written equation: 342 + 30 = 372.

342 + 30 = 372

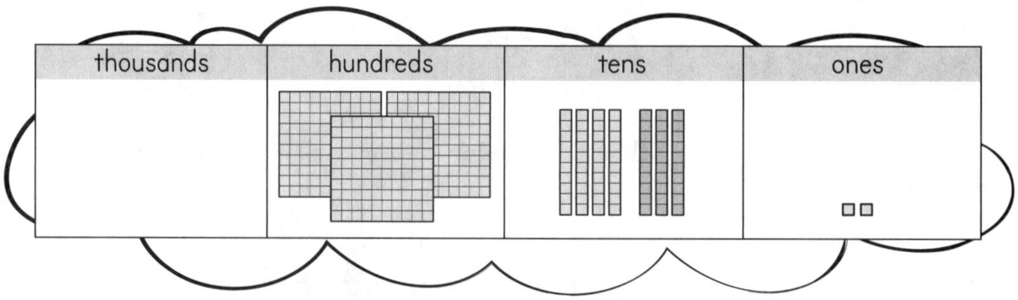

Write "342 + 300 =" on a piece of paper. **This time, imagine adding 3 hundreds to the Place-Value Chart. What would the total be?** *642*. If your child is not sure, have her add 3 flats to the Place-Value Chart. Have her complete the written equation: 342 + 300 = 642.

342 + 300 = 642

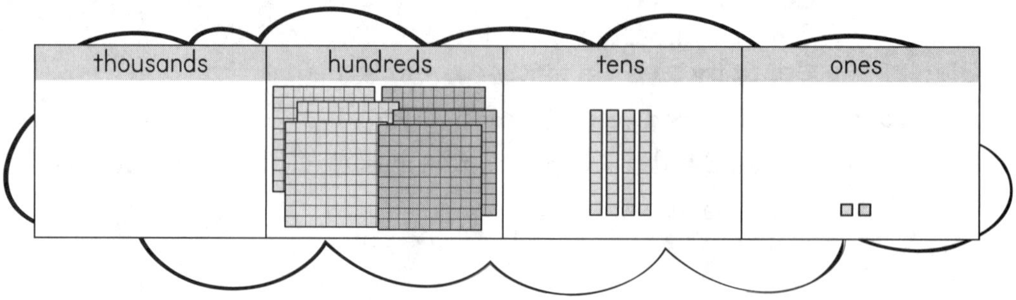

Activity: Complete a Hundred to Add

Earlier this year, you learned how to complete a ten to add in your head. Write "49 + 3 =" on a piece of paper. **To find 49 plus 3, you learned to add in two steps. 49 plus 1 is 50. 50 plus 2 is 52. So, 49 plus 3 equals 52.**

49 + 3 = 52

You can use the same approach to add greater numbers. You just complete a hundred instead of a ten. Write "399 + 2 =" on a piece of paper. Have your child model 399 with base-ten blocks.

399 + 2 =

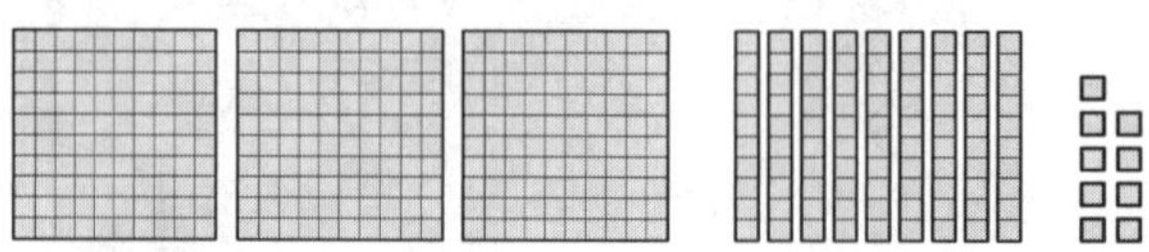

I'll add in two steps. First, I complete the hundred. 399 plus 1 equals 400. Add 1 unit block to the block arrangement. Push the rods and units together so that they look like a flat. **400 plus 1 equals 401.** Add 1 more unit block. **So, 399 plus 2 equals 401.** Have your child complete the written equation: 399 + 2 = 401.

399 + 2 = 401

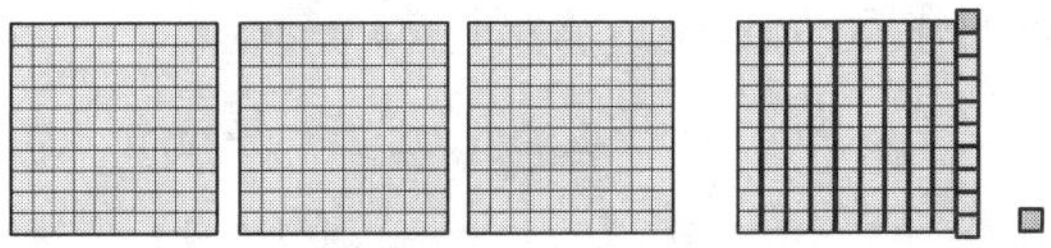

You do not need to trade the 9 rods and 10 units for a flat.

Have your child use the same method to solve the following problems.

498 + 4 = 502

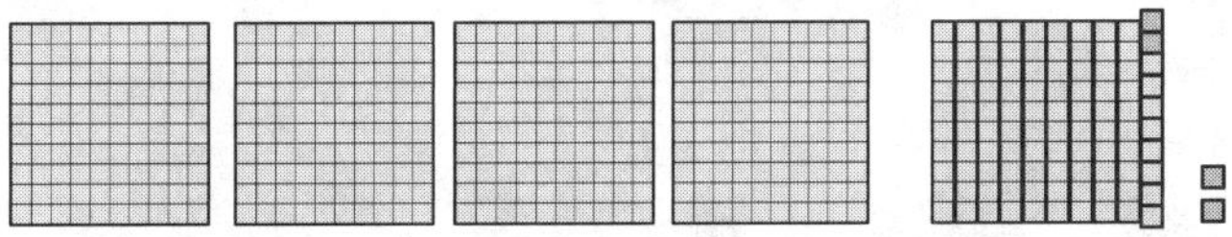

699 + 5 = 704

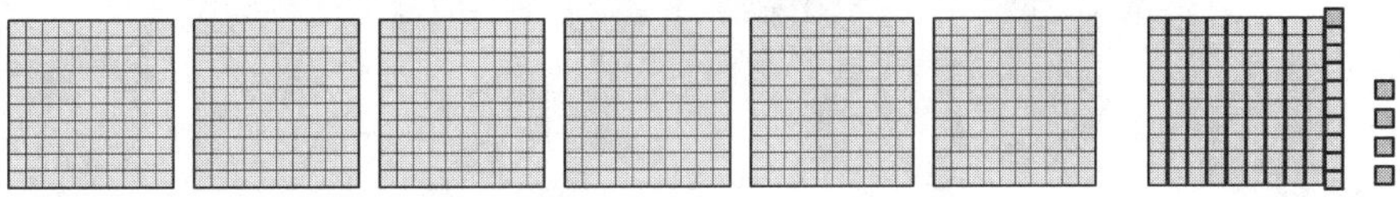

Activity: Play Race to 1000

Play Race to 1000.

If your child had trouble with the simpler mental addition problems in the first activity, modify the game to provide more support. After she flips over each card, have her take the corresponding base-ten block (either 1 unit, 1 rod, or 1 flat). Then, have her count her base-ten blocks to find her new total.

Race to 1000

Materials: Aces, 10s, and face cards from two decks of cards (40 cards total);

Object of the Game: Be the first player to reach 1000.

Shuffle the cards and place them in a face-down pile. Make a simple scorecard to record the score.

Abby	
Mom	

Each player starts with zero points. On your turn, flip over a card.

- If you flip over a 1, add 1 to your score.
- If you flip over a 10, add 10 to your score.
- If you flip over a face card, add 100 to your score.

Record your score in the chart.

Abby	100
Mom	

Sample first play.

Take turns flipping over a card, finding your new sum, and recording your score. Continue until one player reaches 1000 or goes over 1000.

Workbook: Mental Addition and Review

Have your child complete workbook pages 29.1A and 29.1B.

The exercises at the top of 29.1B include practice with both the addition and subtraction algorithms so that your child gets used to switching from one process to the other. This is the first time your child will encounter both algorithms on the same worksheet, so you may want to prompt her to pay extra attention to the signs in these problems.

Lesson 29.2
Mental Subtraction with Numbers to 1000

	Purpose	Materials
Warm-up	• Count by 2s • Practice memory work • Review identifying even and odd numbers	• None
Activities	• Use place-value thinking to subtract ones, tens, or hundreds from three-digit numbers • Subtract one-digit numbers from multiples of 100 (like 300, 500, or 900)	• Base-ten blocks • Playing cards
Workbook	• Practice mental subtraction with numbers to 1000	• Workbook pages 29.2A and 29.2B

Warm-up: Counting, Memory Work, and Review

- Have your child count forward by 2s from the following numbers. Prompt him as needed, and stop him after he reaches the last number listed.
    - × **Count by 2s from 654:** *654, 656, 658, 660, 662.*
    - × **Count by 2s from 480:** *480, 482, 484, 486, 488.*
    - × **Count by 2s from 896:** *896, 898, 900, 902, 904.*
- **How many hundreds equal 1 thousand?** *10.*
- Have your child tell whether the following numbers are even or odd.
    - × 380. *Even.*
    - × 611. *Odd.*
    - × 923. *Odd.*
    - × 234. *Even.*
    - × 706. *Even.*

Activity: Use Place-Value Thinking to Subtract Ones, Tens, or Hundreds

In the last lesson, you used place-value thinking to add. Today, you'll use place-value thinking to subtract. Write "657 – 3 =" on a piece of paper. Model 657 with base-ten blocks on the Place-Value Chart.

657 - 3 =

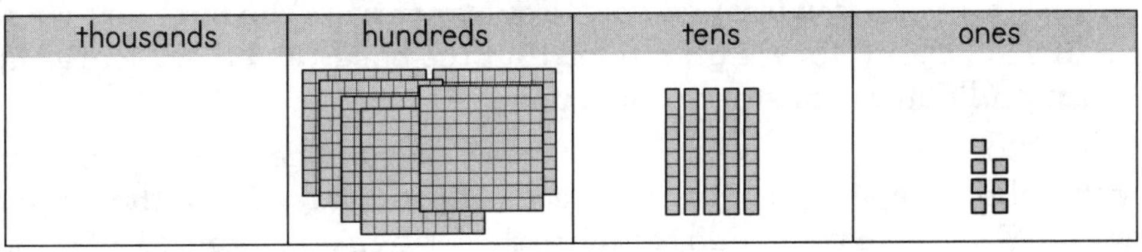

Imagine subtracting 3 ones from the Place-Value Chart. What would be the new value of the blocks? *654.* If your child is not sure, have him remove 3 units from the Place-Value Chart. Have him complete the written equation: 657 – 3 = 654.

657 - 3 = 654

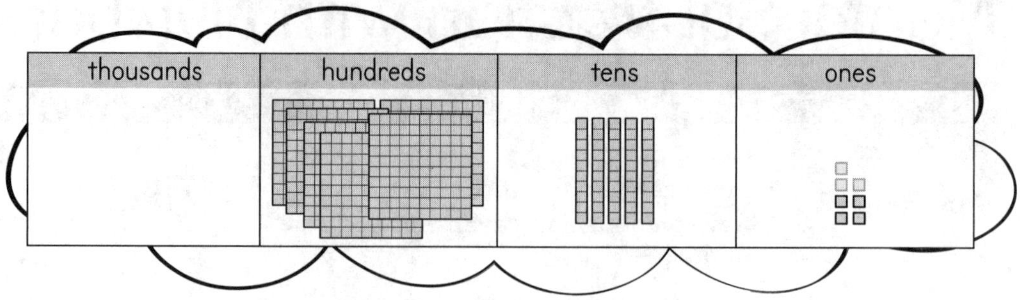

Write "657 – 30 = " on a piece of paper. **This time, imagine subtracting 3 tens from the Place-Value Chart. What would be the new value of the blocks?** *627.* If your child is not sure, have him remove 3 rods from the Place-Value Chart. Have him complete the written equation: 657 – 30 = 627.

657 - 30 = 627

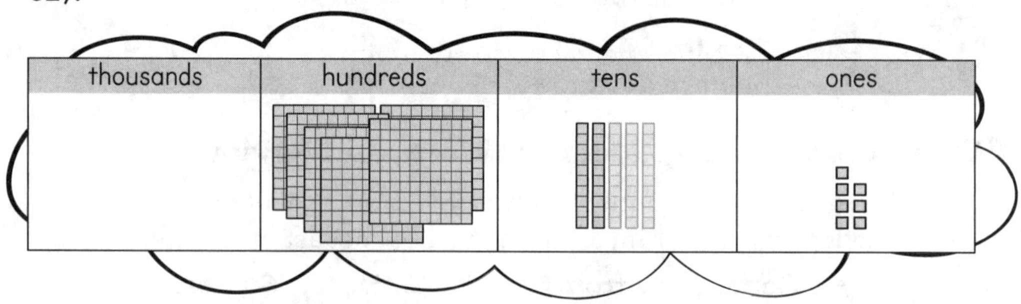

Write "657 – 300 = " on a piece of paper. **This time, imagine subtracting 3 hundreds from the Place-Value Chart. What would be the new value of the blocks?** *357.* If your child is not sure, have him remove 3 flats from the Place-Value Chart. Have him complete the written equation: 657 – 300 = 357.

657 - 300 = 357

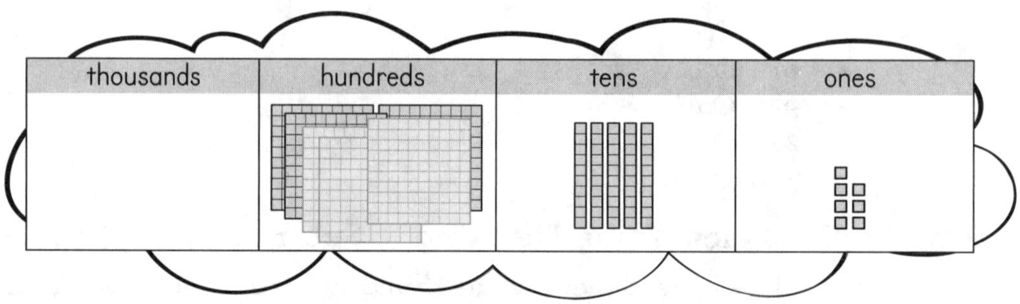

Activity: Subtract One-Digit Numbers from Multiples of 100

Earlier this year, you learned how to subtract from the numbers we say when we count by 10, like 50, 80, or 40. We pretended that the base-ten blocks were chocolate bars and a hungry alligator came to eat them up!

Write "80 – 2 =" on a piece of paper. Place 8 rods on the table. Cover 2 of the units on 1 rod with a slip of paper. **There are 80 pieces of chocolate. Then, the alligator eats 2. How many are left?** *78.* Have your child complete the written equation: 80 – 2 = 78.

80 - 2 =

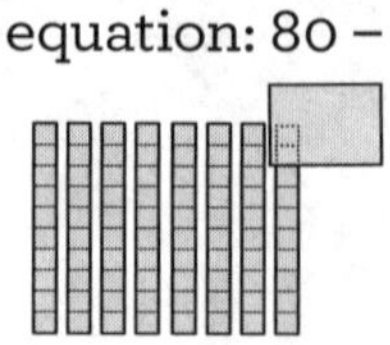

You can use the same way to subtract from the numbers we say when we count by hundreds, like 300, 600, or 700. Write "300 – 4 =" on a piece of paper. Place 3 flats on the table. Use a slip of paper to cover 4 of the units on the flat. **300 minus 4 equals what?** *296.*

300 - 4 = 296

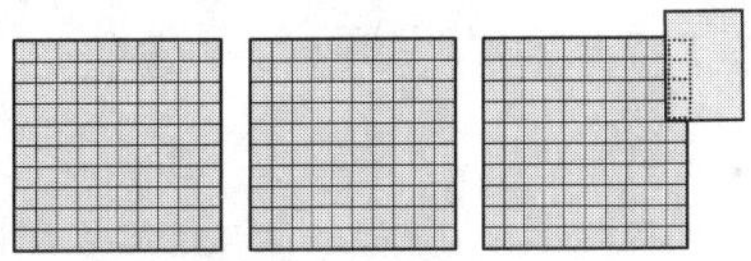

Have your child use the same approach to solve the following problems.

400 - 5 = 395

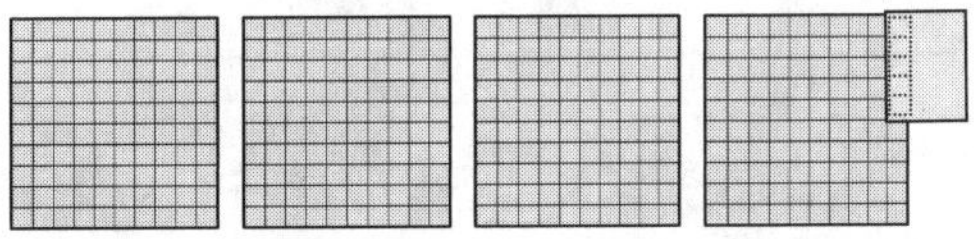

800 - 1 = 799

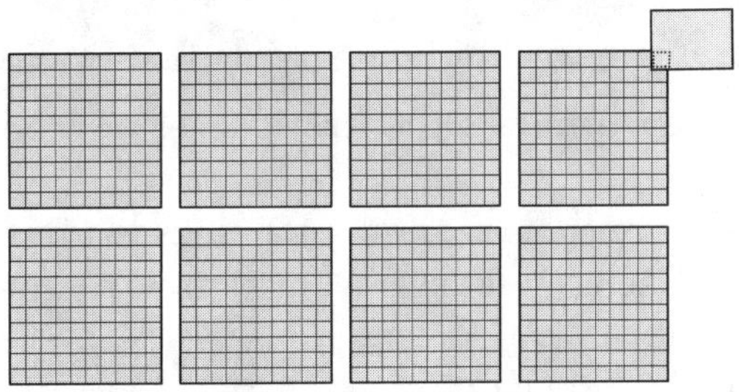

900 - 8 = 892

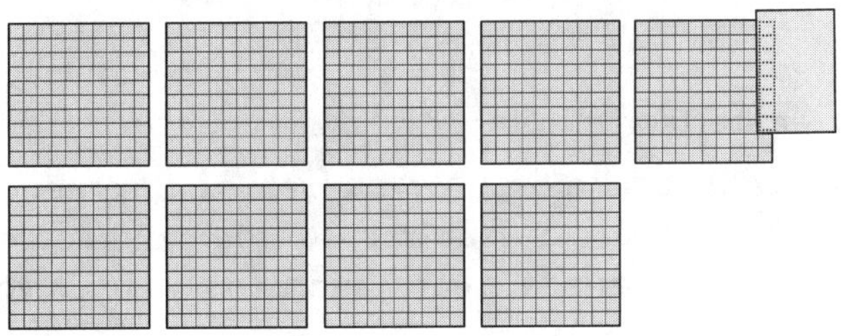

Activity: Play Race to Zero (Advanced Version)

Play Race to Zero (Advanced Version).

This game is similar to Race to Zero from Lesson 18.3, but it involves more challenging numbers.

If your child had trouble with the simpler mental subtraction problems in the first activity, modify the game to provide more support. Have him start the game with 10 flats. After he flips over each card, have him remove the corresponding base-ten block from his pile. Help him trade his base-ten blocks as needed.

Race to Zero (Advanced Version)

Materials: Aces, 10s, and face cards from two decks of cards (40 cards total)
Object of the Game: Be the first player to reach zero.

Shuffle the cards and place them in a face-down pile. Make a simple scorecard to record the score. Each player starts with 1000 points.

Sebastian	1000
Mom	1000

Each player starts with 1000 points. On your turn, flip over a card.

- If you flip over a 1, subtract 1 from your score.
- If you flip over a 10, subtract 10 from your score.
- If you flip over a face card, subtract 100 from your score.

Record your new score in the chart.

Sebastian	1000	990
Mom	1000	

Sample first play.

Take turns flipping over a card, finding your new score, and recording your score. Continue until one player reaches zero or draws a card that is worth more than his current score.

Workbook: Mental Subtraction and Review

Have your child complete workbook pages 29.2A and 29.2B.

Lesson 29.3
Pairs That Make 1000

	Purpose	Materials
Warm-up	• Count by 5s • Practice memory work • Review mental addition	• Playing cards
Activities	• Add and subtract hundreds • Find pairs that make 1000	• Play money
Workbook	• Add and subtract hundreds • Find pairs that make 1000	• Workbook pages 29.3A and 29.3B

Warm-up: Counting, Memory Work, and Review

- Have your child count forward by 5s from the following numbers. Prompt her as needed, and stop her after she reaches the last number listed.
    - **Count by 5s from 655:** *655, 660, 665, 670, 675.*
    - **Count by 5s from 700:** *700, 705, 710, 715, 720, 725.*
    - **Count by 5s from 480:** *480, 485, 490, 495, 500.*
- **How many inches equal 1 foot?** *12.* **How many feet equal 1 yard?** *3.* **How many inches equal 1 yard?** *36.*
- Play Race to 1000. See Lesson 29.1 (page 465) for directions.

Activity: Add and Subtract Hundreds with Play Money

In the last two lessons, you learned how to mentally add and subtract. Today, you'll learn how to add and subtract hundreds. We'll also find pairs that make 1000.

Let's pretend that you have $300. Give your child 3 hundred-dollar bills. **Then, you get $500.** Give your child 5 more hundred-dollar bills. **How much money do you have now?** *$800.* Write 300 + 500 = 800 on a piece of paper.

300 + 500 = 800

If your child has trouble, encourage her to use what she knows about addition to find the answer: **You know that 3 apples plus 5 apples equal 8 apples. So, what do 3 hundreds plus 5 hundreds equal?** *8 hundreds.*

Now, you have $800. Then, you spend $200. Have your child give you 2 hundred-dollar bills. **How much money do you have now?** *$600.* Write 800 – 200 = 600 on a piece of paper.

800 - 200 = 600

Have your child solve the following addition and subtraction problems. Use play money as needed.

- 500 + 400 = *900*
- 300 + 600 = *900*
- 200 + 800 = *1000*
- 600 - 500 = *100*
- 900 - 400 = *500*
- 1000 - 300 = *700*

Activity: Find Pairs that Make 1000

Let's pretend that we have $1000 to share. How many hundred-dollar bills equal $1000? *10.* Place 10 hundred-dollar bills on the table. **If we share the money equally, how much money do we each get?** *$500.*

If your child isn't sure, point out that there are 10 hundred-dollar bills. **What's half of 10?** *5.* **So, we each get 5 hundred-dollar bills.**

Start a simple chart to record how you split the money.

Rebekah	500
Mom	500

What's another way we could split the money? Have your child find several other ways to split the 10 hundred-dollar bills and record them on the chart. Encourage her to use the pairs that make 10 to reason about the hundred-dollar bills. For example: **3 and 7 make 10. So, if I get $300, how much money do you get?** *$700.*

Rebekah	500	700	900	200
Mom	500	300	100	800

Sample answers.

We could also trade 1 hundred-dollar bill for 10 ten-dollar bills. Trade 1 hundred-dollar bill for 10 ten-dollar bills.

Now we have many more ways to share the money! Here's one way. Give your child 1 ten-dollar bill and keep the rest for yourself. How much money do each of us get? *I get $10, but you get $990!* Have your child find several other ways to split the money. Record the amounts in the chart.

Rebekah	500	700	900	200	10	870	650
Mom	500	300	100	800	990	130	350

Sample answers.

Trade 1 ten-dollar bill for 10 one-dollar bills. Have your child find several more ways to split the money. Record the amounts in the chart.

Rebekah	500	700	900	200	10	870	650	572	199	754
Mom	500	300	100	800	990	130	350	428	801	246

Sample answers.

Your child will practice identifying the multiples of 100 that equal 1000 (like 600 and 400, or 100 or 900) so that she knows them by the end of the year. She is not expected to be able to find other pairs that make 1000 mentally in second grade.

Workbook: Pairs That Make 1000 and Review

Have your child complete workbook pages 29.3A and 29.3B.

Lesson 29.4
Count Money to $1000

	Purpose	Materials
Warm-up	• Count by 10s • Practice memory work • Review mental subtraction	• Playing cards
Activities	• Count money combinations • Count out money to match a price	• Play money • 5 slips of paper
Workbook	• Count money • Use mental math to reason about prices	• Workbook pages 29.4A and 29.4B

Warm-up: Counting, Memory Work, and Review

- Have your child count forward by 10s from the following numbers. Prompt him as needed, and stop him after he reaches the last number listed.
    - × **Count by 10s from 300:** 300, 310, 320, 330, 340.
    - × **Count by 10s from 750:** *750, 760, 770, 780, 790.*
    - × **Count by 10s from 880:** *880, 890, 900, 910, 920.*
- **How many months are in a year?** *12.* **How many days are in a week?** *7.*
- Play Race to Zero (Advanced Version). See Lesson 29.2 (page 470) for directions.

Activity: Count Money Combinations to 1000

You have learned a lot about the numbers to 1000. Today, you'll practice counting money amounts up to $1000. Then, we'll go shopping at the Pretend Furniture Store.

Counting larger amounts of money is just like counting smaller amounts of money. We follow the same 3 steps: sort, order, and count.

Mix up 5 hundred-dollar bills, 4 ten-dollar bills, and 2 five-dollar bills on the table. Have your child sort the bills by type and put them in order from greatest value to least value. Then, show your child how to count by 100s, 10s, and 5s to find their value: **100, 200, 300, 400, 500, 510, 520, 530, 540, 545, 550.**

Have your child find the value of the following money combinations.

- 2 hundred-dollar bills, 3 ten-dollar bills, and 3 one-dollar bills. *$233.*
- 4 hundred-dollar bills, 4 ten-dollar bills, 1 five-dollar bill, and 2 one-dollar bills. *$447.*
- 8 hundred-dollar bills, 7 ten-dollar bills, and 6 five-dollar bills. *$900.*

Activity: Pretend Furniture Store

Let's play Pretend Furniture Store! Write $279, $483, $507, $850, and $913 on small slips of paper to make price tags. Place them on 5 pieces of furniture around your house.

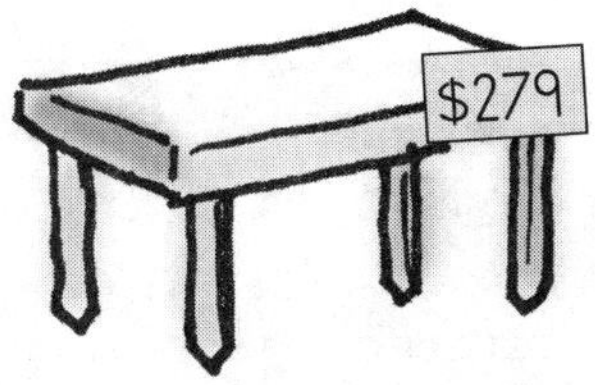

Give your child play money. Have him pretend to be the customer and "buy" the furniture. Help as needed to count out the correct bills for each purchase.

Workbook: Count Money and Review

Have your child complete workbook pages 29.4A and 29.4B.

Lesson 29.5
Enrichment and Review (Optional)

	Purpose	Materials
Warm-up	• Count from 300 to 400 by 1s, 2s, 5s, or 10s • Review memory work • Review your child's favorite or most challenging activities from Week 29	• Varies, depending on the activities you choose
Picture Book	• Understand place value in the context of grouping guests at a party	• *Sir Cumference and All the King's Tens: A Math Adventure,* written by Cindy Neuschwander and illustrated by Wayne Geehan
Enrichment Activity	• Count by 5s to make a dot-to-dot page	• Paper • Tape

Warm-up: Counting, Memory Work, and Review

- Have your child count from 300 to 400 by 1s, 2s, 5s, or 10s. (Choose whichever counting sequence your child needs to practice the most.)
- Quiz your child on the all the memory work for the year. See page 523 for the full list.
- If you have time, repeat one or two of the activities from this week's lessons. Choose activities your child especially enjoyed or found challenging.

Math Picture Book: *Sir Cumference and All the King's Tens: A Math Adventure*

Read *Sir Cumference and All the King's Tens: A Math Adventure,* written by Cindy Neuschwander and illustrated by Wayne Geehan. As you read, discuss how the characters use groups of 10, 100, and 1000 to organize the party guests.

This book includes numbers greater than 1000, but your child is not expected to fully understand these numbers at this point. She will learn more about numbers to 10,000 in third grade.

Enrichment Activity: Make a Count-by-5s Dot-to-Dot

Have your child draw an outline of a simple shape or object on a piece of paper. (Have her use a dark writing utensil so that it will be easy to trace the design in the next step.)

Tape the drawing to a bright window, and tape another piece of paper over it. Have your child mark 10-15 dots around the outline.

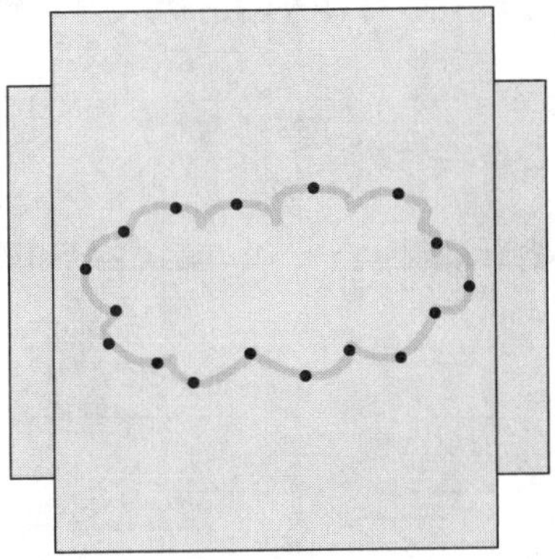

Once she's marked the dots, have her label the first dot "500" and count by 5s to number the rest of the dots in order. She can complete the dot-to-dot herself, or challenge another family member to complete it.

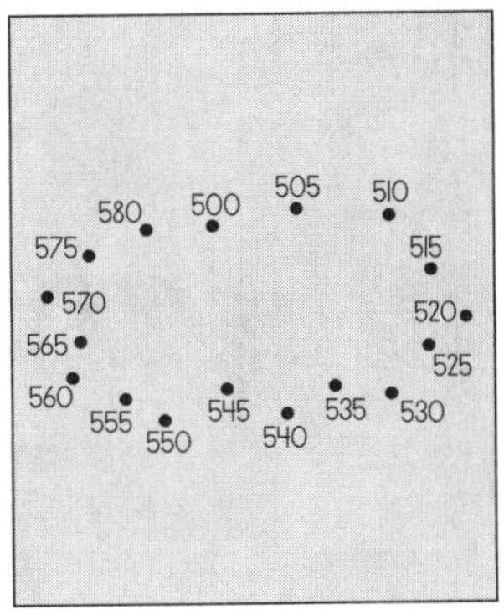

Week 29 Answer Key

29.1A

Complete.

328 + 1 =	329	739 + 1 =	740
328 + 10 =	338	739 + 10 =	749
328 + 100 =	428	739 + 100 =	839
645 + 2 =	647	562 + 3 =	565
645 + 20 =	665	562 + 30 =	592
645 + 200 =	845	562 + 300 =	862

Match.

499 + 2	500	498 + 2
497 + 6	501	496 + 6
498 + 4	502	495 + 6
494 + 6	503	499 + 3

29.1B

Complete.

	1	4	8
-		9	2
		5	6

	1	8	1
-		2	7
	1	5	4

	6	7
+	2	5
	9	2

Complete.

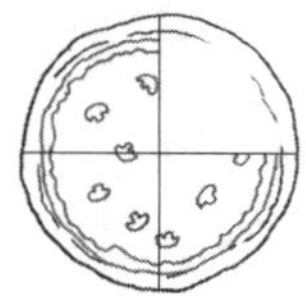

$\frac{3}{4}$ of the pizza is left.

$\frac{1}{4}$ of the pizza has been eaten.

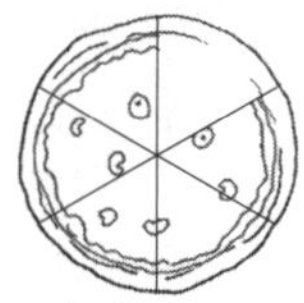

$\frac{5}{6}$ of the pizza is left.

$\frac{1}{6}$ of the pizza has been eaten.

Write a.m. or p.m. for each time.

Storytime 11:00 a.m.

Soccer Practice 4:30 p.m.

Sunset 7:15 p.m.

29.2A

Complete.

328 - 1 =	327	739 - 1 =	738
328 - 10 =	318	739 - 10 =	729
328 - 100 =	228	739 - 100 =	639
645 - 2 =	643	562 - 3 =	559
645 - 20 =	625	562 - 30 =	532
645 - 200 =	445	562 - 300 =	262

Match.

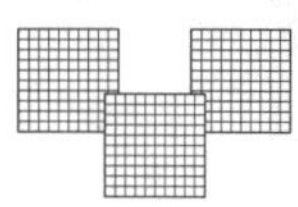

300 - 1 =	299
300 - 5 =	295
300 - 6 =	294
300 - 9 =	291

400 - 2 =	398
400 - 4 =	396
400 - 8 =	392
400 - 3 =	397

29.2B

Complete.

	1	2	9
-		7	5
		5	4

		7	3
+		8	2
	1	5	5

	1	3	0
-		5	4
		7	6

Match.

385	odd	441
750		536
363		198
412	even	629
907		724

Write the time.

8:59

9:00

9:01

Week 29 Answer Key

29.3A

Complete.

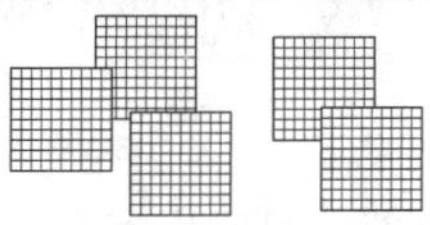

300 + 200 = 500

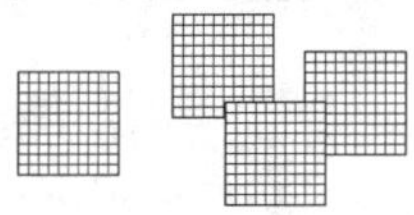

100 + 300 = 400

500 + 200 = 700	400 + 400 = 800
100 + 800 = 900	600 + 200 = 800
300 + 400 = 700	200 + 700 = 900

Match the pairs that make 1000.

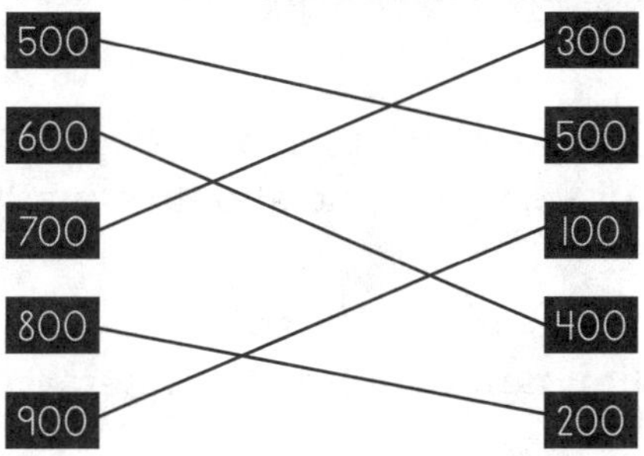

29.3B

Complete.

$67 + 33 = 100$

$68 + 49 = 117$

$92 - 53 = 39$

Complete the sequences.

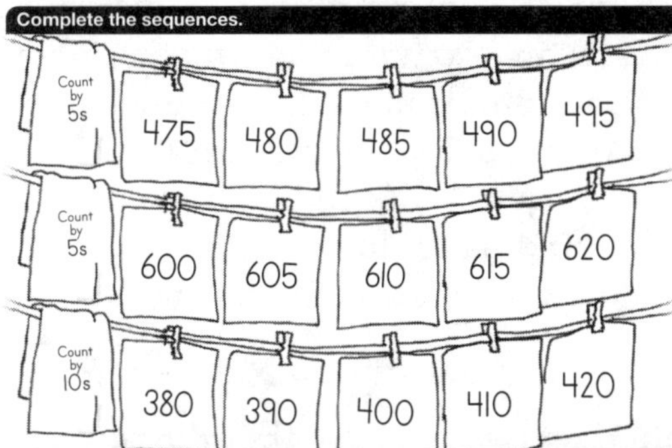

Complete the circles with <, >, or =.

516 < 517	500 > 499	345 > 254
500 = 500	890 > 809	708 < 808
275 < 396	600 < 900	999 < 1000

29.4A

Complete.

$ 235

$ 410

$ 315

$ 230

Use the clues to complete the chart.

- The table costs $200 less than the bed.
- The bookcase costs $1 more than the table.
- The desk costs $5 less than the bookcase.
- The lamp costs $300 less than the desk.

Furniture Sale

Item	Price
Bed	$ 699
Table	$ 499
Bookcase	$ 500
Desk	$ 495
Lamp	$ 195

29.4B

Complete.

$186 - 75 = 111$

$94 - 49 = 45$

$47 + 63 = 110$

Write how many.

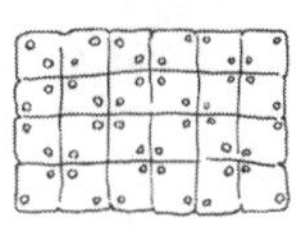

24 tiles

25 tiles

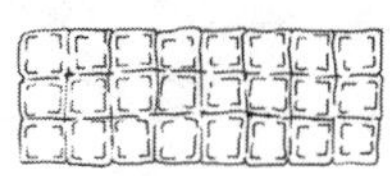

24 tiles

Solve.

Mateo has $46. He spends $24 on a toy. How much money does he have left?

$46 - 24 = 22$

$ 22

Emerson has $41. She spends $17 on a toy. How much money does she have left?

$41 - 17 = 24$

$ 24

Unit 13 Checkpoint

What to Expect at the End of Unit 13

By the end of Unit 13, most children will be able to do the following:

- Read, write, and compare numbers to 1000 and understand place value in numbers to 1000.
- Identify even and odd numbers to 1000 and write numbers to 1000 in expanded form.
- Count by 1s, 2s, 5s, or 10s to 1000. Some children will still have some trouble counting across a century. (For example, when counting by 5s, your child might have to pause and think to figure out what number comes after 395.)
- Solve simple mental addition and subtraction problems with the numbers to 1000.
- Identify pairs that make 1000. Most children will be able to identify pairs of multiples that equal 1000 (like 800 and 200) but will need base-ten blocks to identify more challenging pairs (like 195 and 805).
- Count money amounts up to $1000.

Is Your Child Ready to Move on?

Your child will learn to use the addition and subtraction algorithms to add and subtract three-digit numbers in Unit 14. Before moving on to Unit 14, your child should already be quite comfortable with the following skills:

- Use the addition algorithm to add two-digit numbers, mostly fluently.
- Use the subtraction algorithm to subtract two-digit numbers from numbers to 200, mostly fluently.

It's okay if your child still sometimes has trouble remembering a few of the facts or occasionally forgets one of the steps in the algorithms.

What to Do If Your Child Needs More Practice

If your child needs more practice with the addition or subtraction algorithms, spend a few days practicing adding and subtracting two-digit numbers before you move on to Unit 14.

Unit 14
Addition and Subtraction to 1000

Overview

Your child will integrate all that he has learned about addition, subtraction, and the numbers to 1000 as he adds and subtracts three-digit numbers. You'll use familiar contexts and games to help him apply the addition and subtraction algorithms to these more complex problems.

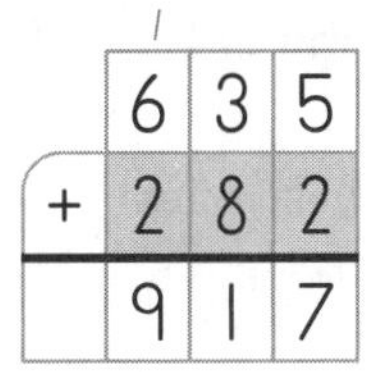

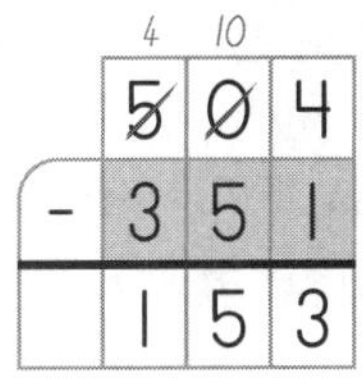

In Week 32, you and your child will review the major concepts and skills he has learned this year and celebrate completing the book.

Week 30	Add Numbers to 1000
Week 31	Subtract Numbers to 1000
Week 32	Review and Celebrate

What Your Child Will Learn

In this unit your child will learn to:

- Use the addition algorithm to add three-digit numbers
- Use the subtraction algorithm to subtract three-digit numbers, including subtracting across a zero

Recommended Math Picture Books (Optional)

These picture books are scheduled in the optional Enrichment and Review lessons at the end of each week.

- *Mapping Penny's World,* by Loreen Leedy. Square Fish, 2003.
- *Christmas Farm,* written by Mary Lyn Ray and illustrated by Barry Root. Harcourt, 2008.

Week 30
Add Numbers to 1000

Overview

Your child will learn to apply the addition algorithm to three-digit numbers. He'll also learn how to use the algorithm to add more than two numbers at a time.

Lesson 30.1	Add Three-Digit Numbers with Base-Ten Blocks
Lesson 30.2	Add Three-Digit Numbers without Base-Ten Blocks
Lesson 30.3	Add 3 or More Addends
Lesson 30.4	Three-Digit Addition Word Problems
Lesson 30.5	Enrichment and Review (Optional)

Teaching Math with Confidence: Extending the Addition Algorithm to Three-Digit Numbers

This week, you'll teach your child how to apply the addition algorithm to three-digit numbers. He may feel intimidated at first by how many digits he needs to add. But, as he works through the problems, you'll show him that he already knows everything needed to solve these problems. The only slight wrinkle is that he needs to add the digits in the hundreds-place after he tackles the tens-place and ones-place.

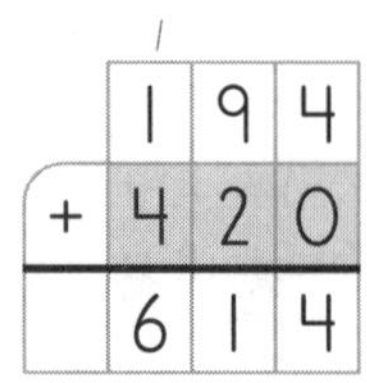

Since your child has already mastered the steps in the addition algorithm, he may resist using base-ten blocks to model the problems. If so, allow him to solve the problems without the blocks as long as it's clear that he understands what he's doing.

Part of the beauty of the addition algorithm is that this simple sequence of steps can be used to add numbers in the millions or billions just as well as it can be used to add miniscule decimals. By developing fluency with the addition algorithm now, your child will be ready to tackle larger numbers and decimals in later grades.

Extra Materials Needed for Week 30

- 12 slips of paper
- 4 children's chapter books, each with 100-250 pages
- For optional Enrichment and Review Lesson:
    - *Mapping Penny's World*, by Loreen Leedy
    - Paper
    - Small toy

Lesson 30.1
Add Three-Digit Numbers with Base-Ten Blocks

	Purpose	Materials
Warm-up	• Count by 5s • Practice memory work • Review the addition algorithm with two-digit numbers	• None
Activities	• Understand how to use the addition algorithm to add three-digit numbers	• Workbook page 30.1A • Base-ten blocks • Place-Value Chart (Blackline Master 5)
Workbook	• Review previously-learned material	• Workbook page 30.1B

Warm-up: Counting, Memory Work, and Review

- Have your child count forward by 5s from the following numbers. Prompt her as needed, and stop her after she reaches the last number listed.
    - **Count by 5s from 335:** *335, 340, 345, 350, 355.*
    - **Count by 5s from 905:** *905, 910, 915, 920, 925.*
    - **Count by 5s from 690:** *690, 695, 700, 705, 710.*
- **How many hundreds equal 1 thousand?** *10.*
- Write the following addition problems on a piece of paper, and have your child use the addition algorithm to solve them:

$$\begin{array}{r} 36 \\ +42 \\ \hline 78 \end{array} \qquad \begin{array}{r} ^{1}\\ 45 \\ +46 \\ \hline 91 \end{array} \qquad \begin{array}{r} 87 \\ +42 \\ \hline 129 \end{array}$$

If your child has trouble keeping the digits aligned in vertical problems, write the problems on a piece of lined paper, turned sideways.

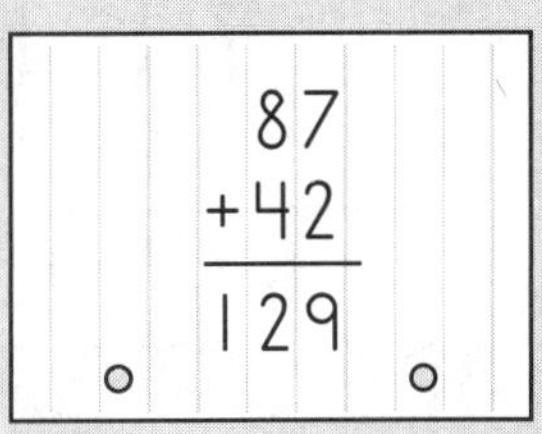

Activity: Add Three-Digit Numbers without Trading

In Unit 10, you learned how to use the addition algorithm to add two-digit numbers. This week, you'll learn how to use the algorithm to add three-digit numbers.

Show your child the Addition Algorithm diagram at the top of workbook page 30.1A. **Remember this diagram? It's the same one we used in Unit 10. You can use the exact same steps to add three-digit numbers that you used to add two-digit numbers.**

Let's pretend again that you're a robot that follows the Addition Algorithm program. Point to the first exercise (213 + 345). Have your child model 213 and 345 with base-ten blocks on the Place-Value Chart.

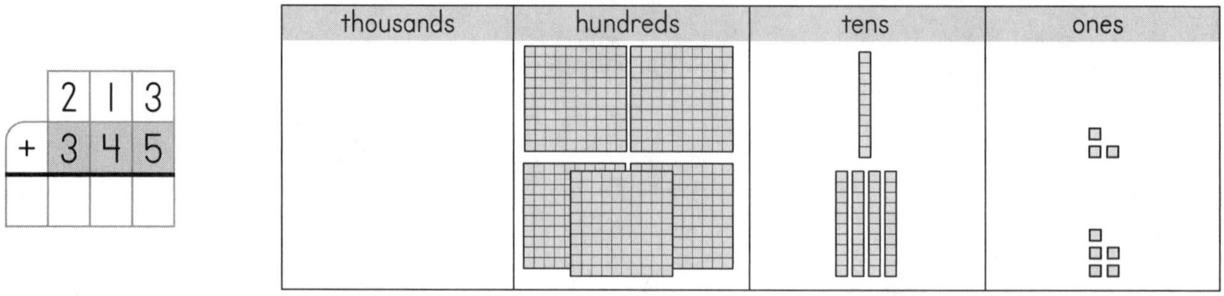

Have your child use the Addition Algorithm to add the digits in the ones-place and tens-place. After she completes the tens-place, ask: **Are we done now?** *No.* **Why not?** *We haven't added the hundreds yet.* Help your child follow the steps in the diagram to add the hundreds. **So, what's 213 + 345?** *558.* **Great job, robot!**

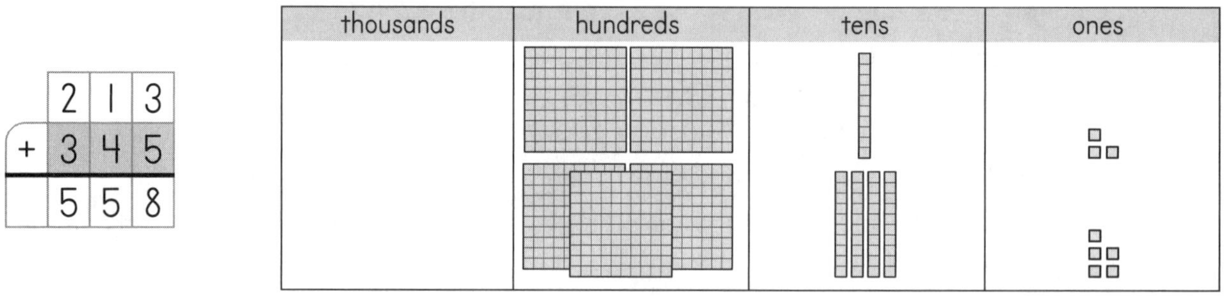

Activity: Add Three-Digit Numbers with Trading

Point to the second exercise (194 + 420). Have your child model 194 and 420 with base-ten blocks on the Place-Value Chart. Have her use the Addition Algorithm to add the digits in the ones-place and tens-place. She will need to trade 10 rods for 1 flat and place the flat in the hundreds-column.

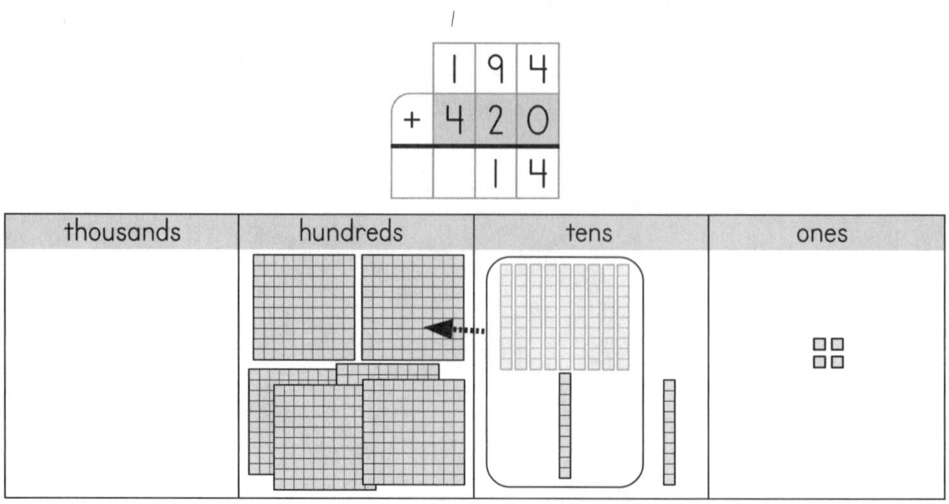

Now, we follow the steps for the hundreds-place. Make sure to add all 3 digits in the hundreds-place. Have your child add the hundreds to complete the problem.

$$\begin{array}{r} \overset{1}{} \\ 194 \\ +\ 420 \\ \hline 614 \end{array}$$

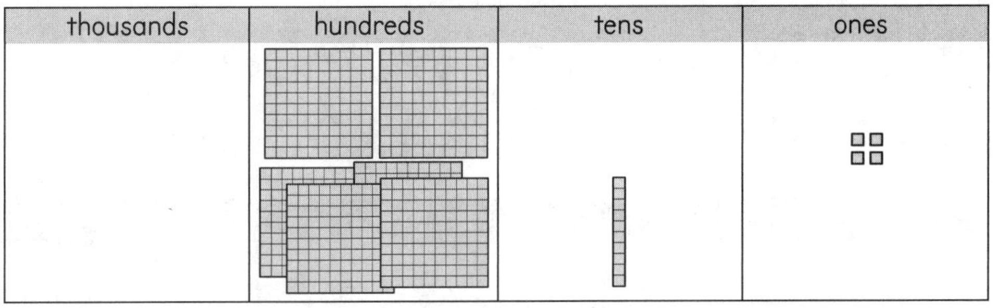

Activity: Add Three-Digit Numbers Like a Robot

Continue in the same way with the rest of the problems on workbook page 30.1A.

$$\begin{array}{r} 616 \\ +\ 175 \\ \hline 791 \end{array} \qquad \begin{array}{r} 681 \\ +\ \ 72 \\ \hline 753 \end{array} \qquad \begin{array}{r} 457 \\ +\ 251 \\ \hline 708 \end{array} \qquad \begin{array}{r} 374 \\ +\ 548 \\ \hline 922 \end{array}$$

> Don't require your child to use base-ten blocks if she can confidently solve the problems without them. See the Week 30 **Teaching Math with Confidence** for more on extending the addition algorithm to three-digit numbers.

For 457 + 251, point out that it's important to record that there are zero tens in the sum: **If you didn't write a zero in the tens-place, the answer would look like 78 instead of 708!**

For 374 + 548, point out that you trade both the ones and the tens: **You traded both the ones and the tens in this problem. Next year, you'll learn how to use the addition algorithm to solve problems where you trade 10 hundreds for 1 thousand.**

Save workbook page 30.1A so your child can refer to the addition algorithm diagram.

Workbook: Review

Have your child complete workbook page 30.1B.

Lesson 30.2
Add Three-Digit Numbers without Base-Ten Blocks

	Purpose	Materials
Warm-up	• Count money • Practice memory work • Review approximating numbers to 1000	• Play money • Book with over 1000 pages
Activities	• Add three-digit numbers on paper, without base-ten blocks	• Base-ten blocks • Place-Value Chart (Blackline Master 5) • Workbook page 30.2A • 12 slips of paper
Workbook	• Review previously-learned material	• Workbook page 30.2B

Your child will begin adding three-digit numbers without base-ten blocks in this lesson. If he has trouble or seems confused, model the problems with base-ten blocks until he feels more confident.

Warm-up: Counting, Memory Work, and Review

- Place 6 hundred-dollar bills, 4 ten-dollar bills, and 3 five-dollar bills on the table. **How much is this money worth?** *$655.*
- **How many minutes equal a half-hour?** *30.*
  How many minutes equal a quarter-hour? *15.*
- Secretly choose a page number between 1 and 1000 in a book with more than 1000 pages. Place a slip of paper in the book to mark the secret page.

I'm thinking of a page number that's greater than 1 and less than 1000. Have your child guess the secret page number. After each guess, tell whether the page number is more or less than his guess. Continue until he figures out the page number. Play several times.

Marking the page with a slip of paper encourages your child to estimate the bookmark's position and helps him begin to approximate numbers to 1000.

Activity: Add Three-Digit Numbers without Base-Ten Blocks

In the last lesson, you learned how to use the addition algorithm to add three-digit numbers. Today, you'll practice more so you can add three-digit numbers fluently, without base-ten blocks.

Point to the first printed problem on workbook page 30.2A (635 + 282). **Try solving this problem with the addition algorithm. While you work, I'll model the problem with base-ten blocks. Once we finish, we'll compare our answers and make sure they match.**

Have your child solve the problem. While she works, model the two addends with base-ten blocks on the Place-Value Chart and trade 10 of the rods for 1 flat. Cover the blocks with a piece of paper.

	1		
	6	3	5
+	2	8	2
	9	1	7

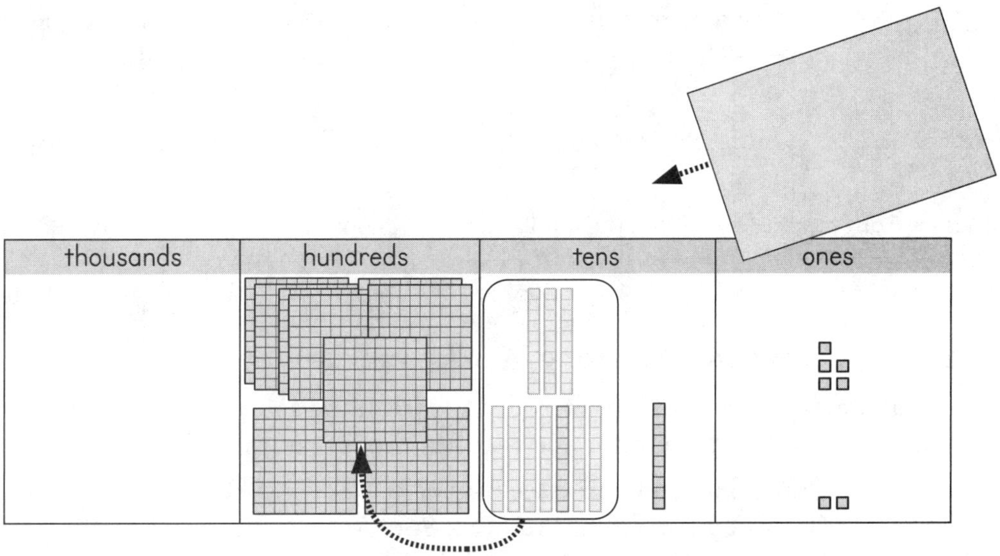

So, what's 635 plus 282? *917.* Remove the cover from the blocks so your child can check whether his answer matches the blocks. If his answer does not match, have him use the blocks to find the correct sum.

Repeat with the other problem (475 + 369).

Activity: Play Snowball Fight

Play Snowball Fight. See Lesson 15.3 (page 246) for general directions. Write the following numbers on slips of paper: 106, 162, 175, 247, 254, 286, 360, 379, 387, 451, 493, 498. Use these slips of paper as your "snowballs" and record the sums in the blank grids on workbook page 30.2A.

	1	1	
	4	7	5
+	3	6	9
	8	4	4

> These addends ensure that your child gets lots of practice with trading, with none of the sums greater than 1000.

Workbook: Review

Have your child complete workbook page 30.2B.

Lesson 30.3
Add 3 or More Addends

	Purpose	Materials
Warm-up	• Count by 10s • Practice memory work • Review adding a series of numbers	• Playing cards
Activities	• Use the addition algorithm to add 3 or more addends	• Play money • Workbook page 30.3A • 4 children's chapter books, each with 100-250 pages
Workbook	• Add 3 or more addends	• Workbook page 30.3A and 30.3B

In this lesson, your child will find the total number of pages in 4 children's chapter books. Each book should have between 100 and 250 pages so that the sum of all the pages is less than 1000. If possible, use books your child has recently read independently or that you've read aloud to her.

Warm-up: Counting, Memory Work, and Review

- Have your child count forward by 10s from the following numbers. Prompt her as needed, and stop her after she reaches the last number listed.
    - **Count by 10s from 620:** *620, 630, 640, 650, 660.*
    - **Count by 10s from 790:** *790, 800, 810, 820, 830.*
    - **Count by 10s from 960:** *960, 970, 980, 990, 1000.*
- **Are times in the afternoon and evening a.m. or p.m.?** *P.m.*
  Are times in the morning a.m. or p.m.? *A.m.*
- Play Make 20 Splat. See Lesson 1.2 (page 16) for directions

  Playing Make 20 Splat prepares your child to add multiple small numbers as she adds digits in this lesson.

Activity: Add 3 or More Addends with Money

In the last two lessons, you learned how to use the addition algorithm to add three-digit numbers. Today, you'll learn how to add more than two numbers at a time.

Point to the first exercise on workbook page 30.3A (354 + 133 + 245). **Let's pretend you have $354. Then, you earn $133. Last, you earn $245.** Have your child model each number with play money and place the bills in the matching columns of the Place-Value Chart.

	3	5	4
	1	3	3
+	2	4	5

Have your child use hundred-dollar bills, ten-dollar bills, and one-dollar bills (rather than twenty-dollar bills or five-dollar bills) so that each bill's value corresponds to its column in the Place-Value Chart.

We could add $354 to $133. Then, we could add the sum to $245 to find the total amount of money. But, it's usually faster and easier to add all the ones, then all the tens, and finally all the hundreds.

First, we add all the ones. Point to each digit in the ones-place as you prompt your child to add them in order. **What's 4 plus 3?** *7.* **Plus 5?** *12.* Have your child trade 10 one-dollar bills for 1 ten-dollar bill. Then, have her write a 1 above the tens-place and a 2 in the sum's ones-place.

		1	
	3	5	4
	1	3	3
+	2	4	5
			2

Next, we add all the tens. Point to each digit in the tens-place as you prompt your child to add them in order. **What's 1 plus 5?** *6.* **Plus 3?** *9.* **Plus 4?** *13.* Have your child trade 10 ten-dollar bills for 1 hundred-dollar bill. Then, have her write 1 above the hundreds-place and 3 in the sum's tens-place.

	1	1	
	3	5	4
	1	3	3
+	2	4	5
		3	2

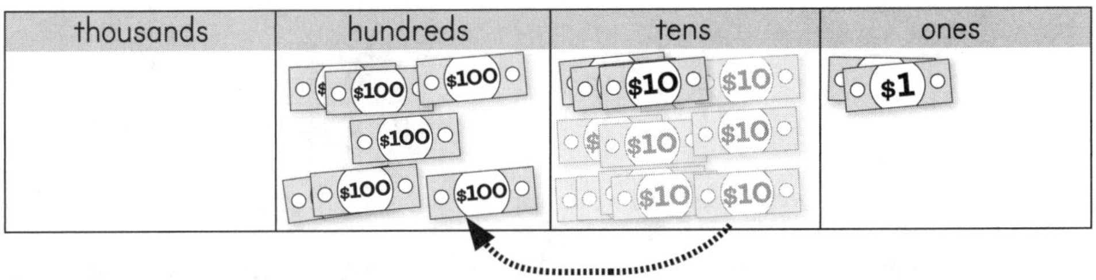

Last, we add all the hundreds. Point to each digit in the hundreds-place as you prompt your child to add them in order. **What's 1 plus 3?** *4.* **Plus 1?** *5.* **Plus 2?** *7.* Have your child write 7 in the sum's hundreds-place. **So, what's 354 plus 133 plus 245?** *732.*

	1	1	
	3	5	4
	1	3	3
+	2	4	5
	7	3	2

Continue in the same way with the rest of the problems in the top row of workbook page 30.3A. Model the problems with play money as needed.

For the third exercise, point out that the addition algorithm works for adding any number of numbers: **We can use the addition algorithm to add as many numbers as we want!** After your child adds the digits in the ones-place, help her trade 20 of the one-dollar bills for 2 ten-dollar bills and write 2 above the tens-place.

	1	1	
	4	0	6
	1	9	8
+	3	6	3
	9	6	7

		2	
	2	4	1
	2	1	8
	2	2	5
+	2	0	7
	8	9	1

Activity: Find the Total Number of Pages in 4 Books

Show your child 4 children's chapter books, each with 100-250 pages. **How many pages do you think are in all 4 books?** *Answers will vary.* Have your child find how many pages are in each book and write the number on a slip of paper.

Let's add up the number of pages in all 4 books to find out! Have your child write each number of pages in the blank grid. Then, have her add to find the total.

	1	2	
	1	7	9
	2	1	2
	1	5	6
+	2	3	8
	7	8	5

Sample addition problem. Use the number of pages in your books as the addends in the problem.

Wow, that's a lot of pages! Discuss how close your child's estimate was to the actual total.

Workbook: Add 3 or More Addends and Review

Have your child complete workbook pages 30.3A and 30.3B.

Lesson 30.4
Three-Digit Addition Word Problems

	Purpose	Materials
Warm-up	• Count by 4s to 40 • Practice memory work • Review pairs that make 1000	• None
Activities	• Solve addition word problems • Correctly line up the digits in vertical addition problems	• Workbook page 30.4A
Workbook	• Review previously-learned material	• Workbook page 30.4B

Warm-up: Counting, Memory Work, and Review

- Have your child count by 4s to 40: *4, 8, 12, 16, 20, 24, 28, 32, 36, 40.*
- **What is another name for 12 p.m.?** *Noon.* **What is another name for 12 a.m.?** *Midnight.*
- Secretly write each of the following equations on a piece of paper and hide the addend indicated with a slip of paper. Have your child use his "x-ray vision" to identify the hidden number in each equation.

$\boxed{500} + 500 = 1000$ $300 + \boxed{700} = 1000$ $800 + \boxed{200} = 1000$

$\boxed{900} + 100 = 1000$ $\boxed{600} + 400 = 1000$

Activity: Solve Three-Digit Addition Word Problems

This week, you have learned how to use the addition algorithm to add three-digit numbers. Today, you'll use the addition algorithm to solve word problems.

Show your child workbook page 30.4A and read the chart at the top of the page. Briefly discuss your child's experiences with bikes. **We'll use the prices in the chart to solve the word problems.**

Read aloud the first word problem: **How much does it cost to buy a kid's bike and adult bike?** Have your child find the cost of each type of bike, write the prices in the blank grid, and add to find the total.

		1	
	2	6	4
+	4	2	8
	6	9	2

Repeat with the rest of the word problems on the page. For the second problem, remind your child as needed to align the digits according to their place value. **Make sure you line up the numbers so that the ones-place for 137 is right above the ones-place for 39. That way, you'll be sure to add the ones to the ones and the tens to the tens.**

How much does it cost to buy a beginner bike and helmet?

		1	
	1	3	7
+		3	9
	1	7	6

How much does it cost to buy 2 beginner bikes?

		1	
	1	3	7
+	1	3	7
	2	7	4

How much does it cost to buy a beginner bike, kid's bike, and adult bike?

	1	1	
	1	3	7
	2	6	4
+	4	2	8
	8	2	9

If your child has trouble with any of the problems on workbook page 30.4A, model the prices with play money as in Lesson 30.3.

Workbook: Review

Have your child complete workbook page 30.4B.

Lesson 30.5
Enrichment and Review (Optional)

	Purpose	Materials
Warm-up	• Count from 500 to 600 by 1s, 2s, 5s, or 10s • Review memory work • Review your child's favorite or most challenging activities from Week 30	• Varies, depending on the activities you choose
Picture Book	• Read and understand maps	• *Mapping Penny's World,* by Loreen Leedy
Enrichment Activity	• Make a map	• Paper • Small toy

Warm-up: Counting, Memory Work, and Review

- Have your child count from 500 to 600 by 1s, 2s, 5s, or 10s. (Choose whichever counting sequence your child needs to practice the most.)
- Quiz your child on the all the memory work for the year. See page 523 for the full list.
- If you have time, repeat one or two of the activities from this week's lessons. Choose activities your child especially enjoyed or found challenging.

Math Picture Book: *Mapping Penny's World*

Read *Mapping Penny's World,* by Loreen Leedy. As you read, discuss the maps in the book and how they match the characters' surroundings.

Enrichment Activity: Make a Treasure Map

Help your child make a simple map of a room in your house. Encourage him to imagine looking at the room from above and drawing the approximate location and size of the main items in the room.

Then, hide a small toy somewhere in the room. Make an X on the map to show your child where to look for the toy. After he follows the map to find the toy, reverse roles: have your child hide the toy and mark the map to help you find it.

Week 30 Answer Key

30.1A

See the Instructor Guide for directions.

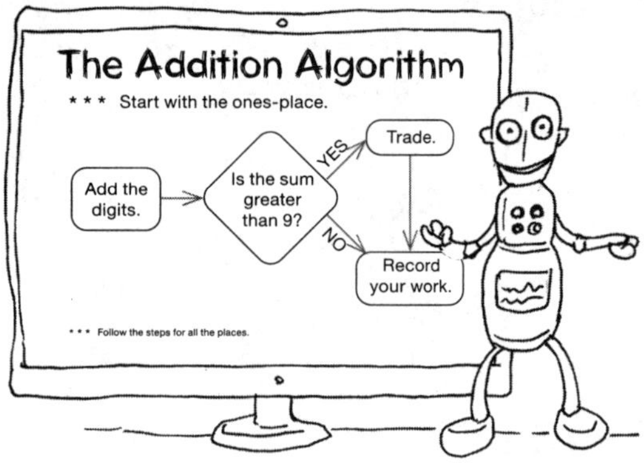

	2	1	3
+	3	4	5
	5	5	8

	1	9	4
+	4	2	0
	6	1	4

	6	1	6
+	1	7	5
	7	9	1

	6	8	1
+		7	2
	7	5	3

	4	5	7
+	2	5	1
	7	0	8

	3	7	4
+	5	4	8
	9	2	2

30.1B

Label the numbers on the number line.

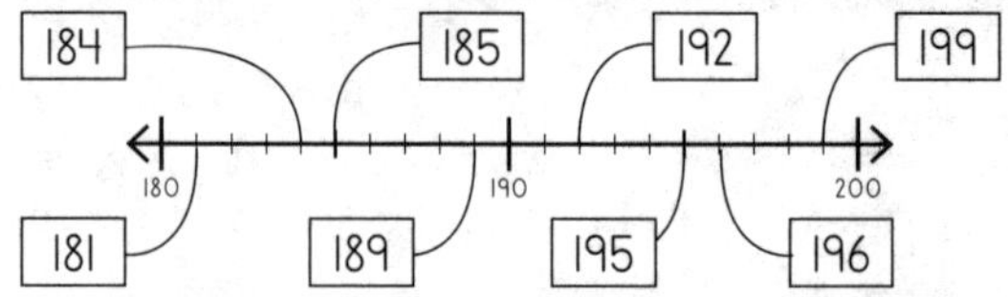

Complete.

425 + 3 = 428	708 - 7 = 701
619 + 20 = 639	840 - 30 = 810
332 + 400 = 732	523 - 200 = 323

Zoe counted some of her toys. Use her chart to make a bar graph.

Toy	Number
Dolls	8
Stuffed Animals	12
Puppets	4

30.2A

See the Instructor Guide for directions.

Snowball Fight

	6	3	5
+	2	8	2
	9	1	7

	4	7	5
+	3	6	9
	8	4	4

175 162 247 254 451 106 379 493 360 387 286 498

30.2B

Use the chart to answer the questions.

Name	Age
Grandma	61
Grandpa	60
Mom	33
Dad	34
Caleb	7

How much older is Grandma than Mom?

	6	1
-	3	3
	2	8

28 years

How much older is Grandpa than Dad?

	6	0
-	3	4
	2	6

26 years

How much younger is Caleb than Grandma?

	6	1
-		7
	5	4

54 years

Color the shapes to match the fractions.

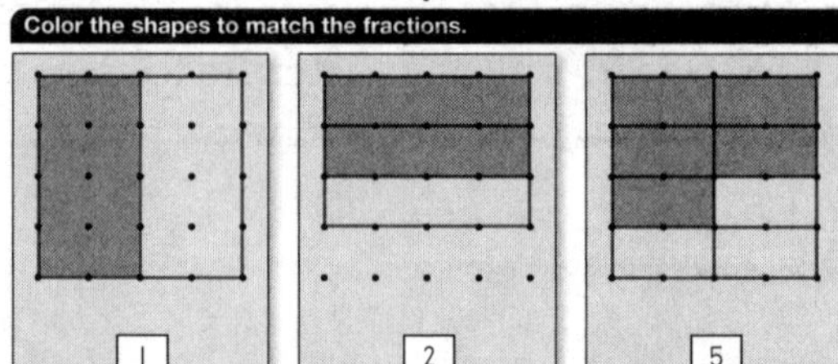

$\frac{1}{2}$ $\frac{2}{3}$ $\frac{5}{8}$

Other ways to color the shapes are possible.

Week 30 Answer Key

30.3A

See the Instructor Guide for directions.

	3	5	4
	1	3	3
+	2	4	5
	7	3	2

	4	0	6
	1	9	8
+	3	6	3
	9	6	7

	2	4	1
	2	1	8
	2	2	5
+	2	0	7
	8	9	1

+			

Complete.

	5	5	0
	1	3	2
+	2	6	4
	9	4	6

	2	2	3
	2	7	1
	2	4	0
+	2	6	1
	9	9	5

	1	5	1
	2	0	9
	1	4	5
	3	2	0
+	1	3	6
	9	6	1

30.3B

Match.

Cylinder | Sphere | Cube | Rectangular prism | Cone

Write the numbers that come before and after.

437	438	439
599	600	601
398	399	400
558	559	560
829	830	831
708	709	710

Use a ruler to draw lines that match the lengths.

4 inches ______________________

12 centimeters ______________________

30.4A

Use the chart to answer the questions.

Bike Shop Prices

Item	Price
Beginner bike	$137
Kid's bike	$264
Adult bike	$428
Helmet	$39

How much does it cost to buy a kid's bike and adult bike?

	2	6	4
+	4	2	8
	6	9	2

$ 692

How much does it cost to buy a beginner bike and helmet?

	1	3	7
+		3	9
	1	7	6

$ 176

How much does it cost to buy 2 beginner bikes?

	1	3	7
+	1	3	7
	2	7	4

$ 274

How much does it cost to buy a beginner bike, kid's bike, and adult bike?

	1	3	7
	2	6	4
+	4	2	8
	8	2	9

$ 829

30.4B

Draw lines to split the shapes into the matching parts.

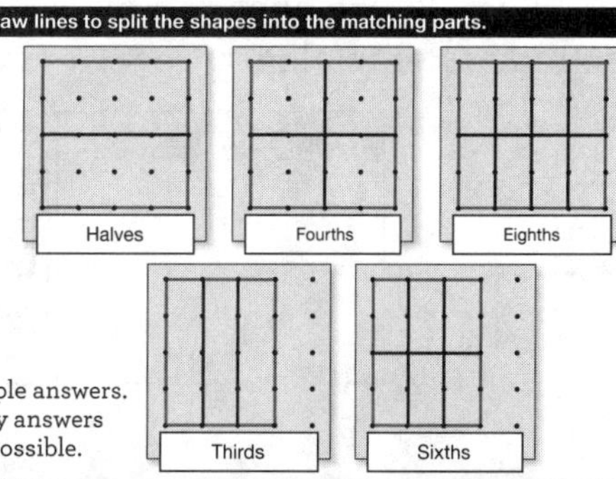

Sample answers. Many answers are possible.

Complete the sequences.

Count by half hours: 9:00, 9:30, 10:00, 10:30, 11:00

Count by quarter hours: 10:00, 10:15, 10:30, 10:45, 11:00

Count by 10 minutes: 12:00, 12:10, 12:20, 12:30, 12:40

Week 31
Subtract Numbers to 1000

Overview

Your child will learn how to use the subtraction algorithm to subtract three-digit numbers. You'll pay special attention to problems in which she needs to subtract across a zero. (See below for more on these problems.)

Lesson 31.1	Subtract Three-Digit Numbers with Base-Ten Blocks
Lesson 31.2	Subtract Across a Zero with Base-Ten Blocks
Lesson 31.3	Subtract Three-Digit Numbers with Money
Lesson 31.4	Three-Digit Subtraction Word Problems
Lesson 31.5	Enrichment and Review (Optional)

Teaching Math with Confidence: The Extra Challenge of Subtracting Across a Zero

This week, you'll teach your child how to apply the subtraction algorithm to three-digit numbers. Most of these problems are quite similar to the two-digit problems that she solved in Unit 12. However, she'll also tackle a new challenge this week: subtracting across a zero. In these problems, your child needs to trade twice in order to have enough ones. First, she needs to trade 1 hundred for 10 tens. Then, she needs to trade 1 ten for 10 ones.

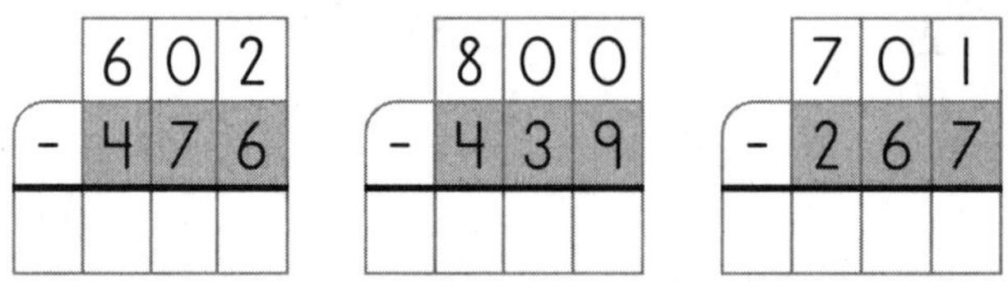

Examples of problems that require subtracting across a zero.

As in Unit 12, you'll use base-ten blocks to help your child concretely understand the steps. You'll also teach her to clearly record and show both trades.

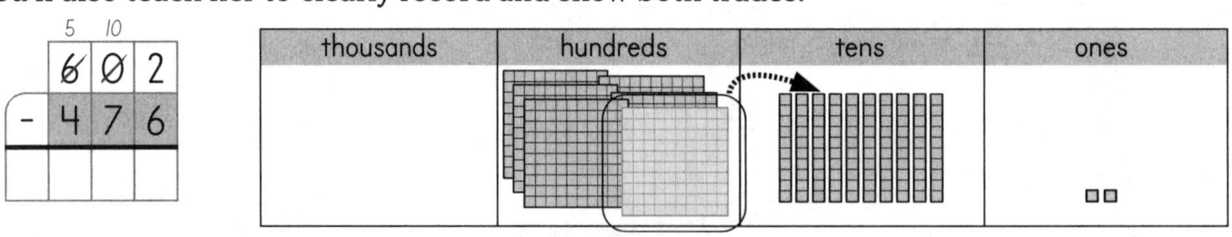

First trade.

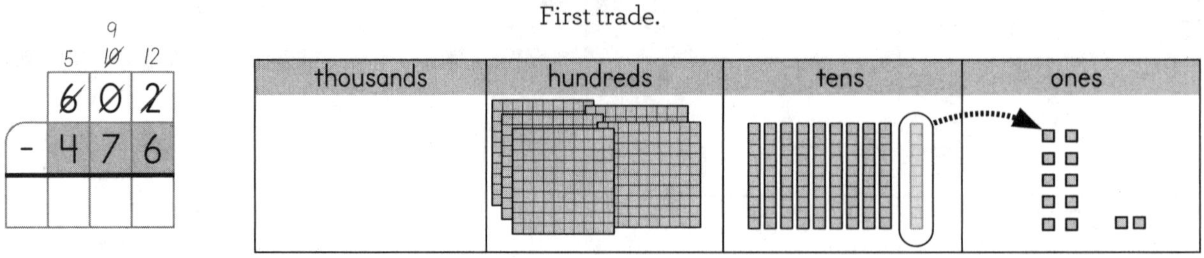

Second trade.

Recording all the trades in this way takes quite a bit of space, but it will help her keep track of all the steps in this complicated process. Once she has made and recorded all the trades, she'll be ready to subtract and complete the problem.

Don't be surprised or worried if your child isn't fully fluent with subtracting across a zero before the end of the year. She'll continue to practice this skill in third grade so that she will eventually become automatic and fluent.

Extra Materials Needed for Week 31

- Paper clip
- For optional Enrichment and Review Lesson:
    - *Christmas Farm,* written by Mary Lyn Ray and illustrated by Barry Root
    - 3 books with 500-1000 pages

Lesson 31.1
Subtract Three-Digit Numbers with Base-Ten Blocks

	Purpose	Materials
Warm-up	• Count backward • Practice memory work • Review the subtraction algorithm	• None
Activities	• Understand how to use the subtraction algorithm to subtract three-digit numbers	• Workbook page 31.1A • Base-ten blocks • Place-Value Chart (Blackline Master 5)
Workbook	• Review previously-learned material	• Workbook page 31.1B

Warm-up: Counting, Memory Work, and Review

- Have your child count backward from the following numbers. Prompt her as needed, and stop her after she reaches the last number listed.
  - × **Count backward from 635:** *635, 634, 633, 632, 631.*
  - × **Count backward from 592:** *592, 591, 590, 589, 588.*
  - × **Count backward from 700:** *700, 699, 698, 697, 696.*
- **How many cents equal 1 dollar?** *100.*
- Write the following problems on a piece of paper. Have your child use the subtraction algorithm to solve them:

6 13	12	13 12
73	125	142
- 46	- 32	- 85
27	93	57

Activity: Use the Subtraction Algorithm to Subtract Three-Digit Numbers

Last week, you learned how to use the addition algorithm to add three-digit numbers. This week, you'll learn how to use the subtraction algorithm to subtract three-digit numbers.

Show your child the Subtraction Algorithm diagram at the top of workbook page 31.1A. **Remember this diagram? It's the same one we used in Unit 11. You can subtract three-digit numbers with the same steps you used to subtract two-digit numbers.**

Let's pretend again that you're a robot that's programmed to follow the Subtraction Algorithm. Point to the first exercise on workbook page 31.1A (786 – 314). Have your child model 786 with base-ten blocks on the Place-Value Chart.

	7	8	6
-	3	1	4

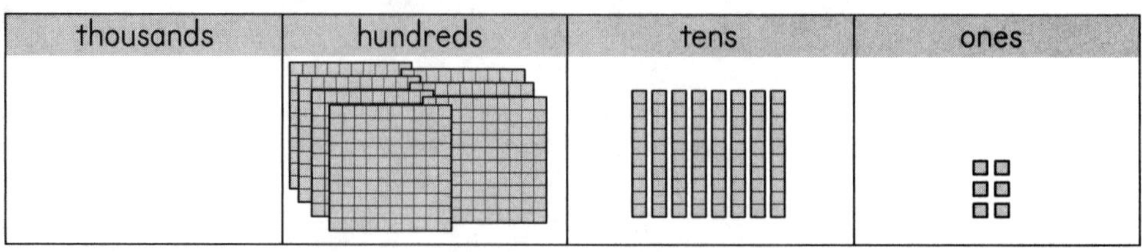

Have your child use the Subtraction Algorithm to subtract the digits in the ones-place and tens-place. After she completes the tens-place, ask: **Are we done now?** *No.* **Why not?** *We haven't subtracted the hundreds yet.* Help your child follow the steps in the diagram to subtract the hundreds.

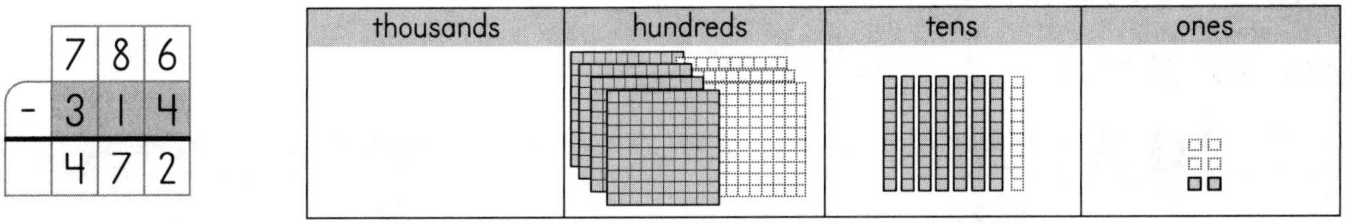

So, what's 786 – 314? *472.* **Great job, robot!**

Activity: Two-Digit Subtraction with Trading

Point to the second exercise (629 – 248). Have your child model 629 with base-ten blocks on the Place-Value Chart.

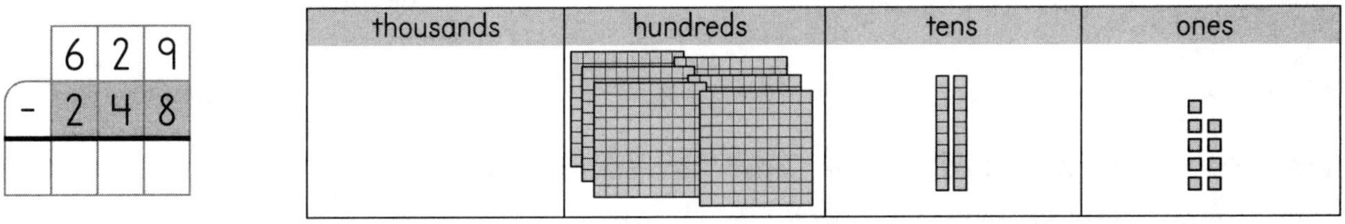

Have your child use the Subtraction Algorithm to subtract the digits in the ones-place and tens-place. For the tens-place, she will need to trade 1 flat for 10 rods.

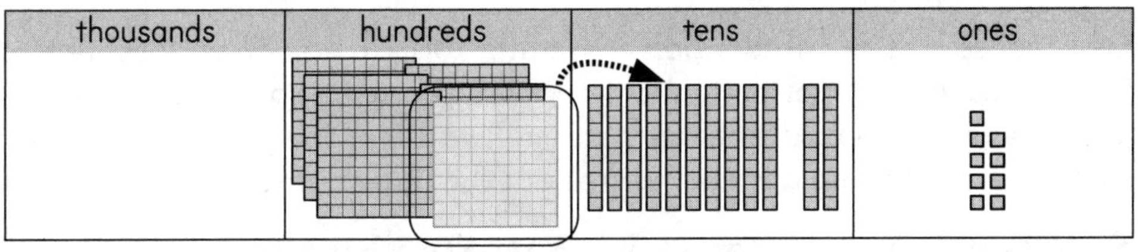

Last, we follow the steps for the hundreds-place. Help your child follow the steps in the Subtraction Algorithm diagram to subtract the hundreds.

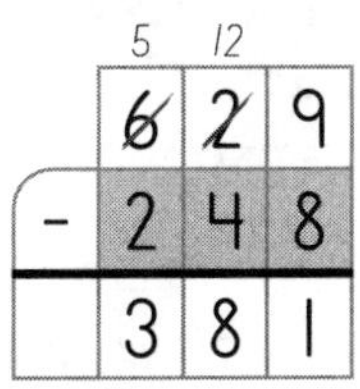

Activity: Subtract Two-Digit Numbers Like a Robot

Continue in the same way with the rest of the problems on the workbook page. Model the problems with base-ten blocks as needed.

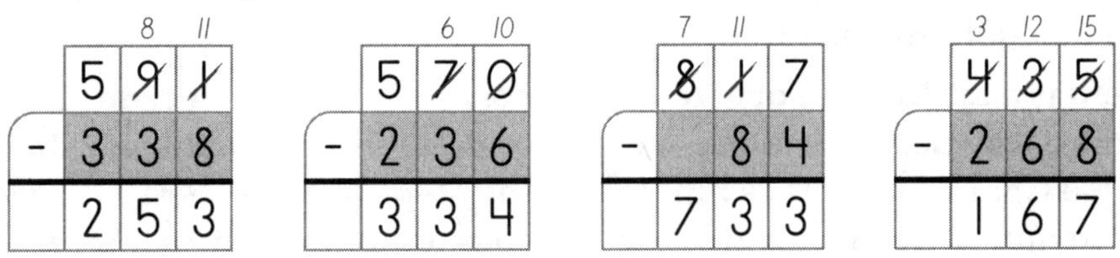

Save workbook page 31.1A so your child can refer to the Subtraction Algorithm diagram.

Workbook: Review

Have your child complete workbook page 31.1B.

Lesson 31.2
Subtract Across a Zero with Base-Ten Blocks

	Purpose	Materials
Warm-up	• Count by 3s to 30 • Practice memory work • Review approximating numbers to 1000	• Play money, optional • Book with over 1000 pages
Activities	• Learn how to use the subtraction algorithm to subtract across zeros in three-digit numbers	• Workbook page 31.2A • Base-ten blocks • Place-Value Chart (Blackline Master 5)
Workbook	• Review previously-learned material	• Workbook page 31.2B

Warm-up: Counting, Memory Work, and Review

- Have your child count by 3s to 30: 3, *6, 9, 12, 15, 18, 21, 24, 27, 30.*
- **How many sides does a triangle have?** *3.* **A quadrilateral?** *4.* **A pentagon?** *5.* **A hexagon?** *6.* **An octagon?** *8.*
- Secretly choose a page number between 1 and 1000 in a book with more than 1000 pages. Place a slip of paper in the book to mark the secret page. Have your child guess the secret page number. After each guess, tell whether the page number is more or less than his guess. Continue until he figures out the page number. Play several times.

Activity: Subtract Across a Zero with Base-Ten Blocks

In the last lesson, you learned how to use the subtraction algorithm to subtract three-digit numbers. Today, you'll learn how to solve three-digit subtraction problems where the greater number has a zero in the tens-place. This is called "subtracting across a zero." Show your child the problems at the top of page 31.2A. Have your child identify the zero (or zeros) in the greater number in each problem.

	504		602		800
−	351	−	476	−	439

Children often find it confusing to subtract across a zero. But if you follow the usual steps in the subtraction algorithm, it's not so hard!

The first problem is a lot like the problems you solved in the last lesson. Point to the first exercise on workbook page 31.2A (504 – 351). Have your child model 504 with base-ten blocks on the Place-Value Chart. Then, have him follow the steps in the subtraction algorithm to find the answer. Guide him as needed, and allow him to refer to the Subtraction Algorithm diagram if he forgets any of the steps.

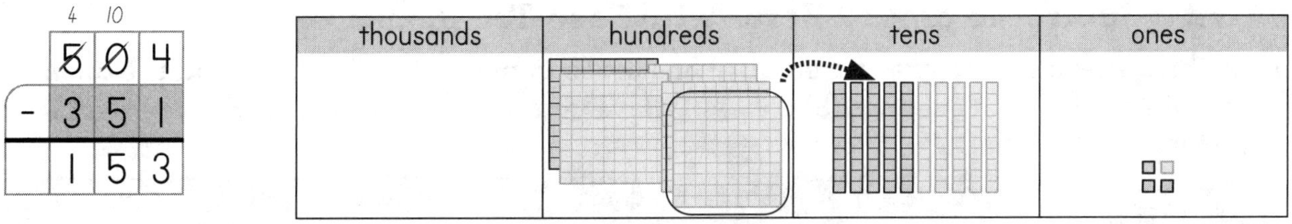

If your child hesitates when he sees a zero in the tens-place, remind him that the zero simply means that there are zero tens. So, he needs to trade 1 hundred for 10 tens and record the trade.

The second exercise is just a little more complicated. Point to the second exercise (602 – 476). Have your child model 602 with base-ten blocks on the Place-Value Chart.

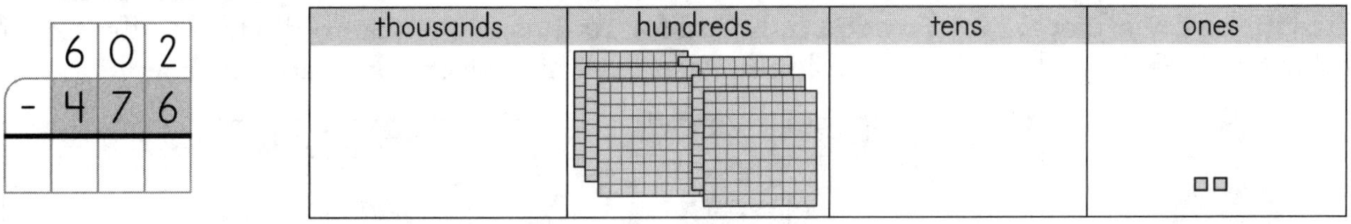

We start with the ones-place again. Is the top digit greater than or equal to the bottom digit? *No.* **So, we need to trade. But, there aren't any tens in the tens-place! How can we get some tens?** *By trading 1 hundred for 10 tens.*

We'll trade in two steps. First, we trade 1 hundred for 10 tens. Have your child trade 1 flat for 10 rods and place the rods in the tens-column. Also have him record the trade as shown.

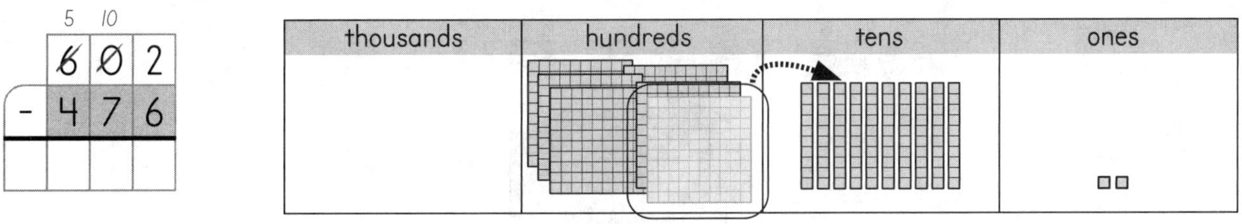

Next, we trade 1 ten for 10 ones. Have your child trade 1 rod for 10 units and place the units in the ones-column. Also have him record the trade as shown.

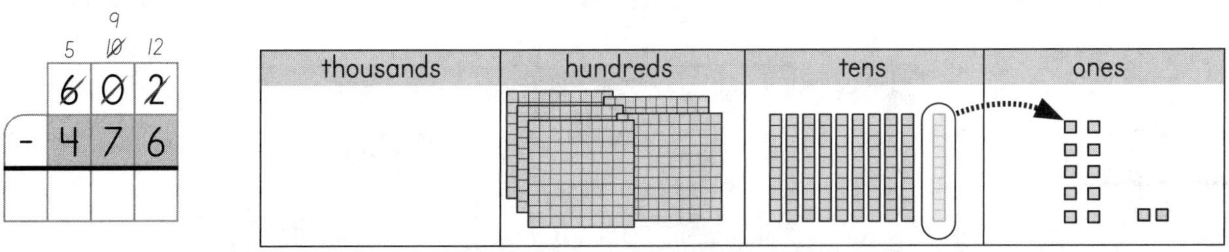

Trading in two steps (and recording each trade separately) may feel inefficient. But, this careful and deliberate approach ensures that your child understands what he's doing and helps prevent mistakes. See the Week 31 **Teaching Math with Confidence** for more on subtracting across a zero.

Now that you've traded, you're ready to subtract. Help your child follow the steps in the subtraction algorithm to complete the problem.

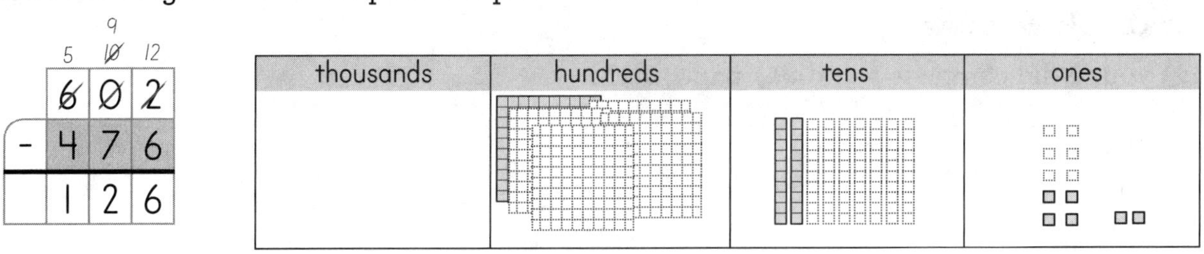

Activity: Subtract Across 2 Zeros with Base-Ten Blocks

In the third exercise, the greater number has zeros in both the tens-place and the ones-place. Point to the third exercise (800 – 439). Have your child model 800 with base-ten blocks on the Place-Value Chart.

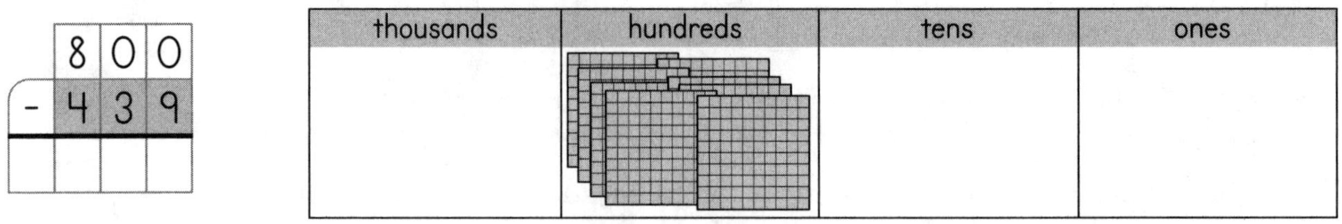

You'll need to trade twice again so that you have some tens in the tens-place and some ones in the ones-place. First, trade 1 hundred for 10 tens. Have your child trade 1 flat for 10 rods and place the rods in the tens-column. Also have him record the trade as shown.

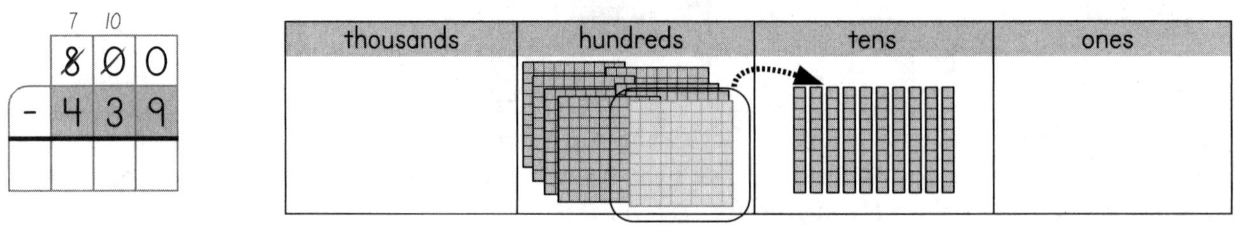

Next, trade 1 ten for 10 ones. Have your child trade 1 rod for 10 units and place the units in the ones-column. Have him record the trade as shown.

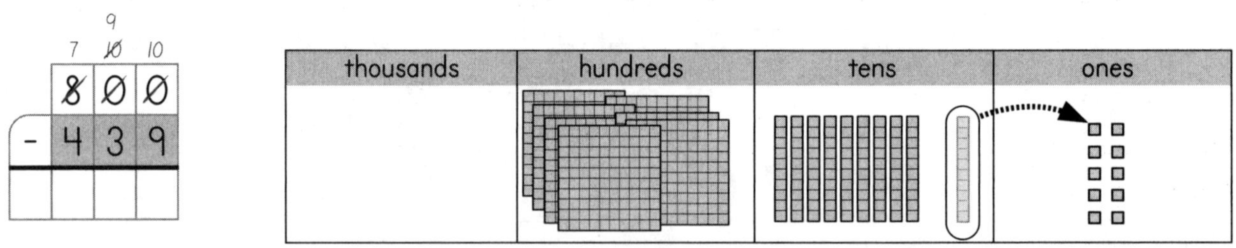

Now, you're ready to subtract. Have your child follow the steps in the subtraction algorithm to complete the problem.

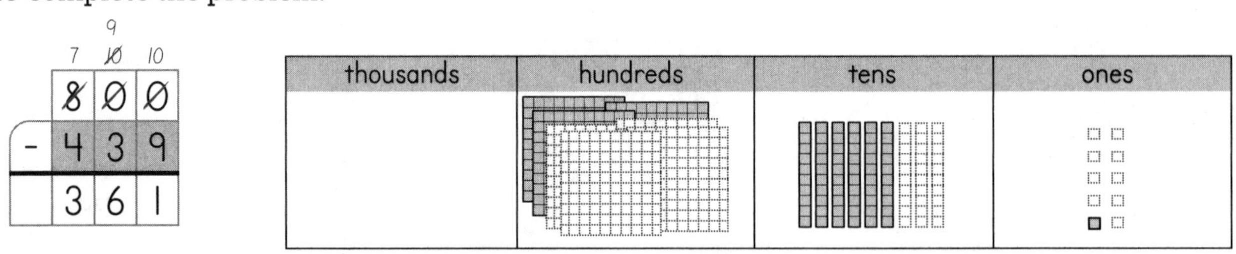

Activity: Play What's the Difference?

Use the bottom part of workbook page 31.2A to play What's the Difference? See Lesson 27.1 (page 434) for directions. Model the problems with base-ten blocks as needed and carefully talk through the trading.

Workbook: Review

Have your child complete workbook page 31.2B.

Lesson 31.3
Subtract Three-Digit Numbers with Money

	Purpose	Materials
Warm-up	• Count money • Practice memory work • Review telling time to the minute	• Play money • Clock
Activities	• Practice subtracting three-digit numbers • Model three-digit subtraction problems with money	• Workbook page 31.3A • Play money • Place-Value Chart (Blackline Master 5) • Paper clip
Workbook	• Review previously-learned material	• Workbook page 31.3A

Warm-up: Counting, Memory Work, and Review

- Place 3 hundred-dollar bills, 10 ten-dollar bills, and 1 one-dollar bill on the table. **How much is this money worth?** *$401.*
- **How many hundreds equal 1 thousand?** *10.*
- Set a clock to the following times: 9:30, 9:45, 10:00, 10:05, 9:55, 9:39, 10:19, 10:30. Have your child tell each time.

Activity: Subtract Three-Digit Numbers with Money

In the last lesson, you learned how to subtract across a zero. Today, we'll use money to practice subtracting three-digit numbers.

Using play money instead of base-ten blocks provides some variety and shows a real-life application for three-digit subtraction.

Point to the first problem on workbook page 31.3A. **Let's pretend you have $928.** Have your child count out $928 in play money and place the bills in the matching columns of the Place-Value Chart.

$$\begin{array}{r} 928 \\ -\ 245 \\ \hline \end{array}$$

thousands	hundreds	tens	ones
			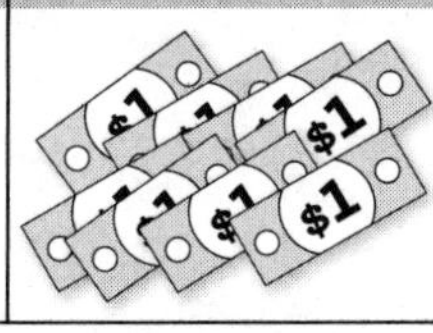

Use 2 ten-dollar bills (and not a twenty-dollar bill) so that each bill's value corresponds to its column in the Place-Value Chart.

Then, you spend $245. Briefly discuss what your child might like to buy with $245. Then, have her use the subtraction algorithm to complete the written problem. Help her model each step with the play money.

	8	12	
	~~9~~	~~2~~	8
-	2	4	5
	6	8	3

Have your child find the answers to the other two subtraction problems at the top of workbook page 31.3A. Model the problems with play money as needed.

		6	12
	8	~~7~~	~~2~~
-	6	0	9
	2	6	3

		9	
	6	~~10~~	11
	~~7~~	~~0~~	~~1~~
-	2	6	7
	4	3	4

Activity: Play Spin to Win

Play Spin to Win. See Lesson 14.2 (page 228) for full directions. Use workbook page 31.3A. On your turn, first spin the paper clip around the top spinner. Write this number on the top line of the first blank grid. Then, move the paper clip and pencil to the bottom spinner. Spin again, and write this number on the next line. Subtract the lesser number from the greater number.

Whoever has the greater difference wins the point. Model the problems with play money as needed.

Workbook: Review

Have your child complete workbook page 31.3B.

Lesson 31.4
Three-Digit Subtraction Word Problems

	Purpose	Materials
Warm-up	• Count by 2s • Practice memory work • Review comparing fractions	• Fraction Bars (Blackline Master 9), cut apart and labeled • Fraction Cards (from Lesson 25.2 and 25.3)
Activities	• Solve subtraction word problems • Correctly line up the digits in vertical subtraction problems	• Workbook page 31.4A • Play money, optional
Workbook	• Review previously-learned material	• Workbook page 31.4B

Warm-up: Counting, Memory Work, and Review

- Have your child count by 2s from the following numbers. Prompt him as needed, and stop him after he reaches the last number listed.
    - **Count by 2s from 718:** 718, 720, 722, 724, 726.
    - **Count by 2s from 496:** *496, 498, 500, 502, 504.*
    - **Count by 2s from 992:** *992, 994, 996, 998, 1000.*
- **How many centimeters equal 1 meter?** *100.*
- Play Fraction War. See Lesson 25.4 (page 409) for directions.

Activity: Solve Three-Digit Subtraction Word Problems

This week, you have learned how to subtract three-digit numbers with the subtraction algorithm. Today, you'll use the subtraction algorithm to solve word problems.

Show your child the chart at the top of workbook page 31.4A. Briefly discuss what your child would want to buy if he were designing his own playset. **We'll use the prices in the chart to solve the word problems.**

Read aloud the first word problem: **How much more does a spiral slide cost than a regular slide?** Have your child find the cost of each type of slide, write the prices in the blank grid, and subtract to find the difference. Model the problem with play money if your child has trouble.

		5	17
	4	~~6~~	~~7~~
-	2	5	8
	2	0	9

Repeat with the rest of the word problems on the page. For the second problem, remind your child to align the digits according to their place value. **Make sure you line up the numbers so that the ones-place for 235 is right above the ones-place for 73. That way, you'll be sure to subtract the ones from the ones and the tens from the tens.**

How much more does a tire swing cost than a regular swing?

	1	13	
	~~2~~	~~3~~	5
-		7	3
	1	6	2

You have $300. You buy a climbing net. How much money do you have left?

		9	
	2	~~10~~	10
	~~3~~	~~0~~	~~0~~
-	2	2	6
		7	4

A baby swing costs $116 less than a tire swing. How much does a baby swing cost?

		2	15
	2	~~3~~	~~5~~
-	1	1	6
	1	1	9

Workbook: Review

Have your child complete workbook page 31.4B.

Lesson 31.5
Enrichment and Review (Optional)

	Purpose	Materials
Warm-up	• Count from 700 to 800 by 1s, 2s, 5s, or 10s • Review memory work • Review your child's favorite or most challenging activities from Week 31	• Varies, depending on the activities you choose
Picture Book	• Understand three-digit subtraction in the context of a Christmas tree farm	• *Christmas Farm,* written by Mary Lyn Ray and illustrated by Barry Root
Enrichment Activity	• Estimate quantities up to 1000 • Use subtraction to find the difference between an estimate and actual quantity	• 3 books with 500-1000 pages

Warm-up: Counting, Memory Work, and Review

- Have your child count from 700 to 800 by 1s, 2s, 5s, or 10s. (Choose whichever counting sequence your child needs to practice the most.)
- Quiz your child on the all the memory work for the year. See page 523 for the full list.
- If you have time, repeat one or two of the activities from this week's lessons. Choose activities your child especially enjoyed or found challenging.

Math Picture Book: *Christmas Farm*

Read *Christmas Farm,* written by Mary Lyn Ray and illustrated by Barry Root. After you enjoy the book, show your child how to use three-digit subtraction to find the number of trees lost throughout the book. For example, subtract 719 from 744 to find that 25 trees are lost in the first winter.

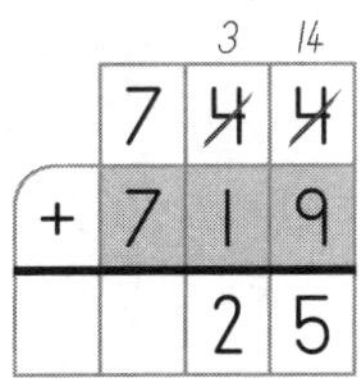

Enrichment Activity: Estimate Page Numbers in Books

Show your child 3 books, each with 500-1000 pages. **All of these books have less than 1000 pages. How many pages do you think are in each book?** *Answers will vary.* Have your child write each estimate on a slip of paper and place it next to the matching book.

Open up one of the books and find its actual number of pages. **We can subtract to find how close your estimate was!** Show your child how to subtract the lesser number from the greater number to find the difference between her estimate and the actual number of pages. For example, if your child guessed 724, and the actual number of pages was 698:

$$\begin{array}{rl} 724 & \leftarrow \text{estimate} \\ -\ 698 & \leftarrow \text{actual number of pages} \\ \hline 26 & \leftarrow \text{difference} \end{array}$$

If the actual number of pages is greater than your child's estimate, reverse the positions of the estimate and actual number of pages.

Repeat with the other two books. Discuss which estimate was closest to the actual number of pages.

Week 31 Answer Key

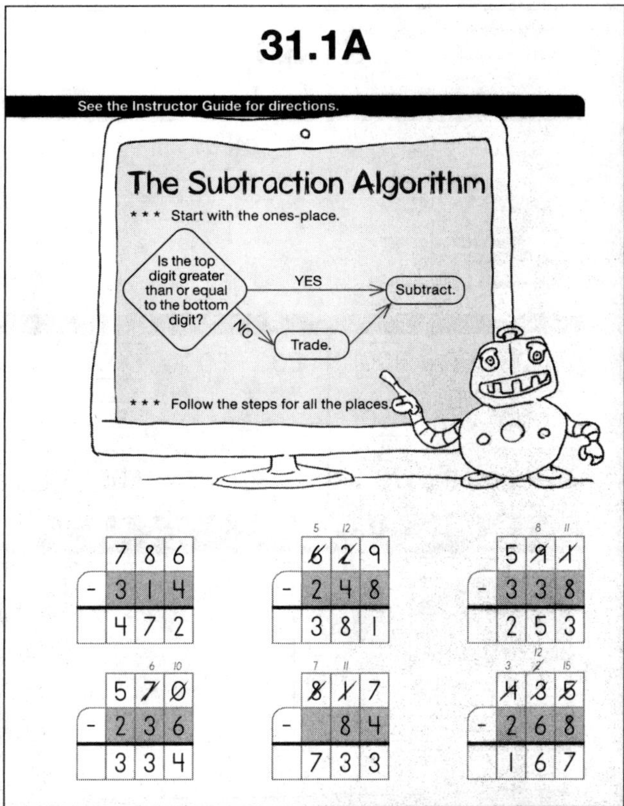

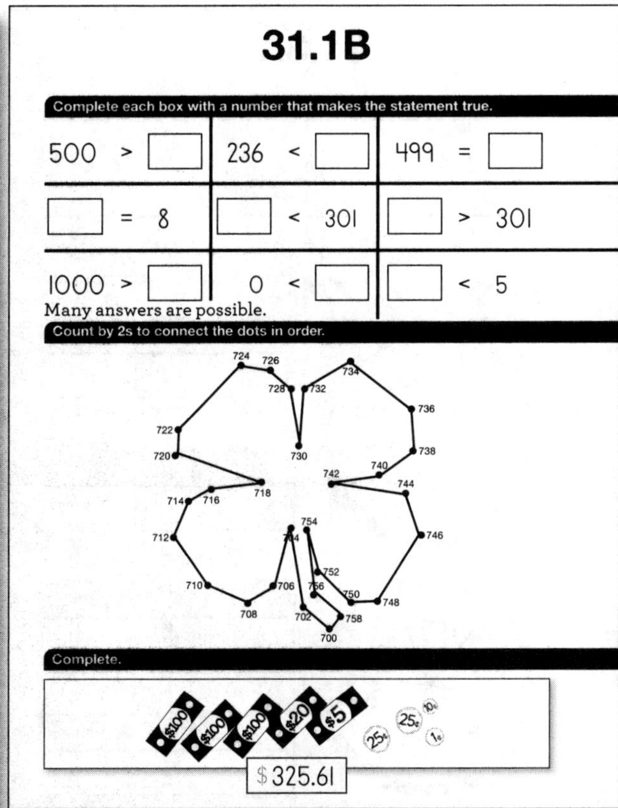

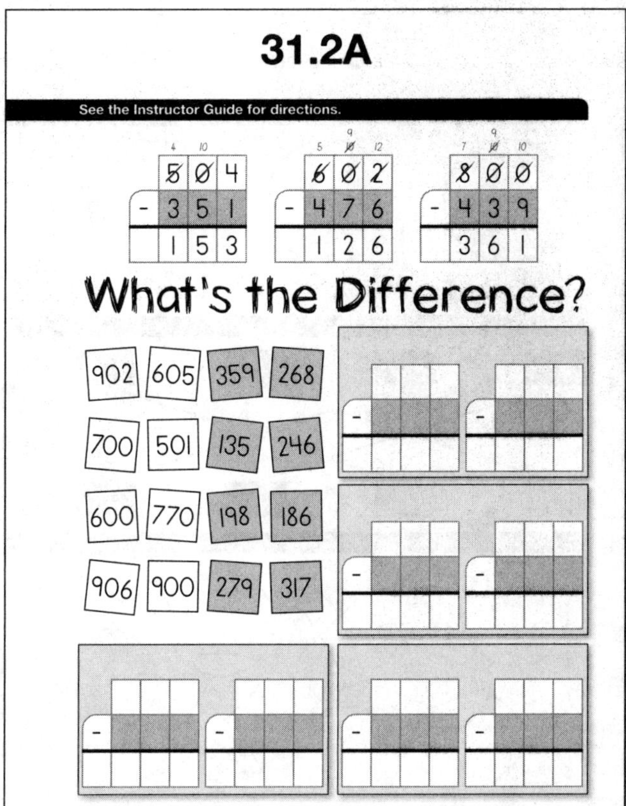

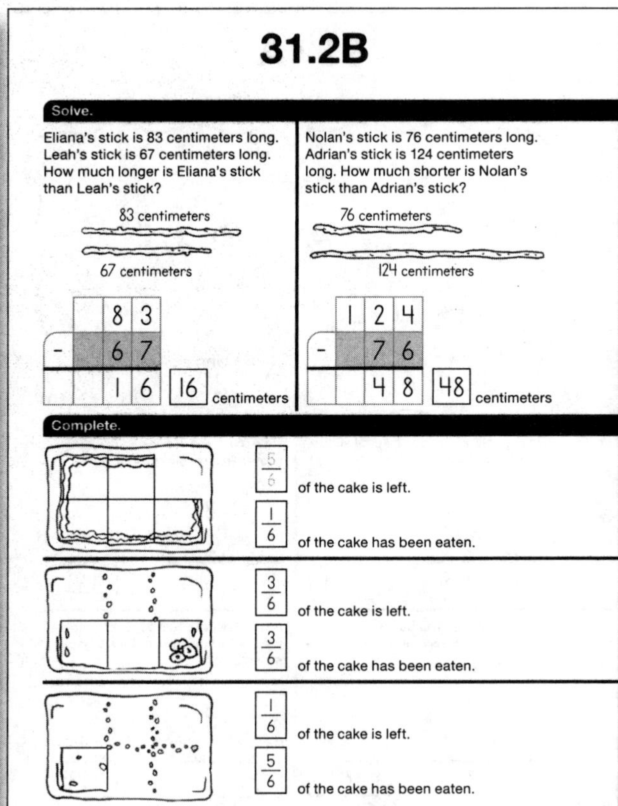

Week 31 Answer Key

31.3A

See the Instructor Guide for directions.

	8	12	
	9̸	2̸	8
-	2	4	5
	6	8	3

	6	12	
	8	7̸	2̸
-	6	0	9
	2	6	3

	6	9 / 1̸0	11
	7̸	0̸	1̸
-	2	6	7
	4	3	4

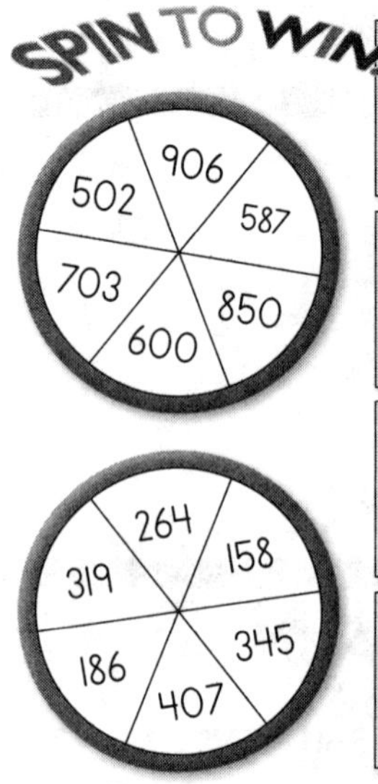

31.3B

Complete.

1 week = 7 days
1 day = 24 hours
1 hour = 60 minutes
1 minute = 60 seconds

1 yard = 3 feet
1 yard = 36 inches
1 foot = 12 inches
1 meter = 100 centimeters

Complete.

400 + 500 = 900	500 + 500 = 1000
400 + 50 = 450	500 + 50 = 550
400 + 5 = 405	500 + 5 = 505

Leila counted how many rainy days there were each month. Use her chart to complete the pictograph.

Month	Minutes
March	10
April	14
May	8

31.4A

Use the chart to answer the questions.

How much more does a spiral slide cost than a regular slide?

	5	17	
	4	6̸	7̸
-	2	5	8
	2	0	9

$ 209

How much more does a tire swing cost than a regular swing?

	1	13	
	2̸	3̸	5
-		7	3
	1	6	2

$ 162

You have $300. You buy a climbing net. How much money do you have left?

	2	9 / 1̸0	10
	3̸	0̸	0̸
-	2	2	6
		7	4

$ 74

A baby swing costs $116 less than a tire swing. How much does a baby swing cost?

		2	15
	2	3̸	5̸
-	1	1	6
	1	1	9

$ 119

31.4B

Write the time.

1:20 7:35 8:55

Match the pairs that equal 1000.

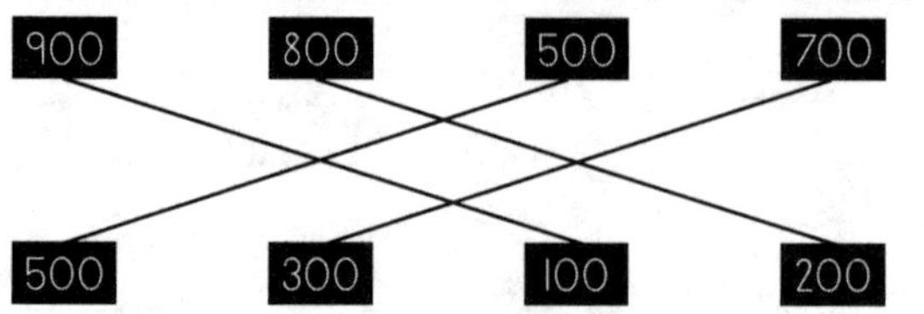

Circle the quadrilaterals. X the shapes that are not quadrilaterals.

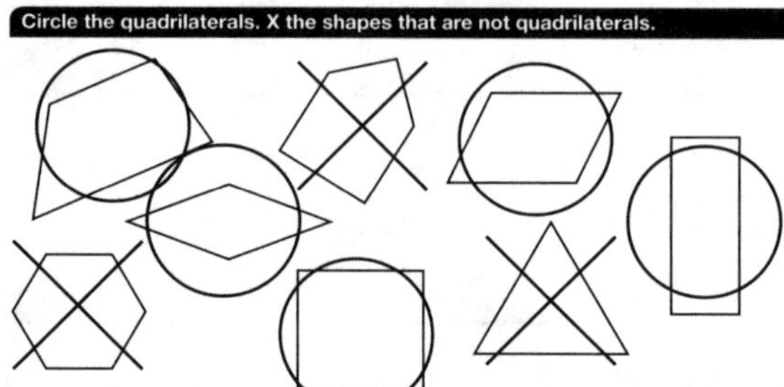

Week 32
Review and Celebrate

Overview

You and your child will look back at how much your child has learned and celebrate the progress he has made. You'll also review some of the key concepts and skills he has learned this year.

Lesson 32.1	Review Numbers to 1000
Lesson 32.2	Review Addition and Subtraction
Lesson 32.3	Review Graphs, Time, Length, Shapes, and Fractions
Lesson 32.4	What I Learned This Year
Lesson 32.5	Enrichment and Review (Optional)

Teaching Math with Confidence: Celebrating Progress

In the daily routine of lessons, it can be easy to forget how much progress your child has made since the start of the year. This week's lessons give both you and your child a chance to look back and celebrate how much he has learned.

Extra Materials Needed for Week 32

- Varies, depending on which activities you choose

Your child can choose his favorite math picture books to reread in Lesson 32.5, so you may want to gather these in advance.

Lesson 32.1
Review Numbers to 1000

	Purpose	Materials
Warm-up	• Count by 2s, 5s, and 10s • Practice memory work • Review adding and subtracting three-digit numbers	• None
Activities	• Celebrate what your child has learned about the numbers to 1000 • Review the numbers to 1000 with your child's favorite activities	• Workbook • Varies, depending on the activities you choose
Workbook	• Review numbers to 1000	• Workbook pages 32.1A and 32.1B

Warm-up: Counting, Memory Work, and Review

- Have your child count by the following numbers. Prompt her as needed, and stop her after she reaches the last number listed.
    - **Count by 2s from 880:** *880, 882, 884, 886, 888.*
    - **Count by 5s from 880:** *880, 885, 890, 895, 900.*
    - **Count by 10s from 880:** *880, 890, 900, 910, 920.*
- **This week, we'll review all the memory work you've learned this year. Today, we'll review the memory work about the numbers to 1000.**
    - Write the < sign. **What does this sign mean?** *Less than.*
      Write the > sign. **What does this sign mean?** *Greater than.*
    - **If a number has 1, 3, 5, 7, or 9 in the ones-place, is the number even or odd?** *Odd.* **If a number has 0, 2, 4, 6, or 8 in the ones-place, is the number even or odd?** *Even.*
    - **How many tens equal 1 hundred?** *10.*
    - **How many hundreds equal 1 thousand?** *10.*
- Write the following problems on a piece of paper, and have your child use the addition or subtraction algorithm to solve them:

$$\begin{array}{r} {\scriptstyle 1\ 1\ \ } \\ 496 \\ +275 \\ \hline 771 \end{array} \qquad \begin{array}{r} {\scriptstyle 7\ 10\ } \\ \not{8}\not{0}7 \\ -434 \\ \hline 373 \end{array}$$

> In this week's warm-ups, your child will practice adding and subtracting three-digit numbers to better cement these skills before the end of the year. Allow your child to use base-ten blocks or play money as needed. If your child has trouble keeping the digits aligned in vertical problems, write the problems on a piece of lined paper, turned sideways.

Activity: Celebrate What Your Child Has Learned About the Numbers to 1000

You have learned so much in math this year! This week, we'll celebrate how much progress you've made. Today, we'll look at how much you've learned about the numbers to 1000.

At the beginning of the year, we started with the numbers to 100. With your child, flip through the Unit 1 workbook pages.

Then, in Unit 3 you used base-ten blocks and the number line to learn about the numbers to 200. You spent a lot of time adding and subtracting numbers to 200 this year. Page through the Unit 3 workbook pages.

Finally, in Unit 13, you learned all about the numbers up to 1000. Look over the Unit 13 workbook pages.

> If you tore out the workbook pages and no longer have them, flip through the matching lessons in the Instructor Guide and have your child look at the workbook page answer keys instead.

Briefly discuss any concepts that were especially difficult for your child, and remind her of how far she has come in her math learning. For example: **Remember how hard it was at first to find numbers on the number line. Now that you've practiced so much, you don't have any trouble!**

Activity: Review Numbers to 1000 with Favorite Activities

Today, we'll review some of your favorite activities with the numbers to 1000. Have your child choose a few of his favorites from the following list and do them together.

- Number Line Bump (Lesson 2.3)
- Race to 100 (Lesson 3.2)
- Find Double or Half with the Number Machine (Lessons 6.1 and 6.2)
- Guess the Secret Number (Lesson 7.2 and warm-up in Lesson 28.3)
- Money War (Lesson 8.2)
- Savings Game (Lesson 8.4)
- Three-Digit War (Lesson 28.1)
- Race to 1000 (Lesson 29.1)
- Race to Zero (Advanced Version) (Lesson 29.2)

Workbook: Review Numbers to 1000

Have your child complete workbook pages 32.1A and 32.1B.

> The Week 32 workbook pages review the most important skills and concepts that your child has learned in *Second Grade Math with Confidence*. They also help you assess your child's learning and growth. If you live in a state that requires you to provide "evidence of progress" or other documentation of your child's learning, you may want to save these pages.

Lesson 32.2
Review Addition and Subtraction

	Purpose	Materials
Warm-up	• Count by 3s to 30 and 4s to 40 • Practice memory work • Review adding and subtracting three-digit numbers	• None
Activities	• Celebrate what your child has learned about addition and subtraction • Review addition and subtraction	• Workbook • Varies, depending on the activities you choose
Workbook	• Review addition and subtraction	• Workbook pages 32.2A and 32.2B

Warm-up: Counting, Memory Work, and Review

- Have your child count by 3s to 30 and by 4s to 40.
- **Today, we'll review the memory work about money, addition, and subtraction.**
    - × **What do we call the result when we add numbers together?** *The sum.* **What do we call the result when we subtract a number from another number?** *The difference.*
    - × **How many cents equal 1 dollar?** *100.*
- Write the following problems on a piece of paper, and have your child use the addition or subtraction algorithm to solve them:

$$\begin{array}{r} {\scriptstyle 1\ \ \ } \\ 520 \\ +191 \\ \hline 711 \end{array} \qquad \begin{array}{r} {\scriptstyle \ \ 9\ \ } \\ {\scriptstyle 5\ \cancel{10}\ 10} \\ \cancel{6}\cancel{0}\cancel{0} \\ -362 \\ \hline 238 \end{array}$$

Activity: Celebrate What Your Child Has Learned About Addition and Subtraction

In the last lesson, we reviewed what you learned this year about the numbers to 1000. Today, we'll celebrate how much you've learned about addition and subtraction.

At the beginning of the year, we started with the addition facts and subtraction facts to 20. With your child, flip through the Unit 2 and Unit 4 workbook pages.

Then, in Units 6 and 8, you learned how to mentally add and subtract numbers up to 100. Page through the Unit 6 and Unit 8 workbook pages.

In Units 10 and 12, you learned how to use the addition and subtraction algorithms to add and subtract numbers up to 200. Look over the Unit 10 and Unit 12 workbook pages.

Finally, in Unit 14, you learned how to add and subtract with numbers up to 1000. Look over the Unit 14 workbook pages. **You'll learn more about adding and subtracting in third grade. You'll also learn about multiplication and division!**

Briefly discuss any concepts that were especially difficult for your child, and remind him of how far he has come in his math learning. For example: **Remember how hard it was for you to remember the steps in the subtraction algorithm at first? Now that you've practiced it so much, it's no problem!**

Activity: Review Addition and Subtraction

Today, we'll review addition and subtraction with some of your favorite games. Have your child choose a few of his favorite games and play them together.

- Addition Climb and Slide (Lesson 1.1)
- Make 20 Splat (Lesson 1.2)
- Subtraction Climb and Slide (Lesson 1.3)
- Addition Crash, +9 Version (Lesson 4.1)
- Addition Crash, +8 Version (Lesson 4.3)
- Addition Bingo (+7 Version) (Lesson 5.1)
- Addition Bingo (+6 Version) (Lesson 5.3)
- Difference War (Lesson 9.1)
- Subtraction Race (-9 Version) (Lesson 9.2)
- Subtraction Race (-8 Version) (Lesson 9.4)
- Treasure Hunt (Lesson 10.2)
- Four in a Row (-2, -3, -4, -5 Facts) (Lesson 11.1)
- Two-Digit Plus One-Digit War (Lesson 14.3)
- Four in a Row (Lesson 18.1)
- Race to Zero (Lesson 18.3)
- Four in a Row (Two-Digit Subtraction) (Lesson 19.1)
- Two-Digit Plus Two-Digit War (Lesson 22.4)

Workbook: Review Addition and Subtraction

Have your child complete workbook pages 32.2A and 32.2B.

Lesson 32.3
Review Graphs, Time, Length, Shapes, and Fractions

	Purpose	Materials
Warm-up	• Count by quarter-hour intervals • Practice memory work • Review adding and subtracting three-digit numbers	• Clock
Activities	• Celebrate what your child has learned about graphs, time, length, shapes, and fractions • Review graphs, time, length, shapes, and fractions	• Workbook • Varies, depending on the activities you choose
Workbook	• Review graphs, time, length, shapes, and fractions	• Workbook pages 32.3A and 32.3B

Warm-up: Counting, Memory Work, and Review

- Set the clock to 11:00. Have your child count by quarter-hour intervals from 11:00 to 1:00: *11:00, 11:15, 11:30, 11:45, 12:00, 12:15, 12:30, 12:45, 1:00.* Have her turn the clock's hands to match each time.
- **Today, we'll review the memory work about time.**
  - **How many months are in a year?** *12.* **How many days are in a week?** *7.*
  - **How many hours are in a day?** *24.* **How many minutes are in an hour?** *60.* **How many seconds are in a minute?** *60.*
  - **Are times in the morning a.m. or p.m.?** *A.m.* **Are times in the afternoon and evening a.m. or p.m.?** *P.m.*
  - **What is another name for 12 a.m.?** *Midnight.* **What is another name for 12 p.m.?** *Noon.*
  - **How many minutes equal a half-hour?** *30.* **How many minutes equal a quarter-hour?** *15.*
- Write the following problems on a piece of paper, and have your child use the addition or subtraction algorithm to solve them:

$$\begin{array}{r} 621 \\ +\,378 \\ \hline 999 \end{array} \qquad \begin{array}{r} {\scriptstyle 3\;10} \\ 7\not{4}\not{0} \\ -\,128 \\ \hline 612 \end{array}$$

Activity: Celebrate What Your Child Has Learned About Graphs, Time, Length, Shapes, and Fractions

In the last lesson, we reviewed what you learned this year about adding and subtracting. Today, we'll celebrate what you've learned about graphs, time, length, shapes, and fractions.

In Unit 5, you learned how to make and interpret bar graphs, pictographs, and line graphs. Flip through the Unit 5 workbook pages.

Then, in Unit 7 you learned how to tell time to the minute. Page through the Unit 7 workbook pages.

In Unit 9, you learned how to measure length in inches and centimeters. You also learned how to use addition and subtraction to solve word problems about length. Look over the Unit 9 workbook pages.

In Unit 11, you learned about shapes and learned how to read and write fractions. Look over the Unit 11 workbook pages.

Briefly discuss any concepts that were especially difficult for your child, and remind her of how far she has come in her math learning. For example: **Remember how hard it was to tell time to the minute at first? You worked really hard at that, and now you can do it!**

Activity: Review Graphs, Time, Length, Shapes, and Fractions

Today, we'll review these topics with some of your favorite activities from the year. Have your child choose a few of her favorite activities from the following list and do them together.

- Make a Dice Sum Bar Graph (Lesson 12.1)
- Flip Coins and Make a Bar Graph (Lesson 12.2)
- Measurement Tag in Inches or Centimeters (Lessons 20.1 or 21.1)
- 1 Yard Scavenger Hunt (Lesson 20.4. Or, do a scavenger hunt with inches, feet, centimeters, or meters.)
- Measure in Centimeters to Make a Rainbow Craft (Lessons 21.1 and 21.2)
- Polygon Four in a Row (Lesson 24.3)
- Fraction Bump (Lesson 25.2)
- Fraction War (Lesson 25.4)

Workbook: Review Graphs, Time, Length, Shapes, and Fractions

Have your child complete workbook pages 32.3A and 32.3B.

Lesson 32.4
What I Learned This Year

	Purpose	Materials
Warm-up	• Count money • Practice memory work • Review adding and subtracting three-digit numbers	• Play money
Activities	• Reflect on the year and look ahead to third grade • Revisit favorite activities	• Workbook page 32.4A • Varies, depending on which activities your child chooses
Workbook	• Celebrate completing the workbook	• Workbook page 32.4B

Warm-up: Counting, Memory Work, and Review

- Place 9 hundred-dollar bills, 6 ten-dollar bills, 7 five-dollar bills, and 5 one-dollar bills on the table. **How much is this money worth?** *$1000.*
- **Today, we'll review the memory work about measurement and polygons.**
  - **How many inches equal 1 foot?** *12.* **How many feet equal 1 yard?** *3.* **How many inches equal 1 yard?** *36.*
  - **How many centimeters equal 1 meter?** *100.*
  - **How many sides does a triangle have? 3. A quadrilateral?** *4.* **A pentagon?** *5.* **A hexagon?** *6.* **An octagon?** *8.*
- Write the following problems on a piece of paper, and have your child use the addition or subtraction algorithm to solve them:

$$\begin{array}{r} {\scriptstyle 1\ 1\ \ } \\ 495 \\ +405 \\ \hline 900 \end{array} \qquad \begin{array}{r} {\scriptstyle 10\ \ } \\ {\scriptstyle 5\ \not{0}\ 11} \\ \not{6}\not{1}\not{1} \\ -537 \\ \hline 74 \end{array}$$

Activity: Reflect on the Year

This week, we've looked back on all you've learned this year. Today, we'll reflect on the year and do a few more of your favorite activities.

Read the sentence starters on workbook page 32.4A to your child. Have your child complete the sentences, or scribe his answers for him.

Then, have your child draw a picture of his favorite math activity from the year at the bottom of the page.

Activity: Choice Review Activity

Have your child choose a few of his favorite activities from the year to revisit. Look at the lists in Lessons 32.1, 32.2, and 32.3 for suggestions.

Workbook: Complete Certificate

Complete the certificate on workbook page 32.4B and present it to your child.

Lesson 32.5
Enrichment and Review (Optional)

	Purpose	Materials
Warm-up	• Count from 900 to 1000 by 1s, 2s, 5s, and 10s • Review memory work	• None
Picture Book	• Reread your child's favorite math picture books	• Varies, depending on which books you choose
Enrichment Activity	• Revisit your child's favorite enrichment activity	• Varies, depending on the activities you choose

Warm-up: Counting, Memory Work, and Review

- Have your child count from 900 to 1000 by 1s, 2s, 5s, and 10s.
- Quiz your child on the all the memory work for the year. See page 523 for the full list.

Math Picture Book: Child's Choice

Reread some of your child's favorite math books from the year.

Enrichment Activity: Child's Choice

Repeat one of your child's favorite enrichment activities from the year.

Week 32 Answer Key

32.1A

Write the expanded form for each number.

352 = 300 + 50 + 2	671 = 600 + 70 + 1
499 = 400 + 90 + 9	908 = 900 + 8

Complete the circles with <, >, or =.

146 > 140	964 > 469	399 < 400
200 < 201	328 < 519	602 < 609
607 < 670	564 = 564	987 > 978

Complete the sequences.

32.1B

Complete.

$ 52.46

$ 460

175 ¢

Color the even numbers yellow. Color the odd numbers red.

32.2A

Complete.

	3	7	2
+	4	5	6
	8	2	8

	6	0	8
+	2	4	8
	8	5	6

	4	9	3
+	3	6	7
	8	6	0

	6	8	4
-	2	3	5
	4	4	9

	7	5	3
-	4	8	8
	2	6	5

	8	0	9
-	2	5	4
	5	5	5

Match.

352+2	354	384-60
200+300	364	600-100
300+100	324	564-200
304+20	400	358-4
264+100	500	800-400

(Matches drawn: 352+2 → 354; 200+300 → 500; 300+100 → 400; 304+20 → 324; 264+100 → 364; 354 → 358-4; 364 → 564-200; 324 → 384-60; 400 → 800-400; 500 → 600-100)

32.2B

Aaron made a sketch about his family's summer road trip. Use his sketch to answer the questions.

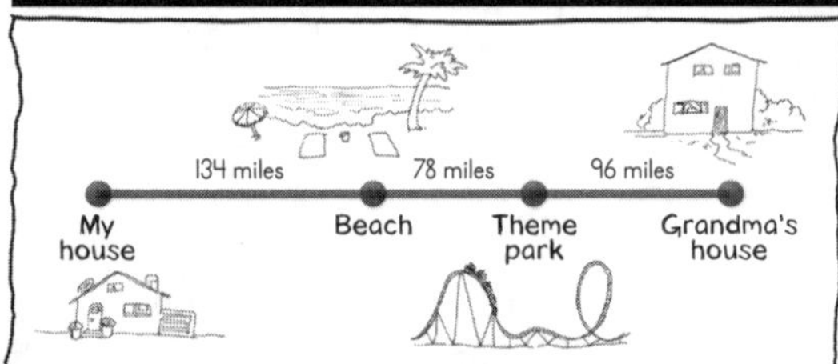

How far is it from Aaron's house to the theme park?

	1	3	4
+		7	8
	2	1	2

212 miles

How much longer is the distance from Aaron's house to the beach than the distance from the beach to the theme park?

	1	3	4
-		7	8
		5	6

56 miles

How much shorter is the distance from the beach to the theme park than the distance from the theme park to Grandma's house?

		9	6
-		7	8
		1	8

18 miles

How far is it from Aaron's house to Grandma's house?

	1	3	4
		7	8
+		9	6
	3	0	8

308 miles

Week 32 Answer Key

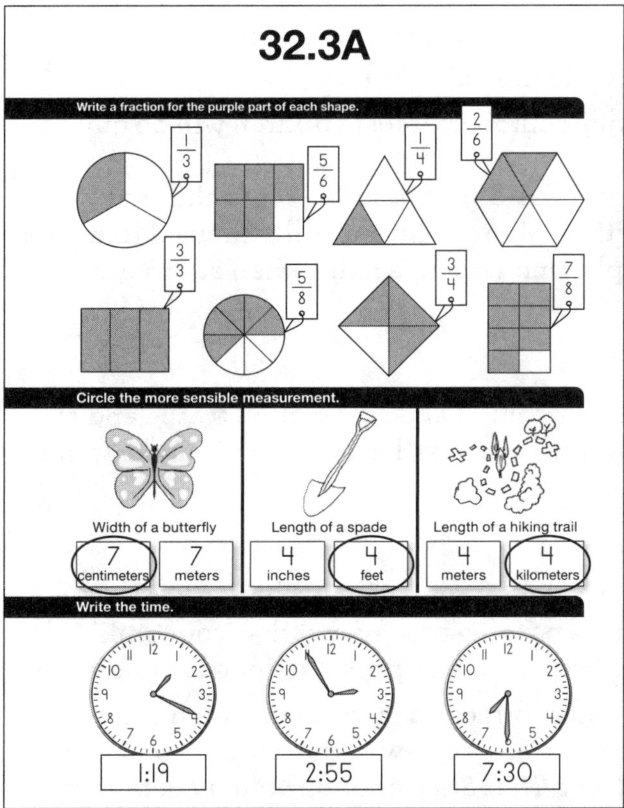

32.3A

Write a fraction for the purple part of each shape.

1/3 · 5/6 · 1/4 · 2/6

3/3 · 5/8 · 3/4 · 7/8

Circle the more sensible measurement.

Width of a butterfly		Length of a spade		Length of a hiking trail	
7 centimeters (circled)	7 meters	4 inches	4 feet (circled)	4 meters	4 kilometers (circled)

Write the time.

1:19 · 2:55 · 7:30

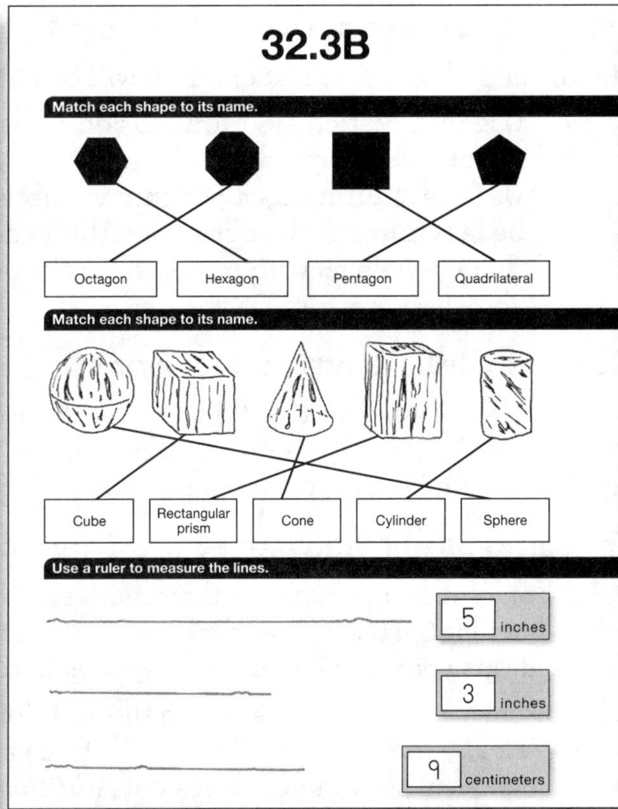

32.3B

Match each shape to its name.

Octagon · Hexagon · Pentagon · Quadrilateral

Match each shape to its name.

Cube · Rectangular prism · Cone · Cylinder · Sphere

Use a ruler to measure the lines.

5 inches

3 inches

9 centimeters

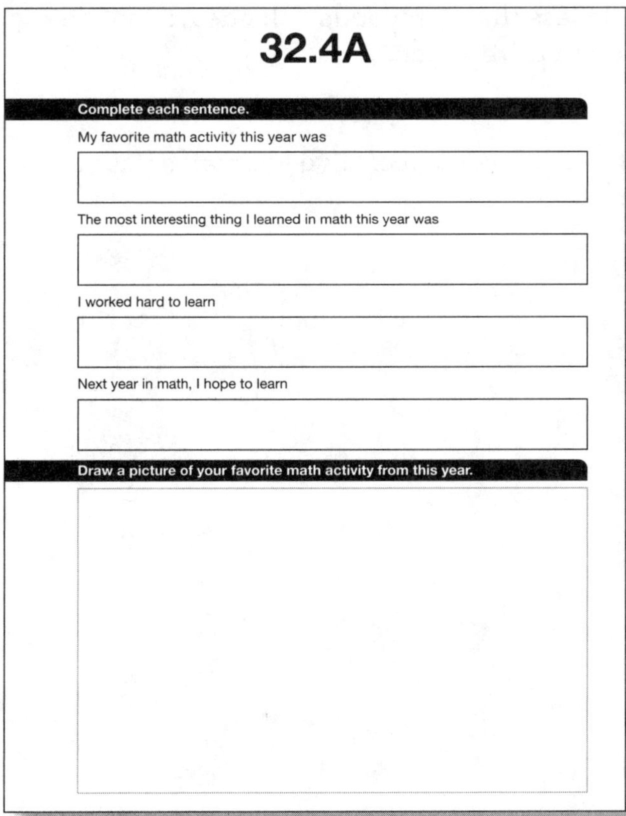

32.4A

Complete each sentence.

My favorite math activity this year was

The most interesting thing I learned in math this year was

I worked hard to learn

Next year in math, I hope to learn

Draw a picture of your favorite math activity from this year.

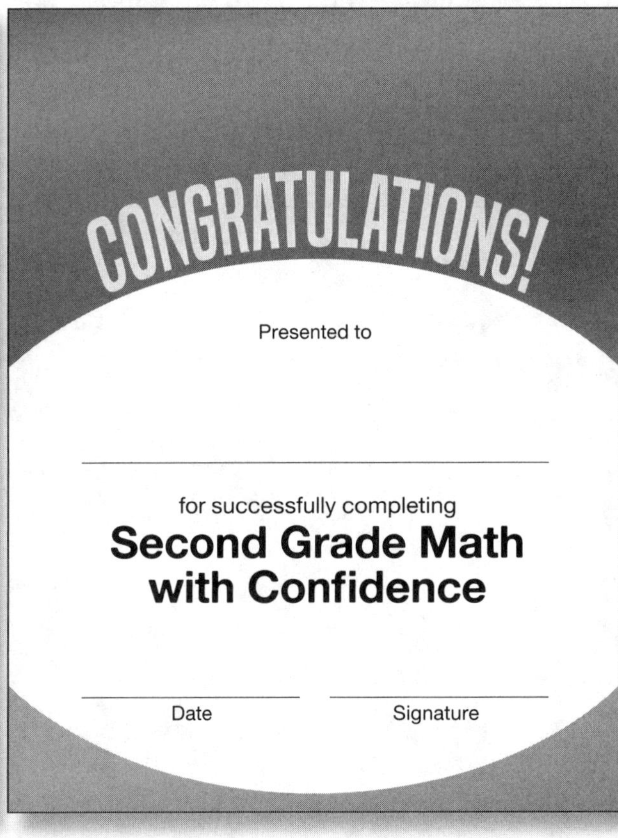

CONGRATULATIONS!

Presented to

for successfully completing

Second Grade Math with Confidence

Date

Signature

Unit 14 Checkpoint

What to Expect at the End of Unit 14

By the end of Unit 14, most children will be able to do the following:

- Use the addition algorithm to add three-digit numbers. Most children will be quite fluent at solving these problems.
- Use the subtraction algorithm to subtract three-digit numbers. Most children will be less fluent with subtraction than addition. Many children will still need to model these problems with base-ten blocks or play money, especially when subtracting across a zero.

Is Your Child Ready to Move on?

Your child does not need to fully master three-digit addition and subtraction by the end of second grade. He will review these techniques in third grade as he deepens his understanding of the numbers to 1000.

Keeping Skills Sharp over the Summer

Children often forget some of their math skills over the summer. If you'd like to keep your child's skills sharp, play math games a couple times per week to review what your child learned this year. You'll find all the games in this book listed on page 530 for easy reference.

If your child is not fully fluent with the addition and subtraction facts, make math fact practice a priority this summer. If you'd like to do a methodical review of the addition or subtraction facts over the summer, check out *Addition Facts That Stick* or *Subtraction Facts That Stick*. You'll find many games (some familiar and some new), as well as workbook pages to help your child further increase his speed and fluency with the math facts. Knowing the answers to all the addition and subtraction facts in less than 3 seconds will ensure that he's well-prepared to tackle multiplication and division in third grade.

Congratulations!

Congratulations on finishing *Second Grade Math with Confidence!* Give yourself a pat on the back for all that you've taught your child this year.

Complete Memory Work List

Week	Memory Work
2	• **What do we call the result when we add numbers together?** *The sum.* • **What do we call the result when we subtract a number from another number?** *The difference.*
4	• Write the < sign. **What does this sign mean?** *Less than.* • Write the > sign. **What does this sign mean?** *Greater than.*
6	• **How many tens equal 1 hundred?** *10.*
8	• **If a number has 1, 3, 5, 7, or 9 in the ones-place, is the number even or odd?** *Odd.* • **If a number has 0, 2, 4, 6, or 8 in the ones-place, is the number even or odd?** *Even.*
10	• **How many cents equal 1 dollar?** *100.*
12	• **How many months are in a year?** *12.* • **How many days are in a week?** *7.*
14	• **How many hours are in a day?** *24.* • **How many minutes are in an hour?** *60.* • **How many seconds are in a minute?** *60.*
16	• **Are times in the morning a.m. or p.m.?** *A.m.* • **Are times in the afternoon and evening a.m. or p.m.?** *P.m.*
18	• **What is another name for 12 a.m.?** *Midnight.* • **What is another name for 12 p.m.?** *Noon.*
20	• **How many minutes equal a half-hour?** *30.* • **How many minutes equal a quarter-hour?** *15.*
22	• **How many inches equal 1 foot?** *12.* • **How many feet equal 1 yard?** *3.* • **How many inches equal 1 yard?** *36.*
24	• **How many centimeters equal 1 meter?** *100.*
26	• **How many sides does a triangle have?** *3.* • **A quadrilateral?** *4.* • **A pentagon?** *5.* • **A hexagon?** *6.* • **An octagon?** *8.*
28	• **How many hundreds equal 1 thousand?** *10.*

No new memory work is introduced after Week 28 so that your child has enough time to memorize all these items before the end of the year.

Scope and Sequence

Unit	Objectives
Unit 1 Review	• Solve addition and subtraction facts with numbers to 10 • Write addition and subtraction fact families • Use the <, >, and = signs to compare numbers • Identify numbers on the number line • Represent numbers to 100 with base-ten blocks and understand their digits' place value • Identify pairs that make 100 (like 99 and 1, or 60 and 40) • Use place value to solve simple mental addition and subtraction problems (like 45 + 3 or 87 – 20)
Unit 2 Addition Facts and Word Problems	• Solve addition facts up to 10 + 10 • Write and solve equations to match simple addition and subtraction word problems • Solve word problems that involve finding how many more of an item is needed • Solve word problems with 3 or more addends
Unit 3 Numbers to 200	• Use base-ten blocks to double or find half of numbers • Identify even and odd numbers • Use repeated addition to find the number of objects in an array • Read, write, and compare numbers to 200 • Understand place value in numbers to 200 • Write numbers to 200 in expanded form • Solve simple mental addition and subtraction problems with the numbers to 200 • Write money amounts with a dollar sign and decimal point, or with a cents sign • Count combinations of bills and coins (including twenty-dollar bills and quarters)
Unit 4 Subtraction Facts and Word Problems	• Solve subtraction facts with numbers to 20 • Solve take-away and take-apart word problems • Use subtraction to compare quantities and ages • Solve word problems involving *more* or *fewer*
Unit 5 Graphs	• Create bar graphs, pictographs, and line graphs • Interpret bar graphs, pictographs, and line graphs with increments of 1 or 10 • Use addition and subtraction to draw conclusions from graphs
Unit 6 Mental Addition to 100	• Mentally add one- or two-digit numbers to two-digit numbers (with sums less than 100)

Unit	Objectives
Unit 7 Time	• Identify times of day as a.m. and p.m. • Be familiar with half hours and quarter hours • Identify the hour and tell time to the minute on clocks with hands
Unit 8 Mental Subtraction to 100	• Mentally subtract one- or two-digit numbers from two-digit numbers
Unit 9 Length	• Approximate the length of an inch, foot, yard, centimeter, and meter • Estimate and measure length in inches, feet, yards, centimeters, and meters • Measure an object's length when the object is not aligned with the ruler's endpoint • Choose appropriate units for measuring in real-life situations
Unit 10 Written Addition to 200	• Understand the steps in the written addition process and model them with base-ten blocks • Fluently add two-digit numbers, with a sum up to 200
Unit 11 Geometry and Fractions	• Name, describe, and draw polygons with different numbers of sides (triangles, quadrilaterals, pentagons, hexagons, and octagons) • Name three-dimensional solids (spheres, cones, cubes, cylinders, and rectangular prisms) • Reason about polygons and use spatial skills to complete puzzles • Split shapes into halves, thirds, fourths, sixths, and eighths, and read and write fractions to describe fractional parts • Use hands-on materials to compare fractions
Unit 12 Written Subtraction to 200	• Understand the steps in the written subtraction algorithm and model them with base-ten blocks • Fluently subtract two-digit numbers from numbers up to 200
Unit 13 Numbers to 1000	• Read, write, and compare numbers to 1000 • Write numbers to 1000 in expanded form • Identify even and odd numbers to 1000 • Count by 1s, 2s, 5s, or 10s to 1000 • Solve simple mental addition and subtraction problems with numbers to 1000 • Identify pairs that make 1000 • Count money amounts up to $1000
Unit 14 Addition and Subtraction to 1000	• Use the addition algorithm to add three-digit numbers • Use the subtraction algorithm to subtract three-digit numbers, including subtracting across a zero

Complete Picture Book List

Reading math picture books together is a fun, cozy, and delightful way to simply enjoy math. Most of these books relate to what your child will learn each week, but some expose your child to other interesting or fun math topics. These picture books are not required. You do not need to buy every book or track down every book in your library system. It's also perfectly fine to use a book on a similar topic as a substitute.

Week	Book
1	*Math-terpieces: The Art of Problem-Solving,* by Greg Tang. Scholastic Press, 2003.
2	*Your Fantastic Elastic Brain: Stretch It, Shape It,* by JoAnn Deak. Little Pickle Press, 2010.
3	*Biggest, Strongest, Fastest,* by Steve Jenkins. HMH Books for Young Readers, 1995.
4	*If You Were a Plus Sign,* written by Trisha Speed Shaskan and illustrated by Francesca Carabelli. Picture Window Books, 2008.
5	*Each Orange Had 8 Slices,* written by Paul Giganti Jr. and illustrated by Donald Crews. Greenwillow Books, 1992.
6	*One Grain of Rice: A Mathematical Folktale,* by Demi. Scholastic Press, 1997.
7	*How Many Seeds in a Pumpkin?,* written by Margaret McNamara and illustrated by G. Brian Karas. Schwartz & Wade, 2007.
8	*Lemonade in Winter,* written by Emily Jenkins and illustrated by G. Brian Karas. Schwartz & Wade, 2012.
9	*If You Were a Minus Sign,* written by Trisha Speed Shaskan and illustrated by Francesca Carabelli. Picture Window Books, 2008.
10	*What's the Difference? An Endangered Animal Subtraction Story,* written by Suzanne Slade and illustrated by Joan Waites. Sylvan Dell Publishing, 2010.
11	*Subtraction Action,* by Loreen Leedy. Holiday House, 2000.
12	*Lemonade for Sale,* written by Stuart J. Murphy and illustrated by Tricia Tusa. HarperCollins, 1998.
13	*The Great Graph Contest,* by Loreen Leedy. Holiday House, 2005.
14	*Night Noises,* written by Mem Fox and illustrated by Terry Denton. HMH Books for Young Readers, 1992.
15	*A Fair Bear Share,* written by Stuart J. Murphy and illustrated by John Speirs. HarperCollins, 1998.
16	*It's About Time, Max!,* written by Kitty Richards and illustrated by Gioia Fiammenghi. Kane Press, 2006.

Week	Book
17	*Pigs on a Blanket,* written by Amy Axelrod and illustrated by Sharon McGinley-Nally. Aladdin, 1998.
18	*Is a Blue Whale the Biggest Thing There Is?,* by Robert E. Wells. Albert Whitman and Company, 1993.
19	*Nothing Stopped Sophie: The Story of Unshakable Mathematician Sophie Germain,* written by Cheryl Bardoe and illustrated by Barbara McClintock. Little, Brown, and Company, 2018.
20	*Actual Size,* by Steve Jenkins. HMH Books for Young Readers, 2004.
21	*Polly's Pen Pal,* written by Stuart J. Murphy and illustrated by Rémy Simard. HarperCollins, 2005.
22	*Blockhead: The Life of Fibonacci,* written by Joseph D'Agnese and illustrated by John O'Brien. Henry Holt and Company, 2010.
23	*Dozens of Doughnuts,* written by Carrie Finison and illustrated by Brianne Farley. G.P. Putnam, 2020.
24	*Perfect Square,* by Michael Hall. Greenwillow Books, 2011.
25	*If You Were a Fraction,* written by Trisha Speed Shaskan and illustrated by Francesca Carabelli. Picture Window Books, 2008.
26	*Shark Swimathon,* written by Stuart J. Murphy and illustrated by Lynne Cravath. HarperCollins, 2001.
27	*Infinity and Me,* written by Kate Hosford and illustrated by Gabi Swiatkowska. Carolrhoda Books, 2012.
28	*How Much is a Million?,* written by David M. Schwartz and illustrated by Steven Kellogg. Mulberry Books, 1985.
29	*Sir Cumference and All the King's Tens: A Math Adventure,* written by Cindy Neuschwander and illustrated by Wayne Geehan. Charlesbridge, 2009.
30	*Mapping Penny's World,* written by Loreen Leedy. Henry Holt, 2000.
31	*Christmas Farm,* written by Mary Lyn Ray and illustrated by Barry Root. Harcourt, 2008.
32	Reread favorite picture books from the year.

Materials List

What You'll Need in Your Math Kit

You'll use the following materials regularly in *Second Grade Math with Confidence*. Stash them in a box or basket and always keep them ready for your next lesson. (See pages 7-8 in the Introduction for more detailed descriptions of each item.)

- Base-ten blocks (at least 100 units, 20 rods, 10 flats, and 1 large cube)
- 50 small counters
- Coins (20 pennies, 20 nickels, 10 dimes, 8 quarters)
- Play money (10 each of one-dollar bills, five-dollar bills, ten-dollar bills, twenty-dollar bills, and hundred-dollar bills)
- Clock with hands
- 1-foot (or 30-centimeter) ruler, labeled with both inches and centimeters
- Two packs of playing cards and two regular, six-sided dice
- Blank paper
- Pencils
- 3 page protectors
- Dry-erase marker
- Binder with page protectors, optional

Other Supplies

Besides your Math Kit, you'll also need the following household items. You'll only need most of them once or twice, so you don't need to gather them ahead of time or store them separately. Check the weekly previews for the specific household items you'll need for each week's lessons.

Items marked with an asterisk are needed for the optional enrichment lessons (the fifth lesson each week).

- *20 items from your child's favorite collection, such as stuffed animals, marbles, toy cars, ponies, or plastic figurines
- Two toothpicks, narrow strips of paper, or crayons
- Scissors
- Tape
- *Chalk, masking tape, or a long strip of paper
- Napkin
- *Chutes and Ladders, Rack-O, or 100 Chart (Blackline Master 4), die, and counters
- 5-6 small toys
- Mirror (hand mirror preferred, but wall-mounted is fine)
- *20 small snack items, such as raisins, pieces of cereal, or blueberries
- 6 forks
- Construction paper or cardstock
- Crayons or colored pencils
- 25 square or rectangular blocks, any size or material

- Rubber band
- *100-200 small food items (such as popcorn kernels, grains of rice, or sunflower seeds)
- *Bills and coins to spend
- *Art supplies, such as construction paper, paint, markers, crayons, or colored pencils
- Cup
- *Graph of your town's average monthly rainfall, either printed or online
- Paper clip
- *Large piece of posterboard (or 9 sheets of paper and tape)
- *Two beanbags, crumpled wads of paper, or soft, unbreakable toys
- Timer
- *Online or streaming video with child-appropriate content, any length
- *Calculator (or calculator app)
- *Map of your local area (or map app)
- 6 narrow paper strips, about 11 inches long and ½-inch wide (or 28 cm long and 1 centimeter wide)
- Stapler
- *1-cup measuring cup or 1-liter measuring cup
- *Ingredients for your choice of recipe involving cups or liters. (See Lesson 21.5 (page 345) for sample recipes.)
- *Egg carton
- 8 toothpicks, popsicle sticks, straws, or other long, narrow objects
- Household items in the shape of a sphere, cone, cylinder, cube, and rectangular prism. Suggested items:
    - Sphere: basketball, baseball, globe
    - Cone: party hat, sports cone, ice cream cone
    - Cylinder: can, oatmeal canister, toy drum
    - Cube: Rubik's cube, dice, sugar cube
    - Rectangular prism: cereal box, shipping box, stick of butter
- Empty cardboard box
- *Several sheets of construction paper, origami paper, or copy paper
- *Glue, optional
- *Large sheets of paper, optional
- *Children's book with more than 100 pages and fewer than 200 pages
- *Toy catalog or access to a website with items your child would like to buy
- Book with over 1000 pages
- *Felt-tip marker or bingo dotter, optional
- *Posterboard or construction paper, optional
- 4 children's chapter books, each with 100-250 pages
- *3 books with 500-1000 pages

Game List and Extra Game Boards

All of these games are scheduled in the lessons, but you can also use them for review, extra practice, or days you don't have time for a full lesson. (This list does not include games in which you write your answers on a workbook page, since these games cannot be reused.)

Games marked with an asterisk require a printed game board. You'll find full-color versions of these game boards on the corresponding workbook pages in the Student Workbook.

Black-and-white versions of all of the game boards are available at welltrainedmind.com/mwc if you need one.

Game	Math Skill Focus	Directions
*Addition Climb and Slide	Addition facts to 10	1.1
Make 20 Splat	Add small numbers to 20	1.2
*Subtraction Climb and Slide	Subtraction facts to 10	1.3
Number Line Bump	Identify numbers on number line	2.3
Race to 100	Place-value to 100	3.2
*Addition Crash (+9 Version)	+9 addition facts	4.1
*Addition Crash (+8 Version)	+8 addition facts	4.3
*Addition Bingo (+7 Version)	+7 addition facts	5.1
*Addition Bingo (+6 Version)	+6 addition facts	5.3
Guess the Secret Number (101-200)	Compare numbers to 200	7.2
Money War	Count money	8.2
*Savings Game	Count money	8.4
Difference War	Subtraction facts to 10	9.1
*Subtraction Race (-9 Version)	-9 subtraction facts	9.2
*Subtraction Race (-8 Version)	-8 subtraction facts	9.4

Game	Math Skill Focus	Directions
*Treasure Hunt	-6 and -7 subtraction facts	10.2
*Four in a Row (-2, -3,-4, and -5 Facts)	-2, -3, -4, and -5 subtraction facts	11.1
Two-Digit Plus One-Digit War	Mental addition	14.3
*Four in a Row (Subtract from Multiples of 10)	Mental subtraction	18.1
Race to Zero	Mental subtraction	18.3
*Four in a Row (Two-Digit Subtraction)	Mental subtraction	19.1
Measurement Tag	Measure length	20.1
Two-Digit Plus Two-Digit War	Written addition	22.4
*Polygon Four in a Row	Identify polygons	24.3
*Fraction Bump	Read fractions	25.2
Fraction War	Compare fractions	25.4
Three-Digit War	Compare three-digit numbers	28.1
Race to 1000	Mental addition with three-digit numbers	29.1
Race to Zero (Advanced Version)	Mental subtraction with three-digit numbers	29.2

Double Ten-frames (Blackline Master 1)

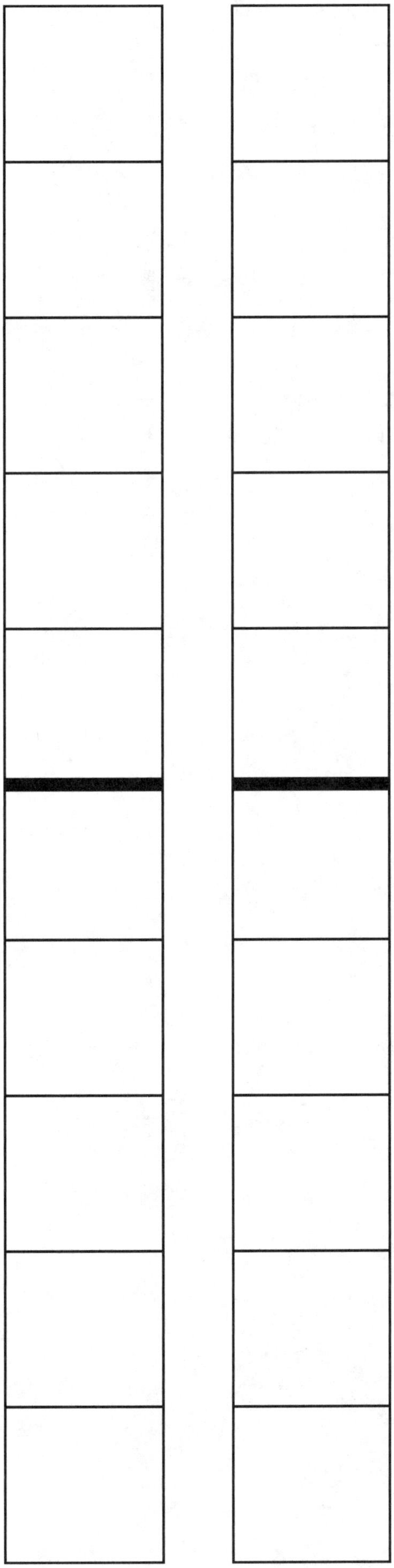

Part-Total Mat (Blackline Master 2)

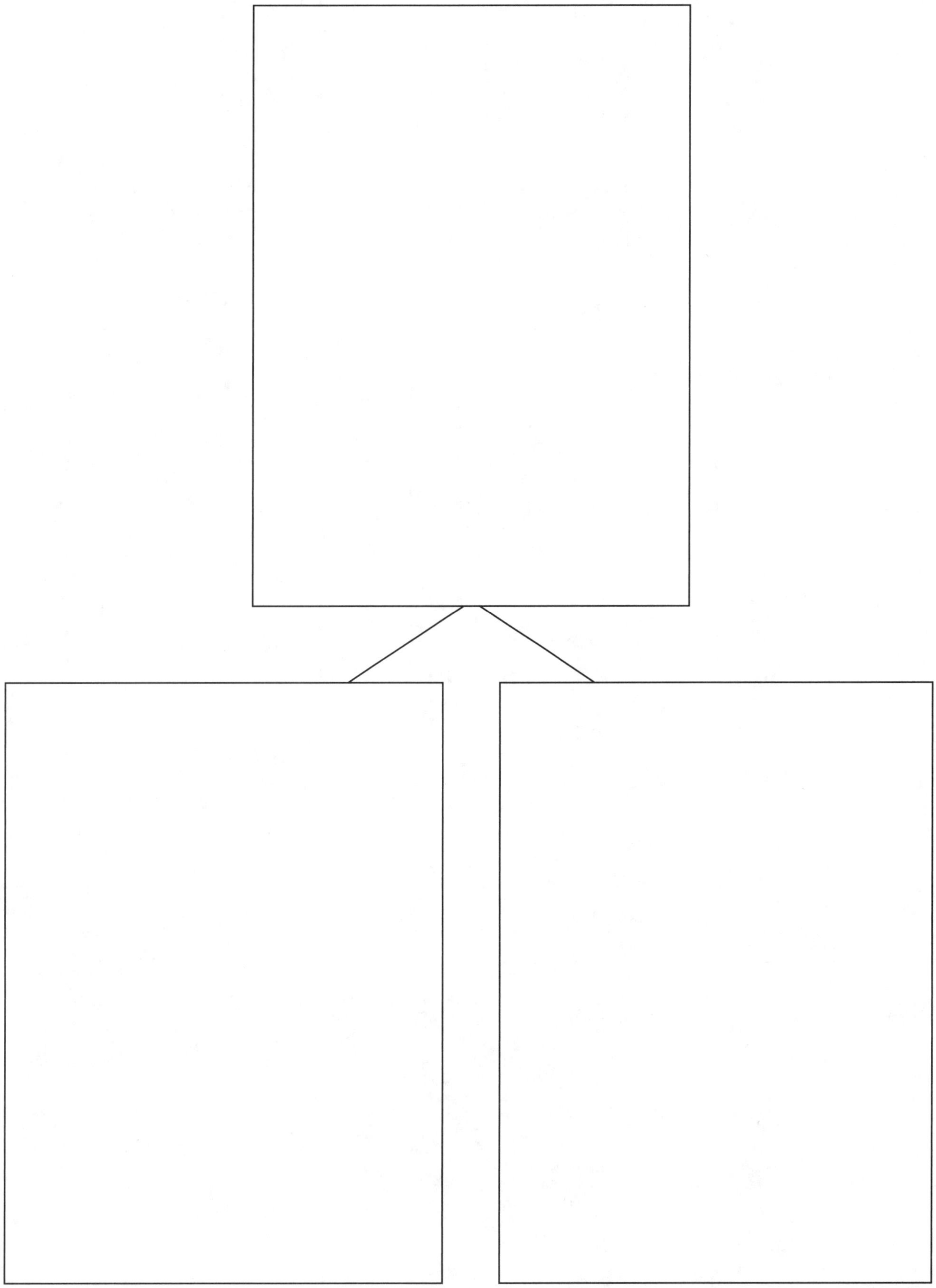

Blank Number Line (Blackline Master 3)

Directions: Cut on the dotted line. Then, tape Edge A to Edge B. Try to line up the two edges without overlapping the paper, and place a piece of transparent tape on both the front and back of the joined edges. This will make it easier to fold the number line for storage. You may want to laminate the number line or cover it with packing tape so that you can label it with a dry erase marker.

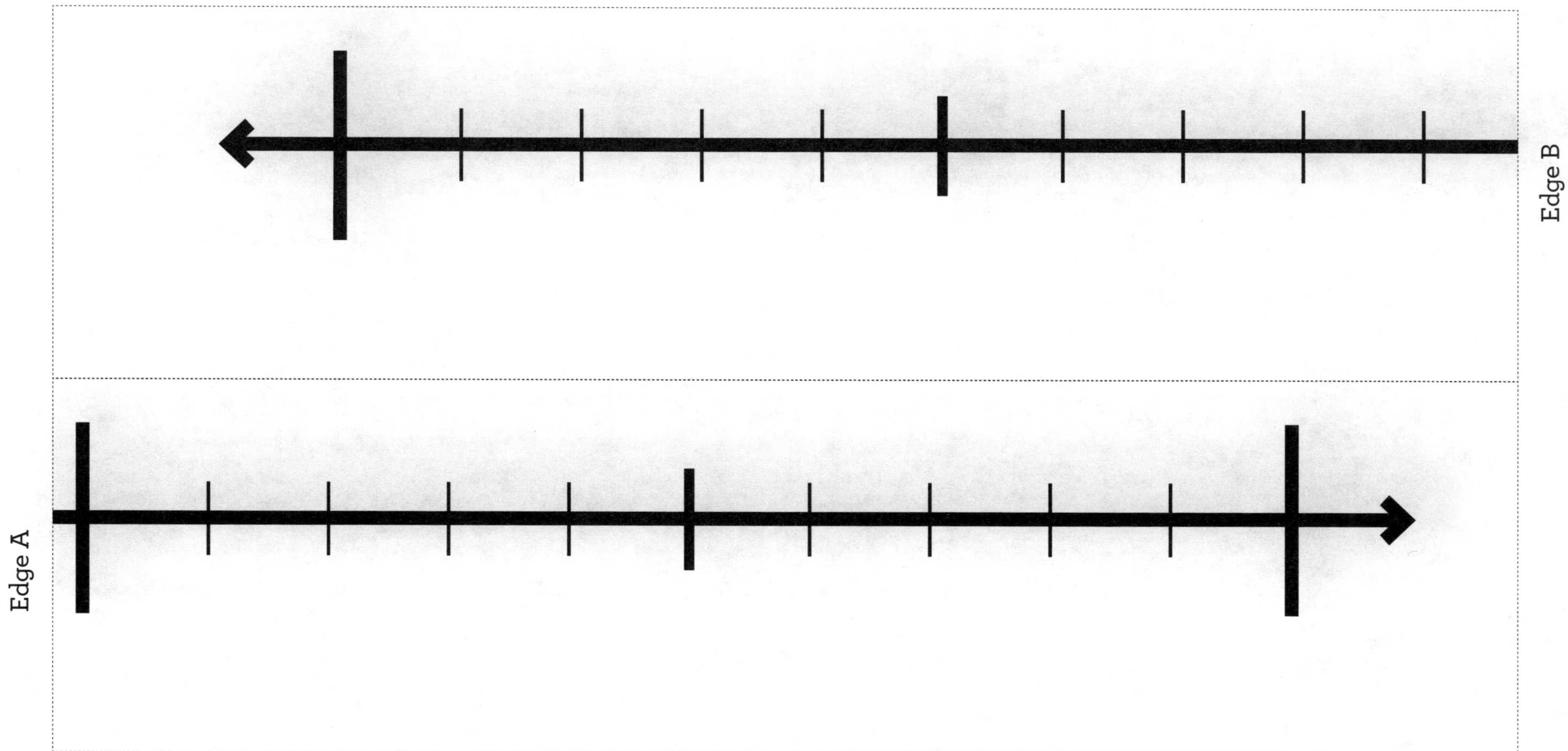

100 Chart (Blackline Master 4)

1	2	3	4	5	6	7	8	9	10
11	12	13	14	15	16	17	18	19	20
21	22	23	24	25	26	27	28	29	30
31	32	33	34	35	36	37	38	39	40
41	42	43	44	45	46	47	48	49	50
51	52	53	54	55	56	57	58	59	60
61	62	63	64	65	66	67	68	69	70
71	72	73	74	75	76	77	78	79	80
81	82	83	84	85	86	87	88	89	90
91	92	93	94	95	96	97	98	99	100

Place-Value Chart (Blackline Master 5)

tens	ones

thousands	hundreds

Dot Array and L-Cover (Blackline Master 6)

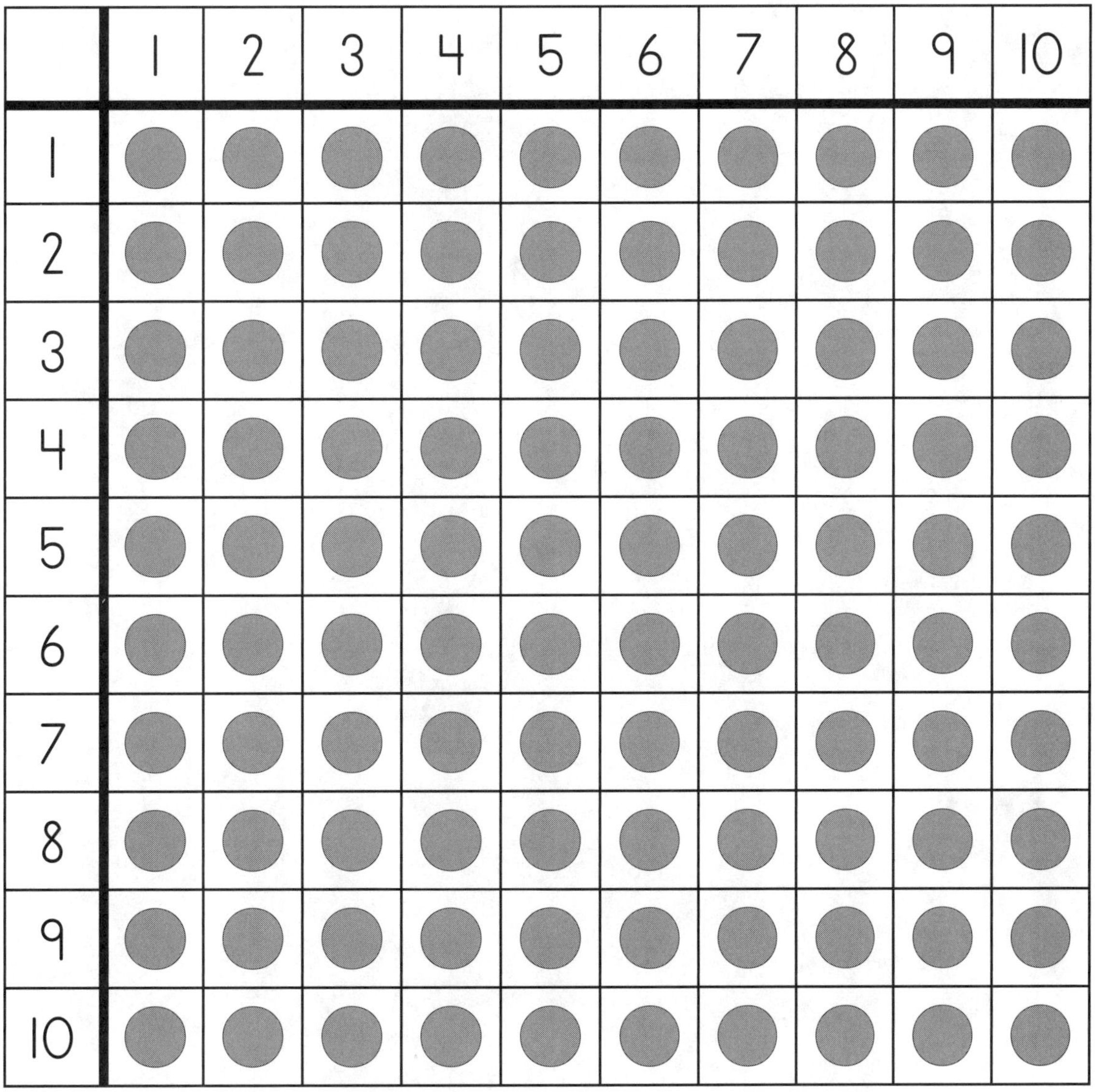

Directions: Cut on the dotted line. You will be left with a gray L.

200 Chart (Blackline Master 7)

101	102	103	104	105	106	107	108	109	110
111	112	113	114	115	116	117	118	119	120
121	122	123	124	125	126	127	128	129	130
131	132	133	134	135	136	137	138	139	140
141	142	143	144	145	146	147	148	149	150
151	152	153	154	155	156	157	158	159	160
161	162	163	164	165	166	167	168	169	170
171	172	173	174	175	176	177	178	179	180
181	182	183	184	185	186	187	188	189	190
191	192	193	194	195	196	197	198	199	200

Mosaic Puzzle Pieces (Blackline Master 8)

Directions: Cut out the pieces carefully so that they will fit together properly. If possible, copy this blackline master onto cardstock before cutting to make the pieces sturdier. Don't laminate them, as plastic coating will make them slide around too much.

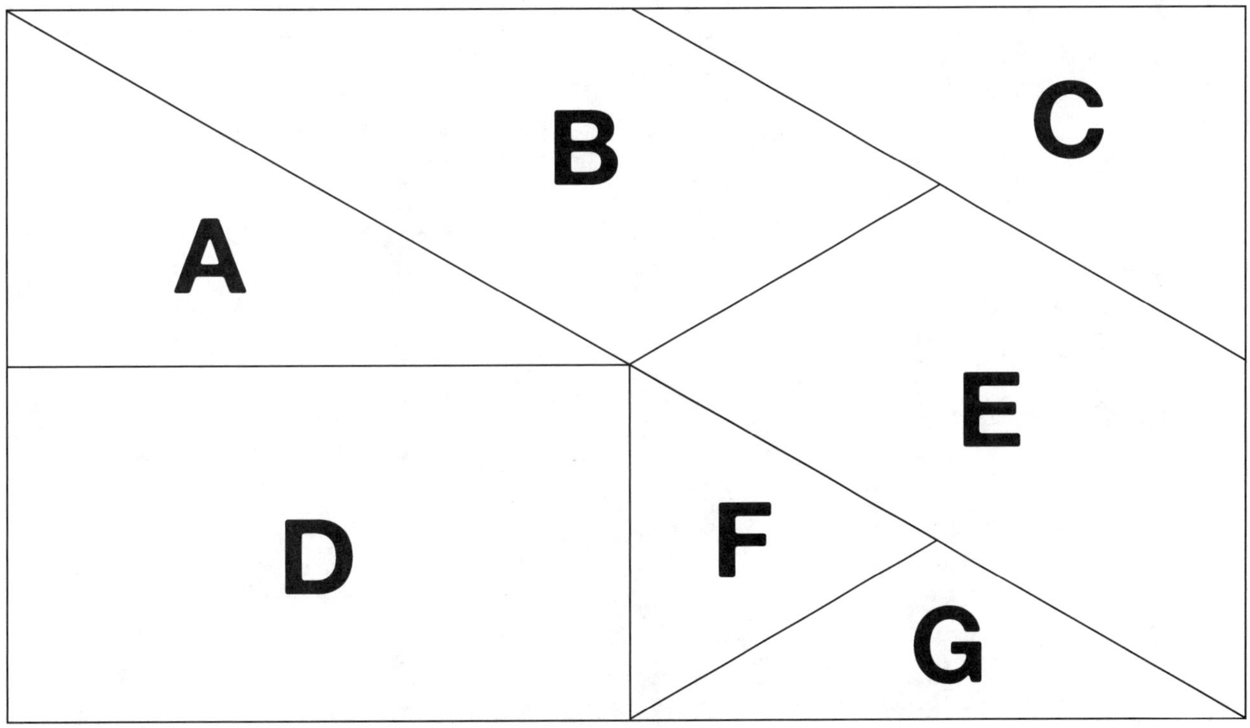

Fraction Bars (Blackline Master 9)

Directions: Copy this page on sturdy paper and cut out the bars on the solid lines. (Your child will cut the dotted lines during Week 25).

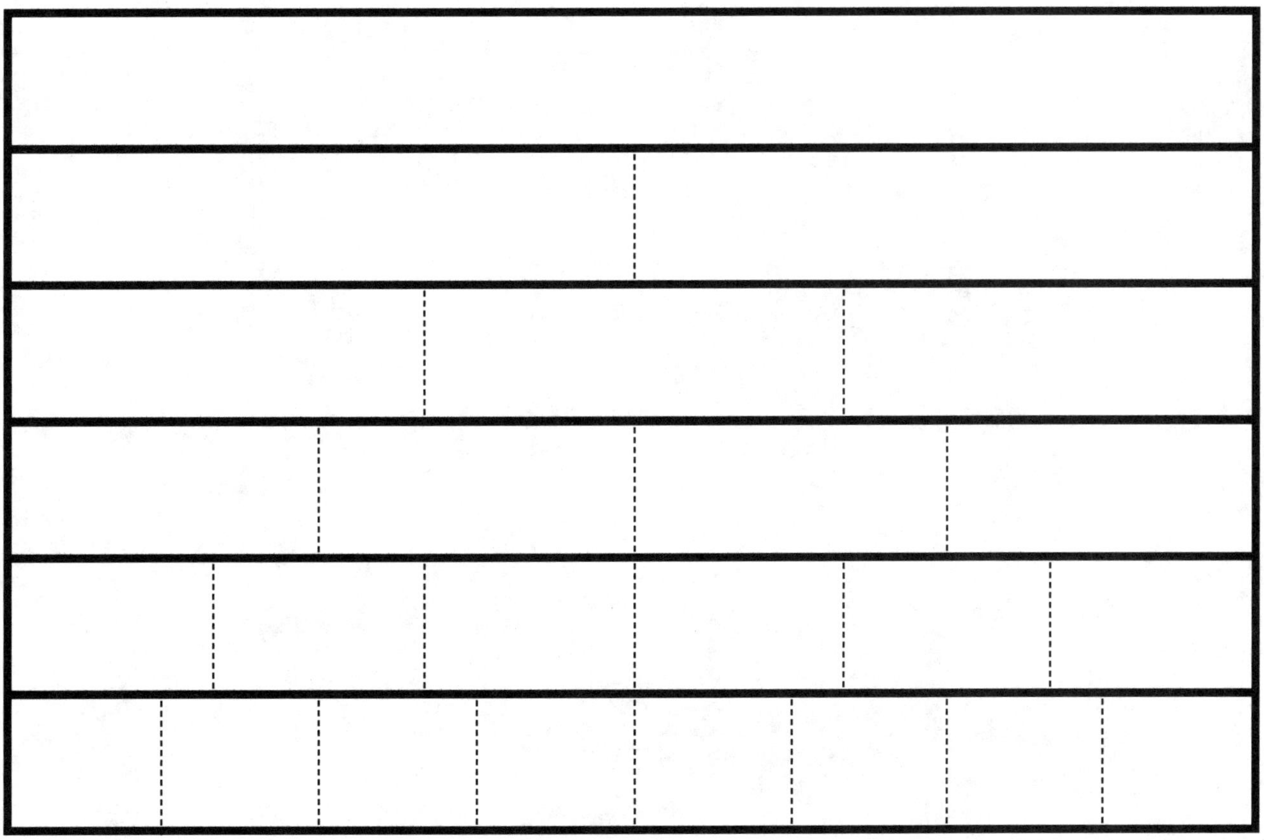

Play Paper Bills for Families Outside the US (Blackline Master 10)

You do not need these if you have other play money, either from a toy cash register or board game.

Directions: Make 2 copies of this page on sturdy paper and cut out the paper bills.

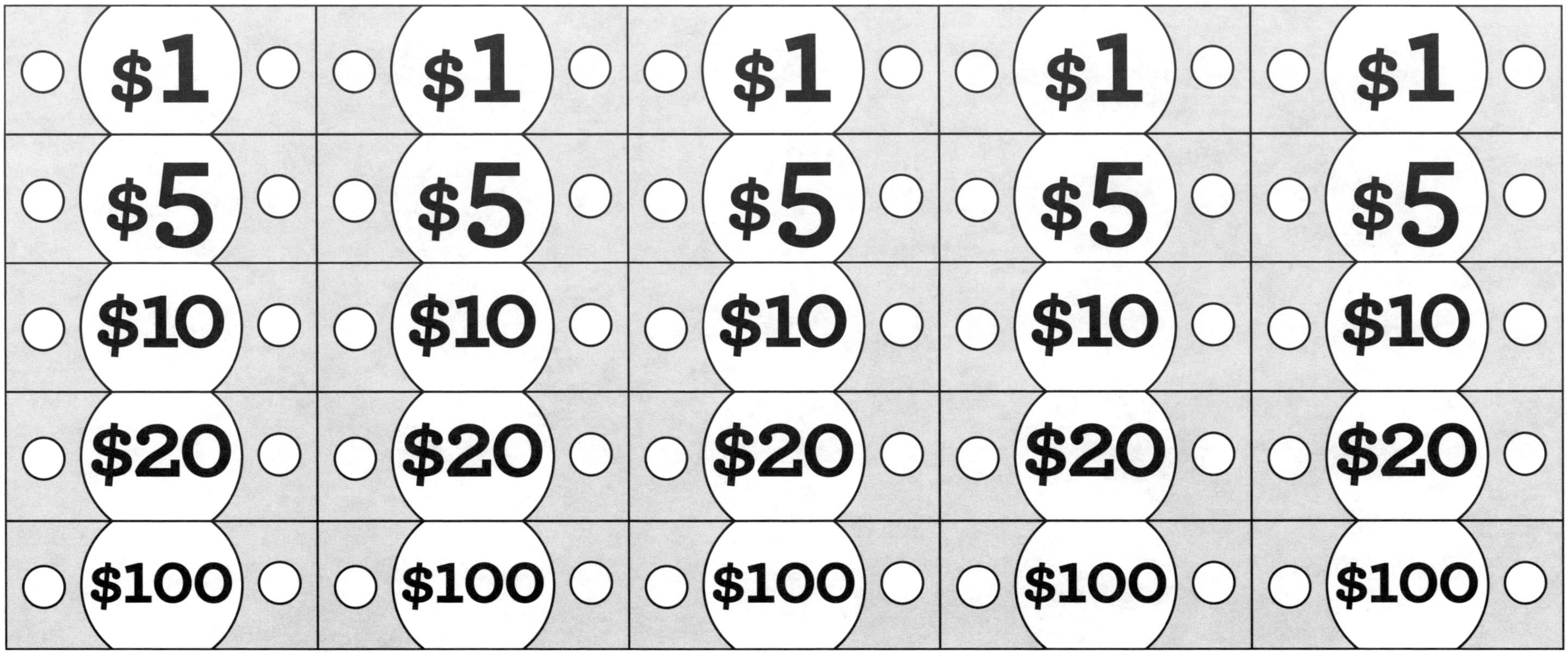

Base-Ten Blocks (Blackline Master 11)

You do not need these if you have real base-ten blocks.

Directions: Make 5 copies of this page on sturdy paper. Cut out the blocks on the dark lines.

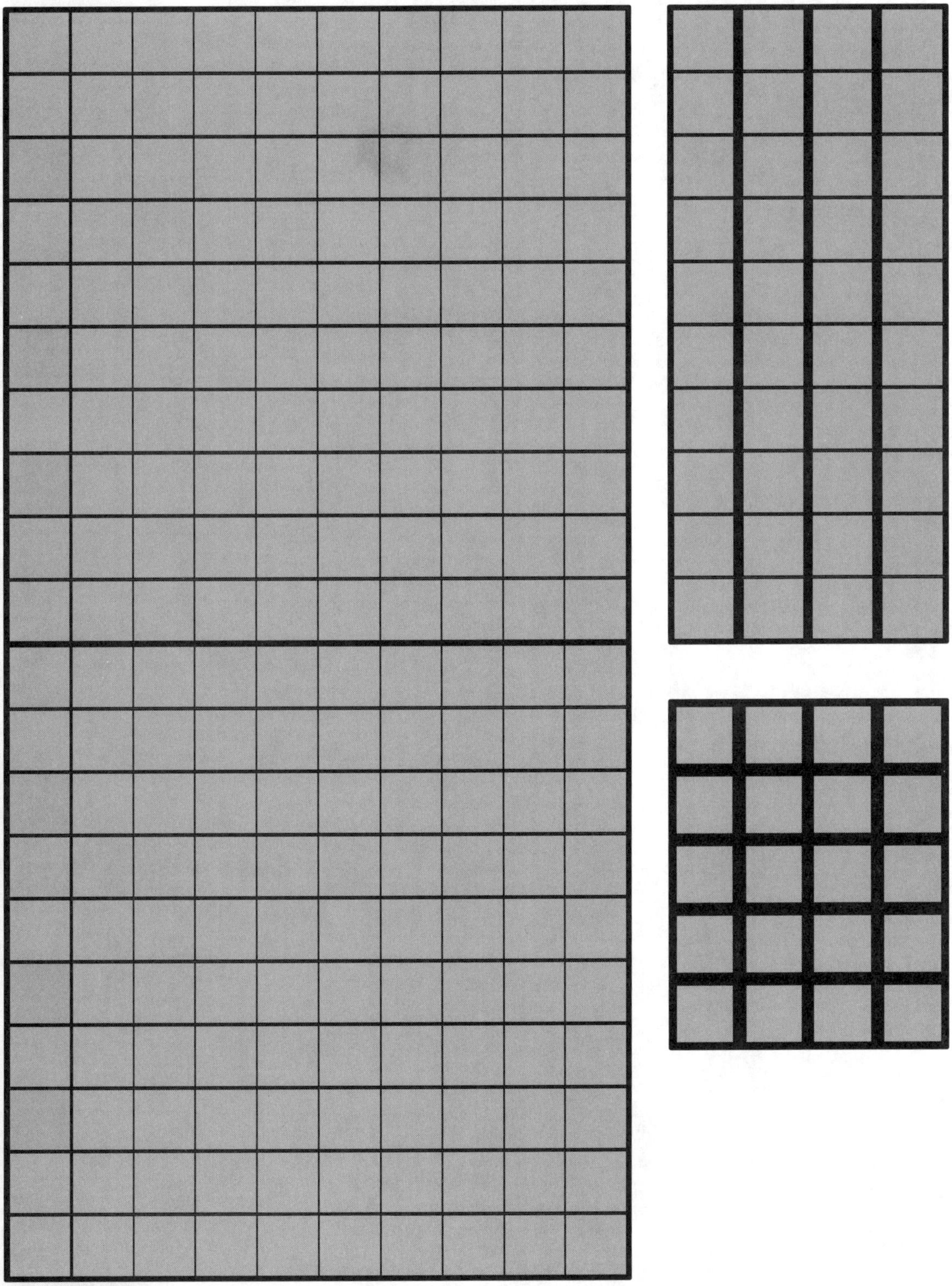

Acknowledgements

Thanks to Itamar Katz, whose design and illustration skills transformed my Word document and sloppy sketches into this clear, easy-to-read Instructor Guide and colorful, whimsical Student Book. These books wouldn't be the same without you, Itamar!

To Bethany Lake, whose close reading and thoughtful suggestions helped me find the balance between mathematical rigor and developmental appropriateness. To Shane Klink, who designed the wonderful covers for the series. And, to Rebecca Fields, who fixed all my typos and made sure that every *i* was dotted and *t* was crossed.

To Susan Wise Bauer, for her guidance and advice as I honed the vision for the *Math with Confidence* series. To Justin Moore, for his thoughtful clarifying questions and indefatigable copy-editing. And to Melissa Moore, both for her expert project management and also for her support, encouragement, and friendship.

Finally, many thanks to the members of the *Second Grade Math with Confidence* pilot-test group. Thank you for finding the activities that didn't work, the lessons that went too long, and the workbook pages that were too boring. This program is better because of you, and I appreciate all the time you spent giving me feedback, answering my questions, and helping me understand how your kids responded to the lessons. Beyond these practical matters, thank you for your overall encouragement and support as I wrote *Second Grade Math with Confidence*. Your commitment to giving your kids an excellent math education motivates and inspires me, and it is an honor to be part of that journey with you.

Meghan Akridge
Megan Anderson
Jacquelyn Beaumont
Nettie Black
Bettina Gentry
DeDi Goss
Janelle H.
Lisa Healy
Joanna Guiao Hidalgo
Rhebeka Hyland
Alexis Jaeger
Jane Kim
Rachel King
Emily Kuhl
Amy Lerner
Melissa Mackey
Rebekah Martin
Sarah McCormick
Jami McCreary
Kate Nicolaus
Katie O'Farrell
Jenna R.
Heather Reynaldo-Casanova
Ashley Scofield
LuAnn Simons
Lynna Sutherland
Jennifer Tierney
Lindsay Toth
Amanda Troxell
Monique Tyson
Duski Van Fleet
Allison vanKlinken
Sara Watson
Elizabeth Wenzel
Valerie Winkley
Amanda Yeary